Thirteenth Workshop on Innovative Use of NLP for Building Educational Applications 2018

New Orleans, Louisiana, USA
5 June 2018

ISBN: 978-1-5108-6354-5

NAACL HLT 2018

**Innovative Use of NLP for
Building Educational Applications**

Proceedings of the Thirteenth Workshop

June 5, 2018
New Orleans, Louisiana

Gold Sponsors

Silver Sponsors

Bronze Sponsors

Introduction

Every year, as we send out the call for papers for the *Workshop on Innovative Use of NLP for Building Educational Applications*, we wonder which subfield of educational applications will be prevalent in the submissions. One year it is speech recognition for automated evaluation, the next it may be grammatical error correction, another year the focus may be on automated scoring of textual assessments. Inevitably, even with more than 130 Program Committee members, we find ourselves scrambling to recruit more reviewers for that year's hot topic.

There was no clear winner this year. The majority of the 2018 submissions were primarily automated writing assessment, automated test generation, and reading. Overall, there was a nice mix of all of the topics above and more.

This year we received 41 submissions and accepted 8 papers as oral presentations and 18 as poster presentations, for an overall acceptance rate of 63 percent. Each paper was reviewed by three members of the Program Committee who were believed to be most appropriate for each paper. We continue to have a strong policy to deal with conflicts of interest. First, we made a concerted effort to not assign papers to reviewers to evaluate if the paper had an author from their institution. Second, organizing committee members recused themselves from discussions of papers when there was a conflict of interest.

We do recognize that there is a core group of institutions and researchers who work in this area. With a higher acceptance rate, we were able to include papers from a wider variety of topics and institutions. The papers accepted were selected on the basis of several factors, including the relevance to a core educational problem space, the novelty of the approach or domain, and the strength of the research. The accepted papers were highly diverse – an indicator of the growing variety of foci in this field. We continue to believe that the workshop framework designed to introduce work in progress and new ideas needs to be revived, and we hope that we have achieved this with the breadth and variety of research accepted for this workshop, a brief description of which is presented below.

The BEA13 workshop has presentations on automated writing evaluation, item generation, readability, dialogue, annotation, speech and grammatical error correction (GEC), annotation and resources:

Automated Writing Evaluation (AWE):

Zhang and Litman present an investigation of using a co-attention based neural network for scoring essays. Horbach et al. investigate the feasibility of cross-lingual content scoring. Gao et al. examine how and why automated content analysis can be used to assess precis writing by university students. Zhang et al. use other texts written by an examinee, in the same test, as extra references in an automated scoring system.

Automated Item Generation (AIG):

Flor and Riordan present a novel rule-based system for automatic generation of factual questions using semantic role labeling. Jiang et al. generate a CLOZE test for Chengyu, a special kind of Chinese idiom. Finally, there are two papers on generating distractors for multiple choice questions. Ha and Yaneva use the question (stem) and the correct answer as input to produce a ranked list of possible distractors. Liang et al. use machine learning models to select distractors that resemble those in actual exam questions.

Reading and Text Complexity:

Bingel et al. predict reading mistakes by children who have reading difficulties by using eye-tracking data. Chinkina et al. automate the selection of reading passages to support teachers. Holz et al. present a web-based application to automatically enhance syllable structure, word stress, and spacing in texts.

Three papers focus specifically on text complexity. Nadeem and Ostendorf propose a neural approach for automated text complexity analysis. Alfter and Volodina investigate the usefulness of previously created word lists to the task of single-word lexical complexity analysis and prediction. Vajjala and Rama explore a universal Common European Framework of Reference (CEFR) classification system.

Dialogue:

When interpreting questions in a virtual patient dialogue system, Jin et al. tackle the challenge of interpreting a long tail of relatively infrequently asked questions. Ramanarayanan and LaMar look at the psychometrics and validity of CALL technologies when evaluating and providing feedback on student learning and conversational ability. Kulkarni and Boyer explore the possibility of building a tutorial question-answering system for Java programming from data sampled from a community-based forum.

Speech:

Loukina et al. look at a new way to test speech systems. As well as training and evaluating against human scores, they report on a system that evaluates a speech scoring engine against corpora.

Grammatical Error Correction (GEC) – the next steps:

None of these papers report on GEC per se. Instead, they are looking ahead to the next steps. Bryant and Briscoe re-examine the use of language modeling in GEC and argue that it is possible to build a simple system that requires minimal annotated data. Rudzewitz et al. develop an approach to provide feedback for second language learners. Finally, Afrin and Litman focus on the quality of revisions in writing. They introduce a corpus of between-draft revisions of student essays that are annotated as to whether each revision improves essay quality.

Annotation:

Two very interesting novel annotation schemas are presented. King and Dickinson investigate issues of variability and acceptability in written text, for both native and non-native speakers, using a dataset of picture description task responses. They define and annotate a handful of features pertaining to form and meaning in order to capture the multi-dimensional ways in which responses can vary. Lugini et al. annotate student talk in text-based (English Language Arts) classroom discussions. They focus on three aspects of student talk: argumentation, specificity, and knowledge domain.

Resources:

Three new resources are being introduced this year. Del Rio Gayo et al. present NLI-PT, the first Portuguese dataset compiled for Native Language Identification. Tack et al. introduce NT2Lex, a lexical resource for Dutch as a foreign language. Vajalla and Lucic describe the collection and compilation of the OneStopEnglish corpus, a collection of texts written at three reading levels.

In addition, this year the BEA Workshop is sponsoring two shared tasks.

Shared Task on Second Language Acquisition Modeling (SLAM):

Settles et al. present the *Second Language Acquisition Modeling* shared task.[1] Given a history of errors made by learners of a second language, the task is to predict errors that they are likely to make in the future. They describe a large corpus of more than 7M words produced by more than 6k learners of English, Spanish, and French using Duolingo, a popular online language-learning app. Then they report on the results of the challenge. Fifteen teams took part in the task and reports appear in these proceedings.

The Second Shared Task on Complex Word Identification (CWI):

---

[1] http://sharedtask.duolingo.com

Yimam et al. report the findings of the *Second Complex Word Identification* shared task.[2] This shared task features multilingual and multi-genre datasets divided into four tracks: English monolingual, German monolingual, Spanish monolingual, and a multilingual track with a French test set, and two tasks: binary classification and probabilistic classification. A total of 12 teams submitted their results in different task/track combinations and 11 of them wrote system descriptions that appear in these proceedings.

On this 13th edition of the workshop, BEA is officially adolescent. Last year saw the creation of the Special Interest Group on Education and NLP (SIGEDU) which is a major step in growing our subfield. SIGEDU held its first elections this winter with over 20 candidates running. The elected SIGEDU officials are all familiar names with respect to the workshop. Jill Burstein is President, Ekaterina Kochmar is Secretary, and Helen Yannakoudakis is Treasurer. The four Board Members are Claudia Leacock, Nitin Madnani, Ildiko Pilan, and Torsten Zesch. Joel Tetreault, who has been the primary contact for the workshop for the last 11 years, and the interim President, chose not to run for office. At the end of this workshop, the reins will be handed over to the new team. Another development from the last year is the creation of a permanent website for the SIGEDU and BEA workshop.[3] Created by Ekaterina Kochmar and Sowmya Vajjala, we hope to develop this into a regularly updated resource and reference site for the community.

We wish to thank everyone who showed interest and submitted a paper, all of the authors for their contributions, the members of the Program Committee for their thoughtful reviews, and everyone who is attending this workshop. We would especially like to thank our sponsors: at the Gold Level, Duolingo, Grammarly®, National Board of Medical Examiners (NBME) and Turnitin®; at the Silver level, Educational Testing Service (ETS®) and iLexIR; at the Bronze level, Cognii. Their contributions help fund workshop extras, such as T-shirts and the dinner, which is a great social and networking event. Also, thanks to Joya Tetreault for designing the t-shirts again this year.

Joel Tetreault, Grammarly
Jill Burstein, Educational Testing Services
Ekaterina Kochmar, University of Cambridge
Claudia Leacock, Grammarly
Helen Yannakoudakis, University of Cambridge

---

[2] https://sites.google.com/view/cwisharedtask2018/
[3] https://ekaterinakochmar.wixsite.com/sig-edu

Organizers:

Joel Tetreault, Grammarly
Jill Burstein, Educational Testing Service
Ekaterina Kochmar, University of Cambridge
Claudia Leacock, Grammarly
Helen Yannakoudakis, University of Cambridge

Program Committee:

Lars Ahrenberg, Linköping University
David Alfter, University of Gothenburg
Dimitris Alikaniotis, Grammarly
Homa B. Hashemi, Intelligent System Program, University of Pittsburgh
Rafael E. Banchs, Institute for Infocomm Research
Sagnik Banerjee, Iowa State University
Rajendra Banjade, Audible inc. (an Amazon company)
Lee Becker, Pearson
Beata Beigman Klebanov, Educational Testing Service
Lisa Beinborn, UKP Lab, Technische Universität Darmstadt
Delphine Bernhard, Université de Strasbourg
Sameer Bhatnagar, Polytechnique Montreal
Serge Bibauw, KU Leuven & Université Catholique de Louvain
Joachim Bingel, University of Copenhagen
Johannes Bjerva, University of Copenhagen
Kristy Boyer, University of Florida
Ted Briscoe, University of Cambridge
Dominique Brunato, Institute of Computational Linguistics (ILC-CNR)
Chris Bryant, University of Cambridge
Aoife Cahill, Educational Testing Service
Andrew Caines, University of Cambridge
Mei-Hua Chen, Tunghai University
Martin Chodorow, Hunter College of CUNY
Shamil Chollampatt, National University of Singapore
Mark Core, University of Southern California
Robert Dale, Language Technology Group
Vidas Daudaravicius, VTEX Research
Kordula De Kuthy, University of Tübingen
Barbara Di Eugenio, University of Illinois at Chicago
Yo Ehara, National Institute of Advanced Industrial Science and Technology
Noureddine Elouazizi, Faculty of Science (Skylight/Dean Office), University of British Columbia
Keelan Evanini, Educational Testing Service
Cédrick Fairon, Université Catholique de Louvain
Youmna Farag, University of Cambridge
Mariano Felice, University of Cambridge
Oliver Ferschke, M*Modal
Michael Flor, Educational Testing Service
Thomas François, UCLouvain
Michael Gamon, Microsoft Research

Dipesh Gautam, University of Memphis
Kallirroi Georgila, University of Southern California
Jonathan Gordon, University of Southern California
Floriana Grasso, University of Liverpool
Gintare Grigonyte, Stockholm University
Iryna Gurevych, UKP Lab, Technische Universität Darmstadt
Na-Rae Han, University of Pittsburgh
Jiangang Hao, Educational Testing Service
Marti Hearst, University of California, Berkeley
Trude Heift, Simon Fraser University
Derrick Higgins, American Family Insurance
Andrea Horbach, University Duisburg-Essen
Chung-Chi Huang, Frostburg State University
Radu Tudor Ionescu, University of Bucharest
Ross Israel, Factual Inc
Lifeng Jin, The Ohio State University
Pamela Jordan, University of Pittsburgh
Marcin Junczys-Dowmunt, Adam Mickiewicz University
John Kelleher, Dublin Institute of Technology
Levi King, Indiana University
Mamoru Komachi, Tokyo Metropolitan University
Sandra Kübler, Indiana University
Girish Kumar, Carousell
Ji-Ung Lee, UKP Lab Technische Universität Darmstadt
John Lee, City University of Hong Kong
Lung-Hao Lee, National Taiwan Normal University
James Lester, North Carolina State University
Wen Li, Indiana University
Maria Liakata, University of Warwick
Chen Liang, Pennsylvania State University
Diane Litman, University of Pittsburgh
Yang Liu, Lingochamp
Peter Ljunglöf, University of Gothenburg and Chalmers University
Anastassia Loukina, Educational Testing Service
Xiaofei Lu, Pennsylvania State University
Luca Lugini, University of Pittsburgh
Nitin Madnani, Educational Testing Service
Montse Maritxalar, University of the Basque Country
Ilia Markov, Center for Computing Research, Instituto Politécnico Nacional
James H. Martin, University of Colorado Boulder
Ditty Mathew, IIT Madras
Julie Medero, Harvey Mudd College
Beata Megyesi, Uppsala University
Detmar Meurers, University of Tübingen
Elham Mohammadi, Concordia University
Maria Moritz, University of Goettingen
Smaranda Muresan, Columbia University
Courtney Napoles, Grammarly
Diane Napolitano, Educational Testing Service
Hwee Tou Ng, National University of Singapore
Huy Nguyen, Graduate Student at University of Pittsburgh

Nobal Bikram Niraula, Boeing Research & Technology
Yoo Rhee Oh, Electronics and Telecommunications Research Institute (ETRI)
Constantin Orasan, University of Wolverhampton
Robert Östling, Stockholm University
Ulrike Pado, Hochschule für Technik Stuttgart
Ted Pedersen, University of Minnesota, Duluth
Isaac Persing, The University of Texas at Dallas
Ildikó Pilán, University of Gothenburg
Patti Price, PPRICE Speech and Language Technology Consulting
Vipul Raheja, Grammarly
Taraka Rama, University of Oslo
Lakshmi Ramachandran, A9.com Inc
Vikram Ramanarayanan, Educational Testing Service R&D and UC San Francisco
Sudha Rao, University of Maryland, College Park
Hanumant Redkar, Indian Institute of Technology Bombay (IIT Bombay)
Marek Rei, University of Cambridge
Robert Reynolds, Brigham Young University
Brian Riordan, Educational Testing Service
Andrew Rosenberg, IBM Research AI
Mark Rosenstein, Pearson
Mihai Rotaru, Textkernel
Alla Rozovskaya, City University of New York
C. Anton Rytting, University of Maryland
Allen Schmaltz, Harvard University
Anders Søgaard, University of Copenhagen
Helmer Strik, Linguistics, Centre for Language Studies (CLS), Centre for Language and Speech
Technology (CLST), Radboud University Nijmegen; NovoLanguage Nijmegen
Jan Švec, Department of Cybernetics, University of West Bohemia
Anaïs Tack, Université Catholique de Louvain & KU Leuven
Yuen-Hsien Tseng, National Taiwan Normal University
Sowmya Vajjala, Iowa State University
Giulia Venturi, Institute of Computational Linguistics "A. Zampolli" (ILC-CNR), Pisa
Aline Villavicencio, Federal University of Rio Grande do Sul and University of Essex
Elena Volodina, University of Gothenburg, Sweden
Shuting Wang, Facebook
Michael White, The Ohio State University
David Wible, National Central University
Alistair Willis, Open University, UK
Michael Wojatzki, University of Duisburg-Essen
Magdalena Wolska, University of Tübingen
Huichao Xue, LinkedIn
Victoria Yaneva, University of Wolverhampton
Zheng Yuan, University of Cambridge
Marcos Zampieri, University of Wolverhampton
Klaus Zechner, Educational Testing Service

Table of Contents

Conference Program

Tuesday, June 5, 2018

08:30–09:00 *Loading of Oral Presentations*

09:00–10:30 Oral Presentations (Speech, Dialogue & Reading)

09:00–09:15 *Opening Remarks*

09:15–09:40 *Using exemplar responses for training and evaluating automated speech scoring systems*
Anastassia Loukina, Klaus Zechner, James Bruno and Beata Beigman Klebanov

09:40–10:05 *Using Paraphrasing and Memory-Augmented Models to Combat Data Sparsity in Question Interpretation with a Virtual Patient Dialogue System*
Lifeng Jin, David King, Amad Hussein, Michael White and Douglas Danforth

10:05–10:30 *Predicting misreadings from gaze in children with reading difficulties*
Joachim Bingel, Maria Barrett and Sigrid Klerke

10:30–11:00 Mid-morning break

11:00–12:30 Oral Presentations (Passage Selection, Text Complexity & Reading; Shared Task Reports)

11:00–11:25 *Automatic Input Enrichment for Selecting Reading Material: An Online Study with English Teachers*
Maria Chinkina, Ankita Oswal and Detmar Meurers

11:25–11:50 *Estimating Linguistic Complexity for Science Texts*
Farah Nadeem and Mari Ostendorf

11:50–12:10 *Second Language Acquisition Modeling*
Burr Settles, Chris Brust, Erin Gustafson, Masato Hagiwara and Nitin Madnani

12:10–12:30 *A Report on the Complex Word Identification Shared Task 2018*
Seid Muhie Yimam, Chris Biemann, Shervin Malmasi, Gustavo Paetzold, Lucia Specia, Sanja Štajner, Anaïs Tack and Marcos Zampieri

12:30–14:00 Lunch

14:00–15:30   **BEA & Shared Task Poster and Demo Session**

14:00–14:45   **Poster Session A**

BEA papers

Towards Single Word Lexical Complexity Prediction
David Alfter and Elena Volodina

COAST - Customizable Online Syllable Enhancement in Texts. A flexible framework for automatically enhancing reading materials
Heiko Holz, Zarah Weiss, Oliver Brehm and Detmar Meurers

Annotating picture description task responses for content analysis
Levi King and Markus Dickinson

Annotating Student Talk in Text-based Classroom Discussions
Luca Lugini, Diane Litman, Amanda Godley and Christopher Olshefski

Toward Automatically Measuring Learner Ability from Human-Machine Dialog Interactions using Novel Psychometric Models
Vikram Ramanarayanan and Michelle LaMar

Generating Feedback for English Foreign Language Exercises
Björn Rudzewitz, Ramon Ziai, Kordula De Kuthy, Verena Möller, Florian Nuxoll and Detmar Meurers

NT2Lex: A CEFR-Graded Lexical Resource for Dutch as a Foreign Language Linked to Open Dutch WordNet
Anaïs Tack, Thomas François, Piet Desmet and Cédrick Fairon

Experiments with Universal CEFR Classification
Sowmya Vajjala and Taraka Rama

Chengyu Cloze Test
Zhiying Jiang, Boliang Zhang, Lifu Huang and Heng Ji

CWI Shared Task papers

LaSTUS/TALN at Complex Word Identification (CWI) 2018 Shared Task
Ahmed AbuRa'ed and Horacio Saggion

Cross-lingual complex word identification with multitask learning
Joachim Bingel and Johannes Bjerva

UnibucKernel: A kernel-based learning method for complex word identification
Andrei Butnaru and Radu Tudor Ionescu

TMU System for SLAM-2018
Masahiro Kaneko, Tomoyuki Kajiwara and Mamoru Komachi

Deep Factorization Machines for Knowledge Tracing
Jill-Jênn Vie

CLUF: a Neural Model for Second Language Acquisition Modeling
Shuyao Xu, Jin Chen and Long Qin

Neural sequence modelling for learner error prediction
Zheng Yuan

15:30–16:00 **Mid-afternoon break**

16:00–17:30 **Oral Presentations (Item Generation, Essay/Content Scoring & Writing)**

16:00–16:25 *Automatic Distractor Suggestion for Multiple-Choice Tests Using Concept Embeddings and Information Retrieval*
Le An Ha and Victoria Yaneva

16:25–16:50 *Co-Attention Based Neural Network for Source-Dependent Essay Scoring*
Haoran Zhang and Diane Litman

16:50–17:15 *Cross-Lingual Content Scoring*
Andrea Horbach, Sebastian Stennmanns and Torsten Zesch

17:15–17:30 *Closing Remarks*

Using exemplar responses for training and evaluating automated speech scoring systems

Anastassia Loukina, Klaus Zechner, James Bruno, Beata Beigman Klebanov
Educational Testing Service
Princeton, NJ, USA
`{aloukina,kzechner,jbruno,bbeigmanklebanov}@ets.org`

Abstract

Automated scoring engines are usually trained and evaluated against human scores and compared to the benchmark of human-human agreement. In this paper we compare the performance of an automated speech scoring engine using two corpora: a corpus of almost 700,000 randomly sampled spoken responses with scores assigned by one or two raters during operational scoring, and a corpus of 16,500 exemplar responses with scores reviewed by multiple expert raters. We show that the choice of corpus used for model *evaluation* has a major effect on estimates of system performance with r varying between 0.64 and 0.80. Surprisingly, this is not the case for the choice of corpus for model *training*: when the training corpus is sufficiently large, the systems trained on different corpora showed almost identical performance when evaluated on the same corpus. We show that this effect is consistent across several learning algorithms. We conclude that evaluating the model on a corpus of exemplar responses if one is available provides additional evidence about system validity; at the same time, investing effort into creating a corpus of exemplar responses for model training is unlikely to lead to a substantial gain in model performance.

1 Introduction

Systems that automatically score constructed responses in an assessment — such as essays or spoken responses — are typically trained and evaluated on a corpus of such test taker responses with scores assigned by trained human raters, considered to be the "gold standard" for both training and evaluation of the automated scoring system (Page, 1966; Attali and Burstein, 2006; Bernstein et al., 2010; Williamson et al., 2012). Human raters follow certain agreed-upon scoring guidelines ("rubrics") that define the characteristics of a response for each discrete score level of the scoring scale. For instance, in the case of speech scoring, human raters may evaluate certain aspects of a test taker's speech production, such as fluency, pronunciation, prosody, vocabulary diversity, grammatical accuracy, content correctness, or discourse organization when determining their score for a given spoken response (Zechner et al., 2009).

Even as assessment companies try their best to ensure high quality of human scores, human raters do not always agree in the scores they assign to a constructed response. One reason is related to properties of the responses themselves: the raters use a unidimensional (holistic) scale to score a multidimensional performance. In this situation different raters may differently weight various aspects of performance (Eckes, 2008) resulting in disagreement. The second reason is related to various imperfections of human raters, e.g., rater fatigue (Ling et al., 2014), differences between novice and experienced raters (Davis, 2016), and the effect of raters' linguistic background on their evaluation of the language skill being measured (Carey et al., 2011).

To guard against such rater inconsistencies, in addition to extensive rater training and monitoring, responses for high-stakes tests are often scored by multiple raters and scores from responses to multiple test questions are used to compute the final score reported to the test taker and other stakeholders, with different responses scored by different raters (Wang and von Davier, 2014; Penfield, 2016). As a result, the final score remains highly reliable despite variation in human agreement at the level of the individual question. However, since automated scoring engines are usually trained using response-level scores, any inconsistencies in such scores due to the variety of reasons outlined above may negatively affect the system

1

Proceedings of the Thirteenth Workshop on Innovative Use of NLP for Building Educational Applications, pages 1–12
New Orleans, Louisiana, June 5, 2018. ©2018 Association for Computational Linguistics

performance.

To monitor rater performance, testing programs sometimes use previously scored responses that are intermixed with the operational responses. These responses are selected from operational responses to represent exemplar cases of each score level and the scores are further reviewed by multiple raters to ensure their accuracy.

In this paper we are examining the effect of using such "exemplar" responses for scoring model training and evaluation in the context of automated speech scoring. In particular, we aim to address the following research questions:

1. How do automated speech scoring models perform when trained on a corpus with randomly selected responses vs. a corpus with exemplar responses?

2. How is performance affected by the choice of evaluation corpus (random response selection vs. exemplar responses)?

Our initial hypothesis about research question (1) is that if the size and score distribution for the training corpora are comparable, we would expect to see the scoring model perform better when trained on the exemplar responses since the model is trained on clear-cut examples (less noise in the data). Similarly, as for research question (2), we hypothesize that when evaluating on clear-cut exemplar responses, scoring model performance should be better than in the default case (random selection) since the machine would likely benefit from the same response properties that also result in more consistent and reliable human scores.

Constructing large corpora of exemplar responses is a very resource-intensive task and therefore little is known about the possible impact of the use of such corpora for training and evaluation of automated scoring models. Our paper uses a very large corpus of spoken responses and an exemplar corpus constructed by experts over the course of multiple years to address this gap and improve our understanding of the effect of training data on the performance of automated scoring models.

2 Related work

Previous studies considered the effect of annotation noise on the performance of various NLP systems (Schwartz et al., 2011; Reidsma and Carletta, 2008; Martínez Alonso et al., 2015; Plank et al., 2014).

In a series of papers, Beigman Klebanov and Beigman (2014; 2009; 2009) studied annotation noise in linguistic data, namely, a situation where some of the data is easy to judge, with clear-cut annotation/classification, whereas some of the data is harder to judge, yielding disagreements among raters.

They show that in a binary classification task, the presence of annotation noise (hard to judge cases) in the evaluation data could skew benchmarking, especially in cases of small discrepancies between competing models. They also show that the presence of hard cases in the training data could compromise system performance on easy-to-judge test cases, a phenomenon they termed *hard case bias*. Using data annotated through crowd-sourcing and across five linguistic tasks, Jamison and Gurevych (2015) extended that work and showed that filtering out low-agreement cases improved performance on test data for some of the tasks without having a substantial detrimental effect on the rest of the cases. They also showed that the filtering of low-agreement instances from the training data ceased being effective if the agreement threshold is set too high, which resulted in too little training data.

In the context of automated scoring, the size of the training set has been shown to have a consistent effect on model performance (Chen, 2012; Heilman and Madnani, 2015; Zesch et al., 2015). At the same time, a number of studies also considered the possibility of training automated systems on a smaller but well-chosen subset of examples. Horbach et al. (2014) simulated a grading approach where responses are clustered automatically, teachers labeled only one item per cluster, and that label was then propagated to the other items in the cluster. They reported a 90% grading accuracy of their system. Zesch et al. (2015) further applied this approach to selecting responses for training automated scoring models for short answer scoring. They used k-means clustering to identify similar responses and trained their classifier on responses closest to the centroid of each cluster. Note that in their study k corresponded to the number of responses to be annotated, not the score levels. They found that the system trained on such responses did not outperform the system trained on the same number of randomly sampled responses. They also found no improvement when the score was propagated to all responses in the cluster and the resulting scores were used to train the model. However, the performance increased when the training data was limited to 'pure' clusters only, that is clusters that contained responses assigned the same score. This system, trained on a subset of responses selected in this fashion, substantially outperformed the system trained on the same number of randomly sampled responses, and in the case of short responses, performed as well as the system trained on the whole training set.

To summarize, previous studies indicate that training NLP systems including automated scoring engines on a selected subset of responses that are either more typical in terms of feature values or easy-to-judge for human annotators may lead to an increase in system performance despite a reduction in the size of the training set.

While previous studies on automated scoring used automated clustering to identify the exemplars, we further extend this work by using a large corpus of exemplar responses identified by experts in assessment to train and evaluate an automated speech scoring engine. We compare the performance of the models to those trained on a large corpus of randomly sampled responses.

3 Description of the data

Both corpora use real responses submitted to a large-scale assessment of English language proficiency. The test takers whose responses were used in this study gave their consent for use of their responses for research purposes during the original test administration. The responses in both corpora were anonymized.

3.1 MAIN corpus

The main corpus in this study contains responses sampled randomly from spoken responses submitted to the same assessment over the course of several years. We selected responses to 6 different types of questions. Each question was designed to elicit spontaneous speech. For some questions test-takers were expected to use the provided materials (e.g., a reading passage) as the basis for their response, other questions were more general such as "What is your favorite food and why?". Depending on the question type, the speakers were given 45 seconds or 1 minute to complete their response. The corpus consisted of 683,694 spo-

Corpus	Total	Per model
MAIN: Train	464,664	77,444
MAIN: Test	219,030	36,505
MAIN* : Train	12,398	2,066
EXEMPLAR:Train	12,390	2,065
EXEMPLAR:Test	4,137	689

Table 1: Characteristics of the corpora used in this study. The table shows the total number of responses in each partition across all 6 question types and the average number of responses used to train/evaluate the model for each question type.

ken responses, 113,949 responses for each question type. For this study, the responses for each question were partitioned randomly into a training (2/3) and evaluation set (1/3).

All responses in the corpus were scored on a scale of 1-4 by human raters. The raters assigned a single holistic score to each response using a scoring rubric that covered three aspects of language proficiency: delivery (pronunciation, fluency), language use (vocabulary, grammar), and content and topical development. Most responses were scored by a single rater, with 8.5% randomly selected responses independently scored by two raters. The average correlation between two human raters for double-scored responses was Pearsons's $r = 0.59$.

3.2 EXEMPLAR responses

The second corpus used in this study contained responses from the same assessment selected for training and monitoring human raters. These responses are expected to be typical examples of the different score levels. They are usually selected from double-scored responses that were assigned the same scores by both raters and then reviewed by multiple experts in human scoring to ensure that the final score is accurate. The corpus only includes responses where all experts agree about the appropriate score. Thus the responses in this corpus have two important characteristics: first, the final score can be considered a true gold standard; second, this final score is not controversial.

The original set of responses had a uniform distribution of human scores. To separate the effect of distribution, in this study we used a subset sampled to match the score distribution in the MAIN corpus. This corpus consisted of 16,527 responses to the same 6 types of questions[1] with on average 2,754 responses per task. This corpus was also randomly partitioned into training and test sets using a 2:1 ratio.

Since the total number of responses in the EXEMPLAR corpus was much smaller than in the MAIN corpus, we randomly sampled 12,398 responses from the training partition of the MAIN corpus matching the score distributions in the other two corpora. We will use this MAIN* corpus to separate the effect of the nature of the training set (random sample vs. exemplar) from the effect of the size of the training set. Table 1 summarizes main properties of each corpus.

4 Automated scoring engine

4.1 Automated speech recognition

All responses were processed using an automated speech recognition system using the Kaldi toolkit (Povey et al., 2011) and the approach described by Tao et al. (2016). The language model was based on tri-grams. The acoustic models were based on a 5-layer DNN and 13 MFCC-based features. Tao et al. (2016) give further detail about the model training procedure.

The ASR system was trained on a proprietary corpus consisting of 800 hours of non-native speech from 8,700 speakers of more than 100 native languages. The speech in the ASR training corpus was elicited using questions similar to the ones considered in this study. There was no overlap of speakers or questions between the ASR training corpus and the corpus used in this paper. We did not additionally adapt the ASR to the speakers or responses in this study.

To estimate the ASR word error rate (WER), we obtained human transcriptions for 480 responses randomly selected from the evaluation partition. The median WER for these responses was 34%.

4.2 Features

For each response, we extracted 77 different features which covered two of the three aspects of language proficiency considered by the human raters: delivery (51 features) and language use (22 features). For this study we did not use any features that cover the content of the response.

Features related to delivery covered general fluency, pronunciation and prosody. Fluency features include general speech rate as well as fea-

tures that capture pausing patterns in the response such as mean duration of pauses, mean number of words between two pauses, and the ratio of pauses to speech. Pronunciation quality was measured using the average confidence scores and acoustic model scores computed by the ASR system for the words in the 1-best ASR hypothesis. Finally, prosody was evaluated by measuring patterns of variation in time intervals between stressed syllables as well as the number of syllables between adjacent stressed syllables and variation in the durations of vowels and consonants.

Features related to language use covered vocabulary, grammar and some aspects of discourse structure. Vocabulary-related features included average log of the frequency of all content words and a comparison between the response vocabulary and several reference corpora. Grammar was evaluated using CVA-based comparison computed based on part-of-speech tags, a range of features which measured occurrences of various syntactic structures and the language model score of response. Finally, a set of features measured the occurrence of various discourse markers.

4.3 Scoring models

To ensure that the results are not an artifact of a particular learning algorithms (hereafter referred to as 'learners'), we used 7 different regressors, both linear and non-linear. For the linear models we used OLS Linear Regression, ElasticNet, Linear SVR, and Huber Regressor. Non-linear models included Random Forest Regressor (RF), Gradient Boosting Regressor (GB), and Multi-layer Perceptron regressor (MLP). In the operational scoring engine the coefficients in the linear models are often restricted to allow only positive values (Loukina et al., 2015). We did not apply such a restriction in this study to allow for a comparison between different types of learners.

We used the *scikit-learn* (Pedregosa et al., 2011) implementation of the learners and the RSMTool toolkit (Madnani et al., 2017) for model training and evaluation. The hyper-parameters for non-deterministic models were optimized using a cross-validated search over a grid with mean squared error (MSE) as the objective function.

The scoring models were trained on the training partition of each of the three corpora. Separate models were trained for each of the 6 question types for a total of 126 models (3 corpora * 6 ques-

---

[1] The actual questions were different across the corpora.

tion types * 7 regressors). Each model was then evaluated on the responses to the same task contained in the evaluation partitions of the MAIN and the EXEMPLAR corpora.

5   Results

5.1   The effect of training set, evaluation set and learner

We used a linear mixed-effect model (Searle et al., 1992; Snijders and Bosker, 2012) fitted using the `statsmodels` Python package (Seabold and Perktold, 2010) to identify statistically significant differences among the various models. We used prediction squared error for each response (N=3,124,338) as a dependent variable, response as a random factor, and learner, training set and test set as fixed effects. We included both the main effects of training and test set as well as their interaction and used the Linear Regression and MAIN corpus as the reference categories.

The average model performance for each model is shown in Table 2. While the model was fitted using squared prediction error, for ease of interpretation and comparison with other studies, we report Pearson's correlation coefficient in the table and in the body of the paper. Corresponding values of root mean squared error (RMSE) are given in the Appendix. Unless stated otherwise, $p < .0001$ for all effects is reported as significant.

The effect of the choice of learner on model performance was statistically significant but very small. Most of the more complex models resulted in higher prediction error than OLS linear regression. Huber regression ($p = 0.007$) and MLP regression gave a slight boost in performance. Random Forest and Linear SVR gave the highest prediction error. In all cases the differences in performance were very small: for RF and SVR the difference between these learners and OLS was 0.03%; in other cases the differences were around 0.01%.

The choice of the evaluation set had the strongest effect on the estimates of model performance. The best model trained on the MAIN corpus of randomly selected responses achieved $r = 0.66$ (MLP) when evaluated on the MAIN corpus. This is consistent with other results reported for similar corpora: Loukina et al. (2017) cite values between 0.60 and 0.67 depending on the question type and system used. This model achieved substantially higher performance on the EXEM-

PLAR corpus with $r = 0.80$. In other words, the corpus that contained typical responses that could be accurately scored by human raters was also accurately scored by the automated engine.

Disappointingly, we did not see any improvement in performance when the models were trained on the EXEMPLAR corpus: the performance on the MAIN corpus was in fact slightly worse than when the models were trained on the MAIN corpus, with the highest correlation being $r = 0.64$ (vs. $r = 0.66$). The performance of these models was also no better than the performance of the models trained on the same amount of randomly sampled responses (MAIN*).

As expected, models trained on EXEMPLAR responses reached high agreement when evaluated on EXEMPLAR responses ($r = 0.79$). The performance of this model was also better than the performance of the model trained on MAIN*. That is, training on EXEMPLAR responses gives an advantage over training on the same number of randomly sampled responses when the model is evaluated on EXEMPLAR responses. However, there was no difference between the model trained on the full training set of the MAIN corpus and the model trained on the EXEMPLAR corpus.

5.2   Size of the training set

To further evaluate whether training on a larger number of EXEMPLAR responses may have lead to better performance on the MAIN corpus, we re-trained the models using all responses pooled across the different question types. Such an approach has been previously used in other studies in situations where all types of questions are scored based on the same or similar rubrics and the scoring models do not include any question-specific features (Higgins et al., 2011; Loukina et al., 2015). A substantial increase in the size of the training set to some extent compensates for loss of information about question-specific patterns. The models were evaluated by question type, as in the rest of this paper.

To obtain the learning curves for different training sets, we trained all models using training sets of varying sizes from 1000 responses to the full training partition of a given corpus. For each N other than where N is the length of full corpus we trained models 5 times using 5 randomly sampled training sets. Figure 1 shows the learning curves for different combinations of training and evalua-

Evaluation set	MAIN			EXEMPLAR		
Training set	MAIN	MAIN*	EXEMPLAR	MAIN	MAIN*	EXEMPLAR
RandomForestRegressor	0.644	0.619	0.616	0.790	0.762	0.777
GradientBoostingRegressor	0.656	0.621	0.630	0.800	0.764	0.784
ElasticNet	0.643	0.634	0.636	0.783	0.772	0.783
LinearSVR	0.635	0.623	0.636	0.767	0.753	0.782
HuberRegressor	0.652	0.635	0.640	0.792	0.771	0.788
MLPRegressor	0.656	0.636	0.640	0.796	0.774	0.787
LinearRegression	0.653	0.633	0.641	0.793	0.771	0.790

Table 2: Average performance (Pearsons's r) across 6 question types from the two corpora in these studies using different combinations of learners and training sets.

tion sets (see Appendix for table with numerical values). All models were trained using OLS linear regression.

The comparison between the two curves showed that when models are evaluated on the MAIN corpus, training on EXEMPLAR responses has a small advantage for a very small training set (N=1000). Once the training set is sufficiently large (for our data, $N > 4,000$) training on randomly sampled responses leads to a slightly higher performance than training on the same number of EXEMPLAR responses.

At the same time, training on EXEMPLAR responses had a clear advantage when models were evaluated on EXEMPLAR responses, although the difference between the two models decreased with the increase in the size of the training set. Thus, our results are consistent with the phenomenon of hard case bias described in Beigman Klebanov and Beigman (2009) – training on noisy data leads to somewhat weaker performance on clear-cut cases.

To conclude, having a larger set of EXEMPLAR responses might have slightly increased the performance of the models on EXEMPLAR responses, but it is unlikely that it would have given a performance boost on the MAIN corpus.

5.3 How similar are predictions from different models?

While differences in training data do not seem to yield consistent differences in performance for the various learners, it is still possible that learners create somewhat different representations when trained on MAIN vs. EXEMPLAR, as was the case, for example, in (Beigman Klebanov and Beigman, 2014). This would, in turn, suggest that the two models could embody different and potentially complementary views of the data, each dealing better with a different subset of the data. It is likewise possible that different learners created usefully different representations. To assess whether this is likely to be a promising direction for further investigation, we compared the predictions generated by different models by computing correlations between the predictions generated by these models. The correlations were very high: the average correlations between predictions generated by *different learners* trained on the *same data sets* were r=0.97 (min r=0.92). Average correlation between predictions generated by the *same learner* trained on *different datasets* was also r=0.98 (min r=0.95). In other words, different learners trained on different corpora seem to be producing essentially the same predictions; this suggests that model combination strategies are unlikely to be very effective.

6 Error analysis

To better understand the source of errors on the MAIN corpus, we conducted qualitative error analysis of 80 responses (20 per score level) with the worst scoring error, based on predictions generated using OLS linear regression.

Inconsistencies in human scoring accounted for discrepancies for 25 of these responses. For an additional 18 responses (11 of these with a human score of 4), the ASR hypothesis was flagged as particularly inaccurate.

For the remaining responses we observed different patterns at different score levels. At lower score points (1 and 2), responses incorrectly scored by the automated scoring engine often contained individually intelligible words or even small chunks of locally grammatical strings but the response as a whole was incoherent or incomprehensible in terms of content. Out of the 37 re-

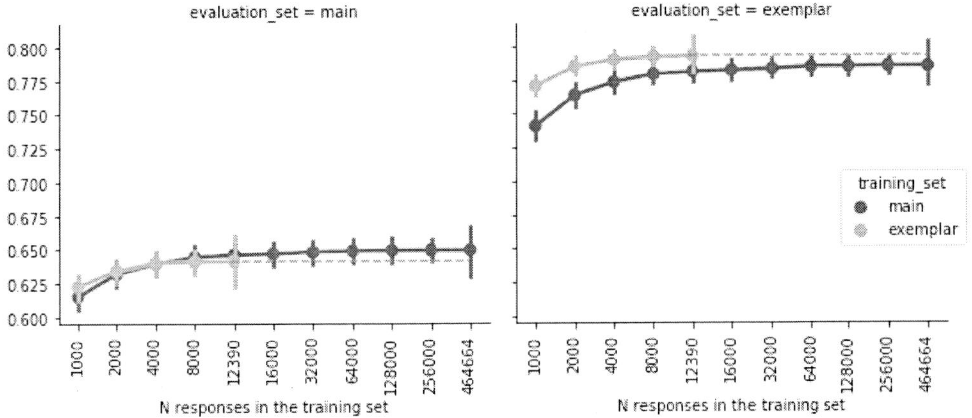

Figure 1: Model performance (r) depending on the size of the training set for different combinations of training and test sets. The dotted line indicates the maximum performance obtained on the EXEMPLAR responses to facilitate comparison with the MAIN set. Note that the x-axis is plotted on a logarithmic scale.

maining responses, 15 fell into this category, most of them for score 1 (13 responses). These responses were over-scored by the automated scoring engine based on fluency features or grammar features that correctly captured local patterns.

The pattern was reversed at score levels 3 and 4: these responses were clear, intelligible and syntactically well-formed, with content that was tightly targeted to the question. Yet the speech was halting, choppy, slow and contained frequent long pauses. Out of the 22 remaining responses, 9 fell into this category. As a result they were scored lower by the automated scoring engine since such fluency patterns are generally more common of responses at lower score levels.

7 Discussion

Based on the results of our evaluations reported in Table 2, our initial hypothesis for research question (1) has to be rejected for the MAIN corpus: the results show that there is no observable effect in scoring model performance based on the training set (the large corpus with randomly selected responses (MAIN) or the EXEMPLAR corpus) — average prediction error and Pearson r correlations vary only minimally for these two evaluation corpora when using the different training corpora for scoring model building. Training on EXEMPLAR responses has a small advantage over training on the same number of randomly sampled responses from the MAIN corpus when the models are evaluated on EXEMPLAR responses, but this advantage disappears by using a training corpus with sufficiently large number of randomly sampled responses.

On the other hand, our initial hypothesis for research question (2) is confirmed, i.e., the system performance increases substantially when evaluating scoring models on the EXEMPLAR corpus vs. the MAIN corpus ($r = 0.80$ vs. $r = 0.66$). Additionally, our results also show that all 7 regressors we used to build scoring models perform similarly on our data, which is also borne out by high correlations between scores generated by the different learners.

In short, we can summarize that while the properties of the *evaluation set* matter substantially, this does not hold for the *training set* (as long as its size is not too small). On the one hand, this is somewhat disappointing since we would have hoped to obtain better scoring models when using exemplar responses for training; on the other hand, it is encouraging to see how well automated scoring models work ($r = 0.80$) when evaluated on data where human raters are in agreement about the response scores (true gold standard data). In some sense, making errors on clear-cut cases is a bigger validity problem for a scoring system than making errors on cases where the correct label is somewhat controversial. Evaluation on clear-cut cases thus provides additional information about the performance of a scoring system.

We now consider possible reasons for the lack of substantial improvement in performance on EXEMPLAR data when trained on EXEMPLAR data vs. a sufficiently large MAIN corpus. Based on Beigman and Klebanov (2009), the potential for hard case bias — namely, a situation where the presence of hard cases in the training data compromises performance on "easy" test data — could arise when the hard cases have an adversarial placement in the feature space for a particular learning algorithm. For example, they show that the clustering of hard cases in an area that is far from the separation plane creates the potential for hard case bias for a system that is trained through hinge-loss minimization. Our results thus represent good news for the feature set: it is apparently rich enough to not represent data in a way that puts a large cluster of hard cases in an unfortunate location, for a variety of learning algorithms. That said, we do observe that Linear SVR suffers from some hard case bias, as it performs somewhat worse on EXEMPLAR responses when trained on MAIN vs. EXEMPLAR (0.767 vs. 0.782). We also note that hard case bias does emerge for Linear Regression when the amount of noisy training data is relatively small; a larger dataset thus seems important for counteracting the detrimental effect of the presence of hard cases in the training data.

We also performed manual error analysis on a small set of highly discrepant machine and human scores and found that a substantial subset of the data investigated had human rater errors that caused score discrepancies (around 30%). In most other cases, the discrepancies between machine and human scores could be attributed to situations where different sub-constructs of speaking proficiency diverged substantially from each other. For instance, we identified responses with locally correct grammar and reasonable fluency but with no meaningful content. For the latter reason, such responses are scored very low by human raters but somewhat higher by the machine, e.g., based on features related to fluency and local grammatical accuracy. We also found the opposite, i.e., responses with very good content but sub-optimal fluency characteristics. Human raters typically award high scores for such responses if the sub-optimal fluency aspects do not interfere substantially with intelligibility of the response, but the machine scores are lower based on the sub-optimal performance in the fluency domain.

For both scenarios, it is important to mention that our scoring models do not contain any features related to content or discourse; developing and adding such features to the automated speech scoring system is an important goal for future work to remediate the score discrepancy in these situations, in addition to the overall goal of providing a comprehensive coverage of the speaking construct in an automated speech scoring system.

8 Conclusion

In this study, we compared the effect of using two different corpora of scored spoken responses for training and evaluation of automated scoring models built using seven different regressor machine learning systems. The MAIN corpus contained a large set of randomly selected responses from an English language assessment. The EXEMPLAR corpus contained responses where multiple human raters had agreed on the scores.

Our main findings were that while the choice of training corpus has no substantial effect on scoring model performance, as long as the noisier training set is sufficiently large, the reverse is true for the choice of evaluation corpus: human-machine score correlations were as high as $r = 0.80$ for the EXEMPLAR corpus, no matter what training corpus was used to build the model or what regressor machine learning system was used. This compares to $r = 0.65$ when using the MAIN corpus for evaluation.

Unfortunately, contrary to our initial assumptions, it is not possible to achieve improvement in performance by simply training the model on the EXEMPLAR corpus, since the model performance in our experiments was only minimally dependent on the training corpus. While we observed that the number of responses necessary to achieve optimal performance is higher when the model is trained on the randomly-selected responses from the MAIN corpus than on the EXEMPLAR corpus, the practical demands of collecting the EXEMPLAR corpus of such quality as used in this study in many real-life situations are likely to outweigh the cost of collecting a larger set of slightly more 'noisy' data, especially considering a very limited gain in performance.

Furthermore, we observed effects of differential profiles of responses in terms of various speaking proficiency sub-constructs: e.g., for responses with low human scores where the content is less well rendered than fluency, machine scores may be inflated; the reverse holds for responses with high human scores where the content is very well rendered but where machine scores can be lower due to lack of fluency.

One main goal for future work derived from our results and the associated error analysis is that features capturing content aspects of the response need to be developed and integrated into the automated speech scoring system to yield a more comprehensive construct coverage and to mitigate the observed effects of responses that exhibit differential performance across various speech subconstructs.

Acknowledgments

We thank Pamela Mollaun for discussing with us many aspects of this work and for helping us obtain the exemplar responses; Matt Mulholland for extracting the features for various corpora used in this study; Keelan Evanini, Su-Youn Yoon, Larry Davis and three anonymous BEA reviewers for their comments and suggestions.

References

Yigal Attali and Jill Burstein. 2006. Automated essay scoring with e-rater®v.2. *Journal of Technology, Learning, and Assessment* 4(3). https://ejournals.bc.edu/ojs/index.php/jtla/article/view/1650/1492.

Eyal Beigman and Beata Beigman Klebanov. 2009. Learning with annotation noise. In *Proceedings of the Joint Conference of the 47th Annual Meeting of the ACL and the 4th International Joint Conference on Natural Language Processing of the AFNLP - ACL-IJCNLP '09*. Association for Computational Linguistics, Morristown, NJ, USA, August, page 280. https://doi.org/10.3115/1687878.1687919.

Beata Beigman Klebanov and Eyal Beigman. 2009. From Annotator Agreement to Noise Models. *Computational Linguistics* 35(4):495–503. https://doi.org/10.1162/coli.2009.35.4.35402.

Beata Beigman Klebanov and Eyal Beigman. 2014. Difficult Cases: From Data to Learning, and Back. In *Proceedings of the 52nd Annual Meeting of the Association for Computational Linguistics*. Baltimore, Maryland, pages 390–396. http://aclweb.org/anthology/P14-2064.

Jared Bernstein, Jian Cheng, and Masanori Suzuki. 2010. Fluency and Structural Complexity as Predictors of L2 Oral Proficiency. *Proceedings of Interspeech 2010, Makuhari, Chiba, Japan* pages 1241–1244. https://www.isca-speech.org/archive/interspeech_2010/i10_1241.html.

M. D. Carey, R. H. Mannell, and P. K. Dunn. 2011. Does a Rater's Familiarity with a Candidate's Pronunciation Affect the Rating in Oral Proficiency Interviews? *Language Testing* 28(2):201–219. https://doi.org/10.1177/0265532210393704.

Lei Chen. 2012. Utilizing cumulative logit models and human computation on automated speech assessment. In *Proceedings of the 7th Workshop on the Innovative Use of NLP for Building Educational Applications*. pages 73–79. http://dl.acm.org/citation.cfm?id=2390393.

Larry Davis. 2016. The influence of training and experience on rater performance in scoring spoken language. *Language Testing* 33(1):117–135. https://doi.org/10.1177/0265532215582282.

Thomas Eckes. 2008. *Rater types in writing performance assessments: A classification approach to rater variability*, volume 25. https://doi.org/10.1177/0265532207086780.

Michael Heilman and Nitin Madnani. 2015. The impact of training data on automated short answer scoring performance. In *Proceedings of the Tenth Workshop on Innovative Use of NLP for Building Educational Applications, BEA@NAACL-HLT 2015, June 4, 2015, Denver, Colorado, USA*. pages 81–85. http://aclweb.org/anthology/W/W15/W15-0610.pdf.

Derrick Higgins, Xiaoming Xi, Klaus Zechner, and David Williamson. 2011. A three-stage approach to the automated scoring of spontaneous spoken responses. *Computer Speech & Language* 25(2):282–306. https://doi.org/10.1016/j.csl.2010.06.001.

Andrea Horbach, Alexis Palmer, and Magdalena Wolska. 2014. Finding a Tradeoff between Accuracy and Rater's Workload in Grading Clustered Short Answers. *Proceedings of the Ninth International Conference on Language Resources and Evaluation (LREC'14)* pages 588–595. http://www.lrec-conf.org/proceedings/lrec2014/pdf/887_Paper.pdf.

Emily K. Jamison and Iryna Gurevych. 2015. Noise or additional information? Leveraging crowdsource annotation item agreement for natural language tasks. In *Proceedings of EMNLP 2015*. Association for Computational Linguistics, Lisbon, Portugal, pages 291–297. http://aclweb.org/anthology/D15-1035.

G. Ling, P. Mollaun, and X. Xi. 2014. A Study on the Impact of Fatigue on Human Raters when Scoring Speaking Responses. *Language Testing* 31:479–499. https://doi.org/10.1177/0265532214530699.

Anastassia Loukina, Nitin Madnani, and Aoife Cahill. 2017. Speech- and Text-driven Features for Automated Scoring of English Speaking Tasks. In

Proceedings of the First Workshop on Speech-Centric Natural Language Processing. Association for Computational Linguistics, Copenhagen, Denmark., pages 67–77. http://www.aclweb.org/anthology/W17-4609.

Anastassia Loukina, Klaus Zechner, Lei Chen, and Michael Heilman. 2015. Feature selection for automated speech scoring. In *Proceedings of the Tenth Workshop on Innovative Use of NLP for Building Educational Applications*. pages 12–19. http://www.aclweb.org/anthology/W15-0602.

Nitin Madnani, Anastassia Loukina, Alina Von Davier, Jill Burstein, and Aoife Cahill. 2017. Building Better Open-Source Tools to Support Fairness in Automated Scoring. In *Proceedings of the First Workshop on ethics in Natural Language Processing, Valencia, Spain, April 4th, 2017*. Association for Computational Linguistics, Valencia, pages 41–52. http://www.aclweb.org/anthology/W17-1605.

Héctor Martínez Alonso, Barbara Plank, Arne Skjærholt, and Anders Søgaard. 2015. Learning to parse with IAA-weighted loss. In *Proceedings of the 2015 Conference of the North American Chapter of the Association for Computational Linguistics: Human Language Technologies*. Association for Computational Linguistics, Denver, Colorado, pages 1357–1361. http://www.aclweb.org/anthology/N15-1152.

Ellis B. Page. 1966. The Imminence of ... Grading Essays by Computer. *The Phi Delta Kappan* 47(5):238–243.

F. Pedregosa, G. Varoquaux, A. Gramfort, V. Michel, B. Thirion, O. Grisel, M. Blondel, P. Prettenhofer, R. Weiss, V. Dubourg, J. Vanderplas, A. Passos, D. Cournapeau, M. Brucher, M. Perrot, and E. Duchesnay. 2011. Scikit-learn: Machine learning in Python. *Journal of Machine Learning Research* 12:2825–2830. http://www.jmlr.org/papers/v12/pedregosa11a.html.

Randall D. Penfield. 2016. Fairness in Test Scoring. In Neil J. Dorans and Linda L. Cook, editors, *Fairness in Educational Assessment and Measurement*, Routledge, pages 55–76.

Barbara Plank, Dirk Hovy, and Anders Søgaard. 2014. Learning part-of-speech taggers with inter-annotator agreement loss. In *Proceedings of the 14th Conference of the European Chapter of the Association for Computational Linguistics*. Association for Computational Linguistics, Gothenburg, Sweden, pages 742–751. http://www.aclweb.org/anthology/E14-1078.

Daniel Povey, Arnab Ghoshal, Gilles Boulianne, Lukas Burget, Ondrej Glembek, Nagendra Goel, Mirko Hannemann, Petr Motlicek, Yanmin Qian, Petr Schwarz, Jan Silovsky, Georg Stemmer, and Karel Vesely. 2011. The Kaldi speech recognition toolkit.

In *Proceedings of the Workshop on Automatic Speech Recognition and Understanding*.

Dennis Reidsma and Jean Carletta. 2008. Reliability Measurement without Limits. *Computational Linguistics* 34(3):319–326. https://doi.org/10.1162/coli.2008.34.3.319.

Roy Schwartz, Omri Abend, Roi Reichart, and Ari Rappoport. 2011. Neutralizing linguistically problematic annotations in unsupervised dependency parsing evaluation. In *Proceedings of the 49th Annual Meeting of the Association for Computational Linguistics: Human Language Technologies - Volume 1*. Association for Computational Linguistics, Stroudsburg, PA, USA, HLT '11, pages 663–672. http://dl.acm.org/citation.cfm?id=2002472.2002557.

Skipper Seabold and Josef Perktold. 2010. Statsmodels: Econometric and statistical modeling with Python. In *Proceedings of the Python in Science Conference*. pages 57–61. https://conference.scipy.org/proceedings/scipy2010/seabold.html.

Shayle R. Searle, George Casella, and Charles E. Mc-Culloch. 1992. *Variance Components*. Wiley-Interscience.

Tom A.B. Snijders and Roel J. Bosker. 2012. *Multilevel Analysis*. Sage, London, 2nd edition.

Jidong Tao, Shabnam Ghaffarzadegan, Lei Chen, and Klaus Zechner. 2016. Exploring deep learning architectures for automatically grading non-native spontaneous speech. In *2016 IEEE International Conference on Acoustics, Speech and Signal Processing (ICASSP)*. IEEE, pages 6140–6144. https://doi.org/10.1109/ICASSP.2016.7472857.

Zhen Wang and Alina von Davier. 2014. Monitoring of scoring using the e-rater automated scoring system and human raters on a writing test. *ETS Research Report Series* 2014(1):1–21. https://doi.org/10.1002/ets2.12005.

David M. Williamson, Xiaoming Xi, and F. Jay Breyer. 2012. A Framework for Evaluation and Use of Automated Scoring. *Educational Measurement: Issues and Practice* 31(1):2–13. https://doi.org/10.1111/j.1745-3992.2011.00223.x.

Klaus Zechner, Derrick Higgins, Xiaoming Xi, and David M. Williamson. 2009. Automatic scoring of non-native spontaneous speech in tests of spoken English. *Speech Communication* 51(10):883–895. https://doi.org/10.1016/j.specom.2009.04.009.

Torsten Zesch, Michael Heilman, and Aoife Cahill. 2015. Reducing Annotation Efforts in Supervised Short Answer Scoring. In *Proceedings of the Tenth Workshop on Innovative Use of NLP for Building Educational Applications*. Denver, Colorado,

pages 124–132. http://www.aclweb.org/
anthology/W15-0615.

A Appendix: supplementary tables

| Evaluation set | MAIN | | | EXEMPLAR | | |
Training set	MAIN	MAIN*	EXEMPLAR	MAIN	MAIN*	EXEMPLAR
MLP Regressor	0.525	0.535	0.538	0.418	0.435	0.421
Huber Regressor	0.526	0.536	0.539	0.422	0.438	0.420
Linear Regression	0.525	0.538	0.539	0.421	0.436	0.419
Elastic Net	0.531	0.536	0.540	0.432	0.438	0.425
Linear SVR	0.535	0.544	0.542	0.443	0.451	0.425
Gradient Boosting Regressor	0.523	0.544	0.543	0.413	0.442	0.423
Random Forest Regressor	0.531	0.545	0.550	0.424	0.448	0.430

Table 3: Corresponding RMSE coefficients for values reported in Table 2.

| Evaluation set | MAIN | | EXEMPLAR | |
| Training set | MAIN | EXEMPLAR | MAIN | EXEMPLAR |
N train				
1000	0.615	0.623	0.741	0.771
2000	0.632	0.634	0.764	0.785
4000	0.639	0.640	0.773	0.790
8000	0.645	0.641	0.779	0.792
12390	0.646	0.641	0.781	0.793
16000	0.647		0.782	
32000	0.648		0.783	
64000	0.649		0.785	
128000	0.649		0.785	
256000	0.649		0.785	
464664	0.649		0.785	

Table 4: The values for the learning curves presented in Figure 1.

Using Paraphrasing and Memory-Augmented Models
to Combat Data Sparsity in Question Interpretation
with a Virtual Patient Dialogue System

Lifeng Jin,[1] David King,[1] Amad Hussein,[2] Michael White,[1] and Douglas Danforth[3]

[1]Department of Linguistics, [2]Department of Computer Science and Engineering,
[3]Department of Family Medicine
The Ohio State University, Columbus, OH, USA
{jin, king, mwhite}@ling.osu.edu
amadh881@gmail.com, doug.danforth@osumc.edu

Abstract

When interpreting questions in a virtual patient dialogue system, one must inevitably tackle the challenge of a long tail of relatively infrequently asked questions. To make progress on this challenge, we investigate the use of paraphrasing for data augmentation and neural memory-based classification, finding that the two methods work best in combination. In particular, we find that the neural memory-based approach not only outperforms a straight CNN classifier on low frequency questions, but also takes better advantage of the augmented data created by paraphrasing, together yielding a nearly 10% absolute improvement in accuracy on the least frequently asked questions.

1 Introduction

To develop skills such as taking a patient history and developing a differential diagnosis, medical students interact with actors who play the part of a patient with a specific medical history and pathology, known as Standardized Patients (SPs). Although SPs remain the standard way to test medical students on such skills, SPs are expensive and can behave inconsistently from student to student. A virtual patient dialogue system aims to overcome these issues as well as provide a means of supplying automated feedback on the quality of the medical student's interaction with the patient (see Figure 1).

In previous work, Danforth et al. (2009, 2013); Maicher et al. (2017) used a hand-crafted pattern-matching system called ChatScript together with a 3D avatar in order to collect chatted dialogues and provide useful student feedback (Danforth et al., 2016). ChatScript matches input text using hand-written patterns and outputs a scripted response for each dialogue turn. With sufficient pattern-writing skill and effort, pattern matching with ChatScript

can achieve relatively high accuracy, but it is unable to easily leverage increasing amounts of training data, somewhat brittle regarding misspellings, and can be difficult to maintain as new questions and patterns are added.

To address these issues, Jin et al. (2017) developed an ensemble of word- and character-based convolutional neural networks (CNNs) for question identification in the system that attained 79% accuracy, comparable to the hand-crafted ChatScript patterns. Moreover, they found that since the CNN ensemble's error profile was very different from the pattern-based approach, combining the two systems yielded a nearly 10% boost in system accuracy and an error reduction of 47% in comparison to using ChatScript alone. Perhaps not surprisingly, the CNN-based classifier outperformed the pattern-matching system on frequently asked questions, but on the least frequently asked questions—where data sparsity was an issue— the CNN performed much worse, only achieving 46.5% accuracy on the quintile of questions asked least often.

In this paper, we aim to combat this data sparsity issue by investigating (1) whether paraphrasing can be used to create novel synthetic training items, examining in particular lexical substitution from several resources (Miller, 1995; Le and Mikolov, 2014; Ganitkevitch et al., 2013; Cocos and Callison-Burch, 2016) and neural MT for back-translation (Mallinson et al., 2017); and (2) whether neural memory-based approaches developed for one-shot learning (Kaiser et al., 2017) perform better on low-frequency questions. We find that the two methods work best in combination, as the neural memory-based approach not only outperforms the straight CNN classifier on low frequency questions, but also takes better advantage of the augmented data created by paraphrasing. Together, the two methods yield nearly

13

Proceedings of the Thirteenth Workshop on Innovative Use of NLP for Building Educational Applications, pages 13–23
New Orleans, Louisiana, June 5, 2018. ©2018 Association for Computational Linguistics

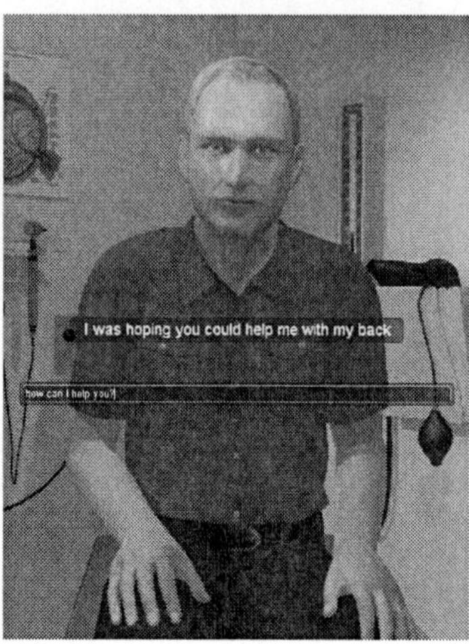

Figure 1: Virtual Patient Dialogue System

a 10% absolute improvement in accuracy on the quintile of least frequently asked questions.

2 Related Work

Question identification is a task that can be approached in at least two ways. One way is to treat it as a multiclass classification problem (e.g., using logistic regression), which can take advantage of class-specific features but tends to require a substantial amount of training data for each class. Formally, letting q be the candidate question, Y be a set of question classes and ϕ a feature extractor, we seek to find the most likely label $\hat{y}$:

$$\hat{y} = \underset{y \in Y}{\operatorname{argmax}} \frac{e^{\phi(q,y)}}{\sum_{y' \in Y} e^{\phi(q,y')}}.$$

Alternatively, a pairwise setup can be used. For example, for each class a binary classification decision can be made as to whether a given question represents a paraphrase of a member of the class, choosing the highest confidence match. More generally, let $q_i^y \in L^y$ be the i-th question variant for label y (where the question variants are the paraphrases of the label appearing in the training data); given some similarity metric σ, we seek to find the label $\hat{y}$ with the most similar question variant $q_i^{\hat{y}}$ in the set $L^{\hat{y}}$ to the candidate question q:

$$\hat{y} = \underset{y \in Y}{\operatorname{argmax}} \max_{q_i^y \in L^y} \sigma(q, q_i^y)$$

Early work on question answering (Ravichandran et al., 2003) found that treating the task as a maximum entropy re-ranking problem outperformed using the same system as a multiclass classifier. By contrast, DeVault et al. (2011) observed that maximum entropy multiclass classifiers performed well with simple n-gram features when each class had a sufficient number of training examples. Jaffe et al. (2015) explored a log-linear pairwise ranking model for question identification in a virtual patient dialogue system and found it outperformed a multiclass baseline along the lines of DeVault et al. (2011). However, Jaffe et al. used a much smaller dataset with only about 915 user turns, less than one-fourth as many as in the current dataset. For this larger dataset, a straightforward logistic regression multiclass classifier outperforms a pairwise ranking model.

In general it appears reasonable to expect that the comparative effectiveness of multiclass vs. pairwise approaches depends on the amount of training data, and that pairwise ranking methods have potential advantages for cross-domain and one-shot learning tasks (Vinyals et al., 2016; Kaiser et al., 2017) where data is sparse or nonexistent. Notably, in the closely related task of short-answer scoring, Sakaguchi et al. (2015) found that pairwise methods could be effectively combined with regression-based approaches to improve performance in sparse-data cases.

Other work involving dialogue utterance classification has traditionally required a large amount of data. For example, Suendermann-Oeft et al. (2009) acquired 500,000 dialogues with over 2 million utterances, observing that statistical systems outperform rule-based ones as the amount of data increases. Crowdsourcing for collecting additional dialogues (Ramanarayanan et al., 2017) could alleviate data sparsity problems for rare categories by providing additional training examples, but this technique is limited to more general domains that do not require special training/skills. In the current medical domain, workers on common crowdsourcing platforms are unlikely to have the expertise required to take a patient's medical history in a natural way, so any data collected with this method would likely suffer quality issues and fail to generalize to real medical student dialogues. Rossen and Lok (2012) have developed an approach for collecting dialogue data for virtual patient systems, but their approach does not directly address the issue that even as the number of dialogues collected increases, there can remain a long

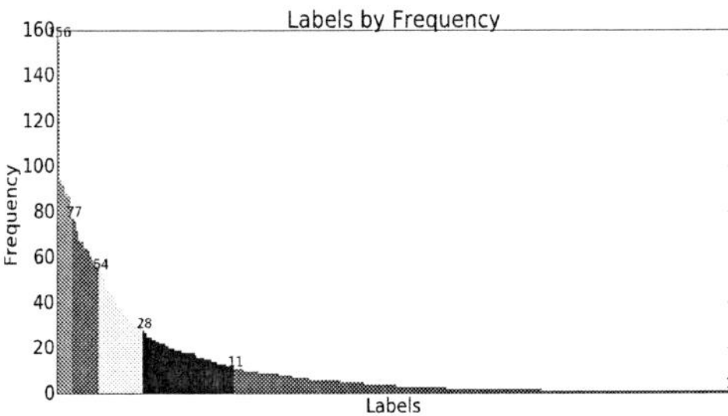

Figure 2: Label frequency distribution is extremely long-tailed, with few frequent labels and many infrequent labels. Values are shown above quintile boundaries.

tail of relevant but infrequently asked questions.

As an alternative to crowdsourcing, we pursue paraphrasing for data augmentation in this paper, focusing on the simplest methods to employ, namely lexical substitution and neural back-translation (see Section 5). The idea is to augment the observed question instances for questions with infrequent labels in the dataset with automatically generated paraphrases, with the aim of making such questions easier to recognize using machine-learned models. In future work, we plan to explore more complex paraphrasing methods, including syntactic paraphrasing (Duan et al., 2016) and inducing paraphrase templates from aligned paraphrases (Fader et al., 2013).

3   Data Imbalance

Our dataset currently consists of 4330 question-answer pairs from 94 dialogues between first year medical students and the virtual patient. After classifying an asked question as having a certain label, the virtual patient replies with the canned response for that label, as illustrated in Table 1. Unfortunately, the labels do not have a uniform distribution with regards to the number of variants each label has (that is, the number of question instances for that label in the dataset). In fact, most of the labels are underrepresented.

On average, each question label has 12 variants, but 8 labels account for nearly 20% of the data, while 256 labels account for the bottom 20% (Figure 2). We define a rare label to be any label that is in that set of 256 infrequent labels. Supplementing the data to account for this imbalance is the primary focus of our work.

4   Memory-Augmented CNN Classifier

Because of the data sparsity issue, we cast the problem of sentence classification for infrequent labels as a problem of few-shot learning. In particular, we use Kaiser et al.'s (2017) memory module together with a CNN encoder (Kim, 2014; Jin et al., 2017) as our main model, the memory-augmented CNN classifier (MA-CNN). Our aim is to take advantage of the MA-CNN's one-shot learning capability to mitigate the issue of data sparsity and also to make better use of data augmentation to achieve better performance.

4.1   The CNN encoder

The CNN encoder follows Kim (2014) and Jin et al. (2017). We briefly summarize the architecture here and direct interested readers to these two papers for implementation details. There are four layers in the encoder: an embedding layer, a convolution layer, a max-pooling layer and a linear layer. Let $\mathbf{x}_i \in \mathbb{R}^k$ be a k-dimensional embedding for the i-th element of the sentence s. We concatenate all of the element embeddings to get $\mathbf{S} \in \mathbb{R}^{|s| \times k}$ as the representation of the whole sentence.

The convolution layer may have many kernels, which are defined as weight matrices $\mathbf{w}_j \in \mathbb{R}^{hk}$, where h is the width of the kernel. They slide across the sentence representation and then pass through a nonlinearity to produce a feature map $\mathbf{c}_j \in \mathbb{R}^{|s|-h+1}$. Then the max-pooling layer uses max-over-time pooling (Collobert et al., 2011) on the feature maps to ensure fixed-dimensional outputs.

Finally, we concatenate all the outputs from all the kernels into a single vector $\mathbf{o}$, multiply it with the weight matrix $\mathbf{W}_l$ and apply $p2$-normalization to it as the final fully-connected neural network layer for the CNN encoder:

$$\mathbf{e} = \frac{\mathbf{o} \cdot \mathbf{W}_l + \mathbf{b}_l}{\|\mathbf{o} \cdot \mathbf{W}_l + \mathbf{b}_l\|} \tag{1}$$

Here $\mathbf{W}_l$ and $\mathbf{b}_l$ are the weight matrix and the bias term for the final layer, respectively.

4.2   The memory module

We follow Kaiser et al. (2017) for implementation of our memory module. The memory module is a tuple of three matrices $\mathbf{K}$, $\mathbf{V}$ and $\mathbf{A}$, which stores

Student question	Label detected	Canned response
hello mr. wilkins	hello mr	hello doctor. i am so glad to see you.
can you tell me a little about your issue	<None>	i'm sorry, i don't understand that question. would you restate it?
what brings you in today	what brings you in today	i was hoping you could help me with my back pain, it really hurts! it has been awful.

Table 1: Sample interactions between a first year medical student and the virtual patient. The virtual patient's task is to accurately detect the kind of question the medical student is asking and then reply with the appropriate canned response.

one key, one label and one age of one memory entry in each corresponding row. A key is an encoded presentation of a training item, a label is the class identifier that the key belongs to, and the age is the number of memory updates that have taken place since the key was inserted or updated. To use the memory, a normalized query item $\mathbf{q}$ is multiplied by the key matrix

$$\mathbf{s}^{\top} = \mathbf{q} \cdot \mathbf{K} \qquad (2)$$

to yield a vector of cosine similarities $\mathbf{s}$ between the query and every entry in the memory. The prediction made by the memory is then $\hat{v} = \mathbf{V}[\hat{n}]$, where $\hat{n} = \mathrm{argmax}(\mathbf{s})$ and $\hat{v}$ is the predicted class label.

The memory operations include insert, update and erase, and loss calculation of the memory depends on the memory operations, therefore we briefly summarize them here. Let $\hat{n}$ be the row index in $\mathbf{s}$ with the highest similarity score such that $\mathbf{V}[\hat{n}]$ is the true label of the query, $\tilde{n}$ be the row index of the entry with the highest similarity score that has a different label from the true label, and v be the true label. When $\mathbf{s}[\hat{n}] > \mathbf{s}[\tilde{n}]$, the memory loss is a margin loss between the similarity scores at $\hat{n}$ and at $\tilde{n}$ with some margin α:

$$\mathrm{loss} = [\mathbf{s}[\tilde{n}] - \mathbf{s}[\hat{n}] + \alpha]_{+} \qquad (3)$$

In this case, the memory entry at $\hat{n}$ will be updated by replacing it with the normalized average of itself and the query:

$$\mathbf{K}[\hat{n}] \leftarrow \frac{\mathbf{q} + \mathbf{K}[\hat{n}]}{\|\mathbf{q} + \mathbf{K}[\hat{n}]\|} \qquad (4)$$

When $\mathbf{s}[\hat{n}] < \mathbf{s}[\tilde{n}]$, the memory loss is:

$$\mathrm{loss} = [\mathbf{s}[\hat{n}] - \mathbf{s}[\tilde{n}] + \alpha]_{+} \qquad (5)$$

In this case, a new entry is inserted at a previously empty row n':

$$\mathbf{K}[n'] \leftarrow \mathbf{q} \quad \mathbf{V}[n'] \leftarrow v \qquad (6)$$

In both cases, the entry in $\mathbf{A}$ at the update or insert site will be replaced by 0, and all the other entries in $\mathbf{A}$ will add 1. When the memory is full, a new insertion will take place where $A[n']$ is the biggest.

Finally, if there is no entry in $\mathbf{K}$ that has the true label v, the insert operation is carried out without any loss calculation. The erase operation is to reset all three matrices to empty, which is used at the end of a training episode.

4.3 Episodic training and evaluation

We train our memory-augmented CNN classifier using a novel episodic training scheme based on the episodic training scheme used in one-shot learning (Vinyals et al., 2016; Kaiser et al., 2017). The main difference is that in one-shot learning, most tasks offer a balanced dataset with many classes but small numbers of instances per class. In our scenario, the dataset is imbalanced, and some classes may have a large number of instances. Moreover, in evaluation, there are no unseen classes in our case. We modify the episodic training scheme to accommodate these differences.

Episodic training

In training, we define an episode to be a complete k-shot learning trial with gradient updates. At the beginning of each episode, a batch of $|C| \times (k + 1)$ samples, where $|C|$ is the number of classes, is sampled from the training data. The first sample of each class is then encoded and inserted into the memory with no loss calculated, which we call loading the memory. From the second sample on, the encoder encodes each sample, and the memory calculates its loss according to its prediction. After all classes have had one sample to complete this process, the encoder is updated by the gradients calculated with the memory loss. The memory is then updated according to the operations corresponding to its predictions of the seen samples in each shot. When all k shots have been processed, the memory is completely erased ready for the next episode (though naturally the updates to the encoder remain in effect).

It is easy to see that this process involves oversampling, which is a known technique for rebalancing imbalanced datasets. Because each class must have $k + 1$ samples for each episode, the minority classes have to be oversampled. However, experiments show that oversampling itself does not lead to better performance.

Episodic evaluation

In evaluation, we define a support set to be a batch of $|C| \times k$ samples from the training data. For a given test set, we first load the memory, then compare each test item to all the entries in the memory in order to generate the memory prediction for the test item based on the most similar memory entry. This forms the model's 1-shot predictions. Then we update the memory with the second sample for each class and redo the prediction step. We now have the model predictions with 2 shots. We continue to follow this routine until predictions from all k shots have been collected.

Because there is some randomness in how a support set is sampled from the data, we use multiple support sets in evaluation. Since some of the classes have a large number of instances, each randomly sampled support set tends to be sufficiently different from other support sets that using multiple support sets becomes analogous to ensembling different models.

Finally, letting p be the number of support sets, we have $k \times p$ predicted labels for each item in the test set. We use majority voting across all the predicted labels to get the final model prediction. This capitalizes on the ensembled support sets and reduces the variance of the model predictions.

5 Data Augmentation

Since previous work (Jin et al., 2017) showed that the majority of labels in our dataset have 11 variants or fewer, we explore using lexical substitution (McCarthy and Navigli, 2009) and neural machine translation (NMT) back-translation (Mallinson et al., 2017) for data augmentation. The main difference in our use of lexical substitution and previous works' is that our setup is unsupervised, as we have no gold test set for determining acceptable paraphrases. Similarly for the NMT system, we do not know which outputs are

acceptable. To mediate this, we employ the use of both human and automatic filtering of the generated paraphrases with the end-goal of facilitating question label identification for infrequent labels.

5.1 Paraphrase generation

We exploit advances in lexical substitution and NMT to automatically produce paraphrases. We also combine these approaches to determine their collective effectiveness in our downstream label identification task.

Lexical substitution

Lexical substitution has often been held up as a exemplary task for paraphrase generation. In its simplest form, one must simply replace a given word with an appropriate paraphrase, i.e. one that retains most of the original sentence's meaning. As an example, in the question *have you ever been seriously ill?*, *seriously* could be replaced with *severely*, and we would consider this to be an appropriate substitution. However, if we instead substituted *solemnly* for the same word, we would not accept this as the meaning would have deviated too far.

For generating paraphrases, we employ three resources: WordNet (Miller, 1995), Word2Vec (Le and Mikolov, 2014), and paraphrase clusters from Cocos and Callison-Burch (2016). To evaluate these resources, we took the mean average precision (MAP) of a given resource's ability to produce a lexical substitution which matched a word that already existed in another variant for the same label. That is, if the label *how has the pain affected your work?* had only two variants, *has the injury made your job difficult?* and *is it hard for you to do your job?*, and a resource successfully produces the swap of *hard → difficult* (producing the sentence *is it difficult for you to do your job?*), this would positively affect a resource's MAP score. We only performed this evaluation on labels with 30 or more variants as this form of evaluation disproportionately penalizes labels with fewer variants.

These preliminary experiments indicated that pooling candidates from all three resources performed better than any given one alone did. We also found that in the case of multiple word senses (e.g. *bug* meaning an insect, an illness, or a flaw in a program), simply picking the first sense produced a higher MAP score than a variety of other selection algorithms. This is not surprising since, in the case of WordNet, the first synset is the most frequently used sense of a given word. For Cocos and Callison-Burch's semantic clusters, these were ordered by a given cluster's average mutual paraphrase score as annotated in the Paraphrase Database (Ganitkevitch et al., 2013). Although our domain is medical, the dialogues are patient directed, less technical, and more colloquial, allowing us to use such a simple selection method for word sense disambiguation.

For augmenting the data in a way that would help the most sparse labels, we focused our lexical substitution task on labels with less that 11 variants. After pooling all the lexical substitution candidates from each resource, we ranked the substitutions by subtracting the original sentence's n-gram log probability from its paraphrase's.[1] We then extracted the top 100 scoring paraphrases for our initial unfiltered data set.

Neural machine translation

We additionally use Neural Machine Translation (NMT) to generate paraphrases by pivoting between languages. In multiple back-translation, a method developed in Mallinson et al. (2017), we take a given English source sentence and generate n-best translations into a pivot language. This is the forward step. For each pivot translation we generate an m-best list of translations back into English. Thus this backward step yields $n \times m$ paraphrases for a given source sentence, where each paraphrase within this final set has a weight based on which of the original n translations it came from in the forward step and its ranking among the m translations in the back step. Any duplicates within this final set are collapsed and their weights are combined before the set is ranked according to weight. This method favors translations which come from high quality sources (high-ranking translations in the lists n and m) as well as translations which occur multiple times.

In our work we translated each given source sentence into 10-best forward translations and 10-best back translations before finally collapsing and ranking the 100 paraphrases. We used a model from Sennrich et al. (2016) and chose German as our pivot language given the quality of the translations and paraphrases we observed.[2]

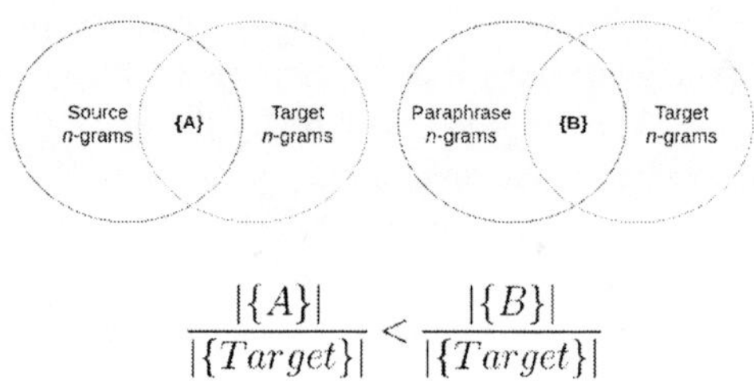

$$\frac{|\{A\}|}{|\{Target\}|} < \frac{|\{B\}|}{|\{Target\}|}$$

Figure 3: A graphical representation of the pseudo-oracle selection process. For a given test item (here *Target*), the n-gram overlap with the paraphrase must be greater than the overlap with the source sentence that paraphrase was derived from.

5.2 Filtering

Since both the lexical substitution and NMT methods generate helpful and unhelpful paraphrases, we needed a way to select useful paraphrases. Although a typical next step might be to manually filter each system's output by hand, we were unsure if expensive human filtering would produce any gain in downstream performance. To explore this question, we experimented with a fully automatic *pseudo*-oracle.

The pseudo-oracle is an automatic filter which we designed to look at a particular test item in a cross-validation setup and select the paraphrases whose n-gram recall with that test item was higher than the original source sentence's, as illustrated in Figure 3. In using this initial step of filtering, we are able to isolate the paraphrases which are most likely to be helpful for classifying question labels. In preliminary experiments using logistic regression, we tested the performance of the pseudo-oracle selection process on the downstream classification task, where we found that the pseudo-oracle was able to facilitate classifying question labels, whereas using all the outputs from the lexical substitution and NMT paraphrase generations systems (without filtering) led to a drop in performance.

Thus, to lessen the expense of human filtering, we used the pseudo-oracle as an automated first step, under the assumption that the selected paraphrases would mostly be kept as well using manual filtering. Next, using the same Gigaword trained language model from Section 5.1, we ranked the lexical substitution and NMT out-

---

[1] We used a 5-gram language model with back off, trained on the Gigaword (Parker et al., 2011).

[2] We found that the pretrained model for German produced the best back-translations when compared to other pretrained models. In future work, we plan to train our own models across various pivot languages to produce an increased variety of paraphrases.

puts. From these ranked lists, we extracted the highest scoring subsets such that each paraphrase not only had a high log probability, but also contributed a unique n-gram (i.e., if two paraphrases contributed the same new n-gram, only the highest scoring paraphrase was selected). This diversity-enhancing filtering reduced the size of the dataset to around 20% of the original raw lexical substitution output and 2.5% of the raw NMT output, greatly lessening human annotation costs.

Since we instructed the annotators (a subset of the authors) to only select useful paraphrases which contributed novel n-grams not present in any other variant, their task was necessarily different from the pseudo-oracle's. Annotators required 16 hours per annotator to manually filter the data. We found that the annotators selected paraphrases which might not necessarily help the downstream task in a cross-validation setup, but which could be expected to help with completely unseen data. For this reason, we chose to combine the pre-selected paraphrases chosen by the pseudo-oracle together with the human-filtered paraphrases in our evaluation.

6 Experiments

We use the best model in Jin et al. (2017), namely a stacked convolutional neural network (Stacked-CNN), together with the model proposed in this work (MA-CNN) in all of the experiments. Our task is to accurately predict a question's label based solely on the typed input from the medical student. With improved accuracy, the virtual patient will be able to more coherently answer the students' questions.

We shuffle the gold dataset first and use 10-fold cross-validation to evaluate our data augmentation process. We specifically focus our analysis on rare labels since that is also where we concentrate our data augmentation efforts. The model we propose here is targeted at improving performance for the rare labels, therefore we are interested in how the model performs on them. Paraphrases are not added to test sets, and paraphrases derived from those test items are filtered from training. Finally, we compute significance using the McNemar test (McNemar, 1947).

6.1 Hyperparameters

We mostly follow Jin et al. (2017) in setting the hyperparameters of the CNN encoder in MA-

CNN. We only use word-based features in the encoder. Following Jin et al. (2017), we set the number of kernels of the encoder of MA-CNN to be 300. We use kernels of widths 3 to 5 for the CNN encoder. All non-linearities in the models are rectified linear units Nair and Hinton (2010). We use Adadelta (Zeiler, 2012) as the optimizer for the whole MA-CNN, and use the recommended values for its hyperparameters ($\rho = 0.9, \epsilon = 1 \times 10^{-6}, learning\_rate = 1.0$). We initialize the embeddings with Word2Vec but allow them to be tuned by the system (Mikolov et al., 2013).

For episodic training, we set the number of shots to be 10. For the episodic evaluation, we use 5 support sets. For each support set, we also do 10-shot evaluation. Therefore for each test item, there are 50 predictions in total. We combine all predictions with majority voting, weighted by the similarity score of each prediction.

6.2 MA-CNN on rare labels

We first train our model MA-CNN and the stacked CNN model from Jin et al. (2017) using just the original VP dataset and explore how the model architecture affects rare label accuracy. Table 2 shows the test accuracy for both models. MA-CNN performs very well on the rare labels. The performance difference between the stacked CNN model and MA-CNN is highly significant, which shows that the pairwise-classification approach paired with episodic training is really powerful on the items which belong to labels with few training instances. We can also see that MA-CNN does not perform as well as the CNN ensemble on all labels, which is consistent with the previous observation that non-pairwise classifiers work better when training data is large. It is worth noting though that the stacked CNN ensemble consists of 10 CNNs that take in word- and character-based features as their inputs, meanwhile the encoder of the MA-CNN is just a single word-based CNN. This further illustrates how a pairwise system which is designed specifically for dealing with classes with few training instances can help improve performance on those classes by using nearest neighbor comparison and episodic training inspired by one-shot learning.

6.3 Generated paraphrases as training data

We further explore the effect on model performance of using the generated paraphrases along with the gold training data in training. We use the

System	Full Acc	Rare Acc
StackedCNN	79.02	46.54
MA-CNN	75.22	**51.78***

Table 2: Test results for the stacked CNN ensemble (Jin et al., 2017) and the memory-augmented CNN classifier (MA-CNN) without any generated paraphrases. The difference of performance on the rare items is highly significant ($p = 9.5 \times 10^{-5}$, *McNemar's test*).

System	Full Acc	Rare Acc
StackedCNN	78.45	53.04
MA-CNN	75.33	**56.14***

Table 3: Test results for the stacked CNN ensemble and the memory-augmented CNN classifier (MA-CNN) with the manually filtered paraphrases. The gain brought by the adding the automatically generated paraphrases into training data for MA-CNN is highly significant ($p = 1.6 \times 10^{-4}$, *McNemar's test*).

manually filtered dataset with both paraphrasing methods, and train both the stacked CNN ensemble and MA-CNN with it plus the gold set. Table 3 shows the results on the test set. First, we can see that both models benefit in terms of rare label accuracy by using the augmented dataset. The difference between MA-CNN trained with only the gold dataset and the augmented dataset is highly significant, showing that the generated paraphrases are of high quality and help MA-CNN to achieve even better performance on the rare labels. It is interesting to note that for full accuracy, performance of both models does not significantly change, showing that the paraphrases are of high enough quality to not be harmful to the frequent labels.

6.4 Effects of data augmentation

Table 4 shows the effect of using pseudo-oracle and manually filtered data on rare labels. We find that the MA-CNN is able to use the data augmentation in a way that directly benefits the rare labels. Specifically, the MA-CNN benefits from the human filtered data, indicating that it benefits from information provided to it that raw n-gram overlap does not capture. At the same time, however, filtering using the pseudo-oracle evidently provides a reasonable approximation of what improvements in accuracy can be obtained with human filtering of the generated paraphrases.

System	Rare Acc
Pseudo-oracle	54.87
Manual	**56.14**

Table 4: Test results for the memory-augmented CNN classifier (MA-CNN) with different filtering techniques.

Paraphrases	Rare Acc
No paraphrases	51.78
Lexical substitution	53.16
Neural Machine Translation	55.22
Both	**56.14**

Table 5: Test results for the memory-augmented CNN classifier (MA-CNN) with different subsets of the manual filtered paraphrases generated using different paraphrase methods.

6.5 Quality of generated paraphrases

We also want to see how the performance on rare labels is connected to the method with which the paraphrases are generated. We use the individual subsets each of which is generated by a single method to augment the training data. Table 5 shows how these methods compete against each other. Surprisingly, simple lexical substitution is already good at providing information that is helpful to MA-CNN, but the neural machine back translation is an even better method at providing paraphrases that have positive impact on rare label accuracy. We inspect the paraphrases generated by both methods and find that paraphrases from back translation are generally more diverse in phrasal structure and contain more novel words than those generated with lexical substitution. The combined dataset gives further improvement, showing that lexical substitution and neural machine translation are at least partially complementary to each other as generation methods.

6.6 Combining the stacked CNN and the MA-CNN

Given the fact that the MA-CNN performs very well on rare labels, but not so well on all labels, it is interesting to see if a combined system with the stacked CNN and MA-CNN can provide a further performance increase. We here choose a relatively simple logistic regression model as our model combiner, though a more sophisticated model could be used in principle. Using 1-5 grams of words and stemmed words as well as 2-5 grams

System	Full Acc	Rare Acc
StackedCNN	79.02	46.54
MA-CNN	75.33	**56.14**
Combiner	**79.86*****	50.98

Table 6: Test results for the combiner as well as the two combined subsystems: the stacked CNN ensemble trained with gold and the memory-augmented CNN classifier trained with gold and generated paraphrases. The gain compared to stacked CNN on full accuracy is highly significant ($p = 1.9 \times 10^{-9}$, *McNemar's test*).

of characters, we trained the model to predict the rarity of a label for a question, i.e. if a candidate question belongs to a rare label or not. This rarity predictor gets 94.2% accuracy on all labels, and 78.1% accuracy on rare labels. Note that the majority baseline for all labels is 80%, but for rare labels it is 20%. This rarity predictor serves as our combiner; that is, we use the combiner to choose whose result to trust between the two classification systems. If the combiner predicts that an item belongs to a rare label, we choose the prediction from the MA-CNN; if the combiner instead predicts it belongs to a frequent label, we choose the prediction for it from the stacked CNN. This is done with 10-fold cross validation, just like how the classifiers were trained above.

The stacked CNN model we use here is the one trained with only gold training data, which is the model with the best accuracy on all labels. We use the MA-CNN model trained with both gold and generated data. With the combiner, we get 50.98% accuracy on rare labels, and 79.86% accuracy on all labels, as shown in Table 6. The result indicates that the two systems are complementary to each other, and simple combination is already effective in providing a significant performance boost. Although the accuracy on rare labels is not as high as the MA-CNN by itself, it is higher than the stacked CNN model by 5 points, and all of these points are translated into an accuracy increase on all labels that is close to 1 point.

7 Conclusion

In this paper, we have investigated the use of paraphrasing for data augmentation and neural memory-based classification in order to tackle the challenge of a long tail of relatively infrequently asked questions in a virtual patient dialogue system. We find that both lexical substitution and neural back-translation yield paraphrases of ob-

served questions that improve system performance on rare labels once the generated paraphrases are manually filtered down to ones taken to be useful, with neural back-translation contributing more to gains in accuracy than lexical substitution. We also find that neural memory-based classification with a novel method of episodic training outperforms a straight CNN classifier on low frequency questions and takes better advantage of the generated paraphrases, together yielding a nearly 10% absolute improvement in accuracy on the least frequently asked questions. Finally, using a simple logistic regression model to combine the predictions of the straight CNN and memory-based classifier, we find that the combined system performs better on all labels, and the gain is from more accurate predictions of rare labels. We expect these gains to yield increased user engagement and ultimately better learning outcomes. In future work, we plan to investigate using the memory-based classifier for fully automatic paraphrase filtering as well as more advanced methods of paraphrasing, including deep generative paraphrasing, syntactic paraphrasing and using aligned paraphrases to induce paraphrase templates. More powerful models may also be explored to better combine the models.

Acknowledgments

Thanks to Kellen Maicher for creating the virtual environment and to Evan Jaffe, Eric Fosler-Lussier and William Schuler for feedback and discussion. This project was supported by funding from the Department of Health and Human Services Health Resources and Services Administration (HRSA D56HP020687), the National Board of Medical Examiners Edward J. Stemmler Education Research Fund (NBME 1112-064), and the National Science Foundation (NSF IIS 1618336). The project does not necessarily reflect NBME policy, and NBME support provides no official endorsement. We thank Ohio Supercomputer Center (1987) for computation support.

References

Anne Cocos and Chris Callison-Burch. 2016. Clustering paraphrases by word sense. In *Proceedings of the 2016 Conference of the North American Chapter of the Association for Computational Linguistics: Human Language Technologies*, pages 1463–1472.

Ronan Collobert, Jason Weston, Lon Bottou, Michael

Karlen, Koray Kavukcuoglu, and Pavel Kuksa. 2011. Natural Language Processing (Almost) from Scratch. *Journal of Machine Learning Research*, 12:2493–2537.

Douglas Danforth, A. Price, Kellen Maicher, D. Post, Beth Liston, Daniel Clinchot, Cynthia Ledford, D. Way, and Holly Cronau. 2013. Can virtual standardized patients be used to assess communication skills in medical students. In *Proceedings of the 17th Annual IAMSE Meeting, St. Andrews, Scotland*.

Douglas Danforth, Mike Procter, Richard Chen, Mary Johnson, and Robert Heller. 2009. Development of virtual patient simulations for medical education. *Journal For Virtual Worlds Research*, 2(2).

Douglas Danforth, Laura Zimmerman, Kellen Maicher, Holly Cronau, Cynthia Ledford, D. Post, Allison Macerollo, D. Way, and Beth Liston. 2016. Virtual standardized patients can accurately assess information gathering skills in medical students. In *Proceedings of the American Association of Medical Colleges*, Seattle, WA.

David DeVault, Anton Leuski, and Kenji Sagae. 2011. An evaluation of alternative strategies for implementing dialogue policies using statistical classification and rules. In *Proceedings of the 5th International Joint Conference on Natural Language Processing (IJCNLP)*, pages 1341–1345.

Manjuan Duan, Ethan Hill, and Michael White. 2016. Generating disambiguating paraphrases for structurally ambiguous sentences. In *Proceedings of the 10th Linguistic Annotation Workshop held in conjunction with ACL 2016 (LAW-X 2016)*, pages 160–170, Berlin, Germany. Association for Computational Linguistics.

Anthony Fader, Luke Zettlemoyer, and Oren Etzioni. 2013. Paraphrase-driven learning for open question answering. In *Proceedings of the 51st Annual Meeting of the Association for Computational Linguistics (Volume 1: Long Papers)*, pages 1608–1618. Association for Computational Linguistics.

Juri Ganitkevitch, Benjamin Van Durme, and Chris Callison-Burch. 2013. Ppdb: The paraphrase database. In *Proceedings of the 2013 Conference of the North American Chapter of the Association for Computational Linguistics: Human Language Technologies*, pages 758–764.

Evan Jaffe, Michael White, William Schuler, Eric Fosler-Lussier, Alex Rosenfeld, and Douglas Danforth. 2015. Interpreting questions with a log-linear ranking model in a virtual patient dialogue system. In *Proceedings of the Tenth Workshop on Innovative Use of NLP for Building Educational Applications*, pages 86–96.

Lifeng Jin, Michael White, Evan Jaffe, Laura Zimmerman, and Douglas Danforth. 2017. Combining CNNs and Pattern Matching for Question Interpretation in a Virtual Patient Dialogue System. In *Proceedings of the 12th Workshop on Innovative Use of NLP for Building Educational Applications*, pages 11–21.

Lukasz Kaiser, Ofir Nachum, Aurko Roy, and Samy Bengio. 2017. Learning to Remember Rare Events. In *Proceedings of the International Conference on Learning Representations*.

Yoon Kim. 2014. Convolutional Neural Networks for Sentence Classification. *Proceedings of the Conference on Empirical Methods in Natural Language Processing*, pages 1746–1751.

Quoc Le and Tomas Mikolov. 2014. Distributed representations of sentences and documents. In *International Conference on Machine Learning*, pages 1188–1196.

Kellen Maicher, Douglas Danforth, A. Price, Laura Zimmerman, B. Wilcox, Beth Liston, Holly Cronau, Laurie Belknap, Cynthia Ledford, D. Way, D. Post, Allison Macerollo, and Milisa Rizer. 2017. Developing a conversational virtual standardized patient to enable students to practice history taking skills. *Simulation in Healthcare*, 12(2):124–131.

Jonathan Mallinson, Rico Sennrich, and Mirella Lapata. 2017. Paraphrasing revisited with neural machine translation. In *Proceedings of the 15th Conference of the European Chapter of the Association for Computational Linguistics: Volume 1, Long Papers*, volume 1, pages 881–893.

Diana McCarthy and Roberto Navigli. 2009. The english lexical substitution task. *Language resources and evaluation*, 43(2):139–159.

Quinn McNemar. 1947. Note on the sampling error of the difference between correlated proportions or percentages. *Psychometrika*, 12(2):153–157.

Tomas Mikolov, Kai Chen, Greg Corrado, and Jeffrey Dean. 2013. Efficient Estimation of Word Representations in Vector Space. In *Proceedings of the International Conference on Learning Representations*, pages 1–12.

George A Miller. 1995. Wordnet: a lexical database for english. *Communications of the ACM*, 38(11):39–41.

Vinod Nair and Geoffrey E Hinton. 2010. Rectified Linear Units Improve Restricted Boltzmann Machines. In *Proceedings of the 27th International Conference on Machine Learning*, 3, pages 807–814.

The Ohio Supercomputer Center. 1987. Ohio Supercomputer Center.

Robert Parker, David Graff, Junbo Kong, Ke Chen, and Kazuaki Maeda. 2011. English gigaword. *Linguistic Data Consortium*.

Vikram Ramanarayanan, David Suendermann-Oeft, Hillary Molloy, Eugene Tsuprun, Patrick Lange, and Keelan Evanini. 2017. Crowdsourcing multimodal dialog interactions: Lessons learned from the HALEF case. In *Proceedings of the AAAI-17 Workshop on Crowdsourcing, Deep Learning, and Artificial Intelligence Agents*, pages 423–431.

Deepak Ravichandran, Eduard Hovy, and Franz Josef Och. 2003. Statistical qa-classifier vs. re-ranker: What's the difference? In *Proceedings of the ACL 2003 workshop on Multilingual summarization and question answering-Volume 12*, pages 69–75. Association for Computational Linguistics.

Brent Rossen and Benjamin Lok. 2012. A crowdsourcing method to develop virtual human conversational agents. *International Journal of HCS*, 70(4):301–319.

Keisuke Sakaguchi, Michael Heilman, and Nitin Madnani. 2015. Effective feature integration for automated short answer scoring. In *Proceedings of the 2015 Conference of the North American Chapter of the Association for Computational Linguistics: Human Language Technologies*, pages 1049–1054. Association for Computational Linguistics.

Rico Sennrich, Barry Haddow, and Alexandra Birch. 2016. Edinburgh neural machine translation systems for wmt 16. In *Proceedings of the First Conference on Machine Translation*, pages 371–376, Berlin, Germany. Association for Computational Linguistics.

David Suendermann-Oeft, Keelan Evanini, Jackson Liscombe, Phillip Hunter, Krishna Dayanidhi, and Roberto Pieraccini. 2009. From rule-based to statistical grammars: Continuous improvement of large-scale spoken dialog systems. pages 4713–4716.

Oriol Vinyals, Charles Blundell, Timothy Lillcrap, Koray Kavukcuoglu, and Daan Wierstra. 2016. Matching Networks for One Shot Learning. In *Proceedings of Neural Information Processing Systems*, pages 817–825.

Matthew D. Zeiler. 2012. ADADELTA: An Adaptive Learning Rate Method. *CoRR*.

Predicting misreadings from gaze in children with reading difficulties

Joachim Bingel[1] and **Maria Barrett**[2] and **Sigrid Klerke**[3]

[1] Department of Computer Science, University of Copenhagen, Denmark
[2] Centre for Language Technology, University of Copenhagen, Denmark
[3] EyeJustRead, Copenhagen, Denmark
`bingel@di.ku.dk, barrett@hum.ku.dk, sk@eyejustread.com`

Abstract

We present the first work on predicting reading mistakes in children with reading difficulties based on eye-tracking data from real-world reading teaching. Our approach employs several linguistic and gaze-based features to inform an ensemble of different classifiers, including multi-task learning models that let us transfer knowledge about individual readers to attain better predictions. Notably, the data we use in this work stems from noisy readings *in the wild*, outside of controlled lab conditions. Our experiments show that despite the noise and despite the small fraction of misreadings, gaze data improves the performance more than any other feature group and our models achieve good performance. We further show that gaze patterns for misread words do not fully generalize across readers, but that we can transfer some knowledge between readers using multitask learning at least in some cases. Applications of our models include partial automation of reading assessment as well as personalized text simplification.

1 Introduction

Reading disabilities are impairments affecting individuals' access to written sources, with downstream effects such as low self-confidence in the classroom and limited access to higher education. Dyslexia, for instance, while being highly prevalent with estimates reaching up to 17.5% of the entire population of the U.S. (Interagency Committee on Learning Disabilities, 1987), often goes undiagnosed, such that unattributed weaknesses in reading comprehension further intimidate affected persons. Due to these severe and broadranging impacts of reading difficulties, many governments have implemented early screening tests for dyslexia and other reading difficulties and provide special training and assistance for struggling

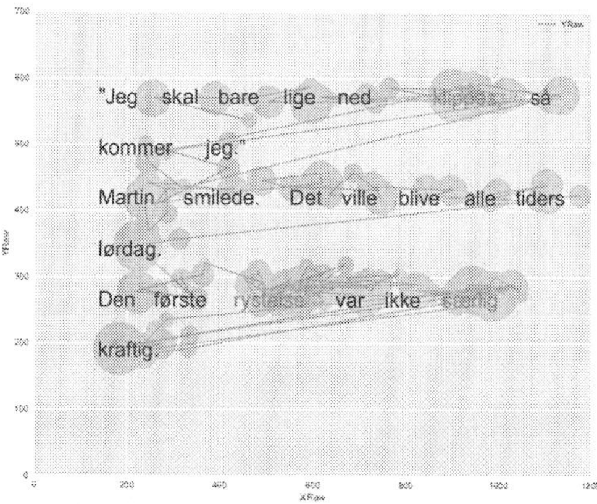

Figure 1: Scanpath and fixations (blue circles) when reading a sentence. This particularly clear example from our dataset shows extended processing time for misread words (marked in red).

readers throughout the educational system and into adulthood.

In Denmark, for example, such programs provide children with specialist training through focused multi-week reading courses in one-on-one or small group settings. Still, the specialized teachers can only attend to one student at a time when closely monitoring their reading, and the quality of any analysis is strictly limited by the human observer's processing "bandwidth" while attending the live reading.

As a possible mitigation, advances in eye-tracking technology–in particular the increased availability of eye trackers–have made it possible to reliably record children's gaze during reading, both allowing teachers to attend to their students' reading post-hoc as well as providing additional insight into reading strategies based on gaze, including the development of these strategies over time. For the teacher to track and keep records of

Proceedings of the Thirteenth Workshop on Innovative Use of NLP for Building Educational Applications, pages 24–34
New Orleans, Louisiana, June 5, 2018. ©2018 Association for Computational Linguistics

reading mistakes (henceforth referred to as *misreadings*), however, the students are still required to read out loud, and the teacher has to review the entire reading and annotate for misreadings.

In this work, we investigate to what extent we can predict misreadings from gaze patterns for individual words. While the aim is not to fully automate reading reviews, being able to successfully predict misreadings from gaze data can be part of a semi-automatic system for reading quality assessment and increase teacher efficiency by pointing out potential misreadings for closer review.

Another motivation for this work comes from text simplification, in particular from the observation that individuals' highly specific reading strengths and weaknesses require text simplification models to be customized to specific users in order to unfold their full potential and truly be helpful. Predicting misreadings in concrete reading scenarios and based on individual gaze patterns can be used as a first step in the typical lexical simplification pipeline (Shardlow, 2014).[1] This task, known as complex word identification, has received a considerable amount of attention in the literature, but has exclusively been approached in a user-agnostic fashion.

The data used in this study are gaze recordings of children with reading difficulties, reading Danish texts assigned by their reading teacher as part of their reading intervention. The recordings stem from EyeJustRead, an eye-tracking based software used in special reading intervention in Danish schools.[2] In Section 3, we discuss further aspects of the treatment of gaze data in general and the collection of the data used in this study in particular.

While the difficulty of processing a word is undoubtedly reflected in the fixation time on that word (Rayner et al., 1989), many other factors affect fixation durations, the most prominent being word length and word frequency, but also predictability and relative position in sentence have strong effects–see Figure 1 for a particularly clear example from our dataset. Notably, almost all analyses of eye-tracking reading data use data collected in research laboratories, where these–

otherwise confounding–factors can be controlled for. We show that we can perform reasonable misreading detection on real-world eye tracking data, including a limited number of textual features to control for these factors.

Contributions a) We present the first work on the automatic detection of misreadings based on gaze patterns of children with reading difficulties. b) This is, to the best of our knowledge, the first attempt at modeling noisy, real-world eye-tracking data from readers. c) We also present, to the best of our knowledge, the first published results using a multi-task learning setup to transfer knowledge between individual readers for personalized, complex word identification.

2 Related Work

Our work is a special case of complex word identification, a task that has recently received a significant amount of interest, including two shared tasks (Paetzold and Specia, 2016; Yimam et al., 2018). The most successful approaches to these tasks had in common that they employed ensembles of classifiers that learned from a number of semantic and psycholinguistic features. Note however, that these previous approaches to complex word identification aimed at developing generic models that took no account of any specifics of a certain user.

Children's eye movements during reading are not as well-studied as adults', and previous studies typically analyze data collected in experiments designed for research. The overall established observations with regards to reading development are: older children have shorter fixation durations, fewer fixations and fewer regressions. They have a higher skipping probability and also higher saccade amplitude. See Blythe and Joseph (2011) for a review. It is not conclusive whether these variations follow chronological age or their increased reading proficiency. Regardless of the underlying cause, due to the observed systematic differences, the standard procedure is to control as closely as possible for age and reading proficiency level when designing reading experiments.

There are several psycholinguistic studies that show that also in children, the typicality and plausibility of sentences (Joseph et al., 2008) as well as temporary sentence ambiguity (Traxler, 2002) can be traced in eye movements, suggesting that also other types of comprehension difficulties are reflected in the reading patterns.

---

[1]While today it may hardly sound plausible to equip each laptop with an eye-tracker in order to track people's reading, further technological advances may well make this possible in the future. Recent development in eye-tracking technology has taken it from expensive research equipment to a gaming interface with a price point as low as $100.

[2]http://www.eyejustread.com

Using gaze data to augment models is a recent addition to NLP. Previous approaches that have used gaze data in the context of natural language processing include the work of Barrett et al. (2016), who aim to improve part-of-speech induction with gaze features, Klerke et al. (2016), where gaze data is used as an auxiliary task in sentence compression, and Klerke et al. (2015b), where gaze data is used to evaluate the output of machine translation. The most related work is Klerke et al. (2015a) and Gonzalez-Garduño and Søgaard (2017). Klerke et al. (2015a) compared gaze from reading original, manually compressed, and automatically compressed sentences. They found that the proportion of regressions to previously read text is sensitive to the differences in human- and computer-induced complexity. Gonzalez-Garduño and Søgaard (2017) show that text readability prediction improves significantly from hard parameter sharing when models try to predict word-based gaze features in a multi-task-learning setup. All of these works, however, use gaze data that was collected under laboratory conditions from skilled, adult readers.

3 Gaze Data

In eye-tracking studies, gaze data is normally sampled under experimental circumstances, where e.g. instructions, location, environment, lighting, participant sampling, textual features, order, duration etc. are controlled for. Our real-world data, on the contrary, lacks all of these controls. While in controlled, cognitive psychology experiments, fixation durations have proven to systematically correlate with cognitive load (see Rayner (1998) for a review), eye movements from-real world applications have been largely understudied, and specific findings from the literature on controlled data may not apply here or may be swamped by extraneous factors. Further, the often-used statistical tests of significant differences between gaze patterns lose some of their legitimacy when data is retrieved under noisy conditions.

3.1 Data collection and preprocessing

The data we use in this work is collected in Danish schools using commercial software specifically developed to record and track children's reading development. The system records the eye movements and voice while the children are reading aloud. The teacher can afterwards replay the read-ing along with the recorded eye movements. The software performs some low-level eye-movement analyses to help the teacher understand how the child processes the text. The teacher can mark which words are erroneously read by the child and later access this and other basic statistics about the reading – see Klerke et al. (2018) for a workflow description. The genre is children's fiction books and the children read contextualized, running text.

As the data is fairly noisy compared to data from laboratory-based eye tracking experiments, we perform thorough cleaning before running any experiments. This cleaning procedure is described below. Table 1 contains a summary of the dataset sizes after each cleaning step. Before any cleaning is performed, the dataset contains 369 reading sessions from 95 unique readers. In total it has 3,161 read pages.

Help word activated on page We start by removing all pages where the reader activated the help word function, which dynamically isolates and enlarges a single word on the screen. This dynamic display generates a series of eye movements that do not resemble typical reading activity. This step removes 94 pages.

Fixation detection We pre-process the raw gaze data by first detecting fixations using a custom implementation of the algorithm of Nyström and Holmqvist (2010). We remove fixations shorter than 40ms and longer than 1.5s.[3] For the calculation of gaze features (see below), we further discard all data points that are not detected as a fixation on text (but instead on images or blank parts of the page). We remove 19 pages where we do not have any fixations on text (e.g. due to the reader just browsing through a book or because of technical issues).

Bad calibration Prior to reading, the student is prompted to calibrate the eye tracker. In the data used in this study, most reading sessions (91%) attain the best calibration score on a five-point scale, while 6% miss a calibration score. The remaining 3% do not have the best calibration score. We remove everything but the 91% with the best calibration score.

Only parts of the readings have been reviewed

---

[3] Removing short fixations also removes the majority of blinks which presents as a sudden downward-upward pattern of saccades separated by a pause in the signal or a short, falsely detected fixation.

Cleaning step	Reading sessions	Unique readers	Read pages	Read words	Misreadings
No cleaning	369	95	3161	73,965	644
Help word activated	366	95	3067	71,911	619
Fixation detection	366	95	3048	64,191	613
Bad calibration	335	87	2865	56,166	565
Marked by teacher	83	44	405	8,681	565

Table 1: Dataset size after each cleaning step

and marked for misreadings by a teacher. However, whether a teacher reviewed a reading or not is not explicitly encoded in the data. Thus, if there are no marked misreadings in some session, we do not know whether this is because this reading was not reviewed or because there actually were no errors. We therefore remove all readings without any marked misreadings, as well as any data before the first marked misreading and after the last marked misreading within marked sessions, assuming that everything between these two points has been marked. Twelve cleaned reading sessions only consist of one misread word – everything before and after was removed. See Figure 2a for an overview of the distribution of number of words per reading after this cleaning step. This leaves us with the subset of the readings that posed most problems for the subjects. Figure 2b shows the distribution of misread words in the cleaned dataset. It is worth noting that since this is not controlled, experimental data, "misread" is not necessarily interpreted equally by all teachers, or even consistently across markings from the same teacher, due to the lack of an annotation protocol. We assume that "misread" means that the pronounced word deviates substantially from the written word. Ultimately, we retain 83 reading sessions from 44 readers with at least one misread word.

3.1.1 Apparatus

The eye tracker used is a Tobii Eye Tracker 4C with a sample rate of 90 Hz. It is an affordable, consumer eye tracker targeted at gaming. The laptop computers to which the trackers are attached, and which run the software, are provided by the different institutions and vary. Screen resolution is locked by the eye tracker software to 1366 x 768, and most systems reportedly run on a 14"–15.6" monitor. The font size is 50pt, which is equivalent to approximately 6mm x-height. Distance between baselines was approximately 18mm with the most commonly used font–otherwise 24mm.

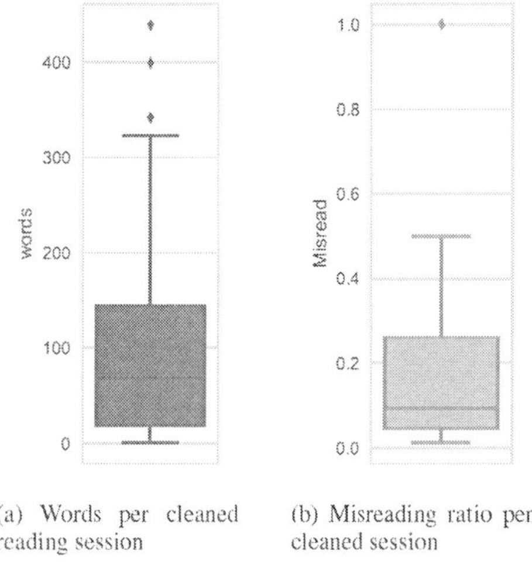

(a) Words per cleaned reading session

(b) Misreading ratio per cleaned session

Figure 2: Distributions of total number of words and misreading ratios per session after cleaning.

3.1.2 Subjects

The cleaned dataset contains 44 unique readers with different reading durations. Readers are probably between 5 and 15 years old, which is the official age of students in the Danish schools, but we do not know their exact ages. To control for reading proficiency, we include the texts' readability scores as a feature in all experiments. All students receive extra reading classes, because they struggle with reading. Many of them are probably dyslexic, but we do not have access to this information. Because this is not experimental data, the students will have received different instructions from the teachers. We do not know if they picked the text themselves or for how long they read prior to each recording. They are not necessarily alone in the room, but it is a fair assumption that they all make an effort to read correctly because they are recorded. The data comes from a number of different systems that we were informed is in the range between 10 and 20, but the actual number of schools and teachers is unknown to us. All children and their parents gave consent that the anonymized eye-tracking data may be used for this research.

3.2 Features

Reading patterns have been shown to be influenced by a number of factors, including textual features and the instructions given to a reader, such as encouraging a specific reading strategy. Readers, or different groups of readers, furthermore display individual reading styles which affect the eye movements (Benfatto et al., 2016). Other factors include the reader's individual skill level, cognitive abilities and mood, among others.

We extract a number of gaze features that have been associated with processing load. Some of our gaze features directly reflect the processing load associated with a word, especially the two correlated measures *total fixation duration* and *number of re-fixations*, but also the *mean fixation duration*. Some gaze features are included to account for preview effects (whether the next or previous word was fixated) as well as the scan path immediately surrounding the word. We split the gaze features into two groups: GAZE (W) for features directly associated with word-level processing and GAZE (C) for features associated with the eye movements on the immediate context of the word. All features are scaled to the $[-1, 1]$ interval.

We further extract a number of basic features that are known to affect gaze features and thus need to be controlled for. These include word length and word frequency (Hyönä and Olson, 1995), but also position in sentence (Rayner et al., 2000) and position on the page have shown to affect reading for adults. We also include a range of linguistic features that we expect to describe word difficulty. All features and feature groups are listed in Table 2 and described below.

Gaze features During reading, the reader performs a series of stable fixations of a couple of hundred milliseconds duration on average. Between fixations, the eyes perform rapid, targeted movements, called *saccades*. All gaze features are computed on the word level and use the application's definition of the area of interest surrounding each word.

For gaze duration, we extract both late and early processing measures. Late measure such as total *fixation duration* and *number of re-fixations* reflect late syntactic and semantic processing in skilled

adult reading (Rayner et al., 1989). For children with reading difficulties, we assume these measures to likely reflect processing difficulty.

For the first three passes over a word, we also extract the direction and the word distance of both the ingoing and outgoing saccade.[4] These six features are expected to map the activity around the word and, for example, show whether some word was part of sequential, forward reading or occurred in a series of erratic saccades.

Four features indicate the *landing positions* of fixations in four equally-sized parts of the display width of a word. This captures whether a word, for instance, has three fixations on the last quarter of its display width, which would be atypical and suggest that the reader is struggling with the ending of this word. We further explicitly encode the landing position of the first and last fixation. Note that because of the anatomy of the eye, eye tracking can never be pixel-accurate, but has at least 2° inaccuracy. For short words (or words printed very small, which does not apply for this study) these features may be misleading.

The data also provides pupil sizes for both eyes. It is well known that the pupil dilates as response to external lighting factors, but there is also evidence that the pupil systematically–but on a much smaller scale–dilates as a response to mental state, emotions or concentration (Beatty et al., 2000). In an experiment collecting pupil size, one would control lighting, which was not possible in the present scenario. For all pupil measures, we subtracted the same side mean of the reading session. We confirmed that all changes larger than 0.6 times the mean were captured when removing short fixations, as they may be caused by the tracker mistaking eyelashes for pupils during blinks.

Basic features The basic features span 16 textual and presentational features that are either directly accessible via the system or easily obtainable. They are included in all our experiments and serve as control features for the gaze features because we expect them to explain some of the variance in the gaze features, e.g. reading changes

---

[4]As we removed everything that was not a fixation on text before calculating the gaze features, intermediary non-text fixations may have occurred between text fixations, such as image fixations. We count the last/next fixated *word*. For example, if a word has index 5, and the first pass incoming saccade is from word index 4, we get a feature value of -1 for first pass ingoing.

BASIC	GAZE ON WORD (W)
Is bold	Number of fixations on word
Is italic	First fixation duration
Is lowercase	Mean fixation duration
Is uppercase	Total fixation duration
Has punctuation	Count of passes over the word
Line index on page	Left pupil size
Word index on line	Right pupil size
Page number	Refixation counts
Position in sentence (relative)	Fixations in first quarter count
Position in sentence (absolute)	Fixations in second quarter count
Sentence length (characters)	Fixations in third quarter count
Sentence length (words)	Fixations in fourth quarter count
Word index	Relative landing position of first fixation
Sentence index	Relative landing position of last fixation
Word length (characters)	Average character index of fixations

GAZE IN CONTEXT (C)	LINGUISTIC
$1st$ pass ingoing saccade dist. and dir.	LIX score for entire text
$1st$ pass outgoing saccade dist. and dir.	Previous occurrences of word stem in text
$2nd$ pass ingoing saccade dist. and dir.	Previous occurrences of word type in text
$2nd$ pass outgoing saccade dist. and dir.	Vowel count
$3rd$ pass ingoing saccade dist. and dir.	Character perplexity
$3rd$ pass outgoing saccade dist. and dir.	Word frequency
Next word fixated	Universal POS tag
Previous word fixated	

Table 2: Overview of the feature groups used in the experiments.

over the course of a line and the course of a sentence (Just and Carpenter, 1980). We further encode the line number a word is located in on a page, as well as its position in that line.

Linguistic features The linguistic features include the absolute vowel count, which in Danish is highly correlated with the number of syllables. Universal POS tags are obtained from the Danish Polyglot tagger.[5] We also include the provided *Läsbarhetsindex* (LIX) (Björnsson, 1968), a Swedish readability metric (commonly also applied to Danish) that considers the mean sentence length and the ratio of long words (more than 6 characters). The log word probability is estimated from a language model we train on the entire Danish Wikipedia (downloaded in November 2017) using KenLM (Heafield, 2011). Frequency

affects processing load and thus fixation duration for adults as well as dyslexic and neurotypical Finnish children (Hyönä and Olson, 1995), but there is conflicting evidence whether text frequencies from adult text explain variance in children's eye movements (Blythe and Joseph, 2011). Character perplexity is estimated using a 5-gram character language model, also using KenLM on the Danish Wikipedia. The previous occurrence of stems and word types is included as reading time for low-frequency words has shown to decrease on later repeats in a text (Rayner et al., 1995). We use NLTK's snowball stemmer for Danish.

4 Model

In preliminary experiments, we observed that the relatively small overall amount of data, as well as the low fraction of positive instances, caused significant variation between repeated random

---

[5] http://polyglot.readthedocs.io

Feature group	F_1	
BASIC	18.78	†
+ GAZE (W)	40.50	*
+ GAZE (C)	18.49	†
+ LINGUISTIC	19.24	†
+ GAZE (W) + GAZE (C)	**41.19**	*
+ GAZE (W) + LINGUISTIC	41.08	*
+ GAZE (W) + LINGUISTIC	18.65	†
All features	40.42	*

Table 3: Performance across feature groups for Experiment 1. Scores are averaged F_1 over ten cross-validation folds. Using an independent t-test, * and † indicate results from ten cross validation rounds significantly different from BASIC and the best feature combination BASIC + GAZE(W) + GAZE(C), respectively.

restarts of various classification algorithms. We thus approach the task of predicting misreadings from gaze with ensemble methods, training N classifiers independently on the same data and letting them vote on the instances in a held-out development set. Using this development set, we then optimize a threshold t, which is the fraction of the number of classifiers that need to cast a positive vote on an item before we accept it as such.

All of our ensembles consist of 10 random forest classifiers and 10 feed-forward neural networks. The random forests, in turn, consist of 100 trees that create splits based on Gini impurity (Breiman, 2001). The neural network models are implemented in Pytorch and trained with the Adam algorithm (Kingma and Ba, 2014), with an initial learning rate of $3 \cdot 10^{-4}$ and a dropout rate of 0.2 on the hidden layers, whose number and sizes we vary in our experiments. We further employ early stopping, monitoring the loss on the development set with a patience of 30 steps.

4.1 Multi-task learning for cross-user knowledge transfer

One of the central questions we investigate in this paper is to what degree gaze patterns for misread words vary between readers, and whether we can learn to transfer knowledge about predictors of misreadings between readers. We address these questions in the experiments reported in Section 5.2, for which we use a multi-task learning

(MTL) model that employs hard parameter sharing. MTL has received significant attention in the natural language processing community over the past years (see Bjerva (2017) for a review). One of the most intriguing properties of MTL is that it allows for the transfer of knowledge between different tasks and datasets, which has been investigated and exploited in a growing number of works (Klerke et al., 2016; Martínez Alonso and Plank, 2017; Bingel and Søgaard, 2017), including work on the identification of complex words (Bingel and Bjerva, 2018).

In this work, we view the different readers as different *tasks*, motivated by Bingel and Bjerva (2018), who interpret different languages as different tasks for cross-lingual complex word identification. We define a feed-forward neural network model with one output layer per reader, all of which are dense projections from a shared hidden layer. In this framework, each training step consists of flipping a coin to sample any of the tasks and retrieving a batch of training data for this task. This batch is then used to optimize both the shared and the respective task-specific parameters. For a detailed definition of the model, see Bingel and Bjerva (2018).

5 Experiments

5.1 Experiment 1: Across entire dataset

As a first experiment, we investigate the performance of our models and the predictiveness of the individual feature groups through 10-fold cross validation across the entire dataset. At each fold, we reserve one tenth of the data for testing and another tenth to monitor validation loss of the network as the early stopping criterion.

Note that we split the data randomly and do not stratify the cross-validation splits in any way. In conjunction with the strong class imbalance, this means that we are likely to encounter very different class distributions across splits. This setup may generally lead to lower performance scores, likely with greater variance. However, this was a deliberate choice as we cannot assume a consistent class distribution across train and test set in the real world, or in fact hardly any prior knowledge with regards to class distribution in the test set. Random splitting also means that data from the same *reading* will likely be distributed across train and test partitions for a certain cross-validation iteration.

We perform a first baseline experiment with

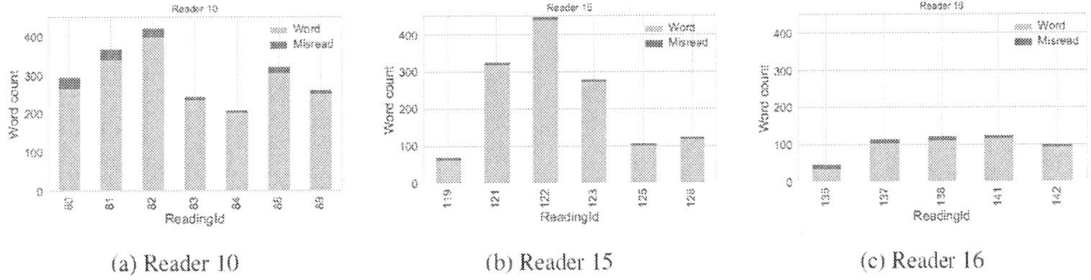

(a) Reader 10   (b) Reader 15   (c) Reader 16

Figure 3: Words and misreading counts for readings of three readers in cross-user experiment

UserId	Number of reading sessions	Words per reading		Thereof misread	
		Mean	std.dev.	Mean	std.dev.
10	7	285.9	67.5	16.6	9.9
15	6	219.2	148.1	5.0	2.3
16	5	91.6	32.7	8.0	3.1

Table 4: Statistics of (misread) words in sessions for the three readers with most readings.

only the basic features that we list in Section 2. On top of this baseline feature set, we perform further experiments, incorporating all combinations over the other feature groups. The results we present in Table 3 are based on the best respective model architecture for each feature combination, evaluated via the average over validation splits.[6]

5.2 Experiment 2: Cross-reader prediction

Without reader's own data In a second experiment, we are interested in how well our model can predict misreadings for specific readers. For this, we identify the three readers with most reading sessions and perform a range of experiments, testing our models on the readings of each of these readers after training them on all other data. We denote the three most active readers by their unique, anonymized IDs as they appear in the dataset: 10, 15 and 16. These readers have 7, 6 and 5 recorded and marked readings, respectively, and we present statistics on these readings in Table 4 and Figure 3. As in the previous experiment, we optimize our model through cross validation to tune hyperparameters and perform early stopping. We report test data results for the model with optimal validation performance in Figure 4, broken down into each reader's different sessions.

Learning from reader's own data Complementing the setup above, we now investigate how data from the same reader, but from different reading sessions, can inform our models. Therefore, we further perform cross-validation experiments across each reader's sessions. More concretely, for a reader with n marked readings, we perform n-fold cross validation, holding out one reading a time as a test set and another to monitor validation loss for early stopping of the neural model, while training on the remaining $n-2$ readings.

MTL As outlined in Section 4.1, we now view readers as tasks in an MTL model. For each of the three readers identified above and for each test reading, we train an ensemble whose neural MTL models define two outputs: one for the reader in question and one combined output for all other readers in the entire dataset. The random forest classifiers are trained on all remaining data except the held-out validation and test readings.

6 Results and Discussion

From Experiment 1, we observe that gaze features of the target word itself contribute strongly to model improvements over the baseline of textual features (see Table 3). Contextual gaze features and linguistic features do so to a lesser degree. The best feature group combination consists of the basic features and both gaze feature groups. Adding the linguistic features to this seems to slightly dilute the model.

---

[6]To address the variation in input dimensionality as we consider different feature group combinations, we train models with different architectures: (i) a single hidden layer with 20 units, (ii) two hidden layers with 20 units each, and (iii) a single hidden layer with 40 units.

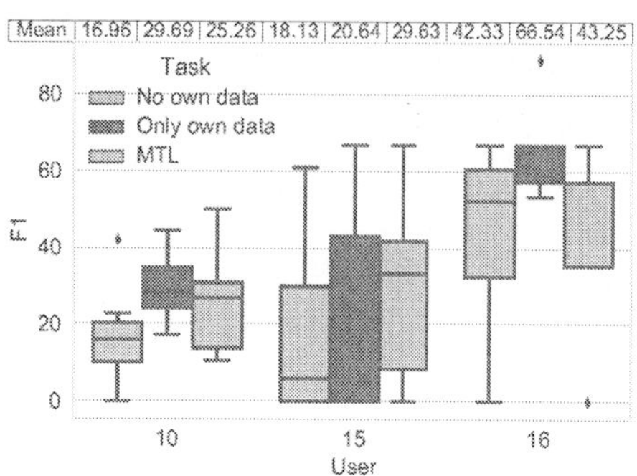

Figure 4: F_1 score distributions across test readings for each of the three readers with most sessions for three tasks.

The results from Experiment 2 in Figure 4 show that, at least for these three readers, there is a considerable degree of specificity attested in the reading patterns of misread words: in the scenario where we learn only from other users' gaze patterns (shown in light blue), performance is generally worse than for the other approaches. The high degree of reader specificity is also reflected in the comparison between learning just across a single user's readings and a multi-task setup that also considers other readers. Here, we observe that the former attains higher mean F_1 scores across readings for readers 10 and 16, although MTL is superior to the single-task setup for reader 15. Another observation is that misreadings can generally be predicted much better for reader 16 than for the other readers, which may in part be due to the higher ratio of misread words in these readings.

As especially our cross-reader experiments show, there is reason to believe that the manifestations of misreadings in gaze differ strongly between these readers. However, since we do not have information on the individual readers' age or general reading proficiency, we cannot confidently conclude whether the better stability of within-user experiments attested in Figure 4 is due to reader-specific idiosyncrasies or group-internal patterns (which would be supported by evidence that readers 10 and 16 were more atypical readers than others in the present dataset). We find some support for the latter hypothesis in literature describing children's reading development, which identifies a range of patterns common to young and low-proficiency readers. These patterns include longer and more frequent fixations, shorter saccadic amplitude and more regressions – all of which are also associated with comprehension difficulties, see Blythe and Joseph (2011) for a review. The presence of group-internal patterns is further supported by the observation that we are still able to successfully transfer knowledge about readings patterns between users in some cases, increasing performance for the readings of user 15.

One disadvantage of noisy, real-world data is that we do not know to what degree similarities and differences in the data, as well as our results, are influenced by chance, or whether they will generalize to other gaze data. The fact that many parameters are outside of our control and also outside of our knowledge means that we cannot describe certain biases in the data (such as age or reading skill) and consider them as causes for statistical variations in model performance.

7 Conclusion

This paper presented first work in the automatic prediction of reading errors in children with dyslexia and other reading difficulties using real-world gaze data. We showed that despite the noisy conditions under which this data was obtained, features we extract from the gaze patterns are predictive of reading mistakes among children. Besides the immediate application in automating some parts of reading teaching, this could be exploited in personalized text simplification, where gaze could be used as feedback to the system.

Our experiments further show that while gaze patterns for misreadings seem to be largely specific to individual readers or groups of readers, we can successfully use MTL to transfer knowledge between readers at least in some cases. Note also that we have very little knowledge of the age and general proficiency of specific readers, including those investigated in our MTL experiments, and we expect that our MTL approach can be much more successful between more similar readers.

Acknowledgements

The authors wish to thank the children using EyeJustRead, as well as their parents, for giving us permission to use their data. We are also grateful to Emil Juul Jacobsen and Janus Askø Madsen for supplying us with the data. We further acknowledge valuable comments by Anders Søgaard as well as by the anonymous reviewers. We acknowledge the support by Trygfonden.

References

Maria Barrett, Joachim Bingel, Frank Keller, and Anders Søgaard. 2016. Weakly supervised part-of-speech tagging using eye-tracking data. In *Proceedings of the 54th Annual Meeting of the Association for Computational Linguistics*, pages 579–584.

Jackson Beatty, Brennis Lucero-Wagoner, et al. 2000. The pupillary system. *Handbook of psychophysiology*, 2:142–162.

Mattias Nilsson Benfatto, Gustaf Öqvist Seimyr, Jan Ygge, Tony Pansell, Agneta Rydberg, and Christer Jacobson. 2016. Screening for dyslexia using eye tracking during reading. *PloS one*, 11(12):e0165508.

Joachim Bingel and Johannes Bjerva. 2018. Cross-lingual complex word identification with multitask learning. In *Proceedings of the Complex Word Identification Shared Task at the 13th Workshop on Innovative Use of NLP for Building Educational Applications*, New Orleans, United States. Association for Computational Linguistics.

Joachim Bingel and Anders Søgaard. 2017. Identifying beneficial task relations for multi-task learning in deep neural networks. *15th Conference of the European Chapter of the Association for Computational Linguistics*.

Johannes Bjerva. 2017. One model to rule them all: Multitask and multilingual modelling for lexical analysis. *arXiv preprint arXiv:1711.01100*.

Carl Hugo Björnsson. 1968. *Läsbarhet*. Liber.

Hazel I Blythe and Holly SSL Joseph. 2011. Children's eye movements during reading. *The Oxford Handbook of Eye Movements*, pages 643–662.

Leo Breiman. 2001. Random forests. *Machine learning*, 45(1):5–32.

Ana Valeria Gonzalez-Garduño and Anders Søgaard. 2017. Using gaze to predict text readability. In *Proceedings of the 12th Workshop on Innovative Use of NLP for Building Educational Applications*, pages 438–443.

Kenneth Heafield. 2011. Kenlm: Faster and smaller language model queries. In *Proceedings of the Sixth Workshop on Statistical Machine Translation*, pages 187–197. Association for Computational Linguistics.

Jukka Hyönä and Richard K Olson. 1995. Eye fixation patterns among dyslexic and normal readers: Effects of word length and word frequency. *Journal of Experimental Psychology: Learning, Memory, and Cognition*, 21(6):1430–40.

Interagency Committee on Learning Disabilities. 1987. Learning Disabilities: A Report to the U.S. Congress. Technical report, Government Printing Office, Washington DC, U.S.

Holly SSL Joseph, Simon P Liversedge, Hazel I Blythe, Sarah J White, Susan E Gathercole, and Keith Rayner. 2008. Children's and adults' processing of anomaly and implausibility during reading: Evidence from eye movements. *Quarterly Journal of Experimental Psychology*, 61(5):708–723.

Marcel A Just and Patricia A Carpenter. 1980. A theory of reading: From eye fixations to comprehension. *Psychological review*, 87(4):329–354.

Diederik P Kingma and Jimmy Ba. 2014. Adam: A method for stochastic optimization. *arXiv preprint arXiv:1412.6980*.

Sigrid Klerke, Héctor Martínez Alonso, and Anders Søgaard. 2015a. Looking hard: Eye tracking for detecting grammaticality of automatically compressed sentences. In *Proceedings of the 20th Nordic Conference of Computational Linguistics (NODALIDA 2015)*, pages 97–105.

Sigrid Klerke, Sheila Castilho, Maria Barrett, and Anders Søgaard. 2015b. Reading metrics for estimating task efficiency with MT output. In *Proceedings of the Sixth Workshop on Cognitive Aspects of Computational Language Learning*, pages 6–13.

Sigrid Klerke, Yoav Goldberg, and Anders Søgaard. 2016. Improving sentence compression by learning to predict gaze. *NAACL*, pages 1528—-1533.

Sigrid Klerke, Janus Askø Madsen, Emil Juul Jacobsen, and John Paulin Hansen. 2018. Substantiating reading teachers with scanpaths.

Héctor Martínez Alonso and Barbara Plank. 2017. When is multitask learning effective? Semantic sequence prediction under varying data conditions. In *15th Conference of the European Chapter of the Association for Computational Linguistics*.

Marcus Nyström and Kenneth Holmqvist. 2010. An adaptive algorithm for fixation, saccade, and glissade detection in eyetracking data. *Behavior research methods*, 42(1):188–204.

Gustavo Paetzold and Lucia Specia. 2016. Semeval 2016 task 11: Complex word identification. In *Proceedings of the 10th International Workshop on Semantic Evaluation (SemEval-2016)*, pages 560–569.

Keith Rayner. 1998. Eye movements in reading and information processing: 20 years of research. *Psychological bulletin*, 124(3):372.

Keith Rayner, Gretchen Kambe, and Susan A Duffy. 2000. The effect of clause wrap-up on eye movements during reading. *The Quarterly Journal of Experimental Psychology Section A*, 53(4):1061–1080.

Keith Rayner, Gary E Raney, and Alexander Pollatsek. 1995. Eye movements and discourse processing. pages 241—-255.

Keith Rayner, Sara C Sereno, Robin K Morris, A Rene Schmauder, and Charles Clifton Jr. 1989. Eye movements and on-line language comprehension processes. *Language and Cognitive Processes*, 4(3-4):SI21–SI49.

Matthew Shardlow. 2014. Out in the open: Finding and categorising errors in the lexical simplification pipeline. In *LREC*, pages 1583–1590.

Matthew J Traxler. 2002. Plausibility and subcategorization preference in children's processing of temporarily ambiguous sentences: Evidence from self-paced reading. *The Quarterly Journal of Experimental Psychology: Section A*, 55(1):75–96.

Seid Muhie Yimam, Chris Biemann, Shervin Malmasi, Gustavo Paetzold, Lucia Specia, Sanja Štajner, Anaïs Tack, and Marcos Zampieri. 2018. A Report on the Complex Word Identification Shared Task 2018. In *Proceedings of the 13th Workshop on Innovative Use of NLP for Building Educational Applications*, New Orleans, United States. Association for Computational Linguistics.

Automatic Input Enrichment for Selecting Reading Material: An Online Study with English Teachers

Maria Chinkina   **Ankita Oswal**   **Detmar Meurers**

Universität Tübingen
Department of Linguistics, ICALL research group*
LEAD Graduate School & Research Network
{mchnkina,aoswal,dm}@sfs.uni-tuebingen.de

Abstract

Input material at the appropriate level is crucial for language acquisition. Automating the search for such material can systematically and efficiently support teachers in their pedagogical practice. This is the goal of the computational linguistic task of automatic input enrichment (Chinkina and Meurers, 2016): It analyzes and re-ranks a collection of texts in order to prioritize those containing target linguistic forms. In the online study described in the paper, we collected 240 responses from English teachers in order to investigate whether they preferred automatic input enrichment over web search when selecting reading material for class. Participants demonstrated a general preference for the material provided by an automatic input enrichment system. It was also rated significantly higher than the texts retrieved by a standard web search engine with regard to the representation of linguistic forms and equivalent with regard to the relevance of the content to the topic. We discuss the implications of the results for language teaching and consider the potential strands of future research.

1   Introduction

Input material at the appropriate level is important for language learners − whether it is a revision of the already acquired linguistic forms or an introduction of the structures to be acquired next, in line with the input hypothesis by Krashen (1977). Automating the search for such material can systematically and efficiently support teachers and is the goal of the computational linguistic task of automatic input enrichment (Chinkina and Meurers, 2016): It provides reading material containing target grammatical and lexical forms by analyzing and re-ranking a collection of texts. Automatic input enrichment systems rely on rigorous NLP analysis of texts

provided either by a search engine or by the user. As a result, the most linguistically appropriate texts are prioritized and presented to the user.

Automatic input enrichment is in essence closely related to the notion of input flood substantially motivated and discussed in second language acquisition research (Trahey and White, 1993) and is a necessary step in providing any type of text-based activities for language learning. It has been shown that a richer representation of target linguistic forms in the input leads to a better acquisition of these forms by the learner (Pigada and Schmitt, 2006). However, the benefits of input flood for language teachers have not been empirically tested so far.

In order to fill this gap, we developed an online study investigating whether English teachers preferred automatic input enrichment, or input flood, over web search when selecting reading material for class. The study implemented a repeated measures design: Participants read and rated 20 news articles on ten different topics. The articles were presented in pairs, with one of them being the top search result retrieved by a standard search engine and the other one provided by an automatic input enrichment system. A topic and a pair of target linguistic forms were kept constant for each pair of articles. The repeated measures design allowed us to collect a sufficient number of responses (n=240) discriminating different types of linguistic forms.

We start by reviewing the relevant research from the field of second language acquisition in Sec. 2 and dwell on the importance of automatic input enrichment for language teaching and its practical implementation in Sec. 3. We then describe the design of the current study and the obtained results in Sec. 4 and discuss the findings in Sec. 5. Finally, we conclude with the implications of the results and ideas for further research in Sec. 6.

35

Proceedings of the Thirteenth Workshop on Innovative Use of NLP for Building Educational Applications, pages 35–44
New Orleans, Louisiana, June 5, 2018. ©2018 Association for Computational Linguistics

2   Motivation and Related Work

Research on second language acquisition has provided insights on effective language teaching and learning techniques. The role of comprehensible input (Krashen, 1977) has been emphasized by many researchers, and extensive exposure to written input has shown positive effects on vocabulary (Krashen, 1989; Waring and Nation, 2004) and grammar acquisition (Pigada and Schmitt, 2006).

While stressing the importance of input, researchers agree that in order for the learner to acquire a linguistic form, it has to be frequent and salient enough in the input (Slobin, 1985). At the same time, the learners should be provided with pedagogical support to notice (Schmidt, 1990) and process the forms (VanPatten, 1990).

The effectiveness of activities targeting certain linguistic forms has been thoroughly investigated by second language acquisition researchers: According to Long (1991), focus on form instruction encourages learners to attend to form within a communicative classroom environment, which has proved to be superior to purely communicative instruction (Leeman et al., 1995). Pointing out the importance of systematic focus on target linguistic forms, VanPatten and Oikkenon (1996) found that contextualized practice activities were more effective than explicit explanations of rules for intermediate learners of Spanish. In a meta-review of research on reading and second language acquisition, Chio (2009) also emphasized the potential of supplementing reading with discussion or interactive activities targeting certain linguistic forms.

Either incidentally drawing learners' attention to certain vocabulary and grammar or providing exercises targeting those, all of the aforementioned approaches rely on the existence of appropriate reading material with a rich representation of linguistic forms for effective language acquisition. The following section provides information on how language teachers can efficiently search for such material.

3   Automatic Input Enrichment for Language Teaching

Automatic provision of reading material for language learners has been guided by text complexity (Vajjala and Meurers, 2012), lexical and grammatical properties (Brown and Eskenazi, 2004; Bennöhr, 2007), and the learner's language proficiency (Collins-Thompson et al., 2011).

We refer to automatic selection of lexically and grammatically appropriate texts as automatic input enrichment and approach it as a web search task (Chinkina and Meurers, 2016). We developed a linguistically aware web search system FLAIR[1] that provides automatic input enrichment of certain lexical and grammatical forms by detecting them in a collection of texts and reordering the texts accordingly. This process can be seen as vocabulary and grammar retrieval.

Vocabulary retrieval is indeed the core of any web search engine: One obtains an appropriate text containing target lexical items by including them in a search query. Grammar retrieval, on the other hand, requires an extension to web search as the user is unlikely to find appropriate texts by simply searching for, e.g., *texts containing present perfect*. Such an extension is implemented in FLAIR as an algorithm detecting linguistic forms relevant for English learners, such as regular and irregular verb forms. The heatmap at the top of Fig. 1 demonstrates that although these two linguistic forms are highly frequent, they are not equally represented across the top 60 search results retrieved by Microsoft Bing.[2] The heatmap at the bottom of the same figure shows the result of automatic input enrichment by FLAIR: a reordered list of the same search results with those containing the best representation of both regular and irregular verbs closer to the top (i.e., to the left in the figure).

FLAIR is built on top of a web search engine Microsoft Bing, relies on third-party tools for text extraction and parsing, detects 87 linguistic forms from the grammar section of the official curriculum of English, and uses a ranking algorithm for prioritizing texts containing the target linguistic forms specified by the user. Once the user has typed in a search query, specified the target linguistic forms and a number of search results to retrieve, they receive a list of web pages, with those that contain the best representation of the target forms at the top of the list. The user can then explore the retrieved texts with the highlighted target linguistic forms and select the texts of appropriate complexity and length (see Fig. 2).

We used FLAIR to find out whether teachers benefit from automatic input enrichment, as compared to a standard web search engine, when

---

[1] www.purl.org/icall/flair
[2] www.bing.com

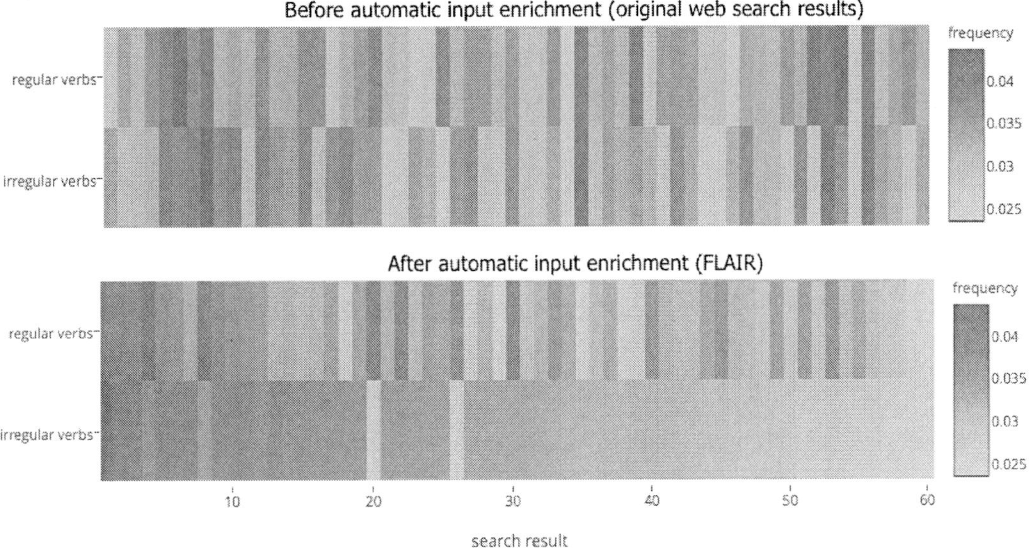

Figure 1: Comparison of the top results retrieved by a standard web search engine before and after automatic input enrichment. The 60 search results are plotted along the X axis, and the two target linguistic forms, regular and irregular verbs, are plotted on the Y axis.

searching for reading material for their students. The following section presents our research questions and hypotheses, the design of the online study, and the results.

4 Automatic Input Enrichment vs. Web Search for Selecting Reading Material

The current study focuses on teachers as media between students and reading material. It assesses teachers' experience and satisfaction with the every-day task of searching for supplementary texts online and provides insights on this process.

The *research questions* of the study address the importance of content and linguistic form and teachers' attitude towards their optimal balance: Does automatic input enrichment succeed in giving teachers the material that:

- is enriched with target linguistic forms relevant in the context of language learning,

- is in line with the information need expressed via a search query, and

- is suitable as a reading assignment for their students?

The online study was designed to operationalize these research questions. In the study, news articles retrieved by the standard web search engine

Microsoft Bing were compared to those provided by the automatic input enrichment system FLAIR. As FLAIR relies on Bing for retrieving web pages, the study in fact evaluates the impact of the NLP-driven re-ranking provided by FLAIR. The following *hypotheses* guided the design and the contents of our study:

H1: Teachers prefer texts provided by FLAIR over those provided by Bing when choosing a reading assignment for their students.

H2: Texts provided by FLAIR are perceived to have a richer representation of target linguistic forms than those provided by Bing.

H3: Texts provided by FLAIR are perceived to be less relevant to the topic than those provided by Bing.

H4: The more infrequent the target linguistic forms are, the more teachers prefer texts provided by FLAIR over those provided by Bing.

4.1 Design of Online Study

In order to address the aforementioned hypotheses, we designed an online study where the participants were asked to rate and compare pairs of news articles: One was the top search result from a standard search engine and the other one was a search result prioritized by FLAIR after specifying the target linguistic forms. Each article had to be rated on two scales: (i) its relevance to a given

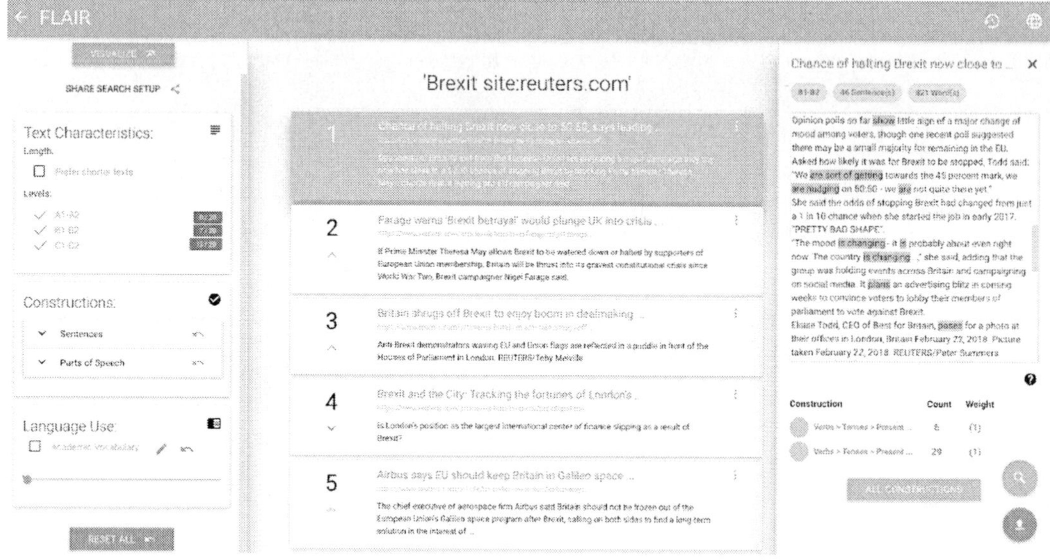

Figure 2: FLAIR interface.

topic and (ii) the representation of given linguistic forms in it. These two criteria are an integral part of language teachers' pedagogical practice: Teachers want to expose their students to language richly containing the structure to be taught or revised using a text that is on a topic that is relevant and motivating to the students.

We opted for a repeated-measures within-subjects design and ensured a random order of news articles retrieved from Bing and FLAIR as well as a random combination of topics and pairs of linguistic forms in the main task. The study proceeded as follows.

Procedure Participants received a message with the link to the online study and were asked to carefully read the information for the participants and the consent form before registering. Upon registration, they filled out a short questionnaire asking for their age, gender, native language(s), English language proficiency, the highest degree in teaching, and the proficiency level(s) of their students. They were also asked whether they used web search to look for reading material for their classes. Once they submitted the answers to the questionnaire, they could read the detailed instructions, which were displayed on every login.

The flow of the main task is demonstrated in Fig. 3: Participants were presented with a topic and a pair of target linguistic forms. They read and rated each of the two provided news articles by an-

swering two questions and were asked to pick one article as a reading assignment for their students with a preference scale from *Definitely Text 1* to *Definitely Text 2*.

Once they have completed the ten topics, participants filled out a debriefing questionnaire, where they explained general strategies for answering each of the questions in the main task (e.g., *How did you decide on the relevance of an article to a given topic?*). Finally, they submitted their email address and received a 20 Euro voucher as reimbursement.

4.2 Implementation of Online Study

We implemented the online study as a Java J2EE web application. To ensure anonymity, the user personal information obtained from the questionnaire was stored separately from their responses. Upon registration, each user was assigned a list of ten topics in a random order. Each topic was randomly matched with one of the three types of linguistic forms (see Sec. 4.3 below), one news article provided by FLAIR and one news article retrieved by Bing. For each topic, the two articles were displayed in a random order, and participants could not change their rating of the first news article once the second one was displayed.

4.3 Data and Participants

The total of 60 news articles were used in the study. The texts were presented in pairs that shared

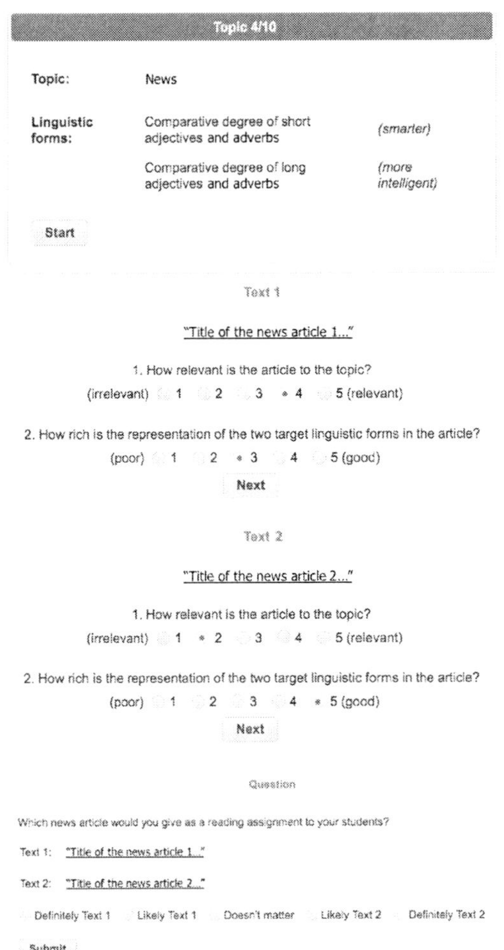

Figure 3: The main task in the online study included reading and rating two news articles and selecting one of them as a reading assignment for class.

the same topic (e.g., *Brexit*) and the same pair of target lingusitic forms (e.g., *the present simple* and *the present continuous tenses*). One article in each pair was obtained by submitting a search query to the web search engine Microsoft Bing and selecting the top search result. The other article in each pair was obtained by submitting the same query to FLAIR, configuring the settings to prioritize texts with the two target linguistic forms and selecting the top search result from the re-ranked list. As FLAIR relies on Microsoft Bing for retrieving the original search results, the only variable that differed between the two conditions was the automatic input enrichment component implemented in FLAIR.

Linguistic forms For the current study, we selected three pairs of linguistic forms (frequent, mixed, and infrequent) based on their document co-occurrence frequency in a corpus of 2400 news articles. Table 1 provides the distribution of their mean relative term frequencies across the texts provided by Bing and FLAIR.

The *frequent* pair was represented by regular (e.g., *typed*) and irregular (e.g., *wrote − written*) verb forms. It had a high document co-occurrence frequency of 95%. This means that these two linguistic forms occur together in 95 out of 100 documents, on average. Both constructions are also highly frequent: in the texts chosen for our study, regular and irregular verbs both had an average relative term frequency of 0.016. We did not count those forms when they occurred in modifier positions (e.g., *is interested, coloured balloons*).

The *mixed* pair of linguistic forms was represented by two grammatical tenses, present simple (e.g., *Kate plays guitar.*) and present continuous (e.g., *Kate is playing guitar now.*). Their respective relative term frequencies in the study were 0.012 and 0.003, with their document co-occurrence frequency being 50%. Predicates containing modal verbs were not counted as the present simple tense (e.g., *He can swim.*), with the exception of the verbs *have to, need,* and *want.* When a form constituted a part of a conditional sentence, it was not counted either (e.g., *I will not go out if it is still raining.*).

The *infrequent* pair was represented by the comparative degree of short adjectives and adverbs (e.g., *nicer*) and that of long adjectives and adverbs (e.g., *more beautiful*). In addition to only co-occurring in 4% of documents, these linguistic forms had low term frequencies of 0.002 and 0.001. When the comparative form *more* occurred as part of a longer form (e.g., *more intelligent*), the whole expression was counted as a long form, and *more* was not additionally counted as a short one.

Texts Using Microsoft Bing, we did a web search for Reuters[3] news articles by expanding the search query with *site:reuters.com.* The following ten topics popular on Bing at the time served as search queries: Game of Thrones, healthcare, street artists, Roger's Cup 2017, SpaceX, electric cars, Bitcoin, Venezuela coup, Brexit, opioid epidemic. The top result for each topic was stored in our database as a Bing result, and the top 20 results

---

[3] www.reuters.com

		Bing	FLAIR
frequent	**regular verbs**	0.012	0.020
	irregular verbs	0.012	0.019
mixed	**present simple**	0.011	0.014
	present continuous	0.001	0.005
infrequent	**comparative d. of short adj. and adv.**	0.001	0.003
	comparative d. of long adj. and adv.	0	0.001

Table 1: Mean relative term frequencies of the linguistic forms used in the study across the top search results provided by Bing and FLAIR.

were used for further reordering.[4] For each topic, we repeatedly configured the FLAIR settings to prioritize texts containing each of the three pairs of linguistic forms presented above and stored the three top hits as FLAIR results. In the end, we had three pairs of news articles per topic: One was the top web search result from Bing and the other one was the top one from FLAIR. The two texts for a given topic and a given pair of linguistic forms were of comparable length (the difference was at most 50% of the shortest article) and at the same or adjacent readability levels calculated using a simple Automated Readability Index (Senter and Smith, 1967).

Participants Twelve English teachers working with upper-intermediate and advanced learners of English in Germany were recruited through university and social media channels. Each participant was reimbursed with a 20 Euro voucher, and all 240 responses were anonymized.

The ages of the participants ranged from 25 to 59 years old, 91% of them being women. The first language of the majority of the participants was German (75%) followed by English (8%), French (8%), and Spanish (8%). All participants had an advanced level of English proficiency and a degree in teaching English. They worked at a secondary school (50%), a high school (42%), or a university (8%). The majority (75%) specified that they were using web search to look for reading material for their students, and 25% said they sometimes used web search for this purpose.

4.4 Results

All the analyses were conducted using R version 3.2.1 (R Core Team, 2009). Packages for individual tests and models are specified in the footnotes.

First, we compared the general preference for FLAIR to that for Bing. The option *Doesn't matter* was selected 25% of the time, and the corresponding responses were not included in the analysis. A chi-square test[5] revealed a significant preference for FLAIR: Participants chose it over Bing 71% of the time; $\chi^2(1) = 16.04$, $p < .001$. They were also more confident in choosing FLAIR: The answer *Definitely* was selected three times more for FLAIR than for Bing; $\chi^2(1) = 12.60$, $p < .001$. Thus, our first hypothesis could be confirmed: Teachers indeed preferred the linguistically enriched texts provided by FLAIR over those provided by Bing when choosing a reading assignment for their students.

We conducted two logistic regression analyses[6] to investigate how texts provided by FLAIR and Bing compared in terms of (i) representation of linguistic forms and (ii) relevance of the content to the topic. In line with the descriptive statistics in Tab. 1, logistic regression models showed that FLAIR ($M = 3.22, SD = 1.07$) was significantly more likely to be rated higher in terms of representation of linguistic forms than Bing ($M = 2.51, SD = 1.15$); $b = 1.89, SE = 0.51$, $p < .001$. Moreover, texts provided by FLAIR ($M = 3.67, SD = 1.08$) were perceived to be slightly more relevant to the topic than those provided by Bing ($M = 3.58, SD = 1.00$) although the difference failed to reach statistical significance; $b = 0.53, SE = 0.74, p = .470$.

In order to test whether the absence of statistical significance was due to chance or texts provided by FLAIR and Bing were indeed comparable with regard to content, we conducted two one-sided tests of equivalence (Schuirmann, 1987).[7] The

---

[4]The number of texts to be retrieved can be configured in the interface. Fig. 1 presented the top 60 results for demonstration purposes. In practice, 20 results are quite heterogeneous and provide a good balance of sufficient variability and speed of analysis.

[5]R native stats package, method *chisq.test()*
[6]R native stats package, method *glm()*
[7]R package *TOSTER*, method *TOSTtwo()*

results were statistically significant ($t_1 = 4.55$, $t_2 = -3.19$, $p_1 < .001$, $p_2 < .001$, 90% CI $[-0.13; 0.31]$), so we could confirm that the samples were equivalent with a medium effect size of 0.5 and an alpha level of .05.

Finally, we used a two-way repeated-measures analysis of variance[8] to test whether the preference for FLAIR depended on the type of linguistic forms. We hypothesized that the more infrequent the target linguistic forms were, the more teachers would prefer texts provided by FLAIR. The first factor was the preference for FLAIR (a five-point scale), and the second factor was the type of linguistic forms (frequent, mixed, or infrequent). ANOVA did not show the tendency that we expected; $F(2, 90) = 0.87, p = .419$; so we inspected the means of all three groups and performed paired samples t-tests.

The biggest mean preference for FLAIR was found for the mixed pair of linguistic forms (present simple and present continuous; $M = 3.92$, $SD = 1.99$), followed by the infrequent group (comparative degree of short adjectives and adverbs; $M = 3.69$, $SD = 1.30$) and the frequent one (regular and irregular verbs; $M = 3.46$, $SD = 1.39$). When we turned the five-point scale into a binary outcome variable (i.e., either selected FLAIR as a reading assignment or not) and calculated the percentage of responses, we found 76% of responses favoring FLAIR in the infrequent group, 75% in the mixed group, and 65% in the frequent one.

As the data in the three groups were not normally distributed (Shapiro-Wilk's normality test[9] yielded significant differences from a normal distribution), we opted for paired two-samples Wilcoxon tests.[10] The paired tests revealed that there was no significant difference between the groups with regard to preference for FLAIR: infrequent and mixed groups, $Z = 128$, $p = .352$; mixed and frequent groups, $Z = 157$, $p = .643$; infrequent and frequent groups, $Z = 217, p = .727$.

5   Discussion

English teachers demonstrated an overall preference for FLAIR over a standard web search engine when choosing a reading assignment for their students. This is in line with our first hypothesis and a strong argument in support of the automatic input enrichment approach.

Feedback from teachers suggested that the relevance of the article to the topic and the content of the article were the decisive factors in choosing one article over the other as a reading assignment. We were, therefore, particularly interested whether there was a trade-off between the content and the representation of linguistic forms in the articles because a large number of the news articles retrieved by FLAIR (40%) were not among the top ten original search results. Thus, we hypothesized that the texts retrieved by FLAIR would have a richer representation of linguistic forms while being less relevant to the topic.

As the number of occurrences of the given linguistic forms in the texts retrieved by FLAIR was higher (see Tab. 1), this indeed resulted in significantly higher teachers' ratings for the representation of linguistic forms. However, counter to our expectations, the texts provided by FLAIR were neither inferior nor superior to those originally retrieved by Bing in terms of content: They were rated slightly, but not significantly, more relevant to the given topic. This suggests that the most appropriate texts for language learners may not appear within the top web search results, and those texts that are not ranked high by standard web search engines can have a higher linguistic and pedagogical potential than the top hits.

As the study showed, automatic input enrichment is particularly beneficial for retrieving texts containing target linguistic forms of lower frequency levels, although the differences were non-significant. This can be explained by document and term frequencies: The high term and document frequencies of frequent linguistic forms make it likely for every retrieved text to contain at least several instances of each form. In this case, the texts prioritized by an automatic input enrichment system may not differ from the original top hits with regard to their linguistic characteristics. Other frequently co-occurring pairs of linguistic forms relevant for language teaching are, for example: adjectives and adverbs (co-occur in 97% of documents), the definite and the indefinite articles (96%), present simple and past simple (93%), *to* infinitives and *ing* verb forms (90%). We propose a way to improve the functionality of automatic input enrichment systems targeting frequent

---

[8]R native stats package, method *aov()*

[9]R package *dplyr*, method *shapiro.test()*

[10]R native stats package, method *wilcox.test()*

linguistic forms in the next section.

Infrequent linguistic forms, on the contrary, appear in few texts together, with a small number of occurrences within each text. The advantage of automatic input enrichment in this case is that it can detect those few texts containing the target infrequent linguistic forms. Other pairs of linguistic forms with a low document co-occurrence frequencies as well as low term frequencies are, for example: the modal verbs *can* and *may* (14%), past perfect and past progressive (12%), future simple and *going to* (9%), wh- questions and yes/no questions (7%), real and unreal conditionals (4%).

In case of mixed pairs of linguistic forms (i.e., the ones consisting of one frequent and one infrequent form), the reordering algorithm pushes the few texts containing the infrequent form to the top. Those texts are at the same time likely to also contain several occurrences of the frequent form because of its high term and document frequencies. Other mixed pairs of linguistic forms relevant for teaching English are: past simple and present perfect (63%), positive and comparative degrees of short adjectives (58%) and adverbs (45%), present simple and future simple (40%), past simple and past continuous (30%). The full list of pairs of linguistic forms with their co-occurrence document frequency was compiled by Chinkina (2015).

The aforementioned results show that, while relying on a standard web search engine for retrieving the results, automatic input enrichment succeeds in providing the texts that are a) enriched with respect to the linguistic forms, b) in line with the information need, and c) suitable as a reading assignment.

6   Conclusion and Outlook

In this paper, we described an online study investigating the effects of automatic input enrichment on English teachers selecting reading material for class. The results of the study show that participants preferred the texts provided by automatic input enrichment over those originally retrieved by a standard web search engine both in terms of representation of linguistic forms and content. The study also provides insights about which linguistic forms benefit the most from automatic input enrichment.

It is important to note that our goal was not to compare automatic input enrichment to web search but to show that the linguistically motivated re-ranking of texts leverages the content and form aspects of the retrieved material. With the abundance of authentic texts available on the web, such reordering does not prioritize texts of low quality but selects the most linguistically appropriate ones in the pool of relevant texts. This means that such systems as FLAIR can rely on standard web search engines for retrieving texts of sound content. Whether automatic input enrichment systems also provide an effective learning environment for language learners should be tested in further end-to-end empirical studies.

Another interesting empirical question would be: For which kind of queries will an input enrichment system find enough texts? Our assumption is that the topics covered in a language classroom are current, prominent, and widely discussed: This is why we selected the texts on popular topics for our online study. However, when searching for texts on more specific topics — or in other less represented languages — fewer relevant texts may be retrieved and the balance of content and form may be skewed. This could be the case for courses targeting English for specific purposes, though for such courses it is likely that special repositories of sample texts from that specific domain would be used. Thus, the automatic analysis and re-ranking can be done on the provided corpus, which is also a capability of the FLAIR system.

Therefore, FLAIR provides an ecologically valid, real-life setting for an empirical evaluation of a number of phenomena discussed in second language acquisition research, such as input flood, input enhancement, structured input activities, and extensive reading. For instance, one could conduct a randomized controlled field study and compare the learning outcomes of two groups of students: one reading and working with the results re-ranked by FLAIR and the other one working with the standard Bing results. In fact, such an experimental yet real-world evaluation in essence only becomes possible thanks to a technology-enabled input enrichment approach such as FLAIR.

Finally, based on the feedback from the English teachers who took part in our study, we identified two strands for potential improvement of automatic input enrichment systems:

1. Providing a variety of contexts in which linguistic forms are used. This challenge can be addressed by the tasks of word and tense

sense disambiguation (Stevenson and Wilks, 2003; Reichart and Rappoport, 2010) that could be expanded to the disambiguation of other linguistic forms. The insights from the task of finding good dictionary examples (Kilgarriff et al., 2008) can help make sure that the contexts in which target linguistic form occur are informative, typical, and intelligible for the learner (Atkins and Rundell, 2008). This could be particularly advantageous for frequent linguistic forms that currently benefit the least from automatic input enrichment as they are richly represented across texts.

2. Integration of a component that automatically generates exercises targeting the selected linguistic forms. The task of automatic question generation has explored generating factual wh- questions (Heilman, 2011), gap sentences (Becker et al., 2012), a combination of those, and grammar-concept questions asking for the meaning of linguistic forms (Chinkina and Meurers, 2017). In line with the idea of providing a variety of contexts, one could generate different types of questions targeting not only different linguistic forms but also different contexts in which those forms occur.

Acknowledgments

This research was funded by the LEAD Graduate School & Research Network [GSC1028], a project of the Excellence Initiative of the German federal and state governments. Maria Chinkina is a doctoral student at the LEAD Graduate School & Research Network.

References

BT Sue Atkins and Michael Rundell. 2008. *The Oxford guide to practical lexicography*. Oxford University Press.

Lee Becker, Sumit Basu, and Lucy Vanderwende. 2012. Mind the gap: Learning to choose gaps for question generation. In *Proceedings of the 2012 Conference of the North American Chapter of the Association for Computational Linguistics: Human Language Technologies*, NAACL HLT '12, pages 742–751, Stroudsburg, PA, USA. Association for Computational Linguistics.

Jasmine Bennöhr. 2007. A web-based personalised textfinder for language learners. In *Data Structures for Linguistic Resources and Applications*, Tübingen. Gunter Narr Verlag.

Jonathan Brown and Maxine Eskenazi. 2004. Retrieval of authentic documents for reader-specific lexical practice. In *InSTIL/ICALL 2004 Symposium on Computer Assisted Learning, NLP and speech technologies in advanced language learning systems*, Venice, Italy. International Speech Communication Association (ISCA).

Maria Chinkina. 2015. Form-focused language-aware information retrieval. M.a. thesis in computational linguistics, Seminar fr Sprachwissenschaft, University of Tbingen.

Maria Chinkina and Detmar Meurers. 2016. Linguistically-aware information retrieval: Providing input enrichment for second language learners. In *Proceedings of the 11th Workshop on Innovative Use of NLP for Building Educational Applications*, pages 188–198, San Diego, CA.

Maria Chinkina and Detmar Meurers. 2017. Question generation for language learning: From ensuring texts are read to supporting learning. In *In Proceedings of the 12th Workshop on Innovative Use of NLP for Building Educational Applications*, page 334.

Kit U Chio. 2009. Reading and second language acquisition. *HKBU Papers in Applied Language Studies*, 13:153–174.

K. Collins-Thompson, P. N. Bennett, R. W. White, S. de la Chica, and D. Sontag. 2011. Personalizing web search results by reading level. In *Proceedings of the Twentieth ACM International Conference on Information and Knowledge Management (CIKM 2011)*.

Michael Heilman. 2011. *Automatic factual question generation from text*. Ph.D. thesis, Carnegie Mellon University.

Adam Kilgarriff, Miloš Husák, Katy McAdam, Michael Rundell, and Pavel Rychlý. 2008. Gdex: Automatically finding good dictionary examples in a corpus. In *Proceedings of EURALEX-08*.

Stephen Krashen. 1977. Some issues relating to the monitor model. *On Tesol*, 77(144-158).

Stephen Krashen. 1989. We acquire vocabulary and spelling by reading: Additional evidence for the input hypothesis. *The modern language journal*, 73(4):440–464.

Jennifer Leeman, Igone Arteagoitia, Boris Fridman, and Catherine Doughty. 1995. Integrating attention to form with meaning: Focus on form in content-based spanish instruction. *Attention and awareness in foreign language learning*, pages 217–258.

Michael H. Long. 1991. Focus on form: A design feature in language teaching methodology. In K. De Bot, C. Kramsch, and R. Ginsberg, editors, *Foreign language research in cross-cultural perspective*, pages 39–52. John Benjamins, Amsterdam.

Maria Pigada and Norbert Schmitt. 2006. Vocabulary acquisition from extensive reading: A case study. *Reading in a foreign language*, 18(1):1.

Development R Core Team. 2009. *R: A Language and Environment for Statistical Computing*. R Foundation for Statistical Computing, Vienna, Austria.

Roi Reichart and Ari Rappoport. 2010. Tense sense disambiguation: a new syntactic polysemy task. In *Proceedings of the 2010 Conference on Empirical Methods in Natural Language Processing*, pages 325–334. Association for Computational Linguistics.

R. Schmidt. 1990. The role of consciousness in second language learning. *Applied Linguistics*, 11:206–226.

Donald J Schuirmann. 1987. A comparison of the two one-sided tests procedure and the power approach for assessing the equivalence of average bioavailability. *Journal of pharmacokinetics and biopharmaceutics*, 15(6):657–680.

RJ Senter and Edgar A Smith. 1967. Automated readability index. Technical report, Cincinatti University Ohio.

D. I. Slobin, editor. 1985. *The crosslinguistic study of language acquisition*. L. Erlbaum Associates, Hillsdale, NJ.

Mark Stevenson and Yorick Wilks. 2003. Word-sense disambiguation. In Ruslan Mitkov, editor, *The Oxford Handbook of Computational Linguistics*, chapter 13, pages 249–265. Oxford University Press.

Martha Trahey and Lydia White. 1993. Positive evidence and preemption in the second language classroom. *Studies in second language acquisition*, 15(02):181–204.

Sowmya Vajjala and Detmar Meurers. 2012. On improving the accuracy of readability classification using insights from second language acquisition. In *In Proceedings of the 7th Workshop on Innovative Use of NLP for Building Educational Applications*, pages 163–173, Montral, Canada. Association for Computational Linguistics.

Bill VanPatten. 1990. Attending to form and content in the input: An experiment in consciousness. *Studies in Second Language Acquisition*, 12(3):287–301.

Bill VanPatten and Soile Oikkenon. 1996. Explanation versus structured input in processing instruction. *Studies in Second Language Acquisition*, 18(04):495–510.

Rob Waring and I.S.P. Nation. 2004. Second language reading and incidental vocabulary learning. *Angles on the English speaking world*, 4:97–110.

Estimating Linguistic Complexity for Science Texts

Farah Nadeem and **Mari Ostendorf**
Dept. of Electrical Engineering
University of Washington
{farahn,ostendor}@uw.edu

Abstract

Evaluation of text difficulty is important both for downstream tasks like text simplification, and for supporting educators in classrooms. Existing work on automated text complexity analysis uses linear models with engineered knowledge-driven features as inputs. While this offers interpretability, these models have lower accuracy for shorter texts. Traditional readability metrics have the additional drawback of not generalizing to informational texts such as science. We propose a neural approach, training on science and other informational texts, to mitigate both problems. Our results show that neural methods outperform knowledge-based linear models for short texts, and have the capacity to generalize to genres not present in the training data.

1 Introduction

A typical classroom presents a diverse set of students in terms of their reading comprehension skills, particularly in the case of English language learners (ELLs). Supporting these students often requires educators to estimate accessibility of instructional texts. To address this need, several automated systems have been developed to estimate text difficulty, including readability metrics like Lexile (Stenner et al., 1988), the end-to-end system TextEvaluator (Sheehan et al., 2013), and linear models (Vajjala and Meurers, 2014; Petersen and Ostendorf, 2009; Schwarm and Ostendorf, 2005). These systems leverage knowledge-based features to train regression or classification models. Most systems are trained on literary and generic texts, since analysis of text difficulty is usually tied to language teaching. Existing approaches for automated text complexity analysis pose two issues: 1) systems using knowledge based features typically work better for longer texts (Vajjala and Meurers, 2014), and 2) complex-

ity estimates are less accurate for informational texts such as science (Sheehan et al., 2013). In the context of science, technology and engineering (STEM) education, both problems are significant. Teachers in these areas have less expertise in identifying appropriate reading material for students as opposed to language teachers, and shorter texts become important when dealing with assessment questions and identifying the most difficult parts of instructional texts to modify for supporting students who are ELLs.

Our work specifically looks at ways to address these two problems. First, we propose recurrent neural network (RNN) architectures for estimating linguistic complexity, using text as input without feature engineering. Second, we specifically train on science and other informational texts, using the grade level of text as a proxy for linguistic complexity and dividing grades k-12 into 6 groups. We explore four different RNN architectures in order to identify aspects of text which contribute more to complexity, with a novel structure introduced to account for cross-sentence context. Experimental results show that when specifically trained for informational texts, RNNs can accurately predict text difficulty for shorter science texts. The models also generalize to other types of texts, but perform slightly worse than feature-based regression models on a mix of genres for texts longer than 100 words. We use attention with all models, both to improve accuracy, and as a tool to visualize important elements of text contributing to linguistic complexity. The key contributions of the work include new neural network architectures for characterizing documents and experimental results demonstrating good performance for predicting reading level of short science texts.

The rest of the paper is organized as follows: section 2 looks at existing work on automated readability analysis and introduces RNN architec-

45

Proceedings of the Thirteenth Workshop on Innovative Use of NLP for Building Educational Applications, pages 45–55
New Orleans, Louisiana, June 5, 2018. ©2018 Association for Computational Linguistics

tures we build on for this work. Section 3 lays out the data sources, section 4 covers proposed models, and section 5 presents results. Discussion and concluding remarks follow in sections 6 and 7.

2   Background

Studies have shown that language difficulty of instructional materials and assessment questions impacts student performance, particularly for language learners (Hickendorff, 2013; Abedi and Lord, 2001; Abedi, 2006). This has lead to extensive work on readability analysis, some of which is explored here. The second part of this section looks at work that leverages RNNs in automatic text classification tasks and the use of attention with RNNs.

2.1   Automated Readability Analysis

Traditional reading metrics including Flesch-Kincaid (Kincaid et al., 1975) and Coleman-Liau index (Coleman and Liau, 1975) are often used to assess a text for difficulty. These metrics utilize surface features such as average length of sentences and words, or word lists (Chall and Dale, 1995). The development of automated text analysis systems has made it possible to leverage additional linguistic features, as well as conventional reading metrics, to estimate text complexity quantified as reading level. NLP tools can be used to extract a variety of lexical, syntactic and discourse features from text, which can then be used with traditional features as input to models for predicting reading level. Some of the models include statistical language models (Collins-Thompson and Callan, 2004), support vector machine classifiers (Schwarm and Ostendorf, 2005; Petersen and Ostendorf, 2009), and logistic regression (Feng et al., 2010). Text coherence has also been explored as a predictor of difficulty level in (Graesser et al., 2004), with an extended feature set that includes syntactic complexity and discourse in addition to coherence (Graesser et al., 2011).

A study conducted in (Nelson et al., 2012) indicates that metrics that incorporate a large set of linguistic features perform better at predicting text difficulty level; the metrics were specifically tested on the Common Core Standards (CCS) texts.[1] Features from second language acquisition complexity measures were used in (Vajjala and Meurers, 2012) to improve readability assessment. This

feature set was further extended to include morphological, semantic and psycholinguistic features to build a readability analyzer for shorter texts (Vajjala and Meurers, 2014). A tool specifically built for text complexity analysis for teaching and assessing is the TextEvaluator™. While knowledge-based features offer interpretability, a drawback is that if the text being analyzed is short, the feature vector is sparse, and prediction accuracy drops (Vajjala and Meurers, 2014). This is particularly true for assessment questions, which are shorter than the samples most models are trained on.

Generally, for any text classification task, the type of text used for training the model is important in terms of how well it performs; training on more representative text tends to improve performance. The work in (Sheehan et al., 2013) shows that traditional readability measures underestimate the reading level of literary texts, and overestimate that of informational texts, such as history, science and mathematics articles. This is due, in part, to the vocabulary specific to the genre. Science texts have longer words, though they may be easier to infer from context. Literary texts, on the other hand, might have simpler words, but more complicated sentence structure. The work demonstrated that more accurate grade level estimates can be obtained by two stage classification: i) classify the text as either literary, informational, or mixed, and then ii) use a genre-dependent analyzer to estimate the level. In an analysis on how well a model trained on news and informational articles generalizes to the categories in CCS, the work in (Vajjala and Meurers, 2014) shows better performance on informational genre than literary texts. Training on more representative text, however, requires genre-specific annotated data.

2.2   Text Classification with RNNs

Recurrent neural networks (RNNs) are adept at learning text representations, as demonstrated by language modeling (Mikolov et al., 2010) and text classification tasks (Yogatama et al., 2017). Additional RNN structures have been proposed for improved representation, including tree LSTMs (Tai et al., 2015) and a hierarchical RNN (Yang et al., 2016). In addition, hierarchical models have been proposed to better represent document structure (Yang et al., 2016).

Attention mechanisms were introduced to improve neural machine translation tasks (Bahdanau et al., 2014), and have also been shown to im-

---

[1] http://www.corestandards.org/

prove the performance of text classification (Yang et al., 2016). In machine translation, attention is computed over the source sequence when predicting the words in the target sequence. This "context" attention is based on a score computed between the target hidden state h_t and a subset of the source hidden states h_s. The score can be computed in several ways, of which a general form is $score(h_t, h_s) = h_t^T W_\alpha h_s^T$ (Luong et al., 2015).

Attention has also been used for a variety of other language processing tasks. In particular, for text classification, attention weights are learned that target the final classification decision. This approach is referred to as "self attention" in (Lin et al., 2017), but will be referred to here as "task attention." The hierarchical RNN in (Yang et al., 2016) uses task attention mechanisms at both word and sentence levels. Since our work builds on this model, it is described in further detail in section 4. In addition, we propose extensions of the hierarchical RNN that leverage attention in different ways, including combining the concept of context attention from machine translation with task attention to capture interdependence of adjoining sentences in a document.

3 Data

For our work we consider grade level as a proxy for linguistic complexity. Within a grade level, there is variability across different genres, which students are expected to learn. Since there is no publicly available data set for estimating grade level and text difficulty aimed at informational texts, we created a corpus using online science, history and social studies textbooks. The textbooks are written for either specific grades, or for a grade range, e.g. grades 6-8. There are a total of 44 science textbooks and 11 history and social studies textbooks, distributed evenly across grades K-12. Given the distribution of textbooks for each grade level, we decide to classify into one of six grade bands: K-1, 2-3, 4-5, 6-8, 9-10 and 11-12. Because of our interest in working with short texts, we split the books into paragraphs, using end line as the delimiter.[2] In addition to the textbooks, we also used the WeeBit corpus (Vajjala and Meurers, 2012) for training, again split into paragraphs.

Grade Level	All chapters	Test set chapters
K-1	25	-
2-3	22	2
4-5	53	9
6-8	165	12
9-10	48	5
11-12	28	3

Table 1: Chapter-based test data split

We have three different sources of test data: i) the CCS appendix B texts, ii) a subset of the online texts that we collected,[3] and iii) a collection of science assessment items.

The CCS appendix B data is of interest because it has been extensively used for evaluating linguistic complexity models, e.g. in (Sheehan et al., 2013; Vajjala and Meurers, 2014). It includes both informational and literary texts. We use document-level samples from the CCS data for comparison to prior work, and paragraph-level samples to provide a more direct comparison to the information test data we created.

For the informational texts, we selected chapters from multiple open source texts. Since we had so few texts at the K-1 level, the test data only included texts from higher grade levels, as shown in table 1. The paragraphs in these chapters were randomly assigned to test and validation sets.

To assess the models on stand alone texts, we assembled a corpora of science assessment questions from (Khot et al., 2015; Clark et al., 2018), AI2 Science Questions Mercury,[4] and AI2 Science Questions v2.1 (October 2017).[5] This test set includes 5470 questions for grades 6-8 from sources including standardized state and national tests. The average length of a question is 49 words.

For training, two data configurations were used. When testing on the CCS data and the science assessment questions, there is no concern about overlap between training and test data, so all text can be used for training. We held out 10% of this data for analysis, and the remaining text is used for the D_1 training configuration. Data statistics are given in table 2. About 20% of the training sam-

---

[2]In splitting the text into paragraphs, we are implicitly assuming that all paragraphs have the same linguistic complexity as the textbook, which is probably not the case. Thus, there will be noise in both the training and test data, so some variation in the predicted levels is to be expected.

[3]Available at `https://tinyurl.com/yc59hlgj`.
[4]`http://data.allenai.org/ai2-science-questions-mercury/`
[5]`http://data.allenai.org/ai2-science-questions/`

Grade Level	Train Samples	Mean Length
K-1	739	24.42
2-3	723	62.05
4-5	4570	63.82
6-8	15940	74.79
9-10	3051	68.24
11-12	2301	75.28

Table 2: Training data (D_1) with mean length of text in words

ples (5152) are from WeeBit, spread across grades 2-12. For testing on all three sets, we defined a training configuration D_2 that did not include any text from chapters overlapping with the test data, so there training set is somewhat smaller than for D_1, except for grades K-1. The same WeeBit training data was included in both cases.

For the elementary grade levels, we have much less data than for middle school, and for high school, we have substantial training data with coarser labels (grades 9-12). To work around both issues, we first used all training samples to train the RNN to predict one of four labels (grades K-3, 4-5, 6-8 and 9-12). We then used the training data with fine labels to train to predict one of six labels. This approach was more effective than alternating the training.

4 Models for Estimating Linguistic Complexity

This section introduces the four RNN structures for linguistic complexity estimation, including: a sequential RNN with task attention, a hierarchical attention network, and two proposed extensions of the hierarchical model using multi-head attention and attention over bidirectional context. In all cases, the resulting document vector is used in a final stage of ordinal regression to predict linguistic complexity. All systems are trained in an end-to-end fashion.

4.1 Sequential RNN

The basic RNN model we consider is a sequential RNN with task attention, where the entire text in a paragraph or document is taken as a sequence. For a document t_i with words K words w_{ik} $k \in \{1, 2, ..., K\}$, a bidirectional GRU is used to learn representation for each word h_{ik}, using a forward run from w_{i1} to w_{iK}, and a backward run from w_{iK} to w_{i1}.

$$\overrightarrow{h_{ik}} = \overrightarrow{GRU}(w_{ik}) \qquad (1)$$
$$\overleftarrow{h_{ik}} = \overleftarrow{GRU}(w_{ik}) \qquad (2)$$
$$h_{ik} = [\overrightarrow{h_{ik}}, \overleftarrow{h_{ik}}] \qquad (3)$$

Attention is computed over the entire sequence α_{ik}, and used to compute the document representation v_i^{seq}:

$$u_{ik} = tanh(W_s h_{ik} + b_s) \qquad (4)$$
$$\alpha_{ik} = \frac{exp(u_{ik}^T u_s)}{\sum_{ik} exp(u_{ik}^T u_s)} \qquad (5)$$
$$v_i^{seq} = \sum_k \alpha_{ik} h_{ik} \qquad (6)$$

The document vector is used to predict reading level. Since the grade levels are ordered categorical labels, we implement ordinal regression using the proportional odds model (McCullagh, 1980). For the reading level labels $j \in \{1, 2, ..., J\}$, the cumulative probability is modeled as

$$P(y \leq j | v_i^{seq}) = \sigma(\beta_j - w_{ord}^T v_i^{seq}), \qquad (7)$$

where $\sigma(.)$ is the sigmoid function, and β_j and w_{ord} are estimated during training by minimizing the negative log-likelihood

$$\mathcal{L}_{ord} = -\sum_i \log(\sigma(\beta_{j(i)} - w_{ord}^T v_i^{seq}) - \qquad (8)$$
$$\sigma(\beta_{j(i)-1} - w_{ord}^T v_i^{seq})).$$

4.2 Hierarchical RNN

While a sequential RNN has the capacity to capture discourse across sentences, it does not capture document structure. Therefore, we also explored the hierarchical attention network for text classification from (Yang et al., 2016). The model builds a vector representation v_i for each document t_i with L sentences s_l, $l \in \{1, 2, .., L\}$, each with T_l words w_{lt}, $t \in \{1, 2, ..., T_l\}$. The first level of the hierarchy takes words as input and learns a representation for each word h_{lt} using a bidirectional GRU. Task attention at the word level α_{lt} highlights words important for the classification task, and is computed using the word level context vector u_w. The word representations are then averaged using attention weights to form a sentence representation s_l

$$\alpha_{lt} = \frac{exp(u_{lt}^T u_w)}{\sum_t exp(u_{lt}^T u_w)} \qquad (9)$$
$$s_l = \sum_t \alpha_{lt} h_{lt}, \qquad (10)$$

where $u_{lt} = tanh(W_w h_{lt} + b_w)$ is a projection of the target hidden state for learning word-level attention. The second level of the hierarchy takes the sentence vectors as input, learns representation h_l for them using a bidirectional GRU. Using a method similar to the word-level attention, a document representation v_i is created using sentence-level task attention α_l which is computed using the sentence level context vector u_s

$$\alpha_l = \frac{exp(u_l^T u_s)}{\sum_l exp(u_l^T u_s)} \qquad (11)$$
$$v_i = \sum_l \alpha_l h_l, \qquad (12)$$

where $u_l = tanh(W_s h_l + b_s)$ is analogous to u_{lt} at the sentence level. The word- and sentence-level context vectors, u_w and u_s, as well as W_w, W_s, b_w and b_s, are learned during training.

4.3 Multi-Head Attention

Work has shown that having multiple attention heads improves neural machine translation tasks (Vaswani et al., 2017). To capture multiple aspects contributing to text complexity, we learn two sets of word level task attention over the word level GRU output. These two sets of sentence vectors feed into separate sentence-level GRUs to give us two document vectors by averaging using task attention weights at the sentence level. The document vectors are then concatenated to form the document representation. The multi-head attention RNN is shown in figure 1.

4.4 Hierarchical RNN with Bidirectional Context

The hierarchical model is designed for representing document structure, however, the sentences within a document are encoded independently. To capture information across sentences, we extend the concept of context attention used in machine translation, using it to learn context vectors for adjoining sentences. We extend the hierarchical RNN by introducing bi-directional context with attention. Using the word level GRU output, a "look-back" context vector $c_{l-1}(w_{lt})$ is calculated using context attention over the preceding sentence, and a "look-ahead" context vector $c_{l+1}(w_{lt})$ using context attention over the following sentence for each word in the current sentence.

$$\alpha_{(l-1)t}(w_{lt}) = \frac{exp(score(h_{lt},h_{(l-1)t}))}{\sum_{t'} exp(score(h_{lt},h_{(l-1)t'}))} \qquad (13)$$
$$c_{l-1}(w_{lt}) = \sum_{t'} \alpha_{(l-1)t'}(w_{lt})h_{(l-1)t'} \qquad (14)$$

$$\alpha_{(l+1)t}(w_{lt}) = \frac{exp(score(h_{lt},h_{(l+1)t}))}{\sum_{t'} exp(score(h_{lt},h_{(l+1)t'}))} \qquad (15)$$
$$c_{l+1}(w_{lt}) = \sum_{t'} \alpha_{(l+1)t'}(w_{lt})h_{(l+1)t'} \qquad (16)$$

where $score(h_{lt}, h_{kt}) = h_{lt} W_\alpha h_{kt}^T$ and a single W_α is used for computing the score in both directions. The context vectors are concatenated with the hidden state to form the new hidden state h'_{lt}.

$$h'_{lt} = [c_{l-1}(w_{lt}), h_{lt}, c_{l+1}(w_{lt})] \qquad (17)$$

The rest of the structure is the same as a hierarchical RNN, using equations 9-12 with h'_{lt} instead of h_{lt}. Figure 2 shows the structure for calculating 'look-back" context.

4.5 Implementation Details

The implementation is done via the Tensorflow library (Abadi et al., 2016).[6] All RNNs use GRUs (Cho et al., 2014) with layer normalization (Ba et al., 2016), trained using Adam optimizer (Kingma and Ba, 2014) with a learning rate of 0.001. Regularization was done via drop out. The validation set was used to do hyper-parameter tuning, with a grid search over drop out rate, number of epochs, and hidden dimension of GRU cells. Good result for all four architectures are obtained with a batch size of 10, a dropout rate of 0.5-0.7, a cell size of 75-250 for the word-level GRU, and a cell size of 40-75 for the sentence-level GRU. For the RNN, we also trained a version with a larger word-level hidden layer cell size of 600.

Pre-trained Glove embeddings[7] are used for all models (Pennington et al., 2014), using a vocabulary size of 65000-75000.[8] The out of vocabulary (OOV) percentage on the CCS test set was 3%, and on the informational test set was 0.5%. All OOV words were mapped to an 'UNK' token. The text was lower-cased, and split into sentences for the hierarchical models using the natural language toolkit (NLTK) (Loper and Bird, 2002).

5 Results and Analysis

We test our models on the two science test sets, as well as on the CCS appendix B document level texts and a paragraph-level version of these texts. We also evaluated the best performing

---

[6]The code and trained models are available at `https://github.com/Farahn/Liguistic-Complexity`.

[7]`http://nlp.stanford.edu/data/glove.840B.300d.zip`

[8]In vocabulary words not present in Glove had randomly initialized word embeddings.

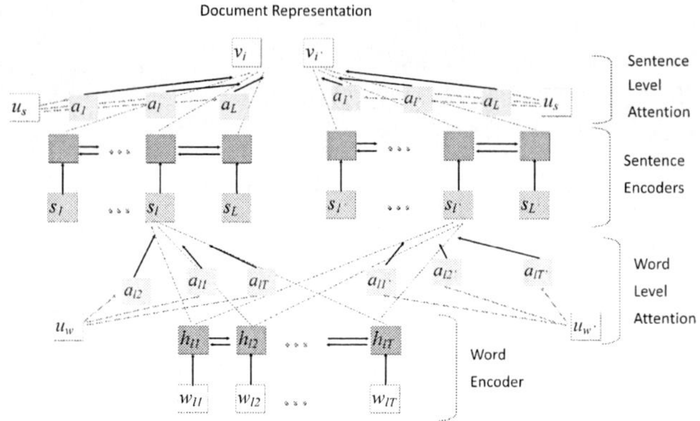

Figure 1: RNN with Multi-Head Attention

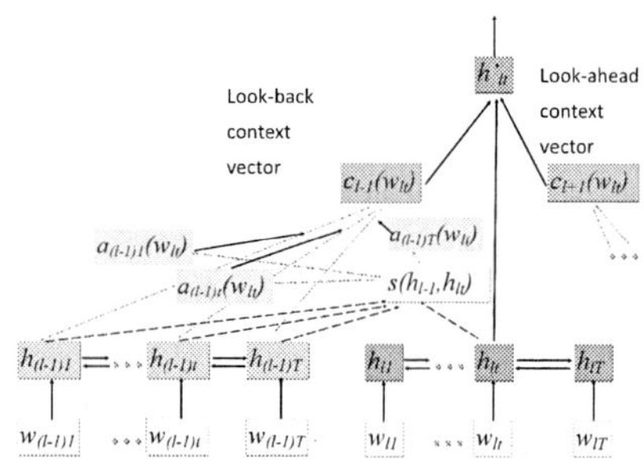

Figure 2: RNN with Bidirectional Context and Attention

model on the middle school science questions data set. Since both the true reading level and predicted levels are ordered variables, we use Spearman's rank correlation as the evaluation metric to capture the monotonic relation between the predictions and the true levels.

As a baseline, we use the WeeBit linear regression system (Vajjala and Meurers, 2014). The WeeBit system uses knowledge-based features as input to a linear regression model to predict reading level as a number between 1 and 5.5, which maps to text appropriate for readers 7-16 years of age. The feature set includes parts-of-speech (e.g. density of different parts-of-speech), lexical (e.g. measurement of lexical variation), syntactic (e.g. the number of verb phrases), morphological (e.g. ratio of transitive verbs to total words) and psycholinguistic (e.g. age of acquisition) features. There are no features related to discourse, thus it is possible to compute features for sentence level texts. The system was trained on a subset of the data that our system was trained on, so it is at a disadvantage. We did not have the capability to

retrain the system.

5.1 Results by Genre

Results for the different models:

- sequential RNN with self attention (RNN),

- large sequential RNN with self attention (RNN 600),

- hierarchical RNN with attention at the word and sentence level (HAN),

- hierarchical RNN with bidirectional context and attention (BCA), and

- multi-head attention (MHA)

are shown in table 3, together with the results for the WeeBit system which has state-of-the-art results on the CCS documents. For the CCS data, both D_1 and D_2 training configurations are used for the neural models; only D_2 is used for the informational test set. For all of these models the hidden layer dimension for the word level was between 125 and 250. We also trained a sequential RNN with a larger hidden layer dimension of 600.

The HAN does better for document level samples than a sequential RNN; the converse is true for paragraph level texts. The RNN with a larger hidden layer dimension performs better for longer texts, while the performance for smaller dimension RNN deteriorates with increasing text length. The BCA model seems to generalize to longer documents and new genres better than the other neural networks.

Figure 3 shows the error distribution for $BCA(D_1)$ in terms of distance from true prediction broken down by genre on the 168 CCS documents. The category of informational texts is often over

Test Set	Model	Samples	WeeBit	RNN	RNN 600	HAN	BCA	MHA
CCS Document	D_1	168	0.69	0.28	0.43	0.47	0.55	0.42
CCS Paragraphs	D_1	1532	0.36	0.30	0.25	0.29	0.32	0.28
CCS Document	D_2	168	0.69	0.34	0.38	0.43	0.48	0.43
CCS Paragraphs	D_2	1532	0.36	0.27	0.26	0.24	0.30	0.29
Informational Paragraphs	D_2	1361	0.22	0.51	0.60	0.60	0.62	0.60

Table 3: Results (Spearman Rank Correlation)

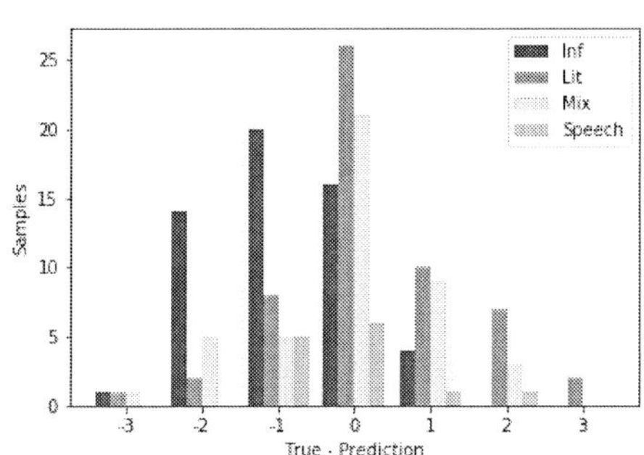

Figure 3: Error distribution for the CCS documents BCA(D_1)

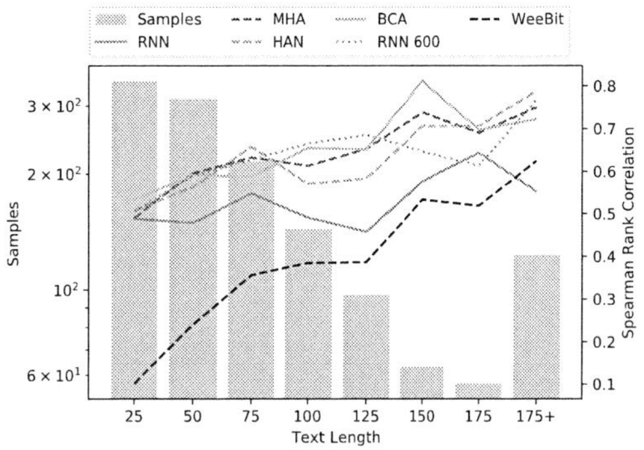

Figure 4: Performance vs. text length for informational paragraphs BCA(D_2)

predicted, which we hypothesize is roughly due to specific articles related to the United States history and constitution. The only training data for our models with that subject is in the grades 6-8 and 9-12 categories. The performance for literary and mixed texts, on the other hand, is roughly unbiased; this shows that the model is better at generalizing to non-informational texts, even when there are no literary text samples in the training data.

5.2 Results by Length

Figures 4 and 5 show the performance of our models and the WeeBit model as a function of document length, both on the informational paragraphs test set and the CCS paragraph level test set. The results indicate that for shorter texts, particularly under 100 words, neural models tend to do better. Even for a mixture of genres, the model with bidirectional context performs better than the feature-based regression model, as shown in figure 5.

It is likely that the WeeBit results results on shorter texts would improve if trained on the same training set that is used for the neural models. However, we hypothesize that the feature-based approach is less well suited for shorter documents because the feature vector will be more sparse.

Comparing the CCS document- and paragraph-level test sets, the average percentage of features that are zero-valued is 28% for document-level texts and 44% for paragraph-level texts. The most sparse vectors are 40% and 81% for document and paragraph-level texts, respectively.

5.3 Results for Science Assessment Questions

Finally, we apply both the baseline WeeBit system and our best model (BCA trained on D_1) to the set of 5470 grade 6-8 science questions. The results are shown in figures 6 and 7, where the grade 6-8 category (ages 11-14) corresponds to predicted level 3 for BCA and predicted level 4 for WeeBit. The results indicate that BCA predictions are better aligned with human rankings than the baseline. As expected, grade 6 questions more likely to be predicted as less difficult than grade 8 questions.

5.4 Attention Visualization

Attention can help provide insight into what the model is learning. In the analyses here, all attention values are normalized by dividing by the highest attention value in the sentence/document to account for different sequence lengths.

Figure 8 shows the word-level attention for the

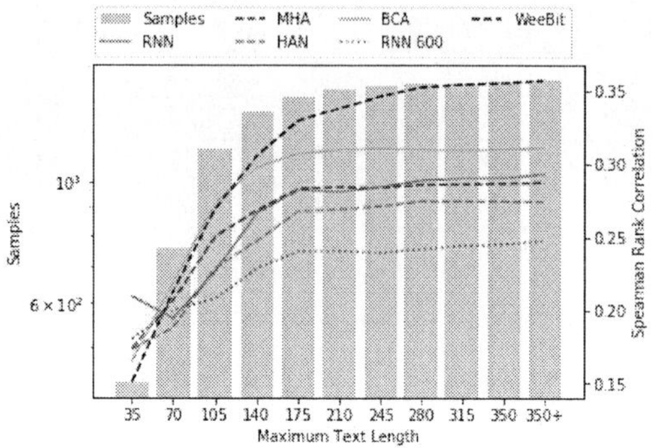

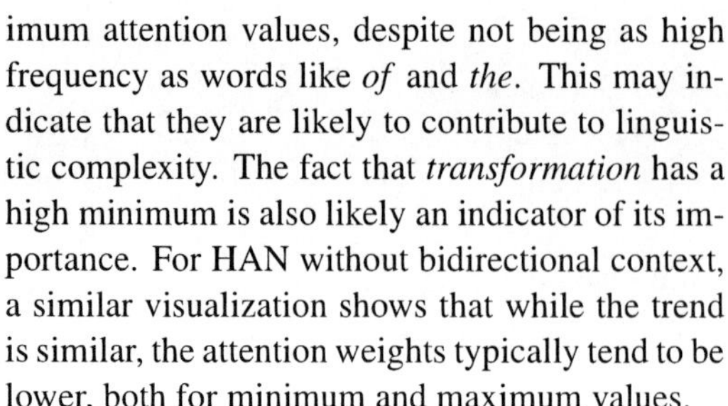

Figure 5: Performance vs. maximum text length for CCS paragraphs BCA(D_1)

BCA and HAN for a sample text from the science assessment questions test set. (Attention weights in the figure are smoothed to reflect the fact that a word vector from a biLSTM reflects the word's context.) The results show that attention weights are more sparse for HAN than for BCA. At the sentence level (not shown here), the BCA sentence weights tend to be more uniformly distributed, whereas HAN weights are again more selective.

Another aspect of the attention is that a word does not have the same attention level for all occurrences in a document. We look at maximum and minimum values of attention as a function of word frequency for each grade band, shown in figure 9 for grade 6-8 science assessment questions.

The pattern is similar for each grade band in the validation and test sets. The minimum attention values assigned to a word drop with increasing word frequency, while the maximum values increase. This suggests that the attention weights are more confident for more frequent words, such as *of*. Words like *fusion* and *m/s* get high max-

imum attention values, despite not being as high frequency as words like *of* and *the*. This may indicate that they are likely to contribute to linguistic complexity. The fact that *transformation* has a high minimum is also likely an indicator of its importance. For HAN without bidirectional context, a similar visualization shows that while the trend is similar, the attention weights typically tend to be lower, both for minimum and maximum values.

We find that sentence-end tokens (period, exclamation and question mark) have high average attention weight, ranging from 0.54 to 0.81, while sentence-internal punctuation (comma, colon and semicolon) get slightly lower weights, ranging from 0.20 to 0.47. The trend is similar for all grades. These high attention values might be due to punctuation serving as a proxy for sentence structure. It is interesting to note that the question mark gets higher minimum attention value than period, despite being high frequency. It may be that questions carry information that is particularly relevant to informational text difficulty.

6 Discussion

Our work differs from existing models that estimate text difficulty since we do not use engineered features. There are advantages and disadvantages to both approaches, which we briefly discuss here. Models using engineered features based on research on language acquisition offer interpretability and insight into which specific linguistic features are contributing to text difficulty. An additional advantage of using engineered features in a regression or classification model is that less training data is required.

However, given both the evolving theories in

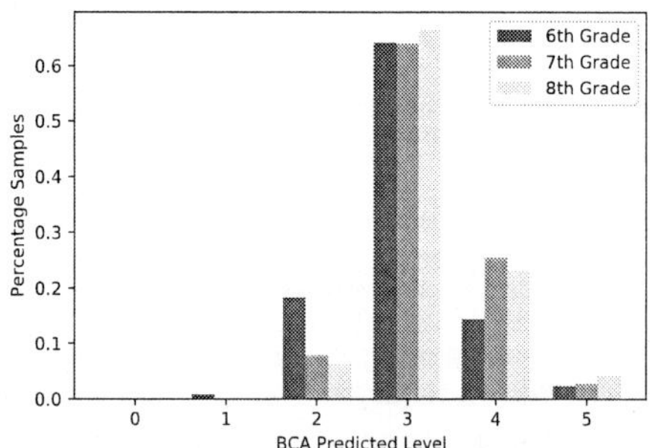

Figure 6: BCA predicted levels for middle school science assessment questions

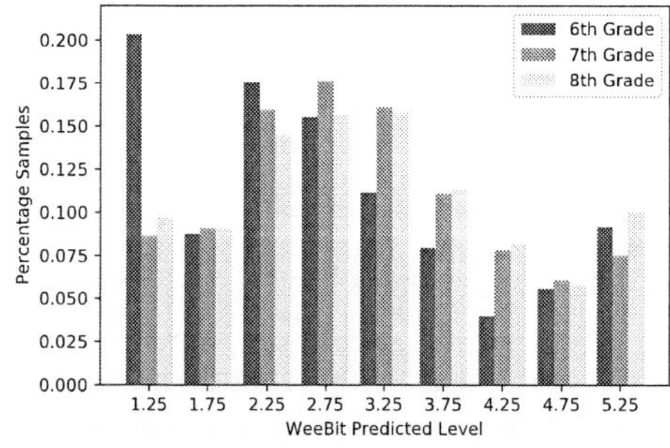

Figure 7: WeeBit predicted levels for middle school science assessment questions

a physicist wants to determine the speed a car must reach to jump over a ramp . the physicist conducts three trials . in trials two and three , the speed of the car is increased by 20 miles per hour . what is the physicist investigating when he changes the speed ? (a) the control (b) the hypothesis statement (c) the dependent (responding) variable (d) the independent (manipulated) variable

a physicist wants to determine the speed a car must reach to jump over a ramp . the physicist conducts three trials . in trials two and three , the speed of the car is increased by 20 miles per hour . what is the physicist investigating when he changes the speed ? (a) the control (b) the hypothesis statement (c) the dependent (responding) variable (d) the independent (manipulated) variable

Figure 8: Word level attention visualization for BCA (top) and HAN (bottom) for a middle school science assessment question

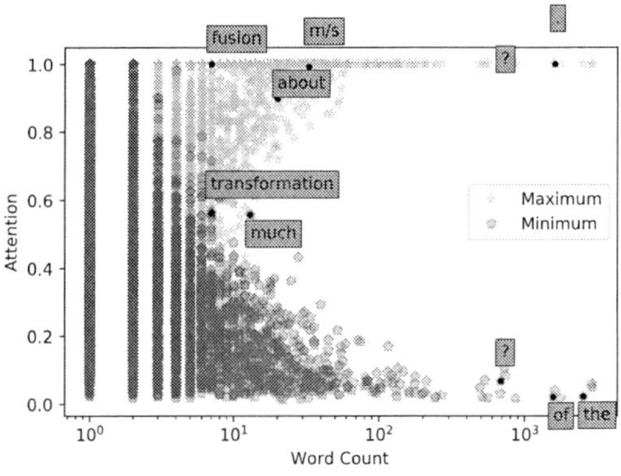

Figure 9: Maximum and minimum values of attention as a function of word count for BCA

language acquisition and the large number of variables that impact second language acquisition, the methodologies used in language acquisition research have certain limitations. For example, the number of variables that can be considered in a study is practically limited, the sample population is often small, and the question of qualitative vs. quantitative methodologies used can influence outcomes (more details in (Larsen-Freeman and Long, 2014; Mitchell et al., 2013)). These limitations can carry into the feature engineering process. Using a model with text as input ensures that these constraints are not inherently part of the model; the performance of the system is not limited by the features provided. Of course, performance is limited by the training data, both in terms of the cost of collection and any biases inherent in the data. In addition, with advances in neural architectures such as attention modeling, there may be opportunities for identifying specific aspects of texts that are particularly difficult, though research in this direction is still in early stages.

7 Conclusion

In summary, this work explored different neural architectures for linguistic complexity analysis, to mitigate issues with accuracy of systems based on engineered features. Experimental results show that it is possible to achieve high accuracy on texts shorter than 100 words using RNNs with attention. Using hierarchical structure improves results, particularly with attention models that leverage bidirectional sentence context. Testing on a mix of genres shows that the best neural model can generalize to subjects beyond what it is trained on, though it performs slightly worse than a feature-based regression model on texts longer than 100 words. More training data from other genres will likely reduce the performance gap. Analysis of attention weights can provide insights into which phrases/sentences are important, both at the aggregate and sample level. Developing new methods for analysis of attention may be useful both for improving model performance and for providing more interpretable results for educators.

Two aspects not considered in this work are explicit representation of syntax and discourse structure. Syntax can be incorporated by concatentating word and dependency embeddings at the token level. Our BCA model was designed to capture cross-sentence coherence and coordination, but it may be useful to extend the hierarchy for longer documents and/or introduce explicit models of the types of discourse features used in Coh-Metrix (Graesser et al., 2004).

Acknowledgments

We thank Dr. Meurers, Professor University of Tubingen, and Dr. Vajjala-Balakrishna, Assistant Professor Iowa State University, for sharing the WeeBit training corpus, their trained readability assessment model and the Common Core test corpus.

References

Martín Abadi, Ashish Agarwal, Paul Barham, Eugene Brevdo, Zhifeng Chen, Craig Citro, Greg S Corrado, Andy Davis, Jeffrey Dean, Matthieu Devin, et al. 2016. Tensorflow: Large-scale machine learning on heterogeneous distributed systems. *arXiv preprint arXiv:1603.04467*.

Jamal Abedi. 2006. Psychometric issues in the ELL assessment and special education eligibility. *Teachers College Record*, 108(11):2282.

Jamal Abedi and Carol Lord. 2001. The language factor in mathematics tests. *Applied Measurement in Education*, 14(3):219–234.

Jimmy Lei Ba, Jamie Ryan Kiros, and Geoffrey E Hinton. 2016. Layer normalization. *arXiv preprint arXiv:1607.06450*.

Dzmitry Bahdanau, Kyunghyun Cho, and Yoshua Bengio. 2014. Neural machine translation by jointly learning to align and translate. *arXiv preprint arXiv:1409.0473*.

Jeanne Sternlicht Chall and Edgar Dale. 1995. *Readability revisited: The new Dale-Chall readability formula*. Brookline Books.

Kyunghyun Cho, Bart Van Merriënboer, Caglar Gulcehre, Dzmitry Bahdanau, Fethi Bougares, Holger Schwenk, and Yoshua Bengio. 2014. Learning phrase representations using rnn encoder-decoder for statistical machine translation. *arXiv preprint arXiv:1406.1078*.

Peter Clark, Isaac Cowhey, Oren Etzioni, Tushar Khot, Ashish Sabharwal, Carissa Schoenick, and Oyvind Tafjord. 2018. Think you have solved question answering? try arc, the ai2 reasoning challenge. *arXiv preprint arXiv:1803.05457*.

Meri Coleman and Ta Lin Liau. 1975. A computer readability formula designed for machine scoring. *Journal of Applied Psychology*, 60(2):283.

Kevyn Collins-Thompson and James P. Callan. 2004. A language modeling approach to predicting reading difficulty. In *Human Language Technology Conference of the North American Chapter of the Association for Computational Linguistics, HLT-NAACL 2004, Boston, Massachusetts, USA, May 2-7, 2004*, pages 193–200.

Lijun Feng, Martin Jansche, Matt Huenerfauth, and Noémie Elhadad. 2010. A comparison of features for automatic readability assessment. In *Proceedings of the 23rd International Conference on Computational Linguistics: Posters*, pages 276–284. Association for Computational Linguistics.

Arthur C. Graesser, Danielle S. McNamara, and Jonna M. Kulikowich. 2011. Coh-metrix. *Educational Researcher*, 40(5):223–234.

Arthur C Graesser, Danielle S McNamara, Max M Louwerse, and Zhiqiang Cai. 2004. Coh-metrix: Analysis of text on cohesion and language. *Behavior Research Methods*, 36(2):193–202.

Marian Hickendorff. 2013. The language factor in elementary mathematics assessments: Computational skills and applied problem solving in a multidimensional irt framework. *Applied Measurement in Education*, 26(4):253–278.

Tushar Khot, Niranjan Balasubramanian, Eric Gribkoff, Ashish Sabharwal, Peter Clark, and Oren Etzioni. 2015. Markov logic networks for natural language question answering. *arXiv preprint arXiv:1507.03045*.

J Peter Kincaid, Robert P Fishburne Jr, Richard L Rogers, and Brad S Chissom. 1975. Derivation of new readability formulas (automated readability index, fog count and flesch reading ease formula) for navy enlisted personnel. Technical report, Naval Technical Training Command Millington TN Research Branch.

Diederik P Kingma and Jimmy Ba. 2014. Adam: A method for stochastic optimization. *arXiv preprint arXiv:1412.6980*.

Diane Larsen-Freeman and Michael H Long. 2014. *An introduction to second language acquisition research*. Routledge.

Zhouhan Lin, Minwei Feng, Cicero Nogueira do Santos, Mo Yu, Bing Ziang, Bowen Zhou, and Yoshua Bengio. 2017. A structured self-attentive sentence embedding. In *Proc. ICLR*.

Edward Loper and Steven Bird. 2002. Nltk: The natural language toolkit. In *Proceedings of the ACL-02 Workshop on Effective tools and methodologies for teaching natural language processing and computational linguistics-Volume 1*, pages 63–70. Association for Computational Linguistics.

Minh-Thang Luong, Hieu Pham, and Christopher D Manning. 2015. Effective approaches to attention-based neural machine translation. *arXiv preprint arXiv:1508.04025*.

Peter McCullagh. 1980. Regression models for ordinal data. *Journal of the royal statistical society. Series B (Methodological)*, pages 109–142.

Tomáš Mikolov, Martin Karafiát, Lukáš Burget, Jan Černockỳ, and Sanjeev Khudanpur. 2010. Recurrent neural network based language model. In *Eleventh Annual Conference of the International Speech Communication Association*.

Rosamond Mitchell, Florence Myles, and Emma Marsden. 2013. *Second language learning theories*. Routledge.

Jessica Nelson, Charles Perfetti, David Liben, and Meredith Liben. 2012. Measures of text difficulty: Testing their predictive value for grade levels and student performance. *Council of Chief State School Officers, Washington, DC*.

Jeffrey Pennington, Richard Socher, and Christopher Manning. 2014. Glove: Global vectors for word representation. In *Proceedings of the 2014 conference on empirical methods in natural language processing (EMNLP)*, pages 1532–1543.

Sarah E Petersen and Mari Ostendorf. 2009. A machine learning approach to reading level assessment. *Computer speech & language*, 23(1):89–106.

Sarah E Schwarm and Mari Ostendorf. 2005. Reading level assessment using support vector machines and statistical language models. In *Proceedings of the 43rd Annual Meeting on Association for Computational Linguistics*, pages 523–530. Association for Computational Linguistics.

Kathleen M Sheehan, Michael Flor, and Diane Napolitano. 2013. A two-stage approach for generating unbiased estimates of text complexity. In *Proceedings of the Workshop on Natural Language Processing for Improving Textual Accessibility*, pages 49–58.

AJ Stenner, Ivan Horabin, Dean R Smith, and Malbert Smith. 1988. The lexile framework. *Durham, NC: MetaMetrics*.

Kai Sheng Tai, Richard Socher, and Christopher D Manning. 2015. Improved semantic representations from tree-structured long short-term memory networks. *arXiv preprint arXiv:1503.00075*.

Sowmya Vajjala and Detmar Meurers. 2012. On improving the accuracy of readability classification using insights from second language acquisition. In *Proceedings of the Seventh Workshop on Building Educational Applications Using NLP*, pages 163–173. Association for Computational Linguistics.

Sowmya Vajjala and Detmar Meurers. 2014. Readability assessment for text simplification: From analysing documents to identifying sentential simplifications. *ITL-International Journal of Applied Linguistics*, 165(2):194–222.

Ashish Vaswani, Noam Shazeer, Niki Parmar, Jakob Uszkoreit, Llion Jones, Aidan N Gomez, Łukasz Kaiser, and Illia Polosukhin. 2017. Attention is all you need. In *Advances in Neural Information Processing Systems*, pages 6000–6010.

Zichao Yang, Diyi Yang, Chris Dyer, Xiaodong He, Alexander J Smola, and Eduard H Hovy. 2016. Hierarchical attention networks for document classification. In *HLT-NAACL*, pages 1480–1489.

Dani Yogatama, Chris Dyer, Wang Ling, and Phil Blunsom. 2017. Generative and discriminative text classification with recurrent neural networks. *arXiv preprint arXiv:1703.01898*.

Second Language Acquisition Modeling

Burr Settles[*]   **Chris Brust**[*]   **Erin Gustafson**[*]   **Masato Hagiwara**[*]   **Nitin Madnani**[†]
[*]Duolingo, Pittsburgh, PA, USA   [†]ETS, Princeton, NJ, USA
{burr,chrisb,erin,masato}@duolingo.com nmadnani@ets.org

Abstract

We present the task of *second language acqui-sition (SLA) modeling*. Given a history of er-rors made by learners of a second language, the task is to predict errors that they are likely to make at arbitrary points in the future. We de-scribe a large corpus of more than 7M words produced by more than 6k learners of English, Spanish, and French using Duolingo, a popular online language-learning app. Then we report on the results of a shared task challenge aimed studying the SLA task via this corpus, which attracted 15 teams and synthesized work from various fields including cognitive science, lin-guistics, and machine learning.

1 Introduction

As computer-based educational apps increase in popularity, they generate vast amounts of student learning data which can be harnessed to drive per-sonalized instruction. While there have been some recent advances for educational software in do-mains like mathematics, learning a language is more nuanced, involving the interaction of lexi-cal knowledge, morpho-syntactic processing, and several other skills. Furthermore, most work that has applied natural language processing to lan-guage learner data has focused on intermediate-to-advanced students of English, particularly in as-sessment settings. Much less work has been de-voted to beginners, learners of languages other than English, or ongoing study over time.

We propose *second language acquisition (SLA) modeling* as a new computational task to help broaden our understanding in this area. First, we describe a new corpus of language learner data, containing more than 7.1M words, annotated for production errors that were made by more than 6.4k learners of English, Spanish, and French, dur-ing their first 30 days of learning with Duolingo (a popular online language-learning app).

Then we report on the results of a "shared task" challenge organized by the authors using this SLA modeling corpus, which brought together 15 re-search teams. Our goal for this work is three-fold: (1) to synthesize years of research in cog-nitive science, linguistics, and machine learning, (2) to facilitate cross-dialog among these disci-plines through a common large-scale empirical task, and in so doing (3) to shed light on the most effective approaches to SLA modeling.

2 Shared Task Description

Our learner trace data comes from Duolingo: a free, award-winning, online language-learning platform. Since launching in 2012, more than 200 million learners worldwide have enrolled in Duolingo's game-like courses, either via the web-site[1] or mobile apps.

Figure 1(a) is a screen-shot of the home screen, which specifies the game-like curriculum. Each icon represents a skill, aimed at teaching themati-cally or grammatically grouped words or concepts. Learners can tap an icon to access lessons of new material, or to review material once all lessons are completed. Learners can also choose to get a per-sonalized practice session that reviews previously-learned material from anywhere in the course by tapping the "practice weak skills" button.

2.1 Corpus Collection

To create the SLA modeling corpus, we sampled from Duolingo users who registered for a course and reached at least the tenth row of skill icons within the month of November 2015. By limit-ing the data to new users who reach this level of the course, we hope to better capture beginners' broader language-learning process, including re-peated interaction with vocabulary and grammar

---

[1]https://www.duolingo.com

56

Proceedings of the Thirteenth Workshop on Innovative Use of NLP for Building Educational Applications, pages 56–65
New Orleans, Louisiana, June 5, 2018. ©2018 Association for Computational Linguistics

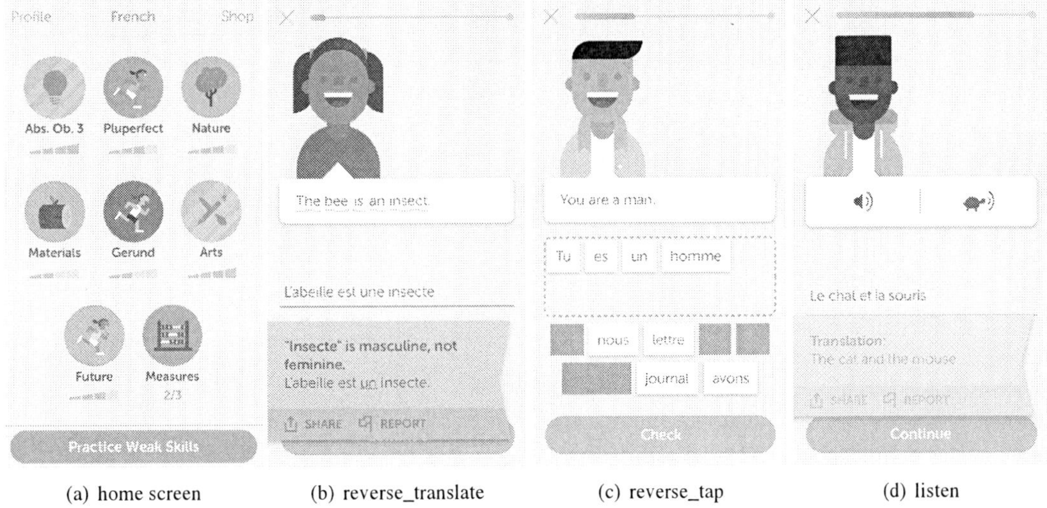

(a) home screen   (b) reverse_translate   (c) reverse_tap   (d) listen

Figure 1: Duolingo screen-shots for an English-speaking student learning French (iPhone app, 2017). (a) The home screen, where learners can choose to do a "skill" lesson to learn new material, or get a personalized practice session by tapping the "practice weak skills" button. (b–d) Examples of the three exercise types included in our shared task experiments, which require the student to construct responses in the language they are learning.

over time. Note that we excluded all learners who took a placement test to skip ahead in the course, since these learners are likely more advanced.

2.2 Three Language Tracks

An important question for SLA modeling is: to what extent does an approach generalize across languages? While the majority of Duolingo users learn English—which can significantly improve job prospects and quality of life (Pinon and Haydon, 2010)—Spanish and French are the second and third most popular courses. To encourage researchers to explore language-agnostic features, or unified cross-lingual modeling approaches, we created three tracks: English learners (who speak Spanish), Spanish learners (who speak English), and French learners (who speak English).

2.3 Label Prediction Task

The goal of the task is as follows: given a history of token-level errors made by the learner in the learning language (L2), accurately predict the errors they will make in the future. In particular, we focus on three Duolingo exercise formats that require the learners to engage in *active recall*, that is, they must construct answers in the L2 through translation or transcription.

Figure 1(b) illustrates a *reverse translate* item, where learners are given a prompt in the language they know (e.g., their L1 or native language), and

learner:	wen	can		help	
reference:	when	can	I	help	?
label:	✗	✓	✗	✓	

Figure 2: An illustration of how data labels are generated. Learner responses are aligned with the most similar reference answer, and tokens from the reference that do not match are labeled errors.

translate it into the L2. Figure 1(c) illustrates a *reverse tap* item, which is a simpler version of the same format: learners construct an answer using a bank of words and distractors. Figure 1(d) is a *listen* item, where learners hear an utterance in the L2 they are learning, and must transcribe it. Duolingo does include many other exercise formats, but we focus on these three in the current work, since constructing L2 responses through translation or transcription is associated with deeper levels of processing, which in turn is more strongly associated with learning (Craik and Tulving, 1975).

Since each exercise can have multiple correct answers (due to synonyms, homophones, or ambiguities in tense, number, formality, etc.), Duolingo uses a finite-state machine to align the learner's response to the most similar reference answer form a large set of acceptable responses, based on token string edit distance (Levenshtein, 1966). For example, Figure 1(b) shows an example of corrective feedback based on such an alignment.

57

Figure 2 shows how we use these alignments to generate labels for the SLA modeling task. In this case, an English (from Spanish) learner was asked to translate, "¿Cuándo puedo ayudar?" and wrote "wen can help" instead of "When can I help?" This produces two errors (a typo and a missing pronoun). We ignore capitalization, punctuation, and accents when matching tokens.

2.4 Data Set Format

Sample data from the resulting corpus can be found in Figure 3. Each token from the reference answer is labeled according to the alignment with the learner's response (the final column: `0` for correct and `1` for incorrect). Tokens are grouped together by exercise, including user-, exercise-, and session-level meta-data in the previous line (marked by the `#` character). We included all exercises done by the users sampled from the 30-day data collection window.

The overall format is inspired by the Universal Dependencies (UD) format[2]. Column 1 is a unique B64-encoded token ID, column 2 is a token (word), and columns 3–6 are morpho-syntactic features from the UD tag set (part of speech, morphology features, and dependency parse labels and edges). These were generated by processing the aligned reference answers with Google SyntaxNet (Andor et al., 2016). Because UD tags are meant to be language-agnostic, it was our goal to help make cross-lingual SLA modeling more straightforward by providing these features.

Exercise meta-data includes the following:
- **user**: 8-character unique anonymous user ID for each learner (B64-encoded)
- **countries**: 2-character ISO country codes from which this learner has done exercises
- **days**: number of days since the learner started learning this language on Duolingo
- **client**: session device platform
- **session**: session type (e.g., lesson or practice)
- **format**: exercise format (see Figure 1)
- **time**: the time (in seconds) it took the learner to submit a response for this exercise.

Lesson sessions (about 77% of the data set) are where new words or concepts are introduced, although lessons also include previously-learned material (e.g., each exercise attempts to introduce only one new word or inflection, so all other tokens should have been seen by the student be-

		TRAIN	DEV	TEST
Track	Users	Tokens (Err)	Tokens (Err)	Tokens (Err)
English	2.6k	2.6M (13%)	387k (14%)	387k (15%)
Spanish	2.6k	2.0M (14%)	289k (16%)	282k (16%)
French	1.2k	927k (16%)	138k (18%)	136k (18%)
Overall	6.4k	5.5M (14%)	814k (15%)	804k (16%)

Table 1: Summary of the SLA modeling data set.

fore). Practice sessions (22%) should contain only previously-seen words and concepts. Test sessions (1%) are mini-quizzes that allow a student to skip out of a single skill in the curriculum (i.e., the student may have never seen this content before in the Duolingo app, but may well have had prior knowledge before starting the course).

It is worth mentioning that for the shared task, we did not provide actual learner responses, only the closest reference answers. Releasing such data (at least in the TEST set) would by definition give away the labels and might undermine the task. However, we plan to release a future version of the corpus that is enhanced with additional meta-data, including the actual learner responses.

2.5 Challenge Timeline

The data were released in two phases. In phase 1 (8 weeks), TRAIN and DEV partitions were released with labels, along with a baseline system and evaluation script, for system development. In phase 2 (10 days), the TEST partition was released without labels, and teams submitted predictions to CodaLab[3] for blind evaluation. To allow teams to compare different system parameters or features, they were allowed to submit up to 10 predictions total (up to 2 per day) during this phase.

Table 1 reports summary statistics for each of the data partitions for all three tracks. We created TRAIN, DEV, and TEST partitions as follows. For each user, the first 80% of their exercises were placed in the TRAIN set, the subsequent 10% in DEV, and the final 10% in TEST. Hence the three data partitions are sequential, and contain ordered observations for all users.

Note that because the three data partitions are sequential, and the DEV set contains observations that are potentially valuable for making TEST set predictions, most teams opted to combine the TRAIN and DEV sets to train their systems in final phase 2 evaluations.

---

[2]http://universaldependencies.org

[3]http://codalab.org

```
# user:XEinXf5+  countries:CO  days:2.678  client:web  session:practice  format:reverse_translate  time:6
oMGsnnH/0101  When     ADV   PronType=Int|fPOS=ADV++WRB                                                    advmod  4  1
oMGsnnH/0102  can      AUX   VerbForm=Fin|fPOS=AUX++MD                                                     aux     4  0
oMGsnnH/0103  I        PRON  Case=Nom|Number=Sing|Person=1|PronType=Prs|fPOS=PRON++PRP                     nsubj   4  1
oMGsnnH/0104  help     VERB  VerbForm=Inf|fPOS=VERB++VB                                                    ROOT    0  0

# user:XEinXf5+  countries:CO  days:5.707  client:android  session:practice  format:reverse_translate  time:22
W+QU2fm70301  He       PRON  Case=Nom|Gender=Masc|Number=Sing|Person=3|PronType=Prs|fPOS=PRON++PRP         nsubj   3  0
W+QU2fm70302  's       AUX   Mood=Ind|Number=Sing|Person=3|Tense=Pres|VerbForm=Fin|fPOS=AUX++VBZ           aux     3  1
W+QU2fm70303  wearing  VERB  Tense=Pres|VerbForm=Part|fPOS=VERB++VBG                                       ROOT    0  0
W+QU2fm70304  two      NUM   NumType=Card|fPOS=NUM++CD                                                     nummod  5  0
W+QU2fm70305  shirts   NOUN  Number=Plur|fPOS=NOUN++NNS                                                    dobj    3  0

# user:XEinXf5+  countries:CO  days:10.302  client:web  session:lesson  format:reverse_translate  time:28
vOeGrMgP0101  We       PRON  Case=Nom|Number=Plur|Person=1|PronType=Prs|fPOS=PRON++PRP                     nsubj   2  0
vOeGrMgP0102  eat      VERB  Mood=Ind|Tense=Pres|VerbForm=Fin|fPOS=VERB++VBP                               ROOT    0  1
vOeGrMgP0103  cheese   NOUN  Degree=Pos|fPOS=ADJ++JJ                                                       dobj    2  1
vOeGrMgP0104  and      CONJ  fPOS=CONJ++CC                                                                 cc      2  0
vOeGrMgP0105  they     PRON  Case=Nom|Number=Plur|Person=3|PronType=Prs|fPOS=PRON++PRP                     nsubj   6  0
vOeGrMgP0106  eat      VERB  Mood=Ind|Tense=Pres|VerbForm=Fin|fPOS=VERB++VBP                               conj    2  1
vOeGrMgP0107  fish     NOUN  fPOS=X++FW                                                                    dobj    6  0
```

Figure 3: Sample exercise data from an English learner over time: roughly two, five, and ten days into the course.

2.6   Evaluation

We use area under the ROC curve (AUC) as the primary evaluation metric for SLA modeling (Fawcett, 2006). AUC is a common measure of ranking quality in classification tasks, and can be interpreted as the probability that the system will rank a randomly-chosen error above a randomly-chosen non-error. We argue that this notion of ranking quality is particularly useful for evaluating systems that might be used for personalized learning, e.g., if we wish to prioritize words or exercises for an individual learner's review based on how likely they are to have forgotten or make errors at a given point in time.

We also report F1 score—the harmonic mean of precision and recall—as a secondary metric, since it is more common in similar skewed-class labeling tasks (e.g., Ng et al., 2013). Note, however, that F1 can be significantly improved simply by tuning the classification threshold (fixed at 0.5 for our evaluations) without affecting AUC.

3   Results

A total of 15 teams participated in the task, of which 13 responded to a brief survey about their approach, and 11 submitted system description papers. All but two of these teams submitted predictions for all three language tracks.

Official shared task results are reported in Table 2. System ranks are determined by sorting teams according to AUC, and using DeLong's test (DeLong et al., 1988) to identify statistical ties. For the remainder of this section, we provide a summary of each team's approach, ordered by the team's average rank across all three tracks. Certain teams are marked with modeling choice indicators ($\Diamond$, $\clubsuit$, $\ddagger$), which we discuss further in §5.

SanaLabs (Nilsson et al., 2018) used a combination of recurrent neural network (RNN) predictions with those of a Gradient Boosted Decision Tree (GBDT) ensemble, trained independently for each track. This was motivated by the observation that RNNs work well for sequence data, while GBDTs are often the best-performing non-neural model for shared tasks using tabular data. They also engineered several token context features, and learner/token history features such as number of times seen, time since last practice, etc.

singsound (Xu et al., 2018) used an RNN architecture using four types of encoders, representing different types of features: token context, linguistic information, user data, and exercise format. The RNN decoder integrated information from all four encoders. Ablation experiments revealed the context encoder (representing the token) contributed the most to model performance, while the linguistic encoder (representing grammatical information) contributed the least.

NYU (Rich et al., 2018) used an ensemble of GBDTs with features engineered based on psychological theories of cognition. Predictions for each track were averaged between a track-specific model and a unified model (trained on data from all three tracks). In addition to the word, user, and exercise features provided, the authors included word lemmas, corpus frequency, L1-L2 cognates, and features indicating user motivation and diligence (derived from usage patterns), and others. Ablation studies indicated that most of the performance was due to the user and token features.

English Track				Spanish Track				French Track		
↑	Team	AUC	F1	↑	Team	AUC	F1	↑	Team	AUC	F1
---	---	---	---	---	---	---	---	---	---	---	---
1	SanaLabs ◇♣	.861	.561	1	SanaLabs ◇♣	.838	.530	1	SanaLabs ◇♣	.857	.573
1	singsound ◇	.861	.559	2	NYU ♣‡	.835	.420	2	singsound ◇	.854	.569
3	NYU ♣‡	.859	.468	2	singsound ◇	.835	.524	2	NYU ♣‡	.854	.493
4	TMU ◇‡	.848	.476	4	TMU ◇‡	.824	.439	4	CECL ‡	.843	.487
5	CECL ‡	.846	.414	5	CECL ‡	.818	.390	5	TMU ◇‡	.839	.502
6	Cambridge ◇	.841	.479	6	Cambridge ◇	.807	.435	6	Cambridge ◇	.835	.508
7	UCSD ♣	.829	.424	7	UCSD ♣	.803	.375	7	UCSD ♣	.823	.442
8	nihalnayak	.821	.376	7	LambdaLab ♣	.801	.344	8	LambdaLab ♣	.815	.415
8	LambdaLab ♣	.821	.389	9	Grotoco	.791	.452	8	Grotoco	.813	.502
10	Grotoco	.817	.462	9	nihalnayak	.790	.338	10	nihalnayak	.811	.431
11	jilljenn	.815	.329	11	ymatusevych	.789	.347	10	jilljenn	.809	.406
12	ymatusevych	.813	.381	11	jilljenn	.788	.306	10	ymatusevych	.808	.441
13	renhk	.797	.448	13	renhk	.773	.432	13	simplelinear	.807	.394
14	zlb241	.787	.003	14	SLAM_baseline	.746	.175	14	renhk	.796	.481
15	SLAM_baseline	.774	.190	15	zlb241	.682	.389	15	SLAM_baseline	.771	.281

Table 2: Final results. Ranks (↑) are determined by statistical ties (see text). Markers indicate which systems include recurrent neural architectures (◇), decision tree ensembles (♣), or a multitask model across all tracks (‡).

TMU (Kaneko et al., 2018) used a combination of two bidirectional RNNs—the first to predict potential user errors at a given token, and a second to track the history of previous answers by each user. These networks were jointly trained through a unified objective function. The authors did not engineer any additional features, but did train a single model for all three tracks (using a track ID feature to distinguish among them).

CECL (Bestgen, 2018) used a logistic regression approach. The base feature set was expanded to include many feature conjunctions, including word n-grams crossed with the token, user, format, and session features provided with the data set.

Cambridge (Yuan, 2018) trained two RNNs—a sequence labeler, and a sequence-to-sequence model taking into account previous answers—and found that averaging their predictions yielded the best results. They focused on the English track, experimenting with additional features derived from other English learner corpora. Hyper-parameters were tuned for English and used as-is for other tracks, with comparable results.

UCSD (Tomoschuk and Lovelett, 2018) used a random forest classifier with a set of engineered features motivated by previous research in memory and linguistic effects in SLA, including "word neighborhoods," corpus frequency, cognates, and repetition/experience with a given word. The system also included features specific to each user, such as mean and variance of error rates.

LambdaLab (Chen et al., 2018) used GBDT models independently for each track, deriving their features from confirmatory analysis of psychologically-motivated hypotheses on the TRAIN set. These include proxies for student engagement, spacing effect, response time, etc.

nihalnayak (Nayak and Rao, 2018) used a logistic regression model similar to the baseline, but added features inspired by research in code-mixed language-learning where context plays an important role. In particular, they included word, part of speech, and metaphone features for previous:current and current:next token pairs.

Grotoco (Klerke et al., 2018) also used logistic regression, including word lemmas, frequency, cognates, and user-specific features such as word error rate. Interestingly, the authors found that ignoring each user's first day of exercise data improved their predictions, suggesting that learners first needed to familiarize themselves with app before their data were reliable for modeling.

jilljenn (Vie, 2018) used a deep factorization machine (DeepFM), a neural architecture developed for click-through rate prediction in recommender systems. This model allows learning from both lower-order and higher-order induced features and their interactions. The DeepFM outperformed a simple logistic regression baseline without much additional feature engineering.

Other teams did not submit system description papers. However, according to a task organizer survey **ymatusevych** used a linear model with multilingual word embeddings, corpus frequency, and several L1-L2 features such as cognates. Additionally, **simplelinear** used an ensemble of some sort (for the French track only). **renhk** and **zlb241** provided no details about their systems.

SLAM_baseline is the baseline system provided by the task organizers. It is a simple logistic regression using data set features, trained separately for each track using stochastic gradient descent on the TRAIN set only.

4 Related Work

SLA modeling is a rich problem, and presents a opportunity to synthesize work from various subfields in cognitive science, linguistics, and machine learning. This section highlights a few key concepts from these fields, and how they relate to the approaches taken by shared task participants.

Item response theory (IRT) is a common psychometric modeling approach used in educational software (e.g., Chen et al., 2005). In its simplest form (Rasch, 1980), an IRT model is a logistic regression with two weights: one representing the learner's ability (i.e., user ID), and the other representing the difficulty of the exercise or test item (i.e., token ID). An extension of this idea is the *additive factor model* (Cen et al., 2008) which adds additional "knowledge components" (e.g., lexical, morphological, or syntactic features). Teams that employed linear models (including our baseline) are essentially all additive factor IRT models.

For decades, tutoring systems have also employed sequence models like HMMs to perform *knowledge tracing* (Corbett and Anderson, 1995), a way of estimating a learner's mastery of knowledge over time. RNN-based approaches that encode user performance over time (i.e., that span across exercises) are therefore variants of *deep knowledge tracing* (Piech et al., 2015).

Relatedly, the *spacing effect* (Dempster, 1989) is the observation that people will not only learn but also forget over time, and they remember more effectively through scheduled practices that are spaced out. Settles and Meeder (2016) and Ridgeway et al. (2017) recently proposed non-linear regressions that explicitly encode the rate of forgetting as part of a decision surface, however none of the current teams chose to do this. Instead, forgetting was either modeled through engineered features (e.g., user/token histories), or opaquely handled by sequential RNN architectures.

SLA modeling also bears some similarity to research in *grammatical error detection* (Leacock et al., 2010) and *correction* (Ng et al., 2013). For these tasks, a model is given a (possibly ill-formed) sequence of words produced by a learner, and the task is to identify which are mistakes. SLA modeling is in some sense the opposite: given a well-formed sequence of words that a learner should be able to produce, identify where they are likely to make mistakes. Given these similarities, a few teams adapted state-of-the-art GEC/GED approaches to create their SLA modeling systems.

Finally, *multitask learning* (e.g., Caruana, 1997) is the idea that machine learning systems can do better at multiple related tasks by trying to solve them simultaneously. For example, recent work in machine translation has demonstrated gains through learning to translate multiple languages with a unified model (Dong et al., 2015). Similarly, the three language tracks in this work presented an opportunity to explore a unified multitask framework, which a few teams did with positive results.

5 Meta-Analyses

In this section, we analyze the various modeling choices explored by the different teams in order to shed light on what kinds of algorithmic and feature engineering decisions appear to be useful for the SLA modeling task.

5.1 Learning Algorithms

Here we attempt to answer the question of whether particular machine learning algorithms have a significant impact on task performance. For example, the results in Table 2 suggest that the algorithmic choices indicated by ($\diamondsuit, \clubsuit, \ddagger$) are particularly effective. Is this actually the case?

To answer this question, we partitioned the TEST set into 6.4k subsets (one for each learner), and computed per-user AUC scores for each team's predictions (83.9k observations total). We also coded each team with indicator variables to describe their algorithmic approach, and used a regression analysis to determine if these algorithmic variations had any significant effects on learner-specific AUC scores.

To analyze this properly, however, we need to determine whether the differences among modeling choices are actually meaningful, or can simply be explained by sampling error due to random variations among users, teams, or tracks. To do this, we use a *linear mixed-effects model* (cf., Baayen, 2008, Ch. 7). In addition to modeling the *fixed* effects of the various learning algorithms, we can also model the *random* effects represented by the

Fixed effects (algorithm choices)	Effect	p-value	
Intercept	.786	<.001	***
Recurrent neural network ($\Diamond$)	+.028	.012	*
Decision tree ensemble ($\clubsuit$)	+.018	.055	.
Linear model (e.g., IRT)	−.006	.541	
Multitask model ($\ddagger$)	+.023	.017	*
Random effects	**St. Dev.**		
User ID	±.086		
Team ID	±.013		
Track ID	±.011		

Table 3: Mixed-effects analysis of learning algorithms.

Features used	Popularity	Effect
Word (surface form)		+.005
User ID		+.014
Part of speech		−.008
Dependency labels		−.011
Morphology features		−.021
Response time		+.028 *
Days in course		+.023 .
Client		+.005
Countries		+.012
Dependency edges		−.000
Session		+.014
Word corpus frequency		+.008
Spaced repetition features		+.013
L1-L2 cognates		+.001
Word embeddings		+.020
Word stem/root/lemma		+.007

Table 4: Summary of system features—both provided (top) and team-engineered (bottom)—with team popularity and univariate mixed-effects estimates.

user ID (learners may vary by ability), the team ID (teams may differ in other aspects not captured by our schema, e.g., the hardware used), and the track ID (tracks may vary inherently in difficulty).

Table 3 presents a mixed-effects analysis for the algorithm variations used by at least 3 teams. The intercept can be interpreted as the "average" AUC of .786. Controlling for the random effects of user (which exhibits a wide standard deviation of ±.086 AUC), team (±.013), and track (±.011), three of the algorithmic choices are at least marginally significant ($p < .1$). For example, we might expect a system that uses RNNs to model learner mastery over time would add +.028 to learner-specific AUC (all else being equal). Note that most teams' systems that were not based on RNNs or tree ensembles used logistic regression, hence the "linear model" effect is negligible (effectively treated as a control condition in the analysis).

These results suggest two key insights for SLA modeling. First, *non-linear algorithms* are particularly desirable[4], and second, *multitask learning* approaches that share information across tracks (i.e., languages) are also effective.

5.2 Feature Sets

We would also like to get a sense of which features, if any, significantly affect system performance. Table 4 lists features provided with the SLA modeling data set, as well as several newly-engineered feature types that were employed by at least three teams (note that the precise details may vary from team to team, but in our view aim to cap-

ture the same phenomena). We also include each feature's popularity and an effect estimate[5].

Broadly speaking, results suggest that feature engineering had a much smaller impact on system performance than the choice of learning algorithm. Only "response time" and "days in course" showed even marginally significant trends.

Of particular interest is the observation that *morpho-syntactic* features (described in §2.4) actually seem to have weakly negative effects. This echoes **singsound**'s finding that their linguistic encoder contributed the least to system performance, and **Cambridge** determined through ablation studies that these features in fact hurt their system. One reasonable explanation is that these automatically-generated features contain too many systematic parsing errors to provide value. (Note that **NYU** artificially introduced punctuation to the exercises and re-parsed the data in their work.)

As for newly-engineered features, word information such as frequency, semantic embeddings, and stemming were popular. It may be that these features showed such little return because our corpus was too biased toward beginners—thus representing a very narrow sample of language—for these features to be meaningful. Cognate features were an interesting idea used by a few teams, and may have been more useful if the data included

---

[4] Interestingly, the only linear model to rank among the top 5 (**CECL**) relied on combinatorial feature conjunctions—which effectively alter the decision surface to be non-linear with respect to the original features. The RNN hidden nodes and GBDT constituent trees from other top systems may in fact be learning to represent these same feature conjunctions.

[5] This is similar to the analysis in §5.1, except that we regress on each feature separately. That is, a feature is the only fixed effect in the model (alongside intercept), while still controlling for user, team, and track random effects.

users from a wider variety of different L1 language backgrounds. Spaced repetition features also exhibited marginal (but statistically insignificant) gains. We posit that the 30-day window we used for data collection was simply not long enough for these features to capture more long-term learning (and forgetting) trends.

5.3 Ensemble Analysis

Another interesting research question is: what is the upper-bound for this task? This can be estimated by treating each team's best submission as an independent system, and combining the results using ensemble methods in a variety of ways. Such analyses have been previously applied to other shared task challenges and meta-analyses (e.g., Malmasi et al., 2017).

The **oracle** system is meant to be an upper-bound: for each token in the TEST set, the oracle outputs the team prediction with the lowest error for that particular token. We also experiment with **stacking** (Wolpert, 1992) by training a logistic regression classifier using each team's prediction as an input feature[6]. Finally, we also pool system predictions together by taking their **average** (mean).

Table 5 reports AUC for various ensemble methods as well as some of the top performing team systems for all three tracks. Interestingly, the oracle is exceptionally accurate ($>.993$ AUC and $>.884$ F1, not shown). This indicates that the *potential* upper limit of performance on this task is quite high, since there exists a near-perfect ranking of tokens in the TEST set based only on predictions from these 15 diverse participating teams.

The stacking classifier produces significantly better rankings than any of the constituent systems alone, while the average (over all teams) ranked between the 3rd and 4th best system in all three tracks. Inspection of stacking model weights revealed that it largely learned to trust the top-performing systems, so we also tried simply averaging the top 3 systems for each track, and this method was statistically tied with stacking for the English and French tracks ($p = 0.002$ for Spanish). Interestingly, the highest-weighted team in each track's stacking model was **singsound** ($+2.417$ on average across the three models), followed

---

[6]Note that we only have TEST set predictions for each team. While we averaged stacking classifier weights across 10 folds using cross-validation, the reported AUC is still likely an over-estimate, since the models were in some sense trained on the TEST set.

System	English	Spanish	French
Oracle	*.995*	*.996*	*.993*
Stacking	.867	.844	.863
Average (top 3)	.867	.843	.863
1st team	.861	.838	.857
2nd team	.861	.835	.854
3rd team	.859	.835	.854
Average (all)	.857	.832	.852
4th team	.848	.824	.843

Table 5: AUC results for the ensemble analysis.

by **NYU** ($+1.632$), whereas the top-performing team **SanaLabs** had a surprisingly lower weight ($+0.841$). This could be due to the fact that their system was itself an ensemble of an RNN and GBDT models, which were used (in isolation) by each of the other two teams. This seems to add further support for the effectiveness of combining these algorithms for the task.

6 Conclusion and Future Work

In this work, we presented the task of *second language acquisition (SLA) modeling*, described a large data set for studying this task, and reported on the results of a shared task challenge that explored this new domain. The task attracted strong participation from 15 teams, who represented a wide variety of fields including cognitive science, linguistics, and machine learning.

Among our key findings is the observation that, for this particular formulation of the task, the choice of learning algorithm appears to be more important than clever feature engineering. In particular, the most effective teams employed sequence models (e.g., RNNs) that can capture user performance over time, and tree ensembles (e.g., GBDTs) that can capture non-linear relationships among features. Furthermore, using a multitask framework—in this case, a unified model that leverages data from all three language tracks—can provide further improvements.

Still, many teams opted for a simpler algorithm (e.g., logistic regression) and concentrated instead on more psychologically-motivated features. While these teams did not always perform as well, several demonstrated through ablation studies that these features can be useful within the limitations of the algorithm. It is possible that the constraints of the SLA modeling data set (beginner language, homogeneous L1 language background, short 30-day time frame, etc.) prevented these features from being more useful across different teams and learning algorithms. It would be interesting to revisit these ideas using a more diverse and longitudinal data set in the future.

To support ongoing research in SLA modeling, current and future releases of our data set will be publicly maintained online at: `https://doi.org/10.7910/DVN/8SWHN0`.

Acknowledgments

The authors would like to acknowledge Bożena Pająk, Joseph Rollinson, and Hideki Shima for their help planning and co-organizing the shared task. Eleanor Avrunin and Natalie Glance made significant contributions to early versions of the SLA modeling data set, and Anastassia Loukina and Kristen K. Reyher provided helpful advice regarding mixed-effects modeling. Finally, we would like to thank the organizers of the NAACL-HLT 2018 Workshop on Innovative Use of NLP for Building Educational Applications (BEA) for providing a forum for this work.

References

D. Andor, C. Alberti, D. Weiss, A. Severyn, A. Presta, K. Ganchev, S. Petrov, and M. Collins. 2016. Globally normalized transition-based neural networks. *CoRR*, abs/1603.06042.

R.H. Baayen. 2008. *Analyzing Linguistic Data: A Practical Introduction to Statistics using R*. Cambridge University Press.

Y. Bestgen. 2018. Predicting second language learner successes and mistakes by means of conjunctive features. In *Proceedings of the NAACL-HLT Workshop on Innovative Use of NLP for Building Educational Applications (BEA)*. ACL.

R. Caruana. 1997. Multitask learning. *Machine Learning*, 28:41–75.

H. Cen, K. Koedinger, and B. Junker. 2008. Comparing two IRT models for conjunctive skills. In *Proceedings of the Conference on Intelligent Tutoring Systems (ITS)*, pages 796–798. Springer.

C.M. Chen, H.M. Lee, and Y.H. Chen. 2005. Personalized e-learning system using item response theory. *Computers & Education*, 44(3):237–255.

G. Chen, C. Hauff, and G.J. Houben. 2018. Feature engineering for second language acquisition modeling. In *Proceedings of the NAACL-HLT Workshop on Innovative Use of NLP for Building Educational Applications (BEA)*. ACL.

A.T. Corbett and J.R. Anderson. 1995. Knowledge tracing: Modeling the acquisition of procedural knowledge. *User Modeling and User-Adapted Interaction*, 4(4):253–278.

F.I.M. Craik and E. Tulving. 1975. Depth of processing and the retention of words in episodic memory. *Journal of Experimental Psychology*, 104:268–294.

E.R. DeLong, D.M. DeLong, and D.L. Clarke-Pearson. 1988. Comparing the areas under two or more correlated receiver operating characteristic curves: a nonparametric approach. *Biometrics*, 44:837–845.

F.N. Dempster. 1989. Spacing effects and their implications for theory and practice. *Educational Psychology Review*, 1(4):309–330.

D. Dong, H. Wu, W. He, D. Yu, and H. Wang. 2015. Multi-task learning for multiple language translation. In *Proceedings of the Association for Computational Linguistics (ACL)*, pages 1723–1732. ACL.

T. Fawcett. 2006. An introduction to ROC analysis. *Pattern Recognition Letters*, 27(8):861–874.

M. Kaneko, T. Kajiwara, and M. Komachi. 2018. TMU system for SLAM-2018. In *Proceedings of the NAACL-HLT Workshop on Innovative Use of NLP for Building Educational Applications (BEA)*. ACL.

S. Klerke, H.M. Alonso, and B. Plank. 2018. Grotoco@SLAM: Second language acquisition modeling with simple features, learners and task-wise models. In *Proceedings of the NAACL-HLT Workshop on Innovative Use of NLP for Building Educational Applications (BEA)*. ACL.

C. Leacock, M. Chodorow, M. Gamon, and J. Tetreault. 2010. Automated grammatical error detection for language learners. *Synthesis Lectures on Human Language Technologies*, 3(1):1–134.

V.I. Levenshtein. 1966. Binary codes capable of correcting deletions, insertions, and reversals. *Soviet Physics Doklady*, 10(8):707–710.

S. Malmasi, K. Evanini, A. Cahill, J. Tetreault, R. Pugh, C. Hamill, D. Napolitano, and Y. Qian. 2017. A report on the 2017 Native Language Identification shared task. In *Proceedings of the EMNLP Workshop on Innovative Use of NLP for Building Educational Applications (BEA)*, pages 62–75, Copenhagen, Denmark. ACL.

N.V. Nayak and A.R. Rao. 2018. Context based approach for second language acquisition. In *Proceedings of the NAACL-HLT Workshop on Innovative Use of NLP for Building Educational Applications (BEA)*. ACL.

H.T. Ng, S.M. Wu, Y. Wu, C. Hadiwinoto, and J. Tetreault. 2013. The CoNLL-2013 shared task on grammatical error correction. In *Proceedings of the Conference on Computational Natural Language Learning (CoNLL)*, pages 1–12. ACL.

S. Nilsson, A. Osika, A. Sydorchuk, F. Sahin, and A. Huss. 2018. Second language acquisition modeling: An ensemble approach. In *Proceedings of the NAACL-HLT Workshop on Innovative Use of NLP for Building Educational Applications (BEA)*. ACL.

C. Piech, J. Bassen, J. Huang, S. Ganguli, M. Sahami, L.J. Guibas, and J. Sohl-Dickstein. 2015. Deep knowledge tracing. In *Advances in Neural Information Processing Systems (NIPS)*, pages 505–513.

R. Pinon and J. Haydon. 2010. The benefits of the English language for individuals and societies: Quantitative indicators from Cameroon, Nigeria, Rwanda, Bangladesh and Pakistan. Technical report, Euromonitor International for the British Council.

G. Rasch. 1980. *Probabilistic models for some intelligence and attainment tests*. The University of Chicago Press.

A. Rich, P.O. Popp, D. Halpern, A. Rothe, and T. Gureckis. 2018. Modeling second-language learning from a psychological perspective. In *Proceedings of the NAACL-HLT Workshop on Innovative Use of NLP for Building Educational Applications (BEA)*. ACL.

K. Ridgeway, M.C. Mozer, and A.R. Bowles. 2017. Forgetting of foreign-language skills: A corpus-based analysis of online tutoring software. *Cognitive Science*, 41(4):924–949.

B. Settles and B. Meeder. 2016. A trainable spaced repetition model for language learning. In *Proceedings of the Association for Computational Linguistics (ACL)*, pages 1848–1858. ACL.

B. Tomoschuk and J. Lovelett. 2018. A memory-sensitive classification model of errors in early second language learning. In *Proceedings of the NAACL-HLT Workshop on Innovative Use of NLP for Building Educational Applications (BEA)*. ACL.

J.J. Vie. 2018. Deep factorization machines for knowledge tracing. In *Proceedings of the NAACL-HLT Workshop on Innovative Use of NLP for Building Educational Applications (BEA)*. ACL.

D.H. Wolpert. 1992. Stacked generalization. *Neural Networks*, 5(2):241–259.

S. Xu, J. Chen, and L. Qin. 2018. CLUF: A neural model for second language acquisition modeling. In *Proceedings of the NAACL-HLT Workshop on Innovative Use of NLP for Building Educational Applications (BEA)*. ACL.

Z. Yuan. 2018. Neural sequence modelling for learner error prediction. In *Proceedings of the NAACL-HLT Workshop on Innovative Use of NLP for Building Educational Applications (BEA)*. ACL.

A Report on the Complex Word Identification Shared Task 2018

Seid Muhie Yimam[1], **Chris Biemann**[1], **Shervin Malmasi**[2], **Gustavo H. Paetzold**[3]
Lucia Specia[3], **Sanja Štajner**[4], **Anaïs Tack**[5], **Marcos Zampieri**[6]

[1]University of Hamburg, Germany, [2]Harvard Medical School, USA
[3]University of Sheffield, UK, [4]University of Mannheim, Germany,
[5]Université catholique de Louvain and KU Leuven, Belgium
[6]University of Wolverhampton, UK
`yimam@informatik.uni-hamburg.de`

Abstract

We report the findings of the second Complex Word Identification (CWI) shared task organized as part of the BEA workshop co-located with NAACL-HLT'2018. The second CWI shared task featured multilingual and multi-genre datasets divided into four tracks: English monolingual, German monolingual, Spanish monolingual, and a multilingual track with a French test set, and two tasks: binary classification and probabilistic classification. A total of 12 teams submitted their results in different task/track combinations and 11 of them wrote system description papers that are referred to in this report and appear in the BEA workshop proceedings.

1 Introduction

The most common first step in lexical simplification pipelines is identifying which words are considered complex by a given target population (Shardlow, 2013). This task is known as complex word identification (CWI) and it has been attracting attention from the research community in the past few years.

In this paper we present the findings of the second Complex Word Identification (CWI) shared task organized as part of the thirteenth Workshop on Innovative Use of NLP for Building Educational Applications (BEA) co-located with NAACL-HLT'2018. The second CWI shared task follows a successful first edition featuring 21 teams organized at SemEval'2016 (Paetzold and Specia, 2016a). While the first CWI shared task targeted an English dataset, the second edition focused on multilingualism providing datasets containing four languages: English, German, French, and Spanish.

In an evaluation paper (Zampieri et al., 2017), it has been shown that the performance of an ensemble classifier built on top of the predictions of the participating systems in the 2016 task degraded, the more systems were added. The low performance of the CWI systems that competed in the first CWI task left much room for improvement and was one of the reasons that motivated us to organize this second edition.

1.1 Task Description

The goal of the CWI shared task of 2018 is to predict which words challenge non-native speakers based on the annotations collected from both native and non-native speakers. To train their systems, participants received a labeled training set where words in context were annotated regarding their complexity. One month later, an unlabeled test set was provided and participating teams were required to upload their predictions for evaluation. More information about the data collection is presented in Section 3.

Given the multilingual dataset provided, the CWI challenge was divided into four tracks:

- **English monolingual CWI;**

- **German monolingual CWI;**

- **Spanish monolingual CWI; and**

- **Multilingual CWI with a French test set.**

For the first three tracks, participants were provided with training and testing data for the same language. For French, participants were provided only with a French test set and no French training data. In the CWI 2016, the task was cast as binary classification. To be able to capture complexity as a continuum, in our CWI 2018 shared task, we

Proceedings of the Thirteenth Workshop on Innovative Use of NLP for Building Educational Applications, pages 66–78
New Orleans, Louisiana, June 5, 2018. ©2018 Association for Computational Linguistics

additionally included a probabilistic classification task. The two tasks are summarized as follows:

- **Binary classification task:** Participants were asked to label the target words in context as complex (1) or simple (0).

- **Probabilistic classification task:** Participants were asked to assign the probability of target words in context being complex.

Participants were free to choose the task/track combinations they would like to participate in.

2   Related Work

Until the appearance of the CWI shared task of 2016, there was no manually annotated and verified CWI dataset. The 2016 shared task brought us one of the largest CWI datasets to that date, consisting of a total of 9,200 sentences manually annotated by 400 different non-native English speakers. In total, 200 sentences are used as a training set where each target is annotated by 20 annotators. The rest of the dataset (9,000 sentences) are used for test set where each target is annotated by a single annotator from the entire pool of 400 annotators.

The approaches used in the first SemEval 2016 Task 11: Complex Word Identification are described in Table 1.

3   Datasets

We have used the *CWIG3G2* datasets from (Yimam et al., 2017b,a) for the complex word identification (CWI) shared task 2018. The datasets are collected for multiple languages (*English, German, Spanish*). The English datasets cover different text genres, namely *News* (professionally written news), *WikiNews* (news written by amateurs), and *Wikipedia articles*. Below, we will briefly describe the annotation process and the statistics of collected datasets. For detail explanation of the datasets, please refer to the works of Yimam et al. (2017b,a)

Furthermore, to bolster the cross-lingual CWI experiment, we have collected a CWI dataset for French. The French dataset was collected through the same method used for the CWIG3G2 corpus (Yimam et al., 2017b,a). The dataset contains Wikipedia texts extracted from a comparable simplified corpus collected by Brouwers et al. (2014). Similar to CWIG3G2, for each article,

all paragraphs containing between 5 and 10 sentences were extracted. From this pool of paragraphs, only the best paragraph was selected via a ranking procedure maximizing sentence length and lexical richness, and minimizing the ratio of named entities and foreign words. From this large selection of best paragraphs per article, an optimal subset of 100 paragraphs was then selected using a greedy search procedure similar to that of Tack et al. (2016), minimizing the vocabulary overlap between pairs of paragraphs using the Jaccard coefficient. Finally, a random test split of 24 paragraphs was selected to be annotated.

3.1   Annotation Process

Annotations were collected using the Amazon Mechanical Turk (MTurk). Instead of showing a single sentence, we presented 5 to 10 sentences to the annotator in a single HIT (Human Intelligence Task) and requested them to highlight words or phrases that could pose difficulty in understanding the paragraph. The annotation system is unique in many aspects such as: 1) The instruction makes clear that the annotators should assume a given target reader such as children, language learners or people with reading impairments. 2) A bonus reward is offered when the user's selection matches at least half of the other annotations to encourage extra care during the complex word or phrase (CP) selection. 3) The maximum number of annotations allowed is limited to 10 so that we could prohibit an arbitrarily large number of selections intending to attain the bonus reward. 4) For the English dataset, more than 20 annotators were able to annotate the same HIT, among which are at least 10 native English speakers and 10 non-native English speakers so that it is possible to investigate if native and non-native speakers have different CWI needs. 5) Complex words are not pre-highlighted, as in previous contributions, so that annotators are not biased to the pre-selection of the complex phrases. 6) In addition to single words, we allowed the annotation of multi-word expressions (MWE), up to a size of 50 characters.

Table 2 shows the total, native, and non-native number of annotators that participated in the annotation task.

3.2   Analysis of Collected Datasets

Table 3 shows statistics of the datasets for the English (combinations of three genres), German, Spanish and French (test set only) CWI tasks.

Team	Approach	System Paper
SV000gg	System voting with threshold and machine learning-based classifiers trained on morphological, lexical, and semantic features	(Paetzold and Specia, 2016b)
TALN	Random forests of lexical, morphological, semantic & syntactic features	(Ronzano et al., 2016)
UWB	Maximum Entropy classifiers trained over word occurrence counts on Wikipedia documents	(Konkol, 2016)
PLUJAGH	Threshold-based methods trained on Simple Wikipedia	(Wróbel, 2016)
JUNLP	Random Forest and Naive Bayes classifiers trained over semantic, lexicon-based, morphological and syntactic features	(Mukherjee et al., 2016)
HMC	Decision trees trained over lexical, semantic, syntactic and psycholinguistic features	(Quijada and Medero, 2016)
MACSAAR	Random Forest and SVM classifiers trained over Zipfian features	(Zampieri et al., 2016)
Pomona	Threshold-based bagged classifiers with bootstrap re-sampling trained over word frequencies	(Kauchak, 2016)
Melbourne	Weighted Random Forests trained on lexical/semantic features	(Brooke et al., 2016)
IIIT	Nearest Centroid classifiers trained over semantic and morphological features	(Palakurthi and Mamidi, 2016)
LTG	Decision Trees trained over number of complex judgments	(Malmasi et al., 2016)
MAZA	Ensemble methods various word frequency features	(Malmasi and Zampieri, 2016)
Sensible	Ensembled Recurrent Neural Networks trained over embeddings	(Gillin, 2016)
ClacEDLK	Random Forests trained over semantic, morphological, lexical and psycholinguistic features	(Davoodi and Kosseim, 2016)
Amrita-CEN	SVM classifiers trained over word embeddings and various semantic and morphological features	(S.P et al., 2016)
AI-KU	SVM classifier trained with word embeddings of the target and surrounding words	(Kuru, 2016)
BHASHA	SVM and Decision Tree trained over lexical and morphological features	(Choubey and Pateria, 2016)
USAAR	Bayesian Ridge classifiers trained over a hand-crafted word sense entropy metric and language model perplexity	(Martínez Martínez and Tan, 2016)
CoastalCPH	Neural Network and Logistic Regression system trained over word frequencies and embedding	(Bingel et al., 2016)

Table 1: SemEval 2016 CWI – Systems and approaches

Language	Native	Non-native	Total
English	134	49	183
German	12	11	23
Spanish	48	6	54
French	10	12	22

Table 2: The number of annotators for different languages

Language	Train	Dev	Test
English	27,299	3,328	4,252
German	6,151	795	959
Spanish	13,750	1,622	2,233
French	-	-	2,251

Table 3: The number of instances for each training, development and test set

An analysis of the English dataset shows that around 90% of complex phrases have been selected by at least two annotators (both native and non-native). When separated by language, the percentage of agreements decreases to 83% at the lowest. This might be because native and non-native annotators have a different perspective what is a complex phrase. Furthermore, we have seen that native annotators agree more within their group (84% and above) than non-native speakers (83% and above). We also see that the absolute agreement between native and non-native annotators is very low (70%), which further indicates that the two user groups might have different CWI needs.

For the German annotation task, we have fewer annotators than the other languages. As it can be seen from Table 2, there are more native annotators, but they participate on fewer HITs than the non-native annotators (on average, 6.1 non-native speakers and 3.9 native speakers participated in a HIT). Unlike the English annotation task, non-native annotators have a higher inter-annotator agreement (70.66%) than the native annotators (58.5%).

The Spanish annotation task is different from both the English and the German annotation tasks since its annotations come almost exclusively from native annotators. In general, Spanish annotators have shown lower agreements than the English and German annotators. Also the Spanish annotators highlight more MWEs than the English and German annotators.

Regarding the French annotation task, we observe a comparable distribution in the number of native and non-native annotators compared to the German annotation task (Table 2). There were slightly more non-native participants than native ones, but the number of native annotators who completed the same number of HITs was considerably larger. This means that although there were more non-native participants, they did not participate equally in all HITs.

		Train		Dev		Test	
		#	%	#	%	#	%
EN		11,253	41	1,388	42	1,787	42
DE		2,562	42	334	42	376	39
ES		5,455	40	653	40	907	41
FR		-		-		657	29

Table 4: The number (#) and ratio (%) of complex instances per language

A striking difference that can be observed in the French dataset pertains to the proportion of identified complex words. Compared to the other languages, we have a considerably lower relative count of complex instances (Table 4). However, this does not necessarily mean that the texts were simpler for French than for the other languages. Looking at the proportion of MWEs annotated as complex (Table 5), we observe that the French dataset contains more MWE annotations than single words compared to the other datasets. One plausible explanation for this could be attributed to the limitation of allowing at most 10 unique annotations per HIT in MTurk. Indeed, a number of annotators highlighted the fact that they sometimes found more than 10 possible annotations of complex words. As a result, in order to account for all of these possibilities, the annotators sometimes grouped nearly adjacent single complex words as one sequence, leading to a larger relative proportion of MWE (3-gram+) annotations. Another explanation for this disparity could be attributed to the lower number of annotators for French compared to English or Spanish. If we had had a similar number of annotators for French, we would probably also have obtained a more varied sample and hence a higher relative amount of different complex word annotations.

		1-gram	2-gram	3-gram+	total
EN	#	10,676	2,760	992	14,428
	%	74.00	19.13	6.87	
DE	#	2,770	307	195	3,272
	%	84.66	9.38	5.96	
ES	#	4,712	1,276	1,027	7,015
	%	67.17	18.19	14.64	
FR	#	414	118	125	657
	%	63.01	17.96	19.03	

Table 5: The distribution of single and MWE annotations of complex words per language

4 System Descriptions and Results

In this section, we briefly describe the systems from all 11 teams that have participated in the 2018 CWI shared task and wrote a system description paper to be presented at the BEA conference. Table 6 and 7 shows the results of all systems for the monolingual and multilingual binary classification tasks while Table 8 and 9 presents the probabilistic classification results for the monolingual and multilingual tracks.

4.1 Baseline Systems

For both the binary and probabilistic classification tasks, we build a simple baseline system that uses only the most basic features described in Yimam et al. (2017b,a), namely only frequency and length features. The Nearest Centroid classifier and the Linear Regression algorithms from the scikit-learn machine learning library are used for the binary and probabilistic classification tasks resp. For the binary classification task, we have used the accuracy and macro-averaged F1 evaluation metrics. For the probabilistic classification task, the Mean Absolute Error (MAE) measure is used. The baseline results are shown in Table 6, 7, 8, and 9 for the monolingual and multilingual tracks.

4.2 Shared Task Systems

UnibucKernel The UnibucKernel (Butnaru and Ionescu, 2018) team participated on the monolingual CWI shared task, specifically on the NEWS, WIKINEWS, and WIKIPEDIA domain datasets.

News	F-1	Rank	WikiNews	F-1	Rank	Wikipedia	F-1	Rank
Camb	0.8736	1	Camb	0.84	1	Camb	0.8115	1
Camb	0.8714	2	Camb	0.8378	2	NILC	0.7965	2
Camb	0.8661	3	Camb	0.8364	4	UnibucKernel	0.7919	3
ITEC	0.8643	4	Camb	0.8378	3	NILC	0.7918	4
ITEC	0.8643	4	NLP-CIC	0.8308	5	Camb	0.7869	5
TMU	0.8632	6	NLP-CIC	0.8279	6	Camb	0.7862	6
ITEC	0.8631	7	NILC	0.8277	7	SB@GU	0.7832	7
NILC	0.8636	5	NILC	0.8270	8	ITEC	0.7815	8
NILC	0.8606	9	NLP-CIC	0.8236	9	SB@GU	0.7812	9
Camb	0.8622	8	CFILT_IITB	0.8161	10	UnibucKernel	0.7804	10
NLP-CIC	0.8551	10	CFILT_IITB	0.8161	10	Camb	0.7799	11
NLP-CIC	0.8503	12	CFILT_IITB	0.8152	11	CFILT_IITB	0.7757	12
NLP-CIC	0.8508	11	CFILT_IITB	0.8131	12	CFILT_IITB	0.7756	13
NILC	0.8467	15	UnibucKernel	0.8127	13	CFILT_IITB	0.7747	14
CFILT_IITB	0.8478	13	ITEC	0.8110	14	NLP-CIC	0.7722	16
CFILT_IITB	0.8478	13	SB@GU	0.8031	15	NLP-CIC	0.7721	17
CFILT_IITB	0.8467	14	NILC	0.7961	17	NLP-CIC	0.7723	15
SB@GU	0.8325	17	NILC	0.7977	16	NLP-CIC	0.7723	15
SB@GU	0.8329	16	CFILT_IITB	0.7855	20	SB@GU	0.7634	18
Gillin Inc.	0.8243	19	TMU	0.7873	19	TMU	0.7619	19
Gillin Inc.	0.8209	24	SB@GU	0.7878	18	NILC	0.7528	20
Gillin Inc.	0.8229	20	UnibucKernel	0.7638	23	UnibucKernel	0.7422	24
Gillin Inc.	0.8221	21	hu-berlin	0.7656	22	hu-berlin	0.7445	22
hu-berlin	0.8263	18	SB@GU	0.7691	21	SB@GU	0.7454	21
Gillin Inc.	0.8216	22	LaSTUS/TALN	0.7491	25	UnibucKernel	0.7435	23
UnibucKernel	0.8178	26	LaSTUS/TALN	0.7491	25	LaSTUS/TALN	0.7402	25
UnibucKernel	0.8178	26	SB@GU	0.7569	24	LaSTUS/TALN	0.7402	25
CFILT_IITB	0.8210	23	hu-berlin	0.7471	26	NILC	0.7360	26
CFILT_IITB	0.8210	23	Gillin Inc.	0.7319	28	hu-berlin	0.7298	27
hu-berlin	0.8188	25	Gillin Inc.	0.7275	30	CoastalCPH	0.7206	28
UnibucKernel	0.8111	28	Gillin Inc.	0.7292	29	LaSTUS/TALN	0.6964	29
NILC	0.8173	27	Gillin Inc.	0.7180	31	Gillin Inc.	0.6604	30
LaSTUS/TALN/TALN	0.8103	29	LaSTUS/TALN	0.7339	27	Gillin Inc.	0.6580	31
LaSTUS/TALN	0.8103	29	Gillin Inc.	0.7083	32	Gillin Inc.	0.6520	32
LaSTUS/TALN	0.7892	31	UnibucKernel	0.6788	33	Gillin Inc.	0.6329	33
UnibucKernel	0.7728	33	SB@GU	0.5374	34	SB@GU	0.5699	34
SB@GU	0.7925	30	-	-	-	CoastalCPH	0.5020	35
SB@GU	0.7842	32	-	-	-	LaSTUS/TALN	0.3324	36
LaSTUS/TALN	0.7669	34	-	-	-	-	-	-
UnibucKernel	0.5158	36	-	-	-	-	-	-
SB@GU	0.5556	35	-	-	-	-	-	-
LaSTUS/TALN	0.2912	37	-	-	-	-	-	-
LaSTUS/TALN	0.1812	38	-	-	-	-	-	-
LaSTUS/TALN	0.1761	39	-	-	-	-	-	-
Baseline	0.7579	-	Baseline	0.7106	-	Baseline	0.7179	-

Table 6: Binary classification results for the monolingual English tracks.

The pipeline consists of feature extraction, computing a kernel matrix and applying an SVM classifier.

The feature sets include low-level features such as character n-grams, and high-level features such semantic properties extracted from lexical resources and word embeddings. The low-level features were extracted based on the target complex word, and include count of characters, count of vowels, count of consonants, count of repeating characters, and count of character n-grams (up to 4 characters).

The first set of word embedding features take into account the word's context which is obtained by computing the cosine similarity between the complex word and each of the other words in the

German	F-1	Rank	Spanish	F-1	Rank	French	F-1	Rank
TMU	0.7451	1	TMU	0.7699	1	CoastalCPH	0.7595	1
SB@GU	0.7427	2	ITEC	0.7637	3	TMU	0.7465	2
hu-berlin	0.6929	4	NLP-CIC	0.7672	2	SB@GU	0.6266	3
SB@GU	0.6992	3	CoastalCPH	0.7458	5	SB@GU	0.6130	4
CoastalCPH	0.6619	5	CoastalCPH	0.7458	5	hu-berlin	0.5738	6
Gillin Inc.	0.5548	10	NLP-CIC	0.7468	4	SB@GU	0.5891	5
Gillin Inc.	0.5459	11	NLP-CIC	0.7419	6	hu-berlin	0.5343	7
Gillin Inc.	0.5398	12	SB@GU	0.7281	7	hu-berlin	0.5238	8
Gillin Inc.	0.5271	14	SB@GU	0.7259	8	hu-berlin	0.5124	9
Gillin Inc.	0.5275	13	CoastalCPH	0.7238	9	-	-	-
CoastalCPH	0.6078	6	hu-berlin	0.7080	11	-	-	-
CoastalCPH	0.5818	7	CoastalCPH	0.7153	10	-	-	-
CoastalCPH	0.5778	8	Gillin Inc.	0.6804	13	-	-	-
CoastalCPH	0.5771	9	Gillin Inc.	0.6784	14	-	-	-
-	-	-	Gillin Inc.	0.6722	15	-	-	-
-	-	-	Gillin Inc.	0.6669	16	-	-	-
-	-	-	Gillin Inc.	0.6547	17	-	-	-
-	-	-	CoastalCPH	0.6918	12	-	-	-
Baseline	0.7546	-	Baseline	0.7237	-	Baseline	0.6344	-

Table 7: Binary classification results for the multilingual German, Spanish and French tracks.

sentence (minimum, maximum and mean similarity values are used). Furthermore, sense embeddings are used, which are computed based on WordNet synsets. Lastly, using word embeddings, additional features were designed based on the location of the complex word in a dimensionally reduced embedding space. For this, they used PCA to reduce the dimension of the embeddings from 300 to 2 dimensions.

Once features are extracted, kernel-based learning algorithms are employed. For the binary classification setup, the SVM classifiers based on the Lib-SVM were used. For the regression setup, they used v-Support Vector Regression (v-SVR). For both setups, different parameters were tuned using the development dataset.

SB@GU systems (Alfter and Pilán, 2018) are adapted from a previous system, which was used to classify Swedish words into different language proficiency levels and participated on the multilingual binary classification part of the shared task. For each target word or MWE, the following set of feature categories were extracted: 1) count and word form features such as length of the target, number of syllables, n-gram probabilities based on Wikipedia, binary features such as "is MWE" or "is number", and so on 2) morphological features, mainly part-of-speech tag and suffix length, 3) semantic features, such as the number of synsets, number of hypernyms, and number of

hyponyms, 4) context features, like topic distributions and word embeddings, and 5) psycholinguistic features, such as British National Corpus frequency, reaction time, bigram frequency, trigram frequency, and so on. For MWE, they averaged the feature values for each word in them.

For English datasets, experiments are conducted with context-free, context-only and context-sensitive features, mainly by excluding word embeddings, using only word embeddings, and combining all features explained above respectively. Classifiers such as Random Forest, Extra Trees, convolutional networks, and recurrent convolutional neural networks were tested. Furthermore, feature selection is performed using the SelectFromModel feature selection method from scikit-learn library. The best performing features includes word frequency, word sense and topics, and language model probabilities.

For the German, Spanish, and French datasets, features such as character-level n-grams were extracted from n-gram models trained on Wikipedia. For the French dataset, the n-gram models from English, German and Spanish were used to obtain n-gram probabilities of each entry. They configured two setups to extract features for the French dataset: 1) Uses English, German and Spanish classifiers and apply majority voting to get the final label, 2) Uses only the Spanish classifier as French and Spanish are both Romance languages.

An Extra Tree classifier with 1000 and 500 estimators was their best classifier.

hu-berlin The systems (Popović, 2018) mainly explored the use of character n-gram features using a multinomial Naive Bayes classifier specifically designed for the multilingual binary classification task. For each target word, all the character n-grams of a given length and their frequencies were extracted and the target word was represented as a "bag of n-grams". Different lengths of n-grams such as a combination of 2-gram, 3-gram, 4-gram, and 5-grams have been experimented with. The experimental results show that the combinations of 2-gram and 4-gram features are the best character level n-gram features for the binary classification task.

For the English datasets, they combined all the training datasets (NEWS, WIKINEWS, and WIKIPEDIA), used 3-gram, 4-gram and 5-gram character level n-gram features in order to maximize performance. The results show that character level n-gram features do not work well for cross-language complex word identification as the performance generally degraded.

For English, two variants of results were submitted, one classified using the corresponding in-domain training corpus and the second one classified using the concatenated training data. For German and Spanish, one result was submitted using the corresponding training data sets. For French, four submissions were made 1) one classified with English Wikipedia training, 2) one classified with all three English datasets, 3) one classified with Spanish data, and 4) one classified with German data.

NILC present systems (Hartmann and dos Santos, 2018) for the monolingual binary and probabilistic classification tasks. Three approaches were created by 1) using traditional feature engineering-based machine learning methods, 2) using the average embedding of target words as an input to a neural network, and 3) modeling the context of the target words using an LSTM.

For the feature engineering-based systems, features such as linguistic, psycholinguistic, and language model features were used to train different binary and probabilistic classifiers. Lexical features include word length, number of syllables, and number of senses, hypernyms, and hyponyms in WordNet. For N-gram features, probabilities of the n-gram containing the target words were computed based on language models trained on the BookCorpus dataset and One Billion Word dataset. Furthermore, psycholinguistic features such as familiarity, age of acquisition, correctness and imagery values were used. Based on these features (38 in total), models were trained using Linear Regression, Logistic Regression, Decision Trees, Gradient Boosting, Extra Trees, AdaBoost, and XGBoost classifiers.

For embedding-based systems, a pre-trained GloVe model (Pennington et al., 2014) was used to get the vector representations of target words. For MWE, the average of the vectors is used. In the first approach, the resulting vector is passed on to a neural network with two ReLu layers followed by a sigmoid layer, which predicted the probability of the target word being complex.

Their experiments show that the feature engineering approach achieved the best results using the XGBoost classifier for the binary classification task. They submitted four systems using XGBoost, average embeddings, LSTMs with transfer learning, and a voting system that combines the other three. For the probabilistic classification task, their LSTMs achieve the best results.

TMU submitted multilingual and cross-lingual CWI systems for both of the binary and probabilistic classification tasks (Kajiwara and Komachi, 2018). The systems use two variants of frequency features from the learner corpus (*Lang-8 corpus*) from Mizumoto et al. (2011) and from the general domain corpus (Wikipedia and WikiNews). The list of features used in building the model include the number of characters in the target word, number of words in the target phrase, and frequency of the target word in learner corpus (Lang-8 corpus) and general domain corpus (Wikipedia and WikiNews).

Random forest classifiers are used for the binary classification task while random forest regressors are used for the probabilistic classification task using the scikit-learn library. Feature ablation shows that both the length, frequency, and probability features (based on corpus statistics) are important for the binary and probabilistic classification tasks. They also discover that features obtained from the learner corpus are more influential than the general domain features for the CWI tasks. The systems perform very well both for the binary and probabilistic classification tasks, winning 5 out of the 12 tracks.

ITEC addresses both the binary and probabilistic classification task for the English and Spanish multilingual datasets (De Hertog and Tack, 2018). They have used 5 different aspects of the target word in the process of feature extractions, namely, word embedding, morphological structure, psychological measures, corpus counts, and topical information. Psychological measures are obtained from the MRC Psycholinguistic Database, which includes age of acquisition, imageability, concreteness, and meaningfulness of the target word. Word frequencies and embedding features are computed based on a web corpus. The word embedding model is computed using the gensim implementation of word2vec, with 300 dimensional embedding space, window-size of 5 and minimum frequency threshold of 20.

They have employed deep learning structure using the keras deep learning library with the tensorflow gpu as a backend. Word embeddings are employed in two input layers, first to replace target words with the appropriate embeddings and second to represent the entire sentences as an input sequence which is considered the topical approximation using contextual cues. The final layer takes into account morphological features based on character embeddings that are trained with a convolutional network. The systems perform reasonably better than the average systems, for both of the binary and probabilistic classification tasks.

Camb describes different systems (Gooding and Kochmar, 2018) they have developed for the monolingual English datasets both for the binary and probabilistic classification tasks. They have used features that are based on the insights of the CWI shared task 2016 (Paetzold and Specia, 2016a) such as lexical features (word length, number of syllables, WordNet features such as the number of synsets), word n-gram and POS tags, and dependency parse relations. In addition, they have used features such as the number of words grammatically related to the target word, psycholinguistic features from the MRC database, CEFR (Common European Framework of Reference for Languages) levels extracted from the Cambridge Advanced Learner Dictionary (CALD), and Google N-gram word frequencies using the Datamuse API The MCR features include word familiarity rating, number of phonemes, thorndike-lorge written frequency, imageability rating, concreteness rating, number of categories, samples, and written frequencies, and age of acquisition.

For the binary classification task, they have used a feature union pipeline to combine the range of heterogeneous features extracted from different categories of feature types. The best performing classification algorithms are obtained based on the ensemble techniques where AdaBoost classifier with 5000 estimators achieves the highest results, followed by the bootstrap aggregation classifier of Random Forest. All the features are used for the NEWS and WIKINEWS datasets, but for the WIKIPEDIA dataset, MCR psycholinguistic features are excluded. For the probabilistic classification task, the same feature setups are used and the Linear Regression algorithm is used to estimate values of targets.

As it can be seen from Tables 6, 7, 8, and 9, most of the systems submitted ranked first for English monolingual binary and probabilistic classification tasks.

CoastalCPH describe systems developed for multilingual and cross-lingual domains for the binary and probabilistic classification tasks (Bingel and Bjerva, 2018). Unlike most systems, they have focused mainly on German, Spanish, and French datasets in order to investigate if multitask learning can be applied to the cross-lingual CWI task. They have devised two models, using language-agnostic approach with an ensemble that comprises of Random Forests (random forest classifiers for the binary classification task and random forest regressors for the probabilistic classification tasks, with 100 trees) and feed-forward neural networks.

Most of the features are similar for all languages except some of them are language-specific features. The set of features incorporated include 1) log-probability features: unigram frequencies as a log-probabilities from language-specific Wikipedia dumps computed using KenLM, character perplexity, number of synsets, hypernym chain. 2) Inflectional complexity: number of suffixes appended to a word stem. 3) Surface features: length of the target and lower-case information. 4) Bag-of-POS: for each tag based on Universal Parts-of-Speech project, count the number of words in a candidate that belong to the respective class. 5) Target-sentence similarity: the cosine similarity between averaged word embeddings for the target word or phrase and the rest of the words

News	MAE	Rank	WikiNews	MAE	Rank	Wikipedia	MAE	Rank
TMU	0.051	1	Camb	0.0674	1	Camb	0.0739	1
ITEC	0.0539	2	Camb	0.0674	1	Camb	0.0779	2
Camb	0.0558	3	Camb	0.0690	2	Camb	0.0780	3
Camb	0.056	4	Camb	0.0693	3	Camb	0.0791	4
Camb	0.0563	5	TMU	0.0704	4	ITEC	0.0809	5
Camb	0.0565	6	ITEC	0.0707	5	NILC	0.0819	6
NILC	0.0588	7	NILC	0.0733	6	NILC	0.0822	7
NILC	0.0590	8	NILC	0.0742	7	Camb	0.0844	8
SB@GU	0.1526	9	Camb	0.0820	8	TMU	0.0931	9
Gillin Inc.	0.2812	10	SB@GU	0.1651	9	SB@GU	0.1755	10
Gillin Inc.	0.2872	11	Gillin Inc.	0.2890	10	NILC	0.2461	11
Gillin Inc.	0.2886	12	Gillin Inc.	0.3026	11	Gillin Inc.	0.3156	12
NILC	0.2958	13	Gillin Inc.	0.3040	12	Gillin Inc.	0.3208	13
NILC	0.2978	14	Gillin Inc.	0.3044	13	Gillin Inc.	0.3211	14
Gillin Inc.	0.3090	15	Gillin Inc.	0.3190	14	Gillin Inc.	0.3436	15
SB@GU	0.3656	16	NILC	0.3203	15	NILC	0.3578	16
NILC	0.6652	17	NILC	0.3240	16	NILC	0.3819	17
Baseline	0.1127	-	Baseline	0.1053	-	Baseline	0.1112	-

Table 8: Probablistic classification results for the monolingual English tracks.

German	MAE	Rank	Spanish	MAE	Rank	French	MAE	Rank
TMU	0.0610	1	TMU	0.0718	1	CoastalCPH	0.0660	1
CoastalCPH	0.0747	2	ITEC	0.0733	2	CoastalCPH	0.0660	1
CoastalCPH	0.0751	3	CoastalCPH	0.0789	3	CoastalCPH	0.0762	2
Gillin Inc.	0.1905	4	CoastalCPH	0.0808	4	TMU	0.0778	3
Gillin Inc.	0.2099	5	Gillin Inc.	0.2513	5	CoastalCPH	0.0866	4
Gillin Inc.	0.2102	6	Gillin Inc.	0.2634	6	-	-	-
Gillin Inc.	0.2122	7	Gillin Inc.	0.2638	7	-	-	-
-	-	-	Gillin Inc.	0.2644	8	-	-	-
-	-	-	CoastalCPH	0.2724	9	-	-	-
-	-	-	CoastalCPH	0.2899	10	-	-	-
Baseline	0.0816	-	Baseline	0.0892	-	Baseline	0.0891	-

Table 9: Probablistic classification results for the multilingual German, Spanish, and French tracks.

in the sentence where out-of-vocabulary problems are addressed using a pre-trained sub-word embeddings (Heinzerling and Strube, 2017).

They have made qualitative and quantitative error analysis, mainly for the cross-lingual French dataset experiments and reported that: 1) The system picks longer targets as positive examples. 2) Short targets are predicted as false negative but they are potentially unknown named entities and technical terms. 3) Complex words are generally longer than simple words. 4) Language models produce lower log-probability for complex words.

The systems submitted performed the best out of all systems for the cross-lingual task (the French dataset) both for the binary and probabilistic classification tasks, showing a promising direction in the creation of CWI dataset for new languages.

LaSTUS/TALN present systems for the monolingual English binary classification task (AbuRa'ed and Saggion, 2018). Two different systems are designed, the first system is based on a set of lexical, semantic and contextual features, and the second system incorporates word embedding features. The word embedding features are obtained from a pre-trained word2vec model[1].

For each sentence, the centroid of the dimensions of the context before the target word, the target word itself, and the context after the target word are computed using word2vec embedding vectors (300 dimensions each), resulting in a total of 900 feature dimensions. Furthermore, two extra features are generated using the embedding vectors, which represent the distance between

---

[1]https://code.google.com/archive/p/word2vec/

the target word and the context before and after the target word respectively. These features are computed using the cosine similarity measures between each pair of the vectors.

A large set of shallow lexical and semantic features are also used in addition to the embedding features. These features include target word length (number of characters), the position of the target word in the sentence, number of words in the sentence, word depth in the dependency tree, parent word length in dependency relation, frequency features based on the BNC, Wikipedia, and Dale and Chall list corpora, number of synsets and senses in WordNet, and so on.

The experiment is conducted using the Weka machine learning framework using the Support vector machine (with linear and radial basis function kernels), Naïve Bayes, Logistic Regression, Random Tree, and Random Forest classification algorithms. The final experiments employ Support Vector Machines and Random Forest classifiers.

CFILT_IITB Developed ensemble-based classification systems for the English monolingual binary classification task (Wani et al., 2018). Lexical features based on WordNet for the target word are extracted as follows: 1) Degree of Polysemy: number of senses of the target word in WordNet, 2) Hyponym and Hypernym Tree Depth: the position of the word in WordNet's hierarchical tree, and 3) Holonym and Meronym Counts: based on the relationship of the target word to its components (meronyms) or to the things it is contained in (Holonym's). Additional feature classes include size-based features such as word count, word length, vowel counts, and syllable counts. They also use vocabulary-based features such as Ogden Basic (from Ogden's Basic Word list), Ogden Frequency (Ogden's Frequent Word List), and Barron's Wordlist (Barron's 5000 GRE Word List).

They have used 8 classifiers namely Random Forest, Random Tree, REP Tree, Logistic Model Tree, J48 Decision Tree, JRip Rules Tree, PART, and SVM. Using these classifiers, a hard voting approach is used to predict a label for the target word. Voting of the positive or negative class is decided if more than 4 classifiers agree on the label. Word-embedding-based classifier is used to decide in the case of a 4-4 tie.

An ablation test shows that size-based features such as word length, vowel counts, and syllable counts, word counts constitute the four top impor-

tant features. Their best system shows an average performance compared to the other systems in the shared task for the monolingual English binary classification track.

NLP-CIC present systems for the English and Spanish multilingual binary classification tasks (Aroyehun et al., 2018). The feature sets include morphological features such as frequency counts of target word on large corpora such as Wikipedia and Simple Wikipedia, syntactic and lexical features, psycholinguistic features from the MRC psycholinguistic database and entity features using the OpenNLP and CoreNLP tools, and word embedding distance as a feature which is computed between the target word and the sentence.

Tree learners such as Random Forest, Gradient Boosted, and Tree Ensembles are used to train different classifiers. Furthermore, a deep learning approach based on 2D convolutional (CNN) and word embedding representations of the target text and its context is employed.

Their best system ranked 10th, 5th, and 16th for the NEWS, WIKINEWS, and WIKIPEDIA monolingual English tracks, which is better than the average systems in the shared task. The system based on the CNN model on the Spanish monolingual dataset ranked 2nd.

5   Conclusions

This paper presented the results and findings of the second CWI shared task. Thirty teams enrolled to participate in the competition and 12 of them submitted their results. Subsequently, 11 teams wrote system description papers that have been reviewed in this report.

Overall, traditional feature engineering-based approaches (mostly based on length and frequency features) perform better than neural network and word embedding-based approaches. However, compared to the SemEval 2016 Task 11 shared task systems presented in Table 1, we have observed that more systems employed deep learning approaches and the results are getting better for the CWI task; the difference is less pronounced for the probabilistic classification tasks.

One of our most important findings is that cross-lingual experimental results are very promising, which we think implies in fundamental progress for CWI research. Despite the fact that we do not provide a training dataset for French, the results obtained have superior or equivalent scores (though they of course cannot be directly compared) to the German and Spanish datasets, when the system uses either one or several training datasets from the other languages.

Acknowledgments

We would like to thank all participants of the CWI shared task, as well as the BEA workshop organizers for hosting and providing all the necessary support for the organization of the shared task. The dataset collection was funded as part of the DFG-SemSch project (BI-1544/3).

References

Ahmed AbuRa'ed and Horacio Saggion. 2018. LaS-TUS/TALN at Complex Word Identification (CWI) 2018 Shared Task. In *Proceedings of the 13th Workshop on Innovative Use of NLP for Building Educational Applications*, New Orleans, United States. Association for Computational Linguistics.

David Alfter and Ildikó Pilán. 2018. SB@GU at the Complex Word Identification 2018 Shared Task. In *Proceedings of the 13th Workshop on Innovative Use of NLP for Building Educational Applications*, New Orleans, United States. Association for Computational Linguistics.

Segun Taofeek Aroyehun, Jason Angel, Daniel Alejandro Prez Alvarez, and Alexander Gelbukh. 2018. Complex Word Identification: Convolutional Neural Network vs. Feature Engineering . In *Proceedings of the 13th Workshop on Innovative Use of NLP for Building Educational Applications*, New Orleans, United States. Association for Computational Linguistics.

Joachim Bingel and Johannes Bjerva. 2018. Cross-lingual complex word identification with multitask learning. In *Proceedings of the 13th Workshop on Innovative Use of NLP for Building Educational Applications*, New Orleans, United States. Association for Computational Linguistics.

Joachim Bingel, Natalie Schluter, and Héctor Martínez Alonso. 2016. CoastalCPH at SemEval-2016 Task 11: The importance of designing your Neural Networks right. In *Proceedings of the 10th International Workshop on Semantic Evaluation (SemEval-2016)*, pages 1028–1033, San Diego, California. Association for Computational Linguistics.

Julian Brooke, Alexandra Uitdenbogerd, and Timothy Baldwin. 2016. Melbourne at SemEval 2016 Task 11: Classifying Type-level Word Complexity using Random Forests with Corpus and Word List Features. In *Proceedings of the 10th International Workshop on Semantic Evaluation (SemEval-2016)*, pages 975–981, San Diego, California. Association for Computational Linguistics.

Laetitia Brouwers, Delphine Bernhard, Anne-Laure Ligozat, and Thomas François. 2014. Syntactic Sentence Simplification for French. In *Proceedings of the 3rd Workshop on Predicting and Improving Text Readability for Target Reader Populations (PITR)*, pages 47–56, Gothenburg, Sweden. Association for Computational Linguistics.

Andrei Butnaru and Radu Tudor Ionescu. 2018. UnibucKernel: A kernel-based learning method for complex word identification . In *Proceedings of the 13th Workshop on Innovative Use of NLP for Building Educational Applications*, New Orleans, United States. Association for Computational Linguistics.

Prafulla Choubey and Shubham Pateria. 2016. Garuda & Bhasha at SemEval-2016 Task 11: Complex Word Identification Using Aggregated Learning Models. In *Proceedings of the 10th International Workshop on Semantic Evaluation (SemEval-2016)*, pages 1006–1010, San Diego, California. Association for Computational Linguistics.

Elnaz Davoodi and Leila Kosseim. 2016. CLaC at SemEval-2016 Task 11: Exploring linguistic and psycho-linguistic Features for Complex Word Identification. In *Proceedings of the 10th International Workshop on Semantic Evaluation (SemEval-2016)*, pages 982–985, San Diego, California. Association for Computational Linguistics.

Dirk De Hertog and Anaïs Tack. 2018. Deep Learning Architecture for Complex Word Identification . In *Proceedings of the 13th Workshop on Innovative Use of NLP for Building Educational Applications*, New Orleans, United States. Association for Computational Linguistics.

Nat Gillin. 2016. Sensible at SemEval-2016 Task 11: Neural Nonsense Mangled in Ensemble Mess. In *Proceedings of the 10th International Workshop on Semantic Evaluation (SemEval-2016)*, pages 963–968, San Diego, California. Association for Computational Linguistics.

Sian Gooding and Ekaterina Kochmar. 2018. CAMB at CWI Shared Task 2018: Complex Word Identification with Ensemble-Based Voting . In *Proceedings of the 13th Workshop on Innovative Use of NLP for Building Educational Applications*, New Orleans, United States. Association for Computational Linguistics.

Nathan Hartmann and Leandro Borges dos Santos. 2018. NILC at CWI 2018: Exploring Feature Engineering and Feature Learning . In *Proceedings of the 13th Workshop on Innovative Use of NLP for Building Educational Applications*, New Orleans, United States. Association for Computational Linguistics.

Benjamin Heinzerling and Michael Strube. 2017. BPEmb: Tokenization-free Pre-trained Sub-word Embeddings in 275 Languages. *CoRR*, abs/1710.02187.

Tomoyuki Kajiwara and Mamoru Komachi. 2018. Complex Word Identification Based on Frequency in a Learner Corpus . In *Proceedings of the 13th Workshop on Innovative Use of NLP for Building Educational Applications*, New Orleans, United States. Association for Computational Linguistics.

David Kauchak. 2016. Pomona at SemEval-2016 Task 11: Predicting Word Complexity Based on Corpus Frequency. In *Proceedings of the 10th International Workshop on Semantic Evaluation (SemEval-2016)*, pages 1047–1051, San Diego, California. Association for Computational Linguistics.

Michal Konkol. 2016. UWB at SemEval-2016 Task 11: Exploring Features for Complex Word Identification. In *Proceedings of the 10th International Workshop on Semantic Evaluation (SemEval-2016)*, pages 1038–1041, San Diego, California. Association for Computational Linguistics.

Onur Kuru. 2016. AI-KU at SemEval-2016 Task 11: Word Embeddings and Substring Features for Complex Word Identification. In *Proceedings of the 10th International Workshop on Semantic Evaluation (SemEval-2016)*, pages 1042–1046, San Diego, California. Association for Computational Linguistics.

Shervin Malmasi, Mark Dras, and Marcos Zampieri. 2016. LTG at SemEval-2016 Task 11: Complex Word Identification with Classifier Ensembles. In *Proceedings of the 10th International Workshop on Semantic Evaluation (SemEval-2016)*, pages 996–1000, San Diego, California. Association for Computational Linguistics.

Shervin Malmasi and Marcos Zampieri. 2016. MAZA at SemEval-2016 Task 11: Detecting Lexical Complexity Using a Decision Stump Meta-Classifier. In *Proceedings of the 10th International Workshop on Semantic Evaluation (SemEval-2016)*, pages 991–995, San Diego, California. Association for Computational Linguistics.

José Manuel Martínez Martínez and Liling Tan. 2016. USAAR at SemEval-2016 Task 11: Complex Word Identification with Sense Entropy and Sentence Perplexity. In *Proceedings of the 10th International Workshop on Semantic Evaluation (SemEval-2016)*, pages 958–962, San Diego, California. Association for Computational Linguistics.

Tomoya Mizumoto, Mamoru Komachi, Masaaki Nagata, and Yuji Matsumoto. 2011. Mining Revision Log of Language Learning SNS for Automated Japanese Error Correction of Second Language Learners. In *Proceedings of 5th International Joint Conference on Natural Language Processing*, pages 147–155, Chiang Mai, Thailand. Asian Federation of Natural Language Processing.

Niloy Mukherjee, Braja Gopal Patra, Dipankar Das, and Sivaji Bandyopadhyay. 2016. JU_NLP at SemEval-2016 Task 11: Identifying Complex Words in a Sentence. In *Proceedings of the 10th International Workshop on Semantic Evaluation (SemEval-2016)*, pages 986–990, San Diego, California. Association for Computational Linguistics.

Gustavo Paetzold and Lucia Specia. 2016a. SemEval 2016 Task 11: Complex Word Identification. In *Proceedings of the 10th International Workshop on Semantic Evaluation (SemEval-2016)*, pages 560–569, San Diego, California. Association for Computational Linguistics.

Gustavo Paetzold and Lucia Specia. 2016b. SV000gg at SemEval-2016 Task 11: Heavy Gauge Complex Word Identification with System Voting. In *Proceedings of the 10th International Workshop on Semantic Evaluation (SemEval-2016)*, pages 969–974, San Diego, California. Association for Computational Linguistics.

Ashish Palakurthi and Radhika Mamidi. 2016. IIIT at SemEval-2016 Task 11: Complex Word Identification using Nearest Centroid Classification. In *Proceedings of the 10th International Workshop on Semantic Evaluation (SemEval-2016)*, pages 1017–1021, San Diego, California. Association for Computational Linguistics.

Jeffrey Pennington, Richard Socher, and Christopher Manning. 2014. Glove: Global Vectors for Word Representation. In *Proceedings of the 2014 Conference on Empirical Methods in Natural Language Processing (EMNLP)*, pages 1532–1543, Doha, Qatar. Association for Computational Linguistics.

Maja Popović. 2018. Complex Word Identification using Character n-grams. In *Proceedings of the 13th Workshop on Innovative Use of NLP for Building Educational Applications*, New Orleans, United States. Association for Computational Linguistics.

Maury Quijada and Julie Medero. 2016. HMC at SemEval-2016 Task 11: Identifying Complex Words Using Depth-limited Decision Trees. In *Proceedings of the 10th International Workshop on Semantic Evaluation (SemEval-2016)*, pages 1034–1037, San Diego, California. Association for Computational Linguistics.

Francesco Ronzano, Ahmed Abura'ed, Luis Espinosa Anke, and Horacio Saggion. 2016. TALN at SemEval-2016 Task 11: Modelling Complex Words by Contextual, Lexical and Semantic Features. In *Proceedings of the 10th International Workshop on Semantic Evaluation (SemEval-2016)*, pages 1011–1016, San Diego, California. Association for Computational Linguistics.

Matthew Shardlow. 2013. A comparison of techniques to automatically identify complex words. In *51st Annual Meeting of the Association for Computational Linguistics Proceedings of the Student Research Workshop*, pages 103–109, Sofia, Bulgaria. Association for Computational Linguistics.

Sanjay S.P, Anand Kumar M, and Soman K P. 2016. AmritaCEN at SemEval-2016 Task 11: Complex Word Identification using Word Embedding. In *Proceedings of the 10th International Workshop on Semantic Evaluation (SemEval-2016)*, pages 1022–1027, San Diego, California. Association for Computational Linguistics.

Anaïs Tack, Thomas François, Anne-Laure Ligozat, and Cédrick Fairon. 2016. Evaluating Lexical Simplification and Vocabulary Knowledge for Learners of French: Possibilities of Using the FLELex Resource. In *Proceedings of the 10th International Conference on Language Resources and Evaluation (LREC 2016)*, pages 230–236, Portorož, Slovenia.

Nikhil Wani, Sandeep Mathias, Jayashree Aanand Gajjam, and Pushpak Bhattacharyya. 2018. The Whole is Greater than the Sum of its Parts: Towards the Effectiveness of Voting Ensemble Classifiers for Complex Word Identification. In *Proceedings of the 13th Workshop on Innovative Use of NLP for Building Educational Applications*, New Orleans, United States. Association for Computational Linguistics.

Krzysztof Wróbel. 2016. PLUJAGH at SemEval-2016 Task 11: Simple System for Complex Word Identification. In *Proceedings of the 10th International Workshop on Semantic Evaluation (SemEval-2016)*, pages 953–957, San Diego, California. Association for Computational Linguistics.

Seid Muhie Yimam, Sanja Štajner, Martin Riedl, and Chris Biemann. 2017a. CWIG3G2 - Complex Word Identification Task across Three Text Genres and Two User Groups. In *Proceedings of the Eighth International Joint Conference on Natural Language Processing (Volume 2: Short Papers)*, pages 401–407, Taipei, Taiwan. Asian Federation of Natural Language Processing.

Seid Muhie Yimam, Sanja Štajner, Martin Riedl, and Chris Biemann. 2017b. Multilingual and Cross-Lingual Complex Word Identification. In *Proceedings of the International Conference Recent Advances in Natural Language Processing, RANLP 2017*, pages 813–822, Varna, Bulgaria. INCOMA Ltd.

Marcos Zampieri, Shervin Malmasi, Gustavo Paetzold, and Lucia Specia. 2017. Complex Word Identification: Challenges in Data Annotation and System Performance. In *Proceedings of the 4th Workshop on Natural Language Processing Techniques for Educational Applications (NLPTEA 2017)*, pages 59–63, Taipei, Taiwan. Asian Federation of Natural Language Processing.

Marcos Zampieri, Liling Tan, and Josef van Genabith. 2016. MacSaar at SemEval-2016 Task 11: Zipfian and Character Features for ComplexWord Identification. In *Proceedings of the 10th International Workshop on Semantic Evaluation (SemEval-2016)*, pages 1001–1005, San Diego, California. Association for Computational Linguistics.

Towards Single Word Lexical Complexity Prediction

David Alfter
Språkbanken
University of Gothenburg
Sweden
david.alfter@gu.se

Elena Volodina
Språkbanken
University of Gothenburg
Sweden
elena.volodina@gu.se

Abstract

In this paper we present work-in-progress where we investigate the usefulness of previously created word lists to the task of single-word lexical complexity analysis and prediction of the complexity level for learners of Swedish as a second language. The word lists used map each word to a single CEFR level, and the task consists of predicting CEFR levels for unseen words. In contrast to previous work on word-level lexical complexity, we experiment with topics as additional features and show that linking words to topics significantly increases accuracy of classification.

1 Introduction

A way of addressing the second-language (L2) acquisition needs of the recent influx of new immigrants to Sweden would be to provide an extensive amount of digitally accessible self-study materials for practice. This could be achieved through the development of specific algorithms for exercise/material generation, but such algorithms generally heavily rely on linguistic resources, such as descriptions of vocabulary and grammar scopes per each stage of language development, so that automatic generation of learning materials would follow some order of increasing complexity.

Vocabulary scope can be described through graded vocabulary lists. These are lexical resources where each lexical item is linked to a level at which the item is appropriate for learners to study, one prominent example being the English Vocabulary Profile (Capel, 2010, 2012). Graded lexical resources are useful, for example, for course book writers, language test designers, language teachers and language learners, since they can inform the users as to what knowledge is to be expected at which proficiency level, as well as which words to teach and test at which levels.

However, any graded list is a finite resource, as it would never be possible to list by levels all items that learners might encounter. We intend, therefore, to use previously compiled graded vocabulary lists to learn from them to predict levels of previously unseen, out-of-vocabulary (OOV), lexical items.

In practical terms, we look at three automatically created corpus-based vocabulary lists, namely Kelly list (Volodina and Kokkinakis, 2012), a resource based on L1 web corpora that identifies frequent vocabulary to guide language learners in their acquisition of vocabulary[1], as well as SVALex (François et al., 2016) and SweLLex (Volodina et al., 2016b), two L2-targeted word lists covering receptive vocabulary and productive vocabulary respectively[2]. The aim of this work is, thus, to create a model that is able to predict the difficulty (i.e. appropriate CEFR[3] level) of any Swedish word with regard to productive and receptive aspects. These graded vocabulary lists are then intended for use in generation of exercises for learners of different levels, though other usage scenarios are also possible.

2 Related Work

There has been some work on the creation and evaluation of automatically graded vocabulary lists (Gala et al., 2013, 2014; Tack et al., 2016b).

Gala et al. (2013) aim at identifying criteria that make words easy to understand, independently of the context in which they appear. Since it has been shown that the concept of difficulty depends on the target group (Blache, 2011; François,

---

[1] Swedish Kelly list is available with CC-BY license from *https://spraakbanken.gu.se/eng/resource/kelly*

[2] Both lists are a part of CEFRLex family of resources, and are available from *http://cental.uclouvain.be/cefrlex/*

[3] Common European Framework of Reference for Languages (Council of Europe, 2001) describes six levels of proficiency, starting from A1 to C2

79

Proceedings of the Thirteenth Workshop on Innovative Use of NLP for Building Educational Applications, pages 79–88
New Orleans, Louisiana, June 5, 2018. ©2018 Association for Computational Linguistics

2012), and thus different combinations of features might model certain groups better than others, they focus on speech productions by patients with Parkinson's disease. Gala et al. (2013) look at 27 intra-lexical and psycholinguistic variables. The intra-lexical variables include number of letters, number of phonemes, number of syllables, syllable structure (CV structure), consistency between graphemes and phonemes, and selected difficult spelling patterns such as double vowels and double consonants. Among psycholinguistic variables are orthographic neighborhood (words that only differ by one letter), lexical frequency and presence/absence from the Gougenheim list, a list of easy-to-understand vocabulary items.

They train a Support Vector Machine (SVM) classifier on the nine (out of initial 27) most predictive features to predict the difficulty level of unseen words. 5-fold cross-validation on the data shows an average accuracy of 62% in the three-way classification. They conclude that syllabic structures and spelling patterns are not very predictive of difficulty and that the most predictive features are the lexical frequency and presence/absence from the Gougenheim list.

Gala et al. (2014) focus on learners of French, both L1 learners and learners of French as a foreign language. They use Manulex (Lété et al., 2004) to model L1 learners' vocabulary and FLELex (François et al., 2014) to model L2 learners' vocabulary. In contrast to Gala et al. (2013), they use 49 features which can be grouped into orthographic features (e.g. number of letters, number of phonemes, number of syllables), morphological features (number of morphemes, affix frequency, compounding), semantic features (degree of polysemy) and statistical features (frequency, Gougenheim list). They train two SVM classifiers, one for L1 learners and one for learners of French as a foreign language. The first one is a three-way classification while the latter is a six-way classification. On the three-way classification, they reach 63% accuracy and on the six-way classification they reach 43% accuracy. As in Gala et al. (2013), they find the most predictive features to be lexical frequency and presence/absence from the Gougenheim list. However, they also find the binary polysemous status, i.e. whether the word polysemous or not, as well as the degree of polysemy to correlate well with the complexity of words. This is an interesting finding, as the degree of polysemy is not directly correlated with frequency.

A related area of work is complex word identification for text simplification. For this task, it is important to identify target *difficult* words or phrases that need simplification (Shardlow, 2013; Paetzold and Specia, 2016; Štajner et al., 2018). However, in contrast to our work, complex word identification is a binary classification and the focus is slightly different, although there are significant overlaps. Tack et al. (2016a) and Tack et al. (2016b) for example aim at identifying and classifying words of a text into known and unknown ones either for an individual learner or for learners of a given proficiency level as a group. They compare different personalized models with a model based on the graded vocabulary list FLELex (François et al., 2014). Their personalized models also use frequency information, CEFR levels of single words as calculated in Gala et al. (2014), number of letters, and number of senses of a word. For the FLELex vocabulary based model and a learner of a given CEFR level, the model considers all words that are of the same or lower level as the learner's level as known and all words that are of higher level as unknown.

Our recent participation in the Complex Word Identification Task 2018 (Štajner et al., 2018) has yielded interesting findings that we hope will further improve the presented system (Alfter and Pilán, 2018).

3   Data

Our data consists of three different word lists for Swedish, namely SVALex (François et al., 2016), SweLLex (Volodina et al., 2016b) and Kelly list (Volodina and Kokkinakis, 2012).

SVALex is compiled from the COCTAILL textbook corpus (Volodina et al., 2014), comprised of reading comprehension texts marked for CEFR levels, and covers receptive vocabulary knowledge. SweLLex is derived from the pilot SweLL learner essay corpus (Volodina et al., 2016a) graded for CEFR levels and covers productive vocabulary knowledge. Kelly list is derived from the Swedish Web-as-Corpus (SweWaC) and contains the 8425 most frequent lemmas appearing in native speaker writing divided into CEFR level according to the frequency of the items and corpus coverage. See table 1 for the overview of the three resources.

While Kelly list already assigns each word to a

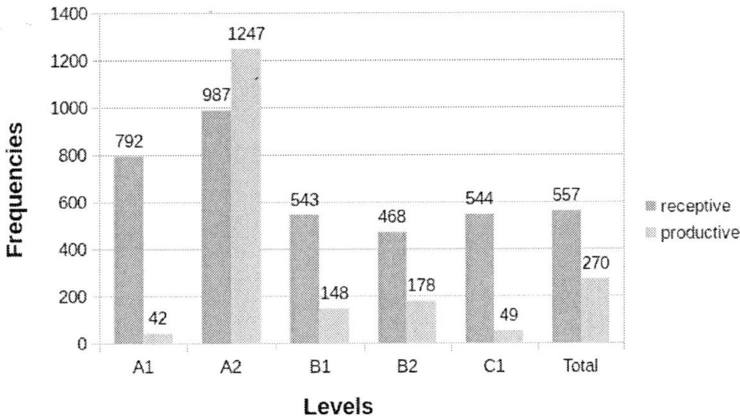

Figure 1: Distribution of the verb *arbeta* 'to work', in receptive and productive resources

	A1	A2	B1	B2	C1	Total
SVALex	968	1973	2761	6223	3697	15 681
SweLLex	602	1258	1317	1024	1248	6 965
Kelly list	1404	1404	1404	1404	2809	8 425

Table 1: Data distribution across lists. In SVALex and SweLLex vocabulary items partially overlap between levels, and hence the total number of items in the list does not equal the sum of items per level.

target CEFR level, SVALex and SweLLex present distributions over CEFR levels, i.e. how often a word occurs at the different CEFR levels, as exemplified in table 2. Since SVALex and SweLLex cover 5 proficiency levels and Kelly list covers 6 proficiency levels, we assimilated the highest level in Kelly list (C2) to the previous level (C1).

To go from distributions to target levels in SweLLex and SVALex, we use the mapping procedures described in Gala et al. (2013), Gala et al. (2014) (first occurrence) and Alfter et al. (2016) (threshold). For *first-occurrence mapping*, we assign each word to the level it first occurs at. For *threshold mapping*, we assign each word to the level where it occurs *significantly* more often than at the preceding level, with the level of significance set at 30%.

Figure 1 shows the distribution of frequencies for the word *arbeta* (Eng. "to work") over the five CEFR levels in SVALex (receptive resource, 1st bar) and SweLLex (productive resource, 2nd bar). According to the *first occurrence* approach, the target level for both receptive and productive competence for the word *arbeta* would be A1, whereas the *threshold* approach suggests that A1 would be the target level for receptive knowledge, and A2

would be the target level for productive level.

We did a comparison of both mapping methods to find out to what degree they agree. Table 3 shows the levels assigned by both methods for the two resources SVALex and SweLLex. By comparing the output of these two mapping methods, we can see that both methods agree to a large extend. When both methods did not agree, they tended to still assign levels that were adjacent, e.g. if one method assigned level B1, the other would assign B2 or A2. This is not a surprise, as the border between different proficiency levels can be fluid. We call this type of disagreement *within one level*. We also see that a certain amount of words were classified as different levels but with the levels assigned being more than one level apart, e.g. one method assigns level A2 and the other method assigns level B2. We call this type of disagreement *more than one level*. Given this finding, and for comparability between studies, e.g. with Gala et al. (2013) and Gala et al. (2014), we have opted to use the first-occurrence approach in the remainder of the study.

The SVALex and SweLLex data is noisy, because, for one, we cannot validate whether the automatically assigned (mapped) levels are accurate

Lemma	Part-of-Speech	A1	A2	B1	B2	C1
beta 'to graze'	VB	0.0	0.0	0.0	19.27	13.21
bo 'to live'	VB	4978.93	2515.92	1252.19	718.53	497.75
hund 'dog'	NN	251.89	81.26	250.26	74.29	98.87

Table 2: Example of word distributions over levels in SVALex

Resource	Same level	Within one level	More than one level
SVALex	12775	1592	1255
SweLLex	5689	706	516

Table 3: Number of items that were assigned the same level, within one level and more than level by both mapping techniques

due to missing gold standard annotations, and secondly because of certain errors resulting from automatic corpus annotation. The data is also sparse, and since the mapping procedure for SVALex and SweLLex very much depends on the data available, this introduces further noise. These are the limitations we are aware of and plan to address in the future by collecting and annotating more data.

4 Features

From each word, including multi-word expressions such as *göra ont* 'to hurt' and *god morgon* 'good morning', we extract features, grouped into count-based features (i), morphological features (ii), semantic features (iii) and context-based features (iv). Table 4 gives an overview of the average values for some selected features per level and resource. As can be seen from this table, words at higher levels tend to be longer, have more syllables, longer suffixes, a higher number of compounds and lower degrees of polysemy and homonymy. Indeed, concerning polysemy, more common words, which are typically found at lower levels, tend to have more different senses than more specialized words found at higher levels.

(i) Count-based and surface form features

- *Length* is the length of the word in characters, our example word *arbeta* (Eng "to work") containing 6 characters. Word length has previously been used to assess linguis-

tic complexity, among others in readability assessment formulas, for example in Smith (1961); Björnsson (1968); O'Regan and Jacobs (1992).

- *Syllable* count is the number of syllables in the word, where *arbeta* contains three syllables. Syllables are counted as number of vowels except for diphthongs ending in 'u' (e.g. 'eu', 'au') which are counted as one syllable. Syllable count has been applied in readability assessment as a measure of increasing text difficulty, e.g. in Flesch (1948); Kincaid et al. (1975), where multi-syllable words have been proven to increase the overall linguistic complexity of a text. By analogy, we assume that the same applies on a single word level.

- *Contains non-alphanumeric characters* is a boolean value that is true if the word contains non-alphanumeric characters, i.e. any character other than A-Z and digits 0-9, for example *13-åring* (Eng. 13-year old).

- *Contains number* is a boolean value that is true if the word contains digits or consists solely of digits.

- The *multi-word* feature indicates whether the lexical expression is made up of more than one single word.

- For *bigrams*, we calculated all character-level bigrams from each word list and retained only the 53 most predictive ones. This feature is a vector indicating the presence or absence of these 53 bigrams in the target word.

- For *n-gram probabilities*, we calculate character-level unigram, bigram and trigram probabilities with a language model based on the Swedish Wikipedia dump from February 2018. We surmise this also implicitly cap-

	A1	A2	B1	B2	C1
Average word length					
SVALex	6.00	7.49	8.51	8.85	9.58
SweLLex	5.10	5.98	7.66	8.89	9.91
Kelly	5.74	7.00	7.54	7.86	7.80
Average syllable count					
SVALex	2.08	2.52	2.88	2.91	3.24
SweLLex	1.80	2.01	2.58	2.94	3.28
Kelly	2.04	2.44	2.62	2.78	2.76
Average suffix length					
SVALex	0.54	0.63	0.77	0.80	0.91
SweLLex	0.47	0.51	0.56	0.63	0.71
Kelly	0.70	0.80	0.86	0.88	0.87
Average number of compounds					
SVALex	0.014	0.037	0.052	0.062	0.067
SweLLex	0.038	0.058	0.112	0.125	0.162
Kelly	0.043	0.095	0.137	0.175	0.167
Average degree of polysemy					
SVALex	0.64	0.51	0.39	0.29	0.24
SweLLex	0.55	0.62	0.46	0.36	0.30
Kelly	0.84	0.73	0.67	0.56	0.56
Average degree of homonymy					
SVALex	1.25	1.11	1.06	1.05	1.02
SweLLex	1.35	1.18	1.10	1.08	1.04
Kelly	1.30	1.13	1.08	1.10	1.05

Table 4: (Selected) feature averages per level and resource

tures information about grapheme-phoneme correspondence, frequency and suffixes.

(ii) Morphological features

- *Part-of-speech* corresponds to the part-of-speech of the word. For multi-word expressions, the part-of-speech of the head noun is taken.

- For *suffix length*, we stem the word using the NLTK stemmer (Bird et al., 2009) and subtract the length of the resulting stem from the length of the original word. In *arbeta*, the final -a is a suffix. Previous work on order of acquisition of inflectional versus derivational morphemes, e.g. Derwing (1976), argue that knowledge of derivational morphology is acquired gradually in the learning progress, thus motivating this feature for our experiments. This intuition also seems to hold when looking at average suffix length by level, as shown in table 4.

- For *compound count*, we run the word through the SPyRo/SALDO pipeline (Östling and Wirén, 2013), which generates possible analyses of the word with regard to compounding. Compound count is the number of possible compounding alternatives. *Arbeta* can theoretically be analyzed as *ar* 'are (unit of measurement)' + *beta* 'to graze' and thus would have a compound count of 1. *Glasskål* on the other hand can be analyzed as *glas* 'glass' + *skål* 'bowl', *glass* 'ice cream' + *skål* 'bowl' and *glass* 'ice cream' + *kål* 'cabbage' and thus would have a compound count of 3. The cognitive load for processing a word, that potentially has several (compounding) interpretations, hypothetically also influences the word's complexity, and hence the level at which it is acquired.

- For *compounds*, we calculate all compound elements, i.e. words that have been identified in compounds, in all lists and selected the 12 most predictive compounds. This feature is a vector indicating the presence or absence of these compounds in the target word.

- *Gender* for nouns is taken from Saldo's morphology (Borin et al., 2008) and encoded numerically as -1 (no information about gender or not applicable), 0 (common gender, aka "en-ord"), 1 (neuter, aka "ett-ord") and 2 (variable gender). For *arbeta* the value would be -1 since gender only applies to nouns. The majority of nouns in Swedish are of common gender (e.g. in the Kelly-list there are 3465 nouns of common gender, while 1065 are neuter).

(iii) Semantic features

- *Degree of polysemy* is calculated by counting the sub-entries of a given dictionary entry in Lexin (Gellerstam, 1999). The verb *arbeta* has only one sub-entry, and is thus non-polysemous. From empirical sources (e.g. various frequency lists), we can observe that non-polysemous words tend to be less used constituting a large bulk of non-frequent words, something that is quite logical given that most word lists are compiled based on lem-grams (e.g. a combination of base form of a word plus its part-of-speech), and not on senses. Usages of several senses of the same lem-gram are thus grouped together in one entry and push the word to the top of the frequency lists. Highly polysemous words, like *komma* 'to come' are thus often learned in the beginning. This seems to be a contradictory trend with regards to our example word, *arbeta* 'to work'. However, if we extend the search to phrasal verbs with *arbeta* in Saldo, there would be seven more entries, and in Lexin four more.

- *Degree of homonymy* is calculated by counting the number of dictionary entries in Lexin with the same orthographic form. An example of a homonym across word classes would be *gift*: it could either be the adjective meaning "married" or the noun meaning "poison". Homonymy within the same word class would be *vara* (Eng. "to last",

"to be"). The example word *arbeta* has only one entry in Lexin. Studies on homonymy within second language learning (Mashhady et al., 2012) show that honomymous words take longer to remember and differentiate between meanings than e.g. several synonyms relating to the same concept, demanding disambiguation of a homonym given the context, which makes homonymy an interesting feature to include into our experiments.

(iv) Context features

- For *topic distributions*, we indicate in which topic lists the target word occurs. Topic lists were extracted from the COCTAILL corpus, where each reading text is assigned one or more topics. We thus extracted all lemmata from reading texts, assigning them to the topics as given in the corpus. We then ran a TF-IDF algorithm over the lists to eliminate words that occurred across all topic lists. This yielded 33 topic lists, such as animals, arts, daily life, food and drink, nature, places, or technology.

Thus, for the verb *arbeta*, we can summarize the above features into the following (simplified) word complexity description: 6-letter 3-syllable non-polysemous non-homonymous verb with one possible suffix, one possible compound analysis, no gender information (since this only applies to nouns), not a multi-word expression and a word used in topics characteristic of presenting people (CEFR levels A1 and A2) which is - supposedly - the reason why the empiric data points out A1 level for receptive and productive knowledge according to *first-occurrence* approach; and A1 for receptive and A2 for productive knowledge if we follow the *threshold* mapping strategy.

5 Classification

In order to check how well the features we have chosen model single word complexity, we use different classifiers and stratified 10-fold cross-validation on the different data sets.

For classification of unseen words, we train classifiers on the available data. We train one classifier for receptive predictions on SVALex and one classifier for productive predictions on SweLLex.

The classification task consists in assigning each word in our word lists a target CEFR level.

	Svalex	Swellex	Kelly
Majority baseline	0.29 ± 0.00	0.29 ± 0.00	0.33 ± 0.00
SVM	0.32 ± 0.02	0.37 ± 0.05	0.39 ± 0.04
MLP	0.32 ± 0.03	0.37 ± 0.04	0.39 ± 0.04
ET	0.27 ± 0.02	0.33 ± 0.05	0.32 ± 0.04
SVM+T	0.44 ± 0.03	$\mathbf{0.41} \pm 0.04$	$\mathbf{0.45} \pm 0.05$
MLP+T	0.53 ± 0.04	0.38 ± 0.05	0.44 ± 0.05
ET+T	$\mathbf{0.55} \pm 0.05$	0.37 ± 0.06	0.43 ± 0.05
SVM+TL	0.48 ± 0.03	0.41 ± 0.05	0.45 ± 0.04
MLP+TL	0.53 ± 0.04	0.39 ± 0.06	0.44 ± 0.03
ET+TL	$\mathbf{0.59} \pm 0.03$	0.37 ± 0.06	0.42 ± 0.03

Table 5: Results: Accuracy and standard deviation using 10-fold cross-validation

For evaluation of the features, accuracy is calculated by comparing the predicted level with the level given by the graded word list. We cannot, at this moment, evaluate classifiers for unseen words, as we would have to have manually graded word lists against which to compare our predictions.

6 Results

Table 5 shows the results of 10-fold cross-validation classification using different algorithms. Majority baseline always predicts the majority class. Since our data is not balanced, this deviates from the expected chance baseline of 0.2 for five-class classification. SVM is a support vector machine with default parameters $C = 1$ and radial basis function (rbf) kernel. MLP is a multilayer perceptron with 100 hidden layers and a learning rate of 0.01. These parameters were chosen based on a randomized grid search over the parameter space. ET is an extra trees classifier, a classifier from the group of random tree classifiers. Preliminary experiments have shown an initial increase in accuracy with an increase in the number of estimators of the ET algorithm but which shows no further improvement after 100 estimators. We thus have fixed the number of estimators for the ET algorithm at 100. SVM+T, MLP+T and ET+T show the accuracies obtained by the same algorithms but with topic distributions added to the data. For comparability, since we have included all word classes in our experiments, we also tried classifying only lexical word classes (nouns, verbs, adjectives and adverbs) as in Gala et al. (2014). The results of these experiments are shown in the rows SVM+TL, MLP+TL and ET+TL.

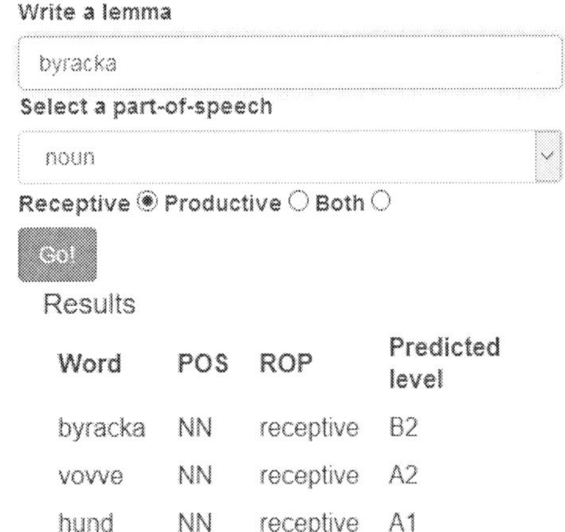

Figure 2: User interface for lexical complexity prediction

In addition, we have created a user interface[4], as shown in figure 2. This user interface can be used for getting predictions of any word, not only words present in the word lists . The input word is transformed into a feature vector as described above and then fed into the classifier, which predicts a label. Figure 2 shows the predictions for *hund* 'dog', *vovve* 'childish or endearing term for dog' and *byracka* 'derogatory term for dog'.

7 Discussion

We found that our features excluding topic distributions barely outperform the majority baseline, yielding even lower scores than the baseline in some cases. Adding topic distributions signifi-

---

[4] https://spraakbanken.gu.se/larkalabb/siwoco

cantly improves accuracy.

In comparison to the results presented in Gala et al. (2014), we can see an expected trend. Indeed, on the L1 resource Manulex and Kelly (which is based on L1 data but intended for L2 audiences), they reach 63% accuracy in a three-way classification while we reach 45% accuracy in a five-way classification. On the L2 textbook corpus resources FLELex and SVALex, they reach 43% accuracy in a six-way classification while we reach 59% accuracy in a five-way classification.

If we are comparing our results without topic distributions, which are more similar to the results presented in Gala et al. (2014) due to the similarity of features, we see that our best system on L2 data performs worse in a five-way classification (0.32) than theirs in a six-way classification (0.43). This is probably due to the size of the corpus that was used to compile these lists. While FLELex was compiled from 28 textbooks and 29 readers, COCTAILL was compiled from 12 textbooks only. As such, their distributions are less sparse and hypotheses about the target level can be made with more certainty.

Another point is that, in contrast to previous work, we have not included information about lexical frequency explicitly. Including such information could possibly further improve accuracy. It can be argued that n-gram probabilities latently encode this information, but it would be interesting to see whether a more explicit approach would lead to better results.

We also ran cross-validated recursive feature elimination (Guyon et al., 2002) to get a ranking of features and discard useless features. This interestingly identified bigram features (presence/absence of most predictive bigrams; not to be confused with bigram frequency) and compound features as useless, but excluding those features does not lead to an increase in accuracy. However, looking at the most predictive bigram and compound files, it seems that something went wrong during calculation of these, since, for example in bigrams, there are only very rare combinations such as 'åä', 'åo', 'xf' and 'xb'. We would like to address this issue in future work. The final model uses 64 features.

One problem for the classifiers could be that representing words as vectors can lead to the same representation for different words with different levels, which leads to a decrease in learnability

since it introduces contradictory data points. We have checked for this and found out that our data contains about 5% of contradictory data points. A possible approach could be to add more disambiguating features.

8 Conclusion and future work

We have presented insights from work-in-progress on single word lexical complexity. In contrast to previous work, we show that adding topic information significantly improves results on the classification task. However, the current topic lists can be further refined, for example by synonym expansion, in the hope of improving accuracy.

For future work, one concern that was also expressed in Gala et al. (2014) is that the current lists do not discriminate between different senses of a word. Thus, words like *glas*, meaning either 'glass' as substance or 'glass' as receptacle for drinks, would be assigned one single level while their different senses clearly should be assigned different levels. We are currently working on recalculating the resources SVALex and SweLLex on the sense level by including a word sense disambiguation component in the pipeline.

Another interesting experiment could be to include number of phonemes in our study, since Swedish has some non-transparent grapheme-to-phoneme correspondences.

There is currently ongoing work concerning the collection and annotation of learner essays, which we hope will alleviate the data sparseness problem that we face at the moment, especially with regard to the learner essay based word list.

We would also like to implicitly crowdsource learner knowledge by embedding words from these automatically mapped lists in automatically generated learner exercises. By monitoring how learners of a given level are dealing with words predicted to be of their level, we hope to be able to draw conclusions about the target level of words, i.e. if learners of intermediate B1 level consistently have problems with certain words that our mapping predicts to be of B1 level, we can assume that the prediction was incorrect.

In the future, we intend to evaluate these resources both with teachers of Swedish as a second language as well as language learners to estimate the validity of the automatic mapping. We would also like to create gold standard annotations, both based on these resources as well as new resources.

9   Acknowledgements

This work has in part been funded by an infrastructure grant from the Swedish Research Council to Swedish National Language Bank. We would also like to thank the anonymous reviewers for their constructive feedback.

References

David Alfter, Yuri Bizzoni, Anders Agebjörn, Elena Volodina, and Ildikó Pilán. 2016. From Distributions to Labels: A Lexical Proficiency Analysis using Learner Corpora. In *Proceedings of the joint workshop on NLP for Computer Assisted Language Learning and NLP for Language Acquisition at SLTC, Umeå, 16th November 2016*, 130, pages 1–7. Linköping University Electronic Press.

David Alfter and Ildikó Pilán. 2018. SB@GU at the Complex Word Identification Task 2018. In *Proceedings of the 13th Workshop on Innovative Use of NLP for Building Educational Applications*.

Steven Bird, Ewan Klein, and Edward Loper. 2009. *Natural language processing with Python: analyzing text with the natural language toolkit*. O'Reilly Media, Inc.

Carl Hugo Björnsson. 1968. *Läsbarhet*. Liber.

Philippe Blache. 2011. A computational model for linguistic complexity.

Lars Borin, Markus Forsberg, and Lennart Lönngren. 2008. The hunting of the BLARK–SALDO, a freely available lexical database for Swedish language technology. *Resourceful language technology. Festschrift in honor of Anna Sågvall Hein*, (7):21–32.

Annette Capel. 2010. A1–B2 vocabulary: insights and issues arising from the English Profile Wordlists project. *English Profile Journal*, 1(1):1–11.

Annette Capel. 2012. Completing the English Vocabulary Profile: C1 and C2 vocabulary. *English Profile Journal*, 3:1–14.

Council of Europe. 2001. *Common European Framework of Reference for Languages: Learning, Teaching, Assessment*. Press Syndicate of the University of Cambridge.

Bruce L Derwing. 1976. Morpheme recognition and the learning of rules for derivational morphology 1. *Canadian Journal of Linguistics/Revue canadienne de linguistique*, 21(1):38–66.

Rudolph Flesch. 1948. A new readability yardstick. *Journal of applied psychology*, 32(3):221.

Thomas François. 2012. *Lexical and syntactic complexities: a difficulty model for automatic generation of language exercises in FFL*. Ph.D. thesis, Université Catholique de Louvain, Louvain-la-Neuve.

Thomas François, Núria Gala, Patrick Watrin, and Cédrick Fairon. 2014. Flelex: a graded lexical resource for french foreign learners. In *LREC*, pages 3766–3773.

Thomas François, Elena Volodina, Ildikó Pilán, and Anaïs Tack. 2016. SVALex: a CEFR-graded Lexical Resource for Swedish Foreign and Second Language Learners. In *LREC*.

Núria Gala, Thomas François, Delphine Bernhard, and Cédrick Fairon. 2014. Un modèle pour prédire la complexité lexicale et graduer les mots. In *TALN 2014*, pages 91–102.

Núria Gala, Thomas François, and Cédrick Fairon. 2013. Towards a French lexicon with difficulty measures: NLP helping to bridge the gap between traditional dictionaries and specialized lexicons. *E-lexicography in the 21st century: thinking outside the paper.*, Tallin, Estonia.

Martin Gellerstam. 1999. LEXIN-lexikon för invandrare. *LexicoNordica*, (6).

Isabelle Guyon, Jason Weston, Stephen Barnhill, and Vladimir Vapnik. 2002. Gene selection for cancer classification using support vector machines. *Machine learning*, 46(1-3):389–422.

J Peter Kincaid, Robert P Fishburne Jr, Richard L Rogers, and Brad S Chissom. 1975. Derivation of new readability formulas (automated readability index, fog count and flesch reading ease formula) for navy enlisted personnel. Technical report, Naval Technical Training Command Millington TN Research Branch.

Bernard Lété, Liliane Sprenger-Charolles, and Pascale Colé. 2004. Manulex: A grade-level lexical database from french elementary school readers. *Behavior Research Methods, Instruments, & Computers*, 36(1):156–166.

Habibollah Mashhady, Behruz Lotfi, and Mahbobeh Noura. 2012. Word Type Effects on L2 Word Retrieval and Learning: Homonym versus Synonym Vocabulary Instruction. *Iranian Journal of Applied Language Studies*, 3(1):97–118.

J Kevin O'Regan and Arthur M Jacobs. 1992. Optimal viewing position effect in word recognition: A challenge to current theory. *Journal of Experimental Psychology: Human Perception and Performance*, 18(1):185.

Robert Östling and Mats Wirén. 2013. Compounding in a Swedish Blog Corpus.

Gustavo Paetzold and Lucia Specia. 2016. SemEval 2016 Task 11: Complex Word Identification. In *SemEval at NAACL-HLT*, pages 560–569.

Matthew Shardlow. 2013. A Comparison of Techniques to Automatically Identify Complex Words. In *ACL (Student Research Workshop)*, pages 103–109.

Edgar A Smith. 1961. Devereux readability index. *The Journal of Educational Research*, 54(8):298–303.

Anaïs Tack, Thomas François, Anne-Laure Ligozat, and Cédrick Fairon. 2016a. Evaluating lexical simplification and vocabulary knowledge for learners of french: Possibilities of using the flelex resource. In *LREC*.

Anaïs Tack, Thomas François, Anne-Laure Ligozat, and Cédrick Fairon. 2016b. Modèles adaptatifs pour prédire automatiquement la compétence lexicale d'un apprenant de français langue étrangère. In *La 23ème Conférence sur le Traitement Automatique des Langues Naturelles (JEP-TALN-RECITAL 2016)*.

Elena Volodina and Sofie Johansson Kokkinakis. 2012. Introducing the Swedish Kelly-list, a new lexical e-resource for Swedish. In *LREC*, pages 1040–1046.

Elena Volodina, Ildikó Pilán, Stian Rødven Eide, and Hannes Heidarsson. 2014. You get what you annotate: a pedagogically annotated corpus of coursebooks for Swedish as a Second Language. In *Proceedings of the third workshop on NLP for computer-assisted language learning at SLTC 2014, Uppsala University*, 107. Linköping University Electronic Press.

Elena Volodina, Ildikó Pilán, Ingegerd Enström, Lorena Llozhi, Peter Lundkvist, Gunlög Sundberg, and Monica Sandell. 2016a. SweLL on the rise: Swedish learner language corpus for european reference level studies. *arXiv preprint arXiv:1604.06583*.

Elena Volodina, Ildikó Pilán, Lorena Llozhi, Baptiste Degryse, and Thomas François. 2016b. SweLLex: second language learners' productive vocabulary. In *Proceedings of the joint workshop on NLP for Computer Assisted Language Learning and NLP for Language Acquisition at SLTC, Umeå, 16th November 2016*, 130, pages 76–84. Linköping University Electronic Press.

Sanja Štajner, Chris Biemann, Shervin Malmasi, Gustavo Paetzold, Lucia Specia, Anaïs Tack, Seid Muhie Yimam, and Marcos Zampieri. 2018. A Report on the Complex Word Identification Shared Task 2018. In *Proceedings of the 13th Workshop on Innovative Use of NLP for Building Educational Applications*, New Orleans, United States. Association for Computational Linguistics.

COAST – Customizable Online Syllable Enhancement in Texts: A flexible framework for automatically enhancing reading materials

Heiko Holz[*] ⬡   **Zarah Weiß**[*]   **Oliver Brehm**   **Detmar Meurers**

LEAD Graduate School & Research Network

ICALL Research Group[†]

University of Tübingen

`{heiko.holz,zarah-leonie.weiss}@uni-tuebingen.de,`
`olibrehm@googlemail.com, dm@sfs.uni-tuebingen.de`

Abstract

This paper presents COAST, a web-based application to easily and automatically enhance syllable structure, word stress, and spacing in texts, that was designed in close collaboration with learning therapists to ensure its practical relevance. Such syllable-enhanced texts are commonly used in learning therapy or private tuition to promote the recognition of syllables in order to improve reading and writing skills.

In a state of the art solutions for automatic syllable enhancement, we put special emphasis on syllable stress and support specific marking of the primary syllable stress in words. Core features of our tool are i) a highly customizable text enhancement and template functionality, and ii) a novel crowd-sourcing mechanism that we employ to address the issue of data sparsity in language resources. We successfully tested COAST with real-life practitioners in a series of user tests validating the concept of our framework.

1 Introduction

Reading and writing disabilities are a pressing issue for today's society – approximately 4–8 % of the German population suffer from dyslexia (Moll and Landerl, 2009; Bundesverband Legasthenie und Dyskalkulie e.V, 2014). Research on reading acquisition has shown that phonological awareness is a crucial skill for successful reading and writing acquisition (Röber-Siekmeyer, 2005). Important dimensions of phonological awareness are syllable synthesis and analysis. Syllable synthesis refers to the ability to blend syllables to a whole word, and syllable analysis to the ability of segmenting a word into its syllables. Experimental studies have shown that syllable synthesis and syllable analysis are essential components of evidence-based reading training (Galuschka and Schulte-Körne, 2016;

Galuschka et al., 2014). Scheerer-Neumann (1981) have shown that specific training of segmenting words into syllables can improve reading accuracy of impaired German primary-school children significantly. Additionally, computer-based programs for primary-school children that sequentially speak and highlight syllables can facilitate the learning process of reading (Jiménez et al., 2007; Olson and Wise, 1992).

Based on these empirical findings, enhanced texts with custom spacing and syllables alternately displayed in different font colors are commonly used in teaching and learning therapy to support acquisition of reading and writing. This so-called *Silbenmethode* (syllable method) (Mildenberer Verlag, 2018) teaches children to focus on and understand syllables and their structures rather than single characters and is commonly used in Germany, which is reflected by popular reading materials , such as *ABC der Tiere* and *Leselöwe*, and by available tools that facilitate the learning process of reading and writing, such as *Celeco Druckstation* and *ABC Silbengenerator.*

While first language acquisition happens through mere exposure, learning to read and write is a learned skill and thus requires explicit instruction, similar to Second Language Acquisition (SLA). In this regard, insights form SLA research on input enhancement relate to reading and writing acquisition. The well-established *Noticing Hypothesis* (Schmidt, 1990) states that learning requires the exposure to salient linguistic constructions that may be recognized by the learner. To facilitate this recognition of relevant linguistic constructions, *Input Enhancement* (Smith, 1993) has been successfully used, in particular in terms of visual enhancement of texts (e.g. colors, font changes, capitalization, spacing), cf. (Rello and Baeza-Yates, 2017; Zorzi et al., 2012; Meurers et al., 2010).

In response to this, we developed COAST.[1]

---

[*] These authors contributed equally to this work.

[†] `http://icall-research.de`

[1] `www.sfs.uni-tuebingen.de/coast/`

Proceedings of the Thirteenth Workshop on Innovative Use of NLP for Building Educational Applications, pages 89–100
New Orleans, Louisiana, June 5, 2018. ©2018 Association for Computational Linguistics

COAST is a web-based application to easily and automatically enhance syllable structure, word stress, and spacing in texts. Its primary focus is on functionality and practicability. In terms of functionality, COAST offers a high degree of customization for text enhancement, supports management of annotation schemes, and includes syllable stress. The performance of detecting syllable stress strongly predicts dyslexia (e.g., Goswami et al. (2013); Landerl (2003)) and correlates highly with reading and writing skills (Sauter et al., 2012) and, thus, is of special importance for dyslexic children. Trainings to improve the awareness of syllable stress are being developed and evaluated (Holz et al., 2017). We extend the approach of text enhancement that are provided by state of the art tools to make syllable structures and stress more salient for German native (dyslexic) speakers using NLP resources. Enhancing the text with such additional linguistic information might boost children's ability to segment words into relevant components and might help them to learn to focus on relevant areas of words – as major orthographic challenges, such as vowel length markers, mainly occur in (conjunction with) stressed syllables (Staffeldt, 2010). To account for practicability, we implement this functionality by collaborating closely with prospective users and in particular teaching practitioners to meet real-life demands.

The remainder of the article is structured as follows: In Section 2, we report findings of a requirement analysis that we conducted in form of expert interviews prior to the system design to determine the wishes and needs of practitioners and compare COAST to two state of the art tools currently used in learning therapy and reading and writing acquisition. In Section 3, we describe the framework of COAST and explain the two core functionalities crowd-sourcing and text enhancement with real-life use cases. In Section 4, we evaluate the usability and user experience of COAST by means of user tests conducted with learning therapists and validate its practical applicability. We conclude by describing the current state of COAST and providing an outlook for its further development in Section 5.

2 Requirements Analysis

2.1 Expert Interviews

As the primary focus of our work was on the design of a tool that allowed for the immediate practical application by language teachers and learning therapists, we performed a requirement analysis for our system preceding its implementation. We conducted four expert interviews with teaching therapists to establish their wishes and requirements for a text-enhancement tool that would facilitate their work. During this process, we identified a series of concrete requests going beyond the tool's basic text analysis functionality. They were centered around four main issues: i) input/output options, ii) flexible customization settings, iii) user profiles and re-usability of settings, and iv) optional expert/user judgments.

Input/Output Options proved to be of particular interest for prospective users. They emphasized the wish to not only be allowed to upload their own texts, but also to be able to flexibly edit them while seeing the syllable enhancement. Therefore, we provide a text box for users in which they may enter and alter their texts. Regarding output options users expressed interest in being able to choose between the formats HTML, MS Word, and PDF/printing, or simply copying texts with enhancements to the clipboard. All of these were incorporated into our system.

Flexible Customization Settings were, aside from the I/O options, one of the most prominent user concerns. We found that the text representations should be customizable not only in terms of the basic text layout, but also preferably in all aspects of the actual syllable enhancement. Thus, users may freely customize the spacing of lines, words, syllables, and characters, as well as different font sizes. Furthermore, the visual syllable enhancement is customizable in terms of the colors used for stressed and unstressed syllables with the additional options to assign a separate color to secondary unstressed syllables. Colors may either be applied to the background or the font. Users may further decide to additionally highlight stressed syllables with bold font. They may also choose to mark syllable boundaries with a freely selectable delimiter. Finally, users can select certain parts-of-speech to be either i) annotated, ii) marked as unstressed, or iii) ignored. Combined, these parameters allow for a highly customizable text design and visual enhancement, that gives users a high degree of freedom regarding the representation of their texts.

User Profiles and Re-Usability became relevant concerns in the course of our expert interviews: Our flexible customization options give users the freedom to design text representations and visual enhancements that are tailored specifically to their purposes. However, users stressed the importance that they could re-use their elaborate customization across sessions, and that they need to be able to switch between various customized enhancement templates. To allow users to save, manage, and re-use their templates, we created user accounts that allow users to locally save their customization. Users may also save the texts they uploaded under a user-defined title in previous sessions.

Expert/User Judgments proved to be a final, pressing issue for prospective users: The option to adjust the automatic analyses in cases where users disagree with the syllabification or stress annotation performed by the system was crucial to our prospective users. To give them complete authority over their analyses, each of both analyses may be altered by the user on click. Furthermore, they asked us to flag words that were unknown to our system and thus more error prone. To facilitate manual corrections, we offer users to review all unknown words consecutively in a separate view, where they are supported by the syllabification and stress suggestions of our systems. All changes conducted by users are saved in their local syllabification data base and used for future analyses. Users may review and edit these new entries in their account settings. A final suggestion of our expert users was to allow the system to learn from user feedback. We thus include a crowd-sourcing based mechanism for updates to the global data base, which is explained in detail in Section 3.2.

2.2 Related Work

There are two dominant syllable enhancement tools for German whose functionality is centered around the so called *Silbenmethode* ("syllable method"), in which reading is taught by focusing on syllables and their pronunciation rather than single characters: the *Silbengenerator* ("syllable generator") and the *Celeco Druckstation* ("Celeco printing station").[2] Table 1 shows a comparison of the tools with *COAST* based on the characteristics that we identified in our expert interviews and some more

System Feature	Silbengenerator	Celeco	COAST
Platform Independent	✗	✗	✓
Web-Based	✗	✗	✓
Freely Available	(✓)	✗	✓
Free Text Input	✓	✓	✓
Text Box	✗	✓	✓
Basic Text Layout Customization	✓	✓	✓
Additional Text Layout Customization	✗	(✓)	✓
Customizable Syllable Enhancement	✗	✓	✓
Configuration Templates	✗	n.a.	✓
Stress Annotation	✗	✗	✓
Syllable Arcs	✗	✓	✗
Customizable Analysis	(✓)	(✓)	✓
Crowd-Sourcing	✗	✗	✓
Exercise Generation	✓	✓	✗

Table 1: Comparison of *ABC Silbengenerator*, *Celeco Druckstation*, and *COAST*.

general usability considerations.

Silbengenerator is a Windows program published by *Mildenberger Verlag (2018)*.[3] It is part of their *ABC der Tiere* ("animal alphabet") series of learning materials based on syllabification as reading aid. Its main functionality is to allow teachers to visually enhance syllables in their reading materials. While the full version has to be purchased, a free demo is freely available for downloads on their web page. The tool allows users to upload own texts for analyses, but not to modify them from within the tool via some form of text box. Supported output formats for enhanced texts are MS Word or PDF/print. The general text layout is adjustable in terms of line spacing, fonts, font sizes, text alignment, line breaks, and background color. However, more advanced changes to the text layout, such as customized syllable, character, or word distances are not supported. The latest customized layout may be re-used upon system restart, but it is not possible to store multiple templates. Syllables are visually enhanced using the conventions of the *ABC der Tiere* materials, which hyphenates syllables and additionally marks alternating syllables with red and blue font. Monosyllabic words default to blue. Word stress is not encoded. To accommodate limited printing capacities, syllables may be enhanced using gray and black instead of red and blue, but further customization is not supported. Users may locally overwrite the syllable boundaries set by the system for individual words by editing a plain text file outside of the program. Changes are applied to all documents upon restart. Changes during run-time or for individual documents are not supported User corrections are not

---

[2]We are not aware of any tools for the English market that provide any syllable enhancement beyond character-based markings.

[3]For details, see: `www.abc-der-tiere.de/index.php?id=388`

re-used to improve the system's syllabification performance. The *Silbengenerator* also includes a limited tutoring functionality, which includes two variations of syllable reading exercises as well as capitalization, vowel, and spelling training.

Celeco Druckstation is a Windows program distributed by *Celeco* (Klische, 2007).[4] Since there is no free demo version, we base our review on the elaborate tool description provided on their web page. It should be pointed out that – unlike the *Silbengenerator* and our system – the *Celeco Druckstation* is distributed as a full fledged diagnosis and therapy tool for reading disorders for learning therapists and home tutoring alike. It thus provides a number of tests and exercises for reading and diagnosis, which are generated from texts specified by the user. This also includes a syllable enhancement facility that allows to load texts into the program, visually enhance syllables, and print them. *Celeco Druckstation* offers to adjust the basic text layout in terms of fonts, font size, font color, and background color. It also supports advanced layout modifications in terms of text segmentation: users may choose to put spaces after every syllable or every 3rd, 4th, or 5th character. Syllables are enhanced with two alternating, freely customizable colors, or with syllable arcs. No special encoding of word stress is offered. Users may provide individual syllable analyses of unknown words. These are saved in a local data base. However, the syllabification of known words can – as far as we could determine – not be altered by the user. We could not determine whether enhancement settings may be saved and re-used as templates.

3   Tool

3.1   System Description

We developed COAST as a platform-independent web-based tool that is deployed with Apache on a server hosted on the Amazon Web Services (AWS).[5] The front-end was developed with HTML, CSS, JavaScript, and AngularDart. [6] The back-end was developed with Python using the frameworks Flask,[7] and SQLAlchemy. [8] We use spaCy (Honnibal and Johnson, 2015) for natural language processing (NLP).

Target Users are on the one hand teaching practitioners, but on the other hand any person with an interest in syllabified reading material, such as tutors or parents. We account for this divide with two separate types of user accounts: regular and expert users. Currently, this distinction is relevant for our crowd-sourcing mechanism, which is discussed in Section 3.2.

Analyzing Input Texts is the core functionality of COAST. Figure 1 shows the workflow of automatic text analysis and enhancement. Before users can enhance texts in the front-end as described in Section 3.2, texts need to be processed accordingly: First, spaCy is used for parsing, tokenization, and part-of-speech (PoS) tagging. The letters of a word and its PoS are used as a combined primary key to query the global and local database stored in SQLite. The global database is initialized with the German version of the language corpus CELEX2 of Baayen et al. (1995) and is available to all users. For the approximately 360,000 lemmas and inflected word forms that are included in CELEX2, we infer primary word stress and syllable structure from CELEX2's orthographic and phonetic transcriptions.The local database consists of manually annotated entries and is only available to the specified user. If an entry was found, the syllabification, syllable stress, and lemma of the word are returned. If no entry was found, the word is marked as unknown and must be manually annotated. Manually annotated entries are automatically stored in the local database of the user and forwarded to the crowd-sourcing mechanism explained in detail in Section 3.2. The annotated information is used afterwards to enhance syllables and words of the text as can be seen in Appendix A, Figure 5. Further linguistic information for each enhanced word may be obtained individually, see Appendix A, Figure 6.

3.2   Features

Crowd-Sourcing is one of *COAST*'s most innovative features. We exploit the crowd-knowledge for long-term improvements of our automatic syllabification and word stress analysis. Currently, the crowd is derived from COAST's active users. To reliably identify not only syllable boundaries but also stress patterns is one of the biggest challenges in automatic syllable enhancement due to limitations of the available linguistic resources. This is especially true for languages other than English and

---

[4] www.celeco.de/
[5] www.aws.amazon.com/
[6] www.angulardart.org/
[7] www.flask.pocoo.org/
[8] www.sqlalchemy.org/

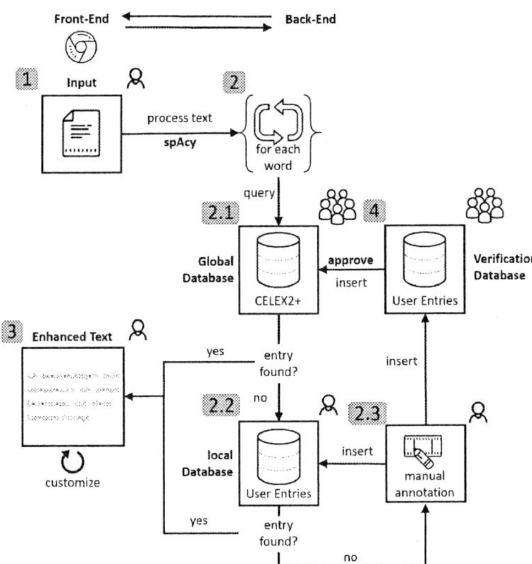

Figure 1: System overview of COAST.

for German this issue is particularly pressing, because irrespective of the size of the underlying data base, morphological composition and derivation are highly productive in German, which makes the occurrence of unknown words more likely. This issue of data sparsity is well-known from other NLP applications such as machine translation or information retrieval, and often addressed in work on compound splitting (Ziering and van der Plas, 2016; Weller et al., 2014). Furthermore, both processes may alter the word stress making the issue more difficult (Féry, 1998).

During the expert interviews it became apparent that prospective users prefer to be alerted to unknown words that may have been mis-analyzed, so they may review and if necessary manually correct them. In this context, we found that users would also prefer the system to learn from their corrections so that they could contribute to making the system more efficient in the long run. Together with our experts we therefore developed a crowdsourcing mechanism, that would allow local corrections of users to be incorporated to our system's global data base after they have been verified by either two more users or an expert user. We derived this role of an expert user to prioritize the votes of learning therapists and linguists over layman judgments. Upon registration, new users may self-identify as experts or as regular users. A verification of this self-assignment remains for future work.Experts may also revoke crowd-induced updates to the data base. With this combined expertise

and additional layer of control through experts, our system may draw from a constantly growing pool of analyses, which ultimately increases its usability and robustness while building a promising resource for future work.

The verification mechanism is located on a separate page that asks users to voluntarily identify syllable boundaries and word stress of words unknown to the system. To facilitate analyses, we provide users with information on how our automatic tools would analyze a word as help as well as with previous analyses of other users. We incorporate the freely accessible MARY-TTS (Schröder and Trouvain, 2003) for automatic suggestions for stress annotation and Pyphen for syllabification. We require users to manually annotate each word unknown to the database due to insufficient performance of automatic stress assignment. This is an extensible framework, which may be expanded with more detailed information in the future.

The following use case illustrates this process: User 1 uploads a text containing two words unknown to the system: *Hitzeschock* ("heat shock") and *Hacken* ("heels"). She is asked to determine the syllable boundaries and stress (marked in bold font) for both words and submits ***Hit**-ze-schock* and ***Hac**-ken*. This syllabification assumes a bisyllabic consonant doubling for both terms. While this is correct for most consonants at syllable boundaries, *ck* is an exception to this rule which is unknown to many laymen. Thus, when our system prompts Users 2 and 3 to verify User 1's analysis, they agree with her and both analyses are updated to the global data base. User 4 uploads another text containing *Hitzeschock*. Afterwards, the word is not flagged as unknown, but analyzed together with all other words that were originally included in the data base. Expert User 5 is asked to review the updates to the data base. She identifies the mistake that has been made and revokes the analysis of *Hacken* to *Ha-cken*. The entry is immediately corrected in the global data base and will be displayed correctly for all future analyses.

Text Enhancement is the core functionality of our tool. We enhance syllable boundaries as well as – unlike other systems – stress. For this, we rely on automatic analyses and manual post-hoc corrections by the user for words that are flagged as unknown: Our expert interviews clearly showed that prospective users not only prefer a high degree of customization in the visual representation

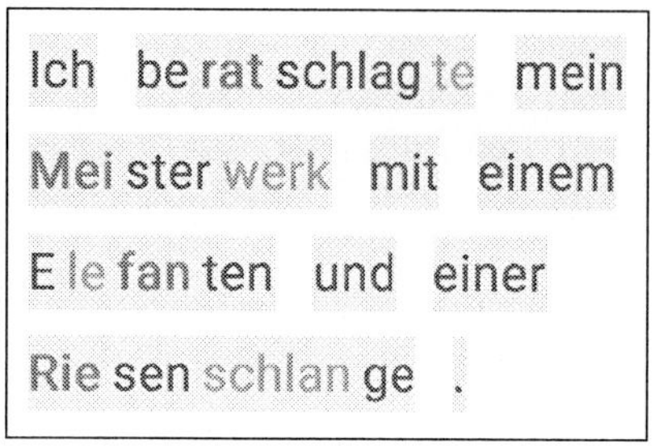

Figure 2: Template inspired by *ABC der Tiere*.

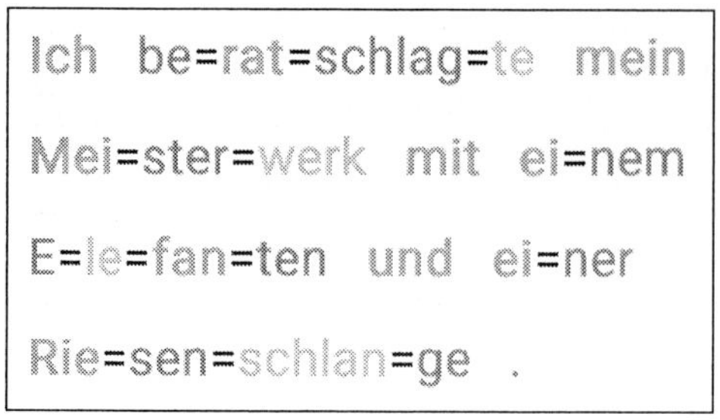

Figure 3: Template inspired by *Leselöwen*.

of their texts, but also want to re-use and switch between templates. Therefore, we not only facilitate advanced customization options for the text and enhancement layout, but also allow users to store various templates, which may be consecutively applied to a text with a simple click.

Our settings feature two main categories: First, they allow to modify the enhancement of syllable stress by allowing users to choose freely the colors assigned to i) stressed syllables, ii) unstressed syllables, and optional iii) the second unstressed syllable. Stressed syllables may be enhanced with bold font. Users can choose whether to apply the color enhancement to the font or the syllables' background. Furthermore, syllable boundaries may be made more salient by using a syllable delimiter character that users may choose freely. Finally, users may specify to which extend certain parts of speech should be analyzed, e.g. they may choose to ignore articles or to default connectives to be enhanced as unstressed. Second, they allow users to customize the text layout independent of the syllable enhancement. This includes basic options such as adjusting font size or line space. However, we also allow to freely choose the distance of words, syllables, and characters. Users may further make word boundaries more salient by choosing a background color for them. The combination of these syllable enhancement and text layout settings may be saved under a descriptive title as a template, which may be re-used and altered at any point across texts or sessions.

The following use case illustrates how this works: User 1 works with children with reading disabilities from two groups: Group A uses the *ABC der Tiere* materials in school. The children are thus used to the blue and red layout, which User 1 wants to alter as little as possible, while still providing her pupils with materials that also mark syllable stress. Therefore, she customizes a template to use the

ABC der Tiere style for her enhancement. Figure 2 shows the result for the sentence *Ich beratschlagte mein Meisterwerk mit einem Elefanten und einer Riesenschlange* ("I consulted my masterpiece with an elephant and a giant snake").

She sets the marking color of stressed syllables to dark red and of unstressed to blue. In order to make the alternation of syllables more salient, secondary unstressed syllables are also marked in red. To clearly distinguish them from stressed syllables, she additionally uses bold font to mark stress and uses a lighter type of red to mark secondary unstressed syllables. Because *ABC der Tiere* colors monosyllabic words in blue, User 1 further sets typically monosyllabic parts of speech, such as articles and prepositions, from the analysis to be analyzed as unstressed. Finally, she makes syllable boundaries more salient by widening the distance between syllables. To make word boundaries more salient, despite this increased syllable distance, she further widens word distance and assigns a beige background color to words.

Children from Group B do not use the *ABC der Tiere* materials at school, but they are reading syllabified stories at home from the *Leselöwen* ("reading lions") materials by the *Loewe* publisher.[9] These materials use three colors to mark alternating syllables and they do not treat monosyllabic words differently from others. For this group, too, User 1 wants to make stressed syllables more salient in her materials, while otherwise not deviating much from the layout the children are already used to. Thus, she designs a second layout which mimics the *Leselöwen* style. The result of applying this template to the same sentence she used for Group A may be seen in Figure 3.

The colors used by *Leselöwen* are green, red, and blue. She assigns stressed syllables the color

---

[9] `www.loewe-verlag.de/` `content-1013-1013/leseloewen/`

green and again additionally marks them with bold font. Unstressed and secondary unstressed syllables are colored red and blue. Because this style already features three colors, she does not want to use a background color for words. At the same time, she wants to make word as well as syllable boundaries more salient. For this, User 1 chooses to mark syllable boundaries with a delimiter (in this case =) but without additional space between syllables and increases the distance between words. While the initial customization took a couple of minutes, User 1 may re-apply her two templates to any text in the future, reducing the time required for customization to mere seconds. She may also alter the templates at any time or add new ones when required.

4 Evaluation

We conducted user tests to evaluate COAST with both practitioners as well as with non-experts. Prior to these, we performed an internal pilot testing to identify runtime issues that are not directly related to the functionality of COAST.

Five scenarios were defined to evaluate the tool's functionality, usability, and user experience. They cover i) account creation, ii) text analysis and enhancement, iii) generation and use of annotation templates, iv) reuse of previously stored texts, and v) verification of user-generated entries ("crowdsourcing").

In the first scenario, the users were asked to create an account with given credentials.

The second scenario consisted of four major steps: First, users were asked to log into the recently created account. Secondly, they had to switch to the *Text Analysis view* of the tool and to analyze and enhance a given text. After analyzing the text, they were told to clarify all words unknown to the system, which are flagged and shaded in red. Finally, users were asked to adjust the annotation settings based on their personal preferences.

The third scenario covered the instructed generation and use of annotation templates. Users were asked to rebuild two annotation schemes by adjusting the annotation settings and save them as new templates.

In the fourth scenario, users were asked to store the analyzed text in their account and re-analyze it by selecting the stored text in the *Account view* of the tool.

In the fifth and final scenario, users were required to verify entries added by other users that are unknown to the global database. In order to do so, they were asked to switch to the *Verification view* (see Figure 7) and approve or edit five entries.

The second, third, and fifth scenario are of special importance as they cover the core-functionality of COAST and can be seen in Figure 8.

User Tests were conducted by seven users from two groups: three experts (learning therapists) to receive subject-specific feedback and four laymen to evaluate the general usability of the tool. The three experts were women aged between 40 and 51 ($M = 45$). The laymen aged between 22 and 27 ($M = 25$) included two men and two women with non-educational professions. The user test was carried out equally for both groups. None of the participants had interacted with the system before.

We used the after-scenario questionnaire (ASQ) by Lewis (1995) for quantitative data analysis. They were answered for each scenario directly after its completion. The ASQ consists of three questions covering ease of use, time efficiency, and documentation of the tool:

1. Overall, I am satisfied with the ease of use of completing the tasks in this scenario

2. Overall, I am satisfied with the amount of time it took to complete the tasks in this scenario

3. Overall, I am satisfied with the support and documentation when completing the tasks

We used a five-point Likert scale ranging from *strongly agree* to *strongly disagree*.

For qualitative analysis, the users were explicitly instructed to "think-aloud" (Rauterberg, 1996) while working on a scenario, thus told to accurately comment each of their actions and to express expectations, thoughts, and critics.

The user test was carried out as follows: Users were free to use their preferred browser for the user test. The default browser was Google Chrome. The user test was conducted on the users' personal laptop if possible, to recreate their home or work environment and to mimic a real-life application as close as possible. If no personal laptop was available, users were provided with one. All input devices were configured according to user preferences. After setting up the work place, users were informed and instructed about the procedure of the user test, its purpose and the think-aloud method.

After clarifying all questions, users processed all scenarios consecutively in fixed order. The user tests were concluded with an interview to get general feedback and to assess the usefulness of the tool with respect to the users' professions.

4.1 Results

The results of the second, third, and fifth scenario are explained in detail due to their relevance, results for scenario one and four can be found in the Table 2.

We normalized the options of the ASQ to range from -2 (strongly disagree) to $+2$ (strongly agree) with 0 (neither) being neutral. In the following, we report positive values (i.e. agree, strongly agree) as positive feedback, negative values (i.e. disagree, strongly disagree) as negative feedback. For a more detailed differentiation of the user feedback, please see Figure 4.

The second scenario was successfully completed by all users. The ease of use ($M = 1.57, SD = 0.53$) and documentation ($M = 1.57, SD = 0.53$) of the tool was rated 100 % positively in the ASQ, time efficiency received 86 % positive and 16 % neutral ratings ($M = 1.57, SD = 0.78$). Some users criticized the layout of the *Text Analysis view*, suggesting a more compact representation of the annotation settings.

The third scenario was completed by five users without help, two needed hints from the investigator to complete all tasks. While the first template could be rebuilt by all users, two users required help with the second template. Error source was the confusion about and between the features *Silbe hervorheben* (enhance syllables), with which either the fore- or background color of syllables could be adjusted accordingly, and *Wort Hintergrundfarbe* (word background color), with which the background color of words could be set (see Figure 5). Three users completed this scenario by trial-and-error. The ease of use of this scenario was

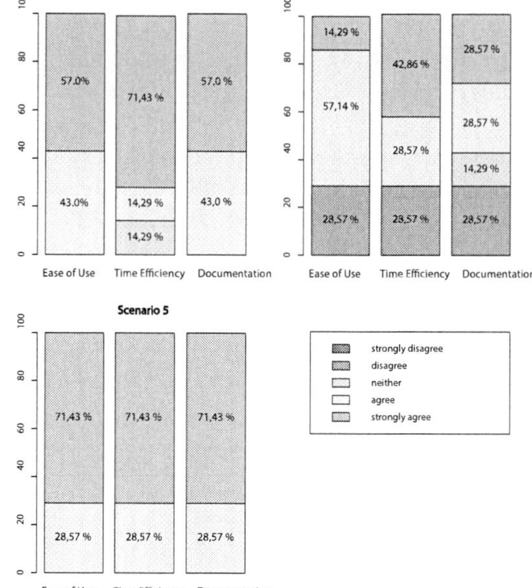

Figure 4: Results of the after-scenario questionnaire completed for scenario 2, 3, and 5.

rated 71.4 % positively and 28.57 % negatively ($M = 0.57, SD = 1.27$), the time efficiency 71% positively and 29 % negatively ($M = 0.86, SD = 1.34$), and 57.2 % positively, 14.3% neutral, and 28.6% negatively in terms of documentation and support ($M = 0.57, SD = 1.14$).

The fifth and last scenario was completed by all users successfully. Ease of use, time efficiency, and documentation of this functionality were rated 100 % positively ($M = 1.71, SD = 0.49$ for each item respectively). Users suggested to design this functionality to be more user friendly by displaying and processing multiple entries at once.

The think-aloud and concluding interviews additionally revealed general layout and design flaws of COAST's visual appearance. While this goes beyond the scope of this paper, we list problems, comments, and feature requests directly linked to the core features of our tool: i) the general navigation of the tool was not very intuitive and self-explaining, ii) some features could only be accessed with scrolling, which was not explicitly visible to the users, iii) some features, e.g. background color of words and syllable enhancement, need explicit documentation/tutorials, iv) some users asked for a simple solution to color syllables alternately independently of syllable stress, v) the feature to not enhance monosyllabic words instead

Question		Rating			
	-2	-1	0	1	2
Scenario 1					
ease of use	0 %	0 %	0 %	29.0 %	71.0 %
time efficiency	0 %	0 %	0 %	0 %	100 %
documentation	0 %	0 %	0 %	29.0 %	71.0 %
Scenario 4					
ease of use	0 %	0 %	0 %	28.6 %	71.4 %
time efficiency	0 %	0 %	0 %	28.6 %	71.4 %
documentation	0 %	0 %	0 %	28.6 %	71.4 %

Table 2: Results of the ASQ for scenario 1 and 4.

of unchecking the annotation of typically monosyllabic parts of speech was requested, vi) fore- and background color of syllables and words should independently be customizable.

5 Conclusion and Outlook

COAST is a highly user-oriented, platform independent, web-based and easily extensible framework for the automatic augmentation of texts with syllable, stress, and word enhancement. It was developed in close collaboration with practitioners and includes a series of features which were explicitly requested by prospective users and that are lacking from currently available, state of the art systems. This paper presents and evaluates its ability to generate appropriate reading materials based on real-life use cases. Additionally, we evaluated the practical applicability of our tool by conducting user tests based on a series of real-life scenarios.

Our exemplary enhanced texts (see Figure 2 and 3) prove that appropriate reading materials can be easily generated automatically, customized, and exported with COAST. The use cases show that the tool meets the requirements deduced from the *a priori* requirement analysis based on our expert interviews. Compared to other tools that support syllable enhancement, COAST offers a higher degree of customization and more features, such as annotating syllable stress, setting spacing of lines, words, syllables, and characters. The automatic analysis of syllable stress and part of speech also make COAST linguistically more informed than other tools. Finally, we carried out user tests with special focus on practical application. These indicate that the majority of users were able to solve the tasks intuitively and time efficiently for each of the scenarios.

We have successfully shown that the current version of COAST allows practitioners to generate enhanced texts as reading materials for their teaching. Being able to save annotation templates and texts has proven to be an especially useful functionality to easily generate new reading materials within the application with little time effort. Furthermore, COAST features a novel crowd-sourcing approach to overcome the pressing issue of limited resources and data sparsity. This is particularly relevant for languages other than English. Currently, our tool illustrates this for the German language. However, the entire framework was designed to be easily extended for any other language for which sufficient resources are available.

Our consultation with prospective users also yielded a series of practical suggestions to optimize user experience further and to include more features. In particular, we aim at including the features discussed in Section 4.1. We also plan to redesign COAST's visual appearance. Furthermore, we intend to elaborate on the current documentation and to provide application-oriented feature tutorials. To improve the reliability of our proposed crowd-sourcing mechanism, we plan to address the verification of user roles, i.e. expert and regular users. In this regard, the need of further user type customization shall be analysed and implemented accordingly. Finally, we intend to carry out user studies to compare COAST's efficiency and efficacy to state of the art tools that support syllable enhancement in texts.

Our ultimate goal is to develop and include a front-end for learners, the *COAST App*. This results in a tutoring system offering reading and spelling exercises optimized for mobile devices. The current *COAST Tool* could be used by practitioners to generate teaching materials to be shared with the *COAST App* and, thus, to supply exercises directly to their pupils.

Acknowledgments

This research was funded by the LEAD Graduate School & Research Network [GSC1028], a project of the Excellence Initiative of the German federal and state governments. Heiko Holz is a doctoral student at the LEAD Graduate School & Research Network.

References

R. Harald Baayen, Richard Piepenbrock, and Léon Gulikers. 1995. CELEX2 LDC96L14. *Web Download. Philadelphia: Linguistic Data Consortium.*

Bundesverband Legasthenie und Dyskalkulie e.V. 2014. Der aktuelle Wissensstand über Legasthenie.

Caroline Féry. 1998. German word stress in optimality theory. *Journal of Comparative Germanic Linguistics*, 2(2):101–142.

Katharina Galuschka, Elena Ise, Kathrin Krick, and Gerd Schulte-Körne. 2014. Effectiveness of Treatment Approaches for Children and Adolescents with Reading Disabilities: A Meta-Analysis of Randomized Controlled Trials. *PLoS ONE*, 9(2):e89900.

Katharina Galuschka and Gerd Schulte-Körne. 2016. The Diagnosis and Treatment of Reading and/or

Spelling Disorders in Children and Adolescents. *Dtsch Arztebl Int.*, 113(16):279–86.

Usha Goswami, Natasha Mead, Tim Fosker, Martina Huss, Lisa Barnes, and Victoria Leong. 2013. Impaired perception of syllable stress in children with dyslexia: A longitudinal study. *Journal of Memory and Language*, 69(1):1–17.

Heiko Holz, Katharina Brandelik, Jochen Brandelik, Benedikt Beuttler, Alexandra Kirsch, and Detmar Meurers. 2017. Prosodiya–a mobile game for german dyslexic children. In *International Conference on Games and Learning Alliance*, volume 10653 of *Lecture Notes in Computer Science*, pages 73–82, Cham. Springer International Publishing.

Matthew Honnibal and Mark Johnson. 2015. An Improved Non-monotonic Transition System for Dependency Parsing. In *Proceedings of the 2015 Conference on Empirical Methods in Natural Language Processing*, pages 1373–1378, Lisbon, Portugal. Association for Computational Linguistics.

Juan E. Jiménez, Isabel Hernández-Valle, Gustave Ramírez, Ma Del Rosario Ortiz, Mercedes Rodrigo, Adelina Estévez, Isabel O'Shanahan, Eduarde García, and María De La Luz Trabaue. 2007. Computer speech-based remediation for reading disabilities: The size of spelling-to-sound unit in a transparent orthography. *Spanish Journal of Psychology*, 10(1):52–67.

Anja Klische. 2007. *Leseschwächen gezielt beheben: Individuelle Diagnose und Therapie mit dem Programm celeco*. Tectum-Verl.

Karin Landerl. 2003. Categorization of vowel length in German poor spellers: An orthographically relevant phonological distinction. *Applied Psycholinguistics*, 24(4):523–538.

James R. Lewis. 1995. IBM Computer Usability Satisfaction Questionnaires: Psychometric Evaluation and Instructions for Use. *International Journal of Human-Computer Interaction*, 7(1):57–78.

Detmar Meurers, Ramon Ziai, Luiz Amaral, Adriane Boyd, Aleksandar Dimitrov, Vanessa Metcalf, and Niels Ott. 2010. Enhancing authentic web pages for language learners. In *Proceedings of the 5th Workshop on Innovative Use of NLP for Building Educational Applications (BEA-5) at NAACL-HLT 2010*, pages 10–18, Los Angeles.

Mildenberer Verlag. 2018. *Eine Einführung in die Silbenmethode*. Mildenberer Verlag.

Mildenberger Verlag. 2018. ABC der Tiere – Silben-Generator für die Grundschule.

Kristina Moll and Karin Landerl. 2009. Double Dissociation Between Reading and Spelling Deficits. *Scientific Studies of Reading*, 13(5):359–382.

Richard K. Olson and Barbara W. Wise. 1992. Reading on the computer with orthographic and speech feedback. *Reading and Writing*, 4(2):107–144.

Matthias Rauterberg. 1996. *Usability Engineering*. Morgan Kaufmann.

Luz Rello and Ricardo Baeza-Yates. 2017. How to present more readable text for people with dyslexia. *Universal Access in the Information Society*, 16(1):29–49.

Christa Röber-Siekmeyer. 2005. Die berücksichtigung des kindlichen sprachwissens für den schrifterwerb. In Hans-Werner Huneke, editor, *Geschriebene Sprache. Strukturen, Erwerb, didaktische Modellbildungen*, pages 129–144. Mattes Verlag, Heidelberg.

Katharina Sauter, Jürgen Heller, and Karin Landerl. 2012. Sprachrhythmus und Schriftspracherwerb. *Lernen und Lernstörungen*, 1(4):225–239.

Gerheid Scheerer-Neumann. 1981. The utilization of intraword structure in poor readers: Experimental evidence and a training program. *Psychological Research*, 43(2):155–178.

R. W. Schmidt. 1990. The Role of Consciousness in Second Language Learning1. *Applied Linguistics*, 11(2):129–158.

M. Schröder and J. Trouvain. 2003. The German Text-to-Speech Synthesis System MARY: A Tool for Research, Development and Teaching. *International Journal of Speech Technology*, 6:365–377.

Michael Sharwood Smith. 1993. Input Enhancement in Instructed SLA. *Studies in Second Language Acquisition*, 15(02):165.

Sven Staffeldt. 2010. *Einführung in die Phonetik, Phonologie und Graphematik des Deutschen Ein Leitfaden für den akademischen Unterricht*. Stauffenburg, Tübingen.

Marion Weller, Fabienne Cap, Stefan Müller, Sabine Schulte im Walde, and Alexander Fraser. 2014. Distinguishing degrees of compositionality in compound splitting for statistical machine translation. In *Proceedings of the 1st Workshop on Computational Approaches to Compound Analysis*, pages 81–90.

Patrick Ziering and Lonneke van der Plas. 2016. Towards Unsupervised and Language-independent Compound Splitting using Inflectional Morphological Transformations. *Proceedings of the 2016 Conference of the North American Chapter of the Association for Computational Linguistics: Human Language Technologies*, pages 644–653.

Marco Zorzi, Chiara Barbiero, Andrea Facoetti, Isabella Lonciari, Marco Carrozzi, Marcella Montico, Laura Bravar, Florence George, Catherine Pech-Georgel, Johannes C Ziegler, and Michael Posner. 2012. Extra-large letter spacing improves reading in dyslexia. *Proceedings of the National Academy of Sciences*, 109(28):11455–11459.

A.1 Screenshots of COAST

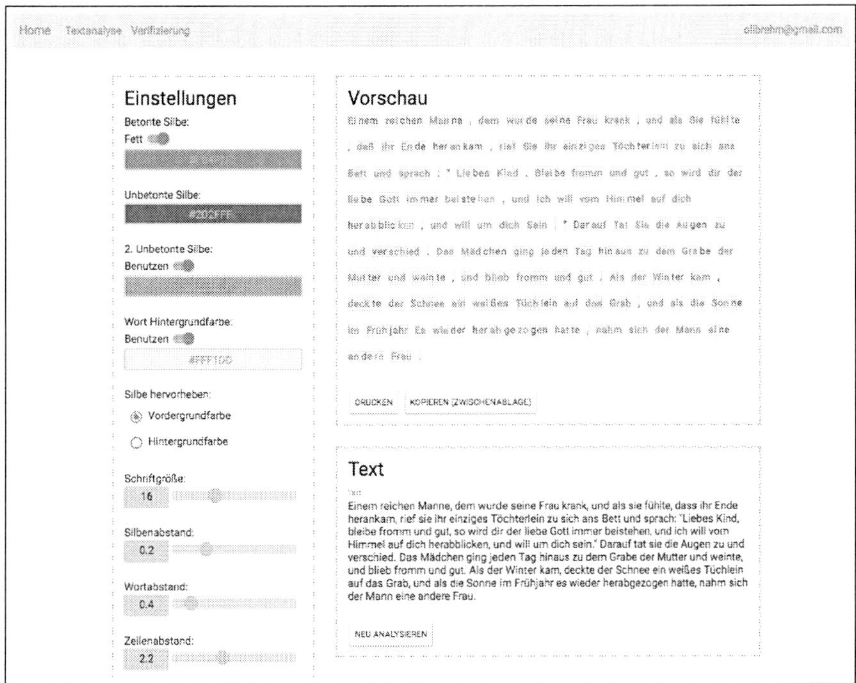

Figure 5: COAST – View for text analysis and enhancement. Users can insert or edit text in the lower text box. The preview of syllable enhancement is given in the upper box. On the left side, users can edit settings regarding syllable annotation: boldness, colors of stressed and unstressed syllables (either background or foreground), background color of words, font size, and spacing between syllables, words, and lines.

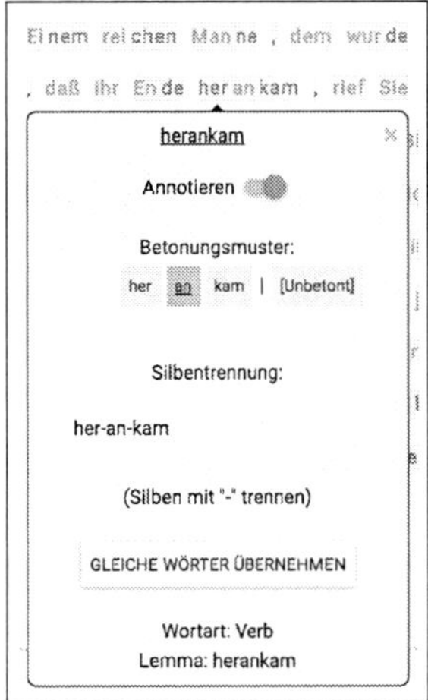

Figure 6: COAST – Word-Popup. Popup with additional information that is invoked when a known word is clicked in the text-view. At the moment, we offer information about syllabification, part of speech, and lemma. Users can additionally manually change the syllabification or stress assignment of the selected word and apply it to the preview.

Figure 7: COAST – Verification-view of entries added by users unknown to the global database. Current word is *geschlossenen* (*ge-schlos-sen-en*, closed). Users can edit stress assignment and syllabification on the left side or agree to a user's judgment or to automatically generated suggestions on the right side.

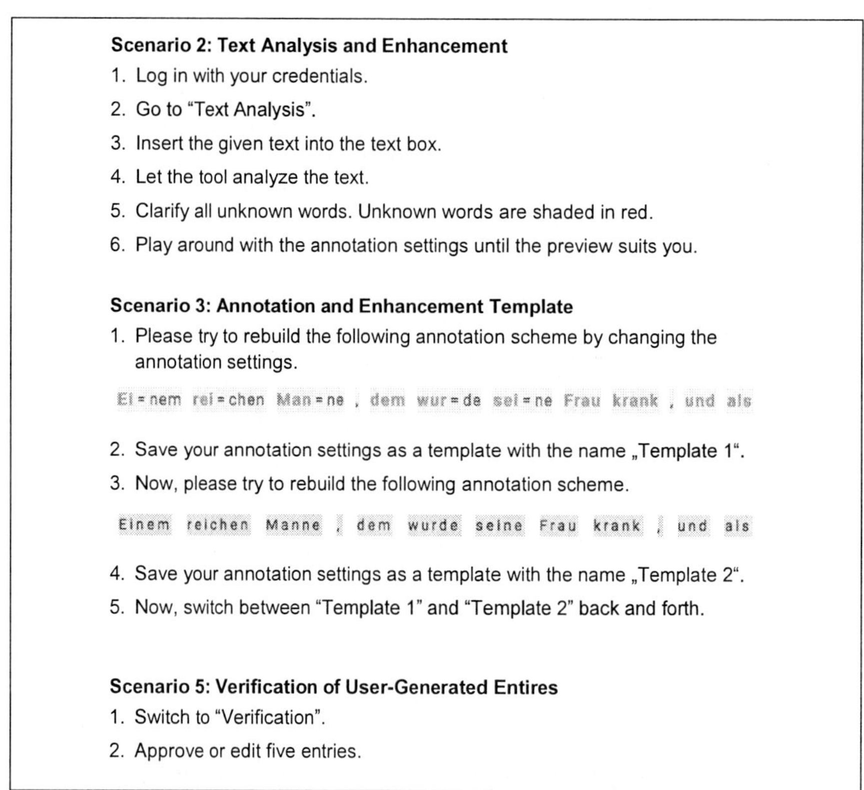

Figure 8: User tests of scenario 2 (text analysis and enhancement), 3 (creation and use of annotation and enhancement templates), and 5 (verification of user-generated entries).

Annotating Picture Description Task Responses for Content Analysis

Levi King
Indiana University
leviking@indiana.edu

Markus Dickinson
Indiana University
md7@indiana.edu

Abstract

Given that all users of a language can be creative in their language usage, the overarching goal of this work is to investigate issues of variability and acceptability in written text, for both non-native speakers (NNSs) and native speakers (NSs). We control for meaning by collecting a dataset of picture description task (PDT) responses from a number of NSs and NNSs, and we define and annotate a handful of features pertaining to form and meaning, to capture the multi-dimensional ways in which responses can vary and can be acceptable. By examining the decisions made in this corpus development, we highlight the questions facing anyone working with learner language properties like variability, acceptability and native-likeness. We find reliable inter-annotator agreement, though disagreements point to difficult areas for establishing a link between form and meaning.

1 Introduction

The (written) data of second language learners poses many challenges, whether it is being analyzed for grammatical errors (Leacock et al., 2014), for linguistic patterns (Kyle and Crossley, 2015), for content analysis (Weigle, 2013), or for interactions with intelligent computer-assisted language learning (ICALL) systems (Amaral and Meurers, 2007). One of the core issues in doing anything with learner data is the inherent amount of variability in how linguistic forms are used to convey meaning (cf., e.g., Meurers and Dickinson, 2017). It may indeed seem like learners can use an infinite variety of forms to express a particular meaning; here we attempt to investigate how large the problem of variability in one particular testing context is for computational processing.

To investigate variability and the mappings between linguistic form and meaning, in this paper we control for meaning by collecting a dataset of picture description task (PDT) responses from a number of NSs and NNSs, and we annotate a handful of features, thereby capturing the multi-faceted ways in which responses can vary and can be acceptable or unacceptable. We call this the SAILS Corpus, for *Semantic Analysis of Image-based Learner Sentences*—our intended use. By examining the decisions made in this corpus development, we highlight the questions facing anyone working with learner language properties such as variability, acceptability and native-likeness.

Given the form-meaning aspect of variability, we are interested in how variable linguistic behavior is *for the same content*, both within and between NS and NNS groups, and the potential use of NS responses to evaluate NNS responses. There is a long-standing notion that systems processing learner data would be wise to constrain the data in some way (e.g., Heift and Schulze, 2007; Somasundaran et al., 2015), but we do not know how much constraint is needed—or whether we sacrifice the possibility of observing particular learner behavior for the sake of a constraint—without knowing more about the ways in which variation happens (cf. Bailey and Meurers, 2008).

The corpus presented here bears some similarities to other task-based learner corpora. Meurers et al. (2011) examined German learner responses to short-answer reading comprehension questions. A target answer was produced by an expert, and annotators used this target to label the meaning of responses as correct or incorrect, along with a more detailed set of labels related to form, meaning, and task appropriateness. In our own previous work (King and Dickinson, 2016, 2013), we annotated a small set of PDT responses as correct or incorrect, with incorrect responses further labeled as errors of form or meaning. Somasundaran and Chodorow (2014) presented work on PDT re-

Proceedings of the Thirteenth Workshop on Innovative Use of NLP for Building Educational Applications, pages 101–109
New Orleans, Louisiana, June 5, 2018. ©2018 Association for Computational Linguistics

sponses in which respondents used provided vocabulary words. Responses were manually annotated on a holistic four point scale, and a set of five features (relating to meaning, relevance and language use) were calculated based on statistical assumptions. Somasundaran et al. (2015) performed a nearly identical analysis with transcribed texts from a six-picture narration task, but neither of these datasets is publicly available.

Our work reverses this mapping by providing manually annotated features, which we hope will be useful for mapping to holistic scores. For example, a response may present the main content of an item correctly but add imaginary details, while another may address background information not asked about in the prompt (see section 3). The acceptability of a response is thus taken as a function of several interacting features, most of which relate the text to the known semantic content. Relating to known content is distinct from typical grammatical error correction (GEC) (Leacock et al., 2014) and from more linguistically driven work such as parsing (e.g., Cahill et al., 2014; Ragheb and Dickinson, 2014), but providing the dimensions of acceptability and elucidating how they are applied provides insight for any enterprise desiring to connect learner text with semantic content, in addition to unpacking the sources of variation and of difficulty in processing a range of learner data.

In section 2 we outline the picture description task (PDT) we use, designed with items that elicit specific types of linguistic behavior. Section 3 outlines the annotation, tackling the five-dimensional scheme; inter-anntotator agreement results are in section 4. While agreement seems reliable, highlighting areas of disagreement showcases difficult areas for establishing a link between form and meaning (cf., e.g., Meurers and Dickinson, 2017).

2 Picture Description Task

2.1 PDT Stimuli

The PDT is built around 30 cartoon-like vector graphics, or **items**. The images were modified to remove any non-essential detail or background; some examples are in Table 1. To factor out the influence of previous linguistic context, images are devoid of any text or symbols, with the exceptions of two images containing numerals, two with music notes, and one with a question mark. Each image depicts an ongoing or imminent action, performed by a person or an animal. The images are divided evenly into canonically intransitive, transitive and ditransitive actions.

Two main versions of the PDT were used. In each version, the first half contains **targeted** items, where questions take the form of *What is <subject> doing?*, with the subject provided (e.g., *the boy, the bird*). The second half contains **untargeted** items, where the question is, *What is happening?*. Collecting both versions allows one to examine response variation with and without a subject constraint, thereby informing approaches to task design and automatic content assessment (Foster and Tavakoli, 2009; Cho et al., 2013). Roughly equal numbers of targeted and untargeted **responses** were collected for each item.

Each half (targeted and untargeted) is introduced with instructions, including an example item with sample responses. The instructions ask participants to focus on the main event depicted in the image and for each response to be one complete sentence. The PDT was presented as an online survey, and all participants typed their responses. Participants were instructed not to use any reference materials, but were permitted to use browser-based spell checking.

2.2 Data Collection

A total of approximately 16,000 responses were collected from 499 participants. Of these, 141 were NNSs, recruited from intermediate and advanced writing courses for English as a Second Language students attending Indiana University. Nearly 90% of these recruits were native speakers of Mandarin Chinese, which could have important implications for conclusions drawn from the corpus. These participants performed the task in a computer lab with the researchers present. They were native speakers of Mandarin Chinese (125), Korean (4), Burmese (3), Hindi (2), and one native speaker each of Arabic, Indonesian Bahasa, German, Gujarati, Spanish, Thai and Vietnamese.

Of the 358 NS participants, 29 were personally known by the researchers. Responses from the remaining 329 NSs were purchased via an online survey platform where participants earn credits they can redeem for gift cards and prizes. Due to length restrictions for purchased surveys, these NSs each completed only half of the task, so their data is equivalent to 164.5 full participants.

In previous similar work (King and Dickinson,

What is the woman doing? [Intrans.]	A1	A2
The woman is running.	1	1
She is wearing a red shirt.	0	0
Trying to run from her bad decisions	1	0

What is the woman doing? [Trans.]	A1	A2
Holding a puppy & looks happy	1	1
She is happy with the dog.	0	0
The lady loves her dog.	1	0

What is the man doing? [Ditrans.]	A1	A2
giving directions to a woman.	1	1
The man is reading a map.	0	0
The man is is telling her where to go	1	0

Table 1: Test sample items and example responses with Core Event annotations from Annotators 1 and 2.

2013), NSs were found to produce less variation than NNSs. Many NSs provided identical responses or ones very similar to the most canonical way of expressing the main action. One purpose of gathering the data is to be able to assess NNS response content by comparing it against the NS responses; thus, NSs were asked to provide two non-identical responses, in the hopes that this would result in more examples of native-like responses

for the NNS responses to compare against.

	Targeted		Untargeted	
Set	NS	NNS	NS	NNS
Intrans	0.628	0.381	0.782	0.492
Trans	0.752	0.655	0.859	0.779
Ditrans	0.835	0.817	0.942	0.936

Table 2: NS and NNS type-to-token ratios (TTR) for complete responses (not words), for all the data.

To examine the degree of variation among the NS and NNS groups in the current study, type-to-token ratios (TTR) were calculated on the response level (ignoring case and final punctuation) for the entire set of items, shown in Table 2. For each data point in the table, the corpus contains roughly 150 NS responses and 70 NNS responses. To control for this imbalance and its effect on the likelihood of seeing new responses, the TTR was calculated for each item based on a random sample of 50 responses. Specifically, we randomly sampled 50 responses, calculated the TTR, and averaged them. The scores in in Table 2 show that, in all cases, the NS set shows a greater degree of response variation, meaning that asking for two responses is an effective way of collecting a broader range of NS responses.

The ratios show the direct relationship between the complexity of the event portrayed (represented here as intransitive, transitive and ditransitive) and the degree of variation elicited. In all cases, TTR increases with this complexity. Interestingly, this trend seems more pronounced in the NNS responses; in the targeted NNS responses, the TTRs for intransitive and ditransitive items are 0.381 and 0.817, respectively, compared to 0.628 and 0.835 for NS responses. The ratios also show that in all cases, variation is greater for untargeted items than it is for targeted items. In other words, asking about a particular subject in the prompt question does constrain the variety of responses.

3 Annotation scheme

The data were annotated with the aim of providing information that would be useful for the automatic assessment of NNS responses via comparison with NS responses. The annotation scheme was developed through an iterative process of annotation, discussion and revision, with input from two annotators and multiple language professionals. The initial scheme was planned as a three-point scale, ranging from *accurate and native-like* (2) to *accurate but not native-like* (1) to *not accurate* (0). This proved problematic, however, as *accuracy* and *native-likeness* could not be adequately defined and applied to the data. For example, in the middle picture of Table 1, it is not clear how accurate or native-like *She is happy with the dog* is. Grammatically, it is native-like, but it does not seem like an appropriate answer to the question, *What is the woman doing?*

To address the specifics of appropriate answers, five binary features were eventually settled on, with each feature having some relation to the original concepts of accuracy and native-likeness. A set of annotation guidelines were produced with definitions, rules and examples for each feature. For most features, the rules for targeted and untargeted items vary slightly; the untargeted rules are generally less strict. The features and brief descriptions are listed here and discussed further in the following sections:

1. **Core Event**: Does the response capture the core event depicted in the image? Core events are not pre-defined but should be fairly obvious given the nature of the images. The response should link an appropriate subject to the event. In the top picture of Table 1, *The woman is running* clearly captures the core event, while *She is wearing a red shirt* is irrelevant to the event happening.

2. **Verifiability**: Does the response contain only information that is true and verifiable based on the image? Inferences should not be speculations and are allowed only when necessary and highly probable, as when describing a familial relationship between persons depicted in the image. For example, in Table 1, *She is wearing a red shirt* conveys information that is irrelevant to the core event but is nonetheless recoverable from the image (annotation=1), while *Trying to run from her bad decisions* has information that cannot be inferred from the picture.

3. **Answerhood**: Does the response make a clear attempt to answer the question? This generally requires a progressive verb. For targeted items, the subject of the question, or an appropriate pronoun, must be used as the subject of the response. For example, *The dog is happy* is answering a question other than *What is the woman doing?* (Table 1).

4. **Interpretability**: Does the response evoke a clear mental image (even if different from the item image)? Any required verb arguments must be present and unambiguous. For example, *The map is hard to read* is too vague to generate a clear mental image (Table 1).

5. **Grammaticality**: Is the response free from errors of spelling and grammar? In our data set, this is a relatively straightforward feature to annotate (see section 4).

Example annotations In Table 3, we see example responses with all five features annotated, illustrating each feature's distinctiveness from the others. For example, for *He is eating food* one can generate a mental picture, e.g., of someone chewing (`interpretability`=1), but the pizza is important to the item image (`core event`=0). As another example, *He may get fat eating pizza* seems to be addressing a question about the consequences of the eating action (`answerhood`=0) and talks about hypotheticals not in the picture (`verifiability`=0). Teasing apart these annotations is the focus of the next section.

4 Agreement

Two annotators participated in the annotation. Both are native speakers of (US) English, and each has several years of language teaching experience with both children and adult learners. Annotator 1 (A1) annotated the complete corpus. Annotator 2 (A2) annotated only the development set and the test set, data subsets described next.

Three items were used as a development set for creating and revising the annotation scheme. These items were also used as examples in the guidelines. They represent one intransitive, one transitive and one ditransitive item. Both annotators annotated portions of the development set multiple times throughout the process, discussing and adjudicating disagreeing annotations before moving on to the test set, which was completed without consultation between the annotators.

The test set parallels the development set and consists of one intransitive, one transitive and one ditransitive item; it is shown in Table 1. Agreement and Cohen's kappa scores are given in Table 4, broken down by different criteria. We will now walk through these results.

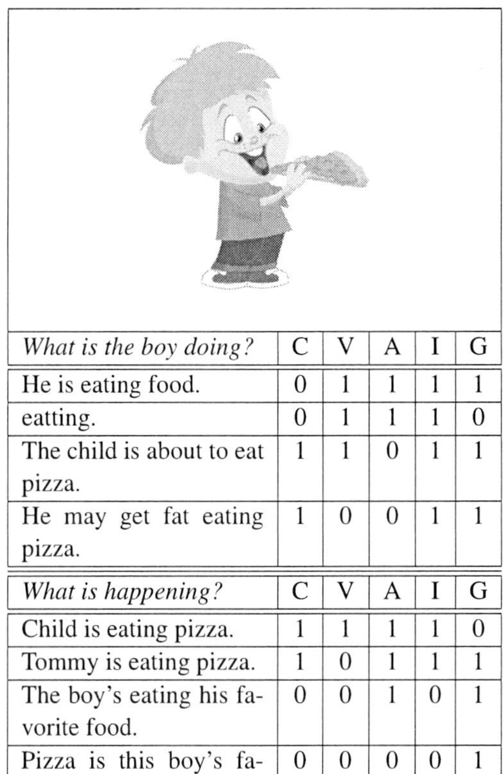

What is the boy doing?	C	V	A	I	G
He is eating food.	0	1	1	1	1
eatting.	0	1	1	1	0
The child is about to eat pizza.	1	1	0	1	1
He may get fat eating pizza.	1	0	0	1	1
What is happening?	C	V	A	I	G
Child is eating pizza.	1	1	1	1	0
Tommy is eating pizza.	1	0	1	1	1
The boy's eating his favorite food.	0	0	1	0	1
Pizza is this boy's favorite food.	0	0	0	0	1

Table 3: Targeted and untargeted sample responses from the development set transitive item, shown with adjudicated annotations for the five features: core event (*C*), verifiability (*V*), answerhood (*A*), interpretability (*I*) and grammaticality (*G*).

4.1 Transitivity

Comparing the intransitive, transitive and ditransitive items reveals an association between agreement and item complexity. The highest raw agreement and Cohen's kappa scores are found with the intransitive item (97.8%, $\kappa = 0.910$) and the lowest with the ditransitive (92.4%, $\kappa = 0.764$).

This is as expected, as ditransitive sentences are longer and have more verbal arguments, making for more opportunities for responses to vary (see Table 2), and thus more opportunities for annotators to disagree on a response. This trend also matches annotator feedback: both ranked the ditransitive item as the most difficult to annotate overall, and the intransitive as the easiest.

4.2 Targeting

Grouping the annotations into targeted and untargeted sets, the raw agreement scores are compara-

ble (94.9% vs. 95.2%). However, despite a greater degree of response variation, the untargeted group has a higher kappa score (0.872 vs. 0.823). When asked to compare the annotations, A2 noted that targeted responses require more concentration and closer consultation of the guidelines. For example, answerhood does not allow for targeted responses to modify the subject provided in the question in any way, whereas in answering *What is happening?*, the respondent is free to speak of characters in the pictures in many different ways. Both A1 and A2 thus describe the annotation of untargeted items as less restrictive.

4.3 Features

Grouped by feature, the annotations all show raw agreement scores above 91% and Cohen's kappa scores above 0.74 (Table 4). For future use of this corpus in content assessment, these kappa scores are comfortably above the 0.67 suggested as a baseline for meaningful, reliable agreement (Landis and Koch, 1977; Artstein and Poesio, 2008). We discuss each feature in turn, highlighting difficulties in coming to an agreement, as such disagreements illustrate some sources of variability.

Core event Isolating whether the main content of the picture is being described or not, the core event feature is the most relevant of the five for content assessment. All five features are skewed toward *yes* annotations, but with an average *yes* rate of 72.5%, core event is the least skewed; i.e., more responses receive a *no* annotation for core event than for any other feature.

Core event has the second lowest interannotator agreement kappa score, at 0.808. This is somewhat lower than expected, as the preadjudication development set score was 0.889. This appears to be largely attributable to the difficulty of the ditransitive item, challenging for both participants and annotators (section 4.1).

The main issue in this case has to do with the amount of specificity required to be the core event. The development set item depicts a man delivering a package to a woman, and most responses describe this as such a transaction, using *give*, *deliver* or *receive*. The test set item shows a man giving directions to a woman (Table 1), and this resulted in a greater degree of variation. Many (particularly NNS) responses portray this not as a canonical *giving directions* event but as *pointing*, *helping a lost person* or *reading a map*, with A2 more

Set	Total	A1Yes	A2Yes	AvgYes	Chance	Agree	Kappa
Intransitive	2155	0.863	0.855	0.859	0.758	0.978	0.910
Transitive	2155	0.780	0.774	0.777	0.653	0.949	0.853
Ditransitive	2155	0.812	0.786	0.799	0.678	0.924	0.764
Targeted	3390	0.829	0.818	0.824	0.709	0.949	0.823
Untargeted	3075	0.806	0.790	0.798	0.678	0.952	0.872
Core Event	1293	0.733	0.717	0.725	0.601	0.923	0.808
Verifiability	1293	0.845	0.817	0.831	0.719	0.968	0.884
Answerhood	1293	0.834	0.831	0.833	0.721	0.982	0.936
Interpretability	1293	0.818	0.787	0.802	0.682	0.919	0.744
Grammaticality	1293	0.861	0.872	0.866	0.768	0.960	0.827

Table 4: Agreement scores broken down by different properties of the test set: total annotations (*Total*), *yes* annotations for Annotator 1 and 2 (*A1Yes, A2Yes*), average *yes* annotations (*AvgYes*), total expected chance agreement for *yes*es and *no*s (*Chance*), actual raw agreement (*Agree*) and Cohen's kappa (*Kappa*).

likely to accept these less specific descriptions.

Similarly, but to a lesser extent, the transitive item, which shows a woman hugging a dog (Table 1), resulted in disagreements where A2 accepts the word *pet* as the object, but A1 rejects such responses as too vague. Despite the acceptable scores for `core event` agreement, the fact that many disagreements hinge on particular word choice or annotators having minor differences in interpretation of the event suggest that greater agreement could be achieved by providing annotators with suggestions about the acceptable content for each response. In other words: by more clearly determining the desired level of specificity of a response—for the verb or its arguments— agreement could be higher. The desired specificity may vary in accordance with the intended use of the annotations; in the current annotations, the standard discussed between annotators and in the guidelines included pragmatic considerations like naturalness, native-likeness and effort.

Verifiability On the flipside of the question of whether the core semantic content is expressed is the question of whether any extraneous content is added, or any content used in a way which cannot be verified from the picture. The average *yes* rate for `verifiability` is 83.1%, making it the third most skewed feature.

The raw agreement score is 96.8%, and the kappa score is 0.884. By both measures, this is the second highest agreement score, after `answerhood`. Of 42 disagreements for `verifiability`, annotators agree that at least eight are avoidable. Of these, five involve the in-

correct use of plurals. For example, A1 accepted *A man is pointing the way for the women*, when the image shows only one woman, but the guidelines reject such responses. Two other errors stem from inaccuracy, with respondents referring to a dog in the illustration as a cat. Each annotator incorrectly accepted one such response. One disagreement involved the misspelling of a crucial object: *The woman is holding the pat.* It is unclear whether *pet* or *cat* was intended. This should render the response unverifiable, but A1 accepted it.

The remaining disagreements are attributable to different opinions about inferences, with A2 being, in general, more strict. For the ditransitive item, for example, both annotators accept responses that refer to the woman as a *hiker*, but only A1 accepts responses where the man and woman are collectively referred to as hikers. For the intransitive item depicting a woman running, A1 accepts multiple responses that refer to this as *a race*, as well as responses that infer the runner's motivation (fitness, leisure, etc.).

Answerhood Capturing the semantic content of the picture isn't the only criterion for determining the quality of a response; the `answerhood` feature was added largely as a way to identify responses that simply do not follow the instructions. Such responses tend to be: i. responses that do not directly answer the given question, perhaps by reframing the perspective so that it seems like a different question was asked; ii. responses that are gibberish or very low-effort and entered only so the participant can proceed to the next item; or iii. "troll" responses that attempt to be funny or obscene at the cost of attempting a direct answer.

The majority of participants do attempt to follow the instructions and answer the question, however, and it is unsurprising that this feature skews strongly toward *yes* annotations and results in the highest raw agreement (98.2%) and kappa (0.936) scores among the five features.

Of 23 disagreements, seven stem from one annotator failing to enforce the requirement that a targeted response subject be either an appropriate pronoun or the exact subject given in the question, without adjectives, relative clauses or other modifiers. Given the question *What is **the woman doing?***, for example, the responses *The **lady** is running* and *The woman **who in pink** is running* were incorrectly accepted by one annotator. While this criterion may seem strict, this subject-identity rule separates the task of identifying an attempt to answer the question from the task of verifying information (see `verifiability` above).

Another ten disagreements involve responses lacking a progressive verb, generally required as an indication that the response refers to the specific action in the image and does not merely describe a state or a general truth (cf., e.g., *The woman is running* vs. *The woman runs*). Annotator fatigue thus accounts for the majority of `answerhood` disagreements.

Interpretability The average *yes* rate for `interpretability` is 0.802; only `core event` is less skewed: responses were thus also more likely to be unacceptable. The raw agreement score is 91.9% and kappa is 0.744, the lowest scores among the five features. This was anticipated, because `interpretability` is perhaps the most difficult to define, leaving room for annotators' personal judgments. Annotators must decide whether a given response evokes a clear mental image, regardless of how well that mental image matches the PDT image. In this way, responses such as *The man is working* which may be completely `verifiable` may still fall short, in that the man could be picking fruit, building a bridge, and so forth.

The guidelines place some restrictions on what it means to be a clear mental image. To begin with, if one were to illustrate the response, the result would be a complete, representational, canonical image. It would not be necessary to guess at major elements, like subjects or objects. All necessary semantic arguments would be identifiable from the

sentence and thus not obscured or out of the frame in the mental image. Vague language should be avoided, but human gender does not need to be specified, especially when a non-gendered word like *doctor* or *teacher* is natural.

Consider a response like *A woman is receiving a package.* By these criteria, the response is annotated as 0 because the person or entity delivering the package is not specified, and an illustrator would need to either guess or compose the image with the deliverer oddly out of the frame. *A man is delivering a package*, on the other hand, would be accepted. An illustrator could simply show a delivery person carrying a package, as an indirect object would not be necessary for the verb *deliver*.

Among the 105 annotator disagreements, fatigue accounts for roughly 30; this is difficult to determine precisely because annotators expressed difficulty in identifying a single root cause for many disagreements. Those that are clearly attributable to annotator error tend to involve responses with some internal inconsistency, as with subject-verb disagreements, where the number of the subject is uninterpretable. Among true disagreements, the level of specificity is often the point of contention, as with `core event`. For example, A1 accepted several transitive item responses with the verb *love*, as in *The woman loves her dog* (Table 1). A2 explained that these are too vague to illustrate as an action; A1 disagreed, and this seems to indicate differing judgments regarding the use of *love* as a dynamic verb.

Grammaticality The `grammaticality` feature is the most heavily skewed one, with an average *yes* rate of 86.6%. As the only non-semantic annotation, this is perhaps not surprising.

Grammaticality has a raw agreement score of 96.0% and a kappa of 0.827. Among 52 disagreements, annotators concurred in discussion that 19 involve an avoidable annotator error. These are primarily responses with typos, misspellings, subject-verb disagreement and bare nouns, all rejected by the annotation rules. Such cases are likely attributable to annotator fatigue.

The remainder reflect an unavoidable level of disagreement. Many of these stem from differing interpretations of bare nouns as either errors or as acceptable mass nouns, as in *The man is giving **direction** to the tourist.* In several cases, annotators disagree over prepositions, which are known to be a common source of disagreement and pose special challenges in the context of learner language (Tetreault and Chodorow, 2008a,b). For example, annotators could not agree on the grammaticality of the prepositions in *The girl is asking for help **to** the man* and *The girl is hugging **with** her cat*.

4.4 NS & NNS responses

Agreement scores were also calculated separately for NS and NNS responses, as shown in Table 5. Comparing the average rate of *yes* annotations shows that the NNSs outperform the NSs by between roughly 8% and 12% on all features except `grammaticality`. It is not surprising that NSs outperform NNSs on this feature (90.2% to 79.3%), but to account for their superior performance on the other features, one must consider the fact that the NNSs were recruited from ESL courses and performed the task with peers and researchers present. The NNSs were more likely to make a good faith effort than the NSs, the majority of whom performed the task anonymously and remotely. Furthermore, with twice as many responses to provide for each item for NSs, fatigue and boredom may have been a contributing factor.

	AvgYes		Kappa	
Set	NS	NNS	NS	NNS
Core	0.686	0.805	0.819	0.767
Verif	0.807	0.882	0.904	0.819
Answer	0.800	0.899	0.928	0.961
Interp	0.764	0.881	0.752	0.697
Gramm	0.902	0.793	0.786	0.863

Table 5: NS and NNS test set responses: average *yes* annotations (*AvgYes*) and Cohen's kappa (*Kappa*).

Raw agreement scores are high among both groups, ranging from 91% to 99.3% (not shown). Notably, for `core event`, `verifiability` and `interpretability`, kappa scores are higher for NS responses than for NNS ones; i.e., annotators agree more on NS responses for these features. It may be no coincidence that these three features are the most closely tied to meaning, while `answerhood` gets at pragmatics and `grammaticality` focuses on form correctness.

The lower kappa score for NS `answerhood` is also attributable to task effects, as a second response (as required of NSs) is more likely to be off topic or in bad faith. For `grammaticality`, kappas for annotator agreement are higher for NNS responses. A relatively low rate of expected (chance) agreement contributes to this fact. Additionally, annotators note that many grammar problems with NNS responses are obvious (e.g., *The **man who in yellow** is showing the way to a girl*, see Table 1), but the few grammar problems in NS data are mostly typos and more easily overlooked due to fatigue (e.g., *The man is giving **ditections***).

5 Conclusion

The SAILS corpus presented here was developed with specific research in mind, but also in the hopes that it may be used to address a broad range of questions. We have demonstrated here a set of binary features that were successfully implemented with reliable levels of inter-annotator agreement. These features were defined with an eye toward content analysis and ICALL, but we believe the annotations and raw responses could find uses in question answering, dialogs, pragmatic modeling, visual references and other challenges in natural language processing. The feature set could also be expanded to better suit other purposes, and the task could easily be extended to include new items. Guidelines, task materials and annotation tools are included with the corpus.[1]

A number of lessons have been learned in this process, and as we intend this work to be extendable, a few suggestions are in order. The inclusion of any symbols or numerals should be avoided as they resulted in response complications; some participants gave clever "meta" responses (*She's breathing in music notes*, rather than *She's singing*), and others focused on the symbols rather than the abstract concepts they represent (*The teacher is teaching '2 + 2 = 4'*, rather than *The teacher is teaching math*). The comparison of crowdsourced NS data with the data of known NS participants and the NNS student data makes it clear that motivations and task environment can affect the quality of responses.

Additionally, more clearly defining acceptable `core events` could lessen the ambiguity for annotators. While we intend the NS responses collected here to be useful for comparing with NNS responses and addressing related research questions, for specific applications like language testing, the use of expert annotators and constructed reference materials or gold standards may be more appropriate (Somasundaran and Chodorow, 2014).

---

[1]https://github.com/sailscorpus/sails

References

Luiz Amaral and Detmar Meurers. 2007. Conceptualizing student models for ICALL. In *Proceedings of the 11th International Conference on User Modeling*, Corfu, Greece.

Ron Artstein and Massimo Poesio. 2008. Survey article: Inter-coder agreement for computational linguistics. *Computational Linguistics*, 34(4).

Stacey Bailey and Detmar Meurers. 2008. Diagnosing meaning errors in short answers to reading comprehension questions. In *The 3rd Workshop on Innovative Use of NLP for Building Educational Applications (ACL08-NLP-Education)*, pages 107–115, Columbus, OH.

Aoife Cahill, Binod Gyawali, and James Bruno. 2014. Self-training for parsing learner text. In *Proceedings of the First Joint Workshop on Statistical Parsing of Morphologically Rich Languages and Syntactic Analysis of Non-Canonical Languages*, pages 66–73, Dublin, Ireland. Dublin City University.

Yeonsuk Cho, Frank Rijmen, and Jakub Novák. 2013. Investigating the effects of prompt characteristics on the comparability of toefl ibt† integrated writing tasks. *Language Testing*, 30(4):513–534.

Pauline Foster and Parvaneh Tavakoli. 2009. Native speakers and task performance: Comparing effects on complexity, fluency, and lexical diversity. *Language learning*, 59(4):866–896.

Trude Heift and Mathias Schulze. 2007. *Errors and Intelligence in Computer-Assisted Language Learning: Parsers and Pedagogues*. Routledge.

Levi King and Markus Dickinson. 2013. Shallow semantic analysis of interactive learner sentences. In *Proceedings of the Eighth Workshop on Innovative Use of NLP for Building Educational Applications*, pages 11–21, Atlanta, Georgia.

Levi King and Markus Dickinson. 2016. Shallow semantic reasoning from an incomplete gold standard for learner language. In *Proceedings of the 11th Workshop on Innovative Use of NLP for Building Educational Applications*, pages 112–121.

Kristopher Kyle and Scott A Crossley. 2015. Automatically assessing lexical sophistication: Indices, tools, findings, and application. *Tesol Quarterly*, 49(4):757–786.

J Richard Landis and Gary G Koch. 1977. The measurement of observer agreement for categorical data. *biometrics*, pages 159–174.

Claudia Leacock, Martin Chodorow, Michael Gamon, and Joel Tetreault. 2014. *Automated Grammatical Error Detection for Language Learners*, second edition. Synthesis Lectures on Human Language Technologies. Morgan & Claypool Publishers.

Detmar Meurers and Markus Dickinson. 2017. Evidence and interpretation in language learning research: Opportunities for collaboration with computational linguistics. *Language Learning. Special Issue on Language learning research at the intersection of experimental, corpus-based and computational methods*, 67(S1):66–95.

Detmar Meurers, Ramon Ziai, Niels Ott, and Janina Kopp. 2011. Evaluating answers to reading comprehension questions in context: Results for german and the role of information structure. In *Proceedings of the TextInfer 2011 Workshop on Textual Entailment*, pages 1–9. Association for Computational Linguistics.

Marwa Ragheb and Markus Dickinson. 2014. The effect of annotation scheme decisions on parsing learner data. In *Proceedings of the 13th International Workshop on Treebanks and Linguistic Theories (TLT13)*, Tübingen, Germany.

Swapna Somasundaran and Martin Chodorow. 2014. Automated measures of specific vocabulary knowledge from constructed responses ('Use these words to write a sentence based on this picture'). In *Proceedings of the Ninth Workshop on Innovative Use of NLP for Building Educational Applications*, pages 1–11, Baltimore, Maryland.

Swapna Somasundaran, Chong Min Lee, Martin Chodorow, and Xinhao Wang. 2015. Automated scoring of picture-based story narration. In *Proceedings of the Tenth Workshop on Innovative Use of NLP for Building Educational Applications*, pages 42–48, Denver, Colorado. Association for Computational Linguistics.

Joel Tetreault and Martin Chodorow. 2008a. Native judgments of non-native usage: Experiments in preposition error detection. In *Coling 2008: Proceedings of the workshop on Human Judgements in Computational Linguistics*, pages 24–32, Manchester, UK. Coling 2008 Organizing Committee.

Joel Tetreault and Martin Chodorow. 2008b. The ups and downs of preposition error detection in ESL writing. In *Proceedings of COLING-08*, Manchester.

Sara Cushing Weigle. 2013. English language learners and automated scoring of essays: Critical considerations. *Assessing Writing*, 18(1):85–99.

Annotating Student Talk in Text-based Classroom Discussions

Luca Lugini, Diane Litman, Amanda Godley, Christopher Olshefski
University of Pittsburgh
Pittsburgh, PA 15260
{lul32,dlitman,agodley,cao48}@pitt.edu

Abstract

Classroom discussions in English Language Arts have a positive effect on students' reading, writing, and reasoning skills. Although prior work has largely focused on teacher talk and student-teacher interactions, we focus on three theoretically-motivated aspects of high-quality student talk: argumentation, specificity, and knowledge domain. We introduce an annotation scheme, then show that the scheme can be used to produce reliable annotations and that the annotations are predictive of discussion quality. We also highlight opportunities provided by our scheme for educational and natural language processing research.

1 Introduction

Current research, theory, and policy surrounding K-12 instruction in the United States highlight the role of student-centered disciplinary discussions (i.e. discussions related to a specific academic discipline or school subject such as physics or English Language Arts) in instructional quality and student learning opportunities (Danielson, 2011; Grossman et al., 2014). Such student-centered discussions – often called "dialogic" or "inquiry-based" – are widely viewed as the most effective instructional approach for disciplinary understanding, problem-solving, and literacy (Elizabeth et al., 2012; Engle and Conant, 2002; Murphy et al., 2009). In English Language Arts (ELA) classrooms, student-centered discussions about literature have a positive impact on the development of students' reasoning, writing, and reading skills (Applebee et al., 2003; Reznitskaya and Gregory, 2013). However, most studies have focused on the role of teachers and their talk (Bloome et al., 2005; Elizabeth et al., 2012; Michaels et al., 2008) rather than on the aspects of student talk that contribute to discussion quality.

Additionally, studies of student-centered discussions rarely use the same coding schemes, making it difficult to generalize across studies (Elizabeth et al., 2012; Soter et al., 2008). This limitation is partly due to the time-intensive work required to analyze discourse data through qualitative methods such as ethnography and discourse analysis. Thus, qualitative case studies have generated compelling theories about the specific features of student talk that lead to high-quality discussions, but few findings can be generalized and leveraged to influence instructional improvements across ELA classrooms.

As a first step towards developing an automated system for detecting the features of student talk that lead to high quality discussions, we propose a new annotation scheme for student talk during ELA "text-based" discussions - that is, discussions that center on a text or piece of literature (e.g., book, play, or speech). The annotation scheme was developed to capture three aspects of classroom talk that are theorized in the literature as important to discussion quality and learning opportunities: *argumentation* (the process of systematically reasoning in support of an idea), *specificity* (the quality of belonging or relating uniquely to a particular subject), and *knowledge domain* (area of expertise represented in the content of the talk). We demonstrate the reliability and validity of our scheme via an annotation study of five transcripts of classroom discussion.

2 Related Work

One discourse feature used to assess the quality of discussions is students' argument moves: their claims about the text, their sharing of textual evidence for claims, and their warranting or reasoning to support the claims (Reznitskaya et al., 2009; Toulmin, 1958). Many researchers view student

Proceedings of the Thirteenth Workshop on Innovative Use of NLP for Building Educational Applications, pages 110–116
New Orleans, Louisiana, June 5, 2018. ©2018 Association for Computational Linguistics

reasoning as of primary importance, particularly when the reasoning is elaborated and highly inferential (Kim, 2014). In Natural Language Processing (NLP), most educationally-oriented argumentation research has focused on corpora of student persuasive essays (Ghosh et al., 2016; Klebanov et al., 2016; Persing and Ng, 2016; Wachsmuth et al., 2016; Stab and Gurevych, 2017; Nguyen and Litman, 2018). We instead focus on multiparty spoken discussion transcripts from classrooms. A second key difference consists in the inclusion of the warrant label in our scheme, as it is important to understand how students explicitly use reasoning to connect evidence to claims.

Educational studies suggest that discussion quality is also influenced by the specificity of student talk (Chisholm and Godley, 2011; Sohmer et al., 2009). Chisholm and Godley found that as specificity increased, the quality of students' claims and reasoning also increased. Previous NLP research has studied specificity in the context of professionally written newspaper articles (Li and Nenkova, 2015; Li et al., 2016; Louis and Nenkova, 2011, 2012). While the annotation instructions used in these studies work well for general purpose corpora, specificity in text-based discussions also needs to capture particular relations between discussions and texts. Furthermore, since the concept of a sentence is not clearly defined in speech, we annotate argumentative discourse units rather than sentences (see Section 3).

The knowledge domain of student talk may also matter, that is, whether the talk focuses on disciplinary knowledge or lived experiences. Some research suggests that disciplinary learning opportunities are maximized when students draw on evidence and reasoning that are commonly accepted in the discipline (Resnick and Schantz, 2015), although some studies suggest that evidence or reasoning from lived experiences increases discussion quality (Beach and Myers, 2001). Previous related work in NLP analyzed evidence type for argumentative tweets (Addawood and Bashir, 2016). Although the categories of evidence type are different, their definition of evidence type is in line with our definition of knowledge domain. However, our research is distinct from this research in its application domain (i.e. social media vs. education) and in analyzing knowledge domain for all argumentative components, not only those containing claims.

3 Annotation Scheme

Our annotation scheme[1] uses argument moves as the unit of analysis. We define an argument move as an utterance, or part of an utterance, that contains an argumentative discourse unit (ADU) (Peldszus and Stede, 2013). Like Peldszus and Stede (2015), in this paper we use transcripts already segmented into argument moves and focus on the steps following segmentation, i.e., labeling argumentation, specificity, and knowledge domain. Table 1 shows a section of a transcribed classroom discussion along with labels assigned by a human annotator following segmentation.

3.1 Argumentation

The argumentation scheme is based on (Lee, 2006) and consists of a simplified set of labels derived from Toulmin's (1958) model: (i) *Claim*: an arguable statement that presents a particular interpretation of a text or topic. (ii) *Evidence*: facts, documentation, text reference, or testimony used to support or justify a claim. (iii) *Warrant*: reasons explaining how a specific evidence instance supports a specific claim. Our scheme specifies that warrants must come after claim and evidence, since by definition warrants cannot exist without them.

The first three moves in Table 1 show a natural expression of an argument: a student first claims that Willy's wife is only trying to protect him, then provides a reference as evidence by mentioning something she said to her kids at the end of the book, and finally explains how not caring about her kids ties the evidence to the initial claim. The second group shows the same argument progression, with evidence given as a direct quote.

3.2 Specificity

Specificity annotations are based on (Chisholm and Godley, 2011) and have the goal of capturing text-related characteristics expressed in student talk. Specificity labels are directly related to four distinct elements for an argument move: (1) it is specific to one (or a few) character or scene; (2) it makes significant qualifications or elaborations; (3) it uses content-specific vocabulary (e.g. quotes from the text); (4) it provides a chain of reasons. Our annotation scheme for specificity includes three labels along a linear scale: (i) *Low*:

---

[1]The coding manual is in the supplemental material.

Move	Stu	Argument Move	Argument	Specificity	Domain
23	S1	She's like really just protecting Willy from everything.	claim	medium	disciplinary
24	S1	Like at the end of the book remember how she was telling the kids to leave and never come back.	evidence	medium	disciplinary
25	S1	Like she's not even caring about them, she's caring about Willy.	warrant	medium	disciplinary
41	S2	It's like she's concerned with him trying to [inaudible] and he's concerned with trying to make her happy, you know? So he feels like he's failing when he's not making her happy like	claim	high	disciplinary
42	S2	"Let's bring your mother some good news"	evidence	high	disciplinary
43	S2	but she knew that, there wasn't any good news, so she wanted to act happy so he wouldn't be in pain.	warrant	high	disciplinary
55	S3	Some people they just ask for a job is just like, some money.	evidence	low	experiential

Table 1: Examples of argument moves and their respective annotations from a discussion of the book *Death of a Salesman*. As shown by the argument move numbers, boxes for students S1, S2, and S3 indicate separate, non contiguous excerpts of the discussion.

statement that does not contain any of these elements. (*ii*) *Medium*: statement that accomplishes one of these elements. (*iii*) *High*: statement that clearly accomplishes at least two specificity elements. Even though we do not explicitly use labels for the four specificity elements, we found that explicitly breaking down specificity into multiple components helped increase reliability when training annotators.

The first three argument moves in Table 1 all contain the first element, as they refer to select characters in the book. However, no content-specific vocabulary, clear chain of reasoning, or significant qualifications are provided; therefore all three moves are labeled as medium specificity. The fourth move, however, accomplishes the first and fourth specificity elements, and is labeled as high specificity. The fifth move is also labeled high specificity since it is specific to one character/scene, and provides a direct quote from the text. The last move is labeled as low specificity as it reflects an overgeneralization about all humans.

3.3 Knowledge Domain

The possible labels for knowledge domain are: (*i*) *Disciplinary*: the statement is grounded in knowledge gathered from a text (either the one under discussion or others), such as a quote or a description of a character/event. (*ii*) *Experiential*: the statement is drawn from human experience, such as what the speaker has experienced or thinks that other humans have experienced.

In Table 1 the first six argument moves are labeled as disciplinary, since the moves reflect knowledge from the text currently being discussed. The last move, however, draws from a student's experience or perceived knowledge about the real world.

4 Reliability and Validity Analyses

We carried out a reliability study for the proposed scheme using two pairs of expert annotators, P1 and P2. The annotators were trained by coding one transcript at a time and discussing disagreements. Five text-based discussions were used for testing reliability after training: pair P1 annotated discussions of *The Bluest Eye*, *Death of a Salesman*, and *Macbeth*, while pair P2 annotated two separate discussions of *Ain't I a Woman*. 250 argument moves (discussed by over 40 students and consisting of over 8200 words) were annotated. Inter-rater reliability was assessed using Cohen's kappa:

Moves	Argumentation (kappa)	Specificity (qwkappa)	Domain (kappa)
169	0.729	0.874	0.980
81	0.725	0.930	1

Table 2: Inter-rater reliability for pairs P1 and P2.

Argumentation	evidence	warrant	claim
evidence	25	5	0
warrant	6	92	12
claim	0	2	27
Specificity	**low**	**medium**	**high**
low	59	5	3
medium	5	25	2
high	1	6	63
Knowledge Domain	**disciplinary**	**experiential**	
disciplinary	138	1	
experiential	0	30	

Table 3: Confusion matrices for argumentation, specificity, and knowledge domain, for annotator pair P1.

unweighted for argumentation and knowledge domain, but quadratic-weighted for specificity given its ordered labels.

Table 2 shows that kappa for argumentation ranges from $0.61 - 0.8$, which generally indicates substantial agreement (McHugh, 2012). Kappa values for specificity and knowledge domain are in the $0.81 - 1$ range which generally indicates almost perfect agreement (McHugh, 2012). These results show that our proposed annotation scheme can be used to produce reliable annotations of classroom discussion with respect to argumentation, specificity, and knowledge domain.

Table 3 shows confusion matrices[2] for annotator pair P1 (we observed similar trends for P2). The argumentation section of the table shows that the largest number of disagreements happens between the claim and warrant labels. One reason may be related to the constraint we impose on warrants - they require the existence of a claim and evidence. If a student tries to provide a warrant for a claim that happened much earlier in the discussion, the annotators might interpret the warrant as new claim. The specificity section shows relatively few low-high label disagreements as com-

pared to low-med and med-high. This is also reflected in the quadratic-weighted kappa as low-high disagreements will carry a larger penalty (unweighted kappa is 0.797). The main reasons for disagreements over specificity labels come from two of the four specificity elements discussed in Section 3.2: whether an argument move is related to one character or scene, and whether it provides a chain of reasons. With respect to the first of these two elements we observed disagreements in argument moves containing pronouns with an ambiguous reference. Of particular note is the pronoun *it*. If we consider the argument move *"I mean even if you know you have a hatred towards a standard or whatever, you still don't kill it"*, the pronoun *it* clearly refers to something within the move (i.e. the standard) that the student themselves mentioned. In contrast, for argument moves such as *"It did happen"* it might not be clear to what previous move the pronoun refers, therefore creating confusion on whether this specificity element is accomplished. Regarding specificity element (4) we found that it was easier to determine the presence of a chain of reasons when discourse connectives (e.g. because, therefore) were present in the argument move. The absence of explicit discourse connectives in an argument move might drive annotators to disagree on the presence/absence of a chain of reasons, which is likely to result in a different specificity label. Additionally, annotators found that shorter turns at talk proved harder to annotate for specificity. Finally, as we can see from the third section in the table, knowledge domain has the lowest disagreements with only one.

We also (Godley and Olshefski, 2017) explored the validity of our coding scheme by comparing our annotations of student talk to English Education experts' evaluations (quadratic-weighted kappa of 0.544) of the discussion's quality. Using stepwise regressions, we found that the best model of discussion quality (R-squared of 0.432) included all three of our coding dimensions: argumentation, specificity, and knowledge domain.

5 Opportunities and Challenges

Our annotation scheme introduces opportunities for the educational community to conduct futher research on the relationship between features of student talk, student learning, and discussion quality. Although Chisholm and Godley (2011) and we found relations between our coding constructs and

---

[2] The class distributions for argumentation and specificity labels vary significantly across transcripts, as can be seen in (Lugini and Litman, 2017) and (Godley and Olshefski, 2017).

discussion quality, these were small-scale studies based on manual annotations. Once automated classifiers are developed, such relations between talk and learning can be examined at scale. Also, automatic labeling via a standard coding scheme can support the generalization of findings across studies, and potentially lead to automated tools for teachers and students.

The proposed annotation scheme also introduces NLP opportunities and challenges. Existing systems for classifying specificity and argumentation have largely been designed to analyze written text rather than spoken discussions. This is (at least in part) due to a lack of publicly available corpora and schemes for annotating argumentation and specificity in spoken discussions. The development of an annotation scheme explicitly designed for this problem is the first step towards collecting and annotating corpora that can be used by the NLP community to advance the field in this particular area. Furthermore, in text-based discussions, NLP methods need to tightly couple the discussion with contextual information (i.e., the text under discussion). For example, an argument move from one of the discussions mentioned in Section 4 stated *"She's saying like free like, I don't have to be, I don't have to be this salesman's wife anymore, your know? I don't have to play this role anymore."* The use of the term *salesman* shows the presence of specificity element (3) (see Section 3.2) because the text under discussion is indeed *Death of a Salesman*. If the students were discussing another text, the mention of the term *salesman* would not indicate one of the specificity elements, therefore lowering the specificity rating. Thus, using existing systems is unlikely to yield good performance. In fact, we previously (Lugini and Litman, 2017) showed that while using an off-the-shelf system for predicting specificity in newspaper articles resulted in low performance when applied to classroom discussions, exploiting characteristics of our data could significantly improve performance. We have similarly evaluated the performance of two existing argument mining systems (Nguyen and Litman, 2018; Niculae et al., 2017) on the transcripts described in Section 4. We noticed that since the two systems were trained to classify only claims and premises, they were never able to correctly predict warrants in our transcripts. Additionally, both systems classified the overwhelming majority of moves as premise,

resulting in negative kappa in some cases. Using our scheme to create a corpus of classroom discussion data manually annotated for argumentation, specificity, and knowledge domain will support the development of more robust NLP prediction systems.

6 Conclusions

In this work we proposed a new annotation scheme for three theoretically-motivated features of student talk in classroom discussion: argumentation, specificity, and knowledge domain. We demonstrated usage of the scheme by presenting an annotated excerpt of a classroom discussion. We demonstrated that the scheme can be annotated with high reliability and reported on scheme validity. Finally, we discussed some possible applications and challenges posed by the proposed annotation scheme for both the educational and NLP communities. We plan to extend our annotation scheme to label information about collaborative relations between different argument moves, and release a corpus annotated with the extended scheme.

Acknowledgements

We want to thank Haoran Zhang, Tazin Afrin, and Annika Swallen for their contribution, and all the anonymous reviewers for their helpful suggestions.

This work was supported by the Learning Research and Development Center at the University of Pittsburgh.

References

Aseel Addawood and Masooda Bashir. 2016. "what is your evidence?" a study of controversial topics on social media. In *Proceedings of the Third Workshop on Argument Mining (ArgMining2016)*, pages 1–11.

Arthur N Applebee, Judith A Langer, Martin Nystrand, and Adam Gamoran. 2003. Discussion-based approaches to developing understanding: Classroom instruction and student performance in middle and high school english. *American Educational Research Journal*, 40(3):685–730.

Richard Beach and Jamie Myers. 2001. *Inquiry-based English instruction: Engaging students in life and literature*, volume 55. Teachers College Press.

David Bloome, Stephanie Power Carter, Beth Morton Christian, Sheila Otto, and Nora Shuart-Faris. 2005. *Discourse analysis and the study of classroom language and literacy events: A microethnographic perspective.* Lawrence Erlbaum.

James S Chisholm and Amanda J Godley. 2011. Learning about language through inquiry-based discussion: Three bidialectal high school students talk about dialect variation, identity, and power. *Journal of Literacy Research*, 43(4):430–468.

Charlotte Danielson. 2011. Evaluations that help teachers learn. *Educational leadership*, 68(4):35–39.

Tracy Elizabeth, Trisha L Ross Anderson, Elana H Snow, and Robert L Selman. 2012. Academic discussions: An analysis of instructional discourse and an argument for an integrative assessment framework. *American Educational Research Journal*, 49(6):1214–1250.

Randi A Engle and Faith R Conant. 2002. Guiding principles for fostering productive disciplinary engagement: Explaining an emergent argument in a community of learners classroom. *Cognition and Instruction*, 20(4):399–483.

Debanjan Ghosh, Aquila Khanam, Yubo Han, and Smaranda Muresan. 2016. Coarse-grained argumentation features for scoring persuasive essays. In *Proceedings of the 54th Annual Meeting of the Association for Computational Linguistics (Volume 2: Short Papers)*, volume 2, pages 549–554.

Amanda Godley and Christopher Olshefski. 2017. The role of argument moves, specificity and evidence type in meaningful literary discussions across diverse secondary classrooms. Unpublished paper presented at Literacy Research Association 67th Annual Conference: Literacy Research for Expanding Meaningfulness.

Pam Grossman, Julie Cohen, Matthew Ronfeldt, and Lindsay Brown. 2014. The test matters: The relationship between classroom observation scores and teacher value added on multiple types of assessment. *Educational Researcher*, 43(6):293–303.

Il-Hee Kim. 2014. Development of reasoning skills through participation in collaborative synchronous online discussions. *Interactive Learning Environments*, 22(4):467–484.

Beata Beigman Klebanov, Christian Stab, Jill Burstein, Yi Song, Binod Gyawali, and Iryna Gurevych. 2016. Argumentation: Content, structure, and relationship with essay quality. In *Proceedings of the Third Workshop on Argument Mining (ArgMining2016)*, pages 70–75.

Carol D Lee. 2006. every good-bye aint gone: analyzing the cultural underpinnings of classroom talk. *International Journal of Qualitative Studies in Education*, 19(3):305–327.

Junyi Jessy Li and Ani Nenkova. 2015. Fast and accurate prediction of sentence specificity. In *Proceedings of the Twenty-Ninth Conference on Artificial Intelligence (AAAI)*, pages 2281–2287.

Junyi Jessy Li, Bridget ODaniel, Yi Wu, Wenli Zhao, and Ani Nenkova. 2016. Improving the annotation of sentence specificity. In *Proceedings of the Tenth International Conference on Language Resources and Evaluation (LREC)*.

Annie Louis and Ani Nenkova. 2011. General versus specific sentences: automatic identification and application to analysis of news summaries. Technical Report MS-CIS-11-07, University of Pennsylvania.

Annie Louis and Ani Nenkova. 2012. A corpus of general and specific sentences from news. In *LREC*, pages 1818–1821.

Luca Lugini and Diane Litman. 2017. Predicting specificity in classroom discussion. In *Proceedings of the 12th Workshop on Innovative Use of NLP for Building Educational Applications*, pages 52–61.

Mary L McHugh. 2012. Interrater reliability: the kappa statistic. *Biochemia medica: Biochemia medica*, 22(3):276–282.

Sarah Michaels, Catherine OConnor, and Lauren B Resnick. 2008. Deliberative discourse idealized and realized: Accountable talk in the classroom and in civic life. *Studies in philosophy and education*, 27(4):283–297.

P Karen Murphy, Ian AG Wilkinson, Anna O Soter, Maeghan N Hennessey, and John F Alexander. 2009. Examining the effects of classroom discussion on students comprehension of text: A meta-analysis. *Journal of Educational Psychology*, 101(3):740.

Huy V Nguyen and Diane J Litman. 2018. Argument mining for improving the automated scoring of persuasive essays. In *Proceedings of the Thirty-Second AAAI Conference on Artificial Intelligence*.

Vlad Niculae, Joonsuk Park, and Claire Cardie. 2017. Argument Mining with Structured SVMs and RNNs. In *Proceedings of ACL*.

Andreas Peldszus and Manfred Stede. 2013. From argument diagrams to argumentation mining in texts: A survey. *International Journal of Cognitive Informatics and Natural Intelligence (IJCINI)*, 7(1):1–31.

Andreas Peldszus and Manfred Stede. 2015. Joint prediction in mst-style discourse parsing for argumentation mining. In *Proceedings of the 2015 Conference on Empirical Methods in Natural Language Processing*, pages 938–948.

Isaac Persing and Vincent Ng. 2016. End-to-end argumentation mining in student essays. In *Proceedings of the 2016 Conference of the North American Chapter of the Association for Computational Linguistics: Human Language Technologies*, pages 1384–1394.

Lauren B Resnick and Faith Schantz. 2015. Talking to learn: The promise and challenge of dialogic teaching. *Socializing Intelligence through academic talk and dialogue*, pages 441–450.

Alina Reznitskaya and Maughn Gregory. 2013. Student thought and classroom language: Examining the mechanisms of change in dialogic teaching. *Educational Psychologist*, 48(2):114–133.

Alina Reznitskaya, Li-Jen Kuo, Ann-Marie Clark, Brian Miller, May Jadallah, Richard C Anderson, and Kim Nguyen-Jahiel. 2009. Collaborative reasoning: A dialogic approach to group discussions. *Cambridge Journal of Education*, 39(1):29–48.

Richard Sohmer, Sarah Michaels, MC OConnor, and Lauren Resnick. 2009. Guided construction of knowledge in the classroom. *Transformation of knowledge through classroom interaction*, pages 105–129.

Anna O Soter, Ian A Wilkinson, P Karen Murphy, Lucila Rudge, Kristin Reninger, and Margaret Edwards. 2008. What the discourse tells us: Talk and indicators of high-level comprehension. *International Journal of Educational Research*, 47(6):372–391.

Christian Stab and Iryna Gurevych. 2017. Parsing argumentation structures in persuasive essays. *Computational Linguistics*, 43(3):619–659.

Stephen Toulmin. 1958. *The uses of argument*. Cambridge: Cambridge University Press.

Henning Wachsmuth, Khalid Al Khatib, and Benno Stein. 2016. Using argument mining to assess the argumentation quality of essays. In *Proceedings of COLING 2016, the 26th International Conference on Computational Linguistics: Technical Papers*, pages 1680–1691.

Toward Automatically Measuring Learner Ability from Human-Machine Dialog Interactions using Novel Psychometric Models

Vikram Ramanarayanan
Educational Testing Service R&D
90 New Montgomery Street, #1500
San Francisco, CA
vramanarayanan@ets.org

Michelle LaMar
Educational Testing Service R&D
90 New Montgomery Street, #1500
San Francisco, CA
mlamar@ets.org

Abstract

While dialog systems have been widely deployed for computer-assisted language learning (CALL) and formative assessment systems in recent years, relatively limited work has been done with respect to the psychometrics and validity of these technologies in evaluating and providing feedback regarding student learning and conversational ability. This paper formulates a Markov decision process based measurement model, and applies it to text chat data collected from crowdsourced native and non-native English language speakers interacting with an automated dialog agent. We investigate how well the model measures speaker conversational ability, and find that it effectively captures the differences in how native and non-native speakers of English accomplish the dialog task. Such models could have important implications for CALL systems of the future that effectively combine dialog management with measurement of learner conversational ability in real-time.

1 Introduction

Advances in multimodal dialog technologies have helped improve the state of the art in interactive computer-assisted language learning (CALL) and educational assessment applications in recent years. However, while much progress has been made with respect to the technology infrastructure and automated processing required in such dialog applications, relatively less work has carefully investigated the efficacy and validity of such assessment instruments, for instance, how well they measure students' capabilities. In other words, there is relatively little investigation into the psychometrics of such CALL applications and dialog-based assessments[1].

Interactive tasks such as multi-turn conversations have had limited use as standardized assessments due in part to the difficulty of evaluating these performances. When such assessment tasks are used, the conversational performance is scored primarily using human raters (take for instance, the IELTS exam[2]). Machine scoring of complex task performances has made substantial progress, especially is the domain of written essays (Shermis, 2014), but has been limited by path complexity in interactive performances such as dialog (Graesser et al., 2005).

While technical language use, (e.g. grammar or pronunciation) might be scorable at the word or phrase grain size, pragmatic conversational ability can only be judged in the context of the conversation history, personal goals, and interpersonal dynamics. In a conversational task, for example, the "correctness" of single utterances cannot be scored independently as their function, and therefore their value, depends upon the current state of the dialog. An utterance at one stage of the conversation might be of high value while the same utterance at a different point would be detrimental. Each utterance must be evaluated based on the speaker's conversational goals, what they have already accomplished in the conversation, and what sequence of interactions might bring them closer to their goal.

Such data is unsuitable to model with traditional psychometric models that assume conditionally independent performance data, such as either classical test theory or item response theory (De Boeck and Wilson, 2004), requiring a more structured and dynamic model (Mislevy et al., 2002). It is this modeling gap that we attempt to bridge in this paper using Markov Decision Process (or MDP)-based measurement modeling (LaMar, 2018). To our knowledge, this is the first attempt at developing a psychometric model for dialog data that explicitly accounts for temporal dependencies in the observed data stream.

---

[1]Psychometrics is the field of study concerned with the theory and technique of psychological measurement, which includes the measurement of knowledge, abilities, attitudes, and personality traits. Psychometricians use a specialized set of statistical tools to create scientifically valid "standardized" assessments of various behaviors. Typically, a test is considered to have been standardized if data have been collected on large numbers of subjects using a set of structured rules for administration and scoring. These data are used to determine the mean score and the standard deviation, which the psychometrician then uses to benchmark the performance of those being tested. For more details, see Association et al. (1999) or Weiss and Zureich (2008).

[2]https://www.ielts.org/

Proceedings of the Thirteenth Workshop on Innovative Use of NLP for Building Educational Applications, pages 117–126
New Orleans, Louisiana, June 5, 2018. ©2018 Association for Computational Linguistics

While the field does need more research into psychometrics and validity of dialog-based summative assessments, there has been substantial work by the learning and formative assessment community in examining learning gains/progressions and modeling cognitive strategies in conversational tutoring applications (see for example Person et al., 2001; VanLehn et al., 2002; Heffernan and Koedinger, 2002; Michael et al., 2003; Pon-Barry et al., 2006; Rus et al., 2013). Researchers have also examined how one can perform adaptive dialog management to personalize the instruction to individual participants over the course of the interaction (Forbes-Riley and Litman, 2011; Vail and Boyer, 2014). This includes using learning progressions, natural language processing and affective computing to adaptively selecting appropriate tasks for the learner to work on, but also adapting the scaffolding while the learner is working on a tasks (Rus et al., 2013).

Such research has important implications for dialog system design as well. Particularly for CALL applications, it is important to integrate formative assessment of student ability into the dialog management process, in order to better adapt instruction to student needs, both in terms of the level of instruction (obtained in real time through measurement models) as well as the content and dialog path (decided by the dialog manager). We envision that future statistical dialog systems could combine statistical dialog management achieved using Partially Observable Markov Decision Processes or POMDPs (see for instance Young, 2006; Williams and Young, 2007; Young et al., 2010) in tandem with statistical measurement (using POMDP-based models) in order to develop more effective conversational language learning applications.

Our work also directly relates to user modeling in dialog systems. While there is plenty of theoretical work on such models (see for example, Kobsa, 1990; Kass, 2012), implemented statistical versions of user models typically estimate the probability of a particular user response given a candidate system response or a interaction history thereof (e.g., Eckert et al., 1997; Levin et al., 2000; Horvitz and Paek, 2001; Pietquin, 2005; Kim et al., 2008). However, the difference in our case is that in order to serve as a measurement model of student performance, our MDP represents the cognitive model of an ideal automated interlocutor. Given a specified set of model parameters, the MDP model can generate action (or response) probabilities for every possible conversational state, depending on a learner/user-specific latent 'conversational ability' parameter which needs to be estimated for each user. Note that for the purposes of *this* paper, we will be broadly looking at conversational ability (in achieving a certain goal), and *not* necessarily technical English language proficiency.

The rest of the paper is organized as follows: Section 2 lays out the mathematical foundations of how MDP models can be used to model learner ability, including the equations for statistical parameter estimation.

Section 3 then describes the dialog infrastructure used along with details regarding the conversational task and crowdsourcing data collection, followed by the formulation of the task-specific MDP for our use case in Section 4. Section 5 analyzes the results of running the model on our dataset and studies how well the model differentiates between native and non-native speakers (who are potential language learners) of English, with example dialogs included for illustration purposes. Finally, we conclude with a discussion of the current state of the art and outstanding issues for future research.

2 Markov Decision Process Measurement Models

As an extension of inverse reinforcement learning, partially observable Markov Decision Processes (POMDPs) have recently been used to represent a cognitive model that describes both human decision making and people's ability to infer the goals and beliefs of others. Baker et al. (2011) describe a "Bayesian theory of mind" in which cognition is modeled as a POMDP. They hypothesize that people act based on their beliefs, modeled by the state space, action set, and transition functions, and in accordance to their desires, which are modeled by the reward structure. With this cognitive framing, POMDPs can be used for measurement within a goal-directed task by comparing actions selected by human participants with the model's predicted probability of those actions (LaMar, 2018). The model and estimation algorithms will be described briefly below; for full details can be found in LaMar (2018). Note that in this work we utilize the more constrained MDP, in which the problem state is assumed to be observable, but extensions to full POMDP models are a natural next step.

2.1 Mathematical Formulation

As a decision model, the MDP defines the probability of selecting of an action $a \in A$ given a specific state of the task $s \in S$. This probability, $p(a|s)$, is known as the policy. Action selection occurs within the context of a reward function $r(s, a, s')$, which specifies the immediate reward for taking action a in state s and entering state s' and a transition model $p(s'|s, a)$, which is the probability of transitioning to a state s' given that action a was taken in state s. An additional parameter $\gamma \in [0, 1]$, known as the discount parameter, represents the relative value of future versus immediate rewards. From this specification, one can calculate the Q function, which is the expected sum of discounted rewards obtained by taking action a while in state s,

$$Q(s,a) = \sum_{s' \in S} p(s'|s,a) \left(r(s,a,s') + \gamma \sum_{a' \in A} p(a'|s') Q(s',a') \right). \tag{1}$$

Note that $\sum_{a' \in A} p(a'|s') Q(s',a')$ is the expected value of the next state, marginalized over the possible next actions. Thus the quantity inside the large parentheses is the sum of the immediate reward and the discounted value of the future state. The expectation of this sum is then taken over all possible states s' that might result from action a in state s. The Q function is recursive, as the value of a state is defined using the Q function itself, but can be calculated using dynamic programming (Howard, 1960).

When MDPs are used in the context of artificial agents, they generally employ an optimal policy which selects the action that maximized Q in each state. To model human performance, however, optimal decision making is not assumed. Instead a Bolzmann policy is used (Baker et al., 2009),

$$p(a|s) \propto e^{\beta Q(s,a)}, \qquad (2)$$

where $\beta \in [0, \infty)$ represents the decision maker's ability to choose actions that will result in higher total rewards. As β increases, the probability choosing an optimal action increases. When β goes to zero, actions are selected uniformly at random from the action set.

2.2 MDPs for Measurement and Inference

Researchers have recently extended the MDP framework to study the quality of inferences that can be made about student/learner cognition based on records of action; for instance, to model learner goals and beliefs (Rafferty et al., 2015; Baker et al., 2009), to model inquiry strategies (LaMar et al., 2017), and to model student decision making ability (LaMar, 2018). Using the Boltzmann policy (Eq. 2), the MDP model can be seen as a generative latent-trait model provided that the latent traits of interest can be formulated as parameters of the model. While elements of the reward function and the transition model can be parameterized for inference about the decision maker's goals and beliefs, here we focus on the capability parameter β_j, a *person-specific* Boltzmann parameter, indicating a person's capability to optimally solve the given problem. The formulation of the Q function remains as in Equation 1, except that we note explicitly the dependency upon the capability parameter β_j. The conditional probability of student j selecting action a when in state s now becomes

$$p(a|s, \beta_j) = \frac{\exp(\beta_j Q(s,a|\beta_j))}{\sum_{a' \in A} \exp(\beta_j Q(s,a'|\beta_j))}. \qquad (3)$$

If the reward and transition parameters are fixed to objectively correct values, the Q function acts as a scoring function, determining the relative value of the actions available in each state. The β_j parameter is then similar to a traditional ability parameter in IRT, measuring the extent to which the highest valued action is taken at each decision point.

2.3 Parameter Estimation

The observed data for student j consist of a sequence of state-action pairs,

$$O_j = \{(s_{1j}, a_{1j}), (s_{2j}, a_{2j}), \dots (s_{N_j j}, a_{N_j j})\}, \qquad (4)$$

where N_j is the total number of actions taken by the student. Each pair indicates a state and the action taken in that state.

The Markov property applies to this model, allowing us to take each action to be conditionally independent, conditioned upon student capability and the system state in which the action was taken. Thus the probability of the observed data can be written as

$$p(O_j|\beta_j, \mu, \sigma) = \prod_{t=1}^{T_j} p(a_{tj}|s_{tj}, \beta_j, \mu, \sigma) \qquad (5)$$

$$= \prod_{t=1}^{T_j} \frac{\exp(Q(s_{tj}, a_{tj}|\beta_j)\beta_j)}{\sum_{a' \in A} \exp(Q(s_{tj}, a'|\beta_j)\beta_j)}.$$

$$\text{where } \beta_j \sim Lognormal(\mu, \sigma^2) \qquad (6)$$

where the optimal value of the person-specific ability parameter, $\hat{\beta}_j$, can be estimated by finding the value of β_j that maximizes this likelihood:

$$\hat{\beta}_j = \underset{\beta_j}{\mathrm{argmax}}\, p(O_j|\beta_j, \mu, \sigma) \qquad (7)$$

To estimate the population parameters of the lognormal distribution[3], μ and σ, we use marginal maximum likelihood (MML), marginalizing over the person-specific parameter distributions. The person-specific β_j can be estimated either using maximum a-posteriori (MAP) or maximum likelihood estimation (MLE) methods. With smaller population sizes the MLE estimation has been found to be more robust and is used for this study. Both the MML and MLE estimations are performed using a two-phase numerical optimization with a global optimization algorithm followed by a local optimization algorithm, both drawn from the *nlopt* library. Gaussian quadrature is used for the approximation of the integrals and the Q-function is approximated using policy iteration methods.

3 Dialog Data

3.1 Dialog System

We use an open-source dialog system[4] to develop a text-based chatbot application. But note that this work is not limited to or dependent on the dialog system being used. Indeed, there are multiple academic (Olympus (Bohus et al., 2007), Alex (Jurčíček et al., 2014), Virtual Human Toolkit (Hartholt et al., 2013), OpenDial[5], etc.) and industrial (Voxeo[6], Alexa [7], etc.) implementations of dialog systems, any of which can be

---

[3] We chose to model β_j using the Lognormal distribution as it has a non-negative range and has been used to describe growth patterns in nature. Moreover, person-specific "ability" can be argued to be the result of a growth process (multiplicative rather than additive).

[4] Link to software anonymized.

[5] http://www.opendial-toolkit.net

[6] https://voxeo.com/prophecy/

[7] https://developer.amazon.com/alexa

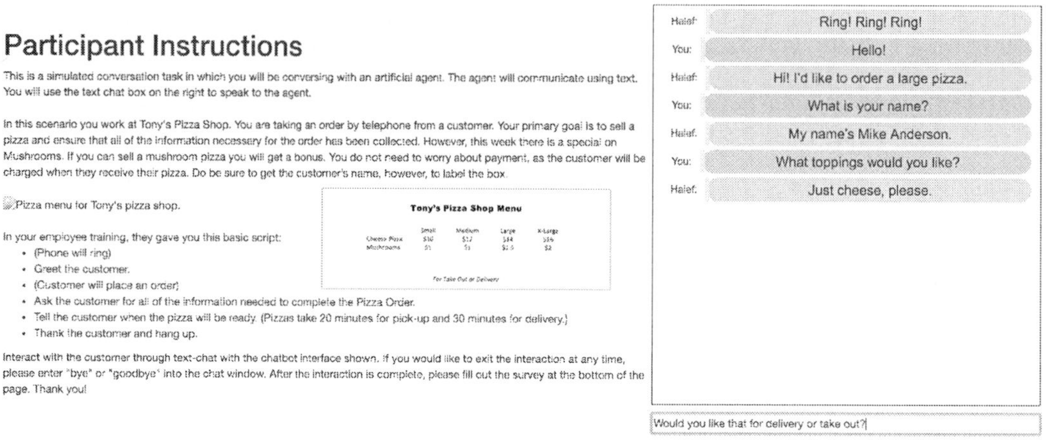

Figure 1: Example webpage screenshot of the text dialog interface that participants might see for the task described in this paper.

used, but many of these often use special architectures, interfaces, and languages paying relatively less attention to existing W3C and other industry standards (see Ramanarayanan et al. (2017) for more details). We however choose to use the *Anonymous* cloud-based dialog system for its standards-compliance, modularity and flexibility in developing both text- and speech-based applications. In this study we will limit ourselves to text-based dialog for simplicity.

3.2 Conversational item design

This study leverages a conversational practice task developed for English language learners, where subjects are asked to pose as a customer services representative at a pizza restaurant, and field an order from an automated customer (played by the dialog system). See Figure 1 for a screenshot of the web-based dialog interface that participants interacted with. Participants are instructed that their primary goal is to sell a pizza while ensuring that they collect all information necessary to complete the order (such as the name of the customer, his address if delivery is requested, etc.). They are further instructed that if they manage to sell the customer mushroom toppings, they will be awarded a bonus for task performance. We used regular expressions to perform the natural language understanding. Figure 2 depicts the dialog flow of the conversational item. Recall that for the purposes of *this* paper, the target of measurement is the student's ability to navigate conversational conventions and achieve the pre-specified task goal (to maximize the pizza sale) through conversation with the automated customer, and not their technical language skills.

3.3 Crowdsourcing data collection

We used Amazon Mechanical Turk for our crowdsourcing data collection experiments. Crowdsourcing has been used in the past for the assessment of dialog systems as well as for collection of dialog interactions (see

for instance (McGraw et al., 2010; Rayner et al., 2011; Jurcicek et al., 2011; Ramanarayanan et al., 2016)). In addition to interacting with the text chatbot interface to complete the conversational task, workers were requested to fill out a 2-3 minute survey regarding different aspects of the interaction, such as their overall experience, how engaged they felt while interacting with the system, how well the system understood them, and basic demographic information. Particularly relevant for this study are callers' self-reported first language, and their ratings of system performance, defined as a qualitative measure of how the system performed as per caller expectations and whether the system responses were appropriate. In all we collected and analyzed dialogs from 390 participants, 54% of which self-reported as native English language speakers and 70% of which were male, primarily in the 20–40 age range. See Tables 3–7 for example dialogs.

4 MDP Model for the Pizza Dialog Task

Table 1: The action set and transition function for the MDP PizzaOrder cognitive model.

Action	Prob	Customer ...
RequestToppings	0.6	requests cheese pizza
RequestToppings	0.4	requests mushroom pizza
SuggestMushroom	0.4	requests cheese pizza
SuggestMushroom	0.6	requests mushroom pizza
AskDelivery	0.5	wants delivery
AskDelivery	0.5	wants take-out
AskName	1.0	gives name
AskSize	1.0	orders large pizza
AskAddress	1.0	gives address
AskPhone	1.0	gives phone number
SayOther	1.0	no effect
EndConversation	1.0	hangs up

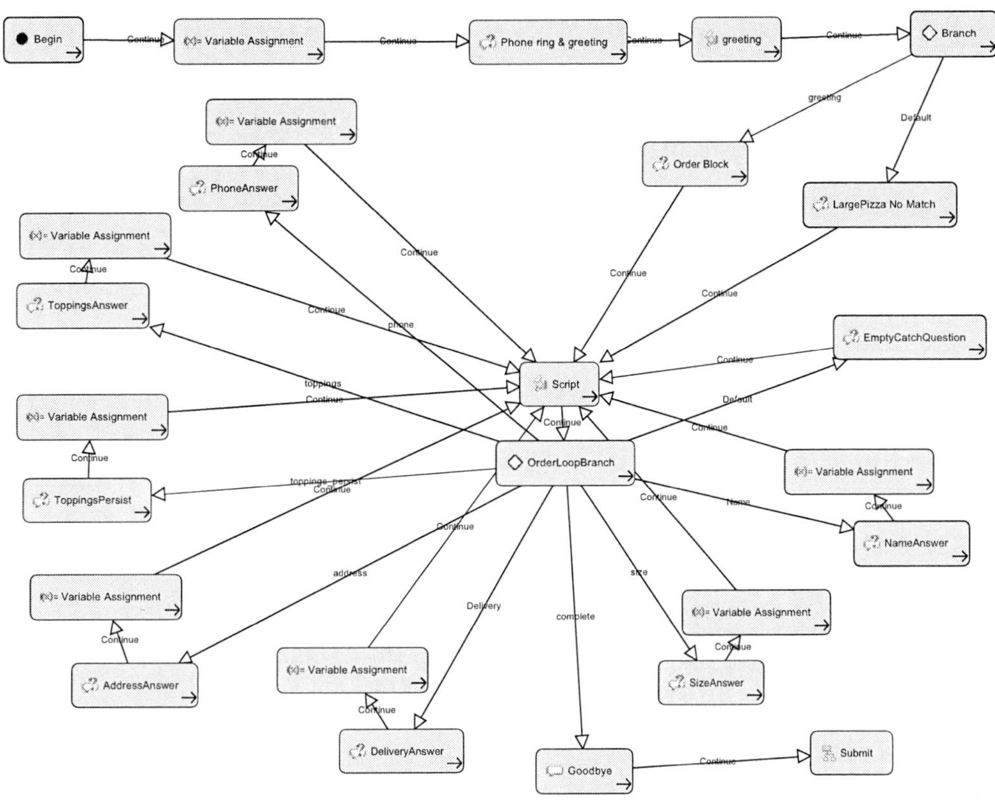

Figure 2: Workflow design of the pizza restaurant-based conversational task deployed and analyzed in this paper. The dialog flow employs a slot-filling structure, where the customer service representative has to ask the automated customer multiple questions in order to fill slots on an order form.

Table 2: The reward table for the simple Pizza Order task

Reward Type	Value	Trigger
PizzaOrdered	3	end-of-call and got all needed info
Mushrooms	1	end-of-call and PizzaOrdered + mushrooms ordered
CompleteInfo	0.5	end-of-call and also got phone #
AngryCustomers	-0.3	any action while customer is annoyed
TimeIsMoney	-0.2	any action

To serve as a measurement model for student performance, the MDP must represent the cognitive model of an ideal pizza shop representative. The full MDP cognitive model consists of a set of actions, a state space, the transition functions, and the reward structure. In Table 1 the action set is listed in the left column, while the transition function is partially illustrated by the probability of effects from each action. The state space is defined by a set of state variables which includes information slot boolean variables such as *gotSize*, *gotAddress*, and *gotCustomerName*. For order information which might affect the choice of future actions, we model the possible values along with a value for "unknown." For example, the *wantsMushroom* variable has three discrete values, 0 for unknown, -1 for "does not want mushrooms," and 1 for "wants mushrooms;" *wantsDelivery* is coded similarly. The possibility of customer annoyance (*isAnnoyed*), which was ommitted from Table 1 for clarity, adds complexity to the dialog task. The cognitive model assumes that every time the customer is asked a question that they have already answered they have a .5 probability of becoming annoyed. This means that while pestering the customer to order mushrooms might result in an mushroom pizza order, it also might result in an annoyed customer. Annoyed customers do not buy pizzas. The final *isSold* state variable gets set to 1 only if all the required information has been gathered:name, topping-preference, size, delivery-or-takeout, and address (in the case of delivery) *and* the customer is not annoyed. Note that the model is intended to reflect the thinking of a competent participant engaging with that task and thus includes stochastic transitions based on "likely" outcomes from different conversational moves. For example, in the test task the customer will always ask for delivery, however the cognitive model for the pizza salesperson gives the probability of the customer wanting delivery as .5, as the representative does not know whether the customer will want delivery until they ask.

The rewards are defined based on actions taken and values of the state variables. Table 2 shows the five reward or cost conditions used for this model. The biggest reward comes from completing the call with a pizza ordered, for a reward of 3 points. An additional point is awarded if the pizza order includes mushrooms and an additional half point is given for collecting the not-required, but nice-to-have phone number of the customer. When customers get annoyed, the whole conversation gets unpleasant causing a cost of 0.3 points (equivalently a reward of -0.3) for every action taken while the customer is annoyed. Finally, each and every action costs 0.2 points. This "time cost" is essential for motivating efficiency in action planning.

Given this specification, the PizzaOrder MDP can generate action probabilities for every possible conversational state, dependent upon the β_j parameter, which we take to be conversational ability as demonstrated by the task.

5 Analyses and Observations

Table 3: Example dialog from a native Hindi speaker $(log(\beta) = -2.75)$.

Speaker	Dialog
Human	Hello, Welcome to Tony's Pizza Shop, How may I help you today?
System	Hi! I'd like to order a large pizza.
Human	Of course. May I know your name please?
System	My name's Mike Anderson.
Human	Sure sir, We have a special on mushroom pizza this week, would you be interested in that?
System	Just cheese, please.
Human	Is that a large or an extra large? A large cheese pizza is $14, andd an extra large is $16.
System	Just cheese, please.
Human	Large cheese pizzza.
System	Just cheese, please.
Human	the pizza will be ready in 30 minutes
System	Alright, thanks! Goodbye!

We ran the MDP measurement model over the full data set of 390 dialogs, estimating the person-specific conversational ability (which, again, is their ability to achieve the pre-specified task goal through conversation, and not their technical language skill) for each dialog as β_j. In our analyses we examine $log(\beta_j)$ which should follow a more familiar normal distribu-

Table 4: Example dialog from a native Tamil speaker $(log(\beta) = -1.26)$.

Speaker	Dialog
Human	hello
System	Hi! I'd like to order a large pizza.
Human	Are you want mushroom pizza?
System	Just cheese, please.
Human	Are you want large one?
System	I'd like a large, please.
Human	It will take 30 minutes to deliver.
System	Alright, thanks! Goodbye!

Table 5: Example dialog from a native Dutch speaker $(log(\beta) = 0.258)$.

Speaker	Dialog
Human	Hi, welcome to Tony's Pizza Shop
System	Hi! I'd like to order a large pizza.
Human	Absolutely, what kind of pizza would you like? We have a special on mushroom pizza, where you can get a medium mushroom pizza for just $1
System	Just cheese, please.
Human	A large cheese pizza is nearly 10 times as expensive as a mushroom
System	Okay, I'd like mushrooms on my pizza as well.
Human	Absolutely, would you like it delivered or do you want to pick it up?
System	Delivery, please.
Human	And what's your name and adress?
System	My name's Mike Anderson.
Human	and your adress?
System	I'm sorry, I didn't catch that. Can you repeat that, please?
Human	and your address?
System	23 Maple Street.
Human	Ok, that will take 30min
System	Alright, thanks! Goodbye!

tion. To evaluate the validity[8] of the resulting estimates, we analyzed them vis-a-vis their reported native language, with the expectation that native-English speakers would generally have higher conversational ability[9]. Recall that our sample included 209 native English speakers, and 181 participants who reported a non-English language as their native tongue.

We observed that participants who reported English as their first language had average $log(\beta_j)$ estimates 0.31 logits higher than players who reported a non-English language as their first language ($t = 3.00, df =$

---

[8]In other words, does this test actually measure what it sets out to measure?

[9]Note that native language is *not* the best variable to use to evaluate validity, merely something that might be a correlate thereof. We used this in lieu of better evidence for establishing validity. Future work will explicitly look into measuring better correlates of validity.

Table 6: Example dialog from a native Indonesian speaker ($log(\beta) = 1.57$).

Speaker	Dialog
Human	Hello, thanks for calling Tony's Pizza. How can I help you?
System	Hi! I'd like to order a large pizza.
Human	Would you like mushrooms on your pizza?
System	Just cheese, please.
Human	Will this be take out or delivery?
System	Delivery, please.
Human	May I have your address?
System	23 Maple Street.
Human	And your phone number?
System	My number's 5550134.
Human	And your name please.
System	My name's Mike Anderson.
Human	Great, we will send the pizza over in 30 minutes.
System	Alright, thanks! Goodbye!

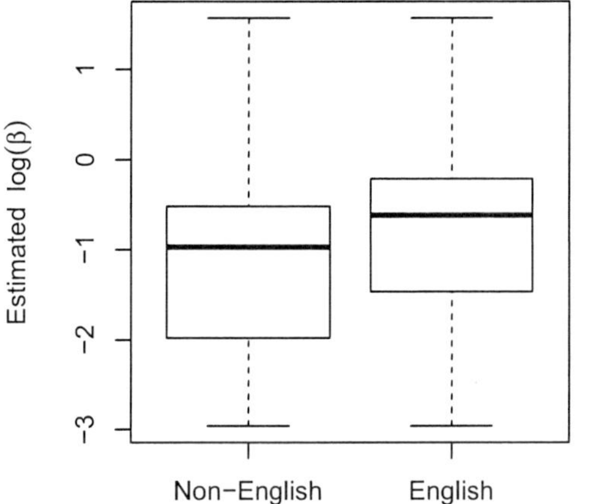

Figure 3: Estimated conversational ability by participant's self-reported primary language.

$374, p = 0.003$). Figure 3 shows a boxplot of the estimated $log(\beta)$ values grouped by native language.

We also compared the dialog-ability estimates to participant-reported satisfaction ratings with respect to the dialog system performance. Here we hypothesize that participants who used phrases that the dialog engine did not recognize would both be dissatisfied with the performance of the system and have low estimated conversational ability. In our sample, 254 participants reported that the system performed well (4 or 5 on a 5-point Likert scale), while 103 participants rated the system at a 3 or lower. Players who rated that the system performed well had an average $log(\beta_j)$ estimate 0.47 logits higher than those who rated the system poorly ($t = 3.64, df = 159.7, p < 0.001$) (Figure 4), which seems to conform with our hypothesis. However, note that these system performance ratings are subjective and might vary depending on the speaker sample and specific conversational item under study.

While these results provide, as yet, only weak validity evidence for the measurement model, they do indicate that the model is performing as expected. We also examined the actual dialogs of different participants interacting with the system in order to better understand how the model of student dialog reflects actual student performance. We have listed example dialogs of non-native participants interacting with the system of different estimated dialog ability and self-reported system performance rating. Note that these are presented as is, without correcting for errors in spelling or grammar. Table 3 shows an example dialog which was assigned a low dialog ability rating ($log(\beta_j)$) as well as a low system performance rating. In this case, while the Hindi speaker mentioned the deal on mushrooms, he asked for the pizza size again even though the automated customer had already given him that information. Per our earlier model specification, this might have 'annoyed' the automated customer. Crucially, though, he failed to ask the automated customer whether he wanted delivery or not, and subsequently his address, which resulted in a low $log(\beta_j)$ score on the task overall. Table 4 shows an example where the automated customer did not get annoyed, but it nonetheless shows clear gaps in the non-native participant's conversational competence in achieving the goal of maximizing the sale. In contrast to these examples, the Indonesian speaker (Table 6) asked the automated customer for each of the requisite pieces of information to complete the task successfully resulting in a successful interaction that received a high $log(\beta_j)$ score, despite the fact that he didn't sell the customer mushrooms. A native speaker of Dutch (Table 5) who performed well on the task in general, but was scored slightly lower ($log(\beta_j) = 0.258$) did persist in selling mushroom toppings to the automated customer while asking for his name and address, but incorrectly spelled the word 'address'. However, the participant caught this error in the next dialog turn, ultimately resulting in successful completion. Note that there were also cases that received a high $log(\beta_j)$ score with low system performance ratings, many of which were due to system natural language understanding issues. Going forward, we will aim to improve this aspect of the system to improve user experience and modeling accuracy.

6   Discussion and Outlook

We have presented a Markov decision process-based measurement model (MDP-MM) for the assessment of of learners' ability to complete a simple customer interaction dialog task. We put forth a formal mathematical description of the model including a maximum likelihood based method to estimate the parameters of the model given input data. On applying the model to crowdsourced customer services dialog interactions at a pizza restaurant, we observed that the model ability ($log(\beta_j)$) estimate is able to differentiate between native and non-native speakers of English and partic-

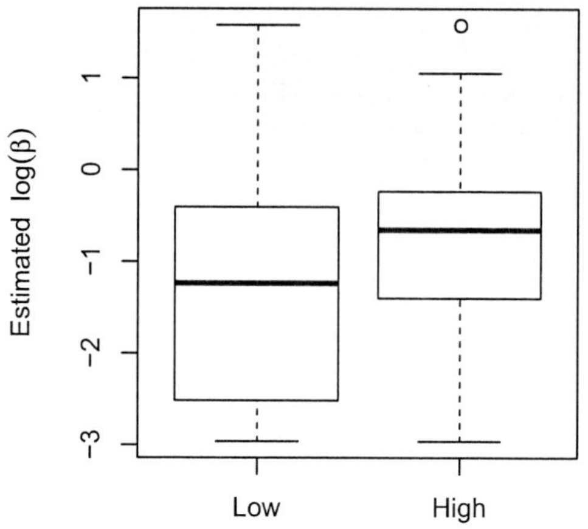

Figure 4: Estimated conversational ability by participant's rating of the system's performance, where "Low" indicates a rating of 1, 2, or 3 and "High" indicates a rating of 4 or 5 on the 5-point Likert scale.

ipant ratings of system performance in a statistically significant manner. Note that the MDP-MM is particularly useful over traditional methods of measurement when the dialogs increase in complexity and branching, and the resulting paths cannot be easily enumerated for scoring.

We plan to investigate several lines of research going forward. First, while we have shown the model's efficacy in capturing conversational ability of participants in successfully completing a given task to a certain extent, neither the degree of nativeness nor their rating of system performance are ideal correlates to establish the validity of the model. A more appropriate variable might be, for instance, an 3rd-party expert rating of their conversational ability (where experts could be English language teachers, for instance). In addition, we hand-crafted a specific set of actions, transition probabilities and rewards for the model presented in this paper based on our subjective expertise. Careful selection of these parameters is important because they directly influence model behavior. Future iterations could benefit from a more scientifically objective method of model specification. We will also need more data from more conversational items and participants to concretely establish the utility of the model and its applicability to a wide variety of dialog use cases in a statistically significant manner.

Second, while this paper has focused on conversational task ability, our longer term goal is to apply such a model to the measurement of conversational language proficiency. This will require modifications to both the task (the goals, dialog flow design, natural language understanding and dialog management logic) as well as the specific variables we measure (such as fluency, language use, vocabulary and grammatical accuracy, prag-

matics and historical discourse context, among others).

Third, while the proposed model assumes that the state of the system is known at every given point of time for simplicity, relaxing this assumption is a natural next step. In such a case, we would have to use a *partially observable* extension of the MDP-MM model (or a POMDP-MM) that explicitly models the uncertainty in the observation process that estimates the state of the system at every time step.

A fourth important future research direction, as mentioned in this paper's introductory paragraphs, involves the integration of statistical measurement of student conversational ability with dialog management, especially for computer-assisted language learning (CALL) or formative assessment applications. Such integration would leverage the measurement of learner conversational ability and/or language proficiency into the dialog manager, allowing one to adapt the conversational instruction flow both based on the content of what the learner said, as well as his/her conversational ability. In addition, popular statistical dialog management modules are based on POMDPs, which might allow for easier combination with the POMDP-based measurement model into a unified model, given that both share the underlying mathematical framework. For example, in such a scenario, one could imagine that the user action model, user goal model and dialog model in a POMDP-based dialog manager (that estimate the user's next action and state, and the next dialog system state, respectively, as described in Young, 2006) would now depend (and be conditional) on the user's conversational ability and/or language proficiency estimate.

Finally, we also plan to evaluate model efficacy and integrability into a full-blown spoken dialog scenario (as opposed to text chat, as in this paper). In addition, the current paper uses simple regular expression-based natural language understanding; incorporating more accurate statistical natural language understanding modules could further improve model performance and estimation accuracy. Such improvements and the early nature of the model notwithstanding, the relative lack of previous work in measuring conversational ability in CALL dialogue and the results presented in this paper speak to the necessity and potential of such measurement models in developing more comprehensive and effective CALL applications.

References

American Educational Research Association, American Psychological Association, and National Council on Measurement in Education. 1999. *Standards for educational and psychological testing*. American Educational Research Association.

C.L. Baker, R. Saxe, and J.B. Tenenbaum. 2009. Action understanding as inverse planning. *Cognition* 113(3):329–349.

C.L. Baker, R.R. Saxe, and J.B. Tenenbaum. 2011. Bayesian theory of mind: Modeling joint belief-desire attribution. In *Proceedings of the Thirty-Third Annual Conference of the Cognitive Science Society*. page 2469–2474.

D. Bohus, A. Raux, T. Harris, M. Eskenazi, and A. Rudnicky. 2007. Olympus: An Open-Source Framework for Conversational Spoken Language Interface Research. In *Proc. of the HLT-NAACL*. Rochester, USA.

P. De Boeck and M. Wilson. 2004. *Explanatory item response models: A generalized linear and nonlinear approach*. Springer Verlag.

Wieland Eckert, Esther Levin, and Roberto Pieraccini. 1997. User modeling for spoken dialogue system evaluation. In *Automatic Speech Recognition and Understanding, 1997. Proceedings., 1997 IEEE Workshop on*. IEEE, pages 80–87.

Kate Forbes-Riley and Diane Litman. 2011. Benefits and challenges of real-time uncertainty detection and adaptation in a spoken dialogue computer tutor. *Speech Communication* 53(9):1115–1136.

Arthur C Graesser, Patrick Chipman, Brian C Haynes, and Andrew Olney. 2005. Autotutor: An intelligent tutoring system with mixed-initiative dialogue. *Education, IEEE Transactions on* 48(4):612–618.

Arno Hartholt, David Traum, Stacy C Marsella, Ari Shapiro, Giota Stratou, Anton Leuski, Louis-Philippe Morency, and Jonathan Gratch. 2013. All together now. In *Intelligent Virtual Agents*. Springer, pages 368–381.

Neil T Heffernan and Kenneth R Koedinger. 2002. An intelligent tutoring system incorporating a model of an experienced human tutor. In *International Conference on Intelligent Tutoring Systems*. Springer, pages 596–608.

Eric Horvitz and Tim Paek. 2001. Harnessing models of users goals to mediate clarification dialog in spoken language systems. In *International Conference on User Modeling*. Springer, pages 3–13.

Ronald A. Howard. 1960. *Dynamic Programming and Markov Processes*. The MIT Press, Cambridge, Mass., 1st edition.

Filip Jurčíček, Ondřej Dušek, Ondřej Plátek, and Lukáš Žilka. 2014. Alex: A statistical dialogue systems framework. In *Text, Speech and Dialogue*. Springer, pages 587–594.

Filip Jurcicek, Simon Keizer, Milica Gašic, Francois Mairesse, Blaise Thomson, Kai Yu, and Steve Young. 2011. Real user evaluation of spoken dialogue systems using amazon mechanical turk. In *Proceedings of INTERSPEECH*. volume 11.

Robert Kass. 2012. Student modeling in intelligent tutoring systems–implications for user modeling. *User Models in Dialog Systems* page 386.

Dongho Kim, Hyeong Seop Sim, Kee-Eung Kim, J Kim, JW Sung, et al. 2008. Effects of user modeling on pomdp-based dialogue systems. In *9th Annual Conference of the International Speech Communication Association, 2008*. Interspeech, pages 1169–1172.

Alfred Kobsa. 1990. User modeling in dialog systems: Potentials and hazards. *AI & society* 4(3):214–231.

M. LaMar, R. S.J.D Baker, and Samuel Greiff. 2017. Methods for assessing inquiry: Machine-learned and theoretical. In *Design recommendations for Intelligent Tutoring Systems: Assessment*, volume 5.

Michelle LaMar. 2018. Markov decision process measurement model. *Psychometrika* .

Esther Levin, Roberto Pieraccini, and Wieland Eckert. 2000. A stochastic model of human-machine interaction for learning dialog strategies. *IEEE Transactions on speech and audio processing* 8(1):11–23.

Ian McGraw, Chia-ying Lee, I Lee Hetherington, Stephanie Seneff, and Jim Glass. 2010. Collecting voices from the cloud. In *LREC*.

Joel Michael, Allen Rovick, Michael Glass, Yujian Zhou, and Martha Evens. 2003. Learning from a computer tutor with natural language capabilities. *Interactive Learning Environments* 11(3):233–262.

Robert J. Mislevy, Russell Almond, Lou Dibello, Frank Jenkins, Linda Steinberg, Duanli Yan, and Deniz Senturk. 2002. Modeling conditional probabilities in complex educational assessments. CSE tech. rep., The National Center for Research on Evaluation, Standards, Student Testing, Cen- ter for Studies in Education, University of California, Los Angeles, Los Angeles, CA.

Natalie K Person, AC Graesser, L Bautista, EC Mathews, Tutoring Research Group, et al. 2001. Evaluating student learning gains in two versions of autotutor. *Artificial intelligence in education: AI-ED in the wired and wireless future* pages 286–293.

Olivier Pietquin. 2005. *A framework for unsupervised learning of dialogue strategies*. Presses univ. de Louvain.

Heather Pon-Barry, Karl Schultz, Elizabeth Owen Bratt, Brady Clark, and Stanley Peters. 2006. Responding to student uncertainty in spoken tutorial dialogue systems. *International Journal of Artificial Intelligence in Education* 16(2):171–194.

Anna N. Rafferty, Michelle M. LaMar, and Thomas L. Griffiths. 2015. Inferring Learners' Knowledge From Their Actions. *Cognitive Science* 39(3):584–618. https://doi.org/10.1111/cogs.12157.

Vikram Ramanarayanan, David Suendermann-Oeft, Patrick Lange, Alexei V Ivanov, Keelan Evanini, Zhou Yu, Eugene Tsuprun, and Yao Qian. 2016. Bootstrapping development of a cloud-based spoken dialog system in the educational domain from scratch using crowdsourced data. *ETS Research Report Series* pages 1–7.

Vikram Ramanarayanan, David Suendermann-Oeft, Patrick Lange, Robert Mundkowsky, Alexei V Ivanov, Zhou Yu, Yao Qian, and Keelan Evanini. 2017. Assembling the Jigsaw: How Multiple Open Standards Are Synergistically Combined in the HALEF Multimodal Dialog System. In *Multimodal Interaction with W3C Standards*, Springer, pages 295–310.

Emmanuel Rayner, Ian Frank, Cathy Chua, Nikolaos Tsourakis, and Pierrette Bouillon. 2011. For a fistful of dollars: Using crowd-sourcing to evaluate a spoken language call application .

Vasile Rus, Sidney DMello, Xiangen Hu, and Arthur Graesser. 2013. Recent advances in conversational intelligent tutoring systems. *AI magazine* 34(3):42–54.

Mark D. Shermis. 2014. State-of-the-art automated essay scoring: Competition, results, and future directions from a United States demonstration. *Assessing Writing* 20:53–76. https://doi.org/10.1016/j.asw.2013.04.001.

Alexandria Katarina Vail and Kristy Elizabeth Boyer. 2014. Adapting to personality over time: examining the effectiveness of dialogue policy progressions in task-oriented interaction. In *Proceedings of the 15th Annual SIGDIAL Meeting on Discourse and Dialogue*. pages 41–50.

Kurt VanLehn, Collin Lynch, Linwood Taylor, Anders Weinstein, Robert Shelby, Kay Schulze, Don Treacy, and Mary Wintersgill. 2002. Minimally invasive tutoring of complex physics problem solving. In *Intelligent Tutoring Systems: 6th International Conference, ITS 2002, Biarritz, France and San Sebastian, Spain, June 2-7, 2002. Proceedings*. Springer, pages 43–55.

Lawrence G. Weiss and Patricia Zureich. 2008. A primer on psychometrics: The important points for speech–language pathologists. *Pearson Education, Inc.* 24:1–12.

Jason D Williams and Steve Young. 2007. Partially observable markov decision processes for spoken dialog systems. *Computer Speech & Language* 21(2):393–422.

Steve Young. 2006. Using POMDPs for dialog management. In *Spoken Language Technology Workshop, 2006. IEEE*. IEEE, pages 8–13.

Steve Young, Milica Gašić, Simon Keizer, François Mairesse, Jost Schatzmann, Blaise Thomson, and Kai Yu. 2010. The hidden information state model: A practical framework for pomdp-based spoken dialogue management. *Computer Speech & Language* 24(2):150–174.

Generating Feedback for English Foreign Language Exercises

Björn Rudzewitz   Ramon Ziai
Kordula De Kuthy   Verena Möller   Florian Nuxoll   Detmar Meurers

Collaborative Research Center 833
Department of Linguistics, ICALL Research Group[*]
LEAD Graduate School & Research Network
University of Tübingen

Abstract

While immediate feedback on learner language is often discussed in the Second Language Acquisition literature (e.g., Mackey 2006), few systems used in real-life educational settings provide helpful, metalinguistic feedback to learners.

In this paper, we present a novel approach leveraging task information to generate the expected range of well-formed and ill-formed variability in learner answers along with the required diagnosis and feedback. We combine this offline generation approach with an online component that matches the actual student answers against the pre-computed hypotheses.

The results obtained for a set of 33 thousand answers of 7th grade German high school students learning English show that the approach successfully covers frequent answer patterns. At the same time, paraphrases and meaning errors require a more flexible alignment approach, for which we are planning to complement the method with the CoMiC approach successfully used for the analysis of reading comprehension answers (Meurers et al., 2011).

1 Introduction

In Second Language Acquisition research and Foreign Language Teaching and Learning practice, the importance of individualized, immediate feedback on learner production for learner proficiency development has long been emphasized (e.g., Mackey 2006). In the classroom, the teacher is generally the only source of reliable, accurate feedback available to students, which poses a well-known practical problem: in a class of 30 students, with substantial individual differences warranting individual feedback to students, it is highly challenging for a teacher to provide feedback in class or, in a timely fashion, on homework.

Intelligent Language Tutoring Systems (ILTS) are one possible means of addressing this problem. For form-focused feedback, ILTS have traditionally relied on online processing of learner language (Heift and Schulze, 2007; Meurers, 2012). They model ill-formed variation either explicitly via so-called mal-rules (e.g., Schneider and McCoy 1998) or by allowing for violations in the language system using a constraint relaxation mechanism (e.g., L'Haire and Faltin 2003).

One problem with such approaches is that they do not take into account what the learner was trying to do with the language they wrote, e.g., which task or exercise they were trying to complete. Yet the potential well-formed and ill-formed variability exhibited by learner language can lead to vast search spaces so that integrating top-down, task information is particularly relevant for obtaining valid interpretations of learner language (Meurers, 2015; Meurers and Dickinson, 2017). Given that incorrect feedback is highly problematic for language learners, ensuring valid interpretations is particularly important. Combining the bottom-up analysis of learner data with top-down expectations, such as those that can be derived from an exercise being completed, can also be relevant for obtaining efficient processing.

In this paper, we present an approach that pursues this idea of integrating task-based information into the analysis of learner language by combining offline hypothesis generation based on the exercise with online answer analysis in order to provide immediate and reliable form-focused feedback. Basing our approach on curricular demands and the exercise properties resulting from these demands, we generate the space of well-formed and ill-formed variability expected of the learner answers, using the well-formed target answers provided for the exercises as a starting point. We thus avoid the problems introduced by directly

---

[*] http://icall-research.de

Proceedings of the Thirteenth Workshop on Innovative Use of NLP for Building Educational Applications, pages 127–136
New Orleans, Louisiana, June 5, 2018. ©2018 Association for Computational Linguistics

analyzing potentially ill-formed learner language. Since generation is done ahead of time, before learners actually interact with the system, we also avoid the performance bottleneck associated with creating and exploring the full search space at run time. The resulting system can be precise and fast in providing feedback on the grammar concepts in a curriculum underlying a given set of exercises.

The paper is organized as follows: Section 2 discusses relevant related work before section 3 introduces our system and section 4 provides an overview on the data we elicit. In section 5, we dive into the feedback architecture and explain both the offline and online component of the mechanism in detail. Section 6 then provides both a quantitative and a qualitative evaluation before section 7 concludes the paper.

2 Related Work

Intelligent Language Tutoring Systems (ILTS) proposed in the literature range from highly ambitious conversation machines (e.g., DeSmedt 1995) to more modest workbook-like approaches (e.g., Heift 2003; Nagata 2002; Amaral and Meurers 2011). However, as discussed by Heift and Schulze (2007), the vast majority of the systems are research prototypes that have never seen real-life testing or use. We therefore limit our discussion here primarily to practical systems that are in use for foreign language learning.

In the domain of general-purpose tools, there are a number of writing aids and grammar checkers available, such as *Grammarly* (http://grammarly.com) and *LanguageTool* (http://languagetool.org). They offer grammar and spelling error correction for arbitrary English text and are intended to assist (non-native) writers of English in composing texts. Such general-purpose systems do not have any information on what the writer is trying to accomplish with the text. As a result, while local grammatical problems such as subject-verb agreement are well-within reach for such tools, the identification of contextually inappropriate forms, such as wrong tense use in a narrative, require task information.

One step further in the direction of task-based language learning, one finds tools such as *duolingo* (von Ahn, 2013). *duolingo* offers exercises for learners of various languages, mainly based on translation into or from the target language. Learners can input free-text answers and obtain immediate feedback from the system. However, while for certain phenomena the feedback is quite explicit and accurate (Settles and Meeder, 2016, p. 1849), cases such as the one in Figure 1 are not handled appropriately.

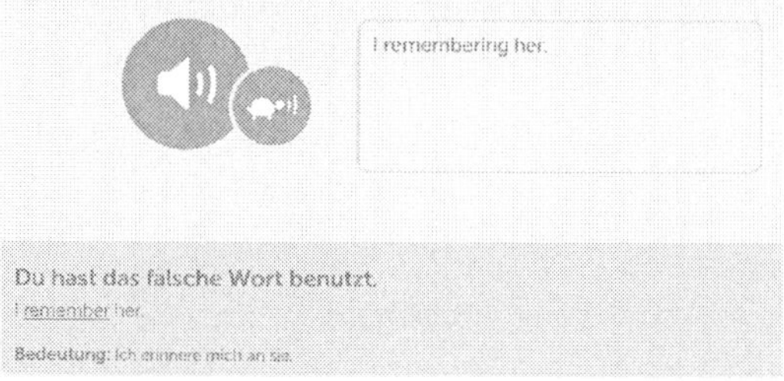

Figure 1: Problematic feedback in duolingo

The learner used the *-ing*-form of the verb *to remember* in place of the simple present. Instead of identifying the form and recognizing that the lemma is the same as that in the expected answer, *duolingo* responds with 'You used the wrong word', which is misleading the learner to select another word. For more appropriate feedback, more metalinguistic information about the identified and the expected form would be needed. However, manually specifying such information quickly becomes infeasible even for relatively closed task types, as shown by Nagata (2009, p. 563) in the context of the *Robo-Sensei* system.

Laarmann-Quante (2016) proposes an approach for the diagnosis of spelling errors in the writing of German children that was independently developed but is conceptually similar to the perspective we pursue in this paper. Instead of attempting to process the erroneous forms directly, Laarmann-Quante obtains phonological analyses for correct spellings and uses rewrite rules that emulate typical misspellings to derive alternatives that can then be matched against actual input. However, the approach is limited to spelling errors and relies heavily on a model of German orthography. It does not target other linguistic levels of analysis, such as morphology and syntax, and the potential interaction of well-formed and ill-formed variability at the sentence level.

3 The Tutoring System

The feedback mechanism discussed in this article is implemented as part of a web-based online workbook *FeedBook* (Rudzewitz et al., 2017; Meurers et al., 2018). The foreign language tutoring system is an adaptation of a paper workbook for a 7th grade English textbook approved for use in German high schools. The FeedBook provides an interface for students to select and work on exercises. For exercises that aim at teaching grammar topics, students receive automatic, immediate feedback by the system informing them whether their answer is correct (via a green check mark) or *why* their answer is incorrect (via red color, highlighting of the error span, and a metalinguistic feedback message). The message is formulated as scaffolding feedback, intended to guide the learner towards the solution, without giving it away. The process of entering an answer and receiving feedback can be repeated, incrementally leading the student to the correct answer. If there are multiple errors in a learner response, the system presents the feedback one at a time.

Students can save and resume work, interact with the system to receive automatic feedback and revise their answers, and eventually submit their final solutions to the teacher. In case the answers are all correct in a selected exercise, the system grades the submission automatically, requiring no work by the teacher. For those answers that are not correct with respect to a given target answer, the teacher can manually annotate the with feedback parallel to the traditional process with a paper workbook. Any such manual feedback is saved in a feedback memory and suggested automatically to the teacher in case the form occurs in another learner response to this exercise. The system provides students with immediate feedback in circumstances where they would normally not receive it, or only after long delay needed for collecting and manually marking up homework assignments, while at the same time relieving teachers from very repetitive and time-consuming work. The exercises are embedded in a full web application with a messaging system for communication, a profile management including e-mail settings, tutorials for using the system, classroom management, and various functions orthogonal to the NLP-related issues (cf. Rudzewitz et al., 2017).

4   Elicited Data

The FeedBook system is being used since October 2016 in several German secondary schools as part of the regular 7th grade English curriculum. The data analysis discussed here is based on a March 2018 snapshot of the data. We collected 6341 submissions of complete exercises by 538 7th grade students from whom we received written permission to use their data in pseudonymized form for research.

From the total of 234 tasks implemented in the system, in the current system version 111 provide the immediate feedback that is introduced and evaluated in this paper. The feedback-enabled tasks include 64 short answer tasks (usually one sentence as input) and 47 fill-in-the-blanks tasks (usually one word to one phrase as input).

The frequency distribution in Figure 2 shows the number of submissions (y-axis) per task in the system, ranked from most frequent to least frequent (x-axis). Blue bars denote that the task provides immediate feedback, and yellow bars indicate that the system does not provide any automatic feedback (these are the tasks where the teacher can manually provide feedback through the system). The figure shows a tendency that more submissions exist for tasks that provide immediate feedback: out of the top 50 most worked on tasks, 36 of them (72%) provide immediate feedback. These 36 tasks are balanced between 17 fill-in-the-blanks and 19 short answer tasks.

Each submission for a feedback-enabled task provides an interaction log that stores intermediate answers and the feedback that the system provided to each answer. In section 6, we use these intermediate answers in an evaluation of the feedback approach, after introducing the architecture in the next section.

5   Feedback Architecture

In this section, we describe the feedback mechanism implemented as part of the tutoring system. The main idea behind our approach is that identifying the well-formed and ill-formed variability of possible learner answers elicited by different tasks is the key to providing precise feedback. Our feedback mechanism thus relies on well-formed target answers available for each task and generates hypothesis about possible learner answers on the basis of these target answers. This is a key difference to the use of traditional mal-rules, which operate on learner language and thus need to analyze the potentially ill-formed interlanguage of students: instead of trying to model learner language, we start from the standard, native language, for which most computational linguistic models have been developed.

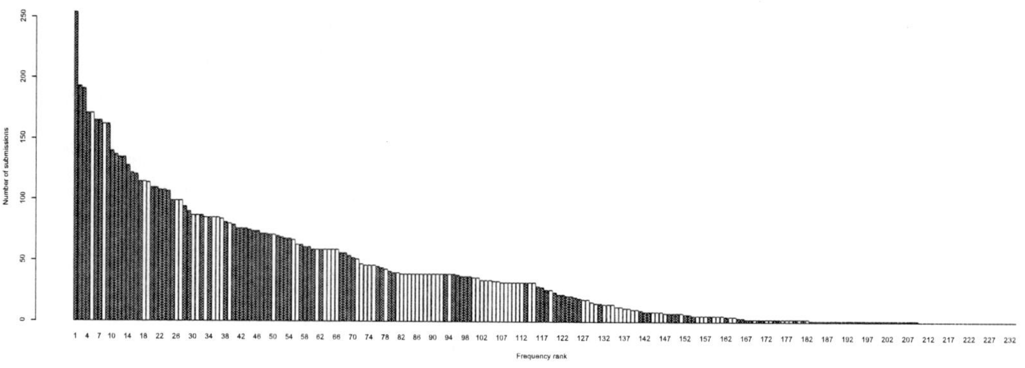

Figure 2: Frequency of submissions per task (blue = immediate feedback support, yellow = no automatic feedback).

The architecture allowing the system to provide immediate feedback consists of two parts: an offline generation process of hypotheses modelling possible well-formed and ill-formed learner answers, and an online matching process that takes the generated hypotheses and matches them in a flexible manner with learner data.

5.1 Offline Hypothesis Generation

The automatic hypothesis generation mechanism works in three steps: i) linguistically analyzing the target answer of an exercise, ii) applying rules to generate alternative forms, and iii) storing the generated forms together with an error diagnosis. In the following, these steps are explained in detail.

As a first step, each target answer of an exercise is analyzed with the help of different NLP tools in order to build a rich linguistic representation as a basis for all further analyses. Table 1 shows the tools employed for analysis.

task	tool
segmentation	ClearNLP
	(Choi and Palmer, 2012)
part-of-speech tagging	ClearNLP
dependency parsing	ClearNLP
lemmatization	Morpha
	(Minnen et al., 2001)
morphological analysis	Sfst (Schmid, 2005)

Table 1: NLP tasks and tools

The analyses are encoded in a UIMA Common Analysis Structure (CAS, Götz and Suhre, 2004). A CAS is a source text with multiple layers of annotations, such as a token annotation layer or a dependency-tree annotation layer. By using a DKPro wrapper (de Castilho and Gurevych, 2014)

around the UIMA annotators, we ensure flexibility and interchangeability of the specific implementations of the NLP tools.

On the CAS representation of the analyses, we run 40 custom UIMA annotators to explicitly annotate further linguistic properties such as complex tenses or irregular comparative forms. The annotators and the subsequently applied rules described below are designed to cover all grammar topics in the 7th grade English curriculum.

The CAS is then used as input to rules that introduce changes modeling the space of well-formed and ill-formed variability. Some rules introduce changes that yield grammatical forms that are not appropriate in this task context, for example changing the tense of verbs. Other rules generate forms that are never grammatical in any context, such as a regular past tense inflection applied to the lemma of an irregular verb.

When introducing a change, the current CAS is first cloned to yield a deep copy. Then this clone is edited by changing the source text and all linguistic analysis layers that refer to the source text. Furthermore a diagnosis denoting both the type and span of the change introduced as well as the category of the original form is added. The diagnosis thus makes it possible to see what change has been introduced related to which part of the data. If a previous diagnosis was present, it is put into a history list and replaced by the new diagnosis.

For rules generating well-formed alternatives, such as tense changes or contraction expansions, we run the NLP tools used for analyzing the initial CAS on the modified clone and then keep the annotations inside the span that has changed in the rule application. For ill-formed alternatives,

130

we manually encode the linguistic analyses of the changed forms. In any case, the result is a minimally modified clone with an updated, full linguistic analysis. This input-output symmetry makes it possible to apply rules to the output of other rules. This is necessary when chains of rules need to be applied, such as first changing the tense and then altering the verbal morphology of this tense's realization. Each rule is self-contained in that it encodes the conditions under which it applies and the complete logic of the changes when applied.

For the purpose of yielding only desired chains of rule applications and to avoid cycles where two or more rules would add and remove the same forms repeatedly, we group rules in so-called "rule layers". A rule layer is a sorted set of rules that are applied in parallel and do not influence each other. Each of the rules in a layer that is applicable yields a minimally modified clone that serves as input to the second layer of rules. By introducing a "self-copy rule" in each layer we ensure that the original, unmodified target answer percolates through all layers and each rule in a deeper layer can be applied to the original answer as well as to the modified clones.

The algorithm is inspired by graph search algorithms, especially breadth-first graph search (Moore, 1959). In our case, the nodes in the network are CAS data structures with a rule application history, and the edges in the graph are instances of rule applications. An edge can only be traversed if the conditions of applicability defined in the corresponding rule are met. We thus restrict the search space based on task information, here: the linguistic analysis of the target answer(s). The depth of the search tree corresponds to our rule layers. Figure 3 illustrates the process of generating target hypotheses from a target answer by combining multiple layers of rule applications. Table 2 shows a small excerpt from the

set of answers generated for a tense and and for a comparative target answer. The table illustrates that the output of any previous layer serves as input to deeper layers. Every hypothesis generated at any layer is saved to the data base.

target	layer 1	layer 2	layer 3
are you doing	are you doing	are you doing	are you doing
	were you doing	were you do	was you do
	have you been doing	have you been do	have you been dos
	had you been doing	had you been do	had you been dos
	will you do	are you do	will you dos
	did you do	…	did you dos
	…		are you dos
			was you doing
			is you dos
			is you doing
			…
friendlier	friendlier	friendlier	friendlier
	more friendly	more friendlier	most friendlier
	friendlyer	more friendlyer	most friendlyer
	…		friendliest
		…	friendlyest
			…

Table 2: Examples for generated answer hypotheses

5.2 From Diagnoses to Feedback Messages

To connect error diagnoses with concrete feedback, a language teacher inspected the data we had collected during one year of system use in schools and compiled a list of most common error types made by students with respect to five areas of grammar topics in the curriculum: tenses, comparatives, gerunds, relative clauses, reflexive pronouns. The teacher then formulated error templates for these error types, which specify precisely what linguistic information needs to be present and the (parameterized) feedback message to be generated. To ensure that the conditions under which a teacher would provide a particular feedback and the formulation of the feedback is as close as possible to the real-life educational settings in schools, our project team includes teachers with experience teaching 7th grade English in German high schools, who reduced their teaching load to take on this research project.

Figure 4 shows an example template listing the

Target form:	SIMPLE PAST
Diagnosed form:	SIMPLE PRESENT
Side conditions:	IF-CLAUSE
Feedback message:	"With conditional clauses (type 2), we use the simple past in the if-clause, not the simple present."

Figure 4: Example error template

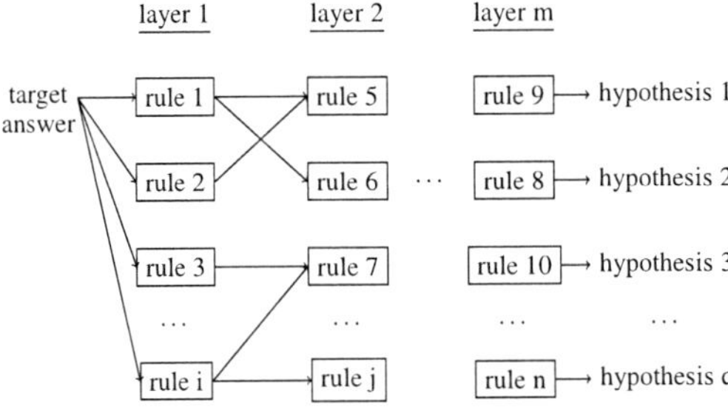

Figure 3: Multi-layered hypotheses generation process

131

required target and diagnosed forms as well as necessary side condition along with the resulting feedback message.

Every error diagnosis generated by the system as described above is associated with the most specific compatible feedback template prior to saving a diagnosis in the data base. The system extracts the diagnosis associated with the CAS and all its side conditions, as, for example, signal words for tense forms. For certain phenomena, such as tense confusions, multiple templates exist with varying degrees of specificity depending on the presence of additional linguistic evidence, so that the template providing the best match with the diagnosis can be selected.

The resulting feedback provided by the system for a typical tense error is illustrated in Figure 5. The learner input *will feel* is not correct with respect to the task context requiring present tense. The will future form *will feel* was generated as one of the target hypothesis for the correct target answer *feel*. The student answer in Figure 5 can thus be matched against this generated target hypothesis and the error template associated with this form is displayed as immediate feedback.

5.3 Flexible Online Matching

The generate-and-retrieve approach described above works well for relatively constrained learner input, as it occurs for example with fill-in-the-blanks tasks. However, there are also more open form-oriented tasks in the workbook, where learners have to enter full sentences to practice certain forms, but the lexical material is constrained by the task instruction. In these tasks, students often use slight variations of our pre-computed hypotheses, but make the same systematic errors. Consider the minimal example of an agreement error, as illustrated by the generated hypothesis *he walk*, into which the learner has inserted an additional adverb in *he always walk*. We tackle this issue by allowing for partial matches of target hypotheses, where the obligatory part of the hypothesis must be matched, but an optional remainder can be varied. In the example, both *he* and *walk* would be obligatory to match, whereas *always* is optional.

Technically, the approach is realized via information retrieval on stored target hypothesis forms. We use Lucene (https://lucene.apache.org) for indexing and retrieval, employing the same linguistic pre-processing as in the hypothesis generation

step in order to ensure comparability of student answers and target hypotheses. Given a list of hits returned by Lucene, we compare the student input to each of the hits and use the first hypothesis where the student answer satisfies all of the matching constraints.

Figure 6 shows an example from a task where students need to enter the correct tenses in conditional clauses. In the example input shown, the student left out the word *more* that is part of the correct answer, and also used pronouns instead of proper names. But since this is not relevant for the diagnosis of the first tense error here, we can still show feedback based on the stored generated hypothesis. Note that the second tense error, simple present *feels* instead of *would feel*, is handled by a subsequent feedback message once the student submits the update answer. This is in line with previous research on the effectiveness of feedback showing that it is preferable to alert the student of one problem at a time (cf., e.g., Heift 2003).

5.4 Individual Immediate Feedback

When students enter an answer into a field of a feedback-enabled exercise, our system executes the algorithm in Figure 7. Using a multi-fallback strategy, the algorithm ensures that more complex feedback retrieval is only tried when simpler strategies (such as a direct match) have failed. Since the student is expected to change their answer upon receiving system feedback, the approach aims at efficiently guiding the student to the correct answer in multiple interactive steps.

6 Evaluation

In this section, we describe an evaluation of the feedback currently given by our system. In a real end-to-end evaluation of a tutoring system, the most interesting evaluation would be to assess the learning gains for the students. We are currently designing a randomized controlled field study for just such an evaluation involving several classes in the coming school year. At this point, however, we can at least report offline evaluation metrics calculated on the student answer data that we collected so far. We plan to make a more comprehensive data set available for research after having conducted the full-year intervention study.

Based on the elicited data introduced in section 4, we selected all individual student answers from the interaction logs of tasks with active, im-

Figure 5: Feedback on tense error

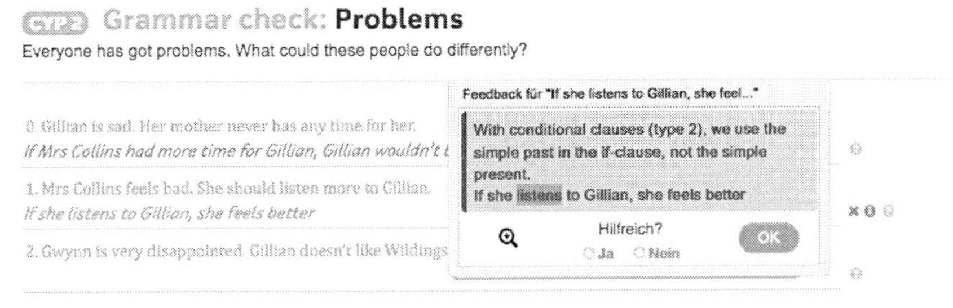

Target answer (for reference):

Figure 6: Student answer including multiple errors with feedback based on a partial hypothesis match

```
if student input == target answer:
  visualize this with green check mark
  -> DONE
else:
  retrieve direct hypothesis matches
  if there are direct matches:
    show associated feedback
  else:
    perform token-level Lucene query
    if there are Lucene hits:
      for every hypothesis:
        if student answer matches criteria:
          show associated feedback
      else:
        show default feedback
```

Figure 7: Feedback algorithm (simplified pseudo-code)

mediate feedback. However, since some of these tasks have meaning-oriented goals (e.g., comprehension, translation), which we do not yet provide feedback on, we excluded data from tasks where the title clearly indicated such a goal (e.g., "Reading: …"). On the other end of the spectrum, we excluded tasks where students only need to enter single characters as part of words.

The remaining set of 33,589 individual student answers (6,755 distinct types) was provided as input to the feedback algorithm of Figure 7.

Note that this data set consists of the authentic learner answers entered into the system at any stage of development. So we run the current version of the feedback algorithm on all the authentic learner data to obtain a complete, current picture of current system performance.

19,809 of the answers were identified as identical to the target answer after basic normalization (upper/lower case, spaces, Unicode punctuation).

Since we do not have gold standard feedback labels for the overall data set, and obtaining them would be a time-consuming annotation task by itself, every student answer that diverges from the target answer must be treated as potentially erroneous and in need of feedback. Note, however, that this diverging set also includes well-formed paraphrases, meaning errors, and form errors we do not intend to provide specific, meta-linguistic feedback on (e.g., spelling).

6.1 Quantitative Results

Table 3 summarizes the results (TA = target answer). We report both answer type counts and answer token counts. For the answers differing from the target answer (i.e., the ones the system provided feedback on), we also report the percentage relative to the total number of answers differing from the target forms.

	# types	# tokens	
identical to TA	342	19,809	
default feedback	5,717	10,297	74.72%
specific feedback	696	3,483	**25.28%**
total	6,755	33,589	

Table 3: Quantitative evaluation results

For the majority of differing answers (74.72%) the system provides default feedback, where a diff with the target answer is shown to the student, as exemplified by Figure 8. As the example illustrates and we will argue in section 6.2, default feedback does not necessarily mean the system missed a potentially relevant error, but can also mean that the default feedback is appropriate or the type of task does not lend itself well to form-focused feedback.

In 25.28% of the differing answers, the system was able to give specific, meta-linguistic feedback, with well-formed and ill-formed tense variation being by far the most productive error pattern. Note that while 696 answer types with specific feedback may seem small, they account for roughly five times as many instances (3,483), showing that it is well worth the effort to model specific, typical error patterns. In comparison, the 10,297 default cases are distributed across 5,717 types, each occurring only about two times, suggesting that there is a long tail of rarely occurring error types that one may not want to model and provide dedicated, meta-linguistic feedback for.

To further analyze this long tail, we calculated the edit distance between the differing answer types and their respective target answers, and investigated the percentage of specific feedback for different edit distance ranges. We found that for the range below the first edit distance tertile, the percentage was at 30.8% and thus higher than the average 25.28%. On the other hand, for the range above the second tertile of edit distances, the percentage of specific feedback is only at 16.6%. The middle range is close to the average, at

25.8%. This suggests that for answers with more variation, including paraphrases and meaning errors, an approach supporting meaning assessment rather than just the form-focused analysis of well-formed and ill-formed variability would be relevant. As a result, we are in the process of integrating the alignment-based CoMiC approach (Meurers, Ziai, Ott, and Bailey, 2011) originally developed for meaning assessment of answers to reading-comprehension questions.

6.2 Qualitative Analysis

Having discussed quantitative results, we now turn to describing several illustrative cases in more detail, using the task displayed in Figure 8.

Example (1) shows a case where the system correctly identifies the systematic problem exhibited by the learner response.

(1) SA: *My brother hates loseing in tennis*
    TA: *My brother hates losing at tennis.*
    FB: *If an infinitive ends in -e, we leave out this -e with -ing-forms.*

The learner may be unaware of the fact that verbs ending in *-e* drop this suffix in the *-ing* form, and since this is a systematic problem covered by the generation mechanism described in section 5, the system is able to inform the student about this particular challenge to help overcome it. A longitudinal learner model recording typical errors by a user could further support the interpretation and scaffolding of such phenomena.

As an example for default feedback that falls short of pointing out the nature of the learner's error, consider (2) where 'SA' is the student answer, 'TA' is the target answer and 'FB' is the system's feedback. The purpose of the exercise in (2) and the following examples is to practice the use of the gerund, as demonstrated by the target answer.

(2) SA: *My brother's hating it if he lose at tennis*
    TA: *My brother hates losing at tennis.*
    FB: *This is not what I am expecting – please try again*

Instead of using a gerund ('losing') in connection with the simple present ('hates'), the learner uses an if-clause together with the present progressive ('s hating'). Additionally, there is an agreement error in the finite verb of the if-clause ('lose' vs. 'loses'). While the general feedback message is not wrong or misleading, a message about the

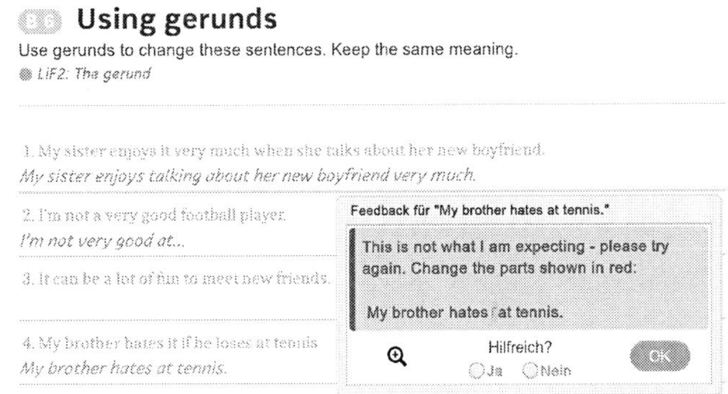

Figure 8: Default feedback example

missing gerund or the incorrect verb forms would have been more helpful.

In (3), a learner has provided a different response to the same exercise.

(3) SA: *My brother hates at tennis.*

    TA: *My brother hates losing at tennis.*

    FB: *This is not what I am expecting – please try again*

Since there is only one error here and it is about the omission of a word ('losing'), the same default feedback that was insufficient in (2) can in fact be helpful enough to guide the student to include a form of the expected word. In a future version, we plan to to include rules targeting the absence of specific grammatical forms, which in this case would enable a more specific message.

7 Conclusion and Outlook

We presented a novel approach to the generation of feedback for English grammar exercises. Building on task properties, we explicitly model the grammar topics targeted by the relevant curriculum (7th grade English) and use a multi-level generation approach to produce the expected range of well-formed and ill-formed variation in student responses to the given tasks. The results of the offline generation process are then used at feedback time in a flexible matching approach in order to account for additional variation in student responses.

Results suggest that the more frequent error patterns are successfully covered by the system, as indicated by the 1:5 ratio of types vs. tokens for which specific feedback is given. In particular, tense-related problems were often diagnosed, which teachers identified as the most challenging grammar topic in the 7th grade curriculum. However, there is also a long tail of infrequent deviations from target answers that do not seem to fall into larger categories. For these, it will be necessary to develop better fallback strategies and evaluate the subjective helpfulness ratings provided by end users at feedback time. Since it is likely that many of the answer deviations occur due to meaning-related issues, our next step will be to integrate meaning error diagnosis into the system. The availability of explicit target answers and the need to diagnose meaning deviations or equivalences between target and student answers suggests that an alignment-based approach such as CoMiC (Meurers et al., 2011) can be effective.

In connection with diagnosing meaning vs. form errors, we also plan to include stronger task modeling into the system. The more we know about the pedagogical goals, the targeted forms, and the range of expected variability, the better we can top-down determine the best feedback strategy before even analyzing a particular student answer.

Finally, we plan to include learner modeling by taking the learners' individual interaction histories into account when providing feedback and for suggesting the next tasks to tackle to provide more practice where needed.

Acknowledgments

We are grateful to our research assistants Madeesh Kannan and Tobias Pütz for their contributions to the implementation of the feedback architecture. We would also like to thank the three anonymous reviewers for their detailed and helpful comments. This work has been funded through a transfer project grant by the Deutsche Forschungsgemeinschaft in connection with the SFB 833.

References

Luis von Ahn. 2013. Duolingo: Learn a language for free while helping to translate the web. In *Proceedings of the 2013 International Conference on Intelligent User Interfaces*, pages 1–2.

Luiz Amaral and Detmar Meurers. 2011. On using intelligent computer-assisted language learning in real-life foreign language teaching and learning. *ReCALL*, 23(1):4–24.

Richard Eckart de Castilho and Iryna Gurevych. 2014. A broad-coverage collection of portable NLP components for building shareable analysis pipelines. In *Proceedings of the Workshop on Open Infrastructures and Analysis Frameworks for HLT (OIAF4HLT)*, pages 1–11, Dublin, Ireland.

Jinho D Choi and Martha Palmer. 2012. Fast and robust part-of-speech tagging using dynamic model selection. In *Proceedings of the 50th Annual Meeting of the ACL*, pages 363–367.

William DeSmedt. 1995. Herr Kommissar: An ICALL conversation simulator for intermediate German. In V. Melissa Holland, Jonathan Kaplan, and Michelle Sams, editors, *Intelligent Language Tutors: Theory Shaping Technology*, pages 153–174. Lawrence Erlbaum Associates Inc., New Jersey.

Thilo Götz and Oliver Suhre. 2004. Design and implementation of the uima common analysis system. *IBM Systems Journal*, 43(3):476–489.

Trude Heift. 2003. Multiple learner errors and meaningful feedback: A challenge for ICALL systems. *CALICO Journal*, 20(3):533–548.

Trude Heift and Mathias Schulze. 2007. *Errors and Intelligence in Computer-Assisted Language Learning: Parsers and Pedagogues*. Routledge.

Ronja Laarmann-Quante. 2016. Automating multilevel annotations of orthographic properties of German words and children's spelling errors. In *Language Teaching, Learning and Technology*, pages 14–22. http://dx.doi.org/10.21437/LTLT.2016-3.

Sébastien L'Haire and Anne Vandeventer Faltin. 2003. Error diagnosis in the FreeText project. *CALICO Journal*, 20(3):481–495.

Alison Mackey. 2006. Feedback, noticing and instructed second language learning. *Applied Linguistics*, 27(3):405–430.

Detmar Meurers. 2012. Natural language processing and language learning. In Carol A. Chapelle, editor, *Encyclopedia of Applied Linguistics*, pages 4193–4205. Wiley, Oxford. http://purl.org/dm/papers/meurers-12.html.

Detmar Meurers. 2015. Learner corpora and natural language processing. In Sylviane Granger, Gaëtanelle Gilquin, and Fanny Meunier, editors, *The Cambridge Handbook of Learner Corpus Research*, pages 537–566. Cambridge University Press. http://purl.org/dm/papers/meurers-15.html.

Detmar Meurers and Markus Dickinson. 2017. Evidence and interpretation in language learning research: Opportunities for collaboration with computational linguistics. *Language Learning*, 67(2). http://dx.doi.org/10.1111/lang.12233.

Detmar Meurers, Kordula De Kuthy, Verena Möller, Florian Nuxoll, Björn Rudzewitz, and Ramon Ziai. 2018. Digitale Differenzierung benötigt Informationen zu Sprache, Aufgabe und Lerner. Zur Generierung von individuellem Feedback in einem interaktiven Arbeitsheft. *FLuL – Fremdsprachen Lehren und Lernen*, 47(2). In press.

Detmar Meurers, Ramon Ziai, Niels Ott, and Stacey Bailey. 2011. Integrating parallel analysis modules to evaluate the meaning of answers to reading comprehension questions. *IJCEELL. Special Issue on Automatic Free-text Evaluation*, 21(4):355–369. http://purl.org/dm/papers/meurers-ziai-ott-bailey-11.html.

Guido Minnen, John Carroll, and Darren Pearce. 2001. Applied morphological processing of English. *Natural Language Engineering*, 7(3):207–233.

Edward F. Moore. 1959. The shortest path through a maze. In *Proceedings of the International Symposium on the Theory of Switching*, pages 285–292. Harvard University Press.

Noriko Nagata. 2002. BANZAI: An application of natural language processing to web-based language learning. *CALICO Journal*, 19(3):583–599.

Noriko Nagata. 2009. Robo-Sensei's NLP-based error detection and feedback generation. *CALICO Journal*, 26(3):562–579.

Björn Rudzewitz, Ramon Ziai, Kordula De Kuthy, and Detmar Meurers. 2017. Developing a web-based workbook for english supporting the interaction of students and teachers. In *Proceedings of the Joint 6th Workshop on NLP for Computer Assisted Language Learning and 2nd Workshop on NLP for Research on Language Acquisition*, pages 36–46. http://aclweb.org/anthology/W17-0305.pdf.

Helmut Schmid. 2005. A programming language for finite state transducers. In *Proceedings of the 5th International Workshop on Finite State Methods in Natural Language Processing*, pages 308–309.

David A. Schneider and Kathleen F. McCoy. 1998. Recognizing syntactic errors in the writing of second language learners. In *Proceedings of the 17th COLING and the 36th Annual meeting of the ACL*, pages 1198–1204, Montreal.

Burr Settles and Brendan Meeder. 2016. A trainable spaced repetition model for language learning. In *Proceedings of the 54th Annual Meeting of the ACL*, volume 1, pages 1848–1858.

NT2Lex: A CEFR-Graded Lexical Resource for Dutch as a Foreign Language Linked to Open Dutch WordNet

Anaïs Tack[1,2,3a]   Thomas François[1,3b]   Piet Desmet[2]   Cédrick Fairon[1]

[1] CENTAL, Université catholique de Louvain, Louvain-la-Neuve, Belgium
[2] ITEC, imec, KU Leuven Campus Kulak, Kortrijk, Belgium
[3] F.R.S.-FNRS [a] Research Fellow, [b] Postdoctoral Researcher

{anais.tack,thomas.francois,cedrick.fairon}@uclouvain.be
{anais.tack,piet.desmet}@kuleuven.be

Abstract

In this paper, we introduce NT2Lex, a novel lexical resource for Dutch as a foreign language (NT2) which includes frequency distributions of 17,743 words and expressions attested in expert-written textbook texts and readers graded along the scale of the Common European Framework of Reference (CEFR). In essence, the lexicon informs us about what kind of vocabulary should be understood when reading Dutch as a non-native reader at a particular proficiency level.

The main novelty of the resource with respect to the previously developed CEFR-graded lexicons concerns the introduction of corpus-based evidence for L2 word sense complexity through the linkage to Open Dutch WordNet (Postma et al., 2016). The resource thus contains, on top of the lemmatised and part-of-speech tagged lexical entries, a total of 11,999 unique word senses and 8,934 distinct synsets.

1 Introduction

In the recent years, a number of graded lexical resources have been developed to further research on first (L1) or second (L2) language complexity. Such a graded lexicon can be defined as a lexical database describing the graded frequency distributions of lexemes as they are attested in authentic pedagogical material along the successive grade levels of a particular language curriculum. The graded lexicons that have been built on these learning scales therefore either specifically pertain to the educational programme of (elementary) school children (Lété et al., 2004) or to the curriculum of foreign language learners (François et al., 2014).

As for the L2 language curriculum in particular, one of the most widespread learning scales which has been used to date is the Common European Framework of Reference for Languages (Council of Europe, 2001) or CEFR scale. The CEFR scale is a general framework that aims to provide a comprehensive description of the types of (written or spoken) discourse a learner at a particular proficiency level[1] should be able to understand or produce. Based on the CEFR scale and as part of the CEFRLex[2] project, a number of graded lexical resources have been developed for French (FLELex, François et al., 2014), Swedish (SVALex, François et al., 2016; SweLLex, Volodina et al., 2016) and English (EFLLex, Dürlich and François, 2018) as a foreign language. These lexicons were compiled from a corpus of L2 learning materials graded per level of the CEFR scale. The materials either include reading activities in textbooks or simplified readers (receptive graded lexicons; François et al., 2014, 2016; Dürlich and François, 2018) or texts written by learners (productive graded lexicons; Volodina et al., 2016). As a result, they inform us about what kind of vocabulary should be understood or produced when reading or writing in a foreign language at a particular proficiency level.

The lexical resources cited above have also found their purpose as components of NLP-driven educational applications. Up to date, we have seen some of the resources being integrated as features of a complex word identification system for French (Tack et al., 2016a,b), as components in a readability-driven learning platform for Swedish (Pilán et al., 2016a) or as part of an automated essay grading system for Swedish as well (Pilán et al., 2016b). It is therefore clear to say that the scope of relevance of the graded lexical resources goes well beyond their apparent usefulness to gain didactic insights into the complexity of the L2 curriculum.

---

[1] The CEFR scale includes six levels ranging from the elementary (A1/A2), to the intermediate (B1/B2) and advanced (C1/C2) levels. See Council of Europe (2001) for more details on the specific learning objectives per level.

[2] http://cental.uclouvain.be/cefrlex/

Proceedings of the Thirteenth Workshop on Innovative Use of NLP for Building Educational Applications, pages 137–146
New Orleans, Louisiana, June 5, 2018. ©2018 Association for Computational Linguistics

The principal aim of this paper is to augment the CEFRLex project by introducing a novel graded receptive lexicon for Dutch as a second or foreign language (*Nederlands tweede taal*, NT2), viz. the NT2Lex resource. Moreover, through the linkage of NT2Lex to Open Dutch WordNet (ODWN) (Postma et al., 2016), our additional objective is to expand upon and to advance the current methodology by introducing the first lexicon with graded frequency distributions for word senses.

The paper is structured as follows. The following section (Section 2) presents a bird's eye review of the literature on L2 receptive vocabulary and on the importance of measuring word sense complexity. In the subsequent sections, we will describe the revised methodology used to generate NT2Lex (Section 3) and we will compare the resource to the other CEFR-graded lexicons (Section 4). In the last section (Section 5), we will analyse the distribution of lexical entries in NT2Lex in light of standard indices of lexical complexity.

2 Background

The construct of receptive vocabulary knowledge has been an important factor when it comes to determining successful reading comprehension in a foreign language. We know that the input conveyed to foreign language learners through reading or listening should be sufficiently comprehensible not only for the message to be understood, but also for subsequent implicit or incidental acquisition to occur (Krashen, 1989). The notion of breadth of vocabulary knowledge (or vocabulary size) in particular plays an important role in predicting adequate comprehension of the L2 input. For reading comprehension, we know that 98% of the running words in the text should be known, which amounts to a vocabulary size of 8,000 word families (Laufer and Ravenhorst-Kalovski, 2010). However, the extent of vocabulary size is also heavily conditioned on the well-known variability in the interlanguage. It is therefore vital to obtain correct and relevant estimates of vocabulary knowledge when defining the lexical adequacy of a specific reading activity.

Various lexicon-based approaches have been considered to estimate the vocabulary knowledge that should be covered when learning or teaching a foreign language.[3] The first approach consists in measuring the vocabulary size based on frequency bands attested in academic word lists drawn from a reference corpus of the target language (Nation and Waring, 1997). A second approach resides in the use of L2-specific pedagogical vocabulary lists, which can be either expert-written such as the CEFR reference level descriptors (Marello, 2012; Milton, 2010) or corpus-based such as the English Vocabulary Profile (Capel, 2010, 2012). Finally, the CEFRLex project proposes a third approach to lexicon-driven evidence of vocabulary knowledge through the use of graded and corpus-based receptive lexicons (François et al., 2014).

An important aspect of vocabulary knowledge that has mostly been overlooked in the lexicon-based approaches concerns the distinction of word senses. Yet, the importance of taking into account form-meaning mappings has been well-evidenced in L2 reading comprehension. Qian (1999), for instance, hightlighted that in the interplay between vocabulary size and reading comprehension, the notion of depth of vocabulary knowledge also plays a significant role. The essential requirements for deep vocabulary knowledge include – besides the surface-level (i.e. spelling and phonetics) and morphological features – a thorough mastery of the various semantic, collocational, discursive and other contextual aspects of the word. Zooming in on the first two aspects in particular, he observed a significant addition of depth of vocabulary to explain the variability in comprehension scores.

The need to account for this semasiological variation when estimating word difficulty can be traced as far back as to Tharp (1939). Indeed, Tharp highlighted the drawbacks of defining word difficulty estimates by tallying the frequency of occurrence of similar word forms that are inherently polysemous. Subsequently, various studies have sought to parameterise the extent of semasiological and onomasiological variation in text-level readability assessment using polysemic, hypernymic and other features based on WordNet (Fellbaum, 1998), the most notable contribution of which relates to Coh-Metrix (Graesser et al., 2004). As for word-level readability assessment, a number of studies on lexical simplification have made advances in the ranking of the difficulty of synonyms based on contextual factors (Jauhar and Specia, 2012) or based on a lexical database of synonyms ranked according to elementary grade levels (Gala et al., 2013).

---

[3]For a more detailed overview on these lexicon-based approaches, we refer the reader to François et al. (2014).

level	A1	A2	B1	B2	C1	total
# tokens	17.878	205.035	153,537	78,439	6,199	461,088
# readers	5	22	11	6	1	45
# documents	53	447	306	110	10	926

Table 1: Corpus statistics

3 Methodology

In view of the need for estimating word sense complexity in L2 learning addressed hereabove, we developed a graded lexical resource for learners of Dutch L2 which includes lexical entries linked to Open Dutch WordNet (ODWN) (Postma et al., 2016). The methodology for compiling a graded lexical resource can be found in Lété et al. (2004); François et al. (2014). Here, we will briefly summarise the method of estimating graded lexical entries, focusing on the particularities for Dutch.

3.1 Data

We used a 461,088-token corpus of CEFR-graded readers and textbooks for Dutch as a foreign language, ranging from the A1 to the C1 levels and with a mixture of writings in Netherlandic and Belgian Dutch (Table 1).

Preprocessing Typographical and language errors as well as other idiosyncracies observed in the OCR-ised texts were manually corrected. Tonic diacritics commonly used to indicate stress in written Dutch (e.g. *veel/véél*, 'many') were also manually removed, excluding the mandatory diaereses (e.g. *efficiënt*, 'efficient') and accents in loan words (e.g. *café*, 'pub'). All texts were lemmatised and part-of-speech tagged and multi-word units were automatically identified with the Frog tagger (van den Bosch et al., 2007).

The tagged texts were then fed to a word-sense disambiguation (WSD) tool[4]. The tool is based on a one-vs.-rest SVM classifier trained on the DutchSemCor (Vossen et al., 2012) and includes a dictionary of 92.617 lexemes and 117.225 senses, of which 52,430 (45%) seem to be matched to ODWN synsets. To increase the tool's coverage with ODWN, we also included all monosemous ODWN entries which were not included in the tool. In total, 76% of all distinct lexical units (adjectives, adverbs, nouns and verbs) were disambiguated for word senses.

3.2 Definition of Lexical Entries

To define the list of lexical entries which make up the resource, we proceeded to some extra correction, simplification and filtering of the previously tagged and word-sense disambiguated texts.

Lemmata We first ruled out all non-alphanumeric entries such as punctuation marks, Arabic numerals, as well as non-standard word forms and abbreviations commonly found in Dutch chatspeak. We also simplified similar alphanumeric numbers (e.g. *4de, 5de*, '4th, 5th') as belonging to the same lexical entry *[digit]de*.

We then resolved some specificities of the Dutch compounding system. On the one hand, we decided to split a number of compounds with an optional parenthesised stem. For a lemma such as *(studie)keuze* ('(study) choice') for instance, we counted the occurrence as two separate lexemes: *keuze* ('choice') and *studiekeuze* ('study choice'). On the other hand, we also resolved the omission of shared stems in a number of coordinated compounds (e.g. *binnenland* vs. *binnen- en buitenland*, 'home and abroad').[5]

Parts of speech The Frog part-of-speech tagger is based on the CGN (*Corpus Gesproken Nederlands*) tagset (Van Eynde, 2004). The CGN tagset is quite extensive in that it counts over 320 tags and thus accounts for a number of detailed lexical and morphological features. However, we found it irrelevant to keep all of these precise features in the resource. We therefore decided to simplify the tagset to a set of 37 tags (Table 2). Consequently, all other special symbols not covered by the tagset were filtered from the resource.

We should note that the multi-word units detected by Frog tagger were not tagged with a specific part of speech, but with a "multi-tag" part of speech (e.g. *door en door*, VZ(fin)_VG(neven)_VZ(fin), 'through and through'). For all of these multi-word units, we also subsequently transposed each one of the individual tags according to our simplified tagset.

Word senses Finally, all lexical entries which were disambiguated for word senses were thus supplemented with a tuple of ODWN sense and

---

[4]The tool was created by Rubén Izquierdo and is available on `http://github.com/cltl/svm_wsd`.

[5]To this end, automatic compound splitting was performed using the publicly available rule-based compound splitter for Dutch (`http://ilps.science.uva.nl/resources/compound-splitter-nl/`)

simplified tag	part of speech	# 37
N(soort/eigen)	noun (common/proper)	# 2
ADJ()	adjective	# 1
WW()	verb	# 1
TW(hoofd/rang)	numeral (card./ord.)	# 2
VNW(...)	pronoun	# 20
LID(bep/onbep)	article (def./indef.)	# 2
VZ(init/fin/versm)	preposition (initial/final/fused)	# 3
VG(neven/onder)	conjunction (coord./subord.)	# 2
BW()	adverb	# 1
TSW()	interjection	# 1
SPEC(deeleigen)	part of proper noun	# 1
LET()	punctuation	# 1

Table 2: List of simplified CGN tags.

corresponding synset ids (e.g. *lezen-v-1*, eng-30-00625119-v, 'to read'). The synset ids include either the WordNet 3.0 offset (*eng-30*) or the ODWN 1.0 offset (*odwn-10*) otherwise. However, we should note that not all WordNet and ODWN synsets included in Open Dutch WordNet have a corresponding lexical entry. We therefore completed those entries with their corresponding sense number (e.g. *overduidelijk*, obvious.a.01) in NLTK's Open Multilingual WordNet (Bird et al., 2009). Finally, in the absence of an ODWN equivalent to DutchSemCor, we decided to keep the original sense id obtained through WSD for the sake of completeness and for future compatibility (e.g. *overbodig*, d_a-415574, 'superfluous').

3.3 Lexical Frequencies and Weighting

After having defined the set of lexical entries, we computed their graded frequency distributions across the five CEFR levels attested in the corpus. The following statistics were computed for each lexical entry and per each level.

Raw frequency The frequency $F_{entry,level}$ is simply computed as the number of times the entry occurs in the level, which amounts to summing up the vector $\mathbf{f}$ of the entry's frequencies of occurrence f in document i for all d documents in that level (see Table 1 on the preceding page).

$$F_{entry,level} = \sum \mathbf{f} = \sum_{i=1}^{d} f_i \quad (3.3.1)$$

Dispersion and adjusted frequencies The exclusive use of raw frequencies to observe lexical distributions has been subjected to much debate in corpus linguistics and especially when applied to mining corpora to futher L2 research. Indeed, Gries (2008) previously stated that the extent of written language proficiency in learner corpora appears to be closely linked to the scope of lexical dispersion: the more dispersed the use of a word, the better it is mastered.

For written language comprehension on the other hand, we could also state that the extent of lexical dispersion in readers and textbooks gives us a better view on what kind of vocabulary is subject to being well-understood at a particular proficiency level. As a consequence, the lexical frequencies we want to use to gain insights in non-native language comprehension should be adjusted to take into account lexical dispersion as well. The following dispersion ($D_{entry,level}$) and adjusted frequency indices ($U_{entry,level}$ and $SFI_{entry,level}$) were computed following Carroll et al. (1971). In the following formulae, N_{level} denotes the number of words in the level and n_i denotes the number of words in document i of all documents d in that level.

$$D = \left[\ln(\textstyle\sum \mathbf{f}) - \left(\frac{\sum_{i=1}^{d} f_i \cdot \ln(f_i)}{\sum \mathbf{f}} \right) \right] \cdot \frac{1}{\ln(d)} \quad (3.3.2)$$

$$U = \frac{10^6}{N_{level}} \left[F \cdot D + (1 - D) \cdot \left(\frac{1}{N_{level}} \sum_{i=1}^{d} f_i \cdot n_i \right) \right] \quad (3.3.3)$$

$$SFI = 10 \cdot [\log_{10}(U) + 4] \quad (3.3.4)$$

4 Resource Description

We compiled two separate versions of NT2Lex. A first version contains only the lemmatised and part-of-speech tagged entries (**NT2Lex-CGN**) and is thus similar to the other graded lexicons previously developed in the CEFRLex project (cf. *supra*). The word-sense disambiguated entries, on the other hand, have been added to a second version of the resource (**NT2Lex-CGN+ODWN**) (see Table 3 for an example). A comparative overview of the number of entries in both versions of NT2Lex and in the other resources can be found in Table 5 on page 6. A more detailed description of the resource is given hereinbelow and in the following section.

NT2Lex-CGN The first version of NT2lex counts 15,227 entries. The total number of entries in the resource is therefore similar to the resources developed for English and Swedish, although slightly lower than for French. Not surprisingly, the majority of the entries contain lexical

lemma	pos	sense-id	synset-id	gloss	U@A1	U@A2	U@B1	U@B2	U@C1	U@total
in zwang	VZ(init) N(soort)	in_zwang-n-1	eng-30-14411884-n	'in vogue'	-	-	-	-	22	0
omgangstaal	N(soort)	omgangstaal-n-1	eng-30-07157123-n	'vernacular'	-	-	-	26	-	3
pakken	WW()	pakken-v-1	odwn-10-101230891-v	'grab'	35	117	101	5	-	99
pakken	WW()	pakken-v-10	eng-30-01100145-v	'defeat'	-	51	12	-	-	28
zijn	VNW(bez,det)	-	-	'his'	3,349	7,900	4,124	3,479	4,308	5,798
zijn	WW()	zijn-v-1	eng-30-02603699-v	'exist'	2,094	1,647	1,423	1,253	1,335	1,601

Table 3: Example of entries in NT2Lex-CGN+ODWN with their graded adjusted frequencies U. A column with glosses was added for illustrative purposes.

words and the number of grammatical entries also remains strongly comparable across all resources.

There is a striking difference however in the number of multi-word entries that are included in NT2Lex and in the other resources. Only 459 of the entries are multi-word units, contrary to 2,038 for French and 1,450 for Swedish. The multi-word units that are included in the resource mostly pertain to well-known named entities (e.g. *Olympische Spelen*, 'Olympic Games') and other phrasal verbs (e.g. *voorzien van*, 'to provide'), adverbs (e.g. *om het even*, 'all the same'), etc.

This difference could be explained by the fact that the majority of the compound words which are multi-word units in other languages (such as in French or English) are one-word units or agglutinative compounds in Dutch (e.g. *afvalverwijderingsstructuur*, 'waste disposal structure'). We observe that 4,431 (31%) of the single-word entries in NT2Lex are in fact compounds. As for the Swedish language, where the compounding system is similar to Dutch, we could attribute this disparity to the fact that different taggers were used to detect multi-word units. Indeed, the recall and precision of multi-word identification depend heavily on the assumptions made by the tagger to resolve the sequential ambiguity, contrary to the agglutinative compounds, which do not need to be disambiguated in this case.

NT2Lex-CGN+ODWN The word-sense disambiguated version of NT2Lex counts 17,743 entries in all, with an extra 2,516 lexical entries and with 1,454 polysemous entries (with at least two senses). Table 4 shows the distribution of polysemous entries across all levels. Although all of these polysemous entries are lexical ones, we should note that some multi-word entries have also been disambiguated for word senses, but none of them are polysemous. The most polysemous entry in the resource is the entry *pakken* (verb, 'to take / grab / defeat / hinder / etc.') which has a total of 10 different senses attested in the resource.

	A1	A2	B1	B2	C1	total
# entries	1,189	7,630	10,160	9,366	1,841	17,743
# senses	849	5,705	7,272	6,517	1,302	11,999
# polysemes	139	828	979	771	118	1,451
# synsets	658	4,450	5,465	4,936	1,046	8,934

Table 4: The number of word senses, polysemes (entries with >1 sense) and unique synsets in NT2Lex-CGN+ODWN

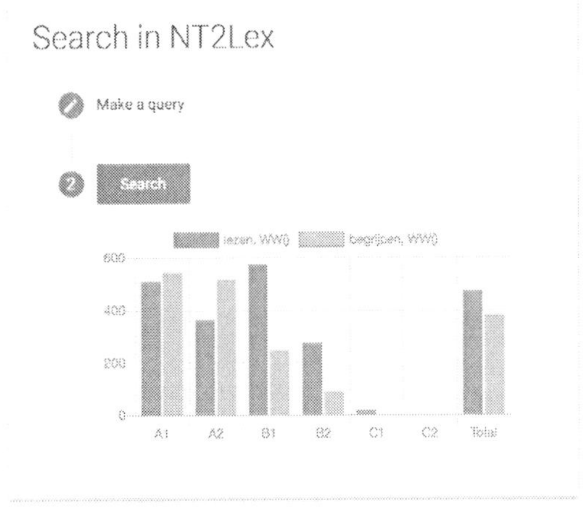

Figure 1: Screenshot of an online query in NT2Lex for the verbs *lezen* ('to read') and *begrijpen* ('to understand')

Table 4 also shows the number of unique concepts (# synsets) included per level and in total. We observe that the resource includes a high variety of concepts, with 8,934 distinct synsets out of 11,999 word senses.

Online query and annotation tools Both versions of the resource will be made available for non-commercial use in the CEFRLex project.[6] Similar to the previous resources, a number of online tools will be made available for teachers and/or researchers to query the lexical database and to annotate a text using NT2Lex (Figure 1).

---

[6] http://cental.uclouvain.be/nt2lex/

resource version	NT2Lex CGN					NT2Lex CGN+ODWN				FLELex CRF		SVALex /		EFLLex /	
# entries	15,227					17,743				17,871		15,681		15,281	
lexical	14,368					16,884				17,404		15,291		14,857	
grammat.	400					400				467		390		424	
multi-w.	459					459				2,038		1,450		3,852	
levels	#	new (%)	compound	hapax	>10	#	new (%)	hapax	>10	#	new (%)	#	new (%)	#	new (%)
A1	953	953 (1.00)	70	313	225	1,189	1,189 (1.00)	427	228	4,976	4,976 (1.00)	1,157	1,157 (1.00)	2,395	2,395 (1.00)
A2	6,220	5,383 (0.87)	1,224	2,482	1,231	7,630	6,580 (0.86)	3,073	1,386	6,995	3,516 (0.50)	3,327	2,432 (0.73)	4,205	2,478 (0.59)
B1	8,559	4,879 (0.57)	1,997	3,936	1,081	10,160	5,571 (0.55)	4,739	1,128	10,780	4,970 (0.46)	6,554	4,332 (0.66)	5,607	2,740 (0.49)
B2	8,172	3,641 (0.45)	1,861	4,362	638	9,366	3,998 (0.43)	5,092	619	7,349	1,653 (0.22)	8,728	4,553 (0.52)	8,228	3,935 (0.48)
C1	1,680	371 (0.22)	252	1,127	63	1,841	405 (0.22)	1,282	62	8,348	2,122 (0.25)	7,564	3,160 (0.41)	9,232	3,733 (0.40)
C2	-	-	-	-	-	-	-	-	-	7,433	634 (0.09)	-	-	-	-

Table 5: A comparative overview of NT2Lex and the other lexicons in terms of the number (#) of entries per level (including new entries, compounds, hapaxes and entries with a frequency greater than 10), as well as the number of lexical (adjectives, adverbs, nouns and verbs), grammatical and multi-word entries.

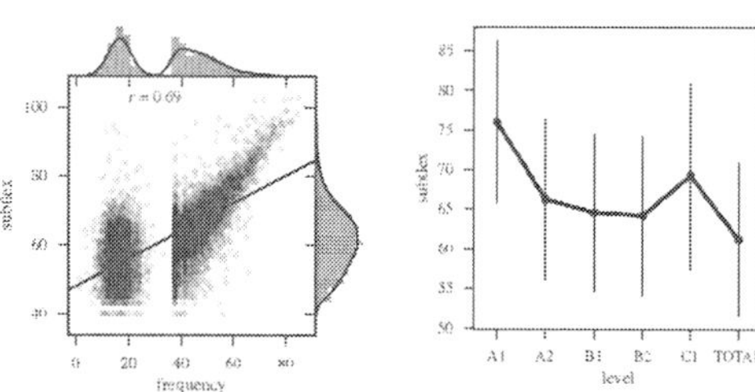

(a) correlation between NT2Lex and Subtlex   (b) median of Subtlex frequencies per level

Figure 2: Comparison of NT2Lex and Subtlex-NL standardised frequencies

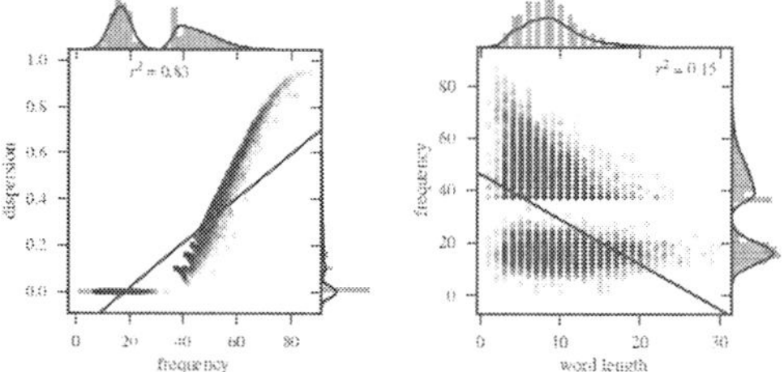

Figure 3: Zipfian effects for adjusted frequencies (*SFI*), dispersions (*D*) and word lengths for all entries in NT2Lex

5 Analysis

In the next sections, we will compare the distribution of lexical entries in NT2Lex in light of a number of standard indices of lexical complexity. We will only report statistics for the most complete version of our resource, i.e. NT2Lex-CGN+ODWN.

5.1 Frequency Effects

As a first means of analysis, we aim to examine the coherence of the frequency distributions in the resource with respect to the word frequency effect in second language processing, which states that words that are more frequent and more familiar are more easily processed by a learner (Ellis, 2002).

Lexical frequency To compare the frequency distributions in the resource, we use the standard frequency index (*SFI*, Formula 3.3.4), which might be best suited to measure the desired effects: a value of 100, 90, 80, ..., 40 on the standard scale indicates that the entry respectively occurs once every $10^0, 10^1, 10^2, ..., 10^6$ entries, and so forth.

When comparing the standardised frequency distributions with Subtlex-NL (Keuleers et al., 2010), we observe a positive value for the Pearson correlation coefficient ($r = .69$, $p < .001$[7]; Figure 2a). This shows us that even though the adjusted frequencies were estimated on a relatively small corpus, they are still very much coherent with the frequencies estimated for the same entries on a reference corpus. Moreover, Figure 2b also illustrates that the average of Subtlex-NL frequencies also decreases per level, with the exception of the C1 level. A possible reason for this is that the C1 subcorpus is the most restricted in size due to the limited availability of C1-level readers.

Dispersion and word familiarity Because of lacking experimental data on actual word familiarity in Dutch L2, we make a simplifying assumption here and use our dispersion metric as a measure of *theoretical* word familiarity: the more the word is dispersed across the L2 documents, the more familiar it should be to a learner in general.

We observe from Figure 3 that this theoretical word familiarity accounts for about 83% in the distribution of the adjusted frequencies. In this respect, we also observe an interesting split in

---

[7]For reasons of comparability with Subtlex, which does not include frequencies for word senses, we report the correlation coefficient for the non-WSD version of the resource.

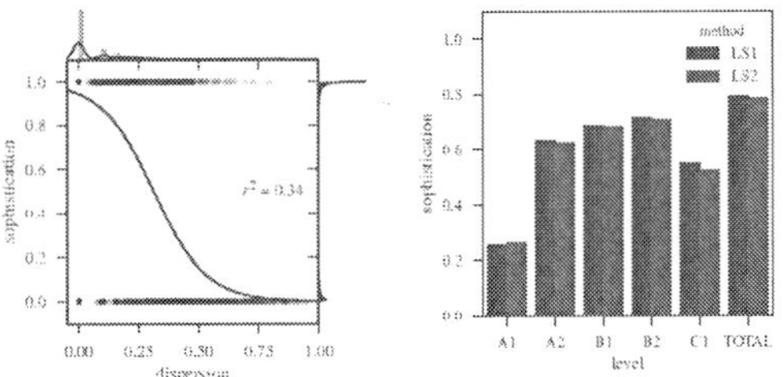

(a) degree of lexical disper- (b) lexical sophistication per
sion and lexical sophistication level based on Lu (2012)'s ratios

Figure 4: The interplay between lexical dispersion and lexical sophistication in NT2Lex

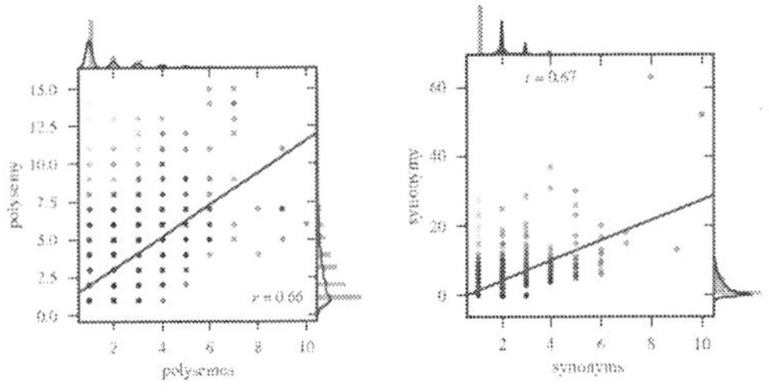

(a) number of polysemes per (b) number of synonyms per
entry in function of ODWN entry in function of ODWN
polysemy   synonymy

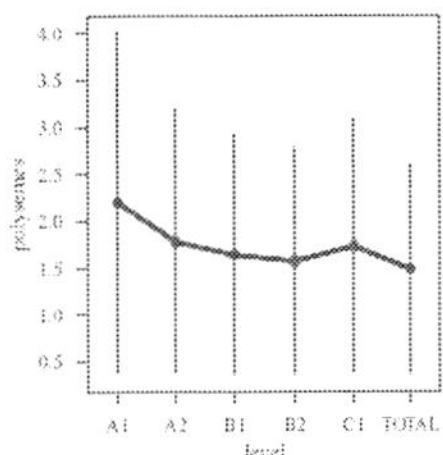

(c) average polysemes / level

Figure 5: Polysemy and synonymy in NT2Lex

the normalised frequency distribution which originates from the way the adjusted frequencies were computed (U; Formula 3.3.3). When $D > 0$, the influence of the raw frequency F increases between $40 < SFI < 100$. Conversely, when $D = 0$, the raw frequencies are not taken into account, but are drawn from a weigthed (Gaussian) frequency distribution ($0 < SFI < 40$) instead.

Zipfian effects From these associations between dispersion and standardised frequencies, we can also observe a number of Zipfian effects. Indeed, for all entries which have a non-zero dispersion (range $40 < SFI < 100$), Zipf's distribution (Zipf, 1949) applies in the standard frequency index. Moreover, these frequencies are in turn negatively correlated with word length: the shorter the word, the more frequent ($r = -.39$; $p < .001$). We take these results as a proof for the consistency of the resource.

Lexical sophistication As a final note on the issue of word frequency, we compare the lexical sophistication ratio of the entries with a basic word list[8] of the 2,000 most frequent Dutch words according to the *Basiswoordenboek Nederlands* (Kleijn and Nieuwberg, 1993).[9] Figure 4a shows that the more dispersed (and hence the more familiar) the entry in the corpus, the least sophisticated the entry is. Moreover, we also observe that the proportion of sophisticated entries (i.e. that go beyond the 2,000 most frequent words) increases per level (Figure 4b), except for the C1 level where

fewer sophisticated words have been attested due to the limitations highlighted earlier.

5.2 Semasio-onomasiological Indices

In addition to the word frequency effect of L2 vocabulary learning, we also investigated the interplay of form-meaning mappings in the resource.

We observe on the one hand that the degree of polysemy and synonymy attested in the resource is strongly correlated to the degree of synonymy and polysemy that is expected in the Open Dutch WordNet (ODWN) (Figure 5). We can therefore conclude that in addition to the correlation between the estimated frequencies and Subtlex-NL (cf. *supra*), the word senses included in the resource are also consistent with the structure of a general semantic network.

However, the lower extent of onomasiological variation (i.e. meaning-to-form mappings) in NT2Lex compared to ODWN synonymy (Figure 5b) might be indicative of the specialised nature of the resource in that for a defined set of concepts it includes a limited range of lexicalizations, which are likely to be specific to the L2.

As for semasiological variation (i.e. form-to-meaning mappings) in NT2Lex, we observe an interesting decreasing trend in the degree of polysemy per level (Figure 5c). This highlights the fact that the lexical stock of elementary L2 texts con-

---

[8] http://www.dikverhaar.nl/wp-content/
uploads/Basiswoordenlijst_2000_
frequente_meest_woorden.pdf

[9] We should note that 61 of the 2,000 basic word forms are not attested in NT2Lex.

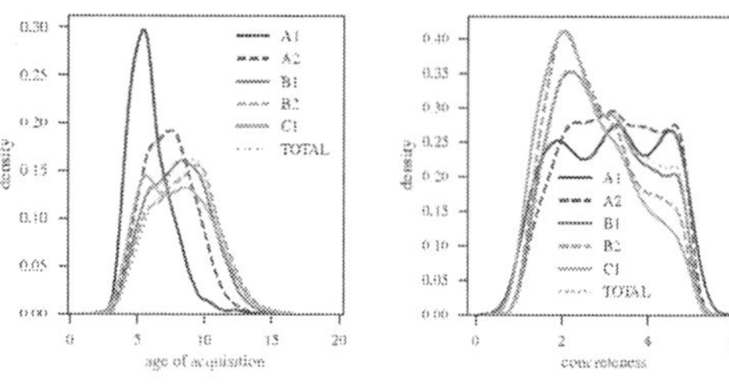

(a) age of acquisition per level   (b) concreteness per level

Figure 6: Psycholinguistic norms in NT2Lex

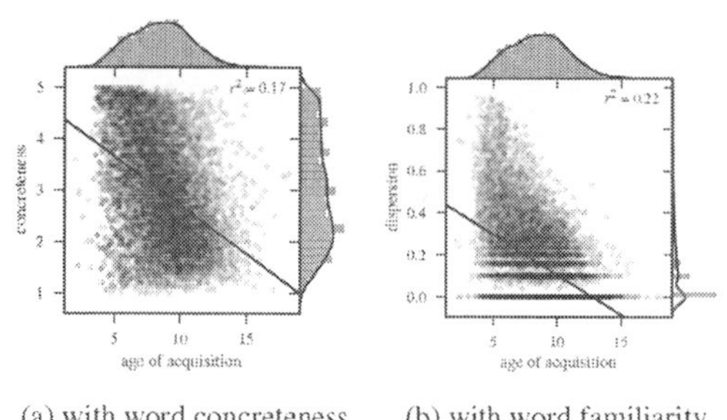

(a) with word concreteness   (b) with word familiarity

Figure 7: Age of acquisition in NT2Lex

tains more ambiguous entries, which in turn tend to be more easily processed (Millis and Bution, 1989). However, no other significant effects in terms of synonymy, polysemy or hypernymy were observed.

5.3 Psycholinguistic Norms

Finally, to investigate the interplay of different psycholinguistic norms in the resource, we use a lexical database of age of acquisition and concreteness norms for Dutch (Brysbaert et al., 2014). Figure 6 shows the distribution of the norms per each attested level in the resource.

Age of acquisition We observe that the vast majority of the lexical stock in the elementary levels (i.e A1/A2) contain words which are acquired the earliest by native speakers as well, approximately around the age of five, whereas the entries in the intermediate levels (i.e. B1/B2) levels are acquired later, approximately between ages 5 and 10. Moreover, the more concrete the word, the earlier it is acquired (Figure 7a), which is consistent with previous observations (Crossley et al., 2009). The earlier the word is acquired, the more familiar it is according to its dispersion in the resource (Figure 7b). As for the C1 level, we observe a similar trend, except for a smaller proportion of entries that are acquired earlier as well (with a higher concentration around the age of 5), which might also explain the higher average of Subtlex frequencies and the lower degree of sophistication attested at this level (cf. *supra*).

Concreteness As regards word concreteness, we observe on the one hand that the highest levels (i.e. B2/C1) contain a considerably higher proportion of abstract (less concrete) words. This observation highlights the fact that, even though the C1 level includes some outliers on the level of

lexical frequency and sophistication, the distribution of the concreteness norms at C1 are similar to what is expected. The most basic levels, on the other hand, contain a lower proportion of abstract words, but the difference between the number of concrete and abstract words appears to be proportionally less clear-cut.

6 Conclusion

In this paper, we presented a new graded lexical resource for Dutch as a foreign language (NT2) based on the proficiency scale of the Common European Framework of Reference (CEFR). Similar to the previous CEFR-graded lexicons for French, Swedish and English, the NT2Lex resource contains graded frequency distributions per lexical entry which are estimated on L2 readers and textbook texts targeting a specific level on the CEFR scale. The novelty of the NT2Lex resource with respect to the common methodology of generating graded lexicons is concerned with the fact that the lexical entries are disambiguated for word senses and are also linked to WordNet synsets. We argued that this linkage gives us a better insight into word sense complexity in a foreign language.

We found that the estimated frequency and word sense distributions are in line with what one expects to observe in the target language. Moreover, the distributions of lexical entries per level in NT2Lex also appeared to be consistent with previous findings in terms of lexical complexity. As regards the features of lexical ambiguity, age of acquisition and concreteness, we observed that the lexical entries in the most basic levels of the resource (i.e. A1/A2) are more polysemous and acquired the earliest by non-native speakers, whereas the lexical entries in the more advanced levels (i.e. B2/C1) portray a significantly higher degree of abstractness and are acquired at a later developmental stage.

We could thus conclude that the resource enables us to get a better grasp on what kind of vocabulary should be understood *a priori* when reading Dutch as a foreign language at a particular proficiency level. Of course, we should highlight that the assumptions that can be drawn are still limited in the sense that they are mainly based on expert knowledge drawn from pedagogical texts. Indeed, we lack extensive experimental data on what vocabulary is effectively understood when reading Dutch at a particular proficiency level and by a specific learner depending on his/her characteristics (e.g. native language, age, experience, etc.). As a future perspective, we therefore aim to contrast the knowledge we gained through the resource with this kind of receptive learner data.

Acknowledgments

This research was funded by an F.R.S.-FNRS research grant. We would like to thank Anne-Sophie Desmet and Dorian Ricci for their helping hand and valuable input in the preparation of the resources and tools.

References

Steven Bird, Ewan Klein, and Edward Loper. 2009. *Natural Language Processing with Python*, 1 edition. O'Reilly, Beijing ; Cambridge Mass.

Antal van den Bosch, Bertjan Busser, Sander Canisius, and Walter Daelemans. 2007. An efficient memory-based morphosyntactic tagger and parser for Dutch. In *Selected Papers of the 17th Computational Linguistics in the Netherlands Meeting*, pages 99–114.

Marc Brysbaert, Michaël Stevens, Simon De Deyne, Wouter Voorspoels, and Gert Storms. 2014. Norms of age of acquisition and concreteness for 30,000 Dutch words. *Acta Psychologica*, 150:80–84.

Annette Capel. 2010. A1–B2 vocabulary: insights and issues arising from the English Profile Wordlists project. *English Profile Journal*, 1(01).

Annette Capel. 2012. Completing the English Vocabulary Profile: C1 and C2 vocabulary. *English Profile Journal*, 3.

John B. Carroll, Peter Davies, and Barry Richman. 1971. *The American Heritage Word Frequency Book*. Houghton Mifflin, Boston.

Council of Europe. 2001. *Common European Framework of Reference for Languages*. Cambridge University Press, Cambridge, UK.

Scott Crossley, Tom Salsbury, and Danielle McNamara. 2009. Measuring L2 Lexical Growth Using Hypernymic Relationships. *Language Learning*, 59(2):307–334.

Luise Dürlich and Thomas François. 2018. EFLLex: A Graded Lexical Resource for Learners of English as a Foreign Language. In *Proceedings of the 11th International Conference on Language Resources and Evaluation (LREC 2018)*, Miyazaki, Japan. To appear.

Nick C. Ellis. 2002. Frequency Effects in Language Processing: A Review with Implications for Theories of Implicit and Explicit Language Acquisition. *Studies in Second Language Acquisition*, 24(2):143–188.

Christiane Fellbaum. 1998. *WordNet: An Electronic Lexical Database*. MIT Press, Cambridge, MA.

Thomas François, Nuria Gala, Patrick Watrin, and Cédrick Fairon. 2014. FLELex: a graded lexical resource for French foreign learners. In *Proceedings of the 9th International Conference on Language Resources and Evaluation (LREC 2014)*, pages 3766–3773, Reykjavik, Iceland. European Language Resources Association (ELRA).

Thomas François, Elena Volodina, Ildikó Pilán, and Anaïs Tack. 2016. SVALex: A CEFR-Graded Lexical Resource for Swedish Foreign and Second Language Learners. In *Proceedings of the 10th International Conference on Language Resources and Evaluation (LREC 2016)*, pages 213–219, Portorož, Slovenia. European Language Resources Association (ELRA).

Nuria Gala, Thomas François, and Cédrick Fairon. 2013. Towards a French lexicon with difficulty measures: NLP helping to bridge the gap between traditional dictionaries and specialized lexicons. In *Electronic lexicography in the 21st century: thinking outside the paper : proceedings of the eLex 2013 conference, 17-19 October 2013, Tallinn, Estonia, 2013, págs. 132-151*, pages 132–151.

Arthur C. Graesser, Danielle S. McNamara, Max M. Louwerse, and Zhiqiang Cai. 2004. Coh-Metrix: Analysis of text on cohesion and language. *Behavior Research Methods, Instruments, & Computers*, 36(2):193–202.

Stefan Th. Gries. 2008. Dispersions and adjusted frequencies in corpora. *International Journal of Corpus Linguistics*, 13(4):403–437.

Sujay Kumar Jauhar and Lucia Specia. 2012. UOW-SHEF: SimpLex – Lexical Simplicity Ranking Based on Contextual and Psycholinguistic Features. In *Proceedings of the First Joint Conference on Lexical and Computational Semantics - Volume 1: Proceedings of the Main Conference and the Shared Task, and Volume 2: Proceedings of the Sixth International Workshop on Semantic Evaluation*, SemEval '12, pages 477–481, Stroudsburg, PA, USA. Association for Computational Linguistics.

Emmanuel Keuleers, Marc Brysbaert, and Boris New. 2010. SUBTLEX-NL: A new measure for Dutch word frequency based on film subtitles. *Behavior Research Methods*, 42(3):643–650.

P. de Kleijn and E. Nieuwberg. 1993. *Basiswoordenboek Nederlands*. Wolters Leuven, Leuven.

Stephen Krashen. 1989. We Acquire Vocabulary and Spelling by Reading: Additional Evidence for the Input Hypothesis. *The Modern Language Journal*, 73(4):440–464.

Batia Laufer and Geke C. Ravenhorst-Kalovski. 2010. Lexical Threshold Revisited: Lexical Text Coverage, Learners' Vocabulary Size and Reading Comprehension. *Reading in a Foreign Language*, 22(1):15–30.

Xiaofei Lu. 2012. The Relationship of Lexical Richness to the Quality of ESL Learners' Oral Narratives. *The Modern Language Journal*, 96(2):190–208.

Bernard Lété, Liliane Sprenger-Charolles, and Pascale Colé. 2004. MANULEX: a grade-level lexical database from French elementary school readers. *Behavior Research Methods, Instruments, & Computers: A Journal of the Psychonomic Society, Inc*, 36(1):156–166.

Carla Marello. 2012. Word lists in Reference Level Descriptions of CEFR (Common European Framework of Reference for Languages). In *Proceedings of the XV Euralex International Congress*, pages 328–335.

Michelle L. Millis and Scoti B. Bution. 1989. The effect of polysemy on lexical decision time: Now you see it, now you don't. *Memory & Cognition*, 17(2):141–147.

James Milton. 2010. The development of vocabulary breadth across the CEFR levels. A common basis for the elaboration of language syllabuses, curriculum guidelines, examinations, and textbooks across Europe. In Inge Bartning, Maisa Martin, and Ineke Vedder, editors, *Communicative proficiency and linguistic development: Intersections between SLA and language testing research*, number 1 in Eurosla Monographs Series, pages 211–232. European Second Language Association.

Paul Nation and Robert Waring. 1997. Vocabulary size, text coverage, and word lists. In Norbert Schmitt and Michael McCarthy, editors, *Vocabulary: description, acquisition and pedagogy*, Cambridge language teaching library. Cambridge Univ. Press, Cambridge.

Ildikó Pilán, Elena Volodina, and Lars Borin. 2016a. Candidate sentence selection for language learning exercises: from a comprehensive framework to an empirical evaluation. *TAL*, 57(3):67–91.

Ildikó Pilán, Elena Volodina, and Torsten Zesch. 2016b. Predicting proficiency levels in learner writings by transferring a linguistic complexity model from expert-written coursebooks. In *Proceedings of the 26th International Conference on Computational Linguistics (COLING'16)*, pages 2101–2111, Osaka, Japan. Association for Computational Linguistics.

M. C. Postma, E. Miltenburg, R. Segers, A. Schoen, and P. T. J. M. Vossen. 2016. Open Dutch WordNet. In *Proceedings of the Eigth Global Wordnet Conference*.

David Qian. 1999. Assessing the Roles of Depth and Breadth of Vocabulary Knowledge in Reading Comprehension. *Canadian Modern Language Review*, 56(2):282–308.

Anaïs Tack, Thomas François, Anne-Laure Ligozat, and Cédrick Fairon. 2016a. Evaluating Lexical Simplification and Vocabulary Knowledge for Learners of French: Possibilities of Using the FLELex Resource. In *Proceedings of the 10th International Conference on Language Resources and Evaluation (LREC 2016)*, pages 230–236, Portorož, Slovenia.

Anaïs Tack, Thomas François, Anne-Laure Ligozat, and Cédrick Fairon. 2016b. Modèles adaptatifs pour prédire automatiquement la compétence lexicale d'un apprenant de français langue étrangère. In *Actes de la 23ème Conférence sur le Traitement Automatique des Langues Naturelles (TALN'16)*, pages 221–234, Paris, France.

James B. Tharp. 1939. The Measurement of Vocabulary Difficulty. *The Modern Language Journal*, 24(3):169–178.

Frank Van Eynde. 2004. Part of speech tagging en lemmatisering van het Corpus Gesproken Nederlands. Technical report, Centrum voor Computerlinguïstiek, KU Leuven, Belgium.

Elena Volodina, Ildikó Pilán, Lorena Llozhi, Baptiste Degryse, and Thomas François. 2016. SweLLex: second language learners' productive vocabulary. In *Proceedings of the joint 5th NLP4CALL and 1st NLP4LA workshops (SLTC 2016)*, pages 76–84, Umeå, Sweden. Linköping University Electronic Press.

Piek Vossen, Attila Görög, Rubén Izquierdo, and Antal Van den Bosch. 2012. DutchSemCor: Targeting the ideal sense-tagged corpus. In *Proceedings of the Eight International Conference on Language Resources and Evaluation (LREC'12)*, pages 584–589, Istanbul, Turkey. European Language Resources Association (ELRA).

George K. Zipf. 1949. *Human Behavior and the Principle of Least Effort*. Addison-Wesley, Cambridge, Massachusetts.

Experiments with Universal CEFR Classification

Sowmya Vajjala
Applied Linguistics and Technology Program
Iowa State University, USA
sowmya@iastate.edu

Taraka Rama
Department of Informatics
University of Oslo, Norway
tarakark@ifi.uio.no

Abstract

The Common European Framework of Reference (CEFR) guidelines describe language proficiency of learners on a scale of 6 levels. While the description of CEFR guidelines is generic across languages, the development of automated proficiency classification systems for different languages follow different approaches. In this paper, we explore universal CEFR classification using domain-specific and domain-agnostic, theory-guided as well as data-driven features. We report the results of our preliminary experiments in monolingual, cross-lingual, and multilingual classification with three languages: German, Czech, and Italian. Our results show that both monolingual and multilingual models achieve similar performance, and cross-lingual classification yields lower, but comparable results to monolingual classification.

1 Introduction

Automated Essay Scoring (AES) refers to the task of automatically grading student essays written in response to some prompt. Different approaches for AES have been proposed in literature, where it is modeled as a regression, ranking or a classification problem (cf. Yannakoudakis et al., 2011; Taghipour and Ng, 2016; Pilán et al., 2016). To our knowledge, all the previous work described approaches that work with a single language (mostly English). Feature representations that can work for multiple languages and those that support cross-lingual AES have not been explored.

At first thought, using an essay scoring model developed for one language to test on another language seems unacceptable. However, CEFR guidelines are not developed for a specific language. This leads us to hypothesize about a common model of "proficiency" that can work across languages. The existence of such a model would also be beneficial for quick prototyping of AES systems for languages that do not have readily available training data.

In this paper, we explore this hypothesis by exploring CEFR-classification for three languages-German, Italian, and Czech, for which CEFR graded data is publicly available. Apart from constructing individual models using generic text classification and AES specific features, we also looked into cross-lingual (i.e., training a model on one language and testing on another) and multilingual classification approaches (i.e., building a single classification model trained on all the three languages at once).

Testing our universal CEFR hypothesis would require a common feature representation across languages. We developed such a representation, by employing features based on part-of-speech tags and dependency relations from the Universal Dependencies (UD)(Nivre et al., 2016) project which provides treebanks for over 60 languages.[1] Therefore, this approach can be easily extended to other languages with available CEFR graded texts and UD treebanks.

In short, the contributions of this paper are as follows:

1. We study AES for multiple languages for the *first* time using CEFR scale.

2. We explore, for the *first* time, the possibility of a Universal CEFR classifier by training a single model consisting of three languages.

3. We also report *first* results on cross-lingual AES.

The rest of this paper is organized as follows: Section 2 describes related work. Section 3 describes our data and methods. Section 4 discuss

---

[1] http://universaldependencies.org/

147

Proceedings of the Thirteenth Workshop on Innovative Use of NLP for Building Educational Applications, pages 147–153
New Orleans, Louisiana, June 5, 2018. ©2018 Association for Computational Linguistics

our experiments and results in detail. Section 5 concludes the paper with pointers to future work.

2 Related Work

AES is a well studied research problem and AES systems are used to automatically grade essays in exams such as GRE® and TOEFL® (Attali and Burstein, 2004). There is a considerable amount of work that explored various aspects of AES research such as: dataset development, feature engineering, multi-corpus studies and the role of prompt and task information (Yannakoudakis et al., 2011; Phandi et al., 2015; Zesch et al., 2015; Alikaniotis et al., 2016; Taghipour and Ng, 2016; Vajjala, 2018).

AES models developed for non-English languages, primarily using the CEFR scale (Hancke 2013 for German, Pilán et al. 2016 for Swedish, Vajjala and Lõo 2014 for Estonian) employ several language specific features and show their relevance for the task. However, to the best of our knowledge, there is no previous work on developing common models and feature representations that work across languages. Against this background, we set out to address the question: "Is there a universal model for language proficiency classification?"

3 Approach

3.1 Dataset

To test our hypotheses, we need corpora graded with CEFR scale for multiple languages. One such multi-lingual corpus is the freely available MERLIN (Boyd et al., 2014) corpus.[2] This corpus consists of 2286 manually graded texts written by second language learners of German (DE), Italian (IT), and Czech (CZ) as a part of written examinations at authorized test institutions. The aim of these examinations is to test the knowledge of the learners on the CEFR scale which consists of six categories – A1, A2, B1, B2, C1, C2 – which indicate improving language abilities. The writing tasks primarily consisted of writing formal/informal letters/emails and essays. MERLIN corpus has a multi-dimensional annotation of language proficiency covering aspects such as grammatical accuracy, vocabulary range, sociolinguistic awareness etc., and we used the "Overall CEFR rating" as the label for our experiments

---

[2]http://merlin-platform.eu/

in this paper. Other information provided about the authors included- age, gender, and native language, and information about the task such as topic, and the CEFR level of the test itself. We did not use these information in the experiments reported in this paper. Further, we removed all Language-CEFR Category combinations that had less than 10 examples in the corpus (German had 5 examples for level C2 and Italian had 2 examples for B2 which were removed from the data). We also removed all the unrated texts from the original corpus. The final corpus had 2266 documents covering three languages, and Table 1 shows the distribution of labels in the final corpus.

CEFR level	DE	IT	CZ
A1	57	29	0
A2	306	381	188
B1	331	393	165
B2	293	0	81
C1	42	0	0
Total	1029	803	434

Table 1: Composition of MERLIN Corpus

3.2 Features

Our feature set consists of features that are commonly used in AES systems, as well as others that can be generalized across languages. They are described below:

1. Word and POS n-grams, which were commonly used in AES models in the past (Yannakoudakis et al., 2011).

2. Task-specific word and character embeddings trained through a softmax layer. Although word embeddings were used in recent neural AES models(Alikaniotis et al., 2016), this paper is the first to explore character embeddings as a cross-linguistic feature for AES model.

3. Dependency n-grams where each unigram is a triplet consisting of dependency relation, POS tag of the dependent, POS tag of the head. To our knowledge, these features were not used in any of the previous work on AES.

4. Linguistic features specific to AES literature:

   (a) Document length: The number of words in a document which is a common feature used in AES literature.

(b) Lexical richness features: Lu (2012) described several lexical richness and language proficiency for English, which were used in previous AES systems (Hancke, 2013). In this paper, we used lexical density, lexical variation, and lexical diversity features that are commonly used in the AES literature.

(c) Error features: Total number of errors and total spelling errors are obtained for German and Italian from an open-source, rule based spelling and grammar checker.[3] To the best of our knowledge, there is no existing tool for Czech grammar check, and hence we did not extract error features for Czech.

We will refer to these as domain features in this paper.

We extracted all n-gram features where $n \in [1, 5]$ and excluded those n-grams that appeared less than 10 times in the corpus. All the POS and dependency relation based features are extracted using the UDPipe parser (Straka et al., 2016) trained on Universal Dependencies treebanks (Nivre et al., 2016).

Feature Combinations: In addition to the above mentioned features, we also explored the effectiveness of combining n-gram features with domain features. The n-gram features are sparse whereas the domain features are dense; therefore, we combined them by training a n-gram feature classifier and using the probability distribution over its cross-validated predictions with domain features to train the final classifier.

3.3 Classification and Evaluation

We compared logistic regression, random forests, multi-layer perceptron, and support vector machines for experiments with non-embedding features and Neural Network models trained on task-specific embedding representations for other experiments. Word embeddings for each language were task-specific are trained only using the MER-LIN corpus. The embeddings are stacked with a softmax layer and trained with categorical cross-entropy loss and Adadelta algorithm. We also experimented by training a softmax classifier with character and word embeddings as input and found that the combined model does not perform as well as a stand-alone word embeddings model.

Considering the space restrictions, we report only the best performing systems in this paper. Due to the unbalanced class distribution across all the three languages in the data, we employed weighted-F1 score to evaluate the performance of our trained models. Weighted F1 is computed as the weighted average of the F1 score for each label, taking label support (i.e., number of instances for each label in the data) into account. For both monolingual and multilingual settings, we report results with 10-fold cross validation. For cross-lingual evaluation, we report results on the test language's data.

All our neural network models are implemented using Keras (Chollet et al., 2015) with Tensor-Flow as the backend (Abadi et al., 2015) and other models were implemented using scikit-learn (Pedregosa et al., 2011; Buitinck et al., 2013).[4]

While it is also possible to model AES as a regression task, we report classification results which is common in CEFR classification tasks. Our initial experiments with linear regression gave Pearson and Spearman correlation in the range of $0.7 - 0.9$ with gold standard scores, which is comparable with previous results on English AES task obtained using regression models (Alikaniotis et al., 2016).

4 Experiments and Results

For all the experiments, we considered a classifier using only document length (number of words per document) as the feature as the baseline. Unless explicitly stated, all the reported results for non-embedding features are based on Random Forest classifier, which was the best performing classifier in our experiments. Numbers with superscript ^{L} indicate performance of results with a Logistic Regression model.

4.1 Monolingual classification

Our classification results with different feature sets for the three languages are summarized in table 2.

All feature representations perform better than the document length baseline, resulting in close to 25% improvement in the macro F1 score in some cases. All the three sets of n-gram features per-

---

[3] https://languagetool.org/

[4]Relevant code, generated results and the parameter settings are available at: https://github.com/nishkalavallabhi/UniversalCEFRScoring

Features	DE	IT	CZ
Baseline	0.497	0.578[L]	0.587[L]
Word ngrams (1)	0.666	0.827	0.721
POS ngrams (2)	0.663	0.825	0.699
Dep. ngrams (3)	0.663	0.813	0.704
Domain features	0.533[L]	0.653[L]	0.663
(1) + Domain	**0.686**	**0.837**	**0.734**
(2) + Domain	**0.686**	0.816	0.709
(3) + Domain	0.682	0.806	0.712
Word embeddings	0.646	0.794	0.625

Table 2: Weighted F1 scores for Monolingual Classification

form comparably in the case of German and Italian. In the case of Czech, word n-grams turn out be a better predictor of CEFR scale than syntactic features. The domain features, by themselves, do not perform well for any of the languages. However, concatenating the domain features with n-gram features yield slightly better classification results. Word embeddings perform poorly for Czech compared to other non-embedding features, and come close to lexical and syntactic features in the case of German and Italian. Whether using embeddings pre-trained on a larger corpus will give us better scores is something that needs to be explored in future.

To our knowledge, Hancke (2013) is the only comparable work which explored CEFR classification for German using the same dataset, but with several language specific morphological and syntactic features. Our results are comparable to the reported results of Hancke (2013), although we primarily rely on data-driven features. To our knowledge, there are no existing results for Czech and Italian.

German, which has a larger dataset, seems to perform poorer than the other two languages. One possible explanation for this could be that we are dealing with a 5 class classification for German, where as it is only a 3 class problem for Czech and Italian. It is also possible that these feature representations are not sufficient to model German language proficiency labeling task. Further experiments (and possibly with other existing CEFR datasets) are needed to understand why the classification results differ between different languages.

4.2 Multilingual classification

In this setup, we combined all the language texts and trained a single universal CEFR classifier. Table 3 shows the results. For the non-neural models, we experimented with and without considering language information as a categorical feature. The neural network model is a multitasking model (Çöltekin and Rama, 2016) that consists of character and word embeddings as input. The model learns to predict both the language of the text (language identification) and the CEFR category simultaneously. The model is trained using categorical cross-entropy and Adadelta algorithm. The table shows results with and without language identification for neural models.

Features	lang (-)	lang (+)
Baseline	0.428[L]	-
Word n-grams	0.721	0.719
POS n-grams	**0.726**	**0.724**
Dependency n-grams	0.703	0.693
Domain features	0.449[L]	0.471[L]
Word + Char embeddings	0.693	0.689

Table 3: Weighted F1 scores for multilingual classification with models trained on combined datasets.

We observe that the document length baseline seems to perform poorer than monolingual models in this case. Further, we can see that the average result on monolingual model as close to the multilingual model in case of POS n-grams, dependency n-grams, and embeddings. However, domain features clearly perform poorly compared to monolingual case. While one could argue that the better performance multilingual model over some monolingual models is due to more training data, this does not seem to be true for some feature groups (baseline, domain features). One inference we can draw is that some feature groups have similarities in terms of proficiency categories assigned for different languages, which lends support to our hypothesis. Although we did not perform a qualitative language specific evaluation yet, the results so far indicate that efforts to build such a universal scoring model is a worthwhile effort.

4.3 Cross-lingual classification

In this setup, we trained a CEFR model on one language and tested it on others. We trained the cross-lingual model only on German data since it has examples for all categories in our corpus. Table 4 summarizes our results. We did not train with word n-grams and word embeddings here as they are lexical and are language specific and are not suitable for this scenario. Table 4 presents the results of the experiments in this setup. The re-

Features	Test:IT	Test:CZ
Baseline	0.553[L]	0.487[L]
POS n-grams	**0.758**	0.649
Dependency n-grams	0.624	**0.653**
Domain features	0.63[L]	0.475

Table 4: Weighted F1 scores for cross-lingual classification model trained on German.

sults show a drop in performance when compared to monolingual models, which is not surprising as the feature weights are tuned to German syntactic features. However, it is interesting to note that the drop is less than 10% in both cases. In the case of Italian, the domain features yield similar results to monolingual results suggesting that there are some possible universal patterns of language use in the progression towards language proficiency. All feature groups perform better than the document length baseline for Italian, and domain features perform poorer than the baseline for Czech. The confusion matrices for these experiments (cf. tables 5a and 5b) suggest that most of the misclassification occurs only between adjacent levels of proficiency.

The results of this experiment indicate that while cross-lingual classification results in a drop in performance, it still captures the proficiency scale meaningfully. So, the next step in this direction would be to explore better representations of the data, and better modeling methods.

5 Conclusion

In this paper, we reported the results of first experiments conducted with the aim of exploring a "universal CEFR classifier". The results so far indicate that cross-lingual and multilingual classifiers yield comparable performance to individual language models. These results provide some evidence for a

→ Pred	A1	A2	B1	B2	C1
A1	5	24	0	0	0
A2	9	311	56	5	0
B1	1	70	279	44	0

(a) DE-Train:IT-Test setup with POS n-gram features

→ Pred	A1	A2	B1	B2	C1
A2	0	129	57	2	0
B1	0	23	101	41	0
B2	0	5	25	51	0

(b) DE-Train:CZ-Test setup with Dependency features

Table 5: Confusion matrices for cross-lingual scoring with Random Forests by training on German data (DE-train).

universal notion of language proficiency and leave open many questions which need to be explored further in future. Our immediate future plans include a systematic exploration of feature representations which are meaningful for the AES context while being portable across languages. Modeling proficiency classification as a domain adaptation problem (where the domain is another language), and doing multi-task learning by considering other annotation dimensions are other interesting directions to pursue in future. Considering that we have publicly available CEFR graded corpora for other languages such as Estonian, it would be interesting to extend this approach to new languages. This would enable us to investigate questions such as the relationship between genetic/typological similarities between languages and cross/multi-lingual CEFR classification task in future.

When it comes to using such methods in real world language testing applications, researchers express concerns about the validity of the chosen feature constructs, and bias and fairness in models. Some recent research (Madnani et al., 2017) in this direction leaves us with some pointers to incorporate these aspects in future research.

Acknowledgments

The second author is supported by BIGMED[5], a Norwegian Research Council funded Lighthouse project, which is gratefully acknowledged.

---

[5] https://bigmed.no

References

Martín Abadi, Ashish Agarwal, Paul Barham, Eugene Brevdo, Zhifeng Chen, Craig Citro, Greg S. Corrado, Andy Davis, Jeffrey Dean, Matthieu Devin, Sanjay Ghemawat, Ian Goodfellow, Andrew Harp, Geoffrey Irving, Michael Isard, Yangqing Jia, Rafal Jozefowicz, Lukasz Kaiser, Manjunath Kudlur, Josh Levenberg, Dan Mané, Rajat Monga, Sherry Moore, Derek Murray, Chris Olah, Mike Schuster, Jonathon Shlens, Benoit Steiner, Ilya Sutskever, Kunal Talwar, Paul Tucker, Vincent Vanhoucke, Vijay Vasudevan, Fernanda Viégas, Oriol Vinyals, Pete Warden, Martin Wattenberg, Martin Wicke, Yuan Yu, and Xiaoqiang Zheng. 2015. TensorFlow: Large-scale machine learning on heterogeneous systems. Software available from tensorflow.org. https://www.tensorflow.org/.

Dimitrios Alikaniotis, Helen Yannakoudakis, and Marek Rei. 2016. Automatic text scoring using neural networks. In *Proceedings of the 54th Annual Meeting of the Association for Computational Linguistics (Volume 1: Long Papers)*. Association for Computational Linguistics, Berlin, Germany, pages 715–725. http://www.aclweb.org/anthology/P16-1068.

Yigal Attali and Jill Burstein. 2004. Automated essay scoring with e-rater® v. 2.0. *ETS Research Report Series* 2004(2).

Adriane Boyd, Jirka Hana, Lionel Nicolas, Detmar Meurers, Katrin Wisniewski, Andrea Abel, Karin Schöne, Barbora Stindlová, and Chiara Vettori. 2014. The merlin corpus: Learner language and the cefr. In *LREC*. pages 1281–1288.

Lars Buitinck, Gilles Louppe, Mathieu Blondel, Fabian Pedregosa, Andreas Mueller, Olivier Grisel, Vlad Niculae, Peter Prettenhofer, Alexandre Gramfort, Jaques Grobler, Robert Layton, Jake VanderPlas, Arnaud Joly, Brian Holt, and Gaël Varoquaux. 2013. API design for machine learning software: experiences from the scikit-learn project. In *ECML PKDD Workshop: Languages for Data Mining and Machine Learning*. pages 108–122.

François Chollet et al. 2015. Keras. https://github.com/keras-team/keras.

Çağrı Çöltekin and Taraka Rama. 2016. Discriminating similar languages with linear svms and neural networks. In *Proceedings of the Third Workshop on NLP for Similar Languages, Varieties and Dialects (VarDial3)*. pages 15–24.

Julia Hancke. 2013. Automatic prediction of cefr proficiency levels based on linguistic features of learner language. *Master's thesis, University of Tübingen* .

Xiaofei Lu. 2012. The relationship of lexical richness to the quality of esl learners' oral narratives. *The Modern Language Journal* 96(2):190–208.

Nitin Madnani, Anastassia Loukina, Alina von Davier, Jill Burstein, and Aoife Cahill. 2017. Building better open-source tools to support fairness in automated scoring. In *Proceedings of the First ACL Workshop on Ethics in Natural Language Processing*. pages 41–52.

Joakim Nivre, Marie-Catherine de Marneffe, Filip Ginter, Yoav Goldberg, Jan Hajic, Christopher D Manning, Ryan T McDonald, Slav Petrov, Sampo Pyysalo, Natalia Silveira, Reut Tsarfaty, and Daniel Zeman. 2016. Universal Dependencies v1: A Multilingual Treebank Collection. In *Proceedings of the Tenth International Conference on Language Resources and Evaluation (LREC 2016)*. pages 1659–1666.

F. Pedregosa, G. Varoquaux, A. Gramfort, V. Michel, B. Thirion, O. Grisel, M. Blondel, P. Prettenhofer, R. Weiss, V. Dubourg, J. Vanderplas, A. Passos, D. Cournapeau, M. Brucher, M. Perrot, and E. Duchesnay. 2011. Scikit-learn: Machine learning in Python. *Journal of Machine Learning Research* 12:2825–2830.

Peter Phandi, Kian Ming A Chai, and Hwee Tou Ng. 2015. Flexible domain adaptation for automated essay scoring using correlated linear regression. In *Proceedings of the 2015 Conference on Empirical Methods in Natural Language Processing*. pages 431–439.

Ildikó Pilán, David Alfter, and Elena Volodina. 2016. Coursebook texts as a helping hand for classifying linguistic complexity in language learners' writings. *CL4LC 2016* page 120.

Milan Straka, Jan Hajic, and Jana Straková. 2016. UDPipe: Trainable Pipeline for Processing CoNLL-U Files Performing Tokenization, Morphological Analysis, POS Tagging and Parsing. In *LREC*.

Kaveh Taghipour and Hwee Tou Ng. 2016. A neural approach to automated essay scoring. In *EMNLP*. pages 1882–1891.

Sowmya Vajjala. 2018. Automated assessment of non-native learner essays: Investigating the role of linguistic features. *International Journal of Artificial Intelligence in Education* 28(1):79–105.

Sowmya Vajjala and Kaidi Lõo. 2014. Automatic cefr level prediction for estonian learner text. In *Proceedings of the third workshop on NLP for computer-assisted language learning at SLTC 2014, Uppsala University*. Linköping University Electronic Press, 107.

Helen Yannakoudakis, Ted Briscoe, and Ben Medlock. 2011. A new dataset and method for automatically grading esol texts. In *Proceedings of the 49th Annual Meeting of the Association for Computational Linguistics: Human Language Technologies*. Association for Computational Linguistics, Portland, Oregon, USA, pages 180–189. http://www.aclweb.org/anthology/P11-1019.

Torsten Zesch, Michael Wojatzki, and Dirk Scholten-
Akoun. 2015. Task-independent features for automated essay grading. In *BEA@ NAACL-HLT*. pages
224–232.

A   Supplemental Material

The code and data relevant for our experiments are available at: `https://zenodo.`
`org/badge/latestdoi/108113378`.

Chengyu Cloze Test

Zhiying Jiang, Boliang Zhang, Lifu Huang and Heng Ji
Computer Science Department
Rensselaer Polytechnic Institute
{jiangz6, zhangb8, huang17, jih}@rpi.edu

Abstract

We present a neural recommendation model for *Chengyu*, which is a special type of Chinese idiom. Given a query, which is a sentence with an empty slot where the Chengyu is taken out, our model will recommend the Chengyu candidate that best fits the slot context. The main challenge lies in that the literal meaning of a Chengyu is usually very different from its figurative meaning. We propose a neural approach to incorporate the definition of each Chengyu as background knowledge. Experiments on both Chengyu cloze test and coherence checking in college entrance exams show that our system achieves 89.5% accuracy on cloze test and outperforms human experts who attended competitive universities in China. We will make all of our data sets and resources publicly available as a new benchmark for research purposes[1].

1 Introduction

Chengyu ("成语", literal translation: "form phrases") is a special type of Chinese idiom, and represents one of the most beautiful, fascinating and unique aspects of the Chinese language. 96% Chengyus consist of four characters each. Chengyus were mainly created from ancient stories, literature and sayings which can be traced back to thousands of years ago. Some examples are shown in Table 1. More than 7,000 Chengyus are still widely used in the modern Chinese, Japanese, Korean and Vietnamese languages. Like idioms in other languages, using Chengyu appropriately makes communication more compelling and engaging because they introduce powerful imagery and figurative meanings that differ from their literal meanings.

When learning Chinese phrases, Chengyus are always the most difficult to understand and mem-

orize. Second-language learners generally have a love-hate relation with Chengyu and tend to avoid it. A typical way to measure a Chinese learner's Chengyu knowledge is "*Cloze Test*", in which the learner is asked to supply the best Chengyu that has been removed from a sentence. It's considered as one of the most difficult problems in Chinese college entrance language and literature exams, and has been the focus of several TV talent shows in China such as the Chinese Idiom Congress by CCTV. This motivated us to develop the first Chengyu recommendation system to assist Chinese learners. Given a context sentence ("*query*") with a Chengyu removed, the system will automatically recommend the best Chengyu to fill in the blank.

The four characters in each Chengyu are often unintelligible without understanding the background story. For example, "沉鱼落雁 *(literal translation: sink fish fall swallow)*" and "闭月羞花 *(literal translation: hide moon shame flower)*" were used to summarize four stories of the top four beauties in ancient China: Xi Shi, Wang Zhaojun, Diao Chan and Yang Yuhuan. They were being so beautiful that fish sank, birds fell from the sky, the moon hid, and flowers were shamed. As a result, we cannot compose the meaning of a Chengyu only based on its four characters. Moreover, each Chengyu is highly succinct, compact and synthetic. For example, "一日三秋 *(literal translation: one day three autums)*" means greatly missing someone so that one day feels as long as three years. However, its key meaning "*missing*" is not in this Chengyu.

To address these challenges, we create a new Chengyu Cloze Test benchmark, which consists of 108,987 query sentences and 7,395 target Chengyus. Each Chengyu is associated with a definition, which describes its general meanings and scenarios where it occurs. Then we develop an

---

[1] https://github.com/bazingagin/chengyu_data

154

Proceedings of the Thirteenth Workshop on Innovative Use of NLP for Building Educational Applications, pages 154–158
New Orleans, Louisiana, June 5, 2018. ©2018 Association for Computational Linguistics

Origin	Query	Recommended Chengyu and Its Definition
Historical Story	文学接受史上经常有这样的现象，某些作品在它的那个时代曾经风行一时，_____。 Throughout history some literary works were extremely popular, so much so that ____.	洛阳纸贵 (Luoyang's paper became expensive) 原指西晋都城洛阳之纸，因大家争相传抄左思的作品《三都赋》，以至一时供不应求，货缺而贵。比喻著作有价值，流传广。 During the Western Jin Dynasty, people kept copying and propagating Zuosi's work "San Du Fu", which caused the supply of paper falling short of demand. Now a metaphor to describe that some great work is valuable and widely disseminated.
Ancient Chinese Literature	三年的高中生活如_____一般转瞬而逝。 The three years of high school life was like ____, time takes wings.	白驹过隙 (time passes quickly like a white pony's shadow across a crevice) 《庄子》："人生天地之间，若白驹之过隙，忽然而已。" Chuang Tzu said ``Human life between heaven and earth is like the white pony seen through a crack in the wall, it's just a moment.
Fable Proverb Saying	_____，各显神通，预示着省楹联艺术家协会成立后必将涌现出成千上万不计其数的佳联妙对。 ____, each with their own special powers. This indicates that thousands of great couplets will emerge and decorate Shanjin beautifully.	八仙过海 (Eight immortals cross the sea) 相传八仙过海时不用舟船，各有一套法术，后比喻各自拿出本领或办法，互相竞赛。 It's said that eight immortals crossed the sea without boats because each of them had special power. Now it's used to describe using one's unique skill to compete.
Foreign Literature	我们喜欢用经济去控制一个国家的命脉，用信仰去控制一个种族，用利益让别人为我们_____。 We like to use economy to control a country's faith, use belief to control a race and use profit to control others so they can ____ for us.	火中取栗 (pull chestnuts from the embers) 出自十七世纪法国寓言诗人拉·封丹的寓言《猴子与猫》。比喻受人利用去冒险，吃了苦头却得不到一点好处。 From the 17 century French fabulist Jean de la Fontaine's "The Monkey and the Cat". Bertrand the monkey persuades Raton the cat to pull chestnuts from the embers amongst which they are roasting, promising him a share. As the cat scoops them from the fire one by one, burning his paw in the process, the monkey gobbles them up. It's used to describe a person used unwittingly or unwillingly by another to accomplish the other's own purpose with his own risk but gets nothing.
Metaphor	这篇小说情节完整生动，人物性格鲜明，但_____，个别语句还欠推敲。 This novel includes a complete and vivid plot, and the characters have distinct personalities. But it's like ____ some sentences need to be further polished.	白璧微瑕 (white jade with a little blemish) 洁白的玉上有些小斑点。比喻很好的人或物有些小缺点，美中不足。 A flaw in a white jade. It's a metaphor for a good person or a good thing with a little defect.

Table 1: Chengyu Examples

attentive neural network architecture to select the most appropriate Chengyu to fit in the slot context of each query. We first encode query sentence and Chengyu definitions using a bi-directional long short-term memory (Bi-LSTM) network (Hochreiter and Schmidhuber, 1997). To better capture the correlation between the query and the definition, we apply a soft attention to assign a weight to each word in the query sentence, and predict a matching score for each candidate Chengyu. Our system significantly outperforms human learners who attended top universities in China.

2 Related Work

Our Chengyu cloze test task is similar to reading comprehension (Hermann et al., 2015; Cui et al., 2016; Chen et al., 2016; Kadlec et al., 2016; Seo et al., 2016). However, it's more challenging because the context includes a sentence instead of a paragraph, the Chengyu phrase itself does not convey its figurative meaning, and there are many more candidate answers. Very few Natural Language Processing techniques have been applied to understand or recommend Chengyu.

Chung (2009) studied a subset of Chinese figurative language, focusing on Chinese five elements and body part terms. Limited efforts have used Chengyu dictionaries to expand Chinese emotion lexicon (Xu et al., 2010) and improve Chinese word segmentation (Chan and Chong, 2008; Sun and Xu, 2011; Wang and Xu, 2017). Chengyus differ from metaphors in other languages (Tsvetkov et al., 2014; Shutova, 2010) because they do not follow the grammatical structure and syntax of the modern Chinese.

3 Approach

Figure 1 shows the overall architecture of our approach. For a query and the definition of a candidate Chengyu, we first apply a word segmentation tool jieba[2] to segment query and definition into words, and apply a Bi-LSTM network to encode each word with a contextual embedding. In order to better capture the correlation between a query and a Chengyu, we further compare the representations of the Chengyu definition and the contextual embedding of each word in the query, and

---

[2]https://github.com/fxsjy/jieba

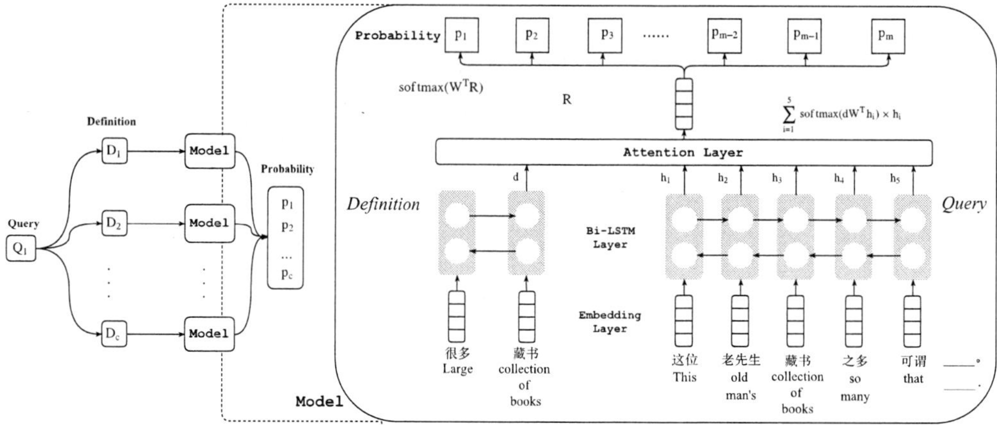

Figure 1: Architecture Overview

take the weighted sum of the query word contextual embeddings as input to a linear function to determine the probability score of the candidate Chengyu. Next we show the approach details.

Encoding Given a query q and a Chenyu definition d_j from the target Chengyu database $D = \{d_1, d_2, ..., d_m\}$, we apply two Bi-LSTM networks to encode them separately. Each Bi-LSTM network leverages long distance features from the whole sentence to capture the context information by using a memory cell (Hochreiter and Schmidhuber, 1997). Each word in q and d_j is assigned a contextual embedding.

Attention To better capture the correlation between a query and each Chengyu definition, we use an attention mechanism (Bahdanau et al., 2014; Sutskever et al., 2014) to compare the semantic relatedness of each word in the query sentence with the meaning of each Chengyu definition.

Given the hidden states $H = h_0, h_1, ..., h_n$ of the Bi-LSTM encoding the query sentence, where h_i denotes the concatenation of the hidden states of word w_i with forward and backward LSTMs, the attention layer sum over h_i with learnable weight α: $\mathbf{R} = \sum_{i=1}^{n} \alpha_i \cdot h_i$, where $\mathbf{R}$ is the weighted sum vector representation of the query. α_i is a learnable weight which is computed by $\alpha_i = \frac{\exp(e_i)}{\sum_{i=1}^{n} \exp(e_i)}$ and $e_i = d^T \cdot \mathbf{W}_\alpha \cdot h_i$, where $\mathbf{W}_\alpha$ is a parameter to capture the relevance between a query and a definition flexibly (Chen et al., 2016). d^T is the last hidden hidden state of the Bi-LSTM encoding the definition.

Training With the weighted sum vector representation of the query $\mathbf{R}$, we apply a softmax function to compute the probability of each candidate Chengyu d_j to be filled into the slot.

$$\mathbf{o}_i = \mathbf{W}_\beta^T \mathbf{R}$$

$$p_i = \frac{\exp(\mathbf{o_i})}{\sum_{j=1}^{m} \exp(\mathbf{o_j})},$$

where $\mathbf{W}_\beta$ maps the final representation of the query into $\mathbb{R}^m$, and m is the number of classes. Then we optimize the log likelihood: $\mathbf{L} = \sum_{j=1}^{m} y_j log(p_j)$, where y_j is 0 or 1 depending on if the truth is Chengyu d_j or not.

Prediction For prediction, we take a query with each Chengyu definition (q, d_j), $1 \leq j \leq m$ as input, and predict a probability matrix $\mathbf{M} \in \mathbb{R}^{m \times m}$, where m is the number of candidates. For example, a choose-one-from-four task will have $m = 4$. The final predicted Chengyu d_j is selected by $argmax(\mathbf{M}[:, j]), 1 \leq j \leq m$.

4 Experiments

4.1 Data and Setting

We crawled 108,987 sentences including 7,395 unique idioms from http://zaojv.com, and the definitions of these idioms from http://cy.5156edu.com. Training and test set contain 108,432 and 555 sentences, and 7,071 and 508 Chengyus respectively. We use the whole Chengyu dataset to train word embeddings. We perform two tests: (1) **cloze test**: for each sentence in the test set, we take out the ground-truth Chengyu, and let the system select a Chengyu

156

TYPE	QUERY	SYSTEM	GROUND TRUTH	ANALYSIS
Incorporating Definition	这事已势不可遏，任何想阻挡他的人都如＿＿＿，简直是不自量力。 This event is unstoppable, anyone who tries to stop it will be like ＿＿＿, almost not recognizing his/her own limited power.	蚍蜉撼树 an ant shaking a tree, to describe one fails to recognize one's limited power	蚍蜉撼树 an ant shaking a tree, to describe one fails to recognize one's limited power	The definition significantly enriches the semantic meanings of Chengyu itself. 蚍蜉撼树(an ant shaking a tree) is a metaphor to describe 自不量力(fail to recognize one's own limited power).
Attention Mechanism	刘备思贤若渴，三请诸葛亮的故事在我国可是＿＿＿，人人皆知的佳话。 It's ＿＿＿ well known by everyone in our country that Liu Bei was eager to recruit talents and invited Zhu Geliang three times.	家喻户晓 well known by every family	家喻户晓 well known by every family	By incorporating the attention mechanism, our approach can better capture the correlations between query context and Chengyu definition. our approach successfully selects 家喻户晓 (well known by every family) to fill in the slot since it shares similar semantic meanings with query context word 知 (known).
World Knowledge	村上春树＿＿＿，29岁才写他的第一部作品。 Haruki Murakami ＿＿＿, he was already at age 29 when he wrote his first works.	画龙点睛 bring the painted dragon to life by putting in the pupils of its eyes	大器晚成 takes a long time to make a great instrument	We need to know "age 29" is relatively late to produce the first works for a writer.
Discourse Coherence	人们面临灾难，不得不＿＿＿，离开他们自己的村落。 When facing disasters, people had to ＿＿＿ and leave their own villages.	逍遥法外 at large	背井离乡 leave one's hometown	Our system focused on the shared meaning of escape/leave while ignored this Chengyu has a specific object "the arm of the law".
Sentiment Analysis	多少人认为一个作家不仅能妙笔生花，也是＿＿＿的。 Many people think that a writer can not only write like an angel but also ＿＿＿.	大言不惭 brag shamelessly	口若悬河 speak eloquently	大言不惭 (brag shamelessly) expresses very negative sentiment while 口若悬河 (speak eloquently) includes positive sentiment.
Negation Detection	你在他面前说那些话，实在是班门弄斧，不知＿＿＿。 The words you said in front of him were really like showing off axe in front of Lu Ban, without knowing ＿＿＿.	孤陋寡闻 with very limited knowledge and scanty information	天高地厚 high as heaven, deep as earth	Our system did not detect negation clues and thus failed to select the right Chengyu antonyms.
Grammatical Structure	写文章先要构思好，不要下笔千言，＿＿＿。 We should think about the plot carefully before write an article, don't write down thousands of words, ＿＿＿	词不达意 the words fail to express the meaning	离题万里 get away from the title ten thousands of miles	When multiple Chengyus appear in the same query sentence, they tend to follow the same grammatical structure.
Rhythm	爱是人性的美的力量，爱是爱你年少时的＿＿＿，更爱你年老时白发苍苍。 Love is the beauty of humanity. To love is to love your youthful vigor like ＿＿＿ as well as your gray hair.	意气风发 high-spirited and vigorous	桃之夭夭 the peach trees in full blossom	Multiple chengyus tend to appear in rhythmical form. In this example, "苍苍"(pronunciation: Cāng Cāng) and "夭夭"(Yāo Yāo) are both reduplication with similar vowel pronunciations.

■ Correct   ▨ Remaining Challenges

Table 2: Detailed Analysis on Correct Examples and Remaining Challenges

from four candidates consisting of the ground-truth and three other randomly selected ones to fill in the slot. (2) **coherence checking in college entrance exam**: we collected 14 problem sets from (1998, 2000) China college entrance exam, where each problem set consists of four sentences including Chengyus. We let the system select the sentence that contains the most appropriate Chengyu that fits into the context in a coherent way. For comparison with human, we asked two Chinese native speakers (not system developers) who attended top universities in China to perform the same tests.

4.2 Results and Analysis

	Cloze Test	Coherence Checking in College Entrance Exam
Human	70%	42.3%
System	89.5%	35.7%

Table 3: System and Human Accuracy Comparison

Table 3 shows our approach achieves comparable performance as human experts. For 18% of our system recommended Chengyus which don't exactly match the ground truth, they are also acceptable choices for the given query contexts.

For example, our system output "白驹过隙*(time passes quickly like a white pony's shadow across a crevice)*" and ground truth "光阴似箭*(time flies)*" are near synonyms. Table 2 shows some correct examples and the remaining challenges that require capabilities beyond lexical semantics.

5   Conclusions and Future Work

We created a new benchmark dataset for a new task of Chengyu cloze test. We also proposed a neural model which leverages the definitions of Chengyu as background knowledge and outperforms human experts. In the future we will explore collective inference to rank multiple Chengyus in the same discourse simultaneously, and incorporate richer linguistic clues based on structures and rhythms.

Acknowledgments

This work was supported by the U.S. DARPA LORELEI Program No. HR0011-15-C-0115 and U.S. ARL NS-CTA No. W911NF-09-2-0053. The views and conclusions contained in this document are those of the authors and should not be interpreted as representing the official policies, either expressed or implied, of the U.S. Government. The U.S. Government is authorized to reproduce and distribute reprints for Government purposes notwithstanding any copyright notation here on.

References

Dzmitry Bahdanau, Kyunghyun Cho, and Yoshua Bengio. 2014. Neural machine translation by jointly learning to align and translate. *arXiv preprint arXiv:1409.0473*.

Samuel W.K. Chan and Mickey W.C. Chong. 2008. An agent-based approach to chinese word segmentation. In *Proceedings of the Sixth SIGHAN Workshop on Chinese Language Processing*.

Danqi Chen, Jason Bolton, and Christopher D Manning. 2016. A thorough examination of the cnn/daily mail reading comprehension task. *arXiv preprint arXiv:1606.02858*.

Siaw-Fong Chung. 2009. A corpus-based study on figurative language through the chinese five elements and body part terms. In *Proceedings of Computational Linguistics and Chinese Language Processing*.

Yiming Cui, Ting Liu, Zhipeng Chen, Shijin Wang, and Guoping Hu. 2016. Consensus attention-based neural networks for chinese reading comprehension. *arXiv preprint arXiv:1607.02250*.

Karl Moritz Hermann, Tomas Kocisky, Edward Grefenstette, Lasse Espeholt, Will Kay, Mustafa Suleyman, and Phil Blunsom. 2015. Teaching machines to read and comprehend. In *Advances in Neural Information Processing Systems*, pages 1693–1701.

Sepp Hochreiter and Jürgen Schmidhuber. 1997. Long short-term memory. *Neural computation*, 9(8):1735–1780.

Rudolf Kadlec, Martin Schmid, Ondrej Bajgar, and Jan Kleindienst. 2016. Text understanding with the attention sum reader network. *arXiv preprint arXiv:1603.01547*.

Minjoon Seo, Aniruddha Kembhavi, Ali Farhadi, and Hannaneh Hajishirzi. 2016. Bidirectional attention flow for machine comprehension. *arXiv preprint arXiv:1611.01603*.

Ekaterina Shutova. 2010. Models of metaphor in nlp. In *Proceedings of the 48th annual meeting of the association for computational linguistics*, pages 688–697. Association for Computational Linguistics.

Weiwei Sun and Jia Xu. 2011. Enhancing chinese word segmentation using unlabeled data. In *Proceedings of the 2011 Conference on Empirical Methods in Natural Language Processing*.

Ilya Sutskever, Oriol Vinyals, and Quoc V Le. 2014. Sequence to sequence learning with neural networks. In *Advances in neural information processing systems*, pages 3104–3112.

Yulia Tsvetkov, Leonid Boytsov, Anatole Gershman, Eric Nyberg, and Chris Dyer. 2014. Metaphor detection with cross-lingual model transfer. In *Proceedings of the 52nd Annual Meeting of the Association for Computational Linguistics (Volume 1: Long Papers)*, volume 1, pages 248–258.

Chunqi Wang and Bo Xu. 2017. Convolutional neural network with word embeddings for chinese word segmentation. In *Proceedings of the The 8th International Joint Conference on Natural Language Processing*.

Ge Xu, Xinfan Meng, and Houfeng Wang. 2010. Build chinese emotion lexicons using a graph-based algorithm and multiple resources. In *Proceedings of the 23rd International Conference on Computational Linguistics (COLING 2010)*.

LaSTUS/TALN at Complex Word Identification (CWI) 2018 Shared Task

Ahmed AbuRa'ed
Universitat Pompeu Fabra
Large Scale Text Understanding
Systems Lab
TALN / DTIC
Barcelona, Spain
ahmed.aburaed@upf.edu

Horacio Saggion
Universitat Pompeu Fabra
Large Scale Text Understanding
Systems Lab
TALN / DTIC
Barcelona, Spain
horacio.saggion@upf.edu

Abstract

This paper presents the participation of the LaSTUS/TALN team in the Complex Word Identification (CWI) Shared Task 2018 in the English monolingual track . The purpose of the task was to determine if a word in a given sentence can be judged as complex or not by a certain target audience. For the English track, task organizers provided a training and a development datasets of 27,299 and 3,328 words respectively together with the sentence in which each word occurs. The words were judged as complex or not by 20 human evaluators; ten of whom are natives. We submitted two systems: one system modeled each word to evaluate as a numeric vector populated with a set of lexical, semantic and contextual features while the other system relies on a word embedding representation and a distance metric. We trained two separate classifiers to automatically decide if each word is complex or not. We submitted six runs, two for each of the three subsets of the English monolingual CWI track.

1 Introduction

Automatic identification of complex words is a core component in several language-related areas of research, including *Text Simplification* (Saggion, 2017), *Lexical Simplification* (Bott et al., 2012), and *Readability Assessment* (Collins-Thompson, 2014).

The Complex Word Identification (CWI) Shared Task 2018 proposes a shared platform for evaluating complex word identification systems under four different tracks: English, Spanish and German monolingual CWI in addition to a multilingual French CWI track with only a test set; the three previously mentioned languages can be used as training for this specific track. The task has two subtasks: binary classification task; to determine if a word is complex or not, and a

probabilistic classification task; the probability of how complex a word is.

In this paper we describe our work for the binary classification task under the English monolingual CWI track in which task participants were provided with a set of sentences to assess. For each sentence, one or more words have been rated as complex or not by 20 human evaluators (ten of which were native speakers).

An example sentence from this dataset is:

A lieutenant who had defected was also killed in the clashes.

In this sentence, the words 'lieutenant' and 'defected' were classified as complex by at least one out of the 20 evaluators, unlike e.g. 'killed', which did not received this label by any of them.

In our participation we cast the identification of complex words as a binary classification problem in which each word is evaluated as complex or not, given the sentence in which it occurs. We designed two systems, the first system modeled each word by a set of lexical, semantic and contextual features and evaluated distinct binary classification algorithms. This system participated from the (CWI) Shared Task 2016 at SemEval (Ronzano et al., 2016) achieving very good performance. The second system modeled each word with its context through a word embedding representation. Our approaches obtained reasonable performance in general but not in comparison with the other participating systems. For evaluation details, the reader is referred to (Yimam et al., 2018).

In Section 2 we provide an overview of relevant research related to Complex Word Identification. Section 3 and 4 respectively introduce the CWI Shared Task 2018 dataset and present the text analysis tools and resources we exploited to characterize complex words. In Section 5 we describe the features we used to build our complex word clas-

159

Proceedings of the Thirteenth Workshop on Innovative Use of NLP for Building Educational Applications, pages 159–165
New Orleans, Louisiana, June 5, 2018. ©2018 Association for Computational Linguistics

sifiers (they have been also reported in (Ronzano et al., 2016)). In Section 6 we present and discuss the performance of our Task 11 system. Finally, in Section 7 we formulate our conclusions and outline future venues of research.

2 Related Work

The identification of complex words constitutes a key aspect of *Text Simplification* (Saggion, 2017) and more specifically of *Lexical Simplification* (Bott et al., 2012). It can be defined as the problem of changing complex words by their simpler synonyms taking into account the specific context in which each word is used. Several techniques have been applied so far to identify complex words. In the context of the PSET Project (Devlin and Tait, 1998), people with aphasia were the target of the first lexical simplification system for English. The system relies on a word difficulty assessment based on psycholinguistic evidence (Quinlan, 1992) in order to decide whether to simplify a word. Recent work compared a corpora of original documents (e.g. English Wikipedia) and their 'simplified' versions (e.g. Simple English Wikipedia pages) to prompt measures which can be used to compare and rank 'quasi-synonymic' word pairs (Yatskar et al., 2010).

Besides lexical simplification, the identification of complex words constitutes a core component of *readability assessment* (Collins-Thompson, 2014), the problem of quantifying the readability of a given text. The more complex words a text has, the harder it becomes to read it. Lists of easy words (Dale and Chall, 1948), word characteristics (Kincaid et al., 1975; Gunning, 1952; Mc Laughlin, 1969), or word use in context (e.g. language models) (Si and Callan, 2001) are all techniques or resources which have been used to support the assessment of text readability: these approaches could also be used to evaluate word complexity.

The CWI Shared Task 2018 is a follow up of the CWI shared task at SemEval 2016 - Task 11 [1] reported by (Paetzold and Specia, 2016a) with the complementary evaluation paper by (Zampieri et al., 2017). 21 teams participated in the task submitting the total of 42 systems. The results concluded that word frequencies are the most reliable predictor of word complexity, also high-

lighted the effectiveness of Decision Trees and Ensemble methods for the task as well.

The best system by (Paetzold and Specia, 2016b) used a voting approach with threshold and machine learning-based classifiers trained on morphological, lexical, and semantic features. TALN (Ronzano et al., 2016) used a Random Forest algorithm over a set of lexical, morphological, semantic and syntactic features.

3 Dataset

The organizers of CWI Shared Task 2018 released a training set and a development set of 27,299 and 3,328 words respectively, together with the sentence in which each word occurs. For each word, the binary complexity judgments of 20 human evaluators were provided (complex word or not complex word); ten of whom where native speakers. Similarly, CWI 2018 task testing dataset consisted of 4,252 words together with the sentence in which each word occurs.

The datasets used in the shared task are described in (Yimam et al., 2017b) and (Yimam et al., 2017a) including the ones for the other tracks in this task.

4 Resources and Tools

In order to identify complex words, we characterize each word by means of a set of lexical, semantic and contextual features, in addition to Word2Vec representations. To this purpose, we analyze both the word and the sentence in which it occurs by means of the language resources and text analysis tools described in what follows.

4.1 Language Resources

To put the word embedding system in use we utilized a pre-trained word2vec model with 300 dimensions representing each vector in the vector space [2]. For the system using engineered features, information about word frequency is important. Therefore, in our complex word identification approach we exploit the word frequency data of two large corpora: (i) a 2014 English Wikipedia Dump and (ii) the British National Corpus (Leech and Rayson, 2014). We also use WordNet (Miller, 1995) to model semantic word features by relying on word senses and synset relations (e.g. hypernymy). Moreover, we use the Dale & Chall list of

---

[1] http://alt.qcri.org/semeval2016/task11/

[2] https://code.google.com/archive/p/word2vec/

3,000 simple words (Dale and Chall, 1948) in order to incorporate the text readability dimension, as this list contains words which 4th grade students considered understandable.

4.2 Text Analysis Tools

We analyze the sentences in which a word to evaluate occurs by means of the Mate dependency parser (Bohnet, 2010). As a result, we obtain a lemmatized and Part-Of-Speech (POS) tagged version of the sentence, along with its syntactic dependencies. Both POS tags and dependency information are used to compute several features as described in the following Section.

We also processed each sentence by the UKB graph-based Word Sense Disambiguation algorithm (Agirre and Soroa, 2009). Specifically, we benefited from the UKB implementation integrated in the Freeling workbench (Padró and Stanilovsky, 2012). In this way, we may disambiguate single or multiword expressions against WordNet 3.0.

5 Method

In order to evaluate the complexity of a word, we designed two systems, each system had different word and sentence representations.

5.1 Word Embedding (WE) System

We utilized word embeddings and modeled each sentence as a Word2Vec representation from a pre-trained model of Google News with 300 dimensions the binary classifier was trained on a set of features.

The set of features is described in the remainder of this Section:

5.1.1 Word and Context representation

Each sentence were handled by calculating the centroid of dimensions of the context before the target word, the target word and the context after the target word, generating a total of 900 features in which each 300 dimensions represent one of the three parts of the sentence. The context surrounding the target word were handled by removing any stop words and only calculating the average of all the tokens that exists in the Google News pre-trained model. Finally, in cases in which there is no context before or after the word a 300 dimensions of zeros were assigned.

5.1.2 Word and Context distance

We generated two extra features to represent the distance between the target word and the context before and after it respectively. The cosine similarity was used to calculate the distance between each pair of vectors in the vector space.

5.2 Lexical, Semantic and Contextual (LSC) features System

We modeled each word as a numeric features vector populated with a set of lexical, semantic and contextual features. In the remainder of this Section we describe the set of word features we used, and motivate their relevance with respect to the characterization of complex words. The approach taken is the same as followed in (Ronzano et al., 2016) which we explain here for the sake of completeness. When presenting word features, we group subsets of related features in the same subsection (Shallow features, Dependency Tree features, etc.). It is important to note that some of the word features presented are computed by considering, besides the target word, also context words in a $[-3, 3]$ window, where position 0 refers to the target word. If the context word at a specific position cannot be determined, the value of the related feature is set to *undefined*.

5.2.1 Shallow Features

We exploited the following set of shallow word features:

- **Word length**: the length of the target word (number of characters).

- **Position of the word**: the position of the target word in the sentence. The value of this feature is normalized in the interval $[0, 1]$ by dividing the the position of the target word in the sentence by the length of the same sentence (number of words). The position of the first word of a sentence is 0.

- **Words in sentence**: the number of tokens in the sentence.

5.2.2 Dependency Tree Features

The following set of features is derived by processing the dependency tree of the sentences that include the word to evaluate:

- **Word depth in the dependency tree**: we considered the depth in the dependency tree of the target word (*position* equal to 0), the three previous words and the three following words.

- **Parent word length**: the length (number of characters) of the parent of the current (target) word in the dependency tree.

5.2.3 Corpus-based Features

Word frequency data derived from the British National Corpus and the 2014 English Wikipedia was used to compute the following set of features:

- **British National Corpus frequency**: we considered the BNC frequency[3] of the target word lemma (*position* equal to 0), the three previous word lemmas and the three following word lemmas.

- **English Wikipedia frequency**: we considered the 2014 English Wikipedia frequency of the target word (*position* equal to 0), the three previous words and the three following words. Word frequencies are computed by tokenizing and lower-casing English Wikipedia contents.

- **Simple word list**: a binary feature to point out the presence of the target word in the Dale & Chall list.

5.2.4 WordNet features

We used WordNet 3.0 to compute the following features. Given a target word, we refer as *target-word-synsets* the set of synsets that have the same POS of the target word and include the target word among their lexicalizations (all the senses of the target word). Note that this set of features is computed without relying on Word Sense Disambiguation.

- **Number of Synsets**: the number of synsets in *target-word-synsets* (i.e. number of senses of the target word).

- **Number of Senses**: the sum of the number of word senses (i.e. the number of lexicalizations) of each *target-word-synset*.

- **Depth in the hypernym tree**: the average depth in the WordNet hypernym hierarchy among all the *target-word-synsets*.

- **Number of Lemmas**: the average number of synset lexicalizations among all the *target-word-synsets*.

- **Gloss length** (WNGloss): the average length of synset Glosses among all the *target-word-synsets*, in terms of number of tokens.

- **Number of relations** (WNRelation): the average number of semantic relations among all the *target-word-synsets*.

- **Number of Distinct POSs** (WNDistinct-POS): the number of distinct POS represented by at least one *target-word-synset*.

- **Part of Speech** (WN_*POS* - 4 features): for each WordNet POS (*POS* equal to Noun, Verb, Adjective and Adverb) we counted the number of synsets with that POS among the *target-word-synsets*, thus generating four features.

5.2.5 WordNet and corpus frequency features

The following set of features was computed by combining WordNet data, the word frequencies of the British National Corpus (BNC) and the results of the UKB WordNet-based Word Sense Disambiguation algorithm applied to the sentences where complex words appear. Thanks to the UKB algorithm, we identify the WordNet 3.0 synset that characterizes the sense of each target word (*WSD-synset*). Besides the target word, each *WSD-synset* usually has other lexicalizations, i.e. other synonyms. We retrieve the BNC frequency of all the lexicalizations of the *target-word-WSD-synset* and compute the following features:

- **Percentage of lexicalizations with higher / lower frequency than target word**: the percentage of the lexicalizations of the *WSD-synset* with a BNC frequency higher / lower than the target word BNC frequency.

- **Ratio of total lexicalizations' frequencies related to lexicalizations with higher / lower frequency than target word**: the ratio between the sum of BNC frequencies of the lexicalizations of the *WSD-synset* with a frequency higher / lower than the target word frequency and the sum of BNC frequencies of all the lexicalizations of the *WSD-synset*.

---

[3] http://ucrel.lancs.ac.uk/bncfreq/lists/1_1_all_fullalpha.txt.Z

We also computed the previous set of 4 features without relying on the results of the UKB Word Sense Disambiguation algorithm: we considered for each target word all the lexicalizations of all the synsets that represent possible senses and have the same POS of the same target word. Similarly to the UKB based features.

With the total of 902 features for the word embedding system and 60 features before applying any filtering to the lexical, semantic and contextual features System, we enabled the training and evaluation of distinct binary classification algorithms tailored to determine whether a word is complex or not. To this end, we relied on the Weka machine learning framework (Witten and Frank, 2000).

6 Results

We evaluated the performance of five classification algorithms: Support Vector Machine (with linear and radial basis function kernels), Naïve Bayes, Logistic Regression, Random Tree and Random Forest. We applied 10 fold-cross validation over the training data, based on the obtained reults we decided to build the classifiers using Random Forest for both systems since they performed best over the whole dataset. The results of the Random Forest system in 10-fold cross validation experiments over the training data can be seen in Table 1.

Table 1: 10-fold cross validation over the training datasets

System	Dataset	P	R	F
WE	News	0.810	0.811	**0.810**
	WikiNews	0.741	0.742	0.736
	Wikipedia	0.708	0.703	0.694
	all	0.803	0.803	**0.803**
LSC	News	0.796	0.793	0.787
	WikiNews	0.747	0.745	**0.738**
	Wikipedia	0.769	0.768	**0.766**
	all	0.785	0.783	0.778

Tables 2, 3 and 4 presents the top 3 systems participating in the evaluation together with our results. We have obtained mixed results: in the English News our Word Embedding (WE) system outperformed the system based on human engineered features (LSC) – eleventh position in the ranking. While the LSC system performed better on WikiNews and Wikipedia, placing the team in the tenth position in the ranking.

Table 2: Comparison with the top three teams for the English News submissions

Team	Accuracy
camb	0.8792
dirkdh	0.8721
TMU	0.8706
WE	0.8172
LSC	0.7785

Table 3: Comparison with the top three teams for the English WikiNews submissions

Team	Accuracy
camb	0.8430
ajason08	0.8368
nathansh	0.8329
LSC	0.7615
WE	0.7374

Table 4: Comparison with the top three teams for the English Wikipedia submissions

Team	Accuracy
camb	0.8115
nathansh	0.7966
andrei.butnaru	0.7920
LSC	0.7414
WE	0.6966

7 Conclusion

In conclusion, we tried to approach the problem of identifying complex words at the CWI shared task 2018 by designing two systems based on binary classifiers, one represents the context as word embedding vectors and the other use a set of lexical, semantic and contextual features. The WE system performed better in the English News part and the LSC system excelled for Wikinews and Wikipedia. For future work we are planning on better analyzing our set of features by applying some feature selection methods e.g. info gain. Afterwards, we will attempt deep-learning neural networks to create our classifiers.

Acknowledgments

This work is (partly) supported by the Spanish Ministry of Economy and Competitiveness under the Maria de Maeztu Units of Excellence Programme (MDM-2015-0502) and by the TUNER project (TIN2015-65308-C5-5-R, MINECO/FEDER, UE).

References

Eneko Agirre and Aitor Soroa. 2009. Personalizing pagerank for word sense disambiguation. In *Proceedings of the 12th Conference of the European Chapter of the Association for Computational Linguistics*, pages 33–41. Association for Computational Linguistics.

Bernd Bohnet. 2010. Very high accuracy and fast dependency parsing is not a contradiction. In *Proceedings of the 23rd International Conference on Computational Linguistics (Coling 2010)*, pages 89–97, Beijing, China. Coling 2010 Organizing Committee.

Stefan Bott, Luz Rello, Biljana Drndarevic, and Horacio Saggion. 2012. Can Spanish Be Simpler? LexSiS: Lexical Simplification for Spanish. In *Proceedings of the 24th International Conference on Computational Linguistics (CoLing 2012)*.

Kevyn Collins-Thompson. 2014. Computational assessment of text readability. a survey of current and future research. *ITL - International Journal of Applied Linguistics 165:2*, 165(2):97–135.

Edgar Dale and Jeanne S. Chall. 1948. The concept of readability. *Elementary English*, 23(24).

Siobhan Devlin and John Tait. 1998. The use of a psycholinguistic database in the simplification of text for aphasic readers. *Linguistic Databases*, pages 161–173.

Robert Gunning. 1952. *The Technique of Clear Writing*. McGraw-Hill.

J. Peter Kincaid, Robert P. Fishburne Jr., Richard L. Rogers, and Brad S. Chissom. 1975. Derivation of New Readability Formulas (Automated Readability Index, Fog Count and Flesch Reading Ease Formula) for Navy Enlisted Personnel. Technical report, Naval Technical Training Command.

Geoffrey Leech and Paul Rayson. 2014. *Word frequencies in written and spoken English: Based on the British National Corpus*. Routledge.

G. Harry Mc Laughlin. 1969. SMOG grading - a new readability formula. *Journal of Reading*, pages 639–646.

George A. Miller. 1995. Wordnet: a lexical database for english. *Communications of the ACM*, 38(11):39–41.

Lluis Padró and Evgeny Stanilovsky. 2012. Freeling 3.0: Towards wider multilinguality. In *Proceedings of the Language Resources and Evaluation Conference (LREC 2012)*, Istanbul, Turkey. ELRA.

Gustavo Paetzold and Lucia Specia. 2016a. SemEval 2016 Task 11: Complex Word Identification. In *Proceedings of the 10th International Workshop on Semantic Evaluation (SemEval-2016)*, pages 560–569, San Diego, California. Association for Computational Linguistics.

Gustavo Paetzold and Lucia Specia. 2016b. Sv000gg at semeval-2016 task 11: Heavy gauge complex word identification with system voting. In *Proceedings of the 10th International Workshop on Semantic Evaluation (SemEval-2016)*, pages 969–974, San Diego, California. Association for Computational Linguistics.

Philip T. Quinlan. 1992. *The Oxford Psycholinguistic Database*. Oxford University Press.

Francesco Ronzano, Ahmed Abura'ed, Luis Espinosa Anke, and Horacio Saggion. 2016. Taln at semeval-2016 task 11: Modelling complex words by contextual, lexical and semantic features. In *Proceedings of the 10th International Workshop on Semantic Evaluation (SemEval-2016)*, pages 1011–1016, San Diego, California. Association for Computational Linguistics.

Horacio Saggion. 2017. *Automatic Text Simplification*. Synthesis Lectures on Human Language Technologies. Morgan & Claypool Publishers.

Luo Si and Jamie Callan. 2001. A statistical model for scientific readability. In *Proceedings of the Tenth International Conference on Information and Knowledge Management*, CIKM '01, pages 574–576, New York, NY, USA. ACM.

Ian H. Witten and Eibe Frank. 2000. *Data Mining: Practical Machine Learning Tools and Techniques with Java Implementations*. Morgan Kaufmann Publishers Inc., San Francisco, CA, USA.

Mark Yatskar, Bo Pang, Cristian Danescu-Niculescu-Mizil, and Lillian Lee. 2010. For the sake of simplicity: Unsupervised extraction of lexical simplifications from Wikipedia. In *Proceedings of the Proceedings of the 49th Annual Meeting of the Association for Computational Linguistics*, pages 365–368.

Seid Muhie Yimam, Chris Biemann, Shervin Malmasi, Gustavo Paetzold, Lucia Specia, Sanja Štajner, Anaïs Tack, and Marcos Zampieri. 2018. A Report on the Complex Word Identification Shared Task 2018. In *Proceedings of the 13th Workshop on Innovative Use of NLP for Building Educational Applications*, New Orleans, United States. Association for Computational Linguistics.

Seid Muhie Yimam, Sanja Štajner, Martin Riedl, and Chris Biemann. 2017a. CWIG3G2 - Complex Word Identification Task across Three Text Genres and Two User Groups. In *Proceedings of the Eighth International Joint Conference on Natural Language Processing (Volume 2: Short Papers)*, pages 401–407, Taipei, Taiwan. Asian Federation of Natural Language Processing.

Seid Muhie Yimam, Sanja Štajner, Martin Riedl, and Chris Biemann. 2017b. Multilingual and Cross-Lingual Complex Word Identification. In *Proceedings of the International Conference Recent Advances in Natural Language Processing, RANLP*

2017, pages 813–822, Varna, Bulgaria. INCOMA Ltd.

Marcos Zampieri, Shervin Malmasi, Gustavo Paetzold, and Lucia Specia. 2017. Complex Word Identification: Challenges in Data Annotation and System Performance. In *Proceedings of the 4th Workshop on Natural Language Processing Techniques for Educational Applications (NLPTEA 2017)*, pages 59–63, Taipei, Taiwan. Asian Federation of Natural Language Processing.

Cross-lingual complex word identification with multitask learning

Joachim Bingel
Department of Computer Science
University of Copenhagen, Denmark
bingel@di.ku.dk

Johannes Bjerva
Department of Computer Science
University of Copenhagen, Denmark
bjerva@di.ku.dk

Abstract

We approach the 2018 Shared Task on Complex Word Identification by leveraging a cross-lingual multitask learning approach. Our method is highly language agnostic, as evidenced by the ability of our system to generalize across languages, including languages for which we have no training data. In the shared task, this is the case for French, for which our system achieves the best performance. We further provide a qualitative and quantitative analysis of which words pose problems for our system.

1 Introduction

Complex word identification (CWI) is the task of predicting whether a certain word might be difficult for a reader to understand and is typically used as a first step in (lexical) simplification pipelines (Shardlow, 2014; Paetzold and Specia, 2015, 2016a). This task has received significant attention from the community over the past few years, leading to two shared tasks and several other publications (Shardlow, 2013a,b).

This paper presents our submission to the CWI 2018 shared task (Yimam et al., 2018), at the 13th Workshop on Innovative Use of NLP for Building Educational Applications. This task includes tracks targeting four languages: English, Spanish, German and French. For each of these languages, the task involves prediction of binary labels of whether any of a range of annotators deemed some word or phrase complex, or prediction of the ratio of those who did. The task further differs from previous approaches to CWI in extending the definition of the target units from the word level to multi-word expressions, such that annotations in the training and test set spanned wider stretches of text than single tokens.

Another difference from previous approaches to CWI is that the data is annotated by a mixture of native and non-native speakers, posing an interesting challenge to reconcile the potentially different complexity assessments of these groups.

One challenge in the CWI 2018 shared task is the fact that one of the languages under consideration (French) does not have any training data available. We approach this problem by exploring a combination of multitask learning and cross-lingual learning. In doing so, we aim to answer the following research questions:

RQ 1 How can multitask learning be applied to the task of cross-lingual CWI?

RQ 2 How can complex words be identified in languages which are not seen during training time?

Our contributions also include a thorough qualitative and quantitative error analysis, which shows that long and infrequent words are very likely to be complex, but that non-complex words that display these properties pose a challenge to our system.

2 Related work

2.1 Multitask Learning

Multitask learning (MTL) is the combined learning of several tasks in a single model (Caruana, 1997). This can be beneficial in a number of scenarios. Previous work has shown benefits, e.g., in cases where one has tasks which are closely related to one another (Bjerva, 2017a,b), when one task can help another escape a local minimum (Bingel and Søgaard, 2017), and when one has access to some unsupervised signal which can be beneficial to the task at hand (Rei, 2017). A common approach to MTL is the application of hard parameter sharing, in which some set of parameters in a model is shared between several tasks. We contribute to previous work in MTL by using a hard parameter sharing approach in which

166

Proceedings of the Thirteenth Workshop on Innovative Use of NLP for Building Educational Applications, pages 166–174
New Orleans, Louisiana, June 5, 2018. ©2018 Association for Computational Linguistics

we share intermediate layers between languages, and use one output-layer per language, thus in a sense seeing languages as tasks, similarly to Bjerva (2017a).

2.2 Cross-lingual learning

Cross-lingual learning is the problem of training a model on a given language, and applying it to another (unseen) language. One common approach is to apply cross-lingual word representations, although this has the disadvantage that it tends to place relatively high demands on availability of parallel text. Another frequently used approach in this context is to use machine translation (MT) so as to obtain a monolingual training set (Tiedemann et al., 2014). However, this approach necessarily increases the complexity of a system, as a fully-fledged MT system needs to be incorporated in the pipeline. Furthermore, this approach bypasses the problem of attempting to find methods or feature sets which can be successful across languages. We therefore follow previous work by, e.g. Bjerva and Östling (2017) in that we use hard parameter sharing with language-agnostic input representations. We build upon this by leveraging language-specific resources which are widely available, such as Wikipedia dumps, and WordNet (see Section 5).

2.3 CWI

Automatic complex word identification has a relatively short history as a research task, with first publications including Shardlow (2013a,b)

A noticeable commonality of the highest-scoring systems in the CWI 2016 shared task was the use of ensemble methods, most notably random forest classifiers, which drew on a range of morphologic, semantic and psycholinguistic features, among others (Paetzold and Specia, 2016b; Ronzano et al., 2016).

Yimam et al. (2017) present first work on CWI that considers languages other than English. They release a German and a Spanish dataset and present first CWI results for these languages. Notably, they also describe first cross-lingual experiments, in which they train on some language and test on another, i.e. without employing any of the common strategies for cross-lingual learning that we outline above.

Recently, Bingel et al. (2018) showed promising results in predicting complex words from gaze patterns of Danish children with reading difficulties,

Language	Training	Dev	Test	Complex
English	27,299	3,328	4,252	42.03%
Spanish	13,750	1,622	2,233	40.61%
German	6,151	795	959	39.21%
French	–	–	2,251	29.18%

Table 1: Data overview. The share of complex words is computed across all data splits.

which opens up possibilities for personalized complex word identification, but it is less certain how well their method generalizes to other languages or demographics.

3 Data

We use the data made available through the shared task (Yimam et al., 2018). Each training instance consists of a sentence, with a marked complex phrase annotation, including the numbers of native and non-native annotators, and the fraction of these who found the phrase to be complex. An overview of the data is given in Table 1. The number of entries which are considered complex is quite skewed, and differs per language as French has substantially fewer complex phrases than English. This is further illustrated in Figure 1.

In addition to the shared task data, we also use external resources in our feature representations (see Section 5).

4 Model

As outlined in Section 2, earlier work has shown the aptitude of ensemble methods for CWI, especially such ensembles that feature random forests. We further choose to address the problem in a cross-lingual fashion, for which we deem multi-task learning models particularly suitable.

Motivated by these observations, we devise an ensemble that comprises a number of random forests as well as feed-forward neural networks with hard parameter sharing. The random forests each consist of 100 trees that create splits based on Gini impurity (Breiman, 2001). They do not implement any form of explicit cross-lingual transfer other than the reliance on language-agnostic features, such that we simply train them on a single language at a time, or on shuffled concatenations of training data for several languages. We use random forest classifiers for the binary task and random-forest regressors for the probabilistic task.

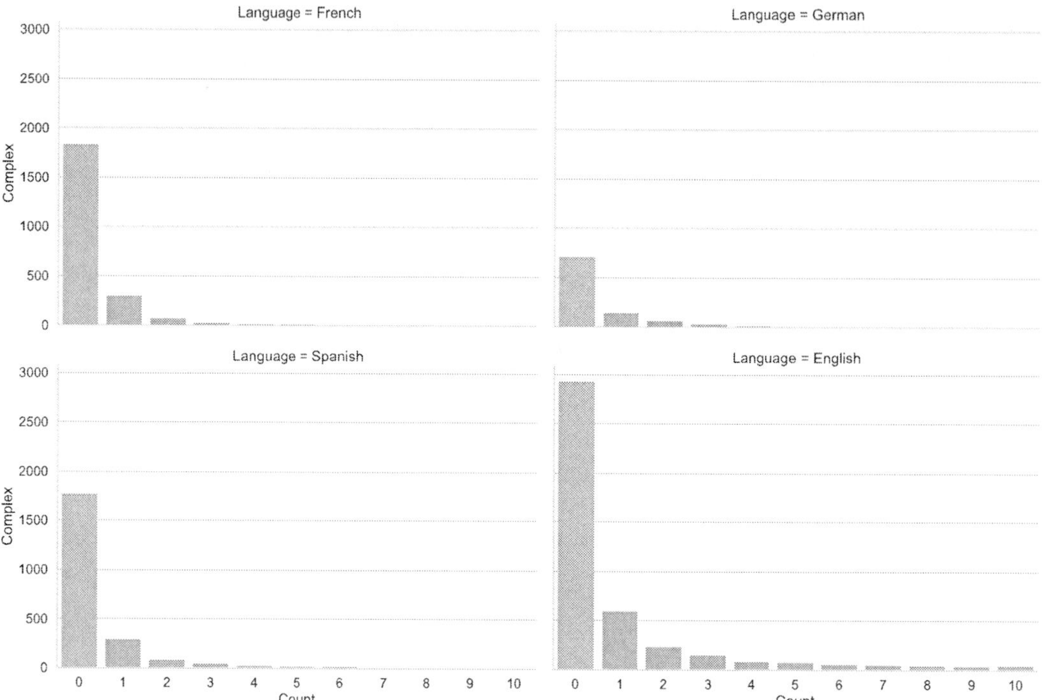

Figure 1: Histogram of numbers sentences (y-axis) which N annotators (x-axis) found to be complex.

Note that our random forests are single-task models, where we cannot define shared or language-specific subparts. Instead, these are always trained on data for the single test language.

The neural MTL models, in contrast, explicitly define parts pertaining to specific languages. Concretely, for each language l, we define a function from a language-specific input layer to a hidden representation h_0 that we share between languages:

$$h_0 = \tanh(x^{(l)} W_{in}^{(l)} + b_{in}^{(l)}) \qquad (1)$$

Here and in the following equations, $W_{(\cdot)}$ and $b_{(\cdot)}$ consistently denote weight matrices and bias vectors, respectively. $W_{in}^{(l)}$ and $b_{in}^{(l)}$ are the weights and bias terms specific to input layer l, and the input $x^{(l)}$ is a vector representation of the features introduced in Sec. 5.

We then compute deeper hidden representations, such that the hidden layer at depth d is defined as follows:

$$h_d = \tanh(h_{d-1} W_d + b_d) \qquad (2)$$

Finally, each language l defines its own output $y^{(l)}$. This output is defined slightly differently for the regression and classification models.

$$y_{reg}^{(l)} = h_D W_{out}^{(l)} + b_{out}^{(l)} \qquad (3)$$

For the former, this is simply a linear transformation of the deepest hidden layer D. The classification model adds a sigmoid activation to this:

$$y_{clf}^{(l)} = \sigma(h_D W_{out}^{(l)} + b_{out}^{(l)}) \qquad (4)$$

4.1 MTL training

Since our multitask model defines several outputs, but our data is only labeled with a single annotation layer (i.e. for a single language or "task"), we need a training strategy that does not require true labels for all tasks. The way this is normally approached is to iteratively optimize for tasks in isolation, e.g. by deciding at random which language we sample a batch of data from at every pass of the forward-backward algorithm we use to train the model.

We employ the above strategy and optimize the regression model with a mean absolute error loss function, as well as cross-entropy for the classification model. We monitor these losses on the validation set as an early stopping criterion.

4.2 Ensemble voting

The different neural and random-forest based model that we train as devised above finally make independent predictions for new examples. For the regression models, we use the median prediction across all systems for a given input to make the final ensemble prediction. For the classifiers, however, we have an additional parameter t that we optimize on a held-out development set. This is a threshold indicating the fraction of classifiers that need to cast a positive vote for us to finally accept an example as complex. All neural and random forest classifiers are weighted equally here, each casting a single binary vote.

4.3 Language identification for cross-lingual prediction

As we expect our system to be able to generate predictions for unseen languages (for which we have no explicit output layer), we implement a further component in our neural model that we optimize to predict the language of some input from the set of available languages with explicit output layers. This is an additional output layer of our model, defined as a dense projection from the first hidden layer followed by a sigmoid.

$$l = \sigma(h_0 W_{lid} + b_{lid}) \tag{5}$$

During training, we then supply a ground truth language identifier $\hat{l}$ as a second target variable and perform optimization under a cross-entropy loss that we add to the CWI loss. At test time, for a language without an explicit output layer, we first predict the most similar language we saw during training using Eq. 5 and then use the output layer for that language to generate CWI predictions. An alternative to this could be to generate predictions from all CWI output layers and ensemble these, possibly weighted, with weights inferred in a similar fashion to language identification.

For the random forest models, which do not define language-specific output functions, we simply concatenate training data from all available languages, leveraging the fact that our feature space is language-independent.

5 Features

Our systems build on the same set of features for all input languages, although some of these are computed from language-specific resources. This means that the distributions of values attained for certain features may differ between languages, which is the motivation for language-specific input layers in our model. We further reduce language idiosyncrasies by normalizing all features to the $[0, 1]$ range. The features are listed below.

Log-probability We compute unigram frequencies for candidates as their log-probabilities in language-specific Wikipedia dumps. For multi-word targets, we use the sum of the log-probabilities of the individual items. Log-probabilities are computed using KenLM (Heafield, 2011).

Character perplexity Based on the same Wikipedia dumps as above, we compute character perplexities over the candidate strings using a smoothed 5-gram character-based language model (again using KenLM).

Number of synsets As a measure of a target's semantic ambiguity, we count the number of synsets that include it. For this, we rely on the language-specific WordNet resources for English (Fellbaum, 1998), Spanish (Gonzalez-Agirre et al., 2012) and French (Sagot and Fišer, 2008). For German, access to GermaNet (Hamp and Feldweg, 1997) was harder to obtain, and we instead automatically translate words from German to English and use the English WordNet.[1] In case of a multi-word target, we take the mean number of synsets across the individual words.

Hypernym chain As a measure of semantic specificity, we further consider the length of the hypernym chain of an item, i.e. the number of hypernyms that can recursively be obtained for a word. These are also obtained using WordNet, and again we average over individual words in a target.

Inflectional complexity As a proxy for inflectional complexity (i.e. the number of suffixes appended to a word stem), we measure the difference in length (character count) between the surface form and the stem of a word. For this, we use language-specific instances of the Snowball stemmer (Porter, 2001) as implemented in NLTK (Bird and Loper, 2004).

Surface features As basic surface features, we include the length of an item (in characters) and whether it is all-lowercase.

---

[1] For the translations, we used a bilingual dictionary (`https://www.dict.cc/`).

Language	MAE	Rank	Δ (system)	F_1	Rank	Δ (system)
French	0.066	1	0.012 (TMU)	0.7595	1	0.013 (TMU)
German	0.075	2	-0.013 (TMU)	0.6621	5	-0.083 (TMU)
Spanish	0.079	3	-0.007 (TMU)	0.7458	5	-0.024 (TMU)

Table 2: Official performance figures of our method for all non-English tracks. The Δ (system) column indicates the difference in performance between our system and the best system in each track except for ours. In accordance with the shared task report, classification performance is measured by macro F_1 between the complex and non-complex class in the official results.

Bag-of-POS   For each tag defined in the Universal Part-of-Speech project (Petrov et al., 2011), we count the number of words in a candidate that belong to the respective class. We obtain POS tags from spacy.[2]

Target-sentence similarity   Motivated by the conjecture that words or phrases are easier to understand if they display higher semantic similarity with their context, we compute the cosine distances between averaged word embeddings for the target word or phrase and the rest of the containing sentence. To mitigate out-of-vocabulary problems, we use pretrained subword embeddings that we retrieve from the BPEemb project (Heinzerling and Strube, 2017).

The data provided for the shared task further includes information on how many of the annotators are native and non-native speakers. While this information is potentially helpful (assuming that non-native speakers would have a stronger bias for annotating as complex), we do not make use of it, considering that access to such information cannot be assumed in a real-world scenario.

6   Results

We present an overview of the results that our method (as well as our best contender) achieved in Table 2 and discuss results for the individual languages below.[3]

6.1   French

Due to the lack of training data for this track, it poses a challenging test for the ability of our models to generalize across languages. While the exact performance figures are at least partly subject to idiosyncrasies in the text samples and annotators,

the results obtained here are a good benchmark of of what we can achieve for languages for which we do not even have validation data to monitor development loss for early stopping.

As Table 2 shows, we achieve the best results of all participating teams for French, both for the classification and for the regression track. We view this as evidence that our cross-lingual MTL approach is an effective means to share knowledge between different data sources and even different languages.

6.2   German/Spanish

Our results for Spanish and German show that, while we did not achieve the best results compared to other participants, our method still performs competitively. Especially for the regression track, while not ranking first, the absolute performance figures place us very close to the winning systems. We see this as a validation of our approach, in particular under the consideration that a gradual assessment of complexity is perhaps more meaningful than a binary one, especially when the definition of the latter makes no distinction between one or all out of 20 annotators judging an item as difficult.

6.3   Analysis

Qualitative error analysis   Table 3 exemplifies some of the correct and incorrect predictions that our system makes for the French test data. We observe that the system picks up on the relatively long targets listed as true positives. Note also that the false positives are relatively long words, which suggests that the system is deceived by this. The targets listed as false negatives are shorter, but they are examples of a (potentially unknown) named entity and a relatively technical term, which might pose difficulties to some readers. The words listed as true negatives are correctly predicted by our

---

[2] https://spacy.io/
[3] We did not submit solutions for the English track.

Il marque néanmoins sa désapprobation en voyant des Juifs prier devant le mur des Lamentations; Einstein commente qu'il s'agit de personnes collées au passé et faisant abstraction du présent.

Rimbaud a donné ses lettres de noblesse à un type de poème en prose distinct d'expériences plus **prosaïques** du type du "Spleen de Paris" de Baudelaire.

Le pays des vallées d'Andorre entre la France et l'Espagne, sur le versant sud des **Pyrénées**, est constitué par deux vallées principales: celle du Valira del Orient et celle du Valira del Nord dont les eaux réunies forment le Valira.

Autres cultures permanentes, la lavande et le lavandin occupent plusieurs milliers d'**hectares** et fournissent plusieurs milliers d'emplois directs.

Beaucoup d'îles des Caraïbes (les Antilles) – par exemple, les Grandes Antilles et les Petites Antilles – sont **situées** au-dessus de la plaque caraïbe, une plaque tectonique avec une topographie diffuse.

Avec un fort penchant à l'hermétisme qu'il partage avec d'autres de ses quasi contemporains (Gérard de Nerval, Stéphane Mallarmé, sinon Paul Verlaine parfois), Rimbaud a le **génie** des visions saisissantes qui semblent défier tout ordre de description du réel.

La **construction** de l'Atomium fut une prouesse technique.
La **proportion** des musulmans, tous sunnites, est inférieure à 1%.

Table 3: Example wins and losses of our model for French. Target words or phrases are marked in bold.

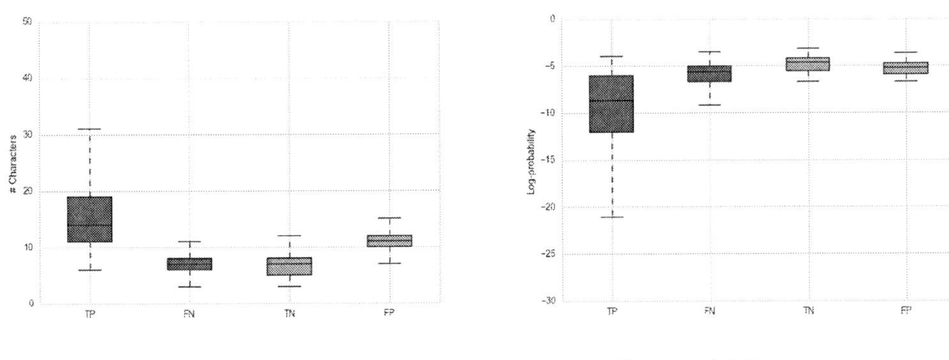

(a) Length in characters per error type   (b) Log-probability per error type

Figure 2: Statistics of character length and language model log-probability for the French test set. The darker-shaded boxes are complex words that we predicted correctly (TP) and incorrectly (FN), respectively. The lighter-shaded boxes are non-complex words, predicted correctly (TN) and incorrectly (FP).

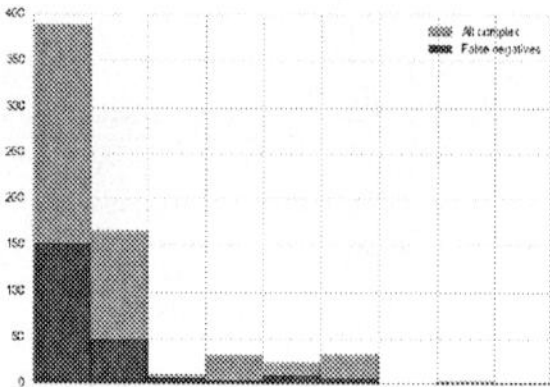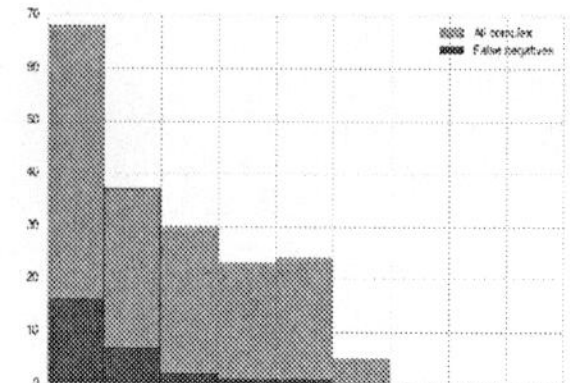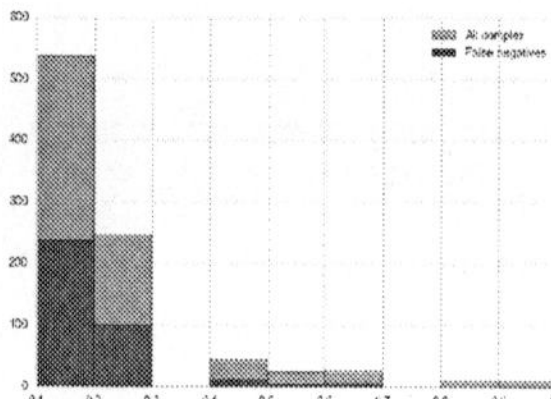

Figure 3: Distributions of false negative predictions per complexity degree as measured by the fraction of annotators that labeled items as complex in the French, German and Spanish test sets (left to right).

system as non-complex, possibly because of their shortness.

Quantitative error analysis Investigating the observations from the previous section in a more quantitative fashion, Figure 2 presents distributions of two basic features across complex vs. non-complex words, and correctly vs. wrongly predicted test set items for French. For item length, we observe a clear pattern that complex words tend to be significantly longer than non-complex ones. Further, the longer they are, the easier it is for our model to detect them as complex. Non-complex words that are relatively long, however, lead to incorrect predictions from our model.

A very similar pattern can be observed for the log-probability of complex and non-complex items. The former are assigned a much lower probability by our language model, and particularly unlikely words are very easy to detect as complex. In turn, non-complex words with relatively low probability pose a challenge for our model.

False negatives per complexity degree We further analyze the influence of the degree of complexity on our model's ability to detect complex words. As stated in the Introduction, an item is labeled as complex in the classification setting if any of the annotators deemed it to be complex. Effectively, no distinction is made in the classification task between a "slightly complex" item that was marked as such by just one out of ten annotators, and one that was unanimously considered complex.

A natural assumption is that our models would more easily pick up on highly complex words and predict false negatives mostly for items with low complex annotation ratios. To verify this assumption, we plot the total number of complex words

in the three non-English test sets against the false negative predictions of our model, grouped by the ratio of annotators who marked an item as complex (Figure 3). The French and Spanish test sets are somewhat inconclusive for our question as they generally contain very few items with a complexity ratio higher than 0.2. The German test set, however, is more balanced, and in fact we observe that items with a complexity ratio above 0.2 are very reliably detected by our model, confirming our hypothesis.

7 Discussion

We approached **RQ 1** by using one output layer per language, and sharing intermediate parameters. This approach was successful, at least in part due to our language-agnostic input representations, which allowed the model to learn similar internal representations for each language. Separate output-layers per language, in turn, allow for the model to make language-specific accommodations. We approached **RQ 2** by using language-agnostic feature representations, and language-specific output layers which were chosen during test time for unseen languages. This approach allowed our model to perform well on the unseen language French, and in fact outperformed our results on other languages. This is, however, not strictly a fair comparison as it is possible that the French test set was somehow easier than the others.

8 Conclusion

We tackled the 2018 Shared Task on CWI with a cross-lingual approach via multitask learning. Our system is highly language-agnostic, as evidenced by our high performance on French, which was not seen during training time. Our analysis confirms that word length and frequency are good, cross-linguistic predictors of complexity. However, the concrete relationships between these features and complexity may differ between languages, which is captured by our multitask learning approach. Our approach is especially promising for the application of CWI to unseen languages, as we do not assume access to any target language training data. Furthermore, this could even substantially facilitate the creation of new CWI datasets, using a bootstrapping or active learning approach.

Acknowledgments

James Thorne wrote much of the Pytorch code that we used in this work. We are grateful to the anonymous reviewer for helpful suggestions. The first author acknowledges the support by Trygfonden.

References

Joachim Bingel, Maria Barrett, and Sigrid Klerke. 2018. Predicting misreadings from gaze in children with reading difficulties. In *Proceedings of the 13th Workshop on Innovative Use of NLP for Building Educational Applications*, New Orleans, United States. Association for Computational Linguistics.

Joachim Bingel and Anders Søgaard. 2017. Identifying beneficial task relations for multi-task learning in deep neural networks. *15th Conference of the European Chapter of the Association for Computational Linguistics*.

Steven Bird and Edward Loper. 2004. Nltk: the natural language toolkit. In *Proceedings of the ACL 2004 on Interactive poster and demonstration sessions*, page 31. Association for Computational Linguistics.

Johannes Bjerva. 2017a. *One Model to Rule them all: Multitask and Multilingual Modelling for Lexical Analysis*. Ph.D. thesis, University of Groningen.

Johannes Bjerva. 2017b. Will my auxiliary tagging task help? Estimating Auxiliary Tasks Effectivity in Multi-Task Learning. In *Proceedings of the 21st Nordic Conference on Computational Linguistics, NoDaLiDa, 22-24 May 2017, Gothenburg, Sweden*, 131, pages 216–220. Linköping University Electronic Press, Linköpings universitet.

Johannes Bjerva and Robert Östling. 2017. Crosslingual Learning of Semantic Textual Similarity with Multilingual Word Representations. In *Proceedings of the 21st Nordic Conference on Computational Linguistics, NoDaLiDa, 22-24 May 2017, Gothenburg, Sweden*, 131, pages 211–215. Linköping University Electronic Press, Linköpings universitet.

Leo Breiman. 2001. Random forests. *Machine learning*, 45(1):5–32.

Rich Caruana. 1997. Multitask learning. *Machine Learning*, 28 (1):41–75.

Christiane Fellbaum. 1998. A semantic network of english verbs. *WordNet: An electronic lexical database*, 3:153–178.

Aitor Gonzalez-Agirre, Egoitz Laparra, and German Rigau. 2012. Multilingual central repository version 3.0. In *LREC*, pages 2525–2529.

Birgit Hamp and Helmut Feldweg. 1997. Germanet-a lexical-semantic net for German. *Automatic Information Extraction and Building of Lexical Semantic Resources for NLP Applications*.

Kenneth Heafield. 2011. Kenlm: Faster and smaller language model queries. In *Proceedings of the Sixth Workshop on Statistical Machine Translation*, pages 187–197. Association for Computational Linguistics.

Benjamin Heinzerling and Michael Strube. 2017. Bpemb: Tokenization-free pre-trained subword embeddings in 275 languages. *arXiv preprint arXiv:1710.02187*.

Gustavo Paetzold and Lucia Specia. 2015. Lexenstein: A framework for lexical simplification. *Proceedings of ACL-IJCNLP 2015 System Demonstrations*, pages 85–90.

Gustavo Paetzold and Lucia Specia. 2016a. Semeval 2016 task 11: Complex word identification. In *Proceedings of the 10th International Workshop on Semantic Evaluation (SemEval-2016)*, pages 560–569.

Gustavo Paetzold and Lucia Specia. 2016b. Sv000gg at semeval-2016 task 11: Heavy gauge complex word identification with system voting. In *Proceedings of the 10th International Workshop on Semantic Evaluation (SemEval-2016)*, pages 969–974.

Slav Petrov, Dipanjan Das, and Ryan McDonald. 2011. A universal part-of-speech tagset. *arXiv preprint arXiv:1104.2086*.

Martin F Porter. 2001. Snowball: A language for stemming algorithms.

Marek Rei. 2017. Semi-supervised multitask learning for sequence labeling. In *Proceedings of the 55th Annual Meeting of the Association for Computational Linguistics (Volume 1: Long Papers)*, pages 2121–2130. Association for Computational Linguistics.

Francesco Ronzano, Luis Espinosa Anke, Horacio Saggion, et al. 2016. Taln at semeval-2016 task 11: Modelling complex words by contextual, lexical and semantic features. In *Proceedings of the 10th International Workshop on Semantic Evaluation (SemEval-2016)*, pages 1011–1016.

Benoît Sagot and Darja Fišer. 2008. Building a free french wordnet from multilingual resources. In *OntoLex*.

Matthew Shardlow. 2013a. A comparison of techniques to automatically identify complex words. In *51st Annual Meeting of the Association for Computational Linguistics Proceedings of the Student Research Workshop*, pages 103–109.

Matthew Shardlow. 2013b. The cw corpus: A new resource for evaluating the identification of complex words. In *Proceedings of the Second Workshop on Predicting and Improving Text Readability for Target Reader Populations*, pages 69–77.

Matthew Shardlow. 2014. Out in the open: Finding and categorising errors in the lexical simplification pipeline. In *LREC*, pages 1583–1590.

Jörg Tiedemann, Željko Agić, and Joakim Nivre. 2014. Treebank translation for cross-lingual parser induction. In *Proceedings of the Eighteenth Conference on Computational Natural Language Learning*, pages 130–140. Association for Computational Linguistics.

Seid Muhie Yimam, Chris Biemann, Shervin Malmasi, Gustavo Paetzold, Lucia Specia, Sanja Štajner, Anaïs Tack, and Marcos Zampieri. 2018. A Report on the Complex Word Identification Shared Task 2018. In *Proceedings of the 13th Workshop on Innovative Use of NLP for Building Educational Applications*, New Orleans, United States. Association for Computational Linguistics.

Seid Muhie Yimam, Sanja Štajner, Martin Riedl, and Chris Biemann. 2017. Multilingual and cross-lingual complex word identification. In *Proceedings of RANLP*, pages 813–822.

UnibucKernel: A kernel-based learning method for complex word identification

Andrei M. Butnaru and **Radu Tudor Ionescu**

University of Bucharest
Department of Computer Science
14 Academiei, Bucharest, Romania
`butnaruandreimadalin@gmail.com`
`raducu.ionescu@gmail.com`

Abstract

In this paper, we present a kernel-based learning approach for the 2018 Complex Word Identification (CWI) Shared Task. Our approach is based on combining multiple low-level features, such as character n-grams, with high-level semantic features that are either automatically learned using word embeddings or extracted from a lexical knowledge base, namely WordNet. After feature extraction, we employ a kernel method for the learning phase. The feature matrix is first transformed into a normalized kernel matrix. For the binary classification task (simple versus complex), we employ Support Vector Machines. For the regression task, in which we have to predict the complexity level of a word (a word is more complex if it is labeled as complex by more annotators), we employ ν-Support Vector Regression. We applied our approach only on the three English data sets containing documents from Wikipedia, WikiNews and News domains. Our best result during the competition was the third place on the English Wikipedia data set. However, in this paper, we also report better post-competition results.

1 Introduction

A key role in reading comprehension by non-native speakers is played by lexical complexity. To date, researchers in the Natural Language Processing (NLP) community have developed several systems to simply texts for non-native speakers (Petersen and Ostendorf, 2007) as well as native speakers with reading disabilities (Rello et al., 2013) or low literacy levels (Specia, 2010). The first task that needs to be addressed by text simplification methods is to identify which words are likely to be considered complex. The complex word identification (CWI) task raised a lot of attention in the NLP community, as it has been addressed as a stand-alone task by some researchers

(Davoodi et al., 2017). More recently, researchers even organized shared tasks on CWI (Paetzold and Specia, 2016a; Yimam et al., 2018). The goal of the 2018 CWI Shared Task (Yimam et al., 2018) is to predict which words can be difficult for a non-native speaker, based on annotations collected from a mixture of native and non-native speakers. Although the task features a multilingual data set, we participated only in the English monolingual track, due to time constraints. In this paper, we describe the approach of our team, UnibucKernel, for the English monolingual track of the 2018 CWI Shared Task (Yimam et al., 2018). We present results for both classification (predicting if a word is simple or complex) and regression (predicting the complexity level of a word) tasks. Our approach is based on a standard machine learning pipeline that consists of two phases: (i) feature extraction and (ii) classification/regression. In the first phase, we combine multiple low-level features, such as character n-grams, with high-level semantic features that are either automatically learned using word embeddings (Mikolov et al., 2013) or extracted from a lexical knowledge base, namely WordNet (Miller, 1995; Fellbaum, 1998). After feature extraction, we employ a kernel method for the learning phase. The feature matrix is first transformed into a normalized kernel matrix, using either the inner product between pairs of samples (computed by the linear kernel function) or an exponential transformation of the inner product (computed by the Gaussian kernel function). For the binary classification task, we employ Support Vector Machines (SVM) (Cortes and Vapnik, 1995), while for the regression task, we employ ν-Support Vector Regression (SVR) (Chang and Lin, 2002). We applied our approach only on the three English monolingual data sets containing documents from Wikipedia, WikiNews and News domains. Our best result during the

175

Proceedings of the Thirteenth Workshop on Innovative Use of NLP for Building Educational Applications, pages 175–183
New Orleans, Louisiana, June 5, 2018. ©2018 Association for Computational Linguistics

competition was the third place on the English Wikipedia data set. Nonetheless, in this paper, we also report better post-competition results.

The rest of this paper is organized as follows. Related work on complex word identification is presented in Section 2. Our method is presented in Section 3. Our experiments and results are presented in Section 4. Finally, we draw our conclusions and discuss future work in Section 5.

2   Related Work

Although text simplification methods have been proposed since more than a couple of years ago (Petersen and Ostendorf, 2007), complex word identification has not been studied as a standalone task until recently (Shardlow, 2013), with the first shared task on CWI organized in 2016 (Paetzold and Specia, 2016a). With some exceptions (Davoodi et al., 2017), most of the related works are actually the system description papers of the 2016 CWI Shared Task participants. Among the top 10 participants, the most popular classifier is Random Forest (Brooke et al., 2016; Mukherjee et al., 2016; Ronzano et al., 2016; Zampieri et al., 2016), while the most common type of features are lexical and semantic features (Brooke et al., 2016; Mukherjee et al., 2016; Paetzold and Specia, 2016b; Quijada and Medero, 2016; Ronzano et al., 2016). Some works used Naive Bayes (Mukherjee et al., 2016) or SVM (Zampieri et al., 2016) along with the Random Forest classifier, while others used different classification methods altogether, e.g. Decision Trees (Quijada and Medero, 2016), Nearest Centroid (Palakurthi and Mamidi, 2016) or Maximum Entropy (Konkol, 2016). Along with the lexical and semantic features, many have used morphological (Mukherjee et al., 2016; Paetzold and Specia, 2016b; Palakurthi and Mamidi, 2016; Ronzano et al., 2016) and syntactic (Mukherjee et al., 2016; Quijada and Medero, 2016; Ronzano et al., 2016) features.

Paetzold and Specia (2016b) proposed two ensemble methods by applying either hard voting or soft voting on machine learning classifiers trained on morphological, lexical, and semantic features. Their systems ranked on the first and the second places in the 2016 CWI Shared Task. Ronzano et al. (2016) employed Random Forests based on lexical, morphological, semantic and syntactic features, ranking on the third place in the 2016 CWI Shared Task. Konkol (2016)

trained Maximum Entropy classifiers on word occurrence counts in Wikipedia documents, ranking on the fourth place, after Ronzano et al. (2016). Wróbel (2016) ranked on fifth place using a simple rule-based approach that considers one feature, namely the number of documents from Simple English Wikipedia in which the target word occurs. Mukherjee et al. (2016) employed the Random Forest and the Naive Bayes classifiers based on semantic, lexicon-based, morphological and syntactic features. Their Naive Bayes system ranked on the sixth place in the 2016 CWI Shared Task. After the 2016 CWI Shared Task, Zampieri et al. (2017) combined the submitted systems using an ensemble method based on plurality voting. They also proposed an oracle ensemble that provides a theoretical upper bound of the performance. The oracle selects the correct label for a given word if at least one of the participants predicted the correct label. The results reported by Zampieri et al. (2017) indicate that there is a significant performance gap to be filled by automatic systems.

Compared to the related works, we propose the use of some novel semantic features. One set of features is inspired by the work of Butnaru et al. (2017) in word sense disambiguation, while another set of features is inspired by the spatial pyramid approach (Lazebnik et al., 2006), commonly used in computer vision to improve the performance of the bag-of-visual-words model (Ionescu et al., 2013; Ionescu and Popescu, 2015).

3   Method

The method that we employ for identifying complex words is based on a series of features extracted from the word itself as well as the context in which the word is used. Upon having the features extracted, we compute a kernel matrix using one of two standard kernel functions, namely the linear kernel or the Gaussian kernel. We then apply either the SVM classifier to identify if a word is complex or not, or the ν-SVR predictor to determine the complexity level of a word.

3.1   Feature Extraction

As stated before, we extract features from both the target word and the context in which the word appears. Form the target word, we quantify a series of features based on its characters. More specifically, we count the number of characters, vowels and constants, as well as the percentage of vowels and constants from the total number of characters in the word. Along with these features, we also quantify the number of consecutively repeating characters, e.g. double consonants. For example, in the word "innovation", we can find the double consonant "nn". We also extract n-grams of 1, 2, 3 and 4 characters, based on the intuition that some complex words tend to be formed of a different set of n-grams than simple words. For instance, the complex word "cognizant" is formed of rare 3-grams, e.g. "ogn" or "niz", compared to its commonly-used synonym "aware", which contains 3-grams that we can easily find in other simple words, e.g. "war" or "are".

Other features extracted from the target word are the part-of-speech and the number of senses listed in the WordNet knowledge base (Miller, 1995; Fellbaum, 1998), for the respective word. If the complex word is actually composed of multiple words, i.e. it is a *multi-word expression*, we generate the features for each word in the target and sum the corresponding values to obtain the features for the target multi-word expression.

In the NLP community, word embeddings (Bengio et al., 2003; Karlen et al., 2008) are used in many tasks, and became more popular due to the *word2vec* (Mikolov et al., 2013) framework. Word embeddings methods have the capacity to build a vectorial representation of words by assigning a low-dimensional real-valued vector to each word, with the property that semantically related words are projected in the same vicinity of the generated space. Word embeddings are in fact a learned representation of words where each dimension represents a hidden feature of the word (Turian et al., 2010). We devise additional features for the CWI task with the help of pre-trained word embeddings provided by *word2vec* (Mikolov et al., 2013). The first set of features based on word embeddings takes into account the word's context. More precisely, we record the minimum, the maximum and the mean value of the cosine similarity between the target word and each other word from the sentence in which the target word occurs. The intuition for using this set of features is that a word can be complex if it is semantically different from the other context words, and this difference should be reflected in the embedding space. Having the same goal in mind, namely to identify if the target word is an outlier with respect to the other words in the sentence, we employ a simple ap-

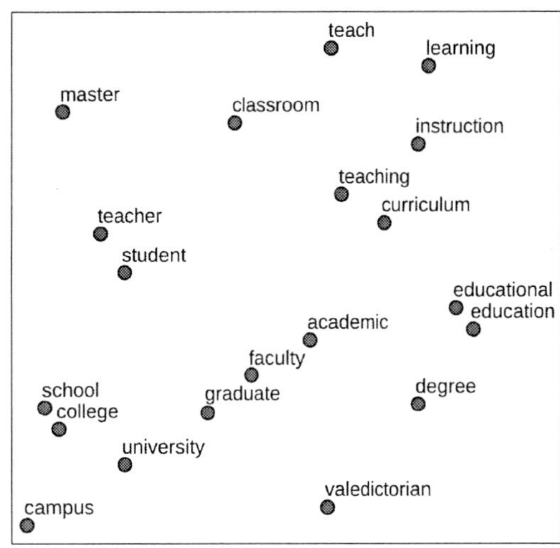

Figure 1: A set of word vectors represented in a 2D space generated by applying PCA on 300-dimensional word embeddings.

proach to compute sense embeddings using the semantic relations between WordNet synsets. We note that this approach was previously used for unsupervised word sense disambiguation in (Butnaru et al., 2017). To compute the sense embedding for a word sense, we first build a *disambiguation vocabulary* or *sense bag*. Based on WordNet, we form the sense bag for a given synset by collecting the words found in the gloss of the synset (examples included) as well as the words found in the glosses of semantically related synsets. The semantic relations are chosen based on the part-of-speech of the target word, as described in (Butnaru et al., 2017). To derive the sense embedding, we embed the collected words in an embedding space and compute the median of the resulted word vectors. For each sense embedding of the target word, we compute the cosine similarity with each and every sense embedding computed for each other word in the sentence, in order to find the minimum, the maximum and the mean value.

Using pre-trained word embeddings provided by the *GloVe* framework (Pennington et al., 2014), we further managed to define a set of useful features based on the location of the target word in the embedding space. In this last set of features, we first process the word vectors in order to reduce the dimensionality of the vector space from 300 components to only 2 components, by applying Principal Component Analysis (PCA) (Hotelling, 1933). Figure 1 illustrates a couple of semanti-

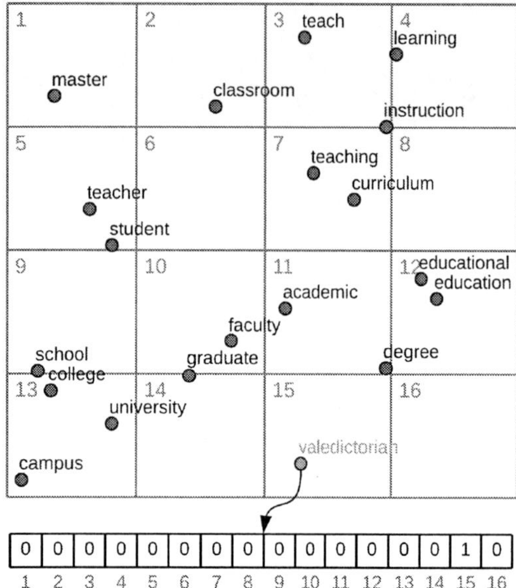

0	0	0	0	0	0	0	0	0	0	0	0	0	0	1	0
1	2	3	4	5	6	7	8	9	10	11	12	13	14	15	16

Figure 2: A grid of 4×4 applied on the 2D embedding space. For example, the word "valedictorian" is located in bin number 15. Consequently, the corresponding one-hot vector contains a non-zero value at index 15.

cally related words, that are projected in the same area of the 2-dimensional (2D) embedding space generated by PCA. In the newly generated space, we apply a grid to divide the space into multiple and equal regions, named bins. This process is inspired by the spatial pyramids (Lazebnik et al., 2006) used in computer vision to recover spatial information in the bag-of-visual-words (Ionescu et al., 2013; Ionescu and Popescu, 2015). After we determine the bins, we index the bins and encode the index of the bin that contains the target word as a one-hot vector. Various grid sizes could provide a more specific or a more general location of a word in the generated space. For this reason, we use multiple grid sizes starting from coarse divisions such as 2×2, 4×4, and 8×8, to fine divisions such as 16×16 and 32×32. In Figure 2, we show an example with a 4×4 grid that divides the space illustrated in Figure 1 into 16 bins, and the word "valedictorian" is found in bin number 15. The corresponding one-hot vector, containing a single non-zero value at index 15, is also illustrated in Figure 2. The thought process for using this one-hot representation is that complex words tend to reside alone in the semantic space generated by the word embedding framework.

We would like to point out that each and every type of features described in this section has a positive influence on the overall accuracy of our framework.

3.2 Kernel Representation

Kernel-based learning algorithms work by embedding the data into a Hilbert space and by searching for linear relations in that space, using a learning algorithm. The embedding is performed implicitly, that is by specifying the inner product between each pair of points rather than by giving their coordinates explicitly. The power of kernel methods (Ionescu and Popescu, 2016; Shawe-Taylor and Cristianini, 2004) lies in the implicit use of a Reproducing Kernel Hilbert Space induced by a positive semi-definite kernel function. Despite the fact that the mathematical meaning of a kernel is the inner product in a Hilbert space, another interpretation of a kernel is the pairwise similarity between samples.

The kernel function offers to the kernel methods the power to naturally handle input data that is not in the form of numerical vectors, such as strings, images, or even video and audio files. The kernel function captures the intuitive notion of similarity between objects in a specific domain and can be any function defined on the respective domain that is symmetric and positive definite. In our approach, we experiment with two commonly-used kernel functions, namely the linear kernel and the Radial Basis Function (RBF) kernel. The *linear kernel* is easily obtained by computing the inner product of two feature vectors x and z:

$$k(x, z) = \langle x, z \rangle,$$

where $\langle \cdot, \cdot \rangle$ denotes the inner product. In a similar manner, the *RBF kernel* (also known as the Gaussian kernel) between two feature vectors x and z can be computed as follows:

$$k(x, z) = exp\left(-\frac{1 - \langle x, z \rangle}{2\sigma^2}\right).$$

In the experiments, we replace $1/(2\sigma^2)$ with a constant value r, and tune the parameter r instead of σ.

A technique that improves machine learning performance for many applications is data normalization. Because the range of raw data can have significant variation, the objective functions optimized by the classifiers will not work properly without normalization. The normalization step gives to each feature an approximately equal contribution to the similarity between two samples. The normalization of a pairwise kernel matrix K containing similarities between samples is obtained by dividing each component to the square root of the product of the two corresponding diagonal elements:

$$\hat{K}_{ij} = \frac{K_{ij}}{\sqrt{K_{ii} \cdot K_{jj}}}.$$

3.3 Classification and Regression

In the case of binary classification problems, kernel-based learning algorithms look for a discriminant function, a function that assigns $+1$ to examples that belong to one class and -1 to examples that belong to the other class. This function will be a linear function in the Hilbert space, which means it will have the form:

$$f(x) = \text{sign}(\langle w, x \rangle + b),$$

for some weight vector w and some bias term b. The kernel can be employed whenever the weight vector can be expressed as a linear combination of the training points, $\sum_{i=1}^{n} \alpha_i\, x_i$, implying that f can be expressed as follows:

$$f(x) = \text{sign}\left(\sum_{i=1}^{n} \alpha_i\, k(x_i, x) + b\right),$$

where n is the number of training samples and k is a kernel function.

Various kernel methods differ in the way they find the vector w (or equivalently the dual vector α). Support Vector Machines (Cortes and Vapnik, 1995) try to find the vector w that defines the hyperplane that maximally separates the images (outcomes of the embedding map) in the Hilbert space of the training examples belonging to the two classes. Mathematically, the SVM classifier chooses the weights w and the bias term b that satisfy the following optimization criterion:

$$\min_{w,b} \frac{1}{n} \sum_{i=1}^{n} [1 - y_i(\langle w, \phi(x_i)\rangle + b)]_+ + \nu ||w||^2,$$

where y_i is the label $(+1/-1)$ of the training example x_i, ν is a regularization parameter and $[x]_+ = \max\{x, 0\}$. We use the SVM classifier for the binary classification of words into simple versus complex classes. On the other hand, we employ

Data Set	Train	Validation	Test
English News	14002	1764	2095
English WikiNews	7746	870	1287
English Wikipedia	5551	694	870

Table 1: A summary with the number of samples in each data set of the English monolingual track of the 2018 CWI Shared Task.

ν-Support Vector Regression (ν-SVR) in order to predict the complexity level of a word (a word is more complex if it is labeled as complex by more annotators). The ν-Support Vector Machines (Chang and Lin, 2002) can handle both classification and regression. The model introduces a new parameter ν, that can be used to control the amount of support vectors in the resulting model. The parameter ν is introduced directly into the optimization problem formulation and it is estimated automatically during training.

4 Experiments

4.1 Data Sets

The data sets used in the English monolingual track of the 2018 CWI Shared Task (Yimam et al., 2018) are described in (Yimam et al., 2017). Each data set covers one of three distinct genres (News, WikiNews and Wikipedia), and the samples are annotated by both native and non-native English speakers. Table 1 presents the number of samples in the training, the validation (development) and the test sets, for each of the three genres.

4.2 Classification Results

Parameter Tuning. For the classification task, we used the SVM implementation provided by Lib-SVM (Chang and Lin, 2011). The parameters that require tuning are the parameter r of the RBF kernel and the regularization parameter C of the SVM. We tune these parameters using grid search on each of the three validation sets included in the data sets prepared for the English monolingual track. For the parameter r, we select values from the set $\{0.5, 1.0, 1.5, 2.0\}$. For the regularization parameter C we choose values from the set $\{10^{-1}, 10^0, 10^1, 10^2\}$. Interestingly, we obtain the best results with the same parameter choices on all three validation sets. The optimal parameter choices are $C = 10^1$ and $r = 1.0$. We use these parameters in all our subsequent classification experiments.

Results. Our results for the classification task on

Data Set	Kernel	Accuracy	F_1-score			Competition Rank	Post-Competition Rank
English News	linear	0.8653	0.8547	0.8111*		12	6
English News	RBF	0.8678	0.8594	0.8178*		10	5
English WikiNews	linear	0.8205	0.8151	0.7786*		10	5
English WikiNews	RBF	0.8252	0.8201	0.8127*		5	4
English Wikipedia	linear	0.7874	0.7873	0.7804*		6	4
English Wikipedia	RBF	0.7920*	0.7919*	0.7919*		3	3

Table 2: Classification results on the three data sets of the English monolingual track of the 2018 CWI Shared Task. The methods are evaluated in terms of the classification accuracy and the F_1-score. The results marked with an asterisk are obtained during the competition. The other results are obtained after the competition.

Data Set	Kernel	Mean Absolute Error	Post-Competition Rank
English News	linear	0.0573	4
English News	RBF	0.0492	1
English WikiNews	linear	0.0724	4
English WikiNews	RBF	0.0667	1
English Wikipedia	linear	0.0846	4
English Wikipedia	RBF	0.0805	2

Table 3: Regression results on the three data sets of the English monolingual track of the 2018 CWI Shared Task. The methods are evaluated in terms of the mean absolute error (MAE). The reported results are obtained after the competition.

the three data sets included in the English monolingual track are presented in Table 2. We would like to note that, before the competition ended, we observed a bug in the code that was used in most of our submissions. In the feature extraction stage, the code produced NaN (not a number) values for some features. In order to make the submissions in time, we had to eliminate the samples containing NaN values in the feature vector. Consequently, most of our results during the competition were lower than expected. However, we managed to fix this bug and recompute the features in time to re-submit new results, but only for the RBF kernel on the English Wikipedia data set. The rest of the results presented in Table 2 are produced after the bug fixing and after the submission deadline. Nevertheless, for a fair comparison with the other systems, we include our F_1-scores and rankings during the competition as well as the post-competition F_1-scores and rankings.

The results reported in Table 2 indicate that the RBF kernel is more suitable for the CWI task than the linear kernel. Our best F_1-score on the English News data set is 0.8594, which is nearly 1.4% lower than the top scoring system, which attained 0.8736 during the competition. On the English WikiNews data set, our best F_1-score (0.8201) is once again about 2% lower than the top scoring system, which obtained 0.8400 during the competition. On the English Wikipedia data set, our best F_1-score is 0.7919. With this score, we

ranked as the third team on the English Wikipedia data set. Two systems performed better on English Wikipedia, one that reached the top F_1-score of 0.8115 and one that reached the second-best scored of 0.7965. Overall, our system performed quite well, but it can surely benefit from the addition of more features.

4.3 Regression Results

Although we did not submit results for the regression task, we present post-competition regression results in this section.

Parameter Tuning. For the regression task, the parameters that require tuning are the parameter r of the RBF kernel and the ν-SVR parameters C and ν. As in the classification task, we tune these parameters using grid search on the validation sets provided with the three data sets included in the English monolingual track. For the parameter r, we select values from the set $\{0.5, 1.0, 1.5, 2.0\}$. For the regularization parameter C we choose values from the set $\{10^{-1}, 10^0, 10^1, 10^2\}$. The preliminary results on the validation sets indicate the best parameter choices for each data set. For the English News data set, we obtained the best validation results using $C = 10^1$ and $r = 1.5$. For the English WikiNews and English Wikipedia data sets, we obtained the best validation results using $C = 10^0$ and $r = 1.5$. For the parameter ν, we leave the default value of 0.5 provided by LibSVM (Chang and Lin, 2011).

Results. The regression results on the three data sets included in the English monolingual track are presented in Table 3. The systems are evaluated in terms of the mean absolute error (MAE). As in the classification task, we can observe that the RBF kernel provides generally better results than the linear kernel. On two data sets, English News and English WikiNews, we obtain better MAE values than all the systems that participated in the competition. Indeed, the best MAE on English News reported during the competition is 0.0510, and we obtain a smaller MAE (0.0492) using the RBF kernel. Similarly, with a MAE of 0.0667 for the RBF kernel, we surpass the top system on English WikiNews, which attained a MAE of 0.0674 during the competition. On the third data set, English Wikipedia, we attain the second-best score (0.0805), after the top system, that obtained a MAE of 0.0739 during the competition. Compared to the classification task, we report better post-competition rankings in the regression task. This could be explained by two factors. First of all, the number of participants in the regression task was considerably lower. Second of all, we believe that ν-SVR is a very good regressor which is not commonly used, surpassing alternative regression methods in other tasks as well, e.g. image difficulty prediction (Ionescu et al., 2016).

5   Conclusion

In this paper, we described the system developed by our team, UnibucKernel, for the 2018 CWI Shared Task. The system is based on extracting lexical, syntatic and semantic features and on training a kernel method for the prediction (classification and regression) tasks. We participated only in the English monolingual track. Our best result during the competition was the third place on the English Wikipedia data set. In this paper, we also reported better post-competition results.

In this work, we treated each English data set independently, due to the memory constraints of our machine. Nevertheless, we believe that joining the training sets provided in the English News, the English WikiNews and the English Wikipedia data sets into a single and larger training set can provide better performance, as the model's generalization capacity could improve by learning from an extended set of samples. We leave this idea for future work. Another direction that could be explored in future work is the addition of more features, as our current feature set is definitely far from being exhaustive.

References

Yoshua Bengio, Réjean Ducharme, Pascal Vincent, and Christian Jauvin. 2003. A neural probabilistic language model. *Journal of Machine Learning Research*, 3(Feb):1137–1155.

Julian Brooke, Alexandra Uitdenbogerd, and Timothy Baldwin. 2016. Melbourne at SemEval 2016 Task 11: Classifying Type-level Word Complexity using Random Forests with Corpus and Word List Features. In *Proceedings of SemEval*, pages 975–981, San Diego, California. Association for Computational Linguistics.

Andrei M. Butnaru, Radu Tudor Ionescu, and Florentina Hristea. 2017. ShotgunWSD: An unsupervised algorithm for global word sense disambiguation inspired by DNA sequencing. In *Proceedings of EACL*, pages 916–926.

Chih-Chung Chang and Chih-Jen Lin. 2002. Training ν-Support Vector Regression: Theory and Algorithms. *Neural Computation*, 14:1959–1977.

Chih-Chung Chang and Chih-Jen Lin. 2011. LibSVM: A Library for Support Vector Machines. *ACM Transactions on Intelligent Systems and Technology*, 2:27:1–27:27. Software available at http://www.csie.ntu.edu.tw/~cjlin/libsvm.

Corinna Cortes and Vladimir Vapnik. 1995. Support-Vector Networks. *Machine Learning*, 20(3):273–297.

Elnaz Davoodi, Leila Kosseim, and Matthew Mongrain. 2017. A Context-Aware Approach for the Identification of Complex Words in Natural Language Texts. In *Proceedings of ICSC*, pages 97–100.

Christiane Fellbaum, editor. 1998. *WordNet: An Electronic Lexical Database*. MIT Press.

Harold Hotelling. 1933. Analysis of a complex of statistical variables into principal components. *Journal of Educational Psychology*, 24(6):417.

Radu Tudor Ionescu, Bogdan Alexe, Marius Leordeanu, Marius Popescu, Dim Papadopoulos, and Vittorio Ferrari. 2016. How hard can it be? Estimating the difficulty of visual search in an image. In *Proceedings of CVPR*, pages 2157–2166.

Radu Tudor Ionescu and Marius Popescu. 2015. PQ kernel: a rank correlation kernel for visual word histograms. *Pattern Recognition Letters*, 55:51–57.

Radu Tudor Ionescu and Marius Popescu. 2016. *Knowledge Transfer between Computer Vision and Text Mining*. Advances in Computer Vision and Pattern Recognition. Springer International Publishing.

Radu Tudor Ionescu, Marius Popescu, and Cristian Grozea. 2013. Local Learning to Improve Bag of Visual Words Model for Facial Expression Recognition. *Workshop on Challenges in Representation Learning, ICML.*

Michael Karlen, Jason Weston, Ayse Erkan, and Ronan Collobert. 2008. Large scale manifold transduction. In *Proceedings of ICML*, pages 448–455. ACM.

Michal Konkol. 2016. UWB at SemEval-2016 Task 11: Exploring Features for Complex Word Identification. In *Proceedings of SemEval*, pages 1038–1041, San Diego, California. Association for Computational Linguistics.

Svetlana Lazebnik, Cordelia Schmid, and Jean Ponce. 2006. Beyond Bags of Features: Spatial Pyramid Matching for Recognizing Natural Scene Categories. *Proceedings of CVPR*, 2:2169–2178.

Tomas Mikolov, Ilya Sutskever, Kai Chen, Gregory S. Corrado, and Jeffrey Dean. 2013. Distributed Representations of Words and Phrases and their Compositionality. *Proceedings of NIPS*, pages 3111–3119.

George A. Miller. 1995. WordNet: A Lexical Database for English. *Communications of the ACM*, 38(11):39–41.

Niloy Mukherjee, Braja Gopal Patra, Dipankar Das, and Sivaji Bandyopadhyay. 2016. JU_NLP at SemEval-2016 Task 11: Identifying Complex Words in a Sentence. In *Proceedings of SemEval*, pages 986–990, San Diego, California. Association for Computational Linguistics.

Gustavo Paetzold and Lucia Specia. 2016a. SemEval 2016 Task 11: Complex Word Identification. In *Proceedings of SemEval*, pages 560–569, San Diego, California. Association for Computational Linguistics.

Gustavo Paetzold and Lucia Specia. 2016b. SV000gg at SemEval-2016 Task 11: Heavy Gauge Complex Word Identification with System Voting. In *Proceedings of SemEval*, pages 969–974, San Diego, California. Association for Computational Linguistics.

Ashish Palakurthi and Radhika Mamidi. 2016. IIIT at SemEval-2016 Task 11: Complex Word Identification using Nearest Centroid Classification. In *Proceedings of SemEval*, pages 1017–1021, San Diego, California. Association for Computational Linguistics.

Jeffrey Pennington, Richard Socher, and Christopher D. Manning. 2014. GloVe: Global Vectors for Word Representation. In *Proceedings of EMNLP*, pages 1532–1543.

Sarah E. Petersen and Mari Ostendorf. 2007. Text Simplification for Language Learners: A Corpus Analysis. In *Proceedings of SLaTE*.

Maury Quijada and Julie Medero. 2016. HMC at SemEval-2016 Task 11: Identifying Complex Words Using Depth-limited Decision Trees. In *Proceedings of SemEval*, pages 1034–1037, San Diego, California. Association for Computational Linguistics.

Luz Rello, Ricardo Baeza-Yates, Stefan Bott, and Horacio Saggion. 2013. Simplify or Help?: Text Simplification Strategies for People with Dyslexia. In *Proceedings of W4A*, pages 15:1–15:10.

Francesco Ronzano, Ahmed Abura'ed, Luis Espinosa Anke, and Horacio Saggion. 2016. TALN at SemEval-2016 Task 11: Modelling Complex Words by Contextual, Lexical and Semantic Features. In *Proceedings of SemEval*, pages 1011–1016, San Diego, California. Association for Computational Linguistics.

Matthew Shardlow. 2013. A Comparison of Techniques to Automatically Identify Complex Words. In *Proceedings of the ACL Student Research Workshop*, pages 103–109.

John Shawe-Taylor and Nello Cristianini. 2004. *Kernel Methods for Pattern Analysis*. Cambridge University Press.

Lucia Specia. 2010. Translating from complex to simplified sentences. In *Proceedings of PROPOR*, pages 30–39.

Joseph Turian, Lev Ratinov, and Yoshua Bengio. 2010. Word representations: a simple and general method for semi-supervised learning. In *Proceedings of ACL*, pages 384–394. Association for Computational Linguistics.

Krzysztof Wróbel. 2016. PLUJAGH at SemEval-2016 Task 11: Simple System for Complex Word Identification. In *Proceedings of SemEval*, pages 953–957, San Diego, California. Association for Computational Linguistics.

Seid Muhie Yimam, Chris Biemann, Shervin Malmasi, Gustavo Paetzold, Lucia Specia, Sanja Štajner, Anaïs Tack, and Marcos Zampieri. 2018. A Report on the Complex Word Identification Shared Task 2018. In *Proceedings of BEA-13*, New Orleans, United States. Association for Computational Linguistics.

Seid Muhie Yimam, Sanja Štajner, Martin Riedl, and Chris Biemann. 2017. CWIG3G2 - Complex Word Identification Task across Three Text Genres and Two User Groups. In *Proceedings of IJCNLP (Volume 2: Short Papers)*, pages 401–407, Taipei, Taiwan.

Marcos Zampieri, Shervin Malmasi, Gustavo Paetzold, and Lucia Specia. 2017. Complex Word Identification: Challenges in Data Annotation and System Performance. In *Proceedings of NLPTEA*, pages 59–63, Taipei, Taiwan. Asian Federation of Natural Language Processing.

Marcos Zampieri, Liling Tan, and Josef van Genabith. 2016. MacSaar at SemEval-2016 Task 11: Zipfian and Character Features for ComplexWord Identification. In *Proceedings of SemEval*, pages 1001–1005, San Diego, California. Association for Computational Linguistics.

CAMB at CWI Shared Task 2018:
Complex Word Identification with Ensemble-Based Voting

Sian Gooding
Dept of Computer Science and Technology
University of Cambridge
shg36@cam.ac.uk

Ekaterina Kochmar
ALTA Institute
University of Cambridge
ek358@cam.ac.uk

Abstract

This paper presents the winning systems we submitted to the Complex Word Identification Shared Task 2018. We describe our best performing systems' implementations and discuss our key findings from this research. Our best-performing systems achieve an F_1 score of 0.8736 on the NEWS, 0.8400 on the WIKINEWS and 0.8115 on the WIKIPEDIA test sets in the monolingual English binary classification track, and a mean absolute error of 0.0558 on the NEWS, 0.0674 on the WIKINEWS and 0.0739 on the WIKIPEDIA test sets in the probabilistic track.

1 Introduction

Poor reading comprehension often caused by the presence of complex technical terms can have serious practical consequences (Dubay, 2004). Although proper text simplification requires a wide range of transformations, it has been shown that application of lexical simplification (LS) techniques alone improves reader understanding and information retention (Leroy et al., 2013). Complex Word Identification (CWI) is concerned with automated identification of words that might present challenge for the target readers and should thus be simplified (Shardlow, 2013a). Early studies on LS (Carroll et al., 1999; Devlin and Tait, 1998) do not consider CWI as part of the simplification pipeline, but recent studies argue that simplification systems benefit from applying CWI as the first step in the LS pipeline (Shardlow, 2014; Paetzold and Specia, 2016b). Inadequate identification of complex words in text might result in an overly difficult text if many potential candidates are missed, or in meaning distortion if many simple words are falsely identified as complex.

CWI can not only be used as a component of LS systems, but also as a stand-alone application within intelligent tutoring systems for second language learners or in reading devices for people with low literacy skills. For instance, Nation (2006) shows that at least 95% of text should be familiar to the reader in order for them to understand the content. A CWI system can help identify the unfamiliar words and provide readers with their definitions even when simpler alternatives are not available. This has the potential to help a wide variety of target reader groups, including general readers of technical texts (Feng, 2008).

Following the SemEval 2016 shared task (Paetzold and Specia, 2016c), the Shared Task 2018 frames CWI as the process of identifying words that are difficult for a given target population (for example, non-native speakers of English) based on the annotation from a sample of that target population (Yimam et al., 2018). We overview the related work in the field in Section 2 and discuss the CWI shared task framework in Section 3. We have participated in the binary and probabilistic classification tasks in the monolingual English track, and scored first in the binary setting on all three data sources, as well as on two out of three data sources in the probabilistic setting. Section 4 presents the implementation details of our systems including features and methods used. In Section 5 we present the results obtained with our systems, and discuss the key findings. Finally, we outline future directions for this research in Section 6.

2 Related Work

The earliest studies that address CWI as an independent task are related to the medical domain: Zeng et al. (2005) predict medical term familiarity based on term occurrence, and show that individualised assessment is possible if the models consider readers' demographics. Elhadad (2006), in addition to corpus frequency, consider using familiarity features from the MRC Psycholinguistic

Proceedings of the Thirteenth Workshop on Innovative Use of NLP for Building Educational Applications, pages 184–194
New Orleans, Louisiana, June 5, 2018. ©2018 Association for Computational Linguistics

Database (Wilson, 1988) and the number of senses from WordNet (Fellbaum, 2005). Zeng-Treitler et al. (2008) improve on the previous methods using contextual information.

Some previous approaches to LS consider all words as potentially complex and try to simplify every word (Devlin and Tait, 1998; Thomas and Anderson, 2012; Bott et al., 2012). This has a number of undesirable effects, including radical changes in the original meaning and the dependence of the simplification process on the availability of alternatives. For instance, the results of Horn et al. (2014) show that such an approach is unable to find a simpler alternative for one third of the complex words in their dataset. Another type of approach introduces a threshold that is typically based on the word frequency (Zeng et al., 2005; Elhadad, 2006; Biran et al., 2011). Until recently (Shardlow, 2013b), the lack of shared data to compare different approaches to CWI has been one of the bottlenecks for this task.

The CW corpus of Shardlow (2013b) is based on the edit histories in Simple Wikipedia, and includes only the sentences where a single word is simplified. Paetzold and Specia (2016c) find that as much as 51.9% of the words in this corpus are annotated as complex by at least one of their annotators and conclude that non-native speakers of English might still find the simplified version of Wikipedia challenging. The quality of Simple Wikipedia and its usefulness for simplification research has been challenged before in Xu et al. (2015). Further experiments in Shardlow (2013a) show that a more resource-intensive threshold-based approach does not perform significantly differently on this dataset to a more naïve technique of simplifying everything, while an SVM classifier performs better in terms of precision but does so at the cost of a much lower recall. These findings inspired further research into classification-based approaches to CWI (Paetzold and Specia, 2016c).

The SemEval 2016 shared task on CWI combines the data from the CW corpus of Shardlow (2013b), the LexMTurk corpus of Horn et al. (2014) and the Simple Wikipedia corpus of Kauchak (2013), all of which rely on Simple Wikipedia data. A set of 400 non-native speakers annotated the content words in the data as simple or complex. The information about annotator's age, native language (L1), education and level of language proficiency has been collected,

but has not been used in the task. The final dataset has a bias towards annotation provided by the non-native speakers of upper levels of language proficiency and, potentially as a result of that, only about 11% of word types (and 3% of word tokens) are annotated as complex (Paetzold and Specia, 2016c). The results of the shared task show that simpler features based on word frequency (Konkol, 2016; Wróbel, 2016; Zampieri et al., 2016) and word presence in certain lexicons (Mukherjee et al., 2016; Wróbel, 2016), work best. A number of systems performing best in terms of G-score used various ensemble-based approaches (Paetzold and Specia, 2016d; Ronzano et al., 2016; Mukherjee et al., 2016; Zampieri et al., 2016). The systems that performed best in terms of F-score used threshold-based approaches (Wróbel, 2016; Malmasi et al., 2016) and frequency features (Malmasi and Zampieri, 2016).

In their analysis of the SemEval 2016 shared task, Zampieri et al. (2017), similarly to Paetzold and Specia (2016c), show that an ensemble of all systems does not outperform the best system or an ensemble of a few best-performing systems. The use of an oracle of the 3 best-performing systems sets the upper bound at 0.60 F-score for the identification of complex words and at 0.98 F-score for the identification of simple words. They also show that the systems more reliably identify those complex words that are annotated as such by the majority of human annotators, arguing that lexical complexity should be seen as a continuum on a spectrum rather than a binary value.

3 CWI Shared Task 2018 Setup

The CWI shared task uses the data from Yimam et al. (2017b), and approaches CWI from two perspectives: under the *binary* (`bin`) view, a word can be either complex or simple, and in the *probabilistic* (`prob`) setting a word receives a score in the range of $[0.0, 1.0]$ reflecting the proportion of annotators that consider the word complex. In this section, we briefly overview the CWI shared task 2018 framework, discuss the data and the annotation, and analyse the challenges the CWI systems are presented with in this task.

3.1 Data

Unlike the previous datasets that rely on the use of Wikipedia and Simple Wikipedia, the CWIG3G2 dataset of Yimam et al. (2017a) uses texts of 3 different genres: professionally written news articles (NEWS), amateurishly written news articles (WIKINEWS), and WIKIPEDIA articles. The dataset includes annotation for content words as well as for phrases. The annotation for the English data is collected from both native and non-native speakers of English. Table 1 presents the statistics on the number of words (w) and phrases (ph) in the training (*train*), development (*dev*) and *test* subsets of the News (NEWS), WikiNews (WINS) and Wikipedia (WIKI) datasets.

Data	Train	Dev	Test
NEWS (w)	11,949	1,502	1,813
NEWS (ph)	2,053	262	282
WINS (w)	6,780	776	1,138
WINS (ph)	966	94	149
WIKI (w)	4,833	606	750
WIKI (ph)	718	88	120
TOTAL	27,299	3,328	4,252

Table 1: Number of instances

3.2 Annotation

The annotation was performed using the Amazon Mechanical Turk platform. The set of annotators comprised 10 native and 10 non-native speakers of English. They were presented with text paragraphs and were asked to select up to 10 lexical items that they found complex. The lexical items included content words (e.g., nouns, verbs, adjectives and adverbs) and phrases up to 50 characters in length. Additional information about the annotators, such as their language proficiency, was collected but was not used in the task.

By allowing the annotators to select phrases as well as individual words, Yimam et al. (2017a) created a more practically useful dataset. By presenting the annotators with whole paragraphs, they replicated a realistic scenario in which words are interpreted in context. By not preselecting target lexical items, they avoided introducing the bias into the annotation, although it may be argued that the limit of 10 lexical items per paragraph restricted the selection options. Finally, since the annotations are provided by both native and non-native speakers, this allows Yimam et al. (2017a) to explore to what extent the needs of non-native speakers can be estimated based on the needs of a wider target population. The analysis in Yimam et al. (2017a) shows that there are quantitative differences between the annotation provided by

the native and non-native speakers, and between the three genres. Further experiments show that the system trained on native speakers' annotations performs better than the system trained on non-native speakers' annotations, both on native and non-native data. Yimam et al. (2017a) also note that the inter-annotator agreement between native speakers is higher than between non-native speakers, which might be due to the fact that, unlike non-native annotators, native speakers share L1 and are of relatively similar language proficiency level. At the same time, these results suggest that the annotation provided by the native speakers can be used to predict the simplification needs of the non-native speakers as well.

The shared task relies on two types of annotation: under the `bin` setting that words and phrases are annotated as complex (label 1) if at least one of the 20 annotators annotated them as such, and simple (label 0) otherwise; and under the `prob` setting that words and phrases receive a label in the range between $[0.0, ..., 1.0]$, with a step of 0.05, reflecting the proportion of annotators who found the lexical item complex.

Table 2 presents the distribution of simple and complex words in the dataset. We present the label break-down in terms of label percentages across the genres (NEWS, WINS, WIKI) and subsets of data (*tr* for training, *dev* for development, and *ts* for test sets). Due to space limitations, for the `prob` setting we present only the percentage of cases annotated as simple ($0_{bin} = 0.0_{prob}$), annotated as complex by a single annotator (0.05_{prob}) and by all 20 annotators (1.0_{prob}).

Data	0_{bin}	1_{bin}	0.05_{prob}	1.0_{prob}
NEWS$_{tr}$	60.41	39.59	13.52	0.39
NEWS$_{dev}$	60.54	39.46	13.83	0.28
NEWS$_{ts}$	61.72	38.28	12.70	0.29
WINS$_{tr}$	58.48	41.52	16.25	0.17
WINS$_{dev}$	59.43	40.57	14.25	0.11
WINS$_{ts}$	57.58	42.42	16.71	0.16
WIKI$_{tr}$	55.07	44.93	16.66	0.52
WIKI$_{dev}$	51.15	48.85	19.31	0.14
WIKI$_{ts}$	49.54	50.46	18.62	0.23

Table 2: Annotation labels break-down (%)

These figures demonstrate that: (1) there is a quantitative difference in the annotation across the three genres, with NEWS being the easier to understand for the annotators (38.28% to 39.59% complex words) and WIKI being the most complex (44.93% to 50.46% complex words), which suggests that systems might perform better if trained and tested within the same genre; (2) the distribution of complex and simple words across training, development and test subsets is consistent for NEWS and WINS with a difference in label distribution of no more than 2.5% – this suggests that the systems for these two genres might generalise better than the one for WIKIPEDIA; (3) about 1/3 of the complex word annotation comes from a single annotator finding a word complex, while the cases where all 20 annotators agree that the word is complex comprise less than 1% in all subsets. Furthermore, we have identified the following challenges presented by the dataset:

Context-specific annotation: Since the lexical items were presented to the annotators in a variety of contexts, the item might have received different annotation depending on the context. Between 3% and 10% of lexical items in the binary setting received different annotation, and in the probabilistic setting a number of words received a wide range of labels: e.g. the labels for *observatory* range from 0.0 to 0.95, and for *tragedy* from 0.0 to 1.0. There are several possible reasons for this effect:

- surrounding context might help or impede understanding of a target word;

- the word might be used in a rare sense;

- the data might show a sequential bias effect (Mathur et al., 2017).

Consider the following example from the WIKI training set:

(1)   Beethoven's $Symphony_{0.6}$ No.7, Bruckner's $Symphony_{0.1}$ No.6   and Mendelssohn's $Symphony_{0.0}$ No.4 comprise a nearly complete list of *symphonies*$_{0.3}$ in this key in the Romantic era.

The first occurrence of the word *symphony* is annotated as complex by 12 annotators, the second one by 2 while the third one is not considered complex by any annotators. This might suggest that (1) by the third occurrence of the same word the annotators perceive the word as familiar, (2) some of them found it unnecessary to annotate a word multiple times, (3) given the restriction of 10 complex items per paragraph they prioritised

other words. The annotation of *symphonies* illustrates that the annotators might find different morphological forms of the same word challenging.

Phrase annotation: The annotators were allowed to select phrases of up to 50 characters in length. At the same time, the component words within the phrase might have been annotated as complex independently by other annotators. This results in cases like (2), where the phrase complexity is a derivative of the component word complexities, as well as (3) where the phrase annotation is independent of the component words:

(2) $future_{0.05} \cup generations_{0.25} = future\ generations_{0.15}$

(3) $traditional_{0.2} \cup connection_{0.0} \cup country_{0.05} \neq traditional\ connection\ to\ that\ country_{0.0}$

Annotation of proper nouns : Proper nouns received a variety of labels: e.g., from 0.0 to 0.45 for *Eurozone*, 0.0 to 0.05 for *Barack*, 0.05 to 0.3 for *Brexit*, and from 0.0 to 0.05 or 0.1 for a number of geographical locations like *Copenhagen*, *Estonia*, *Hungary*, *Warsaw*, etc. The annotation in such cases depends more on world knowledge than on the properties of the words *per se*.

3.3 Evaluation

The systems in the `bin` setting are evaluated using F-score. The systems in the `prob` setting are evaluated using *mean absolute error* (*MAE*) which estimates the average difference between the values in the gold standard and values predicted by the system across all test instances.

4 CAMB systems

This section describes the implementation details of the `CAMB` machine learning framework applied to the shared task data sets.

4.1 Features

The set of features employed in our experiments are based on the insights from the CWI shared task 2016 (Paetzold and Specia, 2016d). In addition, we incorporate (1) the number of words grammatically related to the target one, (2) a range of psycholinguistic features from the MRC Psycholinguistic Database (Wilson, 1988), (3) CEFR levels (Council of Europe, 2011) extracted from the Cambridge Advanced Learner Dictionary

(CALD),[1] and (4) the use of Google N-gram word frequencies sourced using the *Datamuse* API.[2]

4.1.1 Word N-gram and POS

The target word and its syntactic class are represented as matrices of token counts. For words, the token counts represent the whole vocabulary as well as character-based bi-grams contained within the words (*N-gram*). The part of speech tags (*POS*) each correspond to a value within the matrix. The syntactic class of the word is obtained by performing part of speech tagging on all sentences containing target words using the NLPCore pipeline (Manning et al., 2014).

4.1.2 Lexical Features

These features are based on the lexical information about the target word and include:

- *Word length (Len)*: the number of characters in the word.

- *Number of syllables (Syll)*: the syllable count for the target word, collected using the *Datamuse* API.

- *WordNet Features*: number of senses (*Syn*), number of hypernyms (*Hyper*) and hyponyms (*Hypo*) for the word's lemma from WordNet (Fellbaum, 2005).

4.1.3 Dependency Parse Relations

The data was parsed using the NLPCore pipeline, and the number of dependency relations for the target word are extracted and used as a feature (*DepNum*).

4.1.4 Lexicon-Based Features

All but the the last in the following list of features are binary features indicating the presence of the word within a lexicon. CALD returns a CEFR level of the target word on the scale $[1, 6]$:

- *SubIMDB*: a list produced using the SubIMDB corpus (Paetzold and Specia, 2016a). The word frequency in the subtitles from the '*Movies and Series for Children*' section is calculated, and the top $1,000$ words are included in this list.

- *Simple Wikipedia (SimpWiki)*: a list of the top $6,368$ words contained in the Simple Wikipedia (Coster and Kauchak, 2011).

- *Ogden's Basic English*: a list of $1,000$ words from Ogden's Basic English list (Ogden, 1968).

- *Cambridge Advanced Learners Dictionary (CALD)*: the entries contained in the Cambridge Advanced Learner's Dictionary with their CEFR levels.

4.1.5 Word Frequency

The frequency of the target word (*Freq*) is estimated using the Google dataset of syntactic n-grams (Goldberg and Orwant, 2013).

4.1.6 MCR Features

We extract the psycholinguistic features of the target words from the MCR Psycholinguistic Database (Wilson, 1988). As the coverage of this database is relatively low, if a target word is not in the dataset we use a *null* value.

- *Word familiarity rating (FAM)* in the range of $[100, 700]$ is based on a combination of 3 sets of familiarity norms: Pavio (unpublished), Toglia and Battig (1978) and Gilhooly and Logie (1980).

- *Number of phonemes (NPHN)*

- *Thorndike-Lorge written frequency (TLFRQ)* – the frequency of occurrence derived from Thorndike and Lorge (1944).

- *Imageability rating (IMG)*, representing the ease of associating the word with an image, is derived from the same combination of sets as the familiarity rating.

- *Concreteness rating (CNC)* represents the degree to which the concept denoted by a word refers to a perceivable entity based on the norms of Gilhooly and Logie (1980).

- The *number of categories (KFCAT)*, *samples (KFSMP)* and *written frequency (KFFRQ)* are derived from Kučera and Francis (1967).

- *Age of acquisition (AOA)* is based on the norms of Gilhooly and Logie (1980), multiplied by 100 to produce a number in the range of $[100, 700]$ (min 125, max 697, mean 405, SD 120).

4.2 Method

Below we outline how the features are incorporated into the machine learning frameworks for the classification and regression tasks. We use distinct approaches to model word and phrase complexity.

---

[1]Publicly available through http://www.englishprofile.org/wordlists

[2]https://www.datamuse.com/api/

4.2.1 Binary Classification Approach

As a wide range of heterogeneous features are employed by both the classification and regression systems, a feature union pipeline is applied. We use the `sklearn` machine learning framework.[3] The numerical features are normalized using a Standard Scaler, which subtracts the mean and scales the data to unit variance. Text-based features are represented as a matrix of token counts using a Count Vectorizer component.

Experiments on the development set confirm the findings of Paetzold and Specia (2016c) that the best performing classification algorithms for this task are ensemble-based techniques. Of these, the boosting classifier `AdaBoost` with 5000 estimators achieves the highest results, followed by the bootstrap aggregation classifier `Random Forest`. For the WIKIPEDIA and NEWS datasets, the best performance is attained using AdaBoost. However for the WIKINEWS an ensemble voting classifier that combines both the AdaBoost and Random Forest classifiers with equal weightings gives the highest F-Score.

4.2.2 Experimental Setup

Feature Selection

The effectiveness of features varies according to the data set classified. For the WIKINEWS and NEWS all aforementioned features are integrated into the systems. The feature set for WIKIPEDIA does not include MCR psycholinguistic features.

Training Data

The performance of the classifier also varies according to the genre of data used for training. The WIKIPEDIA and WIKINEWS are best classified when all available training data are used (i.e., NEWS, WIKINEWS and WIKIPEDIA combined), whereas the best results are achieved on the NEWS when the system is trained using the NEWS dataset only.

4.2.3 Probabilistic Classification Approach

The probabilistic setting uses the same set of features as the binary classification algorithms. We use the `Linear Regression` algorithm, and the lowest MAE values are achieved with the following settings: we use all features and all training data for the NEWS, all but MRC psycholinguistic features and all training data for the WIKINEWS, and a combination of the

WIKIPEDIA and WIKINEWS training data and all but MRC psycholinguistic features for the WIKIPEDIA.

Since the gold standard labels for the probabilistic classification tasks lie in the range of $[0.0, 1.0]$ with a step of 0.05 reflecting the proportion of annotators, we round the classifier's prediction to the nearest value on this scale.

4.2.4 Phrase Complexity Prediction

Table 1 shows that there are a non-negligible amount of phrases in the data. We implement three binary classification approaches and one probabilistic classification approach to predict phrase complexity.

Binary Classification Techniques

- *CW presence*: Each word within the phrase is first classified using our word-based CW classifier. If the total number of complex words is above a pre-defined threshold then the phrase is marked as complex.

- *N-gram classifier*: The frequency of n-grams contained within phrases is obtained from the Corpus of Contemporary American English (Davies, 2009). An AdaBoost classifier is first trained using these frequencies as features, and then applied to classify new phrase instances.

- *Greedy approach*: The greedy baseline approach simply labels all phrases as complex.

Probabilistic Classification Techniques

For the probabilistic setting, we first apply our word-based CW regression classifier, and then derive the phrase complexity label as the mean of the complexity values within the phrase. Note that this technique helps us correctly predict the phrase complexity for cases similar to example (2) from Section 3, but not for cases similar to example (3).

5 Results

In this Section, we present and discuss the results obtained with the CAMB systems. The systems submitted to the shared task scored first in the binary classification English track on all three text genres, first on the WIKINEWS and WIKIPEDIA test sets and third on the NEWS test set in the probabilistic classification English track. Table 3 presents the results, with those that scored first in the shared task marked in bold.

---

[3] http://scikit-learn.org/stable/

5.1 Test Set Results

	Binary (F-Score)	Probabilistic (MAE)
NEWS	**0.8736**	0.0558
WINS	**0.8400**	**0.0674**
WIKI	**0.8115**	**0.0739**

Table 3: Test set results

The final test files across all genres contain a total of $3,701$ words and 551 phrases. Words are classified using the tailored approaches according to the dataset genre. In the shared task submission, phrases are independently classified using the greedy approach (see Section 4).

5.2 Analysis

Per-Genre Performance

Classification performance as well as feature relevance varies across the datasets. In the binary setting, the highest performance is obtained on the NEWS data when the system is trained on the NEWS data only. In the probabilistic setting, the system performs best on the NEWS data as well. Table 2 suggests that NEWS contains the lowest number of complex words, and Table 4 shows the total number of words, the number of unique words and the percentage of unique words within each genre.

	NEWS	WINS	WIKI
Total	$13,461$	$7,559$	$5,439$
Unique	$3,376$	$3,334$	$3,157$
%	25.08	44.10	58.44

Table 4: Unique words distribution

Table 4 suggests that the NEWS dataset contains the lowest number of unique words, which might be the effect of more restricted vocabulary used in professional news. As a result, the classifier is likely to have multiple exposure to the same word (albeit in different contexts) during training. At the same time, WIKIPEDIA with its 58.44% has the highest ratio of unique words, which might be due to the fact that it covers a very broad range of subjects. Note, that WIKIPEDIA is both more challenging for human annotators (highest percentage of complex words in Table 2) and the classifiers (lowest results in both settings in Table 3). This might explain why the classifiers benefit from training on multiple data sources in this case.

Our CWI systems are context-independent, which means that a word or a phrase receives the same complexity label regardless of a particular context of use. E.g., all three occurrences of the word *Symphony* in the example (1) from Section 3 would receive the same complexity label from our system. This limitation is the biggest source of error for the NEWS dataset (88.94% of the misclassified words in the NEWS test set have multiple labels in the data) and the WIKINEWS dataset (61.31%), while the proportion of such cases in the WIKIPEDIA data is lower (52.78%) which might also be due to the higher ratio of unique words in the WIKIPEDIA data.

Phrase Classification Results

The CAMB submission to the shared task applies a simple *greedy* approach to the phrase classification. We run experiments with more informed approaches overviewed in Section 4 and evaluate whether these approaches improve performance. Table 5 presents the results obtained with the different approaches to the phrase classification in the binary setting. The results of the system submitted to the shared task are marked in bold.

Data	Acc	P	R	F-Score
CW pres.	0.6987	0.8049	0.8231	0.8139
N-gram	0.8004	0.8015	0.9977	0.8889
Greedy	**0.8004**	**0.8004**	**1.000**	**0.8891**

Table 5: Binary classification results for the phrase classification in the test set

The results suggest that the more linguistically informed n-gram classifier is capable of achieving results similar to the baseline greedy approach that simply labels all phrases as complex. To test how it would score in the shared task, we re-run the experiments using the n-gram based phrase classifier, and report the results in Table 6.

Data	Acc	P	R	F-Score
NEWS	0.8535	0.7778	0.8641	0.8479
WINS	0.8423	0.8046	0.8297	0.8392
WIKI	0.8081	0.8254	0.7859	0.8080

Table 6: Test set results using n-gram phrase classifier

We note a drop of 3.13% for the F-score on the NEWS dataset, although the difference in the F-score on the other two datasets is less than 1%.

Features	NEWS	WINS	WIKI
N-grams	0.792	0.789	0.754
POS	0.033	0.035	0.046
Freq	0.029	0.029	0.043
Syn	0.020	0.027	0.013
FAM	0.016	0.008	0.019
Syll	0.013	0.021	0.018
KFSMP	0.012	0.010	0.008
SimpWiki	0.010	0.011	0.005
TLFRQ	0.010	0.009	0.011
CNC	0.009	0.010	0.009

Table 7: Gini coefficient for feature contribution

Individual Feature Contribution

We analyse the contribution of individual features to the classification framework. Table 7 reports the Gini coefficient for the top 10 informative features across different datasets. The Gini coefficient is defined as the total decrease in node impurity, weighted by the probability of reaching that node, averaged over all trees of the ensemble (Breiman, 2015).

We also note that the combination of all features achieves best results on the NEWS and WIKINEWS data sets, but the results on the WIKIPEDIA data decrease when the MCR Psycholinguistic Database features are included. We have noted above that one of the reasons for lower performance on the WIKIPEDIA data is due to the more diverse vocabulary. In addition to that, we note that the MCR Psycholinguistic Database contains values for $150,837$ words, but some measures provide much lower coverage (see Table 8).

Measure	Coverage (words)
AOA	3,503
CNC	8,228
IMG	9,240
FAM	9,392
TLFRQ	25,308
KFCAT/SMP/FRQ	29,778
NPHN	38,438

Table 8: Number of feature instances covered by the MCR Database

As the WIKIPEDIA dataset has the largest proportion of unique words, it is likely that these features do not improve the classification accuracy due to their sparsity.

Performance Across Parts of Speech

Table 9 reports the results achieved by the binary classification algorithm on the different parts of speech in the test files. We include only content words in our analysis.

Data	Size	Acc	P	R	F
Total Test	3,701	0.86	0.82	0.79	0.85
Nouns	2,427	0.86	0.80	0.76	0.84
Verbs	718	0.84	0.83	0.81	0.84
Adjectives	435	0.88	0.86	0.86	0.87
Adverbs	111	0.91	0.89	0.92	0.91

Table 9: POS Classification Metrics

We note that nouns represent the largest proportion of all test items, while showing the lowest precision and recall. We hypothesise that one of the reasons for that might be the dependence of the noun annotation on the context and the context-independent nature of our classifiers. In addition, as we note in Section 3, the complexity of proper nouns largely depends on the world knowledge and is harder to model with a machine learning approach: 12.56% of misclassified instances in the NEWS data, 22.02% in the WIKINEWS and 22.92% in the WIKPEDIA are proper nouns.

6   Conclusion

In this paper, we have presented the implementation of the CAMB systems submitted to the CWI Shared Task 2018, and discussed the key challenges for the systems. Our systems scored first on three text genres in the binary classification track, and on two out of three genres in the probabilistic track. Further analysis of the performance identifies future directions for this research.

First of all, our systems are implemented in a context-independent way, while the context of use clearly affects the perception of word complexity. Future research will look into the ways to include contextual features into the machine learning framework. In addition, future work should investigate how phrase complexity is derived from individual word complexity scores.

Secondly, we believe that the notion of word complexity is dependent on a number of demographic factors such as one's level of education, L1 and level of language competence. These factors should be included both at the data annotation step and at the CW detection step.

Acknowledgments

We are grateful to Cambridge English for supporting this research via the ALTA Institute.

References

Or Biran, Samuel Brody, and Noemie Elhadad. 2011. Putting it Simply: a Context-Aware Approach to Lexical Simplification. In *Proceedings of the 49th Annual Meeting of the Association for Computational Linguistics:shortpapers*, pages 496–501, Portland, Oregon. Association for Computational Linguistics.

Stefan Bott, Luz Rello, Biljana Drndarevic, and Horacio Saggion. 2012. Can Spanish Be Simpler? LexSiS: Lexical Simplification for Spanish. In *Proceedings of COLING 2012: Technical Papers*, pages 357–374, Mumbai. COLING.

Leo Breiman. 2015. Random forests leo breiman and adele cutler. *Random Forests-Classification Description.*

John Carroll, Guido Minnen, Darren Pearce, Yvonne Canning, Siobhan Devlin, and John Tait. 1999. Simplifying Text for Language-Impaired Readers. In *Proceedings of the 9th Conference of the European Chapter of the ACL (EACL'99)*, pages 269–270, Bergen, Norway.

William Coster and David Kauchak. 2011. Simple english wikipedia: a new text simplification task. In *Proceedings of the 49th Annual Meeting of the Association for Computational Linguistics: Human Language Technologies: short papers-Volume 2*, pages 665–669. Association for Computational Linguistics.

Mark Davies. 2009. The 385+ million word corpus of contemporary american english (1990–2008+): Design, architecture, and linguistic insights. *International journal of corpus linguistics*, 14(2):159–190.

Siobhan Devlin and John Tait. 1998. The use of a psycholinguistic database in the simplification of text for aphasic readers. *Linguistic Databases*, pages 161–173.

William H. Dubay. 2004. The Principles of Readability. *Costa Mesa, CA: Impact Information.*

Noemie Elhadad. 2006. Comprehending Technical Texts: Predicting and Defining Unfamiliar Terms. In *AMIA Annual Symposium Proceedings*, pages 239–243.

The Council of Europe. 2011. Common European Framework of Reference for Languages: Learning, Teaching, Assessment.

Christiane Fellbaum. 2005. *Encyclopedia of Language and Linguistics, Second Edition*, chapter WordNet and wordnets. Oxford: Elsevier.

Lijun Feng. 2008. Text simplification: A survey. Technical report, CUNY.

Ken J Gilhooly and Robert H Logie. 1980. Age-of-acquisition, imagery, concreteness, familiarity, and ambiguity measures for 1,944 words. *Behavior research methods & instrumentation*, 12(4):395–427.

Yoav Goldberg and Jon Orwant. 2013. A dataset of syntactic-ngrams over time from a very large corpus of english books. In *Second Joint Conference on Lexical and Computational Semantics (* SEM), Volume 1: Proceedings of the Main Conference and the Shared Task: Semantic Textual Similarity*, volume 1, pages 241–247.

Colby Horn, Cathryn Manduca, and David Kauchak. 2014. Learning a lexical simplifier using Wikipedia. In *Proceedings of the 52nd ACL*, pages 458–463.

David Kauchak. 2013. Improving text simplification language modeling using unsimplified text data. In *Proceedings of the 51st ACL*, pages 1537–1546.

Michal Konkol. 2016. Uwb at semeval-2016 task 11: Exploring features for complex word identification. In *Proceedings of the 10th International Workshop on Semantic Evaluation (SemEval-2016)*, pages 1038–1041, San Diego, California. Association for Computational Linguistics.

Henry Kučera and Winthrop Nelson Francis. 1967. *Computational analysis of present-day American English*. Dartmouth Publishing Group.

Gondy Leroy, James E. Endicott, David Kauchak, Obay Mouradi, and Melissa Just. 2013. User Evaluation of the Effects of a Text Simplification Algorithm Using Term Familiarity on Perception, Understanding, Learning, and Information Retention. *Journal of Medical Internet Research (JMIR)*, 7(15).

Shervin Malmasi, Mark Dras, and Marcos Zampieri. 2016. Ltg at semeval-2016 task 11: Complex word identification with classifier ensembles. In *Proceedings of the 10th International Workshop on Semantic Evaluation (SemEval-2016)*, pages 996–1000, San Diego, California. Association for Computational Linguistics.

Shervin Malmasi and Marcos Zampieri. 2016. Maza at semeval-2016 task 11: Detecting lexical complexity using a decision stump meta-classifier. In *Proceedings of the 10th International Workshop on Semantic Evaluation (SemEval-2016)*, pages 991–995, San Diego, California. Association for Computational Linguistics.

Christopher D. Manning, Mihai Surdeanu, John Bauer, Jenny Finkel, Steven J. Bethard, and David McClosky. 2014. The Stanford CoreNLP natural language processing toolkit. In *Association for Computational Linguistics (ACL) System Demonstrations*, pages 55–60.

Nitika Mathur, Timothy Baldwin, and Trevor Cohn. 2017. Sequence Effects in Crowdsourced Annotations. In *Proceedings of the 2017 Conference on Empirical Methods in Natural Language Processing (EMNLP)*, pages 2860–2865.

Niloy Mukherjee, Braja Gopal Patra, Dipankar Das, and Sivaji Bandyopadhyay. 2016. Ju_nlp at semeval-2016 task 11: Identifying complex words in a sentence. In *Proceedings of the 10th International Workshop on Semantic Evaluation (SemEval-2016)*, pages 986–990, San Diego, California. Association for Computational Linguistics.

I. S. Paul Nation. 2006. How Large a Vocabulary Is Needed For Reading and Listening? *The Canadian Modern Language Review/La Revue canadienne des langues vivantes*, 63(1):59–82.

Charles Kay Ogden. 1968. *Basic English: international second language*. Harcourt, Brace & World.

Gustavo Paetzold and Lucia Specia. 2016a. Collecting and exploring everyday language for predicting psycholinguistic properties of words. In *Proceedings of COLING 2016, the 26th International Conference on Computational Linguistics: Technical Papers*, pages 1669–1679.

Gustavo Paetzold and Lucia Specia. 2016b. Plumberr: An automatic error identification framework for lexical simplification. In *Proceedings of the first international workshop on Quality Assessment for Text Simplification (QATS)*, pages 1–9, Portoroz, Slovenia. European Language Resources Association (ELRA).

Gustavo Paetzold and Lucia Specia. 2016c. SemEval 2016 Task 11: Complex Word Identification. In *Proceedings of the 10th International Workshop on Semantic Evaluation (SemEval-2016)*, pages 560–569, San Diego, California. Association for Computational Linguistics.

Gustavo Paetzold and Lucia Specia. 2016d. Sv000gg at semeval-2016 task 11: Heavy gauge complex word identification with system voting. In *Proceedings of the 10th International Workshop on Semantic Evaluation (SemEval-2016)*, pages 969–974, San Diego, California. Association for Computational Linguistics.

Francesco Ronzano, Ahmed Abura'ed, Luis Espinosa Anke, and Horacio Saggion. 2016. Taln at semeval-2016 task 11: Modelling complex words by contextual, lexical and semantic features. In *Proceedings of the 10th International Workshop on Semantic Evaluation (SemEval-2016)*, pages 1011–1016, San Diego, California. Association for Computational Linguistics.

Matthew Shardlow. 2013a. A comparison of techniques to automatically identify complex words. In *Proceedings of the Student Research Workshop at the 51st Annual Meeting of the Association for Computational Linguistics (ACL)*, pages 103–109, Sofia, Bulgaria. Association for Computational Linguistics (ACL).

Matthew Shardlow. 2013b. The cw corpus: A new resource for evaluating the identification of complex words. In *Proceedings of the 2nd Workshop on Predicting and Improving Text Readability for Target Reader Populations*, pages 69–77, Sofia, Bulgaria. Association for Computational Linguistics (ACL).

Matthew Shardlow. 2014. Out in the open: Finding and categorising errors in the lexical simplification pipeline. In *In Proceedings of the 9th LREC*, pages 1583–1590.

S. Rebecca Thomas and Sven Anderson. 2012. WordNet-Based Lexical Simplification of a Document. In *Proceedings of KONVENS 2012 (Main track: oral presentations)*, Vienna.

Edward L Thorndike and Irving Lorge. 1944. The teacher's wordbook of 30,000 words. new york: Columbia university, teachers college.

Michael P Toglia and William F Battig. 1978. *Handbook of semantic word norms*. Lawrence Erlbaum.

Michael Wilson. 1988. The MRC Psycholinguistic Database: Machine Readable Dictionary, Version 2. *Behavioural Research Methods, Instruments and Computers*, pages 6–11.

Krzysztof Wróbel. 2016. Plujagh at semeval-2016 task 11: Simple system for complex word identification. In *Proceedings of the 10th International Workshop on Semantic Evaluation (SemEval-2016)*, pages 953–957, San Diego, California. Association for Computational Linguistics.

Wei Xu, Chris Callison-Burch, and Courtney Napoles. 2015. Problems in Current Text Simplification Research: New Data Can Help. *Transactions of the Association for Computational Linguistics (TACL)*, 3:283–297.

Seid Muhie Yimam, Chris Biemann, Shervin Malmasi, Gustavo Paetzold, Lucia Specia, Sanja Štajner, Anaïs Tack, and Marcos Zampieri. 2018. A Report on the Complex Word Identification Shared Task 2018. In *Proceedings of the 13th Workshop on Innovative Use of NLP for Building Educational Applications*, New Orleans, United States. Association for Computational Linguistics.

Seid Muhie Yimam, Sanja Štajner, Martin Riedl, and Chris Biemann. 2017a. CWIG3G2 - Complex Word Identification Task across Three Text Genres and Two User Groups. In *Proceedings of the Eighth International Joint Conference on Natural Language Processing (Volume 2: Short Papers)*, pages 401–407, Taipei, Taiwan. Asian Federation of Natural Language Processing.

Seid Muhie Yimam, Sanja Štajner, Martin Riedl, and Chris Biemann. 2017b. Multilingual and Cross-Lingual Complex Word Identification. In *Proceedings of the International Conference Recent Advances in Natural Language Processing, RANLP 2017*, pages 813–822, Varna, Bulgaria. INCOMA Ltd.

Marcos Zampieri, Shervin Malmasi, Gustavo Paetzold, and Lucia Specia. 2017. Complex Word Identification: Challenges in Data Annotation and System Performance. In *Proceedings of the 4th Workshop on Natural Language Processing Techniques for Educational Applications (NLPTEA 2017)*, pages 59–63, Taipei, Taiwan. Asian Federation of Natural Language Processing.

Marcos Zampieri, Liling Tan, and Josef van Genabith. 2016. Macsaar at semeval-2016 task 11: Zipfian and character features for complexword identification. In *Proceedings of the 10th International Workshop on Semantic Evaluation (SemEval-2016)*, pages 1001–1005, San Diego, California. Association for Computational Linguistics.

Qing Zeng, Eunjung Kim, Jon Crowell, and Tony Tse. 2005. *Biological and Medical Data Analysis. ISBMDA 2005. Lecture Notes in Computer Science*, volume 3745 of *ISBMDA 2005*, chapter A Text Corpora-Based Estimation of the Familiarity of Health Terminology. Springer, Berlin, Heidelberg.

Qing Zeng-Treitler, Sergey Goryachev, Tony Tse, Alla Keselman, and Aziz Boxwala. 2008. Estimating Consumer Familiarity with Health Terminology: A Context-based Approach. *Journal of the American Medical Informatics Association: JAMIA*, 15(3):349–356.

Complex Word Identification Based on Frequency in a Learner Corpus

Tomoyuki Kajiwara[††]
[†]Institute for Datability Science
Osaka University
Osaka, Japan
kajiwara@ids.osaka-u.ac.jp

Mamoru Komachi[‡]
[‡]Graduate School of Systems Design
Tokyo Metropolitan University
Tokyo, Japan
komachi@tmu.ac.jp

Abstract

We introduce the TMU systems for the complex word identification (CWI) shared task 2018. TMU systems use random forest classifiers and regressors whose features are the number of characters and words and the frequency of target words in various corpora. Our simple systems performed best on 5 of the 12 tracks. Ablation analysis confirmed the usefulness of a learner corpus for a CWI task.

1 Introduction

Lexical simplification (Paetzold and Specia, 2017) is one of the approaches for text simplification (Shardlow, 2014), which facilitates children and language learners' reading comprehension. Lexical simplification comprises the following steps:

1. Complex word identification

2. Substitution generation

3. Substitution selection

4. Substitution ranking

In this study, we work on complex word identification (CWI) (Shardlow, 2013), a subtask of lexical simplification.

Previous studies (Specia et al., 2012; Paetzold and Specia, 2016a) concluded that the most effective way to estimate word difficulty is to count the word frequency in a corpus. However, they counted the word frequency in corpora written by native speakers, such as Wikipedia. Language learners tend to use simple words as compared to native speakers. Therefore, we expect the word frequency in the learner corpus to be a useful feature for CWI.

Our CWI system considers the word frequency in a learner corpus as well as in corpora written by native speakers. We use the Lang-8 corpus[1] (Mizumoto et al., 2011), a learner corpus that can be used on a large-scale in many languages.

2 CWI Shared Task 2018

In CWI shared tasks, systems predict whether words in a given context are complex or non-complex for a non-native speaker. The first CWI shared task (Paetzold and Specia, 2016a; Zampieri et al., 2017) contained only English data designed for non-native English speakers. Totally, 20 annotators were assigned to each instance in the training set. However, in the test set, only one annotator was assigned to each instance. By contrast, the CWI shared task 2018 (Yimam et al., 2018) used a multilingual dataset (Yimam et al., 2017a,b) having all instances annotated by multiple annotators. This shared task was divided into two tasks (binary and probabilistic classification) and the following four tracks:

- English monolingual CWI

- Spanish monolingual CWI

- German monolingual CWI

- Multilingual CWI with a French test set

The English dataset contained a mixture of professionally written news, non-professionally written news (WikiNews), and Wikipedia articles. Datasets for languages excluding English were from Wikipedia articles. Tables 1 and 2 display the dataset and the number of instances, respectively.

---

[1]http://lang-8.com/

Proceedings of the Thirteenth Workshop on Innovative Use of NLP for Building Educational Applications, pages 195–199
New Orleans, Louisiana, June 5, 2018. ©2018 Association for Computational Linguistics

Sentence	Target	Label	Probability
According to Goodyear, a neighbor heard gun shots.	shots	0	0.00
According to Goodyear, a neighbor heard gun shots.	according to	1	0.05
A lieutenant who had defected was also killed in the clashes.	defected	1	0.45
A bad part of the investigation is we may not get the why.	investigation	1	0.95

Table 1: Example instances of the English dataset.

Dataset		Train	Dev	Test
English	(News)	14,002	1,764	2,095
English	(WikiNews)	7,746	870	1,287
English	(Wikipedia)	5,551	694	870
Spanish	(Wikipedia)	13,750	1,622	2,233
German	(Wikipedia)	6,151	795	959
French	(Wikipedia)	0	0	2,251

Table 2: Number of instances.

	Feature
1	Number of characters
2	Number of words
3	Frequency of target in the Wikipedia corpus
4	Frequency of target in the WikiNews corpus
5	Frequency of target in the Lang-8 corpus
6	Probability of target in the Wikipedia corpus
7	Probability of target in the WikiNews corpus
8	Probability of target in the Lang-8 corpus

Table 3: Our features.

	Wikipedia	WikiNews	Lang-8
English	94,872,197	325,038	3,261,441
Spanish	20,197,778	107,289	185,677
German	44,280,830	145,326	160,110
French	26,224,666	135,845	181,004

Table 4: Number of sentences.

2.1 Binary Classification Task

Labels in the binary classification task were assigned as follows:

0: simple word (none of the annotators marked the word as difficult)

1: complex word (at least one annotator marked the word as difficult)

We evaluated the systems using the macro-averaged F1-score.

2.2 Probabilistic Classification Task

Labels in the probabilistic classification task were assigned as the proportion of annotators identifying the target as complex. Systems were evaluated using the MAE (mean absolute error).

3 TMU Systems

According to previous studies (Specia et al., 2012; Paetzold and Specia, 2016a), we estimated the word difficulty by counting word frequency.

3.1 Classifiers

We used random forest classifiers and random forest regressors for binary classification tasks and probabilistic classification tasks, respectively. We examined all combinations of the following hyper-parameters[2]:

- `n_estimators`: $\{10, 50, 100, 500, 1000\}$
- `max_depth`: $\{5, 10, 15, 20, \infty\}$
- `min_samples_leaf`: $\{1, 5, 10, 15, 20\}$

---

[2]http://scikit-learn.org/

3.2 Features

Table 3 shows all the features used by our systems.

First, we used the heuristics that the longer words are more complex to understand as the first feature. For example, Flesch reading ease (Flesch, 1948), frequently used in research on text simplification, uses this heuristics.

Second, as shown in Table 1, the target includes words and phrases. As long phrases tend to be less frequent, we used the number of words as the second feature.

Others features (3-8) are based on the frequency of targets in a corpus. We counted frequencies from texts written by native speakers and language learners. Language learners are more likely to use simple words than native speakers. Therefore, we expected word frequency in the learner corpus to be a useful feature for CWI. As a text written by native speakers, we counted the frequency from Wikipedia and WikiNews. By contrast, as a text written by language learners, we counted the frequency from the Lang-8 corpus (Mizumoto et al., 2011). The Lang-8 corpus contains texts before and after corrections written by learners and native speakers, respectively. We use the former.

News	Wikipedia	WikiNews	Spanish	German	French
.874 Camb	.812 Camb	.840 Camb	.770 TMU	.745 TMU	.760 CoastalCPH
.864 ITEC	.797 NILC	.831 NLP-CIC	.767 NLP-CIC	.743 SB@GU	.747 TMU
.864 NILC	.792 UnibucKernel	.828 NILC	.764 ITEC	.693 hu-berlin	.627 SB@GU
.863 TMU	.783 SB@GU	.816 CFILT-IITB	.746 CoastalCPH	.662 CoastalCPH	.574 hu-berlin
.855 NLP-CIC	.782 ITEC	.813 UnibucKernel	.728 SB@GU	.555 Gillin Inc.	
.848 CFILT_IITB	.776 CFILT_IITB	.811 ITEC	.708 hu-berlin		
.833 SB@GU	.772 NLP-CIC	.803 SB@GU	.680 Gillin Inc.		
.826 hu-berlin	.762 TMU	.787 TMU			
.824 Gillin Inc.	.745 hu-berlin	.766 hu-berlin			
.818 UnibucKernel	.740 LaSTUS	.749 LaSTUS			
.810 LaSTUS	.721 CoastalCPH	.732 Gillin Inc.			
	.660 Gillin Inc.				

Table 5: Performance on the binary classification task. Systems are ranked by their macro-averaged F1-score.

News	Wikipedia	WikiNews	Spanish	German	French
.051 TMU	.074 Camb	.067 Camb	.072 TMU	.061 TMU	.066 CoastalCPH
.054 ITEC	.081 ITEC	.070 TMU	.073 ITEC	.075 CoastalCPH	.078 TMU
.056 Camb	.082 NILC	.071 ITEC	.079 CoastalCPH	.191 Gillin Inc.	
.059 NILC	.093 TMU	.073 NILC	.251 Gillin Inc.		
.153 SB@GU	.176 SB@GU	.165 SB@GU			
.281 Gillin Inc.	.316 Gillin Inc.	.289 Gillin Inc.			

Table 6: Performance on the probabilistic classification task. Systems are ranked by their MAE score.

3.3 Experimental Settings

The dump data of Wikipedia and WikiNews on December 01, 2017, were downloaded and divided into sentences using WikiExtractor[3] and NLTK[4]. All corpora (Train / Dev / Test and Wikipedia / WikiNews / Lang-8) were tokenized and lower-cased in the script of the statistical machine translation tool Moses[5] (Koehn et al., 2007). Table 4 displays the number of sentences in each corpus.

4 Results

Tables 5 and 6 present the official evaluation results. In Table 5, systems are ranked by their macro-averaged F1-score for the binary classification task. TMU systems ranked first in Spanish and German, and second in French. In Table 6, systems are ranked by their MAE score for the probabilistic classification task. TMU systems ranked first in Spanish, German, and English news track and second in English WikiNews track.

4.1 Ablation Analysis of Freq. and Proba.

Frequency and probability are similar features. Table 7 indicates that although the probability features are more important than the frequency features, systems can yield better performance by considering both features.

4.2 Ablation Analysis of Corpora

We examined which corpus provides important features. Table 8 shows the most important features obtained from the Lang-8 corpus. Remarkably, the largest Wikipedia corpus does not contribute significantly to performance.

5 Related Work

Although our systems (random forest with length and frequency of the target word) are simple, they achieve competitive results. In the first CWI shared task 2016, numerous systems (Brooke et al., 2016; Davoodi and Kosseim, 2016; Mukherjee et al., 2016; Zampieri et al., 2016; Ronzano et al., 2016) used random forest classifiers. The length (Wróbel, 2016; Paetzold and Specia, 2016b; Malmasi and Zampieri, 2016; Malmasi et al., 2016; Zampieri et al., 2016; Ronzano et al., 2016; Palakurthi and Mamidi, 2016; Quijada and Medero, 2016; Konkol, 2016) and frequency (Wróbel, 2016; Paetzold and Specia, 2016b; Brooke et al., 2016; Zampieri et al., 2016; Ronzano et al., 2016; Palakurthi and Mamidi, 2016; Quijada and Medero, 2016; Konkol, 2016; Kauchak, 2016) of the target word were the basic

---

[3]https://github.com/attardi/wikiextractor/
[4]http://www.nltk.org/
[5]https://github.com/moses-smt/mosesdecoder

	News	Wikipedia	WikiNews	Spanish	German	French	Average
Binary Classification Task (macro-averaged F1)							
All Features	0.863	0.762	0.787	0.770	0.745	0.747	0.779
w/o Frequency	0.864	0.770	0.798	0.774	0.742	0.693	0.774
w/o Probability	0.860	0.767	0.803	0.779	0.753	0.663	0.771
Probabilistic Classification Task (MAE)							
All Features	0.051	0.093	0.070	0.072	0.061	0.078	0.071
w/o Frequency	0.052	0.090	0.073	0.071	0.059	0.099	0.074
w/o Probability	0.051	0.094	0.070	0.072	0.061	0.111	0.077

Table 7: Ablation analysis of frequency and probability features.

	News	Wikipedia	WikiNews	Spanish	German	French	Average
Binary Classification Task (macro-averaged F1)							
All Features	0.863	0.762	0.787	0.770	0.745	0.747	0.779
w/o Wikipedia	0.860	0.741	0.790	0.758	0.757	0.748	0.776
w/o WikiNews	0.858	0.750	0.788	0.756	0.748	0.746	0.774
w/o Lang-8	0.859	0.764	0.786	0.743	0.752	0.735	0.773
Probabilistic Classification Task (MAE)							
All Features	0.051	0.093	0.070	0.072	0.061	0.078	0.071
w/o Wikipedia	0.053	0.091	0.072	0.073	0.060	0.079	0.071
w/o WikiNews	0.051	0.092	0.070	0.073	0.061	0.075	0.070
w/o Lang-8	0.052	0.093	0.073	0.075	0.062	0.076	0.072

Table 8: Ablation analysis of corpora.

features of the CWI shared task 2016. These are used as baselines, and a majority of the systems use them as part of their features.

While previous works counted the word frequency in corpora such as Wikipedia, which is written by native speakers, we used corpora written by language learners. As anticipated, the word frequency in the learner corpus proved to be a vital feature in the CWI task.

6 Conclusion

We explained the TMU systems for CWI shared task 2018. Our systems performed best on 5 of the 12 tracks using only simple features.

Previous studies concluded that the most effective way to estimate word difficulty is to count the word frequency in a corpus. However, it was not clear what kind of corpus is useful for counting word frequencies. We discussed the usefulness of a learner corpus for the CWI task for the first time. As anticipated, the word frequency counted from the learner corpus worked better than that from the in-domain corpus written by the native speakers for the CWI task.

Acknowledgements

We would like to thank Xi Yangyang for granting use of extracted texts from Lang-8.

References

Julian Brooke, Alexandra Uitdenbogerd, and Timothy Baldwin. 2016. Melbourne at SemEval 2016 Task 11: Classifying Type-level Word Complexity using Random Forests with Corpus and Word List Features. In *Proceedings of the 10th International Workshop on Semantic Evaluation*, pages 975–981.

Elnaz Davoodi and Leila Kosseim. 2016. CLaC at SemEval-2016 Task 11: Exploring linguistic and psycho-linguistic Features for Complex Word Identification. In *Proceedings of the 10th International Workshop on Semantic Evaluation*, pages 982–985.

Rudolf Flesch. 1948. A new readability yardstick. *Journal of Applied Psychology*, 32:221–233.

David Kauchak. 2016. Pomona at SemEval-2016 Task 11: Predicting Word Complexity Based on Corpus Frequency. In *Proceedings of the 10th International Workshop on Semantic Evaluation*, pages 1047–1051.

Philipp Koehn, Hieu Hoang, Alexandra Birch, Chris Callison-Burch, Marcello Federico, Nicola Bertoldi, Brooke Cowan, Wade Shen, Christine Moran, Richard Zens, Chris Dyer, Ondrej Bojar, Alexandra

Constantin, and Evan Herbst. 2007. Moses: Open Source Toolkit for Statistical Machine Translation. In *Proceedings of the 45th Annual Meeting of the Association for Computational Linguistics*, pages 177–180.

Michal Konkol. 2016. UWB at SemEval-2016 Task 11: Exploring Features for Complex Word Identification. In *Proceedings of the 10th International Workshop on Semantic Evaluation*, pages 1038–1041.

Shervin Malmasi, Mark Dras, and Marcos Zampieri. 2016. LTG at SemEval-2016 Task 11: Complex Word Identification with Classifier Ensembles. In *Proceedings of the 10th International Workshop on Semantic Evaluation*, pages 996–1000.

Shervin Malmasi and Marcos Zampieri. 2016. MAZA at SemEval-2016 Task 11: Detecting Lexical Complexity Using a Decision Stump Meta-Classifier. In *Proceedings of the 10th International Workshop on Semantic Evaluation*, pages 991–995.

Tomoya Mizumoto, Mamoru Komachi, Masaaki Nagata, and Yuji Matsumoto. 2011. Mining Revision Log of Language Learning SNS for Automated Japanese Error Correction of Second Language Learners. In *Proceedings of 5th International Joint Conference on Natural Language Processing*, pages 147–155.

Niloy Mukherjee, Braja Gopal Patra, Dipankar Das, and Sivaji Bandyopadhyay. 2016. JU_NLP at SemEval-2016 Task 11: Identifying Complex Words in a Sentence. In *Proceedings of the 10th International Workshop on Semantic Evaluation*, pages 986–990.

Gustavo Paetzold and Lucia Specia. 2016a. SemEval 2016 Task 11: Complex Word Identification. In *Proceedings of the 10th International Workshop on Semantic Evaluation*, pages 560–569.

Gustavo Paetzold and Lucia Specia. 2016b. SV000gg at SemEval-2016 Task 11: Heavy Gauge Complex Word Identification with System Voting. In *Proceedings of the 10th International Workshop on Semantic Evaluation*, pages 969–974.

Gustavo Paetzold and Lucia Specia. 2017. A Survey on Lexical Simplification. *Journal of Artificial Intelligence Research*, 60:549–593.

Ashish Palakurthi and Radhika Mamidi. 2016. IIIT at SemEval-2016 Task 11: Complex Word Identification using Nearest Centroid Classification. In *Proceedings of the 10th International Workshop on Semantic Evaluation*, pages 1017–1021.

Maury Quijada and Julie Medero. 2016. HMC at SemEval-2016 Task 11: Identifying Complex Words Using Depth-limited Decision Trees. In *Proceedings of the 10th International Workshop on Semantic Evaluation*, pages 1034–1037.

Francesco Ronzano, Ahmed Abura'ed, Luis Espinosa Anke, and Horacio Saggion. 2016. TALN at SemEval-2016 Task 11: Modelling Complex Words by Contextual, Lexical and Semantic Features. In *Proceedings of the 10th International Workshop on Semantic Evaluation*, pages 1011–1016.

Matthew Shardlow. 2013. A Comparison of Techniques to Automatically Identify Complex Words. In *Proceedings of the ACL 2013 Student Research Workshop*, pages 103–109.

Matthew Shardlow. 2014. A Survey of Automated Text Simplification. *International Journal of Advanced Computer Science and Applications, Special Issue on Natural Language Processing*, pages 58–70.

Lucia Specia, Sujay Kumar Jauhar, and Rada Mihalcea. 2012. SemEval-2012 Task 1: English Lexical Simplification. In *Proceedings of the *SEM 2012: The First Joint Conference on Lexical and Computational Semantics*, pages 347–355.

Krzysztof Wróbel. 2016. PLUJAGH at SemEval-2016 Task 11: Simple System for Complex Word Identification. In *Proceedings of the 10th International Workshop on Semantic Evaluation*, pages 953–957.

Seid Muhie Yimam, Chris Biemann, Shervin Malmasi, Gustavo Paetzold, Lucia Specia, Sanja Štajner, Anaïs Tack, and Marcos Zampieri. 2018. A Report on the Complex Word Identification Shared Task 2018. In *Proceedings of the 13th Workshop on Innovative Use of NLP for Building Educational Applications*.

Seid Muhie Yimam, Sanja Štajner, Martin Riedl, and Chris Biemann. 2017a. CWIG3G2 - Complex Word Identification Task across Three Text Genres and Two User Groups. In *Proceedings of the Eighth International Joint Conference on Natural Language Processing*, pages 401–407.

Seid Muhie Yimam, Sanja Štajner, Martin Riedl, and Chris Biemann. 2017b. Multilingual and Cross-Lingual Complex Word Identification. In *Proceedings of the International Conference Recent Advances in Natural Language Processing, RANLP 2017*, pages 813–822.

Marcos Zampieri, Shervin Malmasi, Gustavo Paetzold, and Lucia Specia. 2017. Complex Word Identification: Challenges in Data Annotation and System Performance. In *Proceedings of the 4th Workshop on Natural Language Processing Techniques for Educational Applications*, pages 59–63.

Marcos Zampieri, Liling Tan, and Josef van Genabith. 2016. MacSaar at SemEval-2016 Task 11: Zipfian and Character Features for Complex Word Identification. In *Proceedings of the 10th International Workshop on Semantic Evaluation*, pages 1001–1005.

The Whole is Greater than the Sum of its Parts: Towards the Effectiveness of Voting Ensemble Classifiers for Complex Word Identification

Nikhil Wani[†,⋆], Sandeep Mathias[⋆], Jayashree Aanand Gajjam[♣], Pushpak Bhattacharyya[⋆]

Center for Indian Language Technology
⋆Department of Computer Science and Engineering
♣Department of Humanities and Social Sciences
Indian Institute of Technology Bombay, India,
†`nick.nikhilwani@gmail.com`
⋆`sam,pb{@cse.iitb.ac.in}`, ♣`jayashree_aanand@iitb.ac.in`

Abstract

In this paper, we present an effective system using voting ensemble classifiers to detect contextually complex words for non-native English speakers. To make the final decision, we channel a set of eight calibrated classifiers based on lexical, size and vocabulary features and train our model with annotated datasets collected from a mixture of native and non-native speakers. Thereafter, we test our system on three datasets namely NEWS, WIKINEWS, and WIKIPEDIA and report competitive results with an F1-Score ranging between 0.777 to 0.855 for each of the datasets. Our system outperforms multiple other models and falls within 0.042 to 0.026 percent of the best-performing model's score in the shared task.

1 Introduction

Complex Word Identification (CWI) is an essential sub-task for Lexical Simplification. Lexical Simplification involves substituting a complicated word in the text with a more straightforward synonym. Figure 1 shows the pipeline for Lexical Simplification systems. It is geared for target population like non-native speakers, second-language learners, young learners, and people with language disabilities (like Aphasia and Alexia), with the aim of allowing them to comprehend the presented text completely.

The goal of the shared task is as follows: Given a target word (or phrase) and its context, we are to computationally determine if the target word is complex or not. Unlike the SemEval 2016 shared task, the target words here *could have more than one word* (e.g., *teenage girl*), and the context could stretch over multiple sentences.

The rest of the paper is organized as follows. In Section 2, we mention related work in the area of Complex Word Identification - in particular, the previous shared task at SemEval 2016

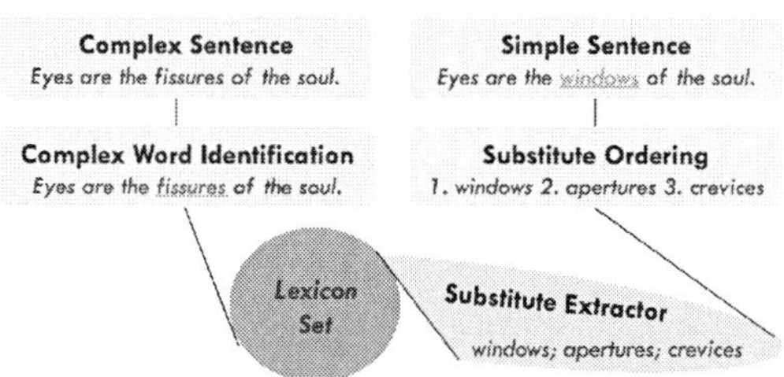

Figure 1: Lexical Simplification Pipeline

(Paetzold and Specia, 2016a). Section 3 describes the dataset of NLP BEA's CWI shared task at NAACL 2018. In Section 4, we describe our system, the features used, and our classification methodology. Moving along we then report our competitive results in Section 5 and discuss them in Section 6. We conclude by recapitulating our paper in Section 7 and identify future work that will be done.

2 Related Work

In SemEval 2016, 21 teams participated in a shared task on complex word identification (Paetzold and Specia, 2016a). The competition involved finding out whether a given word in a sentence was complex or not for a non-native speaker. The dataset used was completely in English.

In this task, the winning team used a soft voting-based approach from the outputs of 21 predictors (either classifiers, threshold-based, or lexical) (Paetzold and Specia, 2016b). This system was the best system according to the G-Score - an evaluation metric designed specifically for this task at SemEval 2016 (Paetzold and Specia, 2016a). The system with the best F1-Score made use of a threshold-based approach that marked a word as complex if its frequency in Simple Wikipedia is above a threshold (Wróbel, 2016).

Other systems at the SemEval 2016 shared

Proceedings of the Thirteenth Workshop on Innovative Use of NLP for Building Educational Applications, pages 200–205
New Orleans, Louisiana, June 5, 2018. ©2018 Association for Computational Linguistics

Dataset	Total Sents.	Unique Sents.
NEWS-TRAIN	14002	1016
NEWS-TEST	2095	175
WIKINEWS-TRAIN	7746	652
WIKINEWS-TEST	1287	105
WIKIPEDIA-TRAIN	5551	387
WIKIPEDIA-TEST	870	61

Table 1: Description of the Dataset. The first column gives the dataset. The next column gives the total number of sentences. The last column gives the number of unique sentences.

task used SVM (Kuru, 2016; Choubey and Pateria, 2016; S P et al., 2016; Zampieri et al., 2016), Random Forest (Davoodi and Kosseim, 2016; Mukherjee et al., 2016; Zampieri et al., 2016; Brooke et al., 2016; Ronzano et al., 2016), Neural Networks (Bingel et al., 2016; Nat, 2016), Decision Trees (Quijada and Medero, 2016; Malmasi et al., 2016; Malmasi and Zampieri, 2016), Nearest Centroid classifier (Palakurthi and Mamidi, 2016), Naive Bayes (Mukherjee et al., 2016), threshold bagged classifiers (Kauchak, 2016) and Entropy classifiers (Konkol, 2016; Martínez Martínez and Tan, 2016).

The features used in most of the systems were common, such as length-based features (like target word length), presence in a corpus (like presence of the target word in Simple English Wikipedia), PoS features of the target word, position features (position of the target word in the sentence), *etc.* However, a few of the systems used some innovative features. One of them was the MRC Psycholinguistic database (Wilson, 1988) used by Davoodi and Kosseim (2016). Another system by Konkol (2016) used **a single feature** namely document frequency of the word in Wikipedia, for classifying using a maximum entropy classifier.

3 Datasets

For this shared task (Yimam et al., 2018), we used only the English monolingual dataset, which made use of data from a number of sources, such as News articles, WikiNews and Wikipedia articles. Table 3 shows details such as total sentences and the number of unique sentences that we computed across all the three datasets. The Wikipedia dataset consisted of sentences from Wikipedia articles. Likewise, the WIKINEWS dataset and the

NEWS dataset contained sentences from news articles. However, the difference between the two is that the articles in the NEWS dataset were written by professional journalists, while lesser experienced writers wrote those in the WIKINEWS dataset.

In a majority of instances, the target words were just a single word. However, there were a few target words that were over a word long. Similarly, in most cases, the context was only one sentence, except for a few instances in which the context was as long as 3 - 4 sentences. The training datasets were annotated by 10 native and 10 non-native English speakers. Even if one amongst them found the word to be difficult, it was annotated as complex.

4 Methodology

In this section, we describe the experiment setup, such as the features used and provide analysis for their selection. This is followed by a detailed system overview which explains the system's architecture.

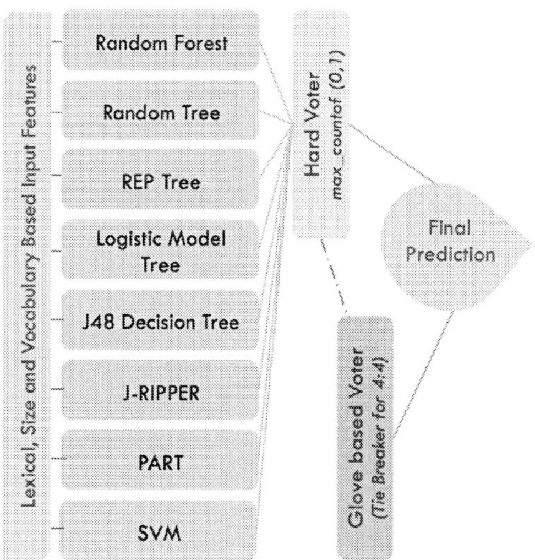

Figure 2: CWI System Architecture

4.1 Feature Sets

We investigated several *intuitive* properties of the target word such as its relevant lexical attributes, length properties and presence in certain word lists.

4.1.1 Lexical Features

The following features were extracted using WordNet (Fellbaum, 1998) for the target word:

- **Degree of Polysemy (DP):** Number of senses of the target word in WordNet (Fellbaum, 1998). This is operationalized by counting the number of Synsets of the target word in WordNet. Words with larger WordNet Synset sizes have several senses and were found to be more unclear.

- **Hyponym (Ho) and Hypernym (He) Tree Depth (TD):** These help in finding lexical relations. To find the position of the word in WordNet's hierarchical tree, we consider capturing its depth. General and simple words tend to be at the top of the tree. By computing the average depth among all the target-word Synsets, we count the number of Hyponyms and Hypernyms as a feature.

- **Holonym Count (HC) and Meronym Count (MC):** An alternative way to traverse Wordnet's hierarchical tree is by considering the relationship of the target word to its components (Meronyms) or to the things it is contained in (Holonyms). Holonyms tend to be more simple than meronyms because meronyms are usually more specific, compared to holonyms, as holonyms are a generalized word for a group of entities, while meronyms refer to specific entities in that group.

- **Verb Entailments (VE):** Verbs being action words often contain entailment relationships. For example, the act of roosting involves the act of sitting, so roosting entails sitting. Target words on average with multiple entailments were found to be relatively complex since they tend to be visually more vivid when trying to comprehend. Hence, the number of verb entailments of the target word was also part of our feature set.

4.1.2 Other Features

In addition to the lexical features, we also make use of size-based features and vocabulary-based features. These features are defined in Table 3.

4.2 System Overview

These input features are converged to the following eight calibrated classifiers, namely Random

Classifier	Precision	Recall	F1-Score
Selected Classifiers			
Random Forest	0.792	0.781	0.787
J48 Decision Tree	0.777	0.777	0.777
Logistic Model Tree	0.778	0.762	0.770
REP Tree	0.768	0.765	0.766
Random Tree	0.796	0.717	0.754
SVM	0.745	0.780	0.762
PART	0.715	0.793	0.752
JRip Rules Tree	0.754	0.737	0.745
Rejected Classifiers ($F1 < 0.70$)			
Decision Table	0.739	0.652	0.693
Decision Stump	0.665	0.696	0.680
Hoeffding Tree	0.686	0.666	0.676
Logistic Regression	0.732	0.591	0.654
SMO	0.751	0.550	0.635
OneR	0.735	0.550	0.629
ZeroR	0.000	0.000	0.000

Table 2: Results of ten-fold cross-validation on the training for each of the classifiers on the **complex class only**. This was used to choose our top classifiers.

Forest, Random Tree, REP Tree, Logistic Model Tree, J48 Decision Tree, JRip Rules Tree, PART, and SVM, from a set of 16 classifiers (7 tree-based classifiers, 5 rule-based classifiers, 1 Bayesian classifier, 1 regression-based classifier, and 2 non-linear classifiers).

SIZE-BASED FEATURES	
Feature	**Definition** *(Number of)*
Word Count (WC)	Words in the target word
Word Length (WL)	Letters in the target word
Vowels Count (VC)	Vowels in the target word
Syllable Count (SC)	Syllables in the target word
VOCABULARY-BASED FEATURES	
Feature	**Definition** *(Word is in)*
Ogden's Basic Lexicons (OB)	Ogden's Basic Word List
Ogden's Freq. Lexicons (OF)	Ogden's Frequent Word List
Barron's Lexicons (BW)	Barron's GRE Word List

Table 3: Size-based and Vocabulary-based features that we use.

These eight classifiers were chosen because they gave the best results on 10-fold cross-validation of the training set. We decided upon these classifiers since each of them had an F1-Score of the **complex class** in excess of 0.70. Table 2 describes the selected and rejected classifiers, along with their Precision, Recall and F1-Score on ten-fold cross-validation of the training data. Since the majority class was the non-

TEAM	DATASET		
	WIKINEWS	WIKIPEDIA	NEWS
camb	0.8430	0.8115	0.8792
ajason08	0.8368	0.7736	0.8625
nathansh	0.8329	0.7996	0.8706
nikhilwani	0.8213	0.7770	0.8554
dirkdh	0.8151	0.7816	0.8721
daalft	0.8050	0.7839	0.8391
TMU	0.7910	0.7621	0.8706
pom	0.7723	0.7460	0.8277
natgillin	0.7498	0.6690	0.8363

Table 4: F1-Score for each of the datasets for the top 10 teams on the corresponding test dataset. The highlighted row corresponds to our submission.

complex class, the ZeroR classifier has a Precision, Recall, and F1-Score of 0.

We use a hard voting approach to predict the class of the target word. If **more than 4 classifiers** classify the target word as either complex or simple, we assign the majority label to that word. In case of a 4-4 tie, (where 4 classifiers say the target word is complex and 4 say that it is simple), we use a word-embedding based classifier to act as a tie-breaker.

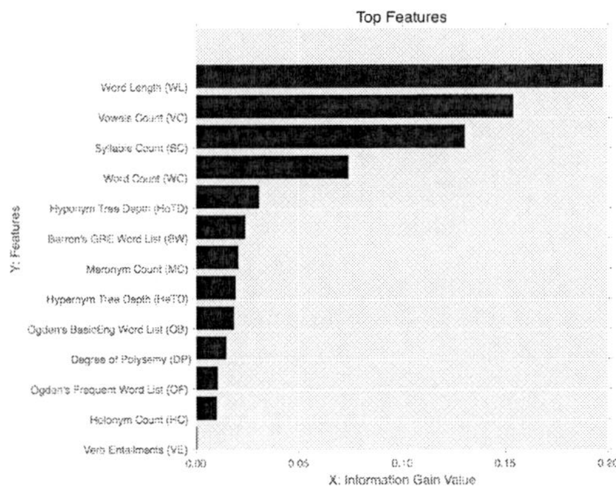

Figure 3: Feature significance observed by ranking them from highest to lowest using Attribute Evaluation based on Information Gain. The length of the bar corresponds to the actual Information Gain value.

For the word-embedding based classifier, we use the GloVe pre-trained word embeddings (Pennington et al., 2014). We first split the target into its constituent words (in most cases, it is a single word, but in a few cases, it is a phrase). We find the most similar word to each of the constituent words in the training set. If any of the given constituent words were tagged as complex, we target the target word as complex as well.

Out of 4252 test points to be classified, 173 times a tie occurred and the ensembled classiferes were unable to make a call. This is almost 4.06% of the predictions, which is significant in the larger scheme of things and further refines the hard voting.

5 Results and Analysis

In this section we discuss the results as well as reflect on the significance of each of the features for this task.

Table 4 gives the results of our experiments on the test set. From the results, our system is placed 4th in the WIKINEWS dataset, 5th in the WIKIPEDIA dataset, and 6th in the NEWS dataset.

Figure 3 delineates important features and ranks them according to their significance. Size based features namely - Word Length, Vowels Count, Syllable Count, Word Count were seen to constitute the first four topmost features. Another useful indicator of a complex word is its presence in Barron's GRE Word List, a list filled with the vocabulary level equivalent to a graduate college student.

6 Discussion

As it is evident from Tables 2 and 4, we see that individual classifiers do not work as well as ensembling them together, which agrees with the expression *"The whole is greater than the sum of its parts"*. Classifier Ensembling would further prove to be an efficacy for contextual documents similarity-based binary classification tasks (Kanojia et al., 2017) which rely heavily on lexical features, as well as it should also potentially cross-pollinate to benefit probabilistic touch classification problems (Wani et al., 2017) where spatial and contextual information has been proven to be pivotal.

7 Conclusion and Future Work

In this paper, we describe our participation to NLP-BEA's CWI 2018 Shared Task at NAACL concerning Complex Word Identification. We presented and evaluated our system across three datasets and showed that Ensemble Classifiers with hard and GloVe Voting are effective by means of lexical, size and vocabulary features for identifying complex words.

As part of our future work, we plan to incorporate Parts of Speech (POS) tags, Named Entity Recognition (NER) tag and word position features to improve our existing effective system.

References

Joachim Bingel, Natalie Schluter, and Héctor Martínez Alonso. 2016. Coastalcph at semeval-2016 task 11: The importance of designing your neural networks right. In *Proceedings of the 10th International Workshop on Semantic Evaluation (SemEval-2016)*, pages 1028–1033, San Diego, California. Association for Computational Linguistics.

Julian Brooke, Alexandra Uitdenbogerd, and Timothy Baldwin. 2016. Melbourne at semeval 2016 task 11: Classifying type-level word complexity using random forests with corpus and word list features. In *Proceedings of the 10th International Workshop on Semantic Evaluation (SemEval-2016)*, pages 975–981, San Diego, California. Association for Computational Linguistics.

Prafulla Choubey and Shubham Pateria. 2016. Garuda & bhasha at semeval-2016 task 11: Complex word identification using aggregated learning models. In *Proceedings of the 10th International Workshop on Semantic Evaluation (SemEval-2016)*, pages 1006–1010, San Diego, California. Association for Computational Linguistics.

Elnaz Davoodi and Leila Kosseim. 2016. Clac at semeval-2016 task 11: Exploring linguistic and psycho-linguistic features for complex word identification. In *Proceedings of the 10th International Workshop on Semantic Evaluation (SemEval-2016)*, pages 982–985, San Diego, California. Association for Computational Linguistics.

Christiane Fellbaum. 1998. *WordNet*. Wiley Online Library.

Diptesh Kanojia, Nikhil Wani, and Pushpak Bhattacharyya. 2017. Is your statement purposeless? predicting computer science graduation admission acceptance based on statement of purpose. In *Proceedings of the 14th International Conference on Natural Language Processing (ICON-2017)*, pages 141–145, Kolkata, India. NLP Association of India.

David Kauchak. 2016. Pomona at semeval-2016 task 11: Predicting word complexity based on corpus frequency. In *Proceedings of the 10th International Workshop on Semantic Evaluation (SemEval-2016)*, pages 1047–1051, San Diego, California. Association for Computational Linguistics.

Michal Konkol. 2016. Uwb at semeval-2016 task 11: Exploring features for complex word identification. In *Proceedings of the 10th International Workshop on Semantic Evaluation (SemEval-2016)*, pages 1038–1041, San Diego, California. Association for Computational Linguistics.

Onur Kuru. 2016. Ai-ku at semeval-2016 task 11: Word embeddings and substring features for complex word identification. In *Proceedings of the 10th International Workshop on Semantic Evaluation (SemEval-2016)*, pages 1042–1046, San Diego, California. Association for Computational Linguistics.

Shervin Malmasi, Mark Dras, and Marcos Zampieri. 2016. Ltg at semeval-2016 task 11: Complex word identification with classifier ensembles. In *Proceedings of the 10th International Workshop on Semantic Evaluation (SemEval-2016)*, pages 996–1000, San Diego, California. Association for Computational Linguistics.

Shervin Malmasi and Marcos Zampieri. 2016. Maza at semeval-2016 task 11: Detecting lexical complexity using a decision stump meta-classifier. In *Proceedings of the 10th International Workshop on Semantic Evaluation (SemEval-2016)*, pages 991–995, San Diego, California. Association for Computational Linguistics.

José Manuel Martínez Martínez and Liling Tan. 2016. Usaar at semeval-2016 task 11: Complex word identification with sense entropy and sentence perplexity. In *Proceedings of the 10th International Workshop on Semantic Evaluation (SemEval-2016)*, pages 958–962, San Diego, California. Association for Computational Linguistics.

Niloy Mukherjee, Braja Gopal Patra, Dipankar Das, and Sivaji Bandyopadhyay. 2016. Ju_nlp at semeval-2016 task 11: Identifying complex words in a sentence. In *Proceedings of the 10th International Workshop on Semantic Evaluation (SemEval-2016)*, pages 986–990, San Diego, California. Association for Computational Linguistics.

Gillin Nat. 2016. Sensible at semeval-2016 task 11: Neural nonsense mangled in ensemble mess. In *Proceedings of the 10th International Workshop on Semantic Evaluation (SemEval-2016)*, pages 963–968, San Diego, California. Association for Computational Linguistics.

Gustavo Paetzold and Lucia Specia. 2016a. SemEval 2016 Task 11: Complex Word Identification. In *Proceedings of the 10th International Workshop on Semantic Evaluation (SemEval-2016)*, pages 560–569, San Diego, California. Association for Computational Linguistics.

Gustavo Paetzold and Lucia Specia. 2016b. Sv000gg at semeval-2016 task 11: Heavy gauge complex word identification with system voting. In *Proceedings of the 10th International Workshop on Semantic Evaluation (SemEval-2016)*, pages 969–974, San Diego, California. Association for Computational Linguistics.

Ashish Palakurthi and Radhika Mamidi. 2016. Iiit at semeval-2016 task 11: Complex word identification using nearest centroid classification. In *Proceedings of the 10th International Workshop on Semantic Evaluation (SemEval-2016)*, pages 1017–1021, San Diego, California. Association for Computational Linguistics.

Jeffrey Pennington, Richard Socher, and Christopher Manning. 2014. Glove: Global vectors for word representation. In *Proceedings of the 2014 Conference on Empirical Methods in Natural Language Processing (EMNLP)*, pages 1532–1543, Doha, Qatar. Association for Computational Linguistics.

Maury Quijada and Julie Medero. 2016. Hmc at semeval-2016 task 11: Identifying complex words using depth-limited decision trees. In *Proceedings of the 10th International Workshop on Semantic Evaluation (SemEval-2016)*, pages 1034–1037, San Diego, California. Association for Computational Linguistics.

Francesco Ronzano, Ahmed Abura'ed, Luis Espinosa Anke, and Horacio Saggion. 2016. Taln at semeval-2016 task 11: Modelling complex words by contextual, lexical and semantic features. In *Proceedings of the 10th International Workshop on Semantic Evaluation (SemEval-2016)*, pages 1011–1016, San Diego, California. Association for Computational Linguistics.

Sanjay S P, Anand Kumar, and Soman K P. 2016. Amritacen at semeval-2016 task 11: Complex word identification using word embedding. In *Proceedings of the 10th International Workshop on Semantic Evaluation (SemEval-2016)*, pages 1022–1027, San Diego, California. Association for Computational Linguistics.

Nikhil Wani, Adarsh Patodi, and Sumit Singh Yadav. 2017. Probabilistic modeling of swarachakra keyboard for improved touch accuracy. In *Adjunct Proceedings of 16th IFIP TC.13 International Conference on Human Computer Interaction (INTERACT 2017 MUMBAI)*, pages 22–27, Industrial Design Centre, IIT Bombay, Mumbai, India.

Michael Wilson. 1988. Mrc psycholinguistic database: Machine-usable dictionary, version 2.00. *Behavior research methods, instruments, & computers*, 20(1):6–10.

Krzysztof Wróbel. 2016. Plujagh at semeval-2016 task 11: Simple system for complex word identification. In *Proceedings of the 10th International Workshop on Semantic Evaluation (SemEval-2016)*, pages 953–957, San Diego, California. Association for Computational Linguistics.

Seid Muhie Yimam, Chris Biemann, Shervin Malmasi, Gustavo Paetzold, Lucia Specia, Sanja Štajner, Anaïs Tack, and Marcos Zampieri. 2018. A Report on the Complex Word Identification Shared Task 2018. In *Proceedings of the 13th Workshop on Innovative Use of NLP for Building Educational Applications*, New Orleans, United States. Association for Computational Linguistics.

Marcos Zampieri, Liling Tan, and Josef van Genabith. 2016. Macsaar at semeval-2016 task 11: Zipfian and character features for complexword identification. In *Proceedings of the 10th International Workshop on Semantic Evaluation (SemEval-2016)*, pages 1001–1005, San Diego, California. Association for Computational Linguistics.

Grotoco@SLAM: Second Language Acquisition Modeling with Simple Features, Learners and Task-wise Models

Sigrid Klerke♣ **Héctor Martínez Alonso**♠ **Barbara Plank**♡♣
♡ Center for Language and Cognition, University of **Gro**ningen, The Netherlands
♠ Thomson Reuters Labs, **To**ronto, Canada
♣ IT University of Copenhagen, **Co**penhagen, Denmark
sigridklerke@gmail.com,hector.martinezalonso@thomsonreuters.com,bplank@gmail.com

Abstract

We present our submission to the 2018 Duolingo Shared Task on Second Language Acquisition Modeling (SLAM). We focus on evaluating a range of features for the task, including user-derived measures, while examining how far we can get with a simple linear classifier. Our analysis reveals that errors differ per exercise format, which motivates our final and best-performing system: a task-wise (per exercise-format) model.

1 Introduction

The shared task on Second Language Acquisition Modeling (SLAM) (Settles et al., 2018) consisted of an error prediction task, i.e., determining whether a language learner (user) made a token-level mistake.[1] Exploring if and how errors can be predicted can provide insights into the learning process and help pinpoint specific constructs that challenge learners of different languages.

The design of each exercise and the time spent on a particular task and language course, which can be expected to influence the performance, are included in the data. The learning context and the learners' background language skills, which would also influence performance, are not known or controlled for. In general, the courses are structured to minimize errors, by providing frequent repetition and only incrementing the difficulty level by small steps. Taken together, this makes the error prediction task a potentially hard task due to a sparse target class and noisy data from the unknown variable of user profiles, besides the temporal dependency.

With data from three language courses, namely English, Spanish and French, it is possible to explore generic and course-specific aspects of the learning problem.

2 Our Approach

With a focus on identifying meaningful feature groups, we use the provided train and development data to train and tune a logistic regression classifier for each language track. We explore features that describe static aspects of the exercise text, features that take the source and target language into account and features that describe the user-specific course trajectory. Due to notable biases in the data, we also experimented training separate classifiers on various data splits, namely for the three distinct exercise formats (listen, reverse tap, reverse translate) and for different days of the course.

Below, we briefly describe the data before detailing each group of features and proceeding to describe the model and results.

2.1 Data

The data splits contain all the same users, and are structured sequentially in time, over a period of 30 learner's days. Roughly the first 80% are given as training data, the next 10% are development data and the last 10% were the held-out test data.

The dataset contains two time variables:

- **days** This is a user-relative "timestamp" (the number of days they have been using Duolingo to learn this language). Monotonically increasing, by user.

- **time** The number of seconds it took the user to construct their response for the current exercise (aka"response time"). Note that this is a measures for the entire response, not for any particular word/token. Some 'null' values are in the dataset due to logging issues.

The data further contains meta-data on the user and the exercise type, besides automatically derived POS tags and dependency trees:

---

[1]Note: we have only access to an error's corrected form.

Proceedings of the Thirteenth Workshop on Innovative Use of NLP for Building Educational Applications, pages 206–211
New Orleans, Louisiana, June 5, 2018. ©2018 Association for Computational Linguistics

COURSE	USERS	TOKENS	ERRORS
en-es	2,593	2,622,958	12%
– Listen	–	–	16%
– Rev. Tap	–	–	4%
– Rev. Transl.	–	–	14%
es-en	2,643	1,973,558	16%
– Listen	–	–	22%
– Rev. Tap	–	–	8%
– Rev. Transl.	–	–	21%
fr-en	1,213	926,657	15%
– Listen	–	–	16%
– Rev. Tap	–	–	6%
– Rev. Transl.	–	–	23%

Table 1: Training set sizes and error rates.

- **format** The task to be solved by the user. One of listen, reverse tap and translate.

- **user** a B64 encoded, 8-digit, anonymized, unique identifier for each user

- **country** country codes from which this user has done exercises

- **client** - the student's device platform (one of: android, ios, or web)

- **session** - the session type (one of: lesson, practice, or test; explanation below)

There were three tracks for learners of English, Spanish, and French. In particular, en-es consists of English learners (who already speak Spanish), es-en are Spanish learners (who already speak English), and fr-en are French learners (who already speak English). We participated in all three. An overview of the data for the three tracks, including number of users, tokens and average error rate is given in Table 1.

The distribution of four attributes of the text and the users are shown in Figure 1. The low values dominating both the token length distribution and the dependency head index distribution reflect a preference for simple sentences. The distribution of the days since course start reveals how user activity declines steeply. The users' individual error distributions reflects the proficiency spread.

2.2 Features

We have mostly limited ourselves to features that could be calculated from the shared task data.

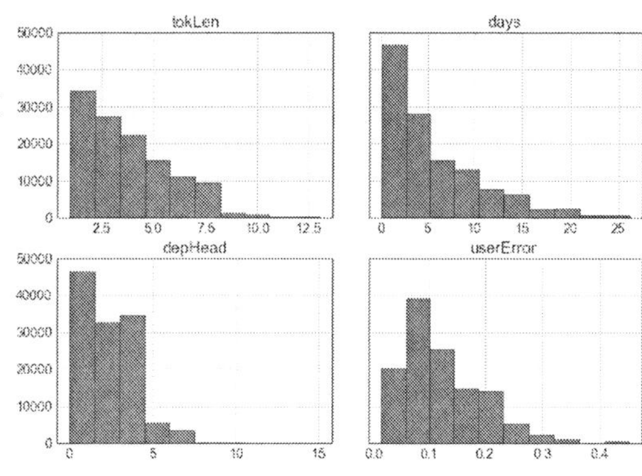

Figure 1: Distribution of token lengths, index of dependency heads, days since course start and users' individual proportion of errors. Based on first 200K tokens of the en-es-track.

Each data instance in our dataset describes a word and its context. For performance reasons, we apply binning to all features, given that many of them are real-valued.

1. **User**, **session** and **client**: Non-linguistic data, but also potential sources of error.

2. **Task format**: Whether a given data point belongs to the *listen*, *reverse tap* or *reverse translate* task format. Each task has a different error prior (Table 1).

3. **Word properties (base)**: Basic word properties, i.e., the word form and its stem. We use the NLTK Snowball stemmers (Loper and Bird, 2002) for the three languages at hand. We add the word's log frequency calculated from Universal Dependencies (UD) 2.1 (Nivre et al., 2016).

4. **Morphosyntax**: We generate part-of-speech (POS) derived features. For instance, the POS of word at hand, the two POS bigrams in which it participates, and the POS trigram centered around it. We also treat the word's morphological features as a set of independent binary features such as *gender=Feminine*, as well as the dependency label of the word, the POS tag of the head, and the distance of head and modifier (in number of tokens). We include sentence properties like cumulative sentence length, and whether the word is the last one in the sequence, to give account for error propagation.

5. **Diacritics**: Whether the word contains any non-ASCII characters. We observed that French and Spanish words with accents were hard to type by English speakers, which motivated this feature.

6. **Cognates and Character similarity (Form)**: Whether the target token exists in the source language. We calculate this feature once for forms and one for stems. We obtain our word lists for each language from the respective UD data. Moreover, letter sequences that are different across languages can be a cause of errors for second language learners. We model this difference by calculating the Kullback-Leibler divergence for the 2-3 grams character distributions of the word (and the previous token) in the source with respect to the target language. We also use a measure of character overlap with tokens in the source language.

7. **Time properties**: The time the exercise was taken since the course start, binned by whole days and by equal log-distance, also cumulatively. The log time taken for the exercise response total and per token, both absolute and cumulative.

8. **User behavior**: We calculate user-dependent characteristics based on the whole training dataset. For a certain word, we calculate whether the user has seen it before, how many times, how many days ago, whether it was an error last, the user's token-error rate, and the days since the last error. When available, we calculate the features' cumulative variant.

9. **Country**: the list of countries in which the user did exercises. Also, whether the country the user is in has the target language as one of its official languages, motivated by the intuition that exposure decreases error rate.

2.3 Model

We use Scikit-learn (Pedregosa et al., 2011) and for computational reasons, we have limited ourselves mostly to single linear classifiers instead of ensemble, kernel or neural methods. Our final system is a logistic regression classifier with $\mathcal{L}_2$ regularization, $C = 0.2$, balanced class-weights and

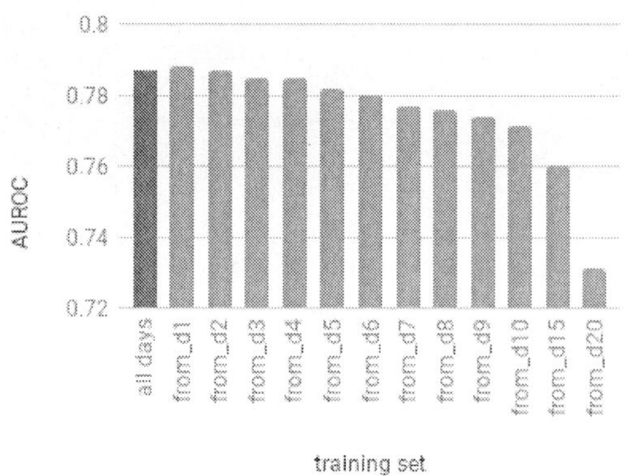

Figure 2: Results for training a single model on all data versus data from later days onwards (`fr-en` dev set).

liblinear as solver. Our code is publicly available.[2]

We also approach each track separately, thus have trained three separate models per language pair, we however believe that creating one joint model is an interesting research direction. Moreover, rather than using format as a feature in one single model, we observed that the error rate prior was strongly determined with the task format, and thus we considered using separate format-wise models, namely by dividing the data by task format, i.e., there is a separate model for English-to-Spanish-Listen, and so on, trained on the task-specific subset of data. At prediction time, the corresponding classifier is applied to each test instance.

3 Results

3.1 Results on dev set

During development, we observed that removing the first day of every user's data was helpful. We claim that first-day errors have more to do with the learning curve of the software, and less with the language itself. Figure 2 illustrates this for one language pair. Removing training instances before day 1 slightly increases performance for all languages. The diminishing data curve shows a pretty flat performance when excluding earlier learner days up to day 4.

3.2 Results on test set

Given the remark that the first day contained more irregular errors, we exclude the first day from the training data, and add the dev section, to train our final classifier.

---

[2] `https://github.com/bplank/slam-2018`

	EN-ES					ES-EN						FR-EN		
r	team	AUC	F1	L	r	team	AUC	F1	L	r	team	AUC	F1	L
1	SanaLabs	0.86	0.56	0.30	1	SanaLabs	0.84	0.53	0.33	1	SanaLabs	0.86	0.57	0.33
9	Lambda	0.82	0.39	0.32	8	Lambda	0.80	0.34	0.35	8	Lambda	0.82	0.41	0.36
10	**Grotoco**	0.82	0.46	0.53	9	**Grotoco**	0.79	0.45	0.54	9	**Grotoco**	0.81	0.50	0.51
11	jilljenn	0.82	0.33	0.33	10	nihalnayak	0.79	0.34	0.36	10	nihalnayak	0.81	0.43	0.37
15	BL	0.77	0.19	0.36	14	BL	0.75	0.18	0.39	15	BL	0.77	0.28	0.40

Table 2: Results on test set. Rank (r), team name, F1, loss (L) for the three language pairs. The table shows the best system (ranked 1), the baseline provided by the organizers (BL), and finally our system with the scores of the immediate higher and lower in ranking for comparison.

We submitted a single system per track, and a task-wise model. The single system, which used all of the features, achieved on average 0.7754 AUROC across the three tasks, while our task-wise model resulted in a considerably better model, reaching 0.79079 AUROC. This supports the hypothesis that errors (and features) are task-specific. Overall, as summarized in Table 2, our final task-wise submission ranked 10 (or 9th) in each of the tracks, which is well above the the SLAM baseline, but also shows that much remains to be done (e.g., integrating forgetting, building a single model for all languages, or integrating dense feature representations).

While we did not further evaluate training more specific task-wise models (with different features), we provide a feature analysis in the next section that could help improve the current model.

3.3 Feature analysis

Figure 3 shows examples of features that differ in prevalence in each class split by task format, both for the gold and predicted labels. Comparing column-wise allows us to compare the feature distribution across languages while row-wise comparison allows us to inspect how similar the predicted and gold label distributions are.

The depicted values are calculated by first determining the feature prevalence as the percentage of data points in each class, where a given feature is 'on' and subtract the prevalence in one class from the other. Only features with a difference in prevalence of at least 5 percentage points and at least 20% prevalence in at least one subgroup are shown (i.e., the feature is active in a fifth or more of at least one language/task-format/class combination)[3]. In feature groups where several subsequent bins fit these criteria, only the most skewed bins were included for the purpose of illustration.

<hr>

[3]This favors features that are active in the smaller positive class, in particular in the easier reverse-tap task.

First we note that prevalence of features is different for the three tasks. For instance, client information as well as time binned features differ per exercise format (listen, reverse tap and reverse translate). Overall, one notable pattern is that the predictions all match the gold splits distribution in shape (row-wise comparison), but tend to split the selected feature values more radically than the gold. A clear example is the two leftmost client-features with more extreme values in the left column of figures (predicted) than the right (gold).

A second notable pattern is that the feature distribution in the gold data (right-hand column) has strong similarities across the three language pairs, which is also reflected by the model output (left-hand column). This indicates that training a single joint model across languages could be fruitful, which we did not consider due to time reasons.

	en-es	es-en	fr-en
all features	**.8158**	.7889	**.8121**
-user	.7637	.7637	.7923
-user-session-client	.7903	.7614	.7895
-base	.8014	.7743	.8000
-pos	.8158	.7889	.8121
-dep	.8151	.7886	.8112
-form	.8147	.7881	.8113
-time	.8108	.7889	.8077
-uvocab	.8097	.7829	.8053
-country	.8157	**.7890**	**.8121**

Table 3: Feature ablation (AUROC) for task-wise model (trained on all train data), results on dev sets.

4   Feature ablation and discussion

Table 3 presents ablation results of our final task-wise model. What sticks out is that the lexical base features (base), timing (time) and user-specific behavioral features (uvocab) are the most predictive. Also knowing the type of session of the exercise and the user's client are very informative, as al-

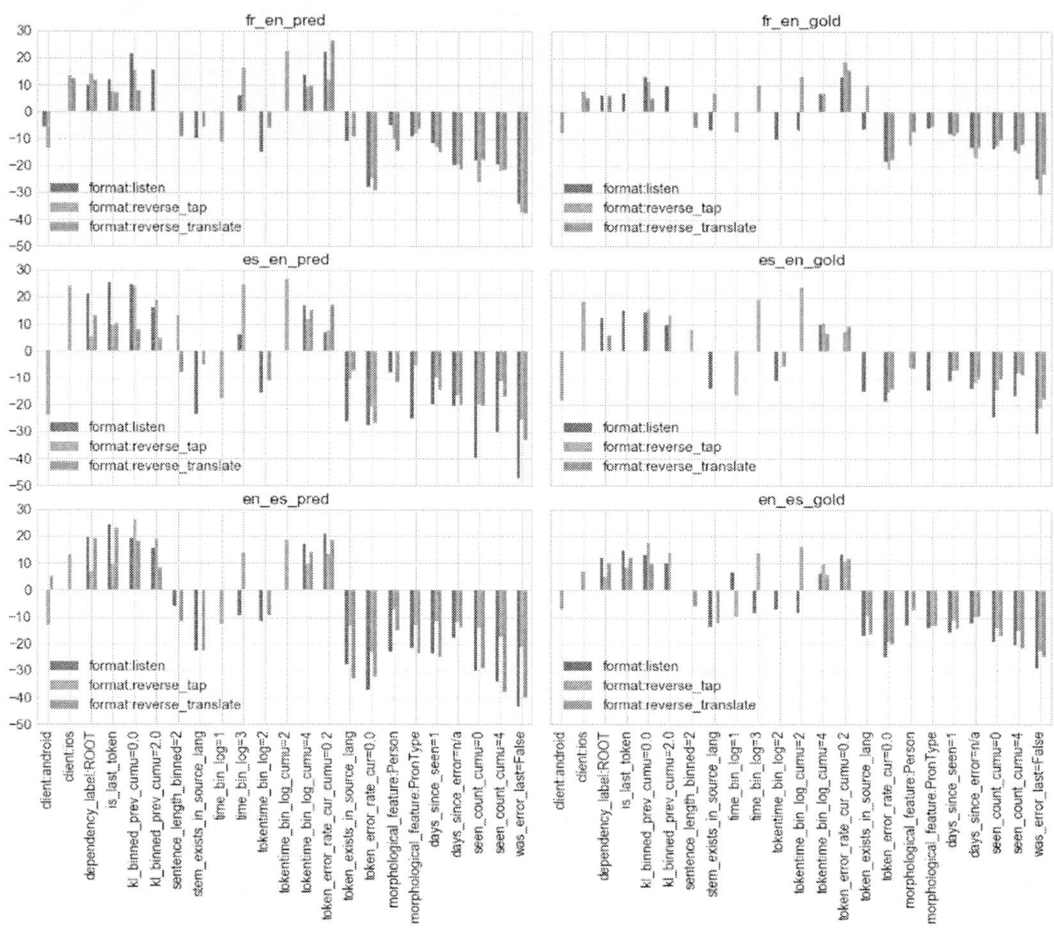

Figure 3: Difference in distribution of feature values in predictions (left-hand side) and in gold labels (right-hand side) by course and task-format based on first 100.000 tokens of development data. Y-axis denotes percentage points over-representation in the classes is-error (positive) or is-correct (negative).

ready found in our earlier analysis. The feature with the least impact is the country information. In fact, removing this feature does not drop performance, rather, improves it by a tiny bit for the Spanish learners. From the morpho-syntactic features we found the POS n-grams and dependency relations are the most helpful.

One key trait of our results is the much higher loss when compared with the systems immediate before and after in the ranking. We attribute this much higher loss to having split the data across task formats, which gives sharped distributions instead of smoother ones. This argument is supported by a higher F1 than that of the surrounding submissions, which indicates that our system is a better 0–1 labeler than a probability estimator.

5   Conclusions

This paper describes the Grotoco contribution to the Second Language Acquisition Modeling shared task. We have presented our architecture, based on format-wise classification models, and lexical features, as well as user- and time-related features. Training separate models per task turned out to be highly beneficial. We found user-specific and time-related features to be the most informative, beside lexical features and session meta-data. We also found that the first experience with the software to be a possible interference, as removing first-day day improved models consistently.

References

Edward Loper and Steven Bird. 2002. NLTK: the natural language toolkit. *CoRR*, cs.CL/0205028.

Joakim Nivre, Marie-Catherine de Marneffe, Filip Ginter, Yoav Goldberg, Jan Hajic, Christopher D. Manning, Ryan McDonald, Slav Petrov, Sampo Pyysalo, Natalia Silveira, Reut Tsarfaty, and Daniel Zeman. 2016. Universal dependencies v1: A multilingual treebank collection. In *Proceedings of the Tenth International Conference on Language Resources and Evaluation (LREC 2016)*, Paris, France. European Language Resources Association (ELRA).

F. Pedregosa, G. Varoquaux, A. Gramfort, V. Michel, B. Thirion, O. Grisel, M. Blondel, P. Prettenhofer, R. Weiss, V. Dubourg, J. Vanderplas, A. Passos, D. Cournapeau, M. Brucher, M. Perrot, and E. Duchesnay. 2011. Scikit-learn: Machine learning in Python. *Journal of Machine Learning Research*, 12:2825–2830.

B. Settles, C. Brust, E. Gustafson, M. Hagiwara, and N. Madnani. 2018. Second language acquisition modeling. In *Proceedings of the NAACL-HLT Workshop on Innovative Use of NLP for Building Educational Applications (BEA)*. ACL.

Context Based Approach for
Second Language Acquisition

Nihal V. Nayak
Stride.AI
Bangalore, India
nihalnayak@gmail.com

Arjun R. Rao
Ramaiah Institute of Technology
Bangalore, India
mailarjunrao@gmail.com

Abstract

SLAM 2018 focuses on predicting a student's mistake while using the Duolingo application. In this paper, we describe the system we developed for this shared task. Our system uses a logistic regression model to predict the likelihood of a student making a mistake while answering an exercise on Duolingo in all three language tracks - English/Spanish (en/es), Spanish/English (es/en) and French/English (fr/en). We conduct an ablation study with several features during the development of this system and discover that context based features play a major role in language acquisition modeling. Our model beats Duolingo's baseline scores in all three language tracks (AUROC scores for en/es = 0.821, es/en = 0.790 and fr/en = 0.812). Our work makes a case for providing favourable textual context for students while learning second language.

1 Introduction

The SLAM 2018 Shared Task is primarily centered around modeling second language acquisition (Settles et al., 2018) of non-native learners of English, Spanish and French. In this shared task, the principal tool used to assess learners is via Duolingo, one of the world's most popular online learning platforms. The data provided as part of the shared task is collected from the way thousands of students performed in over 4 million exercises during their first 30 days on Duolingo. This data consists of annotations at a word level - that indicate errors made by the user in a particular exercise. The task here is to predict mistakes that a learner is likely to make in future, by building a model from the training dataset given. Such a system would thus be able to model the second language acquisition capabilities of non-native learners of these languages.

In this paper, we present our attempt at modelling second language acquisition, primarily by considering context based features. Using these features our system implements a logistic regression model based on the additive conjugate model (Cen et al., 2008) that considers both the instance level features and user's latent ability, that results in reasonably good performance across the three languages being considered.

The rest of this paper is organized as follows. Section 2 highlights some of the existing research in modelling second language acquisition, that we have considered while developing the system. In Section 3, we discuss the features used in our model. We then present our model along with a few alternative approaches we considered (Section 4). An evaluation of our model on the Development and Test datasets is described in Section 5. Finally, scope for future work is discussed in section 6 and we present our conclusions in Section 7.

2 Related work

The process of learning has been thoroughly studied over the years. The forgetting curve (Ebbinghaus, 1885) has been central to these studies, which posits that memory decays exponentially with time. Research suggests that learning a concept in spaced interval helps in long term retention.

Leitner (1972) proposed a strategy (called Leitner's system) which incorporates spaced learning in flashcards. The system accounts for the student's performance and schedules the learning sessions with the help of buckets. For instance, if the student correctly answers the flashcard, it gets promoted to a higher bucket, thereby more spacing is provided between the learning sessions and if the student incorrectly answers the flashcard, then it

Proceedings of the Thirteenth Workshop on Innovative Use of NLP for Building Educational Applications, pages 212–216
New Orleans, Louisiana, June 5, 2018. ©2018 Association for Computational Linguistics

gets demoted to a lower bucket and thus reduces the spacing. Duolingo also implements a variant of the Leitner's system by organizing the cards in virtual buckets.

Apart from the Spacing Effect, there are other theories that have been around for sometime. Experiments by Roediger and Karpicke (2006) indicate that repeated testing increases long term retention. Nayak et al. (2017) developed a flashcard based application which implements the testing effect. They also collect a range of attributes or datapoints (both implicit and explicit data points) from the users.

Data collected from the users can be used for language acquisition modeling. For instance, Duolingo implements HLR (Settles and Meeder, 2016) to implement a trainable model for the forgetting curve. With their model, they attempt to predict the probability of a user correctly recalling a word. In this shared task, the organizers have released a similar dataset.

We posit that, the zone of proximal development (Vygotsky and Cole, 1978) plays a crucial role in language acquisition. The theory suggests that, when a student is in her zone of proximal development, providing appropriate assistance will enable her to complete the task. In language learning, the task is to answer the target word or the exercise given the surrounding words or the context. Therefore, in our work we focus on context based features and explore its effect while answering an exercise.

We use insights from recent works in L2 acquisition from code-switched text as they have focused on learning from context. Labutov and Lipson (2014) carry out experiments to determine the guessability of a word in code switched text. A similar work by Knowles et al. (2016) discuss the factors that can potentially affect the guessability of a German word with English context. We extend these works to model acquisition in multiple languages: English-Spanish, Spanish-English and French-English. For modeling the language acquisition, we make use of an additive conjugate model (Cen et al., 2008), in which we account for both instance level features such as token, part of speech, etc as well as the user's ability. We describe our model in detail in the next sections.

3 Features

In this section, we describe the features we consider in our experiments.

We start looking at the different attributes present in the dataset. These features are selected based on our intuition and past work. For simplicity, we divide the features in 2 categories - baseline features and context features.

3.1 Baseline Features

- **Token (T)** - We preprocess this feature by converting the token to lowercase and store the token as a categorical feature.

- **Part-of-Speech (POS)** - The dataset provides POS information for each token in Universal Dependency format. We use the same POS information without any preprocessing in our model.

- **Morphological Features (M)** - The dataset provides a detailed list of morphological features in Universal Dependency format. We encode each of these features in a separate hash bucket and use it in our model.

- **Dependency Label (D)** - The dataset provides dependency label for each token computed using the language agnostic dependency parser in Google's Syntaxnet.

- **User (U)** - Each user (or student) in the dataset is given a unique identifier. We use this feature to capture the latent ability of the user to answer the exercises.

- **User + Format (UF)** - Duolingo provides 3 formats in their dataset - `reverse_tap`, `reverse_translate` and `listen`. Each exercise can belong to one of the formats. We use a combination of user modelling and exercise format as our feature. The intuition being that the performance of a user depends on the format of the exercise.

- **Session (S)**- In the data, we find that there are 3 types of sessions - lesson, practice and test. We simply encode this information as a feature for our model.

3.2 Context Features

As mentioned in related works section, we use ideas from zone of proximal development and introduce context based features which could assist the student in answering a particular instance in an exercise. We use these context features for all the 3 formats. [1]

- **Previous-Current Token POS and Current-Next Token POS (PCPOS, CNPOS)** - The user may implicitly learn the structure of the language. Therefore, we encode two features - Previous Token POS and Current Token POS as one of the features and Current Token POS and Next Token POS as the other feature.

- **Previous-Current and Next-Current Token Metaphone (PCM, CNM)** - We realize that sounds or phonemes can play a vital role in this task. Therefore, we make use of metaphones to represent the phonemes. Although, we use this feature in all the three tracks, we make use of English language rules to compute the metaphones in other languages as well. We encode the metaphonic combination of Previous Token and Current Token as a feature in our model. We do the same with Current Token and Next Token.

- **Previous-Current Token and Current-Next Token (PCT, CNT)** - We use the combination of Previous and Current instance token as a feature in our model. Likewise, we use a combination of Current instance token and Next instance token in the exercise as a feature.

- **First Token (FT)** - We also investigate the influence of First Token in each exercise. We normalize the First Token by lowering the case and then use it as a categorical feature.

4 Our Model

Recent works in the described in section 3 have encouraged us to use a simple logistic regression model. The equation of logistic regression is as follows:

$$P(y \mid x) = \frac{1}{1 + exp(\vec{w} \cdot \vec{f}(x, y))} \quad (1)$$

---

[1] Our experiments with the development set indicated that Current-Next Token, Current-Next Token POS and Current-Next Token Metaphone feature reduced the AUROC when the format was listen. Therefore, in our model, we consider the above mentioned features only when the format is reverse_tap or reverse_translate.

where $\vec{w}$ is the weight vector and $\vec{f}(x, y)$ is the sparse feature vector.

We use the same model in all three tracks of the competition - English-Spanish, Spanish-English and French-English.

For training the model, we make use of an L2 regularized Stochastic Gradient Descent algorithm to minimize the error, thereby maximizing the likelihood of a class. We also store feature counts to reduce the learning rate of frequently occurring features. Through trial and error, we adjusted the learning rate and prior variance for the model.

Additionally, we also experimented with Hal Daume's MegaM tool[2] through the NLTK interface. The MegaM tool looks to maximize the log likelihood of a class. Our initial results with this approach did not seem as promising as the SGD based logistic regression model. Therefore, we decided to proceed with the former.

5 Evaluation

We experiment with the features mentioned in the section 3 and evaluate the model on the development data of all three languages. Our results in all three languages were promising which encouraged us to make use of the same features with the Test set as well.

5.1 Development

The results for our model with the development set can be found in Table 1. Our results consistently indicate that a context based approach for language acquisition modeling gives good performance.

5.2 Test

We use the development data as part of our training data while evaluating our model on the test data. The results are found in Table 2. Our model beats the Duolingo's baseline model by a good margin in all three language tracks.

We note that our baseline model with all the context features gives best AUROC scores in two tracks. However, there is small dip in the AUROC in French-English track. As a future work, it would be interesting to investigate further into this decrease in performance.

---

[2] http://legacydirs.umiacs.umd.edu/
~hal/megam/version0_3/

Model	en_es	es_en	fr_en
Duolingo's Baseline	0.773	0.746	0.771
Baseline	0.782	0.754	0.779
Baseline + (PCPOS, CNPOS)	0.801	0.776	0.794
Baseline + (PCPOS, CNPOS) + (PCM, CNM)	0.816	0.791	0.811
Baseline + (PCT, CNT) + (PCPOS, CNPOS) + (PCM, CNM)	0.820	0.792	**0.813**
Baseline + (PCT, CNT) + (PCPOS, CNPOS) + (PCM, CNM) + FT	**0.820**	**0.792**	0.812

Table 1: AUROC scores for our model in different language tracks on the development dataset

Model	en_es	es_en	fr_en
Duolingo's Baseline	0.774	0.746	0.771
Baseline + (PCPOS, CNPOS) + (PCM, CNM)	0.817	0.788	0.810
Baseline + (PCT, CNT) + (PCPOS, CNPOS) + (PCM, CNM)	0.821	0.789	**0.812**
Baseline + (PCT, CNT) + (PCPOS, CNPOS) + (PCM, CNM) + FT	**0.821**	**0.790**	0.811

Table 2: AUROC scores for our model in different language tracks on the test dataset

6 Future Work

Recent works in language acquisition through Code-Mixed text have suggested that providing favorable textual context for learners can be an effective strategy. We suggest that a similar strategy would be useful in the Duolingo Application. We would like to extend this line of thought to text readability and text simplification. It would be interesting to see if text simplification techniques could simplify sentences with an intention of assisting language learners to acquire new vocabulary while balancing out the readability of the text.

In our work we show that sound based features can play a vital role while learning. We use metaphones in our work to encode sound features in our model. We would like see if a more expressive method for encoding sound can be used to improve the model's performance. The data does not provide the translation of tokens in the user's native language. By computing the machine translation of these tokens, one could check the effect of cognateness of the word while answering the exercise.

7 Conclusion

In this paper, we show that a simple linear model with context based features gives good performance in modeling language acquisition. In our work, we conduct the feature ablation study and thoroughly evaluate the effect of these context based features in this task. Additionally, we also give direction for future work in text simplification and readability.

Code

To facilitate research and reconstruction of our approach, we have publicly released our code: `https://github.com/iampuntre/slam18`

References

Hao Cen, Kenneth Koedinger, and Brian Junker. 2008. Comparing two irt models for conjunctive skills. *Intelligent Tutoring Systems Lecture Notes in Computer Science*, page 796798.

H Ebbinghaus. 1885. *Memory: A Contribution to Experimental Psychology*. Teachers College, Columbia University, New York, NY, USA.

Rebecca Knowles, Adithya Renduchintala, Philipp Koehn, and Jason Eisner. 2016. Analyzing learner understanding of novel l2 vocabulary. *Proceedings of The 20th SIGNLL Conference on Computational Natural Language Learning*.

Philipp Koehn, Richard Zens, Chris Dyer, Ondej Bojar, Alexandra Constantin, Evan Herbst, Hieu Hoang, Alexandra Birch, Chris Callison-Burch, Marcello Federico, and et al. 2007. Moses. *Proceedings of the 45th Annual Meeting of the ACL on Interactive Poster and Demonstration Sessions - ACL 07*.

Igor Labutov and Hod Lipson. 2014. Generating code-switched text for lexical learning. *Proceedings of the 52nd Annual Meeting of the Association for Computational Linguistics (Volume 1: Long Papers)*.

S Leitner. 1972. *So lernt man lernen. Angewandte Lernpsychologie ein Weg zum Erfolg. Verlag*. Verlag Herder, Freiburg im Breisgau, Germany.

Nihal V Nayak, Tanmay Chinchore, Aishwarya Hanumanth Rao, Shane Michael Martin, Sagar Nagaraj Simha, GM Lingaraju, and HS Jamadagni. 2017. V for vocab: An intelligent flashcard application. In *Proceedings of ACL 2017, Student Research Workshop*, pages 24–29.

Henry L. Roediger and Jeffrey D. Karpicke. 2006. Test-enhanced learning. *Psychological Science*, 17(3):249255.

B. Settles, C. Brust, E. Gustafson, M. Hagiwara, and N. Madnani. 2018. Second language acquisition modeling. In *Proceedings of the NAACL-HLT Workshop on Innovative Use of NLP for Building Educational Applications (BEA)*. ACL.

Burr Settles and Brendan Meeder. 2016. A trainable spaced repetition model for language learning. *Proceedings of the 54th Annual Meeting of the Association for Computational Linguistics (Volume 1: Long Papers)*.

L.S. Vygotsky and M. Cole. 1978. *Mind in Society: Development of Higher Psychological Processes*. Harvard University Press.

Second Language Acquisition Modeling: An Ensemble Approach

Anton Osika, Susanna Nilsson, Andrii Sydorchuk, Faruk Sahin, Anders Huss
Sana Labs, Nybrogatan 8, 114 34 Stockholm, Sweden
{anton, susanna, andrii, faruk, anders}@sanalabs.com

Abstract

Accurate prediction of students knowledge is a fundamental building block of personalized learning systems. Here, we propose a novel ensemble model to predict student knowledge gaps. Applying our approach to student trace data from the online educational platform Duolingo we achieved highest score on both evaluation metrics for all three datasets in the 2018 Shared Task on Second Language Acquisition Modeling. We describe our model and discuss relevance of the task compared to how it would be setup in a production environment for personalized education.

1 Introduction

Understanding how students learn over time holds the key to unlock the full potential of adaptive learning. Indeed, personalizing the learning experience, so that educational content is recommended based on individual need in real time, promises to continuously stimulate motivation and the learning process (Bauman and Tuzhilin, 2014a). Accurate detection of students' knowledge gaps is a fundamental building block of personalized learning systems (Bauman and Tuzhilin, 2014b) (Lindsey et al., 2014). A number of approaches exists for modeling student knowledge and predicting student performance on future exercises including IRT (Lord, 1952), BKT (David et al., 2016) and DKT (Piech et al., 2015). Here we propose an ensemble approach to predict student knowledge gaps which achieved highest score on both evaluation metrics for all three datasets in the 2018 Shared Task on Second Language Acquisition Modeling (SLAM) (Settles et al., 2018). We analyze in what cases our models' predictions could be improved and discuss the relevance of the task setup for real-time delivery of personalized content within an educational setting.

2 Data and Evaluation Setup

The 2018 Shared Task on SLAM provides student trace data from users on the online educational platform Duolingo (Settles et al., 2018). Three different datasets are given representing users responses to exercises completed over the first 30 days of learning English, French and Spanish as a second language. Common for all exercises is that the user responds with a sentence in the language learnt. Importantly, the raw input sentence from the user is not available but instead the best matching sentence among a set of correct answer sentences. The prediction task is to predict the word-level mistakes made by the user, given the best matching sentence and a number of additional features provided. The matching between user response and correct sentence was derived by the finite-state transducer method (Mohri, 1997).

All datasets were pre-partitioned into training, development and test subsets, where approximately the last 10 % of the events for each user is used for testing and the last 10 % of the remaining events used for development . Target labels for token level mistakes are provided for the training and development set but not for the test set. Aggregated metrics for the test set were obtained by submitting predictions to an evaluation server provided by Duolingo. The performance for this binary classification task is measured by area under the ROC curve (AUC) and F1-score.

Although the dataset provided represents real user interactions on the Duolingo platform, the model evaluation setup does not represent a realistic scenario where the predictive modelling would be used for personalizing the content presented to a user. The reason for this is threefold: Firstly, predictions are made given the best matching correct sentence which would not be known prior to the user answering the question for questions that

217

Proceedings of the Thirteenth Workshop on Innovative Use of NLP for Building Educational Applications, pages 217–222
New Orleans, Louisiana, June 5, 2018. ©2018 Association for Computational Linguistics

have multiple correct answers. Secondly, there are a number of variables available at each point in time which represent information from the future creating a form of data leakage. Finally, the fact that interactions from each student span all data partitions means that we can always train on the same users that the model is evaluated for and hence there are never first time users, where we would need to infer student mistakes solely from sequential behaviour. To estimate prediction performance in an educational production setting where next-step recommendations must be inferred from past observations, the evaluation procedure would have to be adjusted accordingly.

3 Method

To predict word-level mistakes we build an ensemble model which combines the predictions from a Gradient Boosted Decision Tree (GBDT) and a recurrent neural network model (RNN). Our reasoning behind this approach lies in the observation that RNNs have been shown to achieve good results for sequential prediction tasks (Piech et al., 2015) whereas GBDTs have consistently achieved state of the art results on various benchmarks for tabular data (Li, 2012). Even though the data in this case is fundamentally sequential, the number of features and the fact that interactions for each user are available during training make us expect that both models will generate accurate predictions. Details of our model implementations are given below.

3.1 The Recurrent Neural Network

The recurrent neural network model that we use is a generalisation of the model introduced by Piech (2015), based on the popular LSTM architecture, with the following key modifications:

- All available categorical and numerical features are fed as input to the network and at multiple input points in the graph of the network (see A.1)

- The network operates on a word level, where words from different sentences are concatenated to form a single sequence

- Information is propagated backward (as well as forward) in time, making it possible to predict the correctness of a word given all the surrounding words within the sentence

- Multiple ordinary- as well as recurrent layers are stacked, with the information from each level cascaded through skip-connections (Bishop, 1995) to form the final prediction

In model training, subsequences of up to 256 interactions are sampled from each user history in the train dataset, and only the second half of each subsequence is included in the loss function. The binary target variable representing word-level mistakes is expanded to a categorical variable and set to *unknown* for the second half of each subsequence in order to match the evaluation setup.

Log loss of predictions for each subsequence is minimised using adaptive moment estimation (Kingma and Ba, 2014) with a batch size of 32. Regularisation with dropout (Srivastava et al., 2014) and L2 regularisation (Schmidhuber, 2014) is used for embeddings, recurrent and feed forward layers. Data points are used once over each of 80 epochs, and performance continuously evaluated on 70 % of the dev data after each epoch. The model with highest performance over all epochs is then selected after training has finished. Finally, Gaussian Process Bandit Optimization (Desautels et al., 2014) is used to tune the hyperparameters learning rate, number of units in each layer, dropout probability and L2 coefficients.

3.2 The Gradient Boosted Decision Tree

The decision tree model is built using the Light-GBM framework (Ke et al., 2017) which implements a way of optimally partitioning categorical features, leaf-wise tree growth, as well as histogram binning for continuous variables (Titov, 2018). In addition to the variables provided in the student trace data we engineer a number of features which we anticipate should have relevance for predicting the word level mistakes

- How many times the current token has been practiced

- Time since token was last seen

- Position index of token within the best matching sentence

- The total number of tokens in the best matching sentence

- Position index of exercise within session

- Preceding token

- A unique identifier of the best matching sentence as a proxy for exercise id

Optimal model parameters are learned through a grid search by training the model on the training set and evaluating on the development set to optimize AUC. The optimal GBDT parameter settings for each dataset can be found in the Supplementary Material A.2.

3.3 Ensemble Approach

The predictions generated by the recurrent neural network model and the GBDT model are combined through a weighted average. We train each model using its optimal hyperparameter setting on the train dataset and generate predictions on the dev set. The optimal ensemble weights are then found by varying the proportion of each model prediction and choosing the weight combination which yields optimal AUC score (Figure 1).

Finally, the RNN and GBDT were trained using their respective optimal hyperparameter settings on the training and development datasets to generate predictions on the test sets. The individual model test set predictions were then combined using the optimal ensemble weights to generate the final test set predictions for task submission.

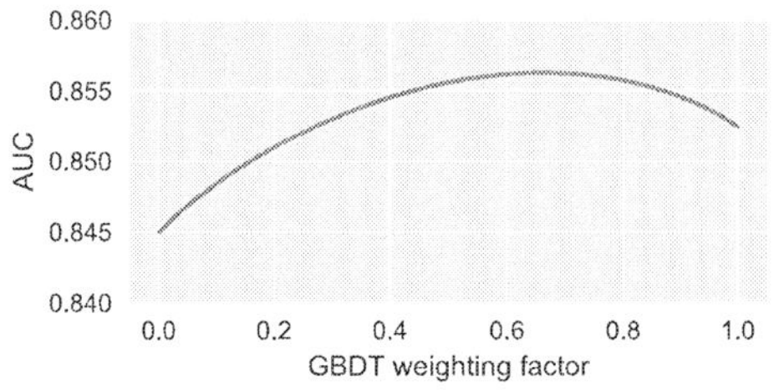

Figure 1: Ensemble model performance as a function of the GBDT ensemble weight parameter for the en_es dataset. 0.0 is equivalent to using only the neural network model while 1.0 is equivalent to using only GBDT.

4 Discussion

Our ensemble approach yielded superior prediction performance on the test set compared to the individual performances of the ensemble components (Table 1). The F1 scores of our ensemble are reported in Table 2. We note that although the within-ensemble prediction correlations are high

(Table 3), the prediction diversity evidently suffices for the ensemble combination to outperform the underlying models. This suggests that the RNN and the GBDT differ in performance on different word mistakes. Most likely, the temporal dynamics modelled by the neural network model complement the GBDT predictions enabling the ensemble to generalise better to unseen user events than its component parts. Notably, none of our individual models would have yielded first place in the Shared Task.

Model	fr_en	es_en	en_es
RNN	0.841	0.830	0.851
GBDT	0.853	0.836	0.856
Ensemble	0.857	0.838	0.861

Table 1: Model AUC scores on the test partition for all datasets.

	fr_en	es_en	en_es
Ensemble	0.573	0.530	0.561

Table 2: Model F1 scores on the test partition for all datasets.

Data partition	fr_en	es_en	en_es
dev	0.881	0.901	0.896
test	0.884	0.894	0.898

Table 3: Pearson correlations coefficients between the GBDT and RNN predictions on the dev and test set for all datasets.

4.1 Feature Importance

Given the predictive power of our model we can use the model components to gain insight into what features are most valuable when inferring student mistake patterns. When ranking GBDT features by information gain, we note that 4 out of 5 features overlap between the three datasets (Figure 4). The unique user identifier is ranked as second on all datasets, suggesting that very often a separate subtree can be built for each user. This implies that generalisation to new users for the GBDT model would result in performance degradation.

4.2 Relevance for Real Time Prediction Delivery

In the setup at hand we have a unique identifier and most of the data available for each user during model training. This means that for example the GBDT can naturally build a subtree representing each individual user. For the model evaluation

fr_en	es_en	en_es
token	*token*	*token*
user	*user*	*user*
format	*format*	*format*
exercise id	*exercise id*	*exercise id*
time	*token attempt*	*time*

Table 4: The top 5 GBDT model features by information gain.

setup where there is no need to generalize to new users this is not an issue. In a production setting however, the model has to serve new users, which would then have to be handled separately. Frequent retraining of the model would also be necessary to prevent performance degradation. This means that the unique user identifier is typically replaced by engineered features that represent the user history. An alternative would be to apply state based models such as Recurrent Neural Networks which by default encode user history without computational overhead or extra engineering effort.

4.3 Error Analysis

Although the predictive power of our model is high, there are mistake patterns that our model is not able to capture. The following sections cover two ways of characterizing subsets of the data where the model performs worse than on average. These observations could potentially be used to improve the overall model performance.

4.3.1 Performance Decay over Time

Due to the sequential partitioning of the training, development and test subsets, the model does not have information about each user's mistakes for the most recent events. In Figure 2 we note that this lack of information results in a degradation in performance as the predictions get further away from the horizon of labeled data points. Effects which drive this phenomenon include:

1. The data is non-stationary, i.e. the distribution it comes from varies over time

2. The model has seen less relevant information about each user when the prediction is far away from the label horizon

3. The model is overconfident far away from the label horizon since it has never experienced missing information on a user level during training

We note that 3 would not be an issue if the model setup did not include a unique user identifier, which would be desirable in a production setting. For models that do include a unique user identifier as a feature, one way to potentially overcome this performance degradation would be to systematically sample subsequences of the training dataset on a user level, train models separately for each sample and then combine the models. In this way each submodel should be less reliant on the most recent exercise answers at any point in time and thus generalise better to the evaluation setup. This is in effect bagging with a sampling strategy taking consecutive time steps into account (Breiman, 1996). We did not attempt to apply this error correction here but leave it for future work.

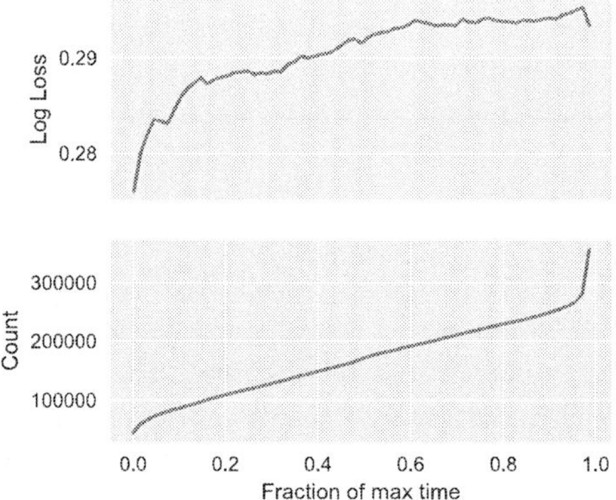

Figure 2: Performance decays as instances further away from the label horizon are considered. Log Loss is computed considering only instances before a given fraction of time, where time is normalized by the maximum time for each user. Here performance decay for the en_es dataset.

4.3.2 The Influence of Rare Words

We note that the 4% of instances with the least common words contribute to 10% of the prediction error measured in Log Loss, Figure 3. This insight gives opportunity to increase prediction performance. Although not attempted here, future work includes building another ensemble component specialized in predicting mistake patterns of words not previously encountered.

In conclusion, we have developed an ensemble approach to modeling knowledge gaps applied here within a second language acquisition setting. Albeit not evaluated in a realistic production environment, our ensemble model achieves high pre-

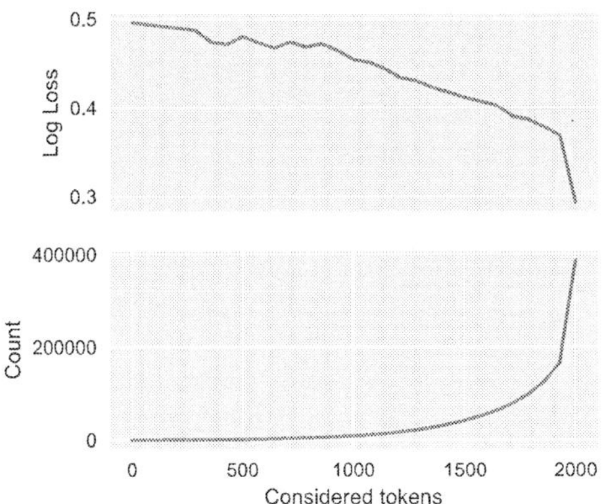

Figure 3: Log loss is high when considering only the x most rare tokens and low when considering all tokens on the en_es dev partition.

dictive performance and allows insights about student mistake patterns. Thus our approach provides a foundation for further research on knowledge acquisition modeling applicable to any educational domain.

References

K. Bauman and A. Tuzhilin. 2014a. Recommending learning materials to students by identifying their knowledge gaps. In *RecSys 2014 Poster Proceedings*, pages 6–10, Foster City, Silicon Valley, USA.

Konstantin Bauman and Alexander Tuzhilin. 2014b. Recommending learning materials to students by identifying their knowledge gaps. In *RecSys Posters*.

Christopher M Bishop. 1995. *Neural networks for pattern recognition*. Oxford university press.

Leo Breiman. 1996. Bagging predictors. *Machine Learning*, 24(2):123–140.

Yossi Ben David, Avi Segal, and Ya'akov Kobi Gal. 2016. Sequencing educational content in classrooms using bayesian knowledge tracing. In *Proceedings of the sixth international conference on Learning Analytics & Knowledge*, pages 354–363. ACM.

Thomas Desautels, Andreas Krause, and Joel W. Burdick. 2014. Parallelizing exploration-exploitation tradeoffs in gaussian process bandit optimization. *Journal of Machine Learning Research*, 15:4053–4103.

Guolin Ke, Qi Meng, Thomas Finley, Taifeng Wang, Wei Chen, Weidong Ma, Qiwei Ye, and Tie-Yan Liu. 2017. Lightgbm: A highly efficient gradient boosting decision tree. In I. Guyon, U. V. Luxburg, S. Bengio, H. Wallach, R. Fergus, S. Vishwanathan, and R. Garnett, editors, *Advances in Neural Information Processing Systems 30*, pages 3146–3154. Curran Associates, Inc.

Diederik P. Kingma and Jimmy Ba. 2014. Adam: A method for stochastic optimization. *CoRR*, abs/1412.6980.

Ping Li. 2012. Robust logitboost and adaptive base class (abc) logitboost. *arXiv preprint arXiv:1203.3491*.

Robert V Lindsey, Jeffery D Shroyer, Harold Pashler, and Michael C Mozer. 2014. Improving students long-term knowledge retention through personalized review. *Psychological science*, 25(3):639–647.

Frederic Lord. 1952. A theory of test scores. *Psychometric monographs*.

Mehryar Mohri. 1997. Finite-state transducers in language and speech processing. *Computational linguistics*, 23(2):269–311.

Chris Piech, Jonathan Spencer, Jonathan Huang, Surya Ganguli, Mehran Sahami, Leonidas J. Guibas, and Jascha Sohl-Dickstein. 2015. Deep knowledge tracing. *CoRR*, abs/1506.05908.

Jürgen Schmidhuber. 2014. Deep learning in neural networks: An overview. *CoRR*, abs/1404.7828.

B. Settles, C. Brust, E. Gustafson, M. Hagiwara, and N. Madnani. 2018. Second language acquisition modeling. In *Proceedings of the NAACL-HLT Workshop on Innovative Use of NLP for Building Educational Applications (BEA)*. ACL.

Nitish Srivastava, Geoffrey Hinton, Alex Krizhevsky, Ilya Sutskever, and Ruslan Salakhutdinov. 2014. Dropout: A simple way to prevent neural networks from overfitting. *Journal of Machine Learning Research*, 15:1929–1958.

Nikita Titov. 2018. LightGBM Features. http://lightgbm.readthedocs.io/en/latest/Features.html. [Online; accessed 23-March-2018].

A   Supplemental Material

A.1   The recurrent neural network model design

Our neural network model desisgn is described below:

1. For each word the network takes as input all available categorical features, excluding morphological features for each word. The exclusion was motivated by the fact that predictive ability added by morphological features was low when evaluated by a decision tree model.

2. Preprocessed numerical features for *days* and *time* are concatenated to an input vector. (Preprocessing in this case means to normalize to mean zero, variance 1, remove outliers that are larger than 100, and concatenate the value itself with the value exponentiated to 0.5 as well as 2.0)

3. The categories *token*, *part_of_speech*, *format*, *correct* and *exercise id* (as described in 3.2), are each mapped to an embedding vector of length 15.

4. The above categorical features are further combined with the feature *correct* by using the cartesian product, and then mapping each category to an embedding vector.

5. All categorical embeddings and numerical features are concatenated together forming an input vector.

6. The input vector is fed through a two layer bidirectional recurrent neural network, where the input to both of the layers are summed with the output, forming a user state vector.

7. Another input vector is formed by concatenating categorical embeddings for the features *token*, *part_of_speech*, *format*, *dependency_label*, *dependency_token*, *user_id* as well as preprocessed numerical features.

8. The user state vector is then projected to two scalars. This is done by dot multiplying it with a vector of trainable variables, as well as dot multiplying it with the second input vector from step 7. The second part accounts for the original operation done by (Piech et al., 2015).

9. We furthermore compute one scalar for each categorical feature, that is specific for the category of the feature, similar to a logistic regression model.

10. Finally, the second input vector together with all computed scalars are concatenated and fed to a 3 layer feed forward neural network.

11. The sum of all scalar values and the output of the feed forward network forms our logit, which is fed through a sigmoid function outputting the probability of a token level mistake.

A.2   GBDT Hyperparameters

Model parameter	fr_en	es_en	en_es
num_leaves	2400	2700	2400
n_estimators	5744	2518	3203
learning_rate	0.002	0.005	0.005
feature_fraction	0.5	0.45	0.4
early_stopping_round	300	100	100

Table 5:   Optimal GBDT parameters for all three datasets.

Modeling Second-Language Learning from a Psychological Perspective

Alexander S. Rich   **Pamela J. Osborn Popp**   **David J. Halpern**
Anselm Rothe   **Todd M. Gureckis**
Department of Psychology, New York University
{asr443,pamop,david.halpern,anselm,todd.gureckis}@nyu.edu

Abstract

Psychological research on learning and memory has tended to emphasize small-scale laboratory studies. However, large datasets of people using educational software provide opportunities to explore these issues from a new perspective. In this paper we describe our approach to the Duolingo Second Language Acquisition Modeling (SLAM) competition which was run in early 2018. We used a well-known class of algorithms (gradient boosted decision trees), with features partially informed by theories from the psychological literature. After detailing our modeling approach and a number of supplementary simulations, we reflect on the degree to which psychological theory aided the model, and the potential for cognitive science and predictive modeling competitions to gain from each other.

1   Introduction

Educational software that aims to teach people new skills, languages, and academic subjects have become increasingly popular. The wide-spread deployment of these tools has created interesting opportunities to study the process of learning in large samples. The Duolingo shared task on Second Lanuage Acquisition Modeling (SLAM) was a competitive modeling challenge run in early 2018 (Settles et al., 2018). The challenge, organized by Duolingo[1], a popular second language learning app, was to use log data from thousands of users completing millions of exercises to predict patterns of future translation mistakes in held-out data. The data was divided into three sets covering Spanish speakers learning English (en_es), English speakers learning Spanish (es_en), and English speakers learning French (fr_en). This paper reports the approach used by our team,

which finished in third place for the en_es data set, second place for es_en, and third place for fr_en.

Learning and memory has been a core focus of psychological science for over 100 years. Most of this work has sought to build explanatory theories of human learning and memory using relatively small-scale laboratory studies. Such studies have identified a number of important and apparently robust phenomena in memory including the nature of the retention curve (Rubin and Wenzel, 1996), the advantage for spaced over massed practice (Ruth, 1928; Cepeda et al., 2006; Mozer et al., 2009), the testing effect (Roediger and Karpicke, 2006), and retrieval-induced forgetting (Anderson et al., 1994). The advent of large datasets such as the one provided in the Duolingo SLAM challenge may offer a new perspective and approach which may prove complementary to laboratory scale science (Griffiths, 2015; Goldstone and Lupyan, 2016). First, the much larger sample sizes may help to better identify parameters of psychological models. Second, datasets covering more naturalistic learning situations may allow us to test the predictive accuracy of psychological theories in a more generalizable fashion (Yarkoni and Westfall, 2017).

Despite these promising opportunities, it remains unclear how much of current psychological theory might be important for tasks such as the Duolingo SLAM challenge. In the field of education data mining, researchers trying to build predictive models of student learning have typically relied on traditional, and interpretable, models and approaches that are rooted in cognitive science (e.g., Atkinson, 1972b,a; Corbett and Anderson, 1995; Pavlik and Anderson, 2008). However, a recent paper found that state-of-the-art results could be achieved using deep neural networks with little or no cognitive theory built in (so

---

[1]http://duolingo.com

Proceedings of the Thirteenth Workshop on Innovative Use of NLP for Building Educational Applications, pages 223–230
New Orleans, Louisiana, June 5, 2018. ©2018 Association for Computational Linguistics

called "deep knowledge tracing", Piech et al., 2015). Khajah, Lindsey, & Mozer (2016) compared deep knowledge tracing (DKT) to more standard "Bayesian knowledge tracing" (BKT) models and showed that it was possible to equate the performance of the BKT model by additional features and parameters that represent core aspects of the psychology of learning and memory such as forgetting and individual abilities (Khajah et al., 2016). An ongoing debate remains in this community whether using flexible models with lots of data can improve over more heavily structured, theory-based models (Tang et al., 2016; Xiong et al., 2016; Zhang et al., 2017).

For our approach to the SLAM competition, we decided to use a generic and fairly flexible model structure that we provided with hand-coded, psychologically inspired features. We therefore positioned our entry to SLAM somewhat in between the approaches mentioned above. Specifically, we used gradient boosting decision trees (GBDT, Ke et al., 2017) for the model structure, which is a powerful classification algorithm that is known to perform well across various kinds of data sets. Like deep learning, GBDT can extract complex interactions among features, but it has some advantages including faster training and easier integration of diverse inputs.

We then created a number of new psychologically-grounded features for the SLAM dataset covering aspects such as user perseverance, learning processes, contextual factors, and cognate similarity. After finding a model that provided the best held-out performance on the test data set, we conducted a number of "lesioning" studies where we selectively removed features from the model and re-estimated the parameters in order to assess the contribution of particular types of features. We begin by describing our overall modeling approach, and then discuss some of the lessons learned from our analysis.

2 Task Approach

We approached the task as a binary classification problem over instances. Each instance was a single word within a sentence of a translation exercise and the classification problem was to predict whether a user would translate the word correctly or not. Our approach can be divided into two components—constructing a set of features that is informative about whether a user will answer an instance correctly, and designing a model that can achieve high performance using this feature set.

2.1 Feature Engineering

We used a variety of features, including features directly present in the training data, features constructed using the training data, and features that use information external to the training data. Except where otherwise specified, categorical variables were one-hot encoded.

2.1.1 Exercise features

We encoded the exercise number, client, session, format, and duration (i.e., number of seconds to complete the exercise), as well as the time since the user started using Duolingo for the first time.

2.1.2 Word features

Using spaCy[2], we lemmatized each word to produce a root word. Both the root word token and the original token were used as categorical features. Due to their high cardinality, these features were not one-hot encoded but were preserved in single columns and handled in this form by the model (as described below).

Along with the tokens themselves we encoded each instance word's part of speech, morphological features, and dependency edge label. We noticed that some words in the original dataset were paired with the wrong morphological features, particularly near where punctuation had been removed from the sentence. To fix this, we reprocessed the data using Google SyntaxNet[3].

We also encoded word length and several word characteristics gleaned from external data sources. Research in psychology has suggested certain word features that play a role in how difficult a word is to process, as measured by how long readers look at the word as well as people's performance in lexical-decision and word-identification tasks. Two such features that have somewhat independent effects are word frequency (i.e., how often does the word occur in natural language; Rayner, 1998) and age-of-acquisition (i.e., the age at which children typically exhibit the word in their vocabulary; Brysbaert and Cortese, 2011; Ferrand et al., 2011). We therefore included a feature that encoded the frequency of each word in the language being acquired, calculated from Speer et al.

---

[2]https://spacy.io/
[3]https://github.com/ljm625/syntaxnet-rest-api

(2017), and a feature that encoded the mean age-of-acquisition (of the English word, in English native speakers), derived from published age-of-acquisition norms for 30,000 words (Kuperman et al., 2012), which covered many of the words present in the dataset. Additionally, words sharing a common linguistic derivation (also called "cognates"; e.g., "secretary" in English and "secretario" in Spanish), are easier to learn than words with dissimilar translations (De Groot and Keijzer, 2000). As an approximate measure of linguistic similarity, we used the Levenshtein edit distance between the word tokens and their translations scaled by the length of the longer word. We found translations using Google Translate[4] and calculated the Levenshtein distance to reflect the letter-by-letter similarity of the word and its translation (Hyyrö, 2001).

2.1.3 User features

Just as we did for word tokens, we encoded the user ID as a single-column, high-cardinality feature. We also calculated several other user-level features that related to the "learning type" of a user. In particular, we encoded features that might be related to psychological constructs such as the motivation and diligence of a user. These features could help predict how users interact with old and novel words they encounter.

As a proxy for motivation, we speculated that more motivated users would complete more exercises every time they decide to use the app. To estimate this, we grouped each user's exercises into "bursts." Bursts were separated by at least an hour. We used three concrete features about these bursts, namely the mean and median number of exercises within bursts as well as the total number of bursts of a given user (to give the model a feature related to the uncertainty in the central tendency estimates).

As a proxy for diligence, we speculated that a very diligent user might be using the app regularly at the same time of day, perhaps following a study schedule, compared to a less diligent user whose schedule might vary more. The data set did not provide a variable with the time of day, which would have been an interesting feature on its own. Instead, we were able to extract for each exercise the time of day relative to the first time a user had used the app, ranging from 0 to 1 (with

0 indicating the same time, 0.25 indicating a relative shift by 6 hours, etc.). We then discretized this variable into 20-minute bins and computed the entropy of the empirical frequency distribution over these bins. A lower entropy score indicated less variability in the times of day a user started their exercises.

The entropy score might also give an indication for context effects on users' memory. A user practicing exercises more regularly is more likely to be in the same physical location when using the app, which might result in better memory of previously studied words (Godden and Baddeley, 1975).

2.1.4 Positional features

To account for the effects of surrounding words on the difficulty of an instance, we created several features related to the instance word's context in the exercise. These included the token of the previous word, the next word, and the instance word's root in the dependency tree, all stored in single columns as with the instance token itself. We also included the part of speech of each of these context words as additional features. When there was no previous word, next word, or dependency-tree root word, a special None token or None part of speech was used.

2.1.5 Temporal features

A user's probability of succeeding on an instance is likely related to their prior experience with that instance. To capture this, we calculated several features related to past experience.

First, we encoded the number of times the current exercise's exact sentence had been seen before by the user. This is informed by psychological research showing memory and perceptual processing improvements for repeated contexts or "chunks" (e.g., Chun and Phelps, 1999).

We also encoded a set of features recording past experience with the particular instance word. These features were encoded separately for the instance token and for the instance root word created by lemmatization. For each token (and root) we tracked user performance through four weighted error averages. At the user's first encounter of the token, each error term E starts at zero. After an encounter with an instance of the token with label L (0 for success, 1 for error), it is updated according to the equation:

$$E \leftarrow E + \alpha(L - E)$$

---

[4]https://cloud.google.com/translate/

where α determines the speed of error updating. The four weighted error terms use $\alpha = \{.3, .1, .03, .01\}$, allowing both short-run and long-run changes in a user's error rate with a token to be tracked. Note that in cases where a token appears multiple times in an exercise, a single update of the error features is conducted using the mean of the token labels. Along with the error tracking features, for each token we calculated the number of labeled, unlabeled, and total encounters; time since last labeled encounter and last encounter; and whether the instance is the first encounter with the token.

In the training data, all instances are labeled as correct or incorrect, so the label for the previous encounter is always available. In the test data, labels are unavailable, so predictions must be made using a mix of labeled and unlabeled past encounters. In particular, for a user's test set with n exercises, each exercise will have between zero and $n - 1$ preceding unlabeled exercises.

To generate training-set features that are comparable to test-set features, we selectively ignored some labels when encoding temporal features on the training set. Specifically, for each user we first calculated the number of exercises n in their true test set[5]. Then, when encoding the features for each training instance, we selected a random integer r in the range $[0, n-1]$, and ignored the labels in the prior r exercises. That is, we encoded features for the instance as though other instances in those prior exercises were unlabeled, and ignored updates to the error averages from those exercises. The result of this process is that each instance in the training set was encoded as though it were between one and n exercises into the test set.

2.2 Modeling

After generating all of the features for the training data, we trained GBDT models to minimize log loss. GBDT works by iteratively building regression trees, each of which seeks to minimize the residual loss from prior trees. This allows it to capture non-linear effects and high-order interactions among features. We used the LightGBM[6] implementation of GBDT (Ke et al., 2017).

For continuous-valued features, GBDT can split a leaf at any point, creating different predicted values above and below that threshold. For categories that are one-hot encoded, it can split a leaf on any of the category's features. This means that for a category with thousands of values, potentially thousands of tree splits would be needed to capture its relation to the target. Fortunately, LightGBM implements an algorithm for partitioning the values of a categorical feature into two groups based on their relevence to the current loss, and create a single split to divide those groups (Fisher, 1958). Thus, as alluded to above, high-cardinality features like token and user ID were encoded as single columns and handled as categories by Light-GBM.

We trained a model for each of the three language tracks of `en_es`, `es_en`, and `fr_en`, and also trained a model on the combined data from all three tracks, adding an additional "language" feature. Following model training, we averaged the predictions of each single-language model with that of the all-language model to form our final predictions. Informal experimentation showed that model averaging provided a modest performance boost, and that weighted averages did not clearly outperform a simple average.

To tune model hyper-parameters and evaluate the usefulness of features, we first trained the models on the `train` data set and evaluated them on the `dev` data set. Details of the datasets and the actual files are provided on the Harvard Dataverse (Settles, 2018). Once the model structure was finalized, we trained on the combined `train` and `dev` data and produced predictions for the `test` data. The LightGBM hyperparameters used for each model are listed in Table 1.

2.3 Performance

The AUROC of our final predictions was .8585 on `en_es`, .8350 on `es_en`, and .8540 on `fr_en`. For reference this placed us within .01 of the winning entry for each problem (.8613 on `en_es`, .8383 on `es_en`, and .8570 on `fr_en`). Also note that the Duolingo-provided baseline model (L2-regularized regression trained with stochastic gradient descent weighted by frequency) obtains .7737 on `en_es`, .7456 on `es_en`, and .7707 on `fr_en`. We did not attempt to optimize F1 score, the competition's secondary evaluation metric.

---

[5]If the size of the test set were not available, it could be estimated based on the fact that it is approximately 5% of each participant's data.

[6]http://lightgbm.readthedocs.io/

Parameter	fr_en	en_es	es_en	all
num_leaves	256	512	512	1024
learning_rate	.05	.05	.05	.05
min_data_in_leaf	100	100	100	100
num_boost_rounds	750	650	600	750
cat_smooth	200	200	200	200
feature_fraction	.7	.7	.7	.7
max_cat_threshold	32	32	32	64

Table 1: Parameters of final LightGBM models. See LightGBM documentation for more information; all other parameters were left at their default values.

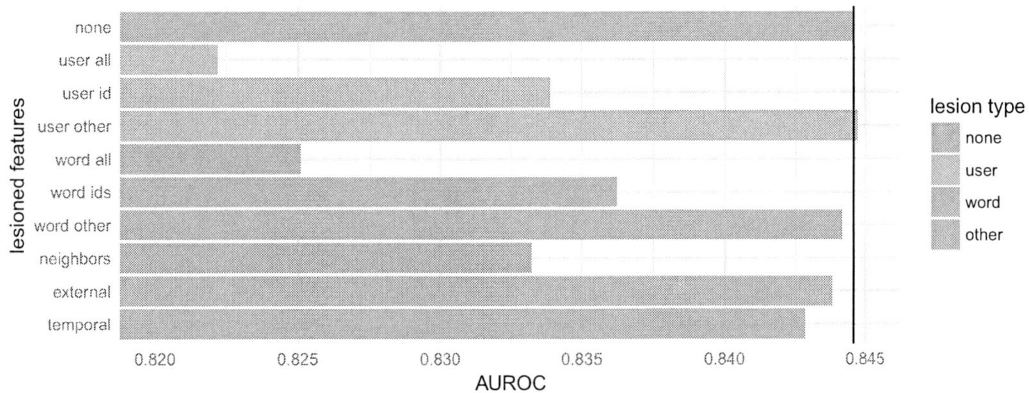

Figure 1: Performance on `dev` of models trained on all `train` data, with different groups of lesioned features. See main text for description of lesion groups

3 Feature Removal Experiments

To better understand which features or groups of features were most important to our model's predictions, we conducted a set of experiments in which we lesioned (i.e., removed) a group of features and re-trained the model on the `train` set, evaluating performance on the `dev` set. For simplicity, we ran each of the lesioned models on all language data and report the average performance. We did not run individual-language models as we did for our primary model. The results of the lesion experiments are shown in Figure 1. The models are as follows.

none: All features are included.

user all: All user-level features, including the user ID and other calculated features like entropy and measures of exercise bursts, are removed.

user id & user other: Only user ID or only the calculated user features, respectively, are removed.

word all: Token and token root IDs; previous, next, and dependency-tree root word IDs; and morphological, part of speech, and dependency tree features are removed. This does not include **external** features listed below.

word id & word other: Only word IDs or only other word features, respectively, are removed. **word other** does not include **external** features listed below.

neighbors: Both word IDs and other word features are removed, but only for the previous, next, and dependency-tree root words. Information about the present word is maintained.

external: External information about the word, including corpus frequency, Levenshtein distance from translation, and age of acquisition, are removed.

temporal: Temporal information, including number and timing of past encounters with the word and error tracking information, is removed.

Interestingly, we found that for both user-level and word-level features, the bulk of the model's predictive power could be achieved using ID's alone, represented as high-cardinality categorical features. Removing other word features, such as morphological features and part of speech, created only a small degradation of performance. In the case of users, removing features such as entropy and average exercise burst length led to a tiny increase of performance. In the case of both users and words, though, we find that in the absence of ID features the other features are helpful and lead to better performance than removing all features. We also found that removing all information about neighboring words and the dependency-parse root word degraded performance. This confirms that word context matters, and suggests that users commonly make errors in word order, subject–verb matching and other grammatical rules.

Our external word features—Levenshtein distance to translation, frequency, and age of acquisition—provided a slight boost to model performance, showing the benefit of considering what makes a word hard to learn from a psychological and linguistic perspective. Adding temporal features about past encounters and errors helped the models, but not as much as we expected. While not included in the final model, we had also tried augmenting the temporal feature set with more features related to massing and spacing of encounters with a word, but found it did not improve performance. This is perhaps not surprising given how small the benefit of the existing temporal features are in our model.

Though not plotted above, we also ran a model lesioning exercise-level features including client, session type, format, and exercise duration. This model achieved an AUROC of .787, far lower than any other lesion. This points to the fact that the manner in which memory is assessed often affects observed performance (e.g., the large literature in psychology on the difference between recall and recognition memory, Yonelinas, 2002).

4 Discussion

When approaching the Duolingo SLAM task, we hoped to leverage psychological insights in building our model. We found that in some cases, such as when using the word's age-of-acquisition, this was helpful. In general, though, our model gained its power not from hand-crafted features but from applying a powerful inference technique (gradient boosted decision trees) to raw input about user IDs, word IDs, and exercise features.

There are multiple reasons for the limited applicability of psychology to this competition. First, computational psychological models are typically designed based on small laboratory data sets, which might limit their suitability for generating highly accurate predictions in big data settings. Because they are designed not for prediction but for explanation, they tend to use a small number of input variables and allow those variables to interact in limited ways. In contrast, gradient boosted decision trees, as well as other cutting-edge techniques like deep learning can extract high-level interactions among hundreds of features. While they are highly opaque, require a lot of data, and are not amenable to explanation, these models excel at prediction.

Second, it is possible that our ability to use theories of learning, including ideas about massed and spaced practice, was disrupted by the fact that the data may have been adaptively created using these very principles (Settles and Meeder, 2016). If Duolingo adaptively sequenced the spacing of trials based on past errors, then the relationship between future errors and past spacing may have substantially differed from that found in the psychological literature (Cepeda et al., 2006).

Finally, if the task had required broader generalization, psychologically inspired features might have performed more competitively. In the SLAM task, there is a large amount of labeled training data for every user and for most words. This allows simple ID-based features to work because the past history of a user will likely influence their future performance. However, with ID-based features there is no way to generalize to newly-encountered users or words, which have an ID that was not in the training set. The learned ID-based knowledge is useless here because there is no way to generalize from one unique ID to another. Theory-driven features, in contrast, can often generalize to new settings because they capture aspects that are shared across (subsets of) users, words, or situations of the learning task. For example, if we were asked to generalize to a completely new language such as German, many parts of our model would falter but word frequency, age of acquisition, and Levenshtein distance to first-language translation would still likely prove to be features which have high predictive utility.

In sum, we believe that the Duolingo SLAM dataset and challenge provide interesting opportunities for cognitive science and psychology. Large-scale, predictive challenges like this one might be used to identify features or variables that are important for learning. Then, complementary laboratory-scale studies can be conducted which establish the causal status of such features through controlled experimentation. Conversely, insights from controlled experiments can be used to generate new features that aid predictive models on naturalistic datasets (Griffiths, 2015; Goldstone and Lupyan, 2016). This type of two-way interaction could lead to long-run improvements in both scientific explanation and real-world prediction.

5 Acknowledgments

This research was supported by NSF grant DRL-1631436 and BCS-1255538, and the John S. McDonnell Foundation Scholar Award to TMG. We thank Shannon Tubridy and Tal Yarkoni for helpful suggestions in the development of this work.

References

Michael C Anderson, Robert A Bjork, and Elizabeth L Bjork. 1994. Remembering can cause forgetting: Retrieval dynamics in long-term memory. *Journal of Experimental Psychology: Learning, Memory, and Cognition*, 20:1063–1087.

R.C. Atkinson. 1972a. Ingredients for a theory of instruction. *American Psychologist*, 27:921–931.

R.C. Atkinson. 1972b. Optimizing the learning of a second-language vocabulary. *Journal of Experimental Psychology*, 96:124–129.

Marc Brysbaert and Michael J Cortese. 2011. Do the effects of subjective frequency and age of acquisition survive better word frequency norms? *Quarterly Journal of Experimental Psychology*, 64(3):545–559.

N.J. Cepeda, H. Pashler, E. Vul, J.T. Wixted, and D. Rohrer. 2006. Distributed practice in verbal recall tasks: A review and quantitative synthesis. *Psychological Bulletin*, 132(3):354–380.

M.M. Chun and E.A. Phelps. 1999. Memory deficits for implicit contextual information in amnesic subjects with hippocampal damage. *Nature Neuroscience*, 2(9):844–847.

AT Corbett and JR Anderson. 1995. Knowledge tracking: Modeling the acquisition of procedural knowledge. *User Modeling and User-Adapted Interaction*, 4:253–278.

Annette De Groot and Rineke Keijzer. 2000. What is hard to learn is easy to forget: The roles of word concreteness, cognate status, and word frequency in foreign-language vocabulary learning and forgetting. *Language Learning*, 50(1):1–56.

Ludovic Ferrand, Marc Brysbaert, Emmanuel Keuleers, Boris New, Patrick Bonin, Alain Méot, Maria Augustinova, and Christophe Pallier. 2011. Comparing word processing times in naming, lexical decision, and progressive demasking: Evidence from chronolex. *Frontiers in psychology*, 2:306.

Walter D Fisher. 1958. On grouping for maximum homogeneity. *Journal of the American statistical Association*, 53(284):789–798.

Duncan R Godden and Alan D Baddeley. 1975. Context-dependent memory in two natural environments: On land and underwater. *British Journal of psychology*, 66(3):325–331.

R.L. Goldstone and G. Lupyan. 2016. Discovering psychological principles by mining naturally occurring data sets. *Topics in Cognitive Science*, 8:548–568.

T.M. Griffiths. 2015. Manifesto for a new (computational) cognitive revolution. *Cognition*, 135:21–23.

Heikki Hyyrö. 2001. Explaining and extending the bit-parallel approximate string matching algorithm of myers. *Technical report in Journal of the ACM*, page 408.

Guolin Ke, Qi Meng, Thomas Finley, Taifeng Wang, Wei Chen, Weidong Ma, Qiwei Ye, and Tie-Yan Liu. 2017. Lightgbm: A highly efficient gradient boosting decision tree. In *Advances in Neural Information Processing Systems*, pages 3149–3157.

Mohammad Khajah, Robert V. Lindsey, and Michael Mozer. 2016. How deep is knowledge tracing? *Proceedings of the Educational Data Mining (EDM)*.

Victor Kuperman, Hans Stadthagen-Gonzalez, and Marc Brysbaert. 2012. Age-of-acquisition ratings for 30,000 english words. *Behavior Research Methods*, 44(4):978–990.

M. C. Mozer, H. Pashler, N. Cepeda, R. Lindsey, and E. Vul. 2009. Predicting the optimal spacing of study: A multiscale context model of memory. In *Advances in Neural Information Processing Systems 22*, pages 1321–1329, La Jolla, CA. NIPS Foundation.

P.I. Pavlik and J.R. Anderson. 2008. Using a model to compute the optimal schedule of practice. *Journal of Experimental Psychology: Applied*, 14(2):101–117.

C. Piech, J. Bassen, J. Huang, S. Ganguli, M. Sahami, L. J. Guibas, and J. Sohl-Dickstein. 2015. Deep knowledge tracing. In *Advances in Neural Information Processing Systems 28*, pages 505–513.

Keith Rayner. 1998. Eye movements in reading and information processing: 20 years of research. *Psychological bulletin*, 124(3):372.

Henry L. Roediger and Jeffrey D. Karpicke. 2006. Test-enhanced learning: Taking memory tests improves long-term retention. *Psychological Science*, 17(3):249–255. PMID: 16507066.

D.C. Rubin and A.E. Wenzel. 1996. One hundred years of forgetting: A quantitative description of retention. *Psychological Review*, 103(4):734–760.

T.C. Ruth. 1928. Factors influencing the relative economy of massed and distributed practice in learning. *Psychological Review*, 35:19–45.

B. Settles, C. Brust, E. Gustafson, M. Hagiwara, and N. Madnani. 2018. Second language acquisition modeling. In *Proceedings of the NAACL-HLT Workshop on Innovative Use of NLP for Building Educational Applications (BEA)*. ACL.

Burr Settles. 2018. Data for the 2018 duolingo shared task on second language acquisition modeling (slam).

Burr Settles and Brendan Meeder. 2016. A trainable spaced repetition model for language learning. In *Proceedings of the 54th Annual Meeting of the Association for Computational Linguistics (Volume 1: Long Papers)*, volume 1, pages 1848–1858.

Robert Speer, Joshua Chin, Andrew Lin, Sara Jewett, and Lance Nathan. 2017. Luminosoinsight/wordfreq: v1.7.

Steven Tang, Joshua C. Peterson, and Zachary A. Pardos. 2016. Deep neural networks and how they apply to sequential education data. In *Proceedings of the Third (2016) ACM Conference on Learning @ Scale*, L@S '16, pages 321–324, New York, NY, USA. ACM.

Xiaolu Xiong, Siyuan Zhao, Eric Van Inwegen, and Joseph Beck. 2016. Going deeper with deep knowledge tracing. In *EDM*, pages 545–550.

T. Yarkoni and J. Westfall. 2017. Choosing prediction over explanation in psychology: Lessons from machine learning. *Persectives in Psychological Science*, 12(6):1100–1122.

Andrew P Yonelinas. 2002. The nature of recollection and familiarity: A review of 30 years of research. *Journal of memory and language*, 46(3):441–517.

Liang Zhang, Xiaolu Xiong, Siyuan Zhao, Anthony Botelho, and Neil T Heffernan. 2017. Incorporating rich features into deep knowledge tracing. In *Proceedings of the Fourth (2017) ACM Conference on Learning@ Scale*, pages 169–172. ACM.

A Memory-Sensitive Classification Model of Errors in Early Second Language Learning

Brendan Tomoschuk and Jarrett T. Lovelett
Department of Psychology
University of California, San Diego
9500 Gilman Drive, La Jolla, CA, 92093-0109
`{btomosch, jlovelet}@ucsd.edu`

Abstract

In this paper, we explore a variety of linguistic and cognitive features to better understand second language acquisition in early users of the language learning app Duolingo. With these features, we trained a random forest classifier to predict errors in early learners of French, Spanish, and English. Of particular note was our finding that mean and variance in error for each user and token can be a memory efficient replacement for their respective dummy-encoded categorical variables. At test, these models improved over the baseline model with AUROC values of 0.803 for English, 0.823 for French, and 0.829 for Spanish.

1 Introduction

Learning a new language is often a challenging task for adults. However, there are many linguistic and cognitive factors that can facilitate (or impair) acquisition of a non-native language, ranging from properties of the languages a learner already knows, to the methods and nature of study. Much work has sought to manipulate these factors in order to both further our understanding of the cognitive systems in play and facilitate learning.

Here, we present a model that explores these factors to predict outcomes for three populations of language learners that use Duolingo, a language learning app that gamifies lessons for a wide variety of to-be-learned languages. We start by describing the various features we developed from the data before describing the random forest model used and the subsequent outcomes.

2 Related Work

Little work has been done building predictive models of adult language acquisition, but many studies have explored the linguistic factors that impact vocabulary learning in a non-native language. Semantic properties of nouns, for example, have been found to impact word learning. Cognates, or words that overlap in form and meaning in both languages (e.g. *lemon* in English and *limón* in Spanish), have been shown to be easier to learn (de Groot & Keijzer, 2000). The same study showed that words that are rated as more concrete (*hat* as opposed to *liberty*) are easier to learn. While perhaps more surprising than the cognate result, this effect is often explained by the fact that more concrete words create more perceptual connections to their conceptual referents (it is easier to imagine a physical hat than the abstract concept of liberty), and it is therefore easier to connect new words to concepts via those connections.

There are likewise many factors than can hinder word learning. For example, interlingual homographs, or words that share surface form but have different meanings (*pan* as something to fry on in English and bread in Spanish) are harder to process and may therefore also be harder to learn (Dijkstra, Timmermans & Schriefers, 2000).

Beyond the linguistic particulars of individual words, the temporal dynamics of learning can powerfully moderate memory. One of the most well established results in cognitive psychology is that two repetitions of a to-be-learned item are best separated by some temporal gap, if the goal is long-term retention (Ebbinghaus 1885/1964, Cepeda, Pashler, Vul, Wixted, & Rohrer, 2006; Cepeda, Vul, Rohrer, Wixted, & Pashler, 2008; Donovan & Radosevich, 1999; T. D. Lee & Genovese, 1988). That is, given a fixed amount of available time to learn something, a learner is better off distributing that time over multiple learning sessions than cramming it all into a single session. Further, the more time that is allowed to pass before a learner encounters a previously learned item again, the longer into the future the learner can

Proceedings of the Thirteenth Workshop on Innovative Use of NLP for Building Educational Applications, pages 231–239
New Orleans, Louisiana, June 5, 2018. ©2018 Association for Computational Linguistics

expect to retain that item (or equivalently, the greater the probability of successful retrieval of that item at a particular future time; but see Cepeda et al. 2008).

Over a century of research has shown this spacing effect to be robust across the human lifespan (e.g. Vander Linde, Morrongiello, & Rovee-Collier, 1985; Ambridge, Theakston, Lieven, & Tomasello, 2006; Carpenter, 2009; Cepeda et al., 2008; Balota, Duchek, & Paullin, 1989), over many varieties of learning tasks (Cepeda et al., 2006; Donovan & Radosevich, 1999; T. D. Lee & Genovese, 1988), and perhaps most strikingly, for nearly every inter-repetition temporal gap that has been investigated, from seconds (Ebbinghaus, 1964), to a range of days (e.g. Cepeda et al., 2008), to years (Bahrick & Phelphs, 1987).

Moreover, the advantage of spacing seems to be enhanced when combined with active retrieval from long-term memory (as compared to passive restudy), making it particularly well-suited to a microtesting-based learning platform like Duolingo (Carpenter & DeLosh, 2006; Cull, 2000; Karpicke & Roediger, 2007; Landauer & Bjork, 1978; Rea & Modigliani, 1985). Crucially for our present purpose, a number of studies have examined the efficacy of spaced repetition specifically in second language learning, where it seems to be effective at least for vocabulary, and perhaps for grammar as well, although further research is needed (for a review, see Ullman & Lovelett, 2018).

3   Data

The data were collected in 2017 from Duolingo, as part of the NAACL HLT 2018 Shared Task on Second Language Acquisition Modeling (SLAM, Settles, Brust, Gustafson, Hagiwara & Madnani, 2018). The data consisted of exercise and phrase level information for three populations of language learners in their first 30 days of using the app: English-speaking learners of Spanish and French as well as Spanish-speaking learners of English.

The data were split into a training set, which consisted of each user's first 80% of sessions, a development set (for testing model generalization before the test phase) that contained the next 10% of each user's data, and a test set that contained the final 10% of exercises for each user. The training data set consisted of 1,882,701 exercises in total (38.9% from learners of Spanish, 43.8% from learners of English and 17.3% from learners of French), while the development data contained 255,383 exercises (45.3% from learners of Spanish, 37.6% learners of from English and 17.1% from learners of French), and the test set contained 249,484 exercises (45.9% from learners of Spanish, 37.4% from learners of English and 16.7% from learners of French).

4   Features

Our approach to modeling errors in second language acquisition was driven primarily by two distinct bodies of research: linguistic effects in second language acquisition, and drivers of robust memory in general. As such we discuss each set of features separately.

4.1   Linguistic features

In this section, we describe the semantic and morpho-syntactic features added to the model. Values for tokens that were not in databases listed below were set to the mean of the feature.

Word length. Orthographic and phonological length (*orthoLength* and *phonLength* respectively) are predictive of word difficulty, and longer written or spoken words generally leave more room for potential errors (Baddeley, Thomon & Buchanan, 1975). Phonological length was taken from the CLEARPOND database (Marian, Bartolotti, Chabal & Shook, 2012).

Word neighbors. A greater number of orthographic and phonological neighbors (*orthoNei* and *phonNei*) for a given word in both the to-be-learned and known languages might cause interference leading to errors. These data were also taken from the CLEARPOND database.

Word Frequency. The log transformed frequency (*logWordFreq*) of the English, Spanish and French words to be learned were also included as predictors, as well as the average log frequency of the phonological (*logOrthoNeiFreq*) and orthographic neighbors (*logPhonNeiFreq*) in the to-be-learned as well as known language.

Edit Distance. Because cognate status impacts language learning, the Levenshtein distance between a given token and its translation to user language (English for Spanish and French learners, and Spanish for English learners) was calculated by feeding single word translations through the Google Translate API and calculating edit distances between the translations. Cognates like *lemon* and *limón* should have a short edit distance, while words like *boy* and *niño* will have relatively longer distances.

Interlingual homographs. Additionally, the interlingual homograph status for each token (whether or not the token shares its surface form with a translation of a different token) were added for each language by using the Google Translate API.

Morphological Complexity. As a proxy for how morphologically complex any given word is, the number of morphological features present in the given morphology columns were summed and treated as a proxy for morphological complexity (*morphoComplexity*).

Concreteness. Mean and standard deviations for concreteness ratings were taken from Brysbaert, Warriner and Kuperman (2014) and added to the model.

4.2 Memory features

Repetition & Experience. Each instance (i.e., each token in each exercise for each user) was labeled with (1) the number of times the current user had encountered that token, up to and including the current instance (*nthOccurrence)* and (2) the number of instances the user had seen in total, up to and including the current instance (*userTrial).*

Spaced Repetition. The amount of time that elapses between successive repetitions of a given item strongly moderate memory for that item (see "Related Work", above). As such, we extracted a number of spacing-related features. To measure the temporal lag, and to capture the power law relationship between time and forgetting, we calculated (separately for each user) the log(*days*) that had elapsed between: (1) each token and its previous occurrence (*tokenLag1*), (2) each token's previous occurrence and its next most recent occurrence (*tokenLag2*), (3) each token's *stem* (e.g. *help,* for *helping*) and its previous occurrence (*stemLag1*), (4) each token's *stem*'s previous occurrence and its next most recent occurrence (*stemLag2*), (5) each token's combination of several morphological features (*number, person, tense, verbform*) and the previous occurrence of that particular combination (*morphoLag1*; to capture any possible spacing effect for verb conjugation skills) and (6) each token's combination of those same morphological features and their next most recent occurrence. Finally, (7) since some evidence suggests that the temporal gap between an item's first and second occurrence is particularly important for retention (Karpicke & Roediger, 2007), we also labeled each instance with the log(*days*) that elapsed between the first and second occurrence of the token's stem (*lagTr1Tr2*).

4.3 Categorical Features

Included in our classifier were a number of categorical features, each encoded as binary indicator variables distributed over a number of columns equal to the number of levels in the category. Importantly, our approach to modeling was constrained by limited computational power and memory, so we chose to include only categorical features with a relatively small number of levels, to reduce the dimensionality of the data. Those features were: *part of speech (pos;* 16 levels), *countries* (94 levels), *session* (3 levels), *format* (3 levels), and all of the morphological features available for each language (46 levels for learners of Spanish, 17 levels for learners of English, and 10 levels for learners of French). *Client* was also included, though we treated iOS and Android as equivalent, preserving only the distinction between web and mobile access to the Duolingo application (2 levels).

Notably, the above listing omits two of the categorical features we considered of greatest potential value in predicting early learner errors: *user* (223 levels for learners of Spanish, 179 levels for learners of English, and 216 levels for learners of French; 618 total) and *token* (2116 levels for learners of Spanish, 1615 in learners of English, 1682 in learners of French). Some users inevitably learn faster and make fewer errors than others, and some tokens are simply harder to learn on average. Instead of encoding these with dummy variables, we elected to replace the *user* feature with two continuous values, determined jointly by the user and the combination of the levels of the features *format, session,* and *client* for each instance: (1) the mean and (2) the variance of the error rate for that user under that combination of feature levels (*userMeanError, userVarError,* respectively), for a total of three values for each user. Similarly, we replaced the token feature with (1) the mean and (2) the variance of the error rate for each combination of the features *token, stem, format,* and *pos,* creating four values per token. This approach allowed us to substantially reduce demands on computational resources while simultaneously capturing much of the predictive power that fully encoding each user and token would have provided. The particular features used to create means within user and token were chosen to maximize potential differences between accuracy in different modalities. Indeed, to foreshadow our results, these features each ranked among the most important for our random forest classifier.

4.4 Interactions

Several interactions between features were also coded into the model. Due to time constraints, only the following interactions were added: *stemLag1* x *stemLag2* and *stemLag1* x *stemLag2* x *lagTr1Tr2*, to capture spacing effects, *lagTr1Tr2* x *morphoComplexity* and *lagTr1Tr2* x *morphoLag1* to capture lag differences between morphological features, *format* x *prevFormat* to capture possible task switching effects, and *orthoNei* x *format* and *phonNei* x *format* and *format* x *client* to capture differences due to listening vs. typing, and finally *morphoComplexity* x *pos* as any complexity effect may be stronger nouns and verbs than function words.

5 Model

In order to focus on feature engineering, random forest techniques were chosen over gradient boosting, logistic regression or other classification techniques. The random forest classifier scales well to large datasets, is not particularly prone to overfitting problems, and requires less parameter tuning.

Random forest classifiers combine the outputs of multiple decision tree classifiers with random features taken in each decision in order to generate one final prediction (Breiman, 2001). Each decision-tree classifier split the data along some number of parameters (equal to the square root of the total number of features in this model) that fits a classifier. Each split of the data was again split along the other included parameters until the leaves of the tree contained only data points with the same label (i.e., only error or only no-error instances). For each learner population, we generated 1000 decision trees to generate predictions. Out-of-bag errors were used to estimate errors in training.

6 Results and Discussion

Figure 1 shows the top 20 importance scores for each language (out of an across-language total of 174 features or interactions). The importance

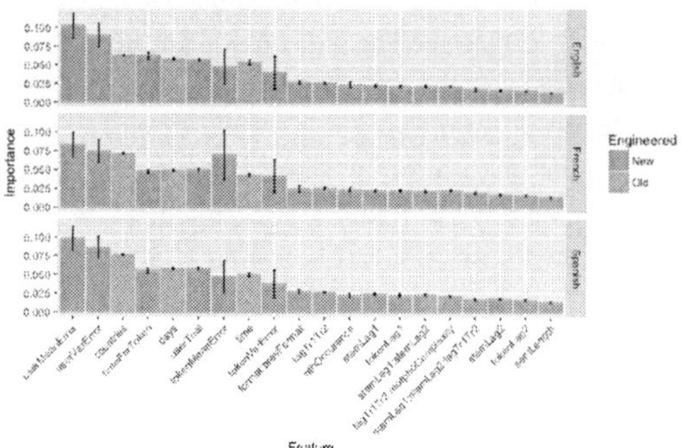

Figure 1: Top 20 importance features grouped by to-be-learned language. Error bars represent standard deviation of the importance of each feature across decision trees. For categorical features, the importances of each level, and their variances (to generate stand deviations), were summed to calculate the overall importance and variability in importance, respectively.

score of a random forest model conveys the predictive power of a given feature relative to the other predictors. Color depicts which features were engineered and which were provided in the raw data. Full importance values, for each language are listed in Appendix A, including the directionality of the relationship between each continuous feature and the error rate. For example, because *userMeanError* is higher on incorrect trials than correct trials, the directionality is considered positive.

The mean and variance in error rate for each user (*userMeanError* and *userVarError*) were the most important features, indicating that each user's history was strongly predictive of their performance at test, and that the variability within each user was nearly as predictive as the difference between users.

Countries, the third most important feature, may have ranked third in all three languages because the importance measure was calculated by summing over each feature level, possibly overstating the value of that feature in total. Nevertheless countries may represent user background information not given in the dataset including their previous language experience (as a Portuguese speaking user from Brazil may be learning Spanish via English, but would likely make different errors than an English monolingual from Canada).

The next most important generated feature was the average time spent on each token within an exercise (*timePerToken*). This likely captures time spent on each exercise better because it accounts for the length of the exercise at the token level.

Next is *userTrial*, which was calculatedly simply as which learning instance a given user is on. This likely captures the experience a user accumulates with the language and perhaps the app more generally.

Next of note is the mean and variance in error rate for each token, showing that each token has some properties that capture difficulty. This is especially true for learners of French, as the importance of *tokenMeanError* is ranked fourth in French as compared to eighth in both English and Spanish.

The interaction between format and previous format shows that there is some cost associated with task switching, perhaps to a slightly higher degree in English and Spanish, as this feature did not quite rank among the top ten in French, but was surpassed in that language by the lag between the first two occurrences of a token's stem.

Finally, the various lag features that reflect recent experience and many of their interactions comprise of the next most important features, indicating that spacing effects are generally predictive of errors of the overall model, the highest of these being the lag between the first two instances of a given token. This is an important and potentially useful feature. A measure of this lag is easy to calculate and necessarily occurs early in learning, making it useful in predictions that are memory intensive and catered to particular users or tokens.

Overall these features, and indeed many of the engineered features, improved the models over baseline, as seen in Table 1. This is particularly noteworthy considering user and token were removed in our model (and replaced with user- and token-level error rates), but were included in the SLAM baseline provided with the data. Indeed, the mean and variance across users and tokens account for ~25% of the importance across all languages. Though the importance of these features aggregate error rates in the training data, the metrics did not differ considerably when evaluated with the development data (AUROC = .824, .818, and .802 for English, French and Spanish respectively). This shows that aggregating is a feasible approach in cases where computational constraints prohibit the exact representation of important high dimensional categorical features. Notably, the within-user variability was an important

	AUROC	F1	Log-loss
SLAM English	.7730	.1899	.3580
English	.8286	.4242	.3191
SLAM French	.7707	.2814	.3952
French	.8228	.4416	.3561
SLAM Spanish	.7456	.1753	.3862
Spanish	.8027	.4353	.3571

Table 1: Final model outcomes in all three metrics as compared to baseline.

feature in our model, but would not automatically be captured by dummy-coding user and token IDs across hundreds or thousands of instances. Thus, substantial computational savings can be achieved using low dimensional summary statistics where significant CPU time and memory resources would be required.

7 Future work

Due to the time-limited nature of this shared modeling task, considerable work remains to be done to both optimize the performance of this model and further understand the cognitive processes involved in early language learning.

To improve the model, we would first refine the relative importance of the current features, by performing ablation tests and model comparisons; some of the current features play little to no role in improving model performance. Furthermore, many interactions in the current feature space,

such as *userMeanAcc* x *tokenMeanAcc*, may be important predictors given each individual feature's importance, and that each user's previous language experience will impact the difficulty associated with any given token. The spacing effect might likewise interact with individual user and token related information.

There is additionally much work to be done in quantifying the benefit of using user- and token-level error rates as opposed to dummy-encoded variables. While these features are a memory and time sensitive solution, we have not yet explored how much model performance is affected by this change relative to a dummy-encoded solution, how much time is saved, and how much data is required to achieve this performance.

Our approach focused on linguistic and cognitive features that are known in their respective literatures to impact learning, and so the bulk of our efforts were devoted to feature engineering. Future work will therefore dedicate more resources to model development. While in the present work only a random forest ensemble classifier was used to generate predictions, logistic regression, deep learning, and/or other modeling approaches may better suit this particular learning task, and should be thoroughly explored.

Finally, there are many more features than can be developed, including word embeddings of tokens and syntactic structure differences. Our work has scratched the surface of linguistic and cognitive theory that might be applied to modeling language learning, but the vast scientific literatures in those and other fields no doubt offer rich possibilities for new features. The relative contribution of all of these features and their interactions to machine learning models of error production is likely to greatly expand our knowledge of early second language learning.

8   Acknowledgements

We thank Ed Vul, Tim Sainburg, Vic Ferreira and the Language Production Lab for their feedback on this project.

References

Ben Ambridge, Anna L. Theakston, Elena V.m. Lieven, and Michael Tomasello. 2006. The distributed learning effect for children's acquisition of an abstract syntactic construction. *Cognitive Development*, *21*(2), 174–193.

Alan D. Baddeley, Neil Thomson, and Mary Buchanan. 1975. Word length and the structure of short-term memory. *Journal of verbal learning and verbal behavior*, *14*(6), 575-589.

Harry P. Bahrick and Elizabeth Phelphs. 1987. Retention of Spanish vocabulary over 8 years. *Journal of Experimental Psychology: Learning, Memory, and Cognition*, *13*(2), 344–349.

David A. Balota, Janet M. Duchek, and Ronda Paullin. 1989. Age-related differences in the impact of spacing, lag, and retention interval. *Psychology and Aging*, *4*(1), 3–9.

Leo Breiman. 2001. Random forests. *Machine Learning*, *45*(1), 5-32.

Marc Brysbaert, Amy Beth Warriner, and Victor Kuperman. 2014. Concreteness ratings for 40 thousand generally known English word lemmas. *Behavior research methods*, *46*(3), 904-911.

Shana K. Carpenter. 2009. Cue strength as a moderator of the testing effect: The benefits of elaborative retrieval. *Journal of Experimental Psychology: Learning, Memory, and Cognition*, *35*(6), 1563–1569.

Shana K. Carpenter and Edward L. DeLosh. 2006. Impoverished cue support enhances subsequent retention: Support for the elaborative retrieval explanation of the testing effect. *Memory and Cognition*, 268-276.

Nicholas J. Cepeda, Harold Pashler, Edward Vul, John T Wixted, and Doug Rohrer. 2006. Distributed practice in verbal recall tasks: A review and quantitative synthesis. *Psychological Bulletin*, *132*(3), 354-380.

Nichlaos J. Cepeda, Edward Vul, Doug Rohrer, John T. Wixted, and Harold Pashler. 2008. Spacing effects in learning: A temporal ridgeline of optimal retention. *Psychological Science*, *19*(11), 1095-1102.

William L. Cull. 2000. Untangling the benefits of multiple study opportunities and repeated testing for cued recall. *Applied Cognitive Psychology*, *14*(3), 215-235.

Annette De Groot and Rineke Keijzer. 2000. What is hard to learn is easy to forget: The roles of word concreteness, cognate status, and word frequency in foreign-language vocabulary learning and forgetting. *Language Learning*, *50*(1), 1-56.

Ton Dijkstra, Mark Timmermans, and Herbert Schriefers. 2000. On being blinded by your other language: Effects of task demands on interlingual homograph recognition. *Journal of Memory and Language*, *42*(4), 445-464.

John J. Donovan and David J. Radosevich. 1999. A meta-analytic review of the distribution of practice effect: Now you see it, now you don't. *Journal of Applied Psychology*, *84*(5), 795-805.

Hermann Ebbinghaus. 1964. Memory: A contribution to experimental psychology (H.A. Ruger, C.E. Bussenius, & E. R. Hilgard, Trans.). New York, NY: Dover. (Original work published in 1885).

Jeffrey D. Karpicke and Henry L. Roediger. 2007. Expanding retrieval practice promotes short-term retention, but equally spaced retrieval enhances long-term retention. *Journal of Experimental Psychology-Learning Memory and Cognition, 33*(4), 704-719.

Thomas K. Landauer and Robert A. Bjork. 1978. Optimum rehearsal patterns and name learning In M. M. Gruneberg, P. E. Morris, & R. N. Sykes 632). London: Academic Press.

Timothy D. Lee and Elizabeth D. Genovese (1988). Distribution of practice in motor skill acquisition: Learning and performance effects reconsidered. *Research Quarterly for Exercise and Sport, 59*(4), 277-287.

Viorica Marian, James Bartolotti, Sarah Chabal, and Anthony Shook. 2012. CLEARPOND: Cross-linguistic easy-access resource for phonological and orthographic neighborhood densities. *PloS one, 7*(8), e43230.

Cornelius P. Rea and Vito Modigliani. 1985. The effect of expanded versus massed practice on the retention of multiplication facts and spelling lists. *Human Learning: Journal of Practical Research and Applications, 4*(1), 11-18.

B. Settles, C. Brust, E. Gustafson, M. Hagiwara, and N. Madnani. 2018. Second Language Acquisition Modeling. In *Proceedings of the NAACL-HLT Workshop on Innovative Use of NLP for Building Educational Applications (BEA)*. ACL.

Michael T. Ullman and Jarrett T. Lovelett. 2016. Implications of the declarative/procedural model for improving second language learning: The role of memory enhancement techniques. *Second Language Research, 39*(1), 39-65.

Eleanor Vander Linde, Barbara A. Morrongiello, and Carolyn Rovee-Collier. 1985. Determinants of retention in 8-week-old infants. *Developmental Psychology, 21*(4), 601–61.

Appendix A.

Feature	English				French				Spanish			
	Import.	SD	Rank	Direc.	Import.	SD	Rank	Direc.	Import.	SD	Rank	Direc.
Case	0.001	0.001	52						0.001	0.000	57	
client	0.004	0.001	44		0.005	0.001	41		0.005	0.001	38	
Concreteness (M)	0.007	0.001	31	+	0.011	0.004	26	-	0.010	0.001	25	+
Concreteness (SD)	0.007	0.001	34	-	0.009	0.003	31	+	0.010	0.001	27	+
countries	0.063	0.001	3		0.071	0.001	3		0.076	0.001	3	
days	0.058	0.001	5	+	0.050	0.001	6	+	0.058	0.001	4	+
Definite	0.000	0.000	55		0.001	0.000	54		0.001	0.000	55	
Degree	0.001	0.000	53						0.000	0.000	61	
dependencyEdgeHead	0.011	0.001	22	-	0.011	0.001	25	+	0.012	0.001	21	-
editDistance	0.007	0.001	32	-	0.010	0.003	29	-	0.010	0.001	26	+
EngPhos	0.005	0.002	43	-	0.006	0.002	38	-	0.002	0.000	50	-
Foreign									0.000	0.000	63	
format	0.006	0.006	36		0.008	0.009	32		0.008	0.008	30	
format:client	0.010	0.006	24		0.012	0.009	22		0.012	0.007	22	
format:prevFormat	0.027	0.002	10		0.025	0.004	11		0.028	0.003	10	
Gender	0.000	0.000	54		0.004	0.001	47		0.004	0.000	42	
Homograph	0.002	0.001	49	-	0.002	0.001	51	-	0.002	0.001	49	-
lagTr1Tr2	0.026	0.001	11	+	0.026	0.001	10	+	0.027	0.001	11	+
lagTr1Tr2:morphoComplex	0.022	0.001	16	+	0.023	0.001	13	+	0.022	0.001	16	+
logEngPhoNeiFreq	0.005	0.001	42	-	0.006	0.002	36	-	0.002	0.000	52	+
logOrthoNeiFreq	0.007	0.001	35	-	0.007	0.002	33	-	0.005	0.001	39	-
logPhonNeiFreq	0.006	0.001	37	-	0.006	0.001	37	-	0.005	0.001	40	-
logWordFreq	0.008	0.002	28	-	0.009	0.003	30	-	0.005	0.001	35	-
Mood	0.002	0.000	50		0.001	0.000	56		0.001	0.000	56	
morphoComplex	0.002	0.000	48	-	0.003	0.002	50	-	0.003	0.000	46	-
morphoComplex:pos	0.006	0.001	38		0.007	0.002	35		0.006	0.001	33	
morphoLag1	0.008	0.000	30	+	0.005	0.000	42	+	0.005	0.000	36	+
morphoLag1:morphoComplex	0.008	0.000	27	+	0.005	0.000	43	+	0.005	0.000	37	+
morphoLag2	0.010	0.000	23	+	0.006	0.000	39	+	0.005	0.000	34	+
nthOccurance	0.024	0.004	12	-	0.024	0.002	12	-	0.023	0.003	15	-
Number	0.002	0.000	47		0.005	0.002	45		0.004	0.001	41	
NumType	0.000	0.000	56						0.000	0.000	59	
orthoLength	0.004	0.002	45	+	0.005	0.001	46	+	0.003	0.001	47	+
OrthoNei	0.005	0.001	39	-	0.006	0.002	40	-	0.004	0.001	43	-
OrthoNei:format	0.010	0.004	26		0.014	0.008	21		0.008	0.003	31	
Person	0.001	0.001	51	+	0.004	0.001	48		0.003	0.000	48	
phoLength	0.004	0.001	46	+	0.004	0.001	49	+	0.003	0.001	45	+
PhonNei	0.005	0.001	41	-	0.005	0.002	44	-	0.003	0.000	44	-
PhonNei:format	0.008	0.004	29		0.011	0.007	24		0.007	0.003	32	

238

Polite									0.000	0.000	64	
pos	0.007	0.001	33		0.012	0.004	23		0.009	0.000	29	
Poss									0.000	0.000	58	
PrepCase									0.000	0.000	60	
PronType					0.002	0.001	52		0.002	0.000	51	
Reflex									0.000	0.000	62	
sentLength	0.013	0.001	20	+	0.014	0.001	20	+	0.013	0.001	20	+
session	0.010	0.001	25		0.011	0.001	28		0.011	0.001	23	
stemLag1	0.023	0.001	13	+	0.023	0.001	14	+	0.025	0.001	12	+
stemLag1:stemLag2	0.022	0.001	14	-	0.022	0.001	16	-	0.023	0.001	13	-
stemLag1:stemLag2:lagTr1Tr2	0.018	0.002	17	+	0.020	0.001	17	+	0.017	0.001	18	-
stemLag2	0.017	0.001	18	+	0.018	0.001	18	+	0.018	0.001	17	+
Tense					0.001	0.000	55		0.001	0.000	54	
time	0.054	0.003	7	+	0.043	0.002	8	+	0.050	0.002	7	+
timePerToken	0.062	0.005	4	+	0.048	0.002	7	+	0.056	0.003	6	+
tokenIndex	0.012	0.001	21	+	0.011	0.001	27	+	0.011	0.001	24	+
tokenLag1	0.022	0.001	15	+	0.023	0.002	15	+	0.023	0.002	14	+
tokenLag2	0.016	0.001	19	+	0.017	0.001	19	+	0.017	0.001	19	+
tokenMeanError	0.048	0.023	8	+	0.070	0.033	4	+	0.047	0.022	8	+
tokenVarError	0.040	0.022	9	+	0.042	0.022	9	+	0.038	0.019	9	+
userMeanError	0.102	0.016	1	+	0.083	0.016	1	+	0.098	0.016	1	+
userTrial	0.058	0.001	6	+	0.050	0.002	5	+	0.058	0.001	5	+
userVarError	0.090	0.015	2	+	0.074	0.015	2	+	0.086	0.015	2	+
VerbForm					0.001	0.000	53		0.001	0.000	53	
wordLength	0.005	0.002	40	+	0.007	0.003	34	+	0.009	0.002	28	+

Annotation and Classification of Sentence-level Revision Improvement

Tazin Afrin
University of Pittsburgh
Pittsburgh, PA 15260
tazinafrin@cs.pitt.edu

Diane Litman
University of Pittsburgh
Pittsburgh, PA 15260
litman@cs.pitt.edu

Abstract

Studies of writing revisions rarely focus on revision quality. To address this issue, we introduce a corpus of between-draft revisions of student argumentative essays, annotated as to whether each revision improves essay quality. We demonstrate a potential usage of our annotations by developing a machine learning model to predict revision improvement. With the goal of expanding training data, we also extract revisions from a dataset edited by expert proofreaders. Our results indicate that blending expert and non-expert revisions increases model performance, with expert data particularly important for predicting low-quality revisions.

1 Introduction

Supporting student revision behavior is an important area of writing-related natural language processing (NLP) research. While revision is particularly effective in response to detailed feedback by an instructor (Paulus, 1999), human writing evaluation is time-consuming. To help students improve their writing skills, various writing assistant tools have thus been developed (Eli Review, 2014; Turnitin, 2014; Writing Mentor, 2016; Grammarly, 2016). While these tools offer instant feedback on a particular writing draft, they typically fail to explicitly compare revisions between drafts.

Our long term goal is to build a system for supporting students in revising argumentative essays, where the system automatically compares multiple drafts and provides useful feedback (e.g., informing students whether their revisions are improving the essay). One step towards this goal is the development of a machine-learning model to automatically analyze revision improvement. Specifically, given only two sentences - original and revised, our current goal is to predict if a revised sentence is better than the original.

In this paper, we focus on predicting revision improvement using non-expert (i.e., student) writing data. We first introduce a corpus of paired original and revised sentences that has been newly annotated as to whether each revision made the original sentence better or not. The revisions are a subset of those in the freely available ArgRewrite corpus (Zhang et al., 2017), with improvement annotated using standard rubric criteria for evaluating student argumentative writing. By adapting NLP features used in previous revision classification tasks, we then develop a prediction model that outperforms baselines, even though the size of our non-expert revision corpus is small. Hence, we explore extracting paired revisions from an expert edited dataset to increase training data. The expert revisions are a subset of those in the freely available Automated Evaluation of Scientific Writing (AESW) corpus (Daudaravicius et al., 2016). Our experiments show that with proper sampling, combining expert and non-expert revisions can improve prediction performance, particularly for low-quality revisions.

2 Related Work

Prior NLP revision analysis work has developed methods for identifying pairs of original and revised textual units in both Wikipedia articles and student essays, as well as for classifying such pairs with respect to schemas of coarse (e.g., syntactic versus semantic) and fine-grained (e.g., lexical vs. grammatical syntactic changes) revision purposes (Bronner and Monz, 2012; Daxenberger and Gurevych, 2012; Zhang and Litman, 2015; Yang et al., 2017). For example, the ArgRewrite corpus (Zhang et al., 2017) was introduced with the goal to facilitate argumentative revision analysis and automatic revision purpose classification. However, purpose classification does not ad-

240

Proceedings of the Thirteenth Workshop on Innovative Use of NLP for Building Educational Applications, pages 240–246
New Orleans, Louisiana, June 5, 2018. ©2018 Association for Computational Linguistics

dress revision quality. For example, a spelling change can both fix as well as introduce an error, while lexical changes can both enhance or reduce fluency. On the other hand, while some work has focused on correction detection in revision (Dahlmeier and Ng, 2012; Xue and Hwa, 2014; Felice et al., 2016), such work has typically been limited to grammatical error detection. The AESW shared task of identifying sentences in need of correction (Daudaravicius et al., 2016) goes beyond just grammatical errors, but the original task does not compare multiple versions of text, and also focuses on scientific writing.

In contrast, Tan and Lee (2014) created a dataset of paired revised sentences in academic writing annotated as to whether one sentence was stronger or weaker than the other. Their work directly sheds light on annotating sentence revision quality in terms of statement strength. However, their corpus focuses on the abstracts and introductions of ArXiv papers. Building on their annotation methodology, we consider paired sentences as our revision unit, but 1) annotate revision quality in terms of argumentative writing criteria, 2) use a corpus of revisions from non-expert student argumentative essays, and 3) move beyond annotation to automatic revision quality classification.

3 Corpora of Revised Sentence Pairs

3.1 Annotating ArgRewrite

The revisions that we annotated for improvement in quality are a subset of the freely available ArgRewrite revision corpus (Zhang et al., 2017)[1]. This corpus was created by extracting revisions from three drafts of argumentative essays written by 60 non-expert writers in response to a prompt[2]. Essay drafts were first manually aligned at the sentence level based on semantic similarity. Non-identical aligned sentences (e.g., modified, added and deleted sentences) were then extracted as the revisions. Our work uses only the 940 modification revisions, as our annotation does not yet consider a sentence's context in its paragraph.

We annotated ArgRewrite revisions for improvement using the labels *Better* or *NotBetter*. *Better* is used when the modification yields an improved sentence from the perspective of argumentative writing, while *NotBetter* is used when the modification either makes the sentence worse or

does not have any significant effect. Binary labeling enables us to clearly determine a gold-standard using majority voting with an odd number of annotators. Binary labels should also suffice for our long term goal of triggering tutoring in a writing assistant (e.g., when the label is *NotBetter*).

Inspired by Tan and Lee (2014), our annotation instructions included explanatory guidelines along with example annotated sentence pairs. The guidelines were crafted to describe improvement in terms of typical argumentative writing criteria. We depend on annotators' judgment for cases not covered by the guidelines. According to the guidelines[3], a revised sentence $S2$ is better than the original sentence $S1$ when: (1) $S2$ provides more information that strengthens the idea/major claim in $S1$; (2) $S2$ provides more evidence/justification for some aspects of $S1$; (3) $S2$ is more precise than $S1$; (4) $S2$ is easier to understand compared to $S1$ because it is fluent, well-structured, and has no unnecessary words; and (5) $S2$ is grammatically correct and has no spelling mistakes.

To provide context, annotators were told that the data was taken from student argumentative essays about electronic communications. We also let the annotators know the identity of the original and revised sentences ($S1$ and $S2$, respectively). Although this may introduce an annotation bias, it mimics feedback practice where instructors know which are the original versus revised sentences.

We collected 7 labels along with explanatory comments for each of the 940 revisions using Amazon Mechanical Turk (AMT). Table 1 shows examples (1, 2, and 3) of original and revised ArgRewrite sentences with their majority-annotated labels. The first revision clarifies a claim of the essay, the second removes some information and is less precise, while the third fixes a spelling mistake. As shown in Table 2, for all 940 revisions, our annotation has slight agreement (Landis and Koch, 1977) using Fleiss's kappa (Fleiss, 1971). If we only consider revisions where at least 5 out of the 7 annotators chose the same label (majority ≥ 5), the kappa values increase to fair agreement, 0.263. Tan and Lee (2014) achieve fair agreement (Fleiss's kappa of 0.242) with 9 annotators labeling 500 sentence pairs for statement strength.

---

[1]http://argrewrite.cs.pitt.edu
[2]Prompt shown in supplemental files.

[3]The guidelines can be found in supplemental files.

	Original Sentence ($S1$)	Revised Sentence ($S2$)	Label
1	The world has *experienced various changes throughout its lifetime.*	The world has *been defined by its revolutions - the most recent one being technological.*	Better
2	Technology is changing the *world, and in particular the* way we communicate.	Technology is changing the way we communicate.	NotBetter
3	...Susan says by to Shelly on the 125th St...	...Susan says by*e* to Shelly on the 125th St...	Better
4	This is numerically expensive but leads to proper results.	This is numerically expensive, but leads to proper results.	Better
5	Section 2 *formulates and solves* the balance equations.	The balance equations *are formulated and solved in* Section 2.	Better

Table 1: Example annotated revisions from ArgRewrite (1,2,3) and AESW (4,5). The label is calculated using majority voting (out of 7 annotators) for ArgRewrite and using expert proofreading edits for AESW.

Data	#Revisions	#Better	#NotBetter	Fleiss's Kappa (κ)
All	940(100%)	784(83.4%)	156(16.6%)	0.201(Slight)
Majority$\geq$ 5	748(79.6%)	658(88.0%)	90(12.0%)	0.263(Fair)

Table 2: Number of revisions, number of *Better* and *NotBetter*, and Fleiss's kappa (κ) per increasing majority voting (out of 7 annotators). Percentage of revisions are shown in parenthesis.

3.2 Sampling AESW

The Automated Evaluation of Scientific Writing (AESW) (Daudaravicius et al., 2016) shared task was to predict whether a sentence needed editing or not. Professional proof-readers edited sentences to correct issues ranging from grammatical errors to stylistic problems, intuitively yielding 'Better' sentences. Therefore, we can use the AESW edit information to create an automatically annotated corpus for revision improvement. In addition, by randomly flipping sentences we can include 'NotBetter' labels in the corpus.

The AESW dataset was created from different scientific writing genres (e.g. Mathematics, Astrophysics) with placeholders for anonymization. We use two random samples of 5000 AESW revisions for the experiments in Section 5. "AESW all" samples revisions from all scientific genres, while "AESW plaintext" ignores sentences containing placeholders (e.g. MATH, MATHDISP) to make the data more similar to ArgRewrite. Table 1 shows two example (4 and 5) AESW revisions.

4 Features for Classification

We adapt many features from prior studies predicting revision purposes (Adler et al., 2011; Javanmardi et al., 2011; Bronner and Monz, 2012; Daxenberger and Gurevych, 2013; Zhang and Litman, 2015; Remse et al., 2016) as well as introduce new features tailored to predicting improvement.

Following prior work, we count each unigram across, as well as unique to, S1 or S2 (Daxenberger and Gurevych, 2013; Zhang and Litman, 2015). However, we also count bigrams and trigrams to better capture introduced or deleted argumentative discourse units.

Another group of features are based on sentence differences similar to those proposed in (Zhang and Litman, 2015), e.g., difference in length, commas, symbols, named entities, etc., as well as edit distance. However, to capture improvement rather than just difference, we also introduce asymmetric distance metrics, e.g. Kullback-Leibler divergence[4]. We also capture differences using BLEU[5] score, motivated by its use in evaluating machine-translated text quality.

Following Zhang and Litman (2015), we calculate the count and difference of spelling and language errors[6], in our case to capture improvement as a result of error corrections.

As stated in the annotation guidelines, one way a revised sentence can be better is because it is more precise or specific. Therefore, we introduce the use of the Speciteller (Li and Nenkova, 2015) tool to quantify the specificity of S1 and S2, and take the specificity difference as a new feature.

Remse et al. (2016) used parse tree based fea-

---

[4] Using scipy.stats.entropy on sentence vectors.
[5] Using *sentence_bleu* from nltk.translate.bleu_score module, with S1 as reference and S2 as hypothesis.
[6] Using python 'language-check' tool.

Experiments	Precision	Recall	F1
Majority baseline	0.417	0.500	0.454
AESW all	0.471*	0.470	0.468
AESW plaintext	0.511*	0.515	0.473
ArgRewrite	0.570*	0.534	0.525*
ArgRewrite + AESW all	0.497*	0.501	0.488*
ArgRewrite + AESW plaintext	**0.574***	**0.555***	**0.551***

Table 3: 10-fold cross-validation performance. * indicates significantly better than majority ($p <$ 0.05). Bold indicates highest column value.

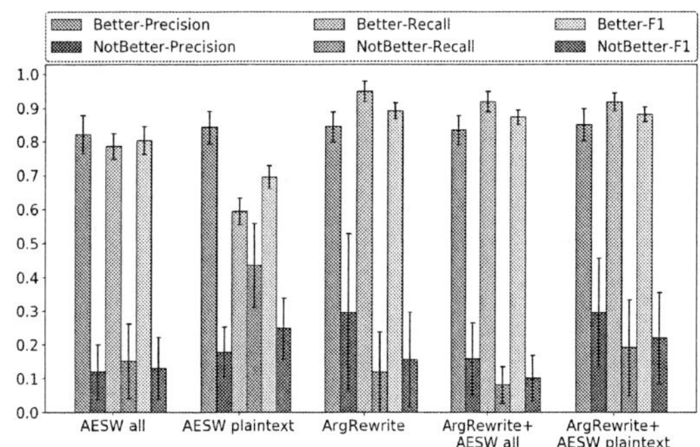

Figure 1: Precision, Recall, and F1 by class label.

tures to capture the readability, coherence, and fluency of a sentence. Inspired by them, we calculate the difference in count of subordinate clauses (SBAR), verb phrases (VP), noun phrases (NP), and tree height in the parse trees[7] of S1 and S2.

5   Experiments and Results

Our goal is to examine whether we can predict improvement for non-expert ArgRewrite revisions, using AESW expert and/or ArgRewrite non-expert revisions for training. Our experiments are structured to answer the following research questions:

Q1: Can we use only non-expert revisions to train a model that outperforms a baseline?

Q2: Can we use only expert revisions to train a model that outperforms a baseline?

Q3: Can we combine expert and non-expert training revisions to improve model performance?

Our machine learning experiments use Random Forest (RF) [8] from Python scikit-learn toolkit (Pedregosa et al., 2011) with 10-fold cross validation. Parameters were tuned using AESW development data. Because of the ArgRewrite class imbalance (Table 2, All row), we used SMOTE (Chawla et al., 2002) oversampling for each training fold. Feature selection was also performed on each training fold. Average un-weighted precision, recall and F1 are reported and compared to majority-class baselines.

To answer Q1, we train a model using only ArgRewrite data. Table 3 shows that this model outperforms the majority baseline, significantly so for Precision and F1. Compared to all other models (Figure 1), this model can identify 'Better' revisions with the highest recall, and can identify 'NotBetter' revisions with the highest precision. However, for our long-term goal of building an effective revision assistant tool, intuitively we will

also need to identify 'NotBetter' revisions with higher recall, which is very low for this model.

To answer Q2, we train only on AESW data but test on the same ArgRewrite folds as above. For both AESW revision samples (before and after removing the placeholders), only Precision is significantly better than the baseline. However, Figure 1 shows that AESW plaintext has significantly higher ($p < 0.05$) Recall than any other model in predicting 'NotBetter' revisions (which motivates Q3 as a way to address the limitation noted in Q1).

To answer Q3, during each run of cross-validation training we inject the AESW data in addition to the 90% ArgRewrite data, then test on the remaining 10% as before. As can be seen from Table 3, AESW plaintext combined with ArgRewrite shows the best classification performance using all three metrics. It also has improved Recall for 'NotBetter' revisions compared to training only on ArgRewrite data. This result indicates that selective extraction of revisions from AESW data helps improve model performance, especially when classifying low-quality revisions.

Finally, to understand feature utility, we compute average feature importance in the 10-folds for each experiment. Top important features include unigrams, trigrams, length difference, language errors, edit distance, BLEU score, specificity difference, and parse-tree features. For example, length difference scores in the top 5 for all experiments. This is intuitive as the annotation guidelines state that adding evidence can make a better revision. Other features such as differences in language errors, specificity scores, and BLEU scores show more importance when training on combined ArgRewrite and AESW data than when training on only ArgRewrite. Surprisingly, spelling error corrections show low importance.

---

[7]https://nlp.stanford.edu/software/lex-parser.shtml

[8]Random Forest outperformed Support Vector Machines.

Original Sentence ($S1$)	Revised Sentence ($S2$)	Label Distribution	Sample Comments
A 1,000-word letter is considered long, and takes days, if not weeks, to reach the recipient.	A 1,000-word letter is considered long, and takes days, if not weeks, to reach the recipient, with risks of getting lost along the way.	3 vs 4	**NotBetter:** S1 is clearer than S2 and the 'risks along the way' could be included as a second sentence to increase readability. **Better:** S2 provides more information that strengthens the idea/major claim in S1.
People can't feel the atmosphere of the conversation.	Also, people can't feel the atmosphere of the conversation.	3 vs 4	**NotBetter:** Either sentence is fine, but sentence two is not any better. **Better:** Assuming this sentence originally came from the context of a larger part of text, I imagine the continuation included here improves the flow of the original context.
With respect to personal life, social networking provides us opportunities to interact with people from different areas, such as Facebook and Twitter.	With respect to personal life, social networkings provide us opportunities to interact with people from different areas, such as Facebook and Twitter.	1 vs 6	**NotBetter:** S2 includes incorrect grammar. **Better:** S1 flows better than S2.

Table 4: Misclassified *NotBetter* revisions from ArgRewrite along with label distribution ($\#Better$ vs $\#NotBetter$) and sample annotator comments.

6 Discussion

Although AESW-plaintext helped classify Not-Better revisions, performance is still low. Table 4 shows some example NotBetter revisions misclassified as Better by most models. The first two examples were also difficult for humans to classify.

In the first example, one annotator for Better (the minority label) points out that the revision provides more information. We speculate that our models might similarly rely too heavily on length and classify longer sentences as Better, since as noted above, length difference was a top 5 feature in all experiments. In fact, for the best model (ArgRewrite+AESW plaintext), the length difference for predicted Better revisions was 4.81, while for predicted NotBetter revisions it was -3.99.

In the second example, one of the annotators who labeled the revision as Better noted that the added word 'Also' indicates a larger context not available to the annotators. This suggests that including revision context could help improve both annotation and classification performance.

The third revision was annotated as NotBetter by 6 annotators. We looked into our features and found that the 'language-check' tool in fact was able to catch this grammatical mistake. Yet only the model using just ArgRewrite for training was able to correctly classify this revision, as all models using AESW data misclassified.

7 Conclusion and Future Work

We created a corpus of sentence-level student revisions annotated with labels regarding improvement with respect to argumentative writing.[9] We used this corpus to build a machine learning model for automatically identifying revision improvement. We also demonstrated smart use of an existing corpus of expert edits to improve model performance.

In the future, we would like to improve inter-rater reliability by collecting expert annotations rather than using crowdsourcing. We would also like to examine how the accuracy of our feature extraction algorithms impacted our feature utility results. Finally, we would like to improve our use of the AESW data, e.g., by automatically clustering revisions for more targeted sampling. Optimizing how many AESW revisions to use and how to balance labels in AESW sampling are also areas for future research.

Acknowledgments

We thank Prof. Rebecca Hwa for her guidance in setting up a pilot predating our current annotation procedure. We would also like to thank Luca Lugini, Haoran Zhang and members of the PETAL group for their helpful suggestions and the anonymous reviewers for their valuable advice. This research is funded by NSF Award 1550635.

References

B. Thomas Adler, Luca de Alfaro, Santiago M. Mola-Velasco, Paolo Rosso, and Andrew G. West. 2011. Wikipedia vandalism detection: Combining natural language, metadata, and reputation features. In

---

[9]Freely available for research usage at: http://www.petal.cs.pitt.edu/data.html

Computational Linguistics and Intelligent Text Processing, CICLing '11, pages 277–288, Berlin, Heidelberg. Springer Berlin Heidelberg.

Amit Bronner and Christof Monz. 2012. User edits classification using document revision histories. In *Proceedings of the 13th Conference of the European Chapter of the Association for Computational Linguistics*, EACL '12, pages 356–366, Avignon, France. Association for Computational Linguistics.

Nitesh V. Chawla, Kevin W. Bowyer, Lawrence O. Hall, and W. Philip Kegelmeyer. 2002. Smote: Synthetic minority over-sampling technique. *Journal of Artificial Intelligence Research*, 16(1):321–357.

Daniel Dahlmeier and Hwee Tou Ng. 2012. Better evaluation for grammatical error correction. In *Proceedings of the 2012 Conference of the North American Chapter of the Association for Computational Linguistics: Human Language Technologies*, NAACL HLT '12, pages 568–572, Stroudsburg, PA, USA. Association for Computational Linguistics.

Vidas Daudaravicius, Rafael E. Banchs, Elena Volodina, and Courtney Napoles. 2016. A report on the automatic evaluation of scientific writing shared task. In *Proceedings of the 11th Workshop on Innovative Use of NLP for Building Educational Applications, BEA@NAACL-HLT 2016, June 16, 2016, San Diego, California, USA*, pages 53–62.

Johannes Daxenberger and Iryna Gurevych. 2012. A corpus-based study of edit categories in featured and non-featured wikipedia articles. In *Proceedings of the 24th International Conference on Computational Linguistics*, COLING '12, pages 711–726, Mumbai, India.

Johannes Daxenberger and Iryna Gurevych. 2013. Automatically classifying edit categories in wikipedia revisions. In *Proceedings of the 2013 Conference on Empirical Methods in Natural Language Processing*, EMNLP '13, pages 578–589, Seattle, Washington, USA. Association for Computational Linguistics.

The Eli Review. 2014. Eli review, https://elireview.com/support/. [online; accessed 03-18-2018].

Mariano Felice, Christopher Bryant, and Ted Briscoe. 2016. Automatic extraction of learner errors in esl sentences using linguistically enhanced alignments. In *Proceedings of COLING 2016, the 26th International Conference on Computational Linguistics: Technical Papers*, pages 825–835.

Joseph L. Fleiss. 1971. Measuring nominal scale agreement among many raters. *Psychological Bulletin*, 76(5):378–382.

Grammarly. 2016. http://www.grammarly.com. [online; accessed 03-18-2018].

Sara Javanmardi, David W. McDonald, and Cristina V. Lopes. 2011. Vandalism detection in wikipedia: A high-performing, feature-rich model and its reduction through lasso. In *Proceedings of the 7th International Symposium on Wikis and Open Collaboration*, WikiSym '11, pages 82–90, New York, NY, USA. ACM.

J. Richard Landis and Gary Koch. 1977. The measurement of observer agreement for categorical data. *Biometrics*, 33(1):159–174.

Junyi Jessy Li and Ani Nenkova. 2015. Fast and accurate prediction of sentence specificity. In *Proceedings of the Twenty-Ninth Conference on Artificial Intelligence (AAAI)*, pages 2281–2287.

Trena M. Paulus. 1999. The effect of peer and teacher feedback on student writing. *Journal of Second Language Writing*, 8(3):265 – 289.

F. Pedregosa, G. Varoquaux, A. Gramfort, V. Michel, B. Thirion, O. Grisel, M. Blondel, P. Prettenhofer, R. Weiss, V. Dubourg, J. Vanderplas, A. Passos, D. Cournapeau, M. Brucher, M. Perrot, and E. Duchesnay. 2011. Scikit-learn: Machine learning in Python. *Journal of Machine Learning Research*, 12:2825–2830.

Madeline Remse, Mohsen Mesgar, and Michael Strube. 2016. Feature-rich error detection in scientific writing using logistic regression. In *Proceedings of the 11th Workshop on Innovative Use of NLP for Building Educational Applications, BEA@NAACL-HLT 2016, June 16, 2016, San Diego, California, USA*, pages 162–171. Association for Computational Linguistics.

Chenhao Tan and Lillian Lee. 2014. A corpus of sentence-level revisions in academic writing: A step towards understanding statement strength in communication. In *Proceedings of the 52nd Annual Meeting of the Association for Computational Linguistics*, volume 2: Short Papers, pages 403–408, Baltimore, MD, USA.

Turnitin. 2014. http://turnitin.com/. [online; accessed 03-18-2018].

The Writing Mentor. 2016. Ets writing mentor, https://mentormywriting.org/, [online; accessed 03-18-2018].

Huichao Xue and Rebecca Hwa. 2014. Improved correction detection in revised esl sentences. In *Proceedings of the 52nd Annual Meeting of the Association for Computational Linguistics (Volume 2: Short Papers)*, pages 599–604, Baltimore, Maryland. Association for Computational Linguistics.

Diyi Yang, Aaron Halfaker, Robert E. Kraut, and Eduard H. Hovy. 2017. Identifying semantic edit intentions from revisions in wikipedia. In *Proceedings of the 2017 Conference on Empirical Methods in Natural Language Processing, EMNLP 2017, Copenhagen, Denmark, September 9-11, 2017*, pages

2000–2010. Association for Computational Linguistics.

Fan Zhang, Homa Hashemi, Rebecca Hwa, and Diane Litman. 2017. A corpus of annotated revisions for studying argumentative writing. In *Proceedings of the 55th Annual Meeting of the Association for Computational Linguistics (Volume 1: Long Papers)*, pages 1568–1578. Association for Computational Linguistics.

Fan Zhang and Diane Litman. 2015. Annotation and classification of argumentative writing revisions. In *Proceedings of the 10th Workshop on Innovative Use of NLP for Building Educational Applications*, pages 133–143, Denver, Colorado. Association for Computational Linguistics.

Language Model Based Grammatical Error Correction
without Annotated Training Data

Christopher Bryant   **Ted Briscoe**

ALTA Institute

Department of Computer Science and Technology

University of Cambridge

Cambridge, UK

{cjb255, ejb1}@cl.cam.ac.uk

Abstract

Since the end of the CoNLL-2014 shared task on grammatical error correction (GEC), research into language model (LM) based approaches to GEC has largely stagnated. In this paper, we re-examine LMs in GEC and show that it is entirely possible to build a simple system that not only requires minimal annotated data ($\sim$1000 sentences), but is also fairly competitive with several state-of-the-art systems. This approach should be of particular interest for languages where very little annotated training data exists, although we also hope to use it as a baseline to motivate future research.

1 Introduction

In the CoNLL-2014 shared task on Grammatical Error Correction (GEC) (Ng et al., 2014), the top three teams all employed a combination of statistical machine translation (SMT) or classifier-based approaches (Junczys-Dowmunt and Grundkiewicz, 2014; Felice et al., 2014; Rozovskaya et al., 2014). These approaches have since come to dominate the field, and a lot of recent research has focused on fine-tuning SMT systems (Junczys-Dowmunt and Grundkiewicz, 2016), reranking SMT output (Hoang et al., 2016; Yuan et al., 2016), combining SMT and classifier systems (Susanto et al., 2014; Rozovskaya and Roth, 2016), and developing various neural architectures (Chollampatt et al., 2016; Xie et al., 2016; Yuan and Briscoe, 2016; Chollampatt and Ng, 2017; Sakaguchi et al., 2017; Yannakoudakis et al., 2017).

Despite coming a fairly competitive fourth in the shared task however (Lee and Lee, 2014), research into language model (LM) based approaches to GEC has largely stagnated. The main aim of this paper is hence to re-examine language modelling in the context of GEC and show that it is still possible to achieve competitive results even with very simple systems. In fact, a notable

strength of LM-based approaches is that they rely on very little annotated data (purely for tuning purposes), and so it is entirely possible to build a reasonable correction system for any language given enough native text. In contrast, this is simply not possible with SMT and other popular approaches which always require (lots of) labelled data.

2 Methodology

The core idea behind language modelling in GEC is that low probability sequences are more likely to contain grammatical errors than high probability sequences. For example, *discuss about the problem* is expected to be a low probability sequence because it contains an error while *discuss the problem* or *talk about the problem* are expected to be higher probability sequences because they do not contain errors. The goal of LM-based GEC is hence to determine how to transform the former into the latter based on LM probabilities.[1]

With this in mind, our approach is fundamentally a simplification of the algorithm proposed by Dahlmeier and Ng (2012a). It consists of 5 steps and is illustrated in Table 1:

1. Calculate the normalised log probability of an input sentence.
2. Build a confusion set, if any, for each token in that sentence.
3. Re-score the sentence substituting each candidate in each confusion set.
4. Apply the single best correction that increases the probability above a threshold.
5. Iterate steps 1-4.

One of the main contributions of this paper is hence to re-evaluate the LM approach in relation to the latest state-of-the-art systems on several benchmark datasets.

---

[1] See Chelba et al. (2014) for more information about popular approaches to language modelling.

Proceedings of the Thirteenth Workshop on Innovative Use of NLP for Building Educational Applications, pages 247–253

New Orleans, Louisiana, June 5, 2018. ©2018 Association for Computational Linguistics

Step	Sentence									Probability
1	I	am	looking	forway	to	see	you	soon	.	-2.71
2 and 3	I	was -2.67 be -3.09 are -3.10 . . .	look -2.91 looks -2.93 looked -2.95 . . .	**forward** **-1.80** Norway -2.36 foray -2.70 . . .	of -2.98 in -2.99 ϵ -3.00 . . .	seeing -3.09 saw -3.25 sees -3.39 . . .	you	sooner -3.05 soonest -3.20	.	-
4	I	am	looking	**forward**	to	see	you	soon	.	-1.80
5	I	am	looking	forward	to	**seeing**	you	soon	.	-1.65

Table 1: A step-by-step example of our approach as described in Section 2. All scores are log probabilities.

2.1 Sequence Probabilities

We evaluate hypothesis corrections in terms of normalised log probabilities at the sentence level. Normalisation by sentence length is necessary to overcome the tendency for shorter sequences to have higher probabilities than longer sequences. Dahlmeier and Ng (2012a) similarly used normalised log probabilities to evaluate hypotheses, but did so as part of a more complex combination of other features. In contrast, Lee and Lee (2014) evaluated hypotheses in terms of sliding five word windows (5-grams).

2.2 Confusion Sets

One of the defining characteristics of LM-based GEC is that the approach does not necessarily require annotated training data. For example, spellcheckers and rules both formed key parts of Dahlmeier and Ng's and Lee and Lee's systems. While Lee and Lee ultimately did make use of annotated training data however, Dahlmeier and Ng instead employed separate classifiers for articles, prepositions and noun number errors trained only on native text.

In this work, we focus on correcting the following error types in English: non-words, morphology, and articles and prepositions.[2]

Non-words: We use CyHunspell[3] v1.2.1 with the latest British English Hunspell dictionaries[4] to generate correction candidates for non-word errors. Non-words include genuine misspellings, such as [*freind* → *friend*], and inflectional errors, such as [*advices* → *advice*]. Although CyHunspell is not a context sensitive spell checker, the proposed corrections are evaluated in a context sensitive manner by the language model.

Morphology: Examples of morphological errors include noun number [*cat* → *cats*], verb tense [*eat* → *ate*] and adjective form [*big* → *bigger*], amongst others. To generate correction candidates for morphological errors, we use an Automatically Generated Inflection Database (AGID),[5] which contains all the morphological forms of many English words. The confusion set for a word is hence derived from this database.

Articles and Prepositions: Since articles and prepositions are closed class words, we defined confusion sets for these error types manually. Specifically, the article confusion set consists of $\{\epsilon, a, an, the\}$, while the preposition confusion set consists of the top ten most frequent prepositions: $\{\epsilon$, about, at, by, for, from, in, of, on, to, with$\}$. Both sets also contain a null character which represents a deletion.

Unlike Dahlmeier and Ng and Lee and Lee, we do not yet handle missing words (∼20% of all errors) because it is often difficult to know where to insert them.

2.3 Iteration

The main reason to iteratively correct only one word at a time is because errors sometimes interact. For example, correcting [*see* → *seeing*] in Table 1 initially reduces the log probability of the input sentence from -2.71 to -3.09. After correcting [*foray* → *forward*] however, [*see* → *seeing*] subsequently increases the probability of the sentence from -1.80 to -1.65 in the second iteration. Consequently, correcting the most serious errors first, in terms of language model probability increase, often helps facilitate the correction of less serious errors later. Dahlmeier and Ng and Lee and Lee both also used iterative correction strategies in their systems, but did so as part of a beam search or pipeline approach respectively.

---

[2]Note that targeting other error types may be more appropriate in other languages; e.g. Mandarin Chinese contains very little morphology.

[3]https://pypi.python.org/pypi/CyHunspell

[4]https://sourceforge.net/projects/wordlist/files/speller/2017.08.24/

[5]http://wordlist.aspell.net/other/

Dataset	Tokenizer	Sents	Coders	Edits
CoNLL-2013	NLTK	1381	1	3404
CoNLL-2014	NLTK	1312	2	6104
FCE-dev	spaCy	2371	1	4419
FCE-test	spaCy	2805	1	5556
JFLEG-dev	NLTK	754	4	10576
JFLEG-test	NLTK	747	4	10082

Table 2: Various stats about the learner corpora we use.

3 Data and Resources

In all our experiments, we used a 5-gram language model trained on the One Billion Word Benchmark dataset (Chelba et al., 2014) with KenLM (Heafield, 2011). While a neural model would likely result in better performance, efficient training on such a large amount of data is still an active area of research (Grave et al., 2017).

Although LM-based GEC does not require annotated training data, a small amount of annotated data is still required for development and testing. We hence make use of several popular GEC corpora, including: CoNLL-2013 and CoNLL-2014 (Ng et al., 2013, 2014), the public First Certificate in English (FCE) (Yannakoudakis et al., 2011), and JFLEG (Napoles et al., 2017).

Since the FCE was not originally released with an official development set, we use the same split as Rei and Yannakoudakis (2016),[6] which we tokenize with spaCy[7] v1.9.0. We also reprocess all the datasets with the ERRor ANnotation Toolkit (ERRANT) (Bryant et al., 2017) in an effort to standardise them. This standardisation is especially important for JFLEG which is not explicitly annotated and so otherwise cannot be evaluated in terms of F-score. Note that results on CoNLL-2014 and JFLEG are typically higher than on other datasets because they contain more than one reference. See Table 2 for more information about each of the development and test sets.

4 Tuning

The goal of tuning in our LM-based approach is to determine a probability threshold that optimises $F_{0.5}$. For example, although the edit [*am* → *was*] in Table 1 increases the normalised sentence log probability from -2.71 to -2.67, this is such a small improvement that it is likely to be a false positive. In order to minimise false positives, we hence set

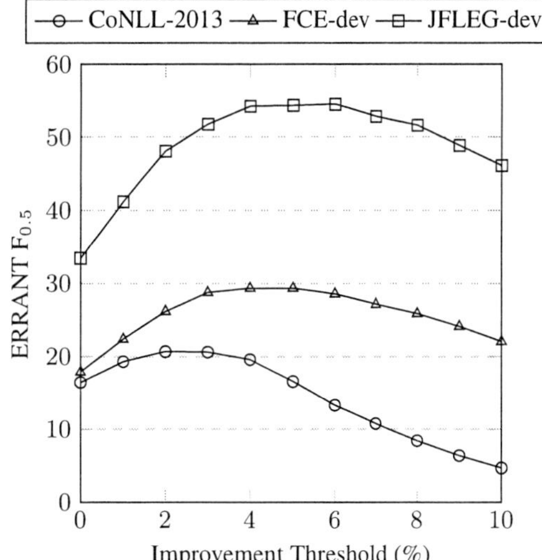

Figure 1: The effect of changing the sentence probability improvement threshold (%) on ERRANT $F_{0.5}$ for each of the development sets.

a threshold such that a candidate correction must improve the average token probability of the sentence by at least X% before it is applied. Although it may be unusual to use percentages in log space, this is just one way to compare the difference between two sentences which we found worked well in practice.

The results of this tuning are shown in Figure 1, where we tried thresholds in the range of 0-10% on three different development sets. It is notable that the optimum threshold for CoNLL-2013 (2%) is very different from that of FCE-dev (4%) and JFLEG-dev (5%), which we suspect is because each dataset has a different error type distribution. For example, spelling errors make up just 0.3% of all errors in CoNLL-2013, but closer to 10% in FCE-dev and JFLEG-dev.

Finally, it should be noted that this threshold is an approximation and it is certainly possible to optimise further. For example, in future, thresholds could be set based on error types rather than globally.

5 Results and Discussion

Before evaluating performance on the test sets, a final post-processing step changed the first alphabetical character of every sentence to upper case if necessary. This improved the scores by about 0.3 $F_{0.5}$ in CoNLL-2014 and FCE-test, but by over 5 $F_{0.5}$ in JFLEG-test. This surprising result once

---

[6]https://ilexir.co.uk/datasets/index.html

[7]https://spacy.io/

Test Set	System	ERRANT			M2 Scorer			GLEU
		P	**R**	$F_{0.5}$	**P**	**R**	$F_{0.5}$	**GLEU**
CoNLL-2014	Lee and Lee (2014)	30.60	20.95	28.02	34.51	21.73	30.88	59.50
	AMU16$_{SMT}$+LSTM	-	-	-	**58.79**	**30.63**	**49.66**	**68.26**
	CAMB16$_{SMT}$+LSTM	-	-	-	49.58	21.84	39.53	65.68
	Our work	36.62	19.93	31.37	40.56	20.81	34.09	59.35
FCE-test	AMU16$_{SMT}$ + LSTM	-	-	-	40.67	17.36	32.06	63.57
	CAMB16$_{SMT}$ + LSTM	-	-	-	**65.03**	**32.45**	**54.15**	**70.72**
	Our work	41.92	13.62	29.61	44.78	14.12	31.22	60.04
JFLEG-test	AMU16$_{SMT}$ + LSTM	-	-	-	60.68	22.65	45.43	42.65
	CAMB16$_{SMT}$ + LSTM	-	-	-	65.86	30.56	53.50	46.74
	Sakaguchi et al. (2017)	-	-	-	65.80	**40.96**	**58.68**	**53.98**
	Our work	73.76	27.61	55.28	**76.23**	28.48	57.08	48.75

Table 3: Our LM-based approach is compared against several state-of-the-art results. AMU16$_{SMT}$+LSTM and CAMB16$_{SMT}$+LSTM were both originally reported by Yannakoudakis et al. (2017), while Lee and Lee (2014) is the system entered by POST in CoNLL-2014. Only our approach does **not** use annotated training data.

again shows that different test sets have very different error type distributions and that even the simplest of correction strategies can significantly affect results.

Our final scores are shown in Table 3 where they are compared with several state-of-the-art systems. Unfortunately, we cannot compare results with Dahlmeier and Ng (2012a) because this system is neither publicly available nor has previously been evaluated on these test sets. Results are reported in terms of M2 $F_{0.5}$ (Dahlmeier and Ng, 2012b), the *de facto* standard of GEC evaluation; ERRANT $F_{0.5}$ (Bryant et al., 2017), an improved version of M2 which we used to develop our system; and GLEU (Napoles et al., 2015), an ngram-based metric designed to correlate with human judgements. Results for ERRANT are not available in all cases because system output is not available.

At this point, it is worth reiterating that our main intention was not to necessarily improve upon the state-of-the-art, but rather quantify the extent to which a simple LM-based approach with minimal annotated data could compete against a much more sophisticated model trained on millions of words of annotated text. This is especially relevant for languages where annotated training data may not be available.

With this in mind, we were firstly pleased to improve upon the previous best LM-based approach by Lee and Lee (2014) in the CoNLL-2014 shared task. This is especially significant given we also did so without any annotated training data (unlike them). Although our system would still have placed fourth overall, the gap between third and

fourth decreased from 3 $F_{0.5}$ to less than 1 $F_{0.5}$.

We were also surprised by the high performance on JFLEG-test, where we not only outperformed two state-of-the-art systems, but also came to within 2 $F_{0.5}$ of the top system. This is especially surprising given our system only corrects a limited number of error types (roughly 14 out of the 55 in ERRANT[8]), and so can maximally correct only 40-60% of all errors in each test set. One possible explanation for this is that unlike CoNLL-2014 and FCE-test, which were only corrected with minimal edits, JFLEG was corrected for fluency (Sakaguchi et al., 2016), and so it intuitively makes sense that LM-based approaches perform better with fluent references.

Although we did not perform as well on CoNLL-2014 or FCE-test, most likely for the same reason, we also note a large discrepancy between state-of-the-art systems tuned on different datasets. For example, while AMU16$_{SMT}$+LSTM tuned for CoNLL achieves the highest result on CoNLL-2014 (49.66 $F_{0.5}$), its equivalent performance on FCE-test (32.06 $F_{0.5}$) is only marginally better than our own (31.22 $F_{0.5}$). We observe a similar effect with CAMB16$_{SMT}$+LSTM tuned for the FCE, and so are wary of approaches that might be overfitting to their training corpora.

We make all our code and system output available online.[9]

---

[8]R:ADJ:FORM, R:DET, R:MORPH, R:NOUN:INFL, R:NOUN:NUM, R:ORTH, R:PREP, R:SPELL, R:VERB:FORM, R:VERB:INFL, R:VERB:SVA, R:VERB:TENSE, U:DET, U:PREP

[9]`https://github.com/chrisjbryant/lmgec-lite`

6 Conclusion

In this paper, we have shown that a simple language model approach to grammatical error correction with minimal annotated data can still be competitive with the latest neural and machine translation approaches that rely on large quantities of annotated training data. This is especially significant given that our system is also limited by the range of error types it can correct. In the future, we hope to improve our system by adding the capability to correct other error types, such as missing words, and also make use of neural language modelling techniques.

We have demonstrated that LM-based GEC is not only still a promising area of research, but one that may be of particular interest to researchers working on languages where annotated training corpora are not yet available. We released all our code and system output with this paper.

References

Christopher Bryant, Mariano Felice, and Ted Briscoe. 2017. Automatic annotation and evaluation of error types for grammatical error correction. In *Proceedings of the 55th Annual Meeting of the Association for Computational Linguistics (Volume 1: Long Papers)*. Association for Computational Linguistics, Vancouver, Canada, pages 793–805. http://aclweb.org/anthology/P17-1074.

Ciprian Chelba, Tomas Mikolov, Mike Schuster, Qi Ge, Thorsten Brants, Phillipp Koehn, and Tony Robinson. 2014. One billion word benchmark for measuring progress in statistical language modeling. In *INTERSPEECH 2014, 15th Annual Conference of the International Speech Communication Association, Singapore, September 14-18, 2014*. pages 2635–2639. http://www.isca-speech.org/archive/interspeech_2014/i14_2635.html.

Shamil Chollampatt, Duc Tam Hoang, and Hwee Tou Ng. 2016. Adapting grammatical error correction based on the native language of writers with neural network joint models. In *Proceedings of the 2016 Conference on Empirical Methods in Natural Language Processing*. Association for Computational Linguistics, Austin, Texas, pages 1901–1911. https://aclweb.org/anthology/D16-1195.

Shamil Chollampatt and Hwee Tou Ng. 2017. Connecting the dots: Towards human-level grammatical error correction. In *Proceedings of the 12th Workshop on Innovative Use of NLP for Building Educational Applications*. Association for Computational Linguistics, Copenhagen, Denmark, pages 327–333. http://www.aclweb.org/anthology/W17-5037.

Daniel Dahlmeier and Hwee Tou Ng. 2012a. A beam-search decoder for grammatical error correction. In *Proceedings of the 2012 Joint Conference on Empirical Methods in Natural Language Processing and Computational Natural Language Learning*. Association for Computational Linguistics, Jeju Island, Korea, pages 568–578. http://www.aclweb.org/anthology/D12-1052.

Daniel Dahlmeier and Hwee Tou Ng. 2012b. Better evaluation for grammatical error correction. In *Proceedings of the 2012 Conference of the North American Chapter of the Association for Computational Linguistics: Human Language Technologies*. Association for Computational Linguistics, Montréal, Canada, pages 568–572. http://www.aclweb.org/anthology/N12-1067.

Mariano Felice, Zheng Yuan, Øistein E. Andersen, Helen Yannakoudakis, and Ekaterina Kochmar. 2014. Grammatical error correction using hybrid systems and type filtering. In *Proceedings of the Eighteenth Conference on Computational Natural Language Learning: Shared Task*. Association for Computational Linguistics, Baltimore, Maryland, pages 15–24. http://www.aclweb.org/anthology/W14-1702.

Édouard Grave, Armand Joulin, Moustapha Cissé, David Grangier, and Hervé Jégou. 2017. Efficient softmax approximation for GPUs. In Doina Precup and Yee Whye Teh, editors, *Proceedings of the 34th International Conference on Machine Learning*. PMLR, International Convention Centre, Sydney, Australia, volume 70 of *Proceedings of Machine Learning Research*, pages 1302–1310. http://proceedings.mlr.press/v70/grave17a.html.

Kenneth Heafield. 2011. KenLM: faster and smaller language model queries. In *Proceedings of the EMNLP 2011 Sixth Workshop on Statistical Machine Translation*. Edinburgh, Scotland, United Kingdom, pages 187–197. https://kheafield.com/papers/avenue/kenlm.pdf.

Duc Tam Hoang, Shamil Chollampatt, and Hwee Tou Ng. 2016. Exploiting n-best hypotheses to improve an smt approach to grammatical error correction. In *Proceedings of the Twenty-Fifth International Joint Conference on Artificial Intelligence (IJCAI-16)*. AAAI Press / International Joint Conferences on Artificial Intelligence, New York, New York, USA, pages 2803–2809. https://www.ijcai.org/Proceedings/16/Papers/398.pdf.

Marcin Junczys-Dowmunt and Roman Grundkiewicz. 2014. The amu system in the conll-2014 shared task: Grammatical error correction by data-intensive and feature-rich statistical machine translation. In

Proceedings of the Eighteenth Conference on Computational Natural Language Learning: Shared Task. Association for Computational Linguistics, Baltimore, Maryland, pages 25–33. http://www.aclweb.org/anthology/W14-1703.

Marcin Junczys-Dowmunt and Roman Grundkiewicz. 2016. Phrase-based machine translation is state-of-the-art for automatic grammatical error correction. In *Proceedings of the 2016 Conference on Empirical Methods in Natural Language Processing*. Association for Computational Linguistics, Austin, Texas, pages 1546–1556. https://aclweb.org/anthology/D16-1161.

Kyusong Lee and Gary Geunbae Lee. 2014. Postech grammatical error correction system in the conll-2014 shared task. In *Proceedings of the Eighteenth Conference on Computational Natural Language Learning: Shared Task*. Association for Computational Linguistics, Baltimore, Maryland, pages 65–73. http://www.aclweb.org/anthology/W14-1709.

Courtney Napoles, Keisuke Sakaguchi, Matt Post, and Joel Tetreault. 2015. Ground truth for grammatical error correction metrics. In *Proceedings of the 53rd Annual Meeting of the Association for Computational Linguistics and the 7th International Joint Conference on Natural Language Processing (Volume 2: Short Papers)*. Association for Computational Linguistics, Beijing, China, pages 588–593. http://www.aclweb.org/anthology/P15-2097.

Courtney Napoles, Keisuke Sakaguchi, and Joel Tetreault. 2017. Jfleg: A fluency corpus and benchmark for grammatical error correction. In *Proceedings of the 15th Conference of the European Chapter of the Association for Computational Linguistics: Volume 2, Short Papers*. Association for Computational Linguistics, Valencia, Spain, pages 229–234. http://www.aclweb.org/anthology/E17-2037.

Hwee Tou Ng, Siew Mei Wu, Ted Briscoe, Christian Hadiwinoto, Raymond Hendy Susanto, and Christopher Bryant. 2014. The CoNLL-2014 shared task on grammatical error correction. In *Proceedings of the Eighteenth Conference on Computational Natural Language Learning: Shared Task*. ACL, Baltimore, Maryland, USA, pages 1–14. http://aclweb.org/anthology/W/W14/W14-1701.pdf.

Hwee Tou Ng, Siew Mei Wu, Yuanbin Wu, Christian Hadiwinoto, and Joel R. Tetreault. 2013. The CoNLL-2013 shared task on grammatical error correction. In *Proceedings of the Seventeenth Conference on Computational Natural Language Learning: Shared Task*. ACL, Sofia, Bulgaria, pages 1–12.

Marek Rei and Helen Yannakoudakis. 2016. Compositional sequence labeling models for error detection in learner writing. In *Proceedings of the 54th Annual Meeting of the Association for Computational Linguistics (Volume 1: Long Papers)*. Association for Computational Linguistics, Berlin, Germany, pages 1181–1191. http://www.aclweb.org/anthology/P16-1112.

Alla Rozovskaya, Kai-Wei Chang, Mark Sammons, Dan Roth, and Nizar Habash. 2014. The illinois-columbia system in the conll-2014 shared task. In *Proceedings of the Eighteenth Conference on Computational Natural Language Learning: Shared Task*. Association for Computational Linguistics, Baltimore, Maryland, pages 34–42. http://www.aclweb.org/anthology/W14-1704.

Alla Rozovskaya and Dan Roth. 2016. Grammatical error correction: Machine translation and classifiers. In *Proceedings of the 54th Annual Meeting of the Association for Computational Linguistics*. Association for Computational Linguistics, Berlin, Germany, pages 2205–2215. http://aclweb.org/anthology/P16-1208.

Keisuke Sakaguchi, Courtney Napoles, Matt Post, and Joel Tetreault. 2016. Reassessing the goals of grammatical error correction: Fluency instead of grammaticality. *Transactions of the Association for Computational Linguistics* 4:169–182. https://tacl2013.cs.columbia.edu/ojs/index.php/tacl/article/view/800.

Keisuke Sakaguchi, Matt Post, and Benjamin Van Durme. 2017. Grammatical error correction with neural reinforcement learning. In *Proceedings of the Eighth International Joint Conference on Natural Language Processing (Volume 2: Short Papers)*. Asian Federation of Natural Language Processing, Taipei, Taiwan, pages 366–372. http://www.aclweb.org/anthology/I17-2062.

Raymond Hendy Susanto, Peter Phandi, and Hwee Tou Ng. 2014. System combination for grammatical error correction. In *Proceedings of the 2014 Conference on Empirical Methods in Natural Language Processing (EMNLP)*. Association for Computational Linguistics, Doha, Qatar, pages 951–962. http://www.aclweb.org/anthology/D14-1102.

Ziang Xie, Anand Avati, Naveen Arivazhagan, Dan Jurafsky, and Andrew Y. Ng. 2016. Neural language correction with character-based attention. *CoRR* abs/1603.09727. http://arxiv.org/abs/1603.09727.

Helen Yannakoudakis, Ted Briscoe, and Ben Medlock. 2011. A new dataset and method for automatically grading esol texts. In *Proceedings of the 49th Annual Meeting of the Association for Computational Linguistics: Human Language Technologies*. Association for Computational Linguistics, Portland, Oregon, USA, pages 180–189. http://www.aclweb.org/anthology/P11-1019.

Helen Yannakoudakis, Marek Rei, Øistein E. Andersen, and Zheng Yuan. 2017. Neural sequence-labelling models for grammatical error correction.

In *Proceedings of the 2017 Conference on Empirical Methods in Natural Language Processing.* Association for Computational Linguistics, Copenhagen, Denmark, pages 2795–2806. `https://www.aclweb.org/anthology/D17-1297`.

Zheng Yuan and Ted Briscoe. 2016. Grammatical error correction using neural machine translation. In *Proceedings of the 2016 Conference of the North American Chapter of the Association for Computational Linguistics: Human Language Technologies.* Association for Computational Linguistics, San Diego, California, pages 380–386. `http://www.aclweb.org/anthology/N16-1042`.

Zheng Yuan, Ted Briscoe, and Mariano Felice. 2016. Candidate re-ranking for smt-based grammatical error correction. In *Proceedings of the 11th Workshop on Innovative Use of NLP for Building Educational Applications.* Association for Computational Linguistics, San Diego, CA, pages 256–266. `http://www.aclweb.org/anthology/W16-0530`.

A Semantic Role-based Approach
to Open-Domain Automatic Question Generation

Michael Flor and **Brian Riordan**
Educational Testing Service
660 Rosedale Road, Princeton, NJ 08541, USA
{mflor, briordan}@ets.org

Abstract

We present a novel rule-based system for automatic generation of factual questions from sentences, using semantic role labeling (SRL) as the main form of text analysis. The system is capable of generating both *wh*-questions and yes/no questions from the same semantic analysis. We present an extensive evaluation of the system and compare it to a recent neural network architecture for question generation. The SRL-based system outperforms the neural system in both average quality and variety of generated questions.

1 Introduction

Automatic generation of questions (AQG) is an important and challenging research area in natural language processing. AQG systems can be useful for educational applications such as assessment of reading comprehension, intelligent tutoring, dialogue agents, and instructional games. Most of the research on AQG focuses on factoid questions – questions that are generated from reading passages and ask about information that is expressed in the text itself (as opposed to, e.g., readers' opinions of the text or external knowledge related to the text).

Traditional architectures for AQG involve syntactic and semantic analysis of text, with rule-based and template-based modules for converting linguistic analyses into questions. Many of these systems employ semantic role labeling (SRL) as an important analytic component (Mazidi and Tarau, 2016; Huang and He, 2016). Recently, neural network architectures have also been proposed for the AQG task (Du et al., 2017; Serban et al., 2016).

In this paper we present an automatic question generation system based on semantic role labeling. The system generates questions directly from semantic analysis, without templates. Our system includes two innovations. While previous SRL-based AQG systems generated only *wh*-questions,

ours is the first reported system that also generates yes/no questions from SRL analysis. It is also the first system that generates questions for copular sentences from their SRL analysis (both yes/no and *wh*-questions).

To evaluate the performance of our system, we compare the quality of its output with that of a state-of-the-art neural network AQG system, over the same set of texts. To the best of our knowledge, ours is the first direct comparison of SRL-based and neural AQG systems.

The rest of this paper is structured as follows. Section 2 presents related work on AQG. Section 3 describes our SRL-based system and section 4 outlines the neural network AQG system. Section 5 describes the annotation study. Results are presented in section 6 and error analysis in section 7.

2 Related work

The bulk of research on automatic question generation from text takes one of two basic approaches: transforming sentences into questions using various intermediate representations, or generating questions from predefined templates, where the appropriate template for each question is selected based on analysis of the text. In both approaches, the analysis of text plays a major role. Text analysis is focused on primarily syntax-based methods or more semantics-based methods.

Syntax-based methods apply a parser to determine the syntactic structure of a sentence, then apply syntactic transformation rules and question word placement (e.g., "where"). The earliest such system was proposed by Wolfe (1976). Contemporary systems use constituent and dependency parsing (Heilman and Smith, 2010a; Varga and Ha, 2010; Kalady et al., 2010; Ali et al., 2010). Yao et al. (2012) proposed a system based on HPSG parsing with semantic analysis. A recent

Proceedings of the Thirteenth Workshop on Innovative Use of NLP for Building Educational Applications, pages 254–263
New Orleans, Louisiana, June 5, 2018. ©2018 Association for Computational Linguistics

example of the syntax-based approach is the system of Danon and Last (2017).

Semantics-based methods place greater emphasis on semantic analysis of texts, although they typically also use some syntactic analysis. Huang and He (2016) present an AQG system that uses the Lexical Functional Grammar representation, including syntactic and semantic layers. Araki et al. (2016) present a study of AQG from richly annotated sources. Many AQG systems rely on semantic role labeling as the main driver of linguistic analysis (Rodrigues et al., 2016; Mazidi and Tarau, 2016; Mazidi and Nielsen, 2015; Lindberg et al., 2013; Mannem et al., 2010), or as a supporting subsystem (Huang and He, 2016).

With recent advances in neural networks, some approaches forgo most linguistic analysis and train neural networks to generate questions from sequences of word tokens (Du et al., 2017; Serban et al., 2016). Using large quantities of paired texts and human-generated questions and the encoder-decoder neural network framework, these systems learn to map from sentences to questions in a manner similar to neural machine translation approaches. Further detail on neural network systems for question generation and the specific benchmark system we use is provided in Section 4.

2.1 Common issues in AQG research

Most research on AQG systems needs to address the following set of common issues: 1) content selection; 2) target identification; 3) simplification; 4) question formulation, and 5) evaluation.

Content selection refers to picking sections of the source text (typically single sentences) for which questions should be generated, i.e. what parts of the text are worth asking a question about (Vanderwende, 2008). Prior research embraced the working assumption that content selection should focus on the most important and salient information in a text. Hence, some AQG systems used automatic extractive summarization for sentence selection (Becker et al., 2012; Agarwal and Mannem, 2011). Recently, Du and Cardie (2017) described a neural architecture for the content selection task in AQG.

Target selection defines what exactly should be asked about the selected content. For example, given a sentence like *The executive arrived at 5pm in a black limousine*, we could ask who arrived,

when, or in what kind of vehicle. Clearly, a variety of questions can be posed, and their selection may heavily depend on the educational task, e.g. assisting in reading comprehension (Gates, 2008), writing literature reviews (Liu et al., 2012), learning online (Lindberg et al., 2013).

Simplification of text has two aspects. Texts often use complex and long sentences, but questions are rarely very long. For a human reader, shorter questions are easier to process. From the perspective of AQG, simplification of the original text is sometimes necessary for applying transformation or matching to predefined templates (Lindberg et al., 2013; Yao et al., 2012; Heilman and Smith, 2010a).

Question formulation involves the actual process of generating a question and producing the final surface-form realization. Systems differ widely in this respect. For factoid questions, syntactic transformations or semantic analysis are often sufficient for question formulation. Template-based methods allow asking questions that can go beyond the explicit information in a text (Mazidi and Tarau, 2016; Lindberg et al., 2013).

Evaluation of AQG systems is a complex task in itself. Common criteria for sentence-based questions are grammaticality (syntactic correctness), relevance to the input sentence, the variety of question types produced, and semantic appropriateness (Godwin and Piwek, 2016; Chali and Golestanirad, 2016; Heilman and Smith, 2010b). Lindberg et al. (2013) add the notion of learning value (pedagogical usefulness) for question evaluation. However, the pedagogical value of questions is tightly related to the goals of the question use (Mazidi and Nielsen, 2014).

3 SRL-based system

Our SRL-based AQG system uses a mostly standard NLP pipeline structure with the following steps: 1) tokenization and sentence boundary detection; 2) POS tagging; 3) detection of verbal groups; 4) semantic role labeling; 5) postprocessing; 6) question generation.

For POS-tagging we use OpenNLP.[1] We use the SENNA system (Collobert et al., 2011) for semantic role labeling, similar to some previous research in AQG (Mazidi and Nielsen, 2015; Lindberg et al., 2013).

---

[1] https://opennlp.apache.org

Given a sentence, SENNA produces semantic role labels according to the Propbank 1.0 specifications (Palmer et al., 2005). Verbs in a sentence are considered as predicates. Semantic roles include the generalized core arguments of verbs – labeled A0, A1, etc. – and a set of adjunct modifiers. Table 1 provides an overview.

Label	Role
A0	proto-agent (often grammatical subject)
A1	proto-patient (often grammatical object)
A2	instrument, attribute, benefactive, amount, etc.
A3	start point or state
A4	end point or state
AM-LOC	location
AM-DIR	direction
AM-TMP	time
AM-CAU	cause
AM-PNC	purpose
AM-MNR	manner
AM-EXT	extent
AM-DIS	discourse
AM-ADV	adverbial
AM-MOD	modal verb
AM-NEG	negation

Table 1: Semantic roles per PropBank 1.0 specification.

Detection of verbal groups. In an English language clause, a verbal group consists of the main lexical verb and its related modifiers – negation, auxiliary verbs, and modals (Palmer, 1987). A sentence with multiple clauses may have several verbal groups. The verbal group does not include the semantic roles or their fillers, although there is some overlap with the Propbank definitions, since Propbank includes Modal and Negation as semantic arguments. Our question generation system includes a rule-based module for detection and analysis of verbal groups in sentences. The module uses POS and lexical patterns to identify verbal groups and analyze tense, grammatical aspect, verb negation, modality, and grammatical voice (passive/active). All of this information is necessary for adequate formulation of questions.

Postprocessing. In the postprocessing step, we correct several issues in the SRL output. The SENNA system tends to assign the A1 role for subjects instead of A0. For example, for *John ar-*

rived today, 'John' is assigned A1. This also often happens for copula sentences, e.g. SENNA produces: $[_{A1}John]$ is $[_{A1}$ *a painter]*. Since we want to treat A1 assignments as direct objects, we automatically remap A1 in objectless clauses to a specially devised category, A01, which, for question generation, is treated the same as A0 arguments (i.e., as grammatical subjects).

Another step in postprocessing is linking the verbal group to the verb of the detected predicate. In the presence of auxiliary verbs, SENNA produces multiple analyses for the same chunk of text, and some of them are systematically incorrect. We are able to correct this by utilizing the separately detected verbal group. For example, for *Joe has sold his house*, SENNA produces both $[_{A0}$ *Joe]* $[_{Predicate}$ *has]* $[_{A1}$ *sold his house]* and $[_{A0}$ *Joe] has $[_{Predicate}$ *sold]* $[_{A1}$ *his house]* A verbal group would indicate that 'has' is an auxiliary of 'sold', and our system would pick up the second analysis.

3.1 Generating constituent questions

Constituent questions (CQ, a.k.a. *wh*-questions) are the most common type of question in AQG research. Semantic role labeling is a natural choice for CQ generation, since SRL basically analyzes a sentence into *who did what to whom, how and when*.... Producing CQ from SRL involves three main steps: a) focusing, b) producing the question word(s), and c) formulating the question.

Focusing. To generate a question for a predicate, we need to choose the focal argument – the argument about which the question will be asked. We create questions from all of the major arguments, and also for the following adjunct arguments:[2] AM-TMP, AM-MNR, AM-CAU, AM-LOC, AM-PNC, AM-DIR. The text of the chosen focal argument becomes the expected answer to the question.

Producing question words involves some intricate decisions. There are at least three broad issues: 1) selecting the appropriate question word for the semantic argument, 2) deciding on *What* vs. *Who*, and 3) handling prepositions.

Selecting the appropriate *wh*-word is aided by the identity of the focused argument. Manner (AM-MNR) invites *How* and location (AM-LOC) invites *Where*. However, the situation is not quite so simple. Consider, for example, semantic role

---

[2] Selecting question focus by semantic roles may be useful for user customization. For example one may wish to focus questions only on manner arguments, cause and purpose, etc.

A4, which is often used for the 'end point' of complex locative constructions. A sentence like *They can fly from here [A4 to any country]*, should generate a question with *Where*. However, a similar construction in *Antarctica doesn't belong [A4 to any country]* should not produce a *Where* question.

A major issue is deciding on whether to use *Who* or *What* (for subject, direct object, and some other cases). Currently we make a rule-based decision, based on examining the POS of the argument, presence of pronouns, a check in a large gazetteer of first and last person names (about 130K entries), and a lookup into a list of person-denoting words derived from WordNet supersenses[3] (Fellbaum, 1998) (e.g., *king, senator*, etc.). If the argument is a whole phrase, a careful analysis is required. For example, *king of the land* is a *Who*, but *a hat for a lady* is a *What*.

The complexity of generating adequate question words is well illustrated with the case of temporal arguments. It is not the case that everything tagged as AM-TMP can have a question with *When* generated for it. Essentially, an SRL designation of AM-TMP is too general. It does not distinguish between time points, durations, and sets (repetitive temporal specifications). (For detailed temporal nomenclature, see, for example, Verhagen et al. (2010)). This is the minimal distinction that is necessary for *When*-questions, as opposed to *How long* and *How often*. As an illustration, consider the following sentences:

1. [A0Peter] *called* [AM−TMP on Monday].

2. [A0Peter] *called* [AM−TMP for six hours].

3. [A0Peter] *called* [AM−TMP every day].

Their corresponding proper questions are: 1) *When did Peter call?* (A: on Monday); 2) *For how long did Peter call?* (A: for six hours); 3) *How often did Peter call?* (A: every day).

Inspired by research on rule-based handling of time-expressions (Chang and Manning, 2013; Strotgen and Gertz, 2010), we designed a rule-based algorithm for subclassification of temporal expressions. Prepositions in time expressions are major clues in this task. For example, 'every' and 'each' hint at *How often*, 'for' hints at *Duration*,

---

[3]Supersenses were also used for this pupose by prior systems, e.g., Huang and He (2016), Heilman and Smith (2010a).

while many other prepositions hint at a time point (or time range) description, which is asked about with *When*. Some prepositions of temporal expressions are retained to be used in the questions, for example *from/until Monday* → `from/until when?`, *for five minutes* → `for how long?`.

Prepositions are sometimes retained for the formation of question word-sequences also for non-temporal semantic arguments. For example *The bird sat on the branch* → `On what did the bird sit?`. The who/what distinction can appear in this context as well. For example: *They rely on him/it* → `On whom/what do they rely?`

For **question formation** we need to select and rearrange the remaining arguments of the predicate. While SRL is a type of semantic analysis, for question formulation we need at least approximate grammatical information, such as the subject and direct object of the clause. For example, for *[A0Danny] dropped [A1 the package]*, with a focus on 'the package', we need to introduce do-support: `What did Danny drop?`. In the current implementation, we presume A0 arguments are subjects and A1 arguments are direct objects. Question formation also checks whether the verbal group is in active or passive voice, to adjust the placing of auxiliary verbs. Presently we do not convert passive sentences into active-voice questions.

3.2 Generating Yes/No questions

We generate a simple yes/no question (YNQ) for every predicate that has a finite verb (thus excluding bare and to-infinitives, and gerunds). If a sentence contains multiple predicates, we generate multiple yes/no questions – one for each predicate.

First, the system selects from a clause all chunks that are role-fillers for the current predicate. Next, the sequential position of SRL arguments may need to be rearranged. For yes/no questions, the standard declarative word order (usually SOV) is preserved. Do-support is provided when needed, based on the analysis of the verbal group (constructions that do not require do-support include copular, modals, and cases when an auxiliary *be/have/do* is already present). Adjunct arguments may be moved relative to the main verb (e.g. *he quickly ate* → `did he eat quickly ?`).

Positivize. For the current application, yes/no questions are always posed in positive mode.

The analyzed verbal group of the predicate will have information about explicit negation of the main verb, including contracted negation, such as 'didn't' and 'couldn't'. The question generation process then avoids transferring the negation into the question, but it also registers that the correct answer is flipped from 'yes/no' to 'no/yes'. For example, from *Johnny didn't know the song*, we derive `Did Johnny know the song?` + Answer='no'. For the copula *The tea isn't sweet enough*, we derive `Is the tea sweet enough?` + Answer='no'.

4 Neural network benchmark system

The neural network system we used for comparison during evaluation is the LSTM-based system described by Du et al. (2017)[4]. The system is trained on a large corpus of question-answer pairs from Wikipedia. Given an input sentence, the system generates a question based on the encoded input and what the model has learned from the training data about plausible question content and form.

The network employs the encoder-decoder framework. An encoder network encodes an input sentence with a bidirectional LSTM. The network uses the encoded sentence to initialize a decoder network for question generation. The decoder generates a question token-by-token. At each time step t, the decoder employs a global bilinear attention mechanism (Luong et al., 2015) over the encoder representation, allowing the network to focus the encoded representation on tokens that are more salient for that time step. The network generates the next token using the decoder's state and the attention-weighted encoding of the input at t.

We use the sentence-oriented model[5] from Du et al. (2017), where only the input sentence is encoded. We use their code without modification.

We trained the network on the preprocessed version of the SQuAD dataset (Rajpurkar et al., 2016) provided by Du et al. (2017). SQuAD consists of 536 articles with more than 100,000 question-answer pairs generated by crowd workers. The corpus was processed with Stanford CoreNLP, and question-answer pairs without any non-stop words in common were filtered out. The model is trained on 80% of the data split at the article level.

The source vocabulary is 45,000 tokens and the target vocabulary is 28,000 tokens. Pretrained GloVe embeddings (Pennington et al., 2014) are used to initialize the token representations and are fixed during network training. The LSTM encoder used 2 layers with 600 dimensions. The decoder uses beam search with a beam size of 3. Of note, in Du et al.'s implementation, generated questions are post-processed by replacing any <UNK> tokens with the token from the input with the highest attention score.

5 Evaluation study

We evaluate the SRL and neural network systems' capacity to produce generally good questions, focusing only on question-generation capabilities. In this respect, our evaluation study differs from some previous studies in which the AQG system was tasked with performing both content selection (picking the 'important' sentences for which questions would be generated) and the question generation process itself. We believe that content selection depends very much on the goals of the educational task for which questions are generated, and should be seen as a separate task. For a similar perspective, see Rus et al. (2010).

Since our focus is on question generation for educational applications, we selected five expository texts. Three of the texts consist of several initial paragraphs from Wikipedia articles[6] and two are complete short articles from an educational website[7]. From those texts, we retained only declarative sentences that have at least five words and do not include conditional (if...then) clauses. Our corpus consists of 171 sentences, with a maximum sentence length of 50 tokens and an average of 17.

Both the neural and the SRL-based systems were tasked with generating questions for each of the 171 sentences.

The SRL-based system generated at least one question for 165 sentences and failed to provide an output for 6 sentences. Overall, the SRL-based system generated 890 questions, with an average of 5.4 questions per sentence. There are two reasons for this abundance. First, the system attempts to generate a yes/no question for each predicate in each sentence. As a result, it generated 236 yes/no questions. Next, the system attempts to generate a constituent question for almost every argument

---

[4]https://github.com/xinyadu/nqg

[5]Du et al. (2017) also propose a paragraph-oriented model.

[6]Fox (animal), Helsinki (city), and Celsius (scientist).

[7]beyondpenguins.ehe.osu.edu/stories-for-students

Sentence	Generated Question	Sys	GR	SEM	REL
The Senate was relocated to Vaasa, although some senators and officials remained in hiding in the capital.	Who remained in hiding in the capital?	SRL	5	5	3
The Sun's temperature is much too hot for anything alive.	What the Sun's temperature is for anything alive?	SRL	2.5	2.5	2
Deep below is a place called the magma chamber.	Did a place call the magma chamber?	SRL	4.5	1.5	2.5
The particles from the Sun also carry an electric charge.	Do the particles from the Sun carry an electric charge?	SRL	5	5	3
Dr. Philip Kyle is one of these scientists.	Who is one of the scientists that is one of the scientists?	NN	2	2	1.5
But the real wonder is inside the volcano's crater itself.	What is the real view of the planet?	NN	4.5	2	1
Other foxes such as fennec foxes, are not endangered.	What are some other animals that are not endangered?	NN	5	5	3

Table 2: Examples of sentences, generated questions and evaluation ratings (average of two raters).

of every predicate. If a sentence contains multiple predicates, even more questions are generated. The system generated 654 constituent questions.

The neural system generated one question for each of 169 sentences (and failed for two sentences). All questions generated by the system resemble constituent questions because the SQuAD dataset does not contain yes/no questions. We investigated whether it was possible to generate more than one question per sentence by retrieving hypotheses from the beam search, but the hypotheses are not fully formed and are small variants of the best question for each sentence.

5.1 Annotation

In total 1,060 questions were automatically generated for evaluation. The questions were annotated by two annotators with expertise in linguistic annotation of English Learning Arts materials and student-produced writing. Each question was rated on three scales: grammar, semantics and relevance.

The *grammar* scale is a five-point scale: 5) grammatically well-formed; 4) mostly well-formed, with slight problems; 3) has grammatical problems; 2) seriously disfluent; 1) severely mangled. The five-point *semantic* scale was intended to check to what extent the question 'understood' the semantics of the original sentence: 5) semantically adequate; 4) mostly semantically adequate, with slight problems; 3) has semantic problems; 2) serious misunderstanding of the original sentence; 1) severely mangled and makes no sense. The *relevance* scale was designed to check to what extent the generated question is about information that was conveyed in the original sentence. This scale had just four levels: 3) is about the sentence; 2) goes beyond the information in the sentence; 1) veers away, is unrelated to the sentence; 0) too mangled to make a reasonable judgment.

The annotators completed a training session with 272 questions that were generated from a separate set of texts.

Upon completion of training, the annotators received the 1060 questions of the main data set (with corresponding sentences, and access to original texts). Each annotator completed annotations individually. We measured inter-annotator agreement with Quadratically-weighted Kappa (QWK). Agreement was high: grammar = 0.75, semantics = 0.77, relevance = 0.48[8].

In our analysis we used the average ratings on each question for each of the categories. In addition, for each question we also computed a *total* rating, which is the sum of grammar, semantics, and relevance ratings. Samples of sentences with corresponding generated questions and ratings are presented in Table 2.

---

[8]The low agreement on relevance stemmed from the tendency of one of the annotators to lower the relevance rating to 0 when a question was 'mangled'.

6   Results

To estimate the quality of the various questions, we compared the average ratings for three groups of questions: yes/no and constituent questions from the SRL-based system (SRL-YNQ and SRL-CQ), and questions from the neural system (NN). We conducted ANOVA analyses for each of the three rating scales and for the total score (with Bonferrroni adjustment for pairwise contrasts). Results are presented in Table 3 and in Figure 1.

SRL-YNQ questions (n=236), are rated significantly higher than SRL-CQ (n=654), which, in turn, are rated significantly higher than questions from the neural system (n=169). All comparisons are statistically significant ($p < .001$), except for SRL-CQ vs. NN on grammar. In other words, the neural system-generated questions achieved a similar level of grammaticality judgment as the SRL system's constituent questions.

Scale	SRL-YNQ	SRL-CQ	NN
Grammar	4.32	3.89	3.75
Semantics	4.34	3.79	2.61
Relevance	2.75	2.52	1.65
Total	11.41	10.20	8.01

Table 3: Average ratings for SRL system yes/no questions (SRL-YNQ), constituent questions (SRL-CQ), and neural network questions (NN). *Total* is the sum of grammar, semantics, and relevance.

We also looked at the 163 sentences that have both a NN question and at least one SRL-CQ question. We picked the best scoring SRL-CQ question for each sentence (using total score values). The mean rating of the best SRL-CQ question per sentence is 12.2, while the mean rating of NN questions is 8.1. The difference is statistically significant (t-test, $p < .0001$). Thus, if we had to pick just one CQ question for each sentence, SRL-based questions are on average much better than NN-generated questions.

We also investigated to what extent the automatically generated questions might be potentially usable in a learning context (e.g. for reading comprehension assessment). We consider a *potentially useful* question to be one that has reasonably good grammar (rating ≥ 4), is semantically sensible in context (rating ≥ 4) and is relevant to the information conveyed in the text (rating ≥ 2). We operationalize these criteria with two measures. First, we look at what proportion of questions have a

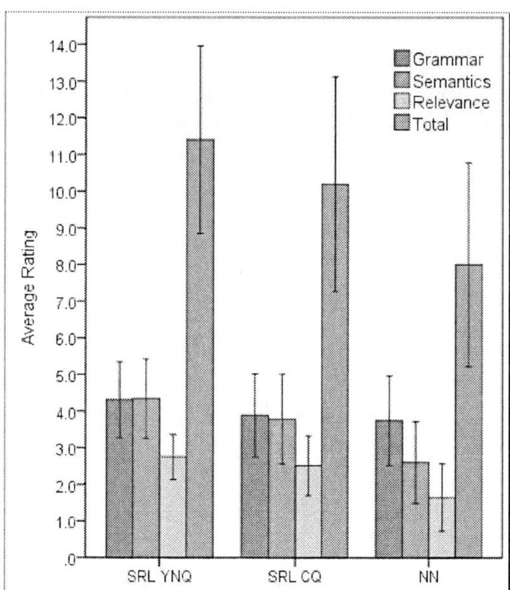

Figure 1: Average ratings and standard deviations for automatically generated questions, by system and question type. Note that score range is 1-5 for Grammar and Semantics, 0-3 for Relevance and 2-13 for Total.

total rating ≥ 10. Among the SRL-YNQ questions, 81% are potentially useful, compared to 64% among SRL–CQ questions, and 29% among questions generated by the neural network. Our second, more stringent, measure is to require that a question meet the criteria above on each of the three scales, i.e. grammar ≥ 4, semantics ≥ 4, and relevance ≥ 2. With this measure, the proportion of potentially useful questions is 71% for SRL-YNQ questions, 50% for SRL-CQ questions, and 15% for the neural network-generated questions.

7   Error analysis

We analyzed patterns of errors in SRL-based questions that received ratings below 4 on grammar and semantics and below 2 on relevance.

Among the constituent questions generated by the SRL-based system, we randomly sampled 30 questions. The most common reason for errors (33%) was incorrect handling of longer and more complicated sentences, including incorrect handling of arguments in subordinate clauses. For example, for the sentence *Red foxes have been introduced into Australia, which lacks similar carnivores...*, one of the generated questions was `What lacks?` This question misses the subject, *Australia*, which only appears in the matrix clause.

Incorrect handling of subordinate clauses is also one of the common reasons for errors among the SRL-based yes/no questions. For example, for the sentence *It's a little like the sound waves bats and dolphins use to find objects in the air and water.*, the system generated `Do bats and dolphins use to find objects in the air and water?`. The proper question should have been: `Do bats...use sound waves...to find...?`. The necessary direct object, *sound waves*, is outside the reduced relative clause and was missed in question generation.

7.1 Analysis of NN system errors

The patterns of ratings for errorful questions from the neural system differed from the SRL system. One pattern, of high grammaticality but low semantic coherence and relevance (22.7%), was attributable to strange substitutions of words in the original sentence. For example, for the sentence *Greater Helsinki has eight universities and six technology parks*, the generated question was: `How many universities does greater Strasbourg have?` Another common pattern was repetition of a word or phrase in the question. For example: `What type of birds do birds usually live?` Word repetition caused poor ratings on all scales. Another notable pattern was high grammaticality but low semantic coherence and relevance. This pattern is sometimes characterized by word substitutions but more generally a lack of analysis of the original sentence. For example, for the sentence *Despite the tumultuous first half of the 20th century, Helsinki continued to develop steadily*, the system generated: `When did the first half of the 20th century occur?`

We also analyzed a sample of sentences that were rated highly across all categories. Many of these sentences were simple declarative sentences. For the most part, the network reused words from the original sentence and created grammatical questions. In a few instances, the network gave hints of an ability to generalize lexical items. For example, for the sentence, *In fact, as the inside walls of the igloo start to melt, they come into contact with...*, the generated question was: `What do the walls of the igloo begin to do?`

8 Discussion

The SRL-based system generates a relatively high percentage of questions that are potentially usable as-is in an application, achieving good ratings for grammaticality, semantic coherence, and relevance. The SRL system was able to generate particularly high quality yes/no questions, as demonstrated by the strong scores from the human raters. Another strength demonstrated by the SRL-based system was the ability to systematically generate multiple constituent questions by focusing on each argument of a predicate in a clause.

The average quality of yes/no questions generated by the SRL system is significantly higher than the average quality of the generated constituent questions. The reason for this is mostly due to the fact that, while both types of questions are generated based on the same SRL analysis, yes/no questions require less complicated processing for generation.

While the questions produced by the SRL system show a promising level of quality, one area where the system falters is in handling long and complicated sentences, particularly those that involve subordinated clauses.

Although we did not focus on augmenting the neural network system for this study, our results demonstrate that the basic neural architecture of LSTM and attention already shows a surprising ability to produce readable questions, as indicated by reasonably high average grammaticality ratings. At the same time, the neural system had difficulty producing semantically adequate and relevant questions. These results point to the need for improved semantic analysis in neural AQG systems.

9 Conclusions

In this work, we described a novel rule-based system for automatic generation of factual questions from sentences that leverages semantic role labeling for text analysis and is capable of generating both *wh*-questions and yes/no questions from the same semantic analysis. Both of these capabilities are likely to prove useful in practical applications, for example to limit generated questions to only certain types of constituents or to generate questions of only certain forms. Another practical advantage of SRL-based AQG is that this approach produces questions with corresponding answers. This can be very useful for downstream applications such as quiz generators or automated scoring of responses.

We presented a detailed evaluation of the system and compared it to a state-of-the-art neural network architecture for question generation. The SRL-based system produced questions with greater variety and higher average quality than the neural system. In future work, we will explore methods for combining the strengths of rule-based and neural methods for text analysis and question generation.

Acknowledgments

Many thanks to our raters, Jennifer Wain and Jeremy Lee. The paper benefited much from the comments of three anonymous BEA reviewers and comments by Aoife Cahill, Ikkyu Choi, Beata Beigman Klebanov, and David Pautler.

References

Manish Agarwal and Prashanth Mannem. 2011. Automatic gap-fill question generation from text books. In *Proceedings of the 6th Workshop on Innovative Use of NLP for Building Educational Applications*, pages 56–64, Portland, OR, USA. Association for Computational Linguistics.

Husam Ali, Yllias Chali, and Sadid A. Hasan. 2010. Automation of question generation from sentences. In *Proceedings of QG2010: The Third Workshop on Question Generation*, pages 58–67.

Jun Araki, Dheeraj Rajagopal, Sreecharan Sankaranarayanan, Susan Holm, Yukari Yamakawa, and Teruko Mitamura. 2016. Generating questions and multiple-choice answers using semantic analysis of texts. In *Proceedings of COLING 2016, the 26th International Conference on Computational Linguistics: Technical Papers*, pages 1125?–1136. Association for Computational Linguistics.

Lee Becker, Sumit Basu, and Lucy Vanderwende. 2012. Mind the gap: Learning to choose gaps for question generation. In *Proceedings of the 2012 Conference of the North American Chapter of the Association for Computational Linguistics: Human Language Technologies*, pages 742–751, Montréal, Canada. Association for Computational Linguistics.

Yllias Chali and Sina Golestanirad. 2016. Ranking automatically generated questions using common human queries. In *Proceedings of The 9th International Natural Language Generation conference*, pages 217–?231. Association for Computational Linguistics.

Angel Chang and Christopher D. Manning. 2013. SUTime: Evaluation in TempEval-3. In *Second Joint Conference on Lexical and Computational Semantics (*SEM), Volume 2: Proceedings of the Seventh International Workshop on Semantic Evaluation (SemEval 2013)*, pages 78–82, Atlanta, Georgia, USA. Association for Computational Linguistics.

Ronan Collobert, Jason Weston, Leon Bottou, Michael Karlen, Koray Kavukcuoglu, and Pavel Kuksa. 2011. Natural language processing (almost) from scratch. *The Journal of Machine Learning Research*, 2011:2493–2537.

Guy Danon and Mark Last. 2017. A syntactic approach to domain-specific automatic question generation. In *linguisarXiv:1712.09827v1*.

Xinya Du and Claire Cardie. 2017. Identifying where to focus in reading comprehension for neural question generation. In *Proceedings of the 2017 Conference on Empirical Methods in Natural Language Processing*, pages 2067–2073, Copenhagen, Denmark. Association for Computational Linguistics.

Xinya Du, Junru Shao, and Claire Cardie. 2017. Learning to ask: Neural question generation for reading comprehension. In *Proceedings of the 55th Annual Meeting of the Association for Computational Linguistics (Volume 1: Long Papers)*, pages 1342–1352, Vancouver, Canada. Association for Computational Linguistics.

Chrisiane Fellbaum, editor. 1998. *WorNet: an electronic lexical database*. The MIT Press, Cambridge, MA, USA.

Donna M. Gates. 2008. Generating look-back strategy questions from expository texts. In *The Workshop on the Question Generation Shared Task and Evaluation Challenge*, Arlington, VA, USA.

Keith Godwin and Paul Piwek. 2016. Collecting reliable human judgements on machine-generated language: The case of the qg-stec data. In *Proceedings of The 9th International Natural Language Generation conference*, pages 212?–216. Association for Computational Linguistics.

Michael Heilman and Noah A Smith. 2010a. Good question! Statistical ranking for question generation. In *Proceedings of the 2010 Annual Conference of the North American Chapter of the Association for Computational Linguistics*, pages 609–?617. Association for Computational Linguistics.

Michael Heilman and Noah A Smith. 2010b. Rating computer-generated questions with mechanical turk. In *In Proceedings of the NAACL HLT 2010 Workshop on Creating Speech and Language Data with Amazon?s Mechanical Turk*, pages 35?–40. Association for Computational Linguistics.

Yan Huang and Lianzhen He. 2016. Automatic generation of short answer questions for reading comprehension assessment. *Natural Language Engineering*, 22(3):457–489.

Saidalavi Kalady, Ajeesh Elikkottil, and Rajarshi Das. 2010. Natural language question generation using syntax and keywords. In *Proceedings of QG2010: The Third Workshop on Question Generation*, pages 1–10.

David Lindberg, Fred Popowich, John Nesbit, and Philip Winne. 2013. Generating natural language questions to support learning on-line. In *Proceedings of the 14th European Workshop on Natural Language Generation*, pages 105?–114. Association for Computational Linguistics.

Ming Liu, Rafael A. Calvo, and Vasile Rus. 2012. G-asks: an intelligent automatic question generation system for academic writing support. *Dialogue and Discourse*, 3(2):101–124.

Thang Luong, Hieu Pham, and Christopher D. Manning. 2015. Effective approaches to attention-based neural machine translation. In *Proceedings of the 2015 Conference on Empirical Methods in Natural Language Processing*, pages 1412–1421, Lisbon, Portugal. Association for Computational Linguistics.

Prashanth Mannem, Rashmi Prasad, and Aravind Joshi. 2010. Question generation from paragraphs at UPenn: QGSTEC system description. In *Proceedings of QG2010: The Third Workshop on Question Generation*, pages 84–91.

Karen Mazidi and Rodney D Nielsen. 2014. Pedagogical Evaluation of Automatically Generated Questions. In Stefan Trausan-Maru, Kristy Elizabeth Boyer, Martha Crosby, and Kitty Panourgia, editors, *Proceededngs of the 12th international conference on Intelligent Tutoring Systems*, pages 294–299. Springer, Honolulu, HI, USA.

Karen Mazidi and Rodney D Nielsen. 2015. Leveraging multiple views of text for automatic question generation. In TBD, editor, *Artificial Intelligence in Education, LNCS*, pages 0–0. Springer, TBD.

Karen Mazidi and Paul Tarau. 2016. Infusing nlu into automatic question generation. In *Proceedings of The 9th International Natural Language Generation conference*, pages 51?–60. Association for Computational Linguistics.

Frank R. Palmer. 1987. *The English Verb*, 2nd edition. Longman, London, UK.

Martha Palmer, Daniel Gildea, and Paul Kingsbury. 2005. The proposition bank: An annotated corpus of semantic roles. *Computational Linguistics*, 31(1):71?106.

Jeffrey Pennington, Richard Socher, and Christopher D. Manning. 2014. Glove: Global Vectors for Word Representation. In *Empirical Methods in Natural Language Processing (EMNLP)*, pages 1532–1543.

Pranav Rajpurkar, Jian Zhang, Konstantin Lopyrev, and Percy Liang. 2016. Squad: 100,000+ questions for machine comprehension of text. In *Proceedings of the 2016 Conference on Empirical Methods in Natural Language Processing*, pages 2383–2392, Austin, Texas. Association for Computational Linguistics.

Hugo Rodrigues, Luisa Coheur, and Eric Nyberg. 2016. Qgasp: a framework for question generation based on different levels of linguistic information. In *Proceedings of The 9th International Natural Language Generation conference*, pages 242?–243. Association for Computational Linguistics.

Vasile Rus1, Brendan Wyse, Paul Piwek, Mihai Lintean, Svetlana Stoyanchev, and Cristian Moldovan. 2010. Overview of The First Question Generation Shared Task Evaluation Challenge. In *Proceedings of QG2010: The Third Workshop on Question Generation*, pages 45–57.

Iulian Vlad Serban, Alberto Garcia-Duran, Caglar Gulcehre, Sungjin Ahn, Sarath Chandar, Aaron Courville, and Yoshua Bengio. 2016. Generating factoid questionswith recurrent neural networks: The 30m factoid question-answer corpus. In *Proceedings of the 54th Annual Meeting of the Association for Computational Linguistics*, pages 588?–598. Association for Computational Linguistics.

Jannik Strotgen and Michael Gertz. 2010. Heideltime: High quality rule-based extraction and normalization of temporal expressions. In *Proceedings of the 5th International Workshop on Semantic Evaluation*, pages 321–324, Uppsala, Sweden. Association for Computational Linguistics.

Lucy Vanderwende. 2008. The importance of being important: Question generation. In *Workshop on the Question Generation, Shared Task and Evaluation Challenge*, pages 1342?–1352.

Andrea Varga and Le An Ha. 2010. WLV: A question generation system for the QGSTEC 2010, task b. In *Proceedings of QG2010: The Third Workshop on Question Generation*, pages 80–83.

Marc Verhagen, Roser Sauri, Tommaso Caselli, and James Pustejovsky. 2010. Semeval-2010 task 13: Tempeval-2. In *Proceedings of the 5th International Workshop on Semantic Evaluation*, pages 57–62, Uppsala, Sweden. Association for Computational Linguistics.

John H. Wolfe. 1976. Automatic question generation from text - an aid to independent study. *ACM SIGCUE Outlook*, 10:104–112.

Xuchen Yao, Gosse Bouma, and Yi Zhang. 2012. Semantics-based question generation and implementation. *Dialogue and Discourse*, 3(2):11–42.

Automated Content Analysis: A Case Study of Computer Science Student Summaries

Yanjun Gao[1], **Patricia M. Davies**[2], and **Rebecca J. Passonneau**[1]

[1]Department of Computer Science and Engineering, Penn State University
[1]*{yug125,rjp49}@cse.psu.edu*
[2]Department of Computer Science, University of Wolverhampton
[2]*Patrica.Davies@wlv.ac.uk*

Abstract

Technology is transforming Higher Education learning and teaching. This paper reports on a project to examine how and why automated content analysis could be used to assess précis writing by university students. We examine the case of one hundred and twenty-two summaries written by computer science freshmen. The texts, which had been hand scored using a teacher-designed rubric, were autoscored using the Natural Language Processing software, PyrEval. Pearsons correlation coefficient and Spearman rank correlation were used to analyze the relationship between the teacher score and the PyrEval score for each summary. Three content models automatically constructed by PyrEval from different sets of human reference summaries led to consistent correlations, showing that the approach is reliable. Also observed was that, in cases where the focus of student assessment centers on formative feedback, categorizing the PyrEval scores by examining the average and standard deviations could lead to novel interpretations of their relationships. It is suggested that this project has implications for the ways in which automated content analysis could be used to help university students improve their summarization skills.

1 Situating Automated Content Analysis in Higher Education

Our present concerns are about CS students having difficulty summarizing or synthesizing texts accurately. Instead of staying focused, some tend to wander away from significant points in written reports. There are also issues relating to CS instructors wasting valuable time on badly written reports, especially in cases when class sizes are very large (with 150 to 250 students). This often results in students not receiving meaningful feedback that could help them to advance their learning. Increasing the availability and quality of timely feedback could significantly improve students' written-communication skills.

The focus of this study is to investigate how PyrEval (Gao et al., 2018a), an existing summary content analysis software tool, might be used to automate the assessment of student summaries, given a small set of reference summaries from which to construct a content model. Scores from an earlier implementation of automated pyramid scoring were shown to have high Pearson correlation of 0.83 with a main ideas rubric applied to 120 community college summaries (Passonneau et al., 2016); on the same summaries PyrEval has even higher correlation of 0.87. As such, the aim is not to examine its correctness here; instead, we seek to understand how it could be adapted for use within Higher Education (HE). In particular, we are interested in exploring how PyrEval might be used for <u>formative</u>, rather than <u>summative</u>, assessment of student work. With this view, the discussions here focus on PyrEval as a tool for helping students to improve written assignments prior to submission, thereby making the time instructors spend marking more beneficial.

Learning in HE, often described as constructivist, involves learners actively constructing knowledge and meaning based on prior experiences (Barr and Tagg, 1995; Bostock, 1998; Brockbank and McGill, 2007; Tess, 2013). In this approach, students create knowledge by connecting what they already know to new subject content encountered in lectures, texts and discussions. This shift in paradigm, from one where the learner retrieves information from the instructors, has prompted recently coined phrases such as, self-directed learning (Hiemestra, 1994) and student-centered learning (Lea et al., 2003). Unfortunately, assessing students' self-directed learning, and providing formative feedback in this learning

Proceedings of the Thirteenth Workshop on Innovative Use of NLP for Building Educational Applications, pages 264–272
New Orleans, Louisiana, June 5, 2018. ©2018 Association for Computational Linguistics

approach, has not developed as rapidly.

Feedback is intended to provide students with information on their current state of learning and performance, and is essential for elevating students' motivation and confidence (Hyland, 2000). Rather than being an evaluation of performance on assigned tasks, formative feedback provides information to help students scaffold their knowledge and accelerate their learning (Sadler, 2010). Therefore, formative assessment applications play an important role by helping students take greater control of their own learning, and moves them towards becoming self-regulated learners.

Within HE, formative feedback is perceived as information communicated to the students about learning-oriented assignments (Race, 2001) such as essays. This feedback can be oral or written, and is often generated by the instructor. Providing feedback remains the responsibility of the instructor, and with much emphasis being placed on evaluating student learning at the end of an instructional unit, instructor feedback is often limited. Some even use custom software, such as E-rater®, used by the Educational Testing Service for automated scoring of essays, which provides a holistic score rather than a narrative. Our present concerns move beyond simply providing a score to examine how and why PyrEval could be used to provide formative feedback on students' summaries. It is distinctive in providing interpretable scores that can be justified by automated identification of important, unimportant and missing content (Passonneau et al., 2016). This study provides a conceptualization for the next steps in the development of the tool towards this end.

The next three sections present the following: background to the study through a review of existing literature; a summarization task given to CS students at a UK university along with a description of how it was assessed by the instructor, one of the authors PyrEval, an automated tool to analyze content of summaries that depends on a reference set of four or more expert summaries.

Section 5 presents our experiments to compare PyrEval scores of the students' summaries with scores assigned by the human scorer using a rubric. The findings show that PyrEval scores correlate moderately well with the rubric, but more importantly, the analysis led to reconsideration of scores for several summaries. Section 6 discusses the benefits and limitations of the automated tool,

and our plans for future work.

2   Related Work

Summarization is an important pedagogical tool for teaching reading and writing strategies in elementary school (Kırmızı, 2009), middle school (Graham and Perin, 2007), community college (Perin et al., 2013), as part of blended instructional methods at the college level (Yang, 2014), and for English language learners (Babinski et al., 2017). Instruction in summarization strategies includes occasional forays into computer-based training (Sung et al., 2008), including intelligent tutoring systems that provide writing practice (Proske et al., 2012)(Roscoe et al., 2015).

Recent work built regression models to predict scores based on several rubrics for summaries from L2 business school students (Sladoljev Agejev and Šnajder, 2017). Features were automatically derived from Coh-Metrix (McNamara et al., 2014), BLEU scores (Papineni et al., 2002) and ROUGE scores (Lin, 2004). In (Srihari et al., 2008), OCR was used to digitize handwritten essays, which were then scored using various automated essay scoring methods, including latent semantic analysis and a feature-based approach. Essays are automatically scored in (Zupanc and Bosni, 2017) after constructing an ontology from model essays using information extraction and logic reasoning. PyrEval constructs a content model from a small set of reference summaries, using latent semantic vectors to represent meanings of phrases.

There has been recent interest in developing automated revision tools for students' written work but none have, hitherto, been reported in the literature. There is existing work on automated revision of short answers for middle school science writing (Tansomboon et al., 2017), and a corpus on automated revision of argumentation (Zhang et al., 2017). What is distinctive about our work is the feasibility of providing automated feedback on summary content, either for teachers or students, which could ultimately lead to the development of an automated revision tool.

3   Task and Educational Rubrics

3.1   The student setting and their task

At the start of this academic year, 159 CS students were enrolled in Academic Skills and Team-based Learning at Bakersview University (a pseudonym)

Scoring rubric

Item	Description of Idea
1	Dont take everything you read for granted. Always ask - says who? so what? what next?
2	Check if the references are accurate.
3	Check the authors' qualifications and experience (academic and practice), and what qualifies them to undertake this work. See if they have published any other works and if they have been cited by others.
4	If they have, it is worthwhile checking out some of those citations to see if they are positive or negative.
5	Check for evidence of how this information could have, or has, had an impact.
6	Ensure the data is provided to back up any arguments.
7	Understand how this information affects what you already know.
8	Check if there any consequences of this information that show the need for further research.
9	Critical thinking helps you identify potential strengths and weaknesses in the text.
10	Critical thinking helps you evaluate what you read and relate it to other information.

Figure 1: Scoring rubric for *Critical Thinking* task. Each of 10 items contributes 1 point.

in the UK. Bakersview is a non-selective university with an agenda to widen participation in higher education, and thus attracts students from a variety of learning backgrounds. Academic Skills and Team-based Learning is a core course taken by all CS freshmen. It aims to develop in students a range of written communication styles and approaches, and the critical reading skills, needed for academic and professional work. The goal is to give these students the opportunity to develop proficiencies and attitudes necessary for success at university and in employment.

The data being used for the present project came from student submissions for one of the assignments in the Academic Skills and Team-based Learning course. First, the students were asked to attend a workshop offered by the university's Library and Information Services. The focus of the workshop was finding information and critical thinking. Presentations and handouts were provided, and students were asked to make notes on the material covered. Following the workshop, they were asked to summarize, in no more than 200 words, what they learned during the workshop about critical thinking and its importance in HE.

3.2 The rubric

One hundred and thirty-nine summaries were submitted. These were then scored by hand using a rubric developed from the presentation given during the workshop. The 10 main points identified in the presentation were used as checkpoints in the rubric, which is shown in Figure 1.

One point was assigned to each of the ideas listed in the rubric; however, the interpretation of what constituted an idea was open to the discretion of the instructor. Each student received a score out of 10 for the assignment. A handful of student summaries did not meet the word-

count requirement, these were not included in the anonymized samples for testing the autoscoring software PyrEval. Thirteen summaries, which received scores of 9 and 10, were used as reference summaries to construct a content model for interpretable scores, and the score justification.

4 System Description

PyrEval constructs a pyramid content model that consists of sets of distinct summary content units (SCUs) found in a set of N reference summaries written by experts or more advanced students, for $4 \leq N \leq 6$. In pyramid summary content evaluation, originally a manual annotation method, an SCU is similar to a set of paraphrases, each paraphrase drawn from a distinct reference summary (Nenkova et al., 2007). A given SCU can be expressed in anywhere from 1 to N summaries, so will consist of from 1 to N contributors from distinct summaries. The number of contributors to an SCU is an importance weight that is assigned to ideas in a new summary being scored. The weights of SCUs in a new summary are summed, and the sum is normalized in different ways, as described further below. A pyramid content model thus consists of all the distinct ideas, or SCUs, in the reference summaries, along with their weights.

To construct the pyramid content model automatically, sentences are first decomposed into distinct clausal or phrasal segments, then each segment is converted to a dense vector representation using Weighted Text Matrix Factorization (WTMF) (Guo et al., 2014). These semantic vectors are then grouped into semantically similar sets to form the SCUs, using a restricted set partition algorithm, EDUA, as noted below (Gao et al., 2018b). A new summary is scored against this content model by first segmenting the sentences and vectorizing them, then matching them to the content model using a weighted set cover algorithm (Sakai et al., 2003). The following subsections describe the preprocessing (segmentation and conversion to dense vectors), pyramid construction, and scoring.

4.1 Preprocessing

The preprocessing step uses a sentence decomposition parser we implemented to produce alternative covering segmentations of each sentence, and WTMF (see above) to produce the dense vector representations. This is a pre-trained process so as to make PyrEval a light-weight tool that can be applied easily to new summarization tasks. The decomposition parser output is derived from constituency parsing and dependency parsing, using Stanford CoreNLP tools (Chen and Manning, 2014). The decomposition parser first locates every tensed verb phrase (VP) in the constituency parse, then uses the subject dependencies from the dependency parser to find each VP subject. The leftover words are reinserted into segments, according to their positions in the original sentence. We use WTMF to convert each segment into a vector representation for semantic similarity evaluation. It has proved to have high accuracy in sentence similarity tasks.

Sentence Decomposition Example

Critical thinking also means you must approach everything you read with a certain level of scepticism and find out if the points that are being made are backed up with evidence.	
Segmentation 1	
Segment 1	that are being made
Segment 2	you read with a certain level of scepticism
Segment 3	if the points are backed up with evidence
Segment 4	you must approach everything and find out
Segment 5	Critical thinking also means .
Segmentation 2	
Segment 1	you Critical thinking also means you must approach everything read with a certain level of scepticism and find out if the,
Segment 2	points that are being made
Segment 3	points are backed up with evidence .

Figure 2: Sentence decomposition parser output showing two alternative segmentations of the same sentence. The full sentence is also considered as a default segmentation.

4.2 Pyramid Construction

The core of PyrEval is an algorithm, *Emergent Discovery of Units of Attraction (EDUA)*, for allocating segments into SCUs according to their semantic similarity.

EDUA builds a graph G where vertices are segments and edges are semantic similarity above a threshold t_{edge}. Similarity values are distributed differently for different sets of summaries, so we define t_{edge} in terms of a selected percentile over the range of observed cosine values for a given set of reference summaries; from past work through grid-search on development sets we use $t_{edge} = 0.83$. An SCU is a connected component of G with at most N vertices, where the average edge weight leads to a high quality pyramid. The quality of an individual SCU is the average similarity (or attraction A_C) of its edges. Given a connected component C with k edges, A_C is defined as:

$$A_C = \frac{\sum_{u,v \in C, u \neq v} similarity(u, v)}{k} \qquad (1)$$

The global attraction over the pyramid is given as:

$$A_P = \max \sum_1^n \left(\frac{1}{|C_n|} \sum_1^{|C_n|} A_C \right) \qquad (2)$$

where n here represents the number of reference summaries, which in turn corresponds to the different sizes of SCUs in the pyramid.

EDUA's objective is to find a set of connected components (SCUs) that achieve the highest A_P, while obeying the constraints that no two segments from the same reference summary can be in the same SCU. We have developed two versions of the algorithm: EDUA-Complete (EDUA-C) and EDUA-Greedy (EDUA-G). EDUA-C performs a Depth First Search in the graph to find the set of SCUs with maximum A_P. EDUA-G takes a greedy approach and imposes a constraint based on the observation that SCU annotation follows a Zipfian distribution (Nenkova et al., 2007): there are a few SCUs that occur in every reference summary (maximum weight), more that occur in all but one, and so on, with a long tail of SCUs that occur in only one reference summary (minimum weight). SCU weight forms a partition over the set of SCUs. EDUA-G finds the SCUs with maximum A_C at each iteration n from N to 1, and allocates them into equivalence class n until the capacity of that class is full, then moves on to the next n. A constraint on the relative size of the equivalence classes requires them to adhere to a Zipfian distribution. Both EDUA variants perform equally well on a machine summarization task (Gao et al., 2018b). However, EDUA-C is computationally expensive. Hence we conducted experiments using EDUA-G.

Pair	Pearson(P-v)	Spearman(P-v)	Pair	Pearson(P-v)	Spearman(P-v)
P_1,R	46.47 (6.88e-08)	44.27 (3.28e-07)	P_1,P_2	73.82 (9.09e-23)	73.50 (1.70e-22)
P_2,R	49.18 (8.75e-09)	46.13 (8.893-08)	P_1,P_t	68.02 (2.69e-18)	68.63 (1.02e-18)
P_t,R	45.85 (1.39e-07)	44.77 (2.95e-07)	P_2,P_t	75.97 (9.67e-25)	77.33 (4.21e-26)

Table 1: Pearson correlation ($\rho \times 100$) and Spearman rank correlation ($r_s \times 100$) of PyrEval scores with rubric R (left columns), and with other PyrEval scores (right columns) given different pyramids. P-values are in parentheses.

4.3 Scoring

For matching segments from a summary to a pyramid, PyrEval applies WMIN, a weighted independent set allocation algorithm (Sakai et al., 2003). The scoring algorithm has proven its reliability to have good correlation with human annotation (Passonneau et al., 2016).

The input to WMIN consists of the vector representations of all segmentations produced by the decomposition parser for each sentence in a new summary. Vertices in the WMIN graph are matches between an SCU and a segment from a new summary, weighted by the product of the SCU weight and the mean cosine similarity of the summary vector to the SCU vectors; we use 0.5 as the similarity threshold (Passonneau et al., 2016). The objective is to find an assignment of SCUs to the new summary that produces the highest sum of SCU weights. WMIN ensures that no SCU is allocated more than once to a summary, and that segments are not allocated from different segmentations of the same sentence.

Four scores are reported by PyrEval: Raw score, quality, coverage and comprehensive. Given a student summary, the raw score is calculated by the sum of all matched content units with their weights. For the quality score, the raw sum is normalized by the maximum sum that the pyramid could assign to the same number of SCUs, using each pyramid SCU no more than once. The coverage score normalizes the raw score by the maximum sum the pyramid could assign given the average number of SCUs in a reference summary. The comprehensive score is the average of the quality and coverage scores.

5 Experiments and Results

5.1 Correlations with Teacher Scores

To see how PyrEval performs in an educational context, we ran PyrEval on the student summaries and compared the resulting scores to those assigned by the instructor. Five of the 136 summaries had received a perfect score of 10 from the instructor; eight additional summaries were nearly as good, each with a score of 9. These, together with a model summary written by the instructor, were used in PyrEval to generate three different pyramid content models as follows: P_1 uses a random selection of six of the thirteen highest-scoring student summaries, and P_2 uses the remaining seven. P_t consists of the five student summaries with perfect scores combined with the instructor's summary. The remaining 122 student summaries are targets to PyrEval scoring.

As shown in Table 1, the highest Pearson correlation between PyrEval scores and the instructor's scores (P_n, R) is 49%, with an average of 47%. The highest Spearman rank correlation is 46%, with an average of 45%. Pyramid model P_t does not show a significant advantage over P_1 and P_2.

Rubrics *Critical thinking helps you identify potential strengths and weaknesses in the text.*
SCU1   5   Critical thinking is the exercise of questioning the material, identifying its strengths and weaknesses and understanding what this changes about your knowledge. SCU1   5   thinking Critical is crucial for academic writing , as it ensures all text read is respected and understood , analysed in depth to identify strengths and weaknesses, evaluated and used to compare to other sources of information. SCU1   5   Critical thinking is the process of understanding , interpreting and questioning the subject at hand, identifying potential strengths and weaknesses within the text. SCU1   5   you To effectively identify the utility of the text , must not trust what is being said; instead evaluating and extracting its strengths , weaknesses and main points. SCU1   5   Critical thinking is about finding your strength and weaknesses in a text, evaluating summarising.

Figure 3: An SCU (SCU1, Wt=5) matched with one rubric checkpoint (See textbox in the top). The SCU format is: SCU_{index}, $Weight$, $Segment$. The segments with the same index belong to the same SCU.

5.2 Quality of Pyramid and Scoring

We examined the quality of pyramid content models built by PyrEval by comparing the 10 ideas in the rubric with high-weighted SCUs from pyramid

P_t, since it includes the instructor's summary.

Rubrics		Don't take everything you read for granted. Always ask —says who, so what? what next?
SCU5	4	for you to evaluate
SCU5	4	Critical thinking involves objective analysis and evaluation.
SCU5	4	thinking involves the evaluation of sources and the ability to extract only the useful information from it
SCU5	4	that students must assess and criticise all work to determine its potential merits and shortcomings before deciding whether to include it in their own work
SCU6	4	In thinking critically , you should always ask: says who, so what and.
SCU6	4	The work in question must be evaluated in respect to one s.
SCU6	4	Critical thinkers should always find answers to these three questions:.
SCU6	4	they have a possible bias, and are these recent Another step in critical thinking

Figure 4: Two SCUs (SCU 5, SCU 6, Wt=4) conveying the same meaning as a rubric checkpoint.

According to the rubric, a perfect score would be 10. With six reference summaries in P_t, the highest weight for an SCU is 6. The important SCUs are those with weights in $[\frac{n}{2},n]$. There are sixteen SCUs with weights greater than 2 generated by PyrEval. Table 2 shows the distribution

Weights	6	5	4	3
Number of SCUs	1	2	4	9

Table 2: Distribution of high-weighted SCUs.

of SCUs associated with different weights. The highest score one could obtain by mentioning all important ideas is 59.

SCU2	5	you read
SCU2	5	what you know
SCU2	5	what you know
SCU2	5	what you read and relate it to other information
SCU2	5	what A text should have information
SCU8	3	what next Check
SCU8	3	What next Are there any points uncovered, critical .
SCU8	3	what is next.

Figure 5: 2 SCUs (SCU 2 and SCU 8) that are less informative.

Next, we focus on comparing the SCUs to the rubric. As seen in Figure 3, PyrEval generates some SCUs that convey the same meaning as the rubric. Figure 4 shows an example SCU from pyramid P_t that corresponds to item 1 in the rubric (cf. Figure 1).

SCU3	4	Critical thinking helps .
SCU3	4	Critical thinking is crucial for academic writing.
SCU3	4	Critical Thinking is to not take everything .
SCU3	4	To be able to think critical

Figure 6: The content in SCU 3 is not included in rubric.

There are some cases when PyrEval produces SCUs based on segments that are too short; these SCUs are actually less informative. In Figure 5, the content of SCU 2 serves as a object in sentences: *...a judgment should be made on if the new information has affected what you know or* ... and SCU 8 is used as transition in the original statement.

We also identified one high-weight SCU not being matched with any checkpoints in rubric. See Figure 6.

Segment: 3 I Content Unit: 1 [Weight: 5]
Segment: .... so any strengths and weaknesses are identified through the evaluation of information and comparison with other sources
Matched Content Unit: *Contributor...........* (1) are they cited by others within the selected discipline is to systematically identify weaknesses and strengths in the various sources ; Does Are they able to give testable verifiable evidence of   *Contributor...........* (2) you identify potential strengths and weaknesses in the text   *Contributor ....* (3) Always it is important to identify the potential strengths and weaknesses from a text and to look for evidence .   *Contributor ....* (4) all text read is respected and understood , analysed in depth to identify strengths and weaknesses , evaluated and used to compare to other sources of information   *Contributor ....* (5) you To effectively identify the utility of the text , must not trust what is being said ; instead evaluating and extracting its strengths , weaknesses and main points .

Figure 7: An scoring example. The first line of top textbox indicates segment 3 from student summary matched with content unit 1 in pyramid, with weight as 5. The second line is the text of student summary segment. The textbox in the bottom shows a matched content unit from pyramid model composed by 5 contributors, denoted as $Contributor, \ldots, Index, Content$.

Finally, Figure 7 shows a match between a segment from a student summary and an SCU. The content in this SCU also corresponds to checkpoint 9 in rubric, as shown in Figure 3.

5.3 Revising the SCUs

The observations mentioned above lead us to question whether some type of post-processing on the

Removal	Pearson (P-v)	Spearman (P-v)
(2, 8)	49.37 (7.52e-09)	48.75 (1.24e-08)
(2, 3, 8)	53.39 (2.40e-10)	52.89 (3.80e-08)

Table 3: Pearson correlations and Spearman correlation of PyrEval scores with teachers' scores after removing the problematic SCUs. SCUs (2, 8) are the uninformative SCUs; Adding SCU 3 includes an irrelevant SCU.

Method	Below Avg	Avg	Above Avg	Total
H	21	76	25	122
P	27	75	20	122
Overlap	8	50	10	68

Table 4: Agreements between H - human using rubric, and P - PyrEval

pyramid models would improve the correlation scores. To test this supposition, we manually removed the three uninformative high-weighted SCUs identified above, and ran the scoring based on the resulting adjusted pyramids.

Table 3 shows that both Pearson and Spearman correlations are improved after removal of uninformative SCUs (49%), or both uninformative and irrelevant SCUs (53%). These slight increases suggest that post-processing, such as removing irrelevant and uninformative SCUs using entropy, could help to improve the quality of a pyramid.

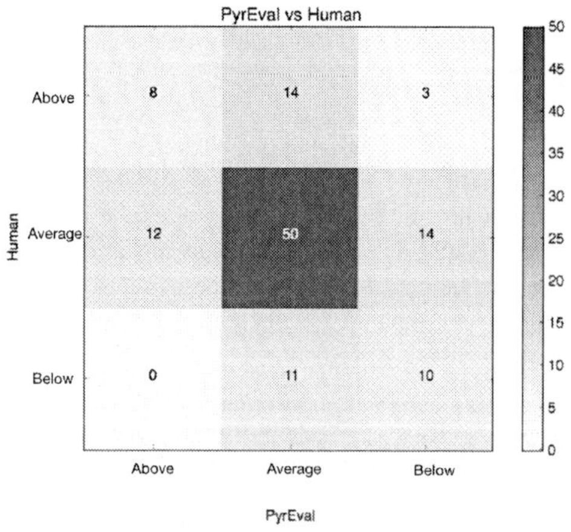

Figure 8: Confusion matrix of disagreements and agreements between human using rubric and PyrEval. Horizontal axis represents PyrEval and vertical axis represents human evaluation.

We took another approach by binning the scores into three ranges: below average, average and above average. Table 4 presents two distributions obtained from both the human and PyrEval scores that are almost identical, and the agreements between two sets of scores. The human and PyrEval scores identify 21 versus 27 student summaries as below average, 25 versus 20 as above average. There are 76 summaries marked as around average by human and 75 by PyrEval. However, among 122 summaries, 68 of these (over 55%) overlap in terms of where they fall in these newly defined categories. Both agreements and disagreements are distributed as shown in Figure 8. In the extreme disagreements, none of the summaries judged as below average by human are evaluated as above average by PyrEval. Additionally, only three summaries PyrEval regards as below average are considered above average by human. PyrEval and educators easily agree on summaries that fall within the medium range, but tend to disagree on both below average summaries and above summaries.

6 Potential Uses and Developments

The three different pyramids returned very similar Pearson and Spearman correlation coefficients. Although they all indicated a moderately positive relationship between the human and PyrEval scores, the similarity in their values led us to consider a different approach for examining the relationships.

The above classification demonstrates how PyrEval could be used accurately to distinguish between good and bad student summaries. In other words, it is highly unlikely that summaries judged to be below average by a human scorer would be regard as above average by PyrEval, and vice versa. As such, the three groupings - below average, average and above average - provide scope for filtering submissions being uploaded to an online repository as follows. Summaries in Group C (below average) are rejected outright, with feedback on what needs improving; those in Group B (average) are accepted and scored by PyrEval but, in addition, given some indication on how the score could be improved; those in Group A (above average) are accepted as ready to be hand scored by the instructor.

What needs to be addressed next is the type of feedback PyrEval might provide each summary, and how. It is possible for the tool to list details of

SCUs missing from the summary, thereby providing the opportunity for students to improve their work. This would make Pyreval very effective as a formative feedback tool, especially if the revised summaries were then resubmitted and checked via the same process. A future project could involve devising a way to provide students with text-based feedback, aimed at helping them address specific areas of concern relating to missing content.

PyrEval's potential for advancing student learning is not limited to helping students write better. It could also be used in ways that significantly cut down on the amount of marking instructors have to do. Using the classification above could mean that papers in Group A are hand scored by the instructor, with an assurance that such papers will include a high percentage of all of the ideas present in the rubric. In certain situations, depending on the assessment criteria, high quality submissions might not need to be hand scored at all. Similarly, those in Group C could be rejected outright, with feedback on how to the text should be improved. Those in Group B could be accepted with a warning about the maximum score attainable, say 70 percent. There could also be an opportunity for the summary to be improved and resubmitted.

There is need to examine the three summaries which the human scorer rated above average but PyrEval classed as below average. Reading these texts over, this time checking for clues that could shed light on the discrepancies, revealed that the human scorer was lenient in all three cases. The reassessment showed that these papers were particularly well written (fluent), even though they did not strictly meet the requirements of the assignment. Reading them might have brought some relief to the human scorer; for example, following a spate of poorly written summaries. It is therefore possible that extra effort was made to match sections of these text to the checkpoints in the rubric, albeit that these matches were not warranted. Human are susceptible to emotion and fatigue, which can in turn affect their scoring behavior while automated scoring will be consistent.

7 Conclusion

The present research project extends current knowledge about the uses of NLP in building educational applications by discussing PyrEval as a formative assessment tool. The discovery of a new typology has enabled us to begin to understand how student self-directed learning could be developed and, indeed, measured. This could have a direct impact on the assessment practices and policies within institutions and, ultimately, on increasing retention and progression in university courses.

A long-term goal is to develop a web-based application, which uses PyrEval to provide formative assessment feedback on student summaries. The ultimate aim is to extend the thematic scope of the research to include other courses, particularly STEM.

Acknowledgments

This work was partly supported by Penn State University's Teaching and Learning with Technology.

References

Leslie M. Babinski, Steven J. Amendum, Steven E. Knotek, Marta Sánchez, and Patrick Malone. 2017. Improving young english learners language and literacy skills through teacher professional development: A randomized controlled trial. *American Educational Research Journal*, 55(1):117–143.

Robert B Barr and John Tagg. 1995. From teaching to learninga new paradigm for undergraduate education. *Change: The magazine of higher learning*, 27(6):12–26.

Stephen J Bostock. 1998. Constructivism in mass higher education: a case study. *British journal of educational technology*, 29(3):225–240.

Anne Brockbank and Ian McGill. 2007. *Facilitating reflective learning in higher education*. McGraw-Hill Education (UK).

Danqi Chen and Christopher Manning. 2014. A fast and accurate dependency parser using neural networks. In *Proceedings of the 2014 Conference on Empirical Methods in Natural Language Processing (EMNLP)*, pages 740–750. Association for Computational Linguistics.

Yanjun Gao, Andrew Warner, and Rebecca J. Passonneau. 2018a. Pyreval: An automated method for summary content analysis. In *Proceedings of the Eleventh International Conference on Language Resources and Evaluation (LREC) 2018*.

Yanjun Gao, Andrew Warner, Chen Sun, and Rebecca J. Passonneau. 2018b. Emergent discovery of content units in summaries. In submission.

Steve Graham and Dolores Perin. 2007. A meta-analysis of writing instruction for adolescent students. *Journal of Educational Psychology*, 99(3):445–476.

Weiwei Guo, Wei Liu, and Mona T Diab. 2014. Fast tweet retrieval with compact binary codes. In *COLING*, pages 486–496.

R. Hiemestra. 1994. Self-directed learning. In T. Husen and T. N. Postlethwaite, editors, *The International Encyclopaedia of Education*, 2nd edition. Pergamon Press, Oxford.

Fiona Hyland. 2000. Esl writers and feedback: Giving more autonomy to students. *Language teaching research*, 4(1):33–54.

Fatma Susar Kırmızı. 2009. The relationship between writing achievement and the use of reading comprehension strategies in the 4th and 5th grades of primary schools. *Procedia - Social and Behavioral Sciences*, 1(1):230–234.

Susan J Lea, David Stephenson, and Juliette Troy. 2003. Higher education students' attitudes to student-centred learning: beyond 'educational bulimia'? *Studies in higher education*, 28(3):321–334.

Chin-Yew Lin. 2004. ROUGE: A package for automatic evaluation of summaries. In *Text summarization branches out: Proceedings of the ACL-04 workshop*, volume 8, pages 74–81. Barcelona, Spain.

Danielle S. McNamara, Arthur C. Graesser, Philip M. McCarthy, and Zhiqiang Cai. 2014. *Automated Evaluation of Text and Discourse with Coh-Metrix*. Cambridge University Press.

Ani Nenkova, Rebecca J. Passonneau, and Kathleen McKeown. 2007. The pyramid method: Incorporating human content selection variation in summarization evaluation. *ACM Transactions on Speech and Language Processing (TSLP)*, 4(2):4.

Kishore Papineni, Salim Roukos, Todd Ward, and Wei-Jing Zhu. 2002. BLEU: A method for automatic evaluation of machine translation. In *Proceedings of the 40th Annual Meeting on Association for Computational Linguistics ACL*, page 311318.

Rebecca J. Passonneau, Ananya Poddar, Gaurav Gite, Alisa Krivokapic, Qian Yang, and Dolores Perin. 2016. Wise crowd content assessment and educational rubrics. *International Journal of Artificial Intelligence in Education*, pages 1–27.

Dolores Perin, Rachel Hare Bork, Stephen T Peverly, and Linda H Mason. 2013. A contextualized curricular supplement for developmental reading and writing. *Journal of College Reading and Learning*, 43(2):8–38.

Antje Proske, Susanne Narciss, and Danielle S. McNamara. 2012. Computer-based scaffolding to facilitate students' development of expertise in academic writing. *Journal of Research in Reading*, 35(2):136–152.

Phil Race. 2001. A briefing on self, peer and group assessment. *LTSN generic centre assessment guides series*.

Rod D. Roscoe, Laura K. Allen, Jennifer L. Weston, Scott A. Crossley, and Danielle S. McNamara. 2015. The Writing Pal intelligent tutoring system: Usability testing and development. *Computers and Composition*, 34:39–59.

D Royce Sadler. 2010. Beyond feedback: Developing student capability in complex appraisal. *Assessment & Evaluation in Higher Education*, 35(5):535–550.

Shuichi Sakai, Mitsunori Togasaki, and Koichi Yamazaki. 2003. A note on greedy algorithms for the maximum weighted independent set problem. *Discrete Applied Mathematics*, 126(2):313–322.

Tamara Sladoljev Agejev and Jan Šnajder. 2017. Using analytic scoring rubrics in the automatic assessment of college-level summary writing tasks in L2. In *Proceedings of the Eighth International Joint Conference on Natural Language Processing (Volume 2: Short Papers)*, pages 181–186, Taipei, Taiwan. Asian Federation of Natural Language Processing.

Sargur Srihari, Jim Collins, Rohini Srihari, Harish Srinivasan, Shravya Shetty, and Janina Brutt-Griffler. 2008. Automatic scoring of short handwritten essays in reading comprehension tests. *Artificial Intelligence*, 172(2):300 – 324.

Yao-Ting Sung, Kuo-En Chang, and Jung-Sheng Huang. 2008. Improving childrens reading comprehension and use of strategies through computer-based strategy training. *Computers in Human Behavior*, 24(4):1552–1571.

Charissa Tansomboon, Libby F. Gerard, Jonathan M. Vitale, and Marcia C. Linn. 2017. Designing automated guidance to promote productive revision of science explanations. *International Journal of Artificial Intelligence in Education*, 27(4):729–757.

Paul A Tess. 2013. The role of social media in higher education classes (real and virtual)–a literature review. *Computers in Human Behavior*, 29(5):A60–A68.

Yu-Fen Yang. 2014. Preparing language teachers for blended teaching of summary writing. *Computer Assisted Language Learning*, 27(3):185–206.

Fan Zhang, Homa B. Hashemi, Rebecca Hwa, and Diane Litman. 2017. A corpus of annotated revisions for studying argumentative writing. In *Proceedings of the 55th Annual Meeting of the Association for Computational Linguistics (Volume 1: Long Papers)*, pages 1568–1578, Vancouver, Canada. Association for Computational Linguistics.

Kaja Zupanc and Zoran Bosni. 2017. Automated essay evaluation with semantic analysis. *Knowledge-Based Systems*, 120:118 – 132.

Toward Data-Driven Tutorial Question Answering with Deep Learning Conversational Models

Mayank Kulkarni and **Kristy Elizabeth Boyer**
Department of Computer & Information Science & Engineering
University of Florida
Gainesville, Florida, USA
mayankk91@ufl.edu, keboyer@ufl.edu

Abstract

There has been an increase in popularity of data-driven question answering systems given their recent success. This paper explores the possibility of building a tutorial question answering system for Java programming from data sampled from a community-based question answering forum. This paper reports on the creation of a dataset that could support building such a tutorial question answering system and discusses the methodology to create the 106,386 question strong dataset. We investigate how retrieval-based and generative models perform on the given dataset. The work also investigates the usefulness of using hybrid approaches such as combining retrieval-based and generative models. The results indicate that building data-driven tutorial systems using community-based question answering forums holds significant promise.

1   Introduction

Question answering in dialogue is a central concern for designing the next generation of dialogue systems. Recent work has made great strides in generating dialogue, for example, with neural conversation models (Vinyals and Le, 2015), persona-based conversation models (Li et al., 2014) and adversarial models (Li et al., 2017). Specifically, for responding to questions, information-retrieval techniques have long been explored (Jeon et al., 2005; Ramos, 2003; Lowe et al., 2015). A critical open question is how to build data-driven systems for specific domains. A challenge that is faced by the community for such systems is the availability of data for those domains. Given that transfer learning has not yet been shown to yield good results (Mou et al., 2016), there has been investigation in the area of partially

data-driven and hand-crafted systems (Williams et al., 2017). However, handcrafted systems face tremendous limitations in authoring. *Data-driven* dialogue systems, which derive their functionality from corpora, have the potential to eliminate this bottleneck.

This work explores the possibility of building a data-driven question-answering system for Java programming. We leverage a promising source of data by drawing from community-based question answering forums of Stack Exchange. Forums typically also have sub-forums, such as Stack Overflow for programming questions and Ask Ubuntu for Ubuntu operating system related questions. Such community-based forums serve as excellent datasets for specific domains, such as programming or IT support, that are otherwise not easily available to the general public. The promise of this data is further demonstrated by other work done using the Stack Exchange data: Campbell and Treude (2017) explore how to use semantic parsing to convert an English sentence or query into a code snippet, while Campos et al. (2016) investigate returning relevant question answer pairs for Swing, Boost and LINQ by using indexing techniques and building feature-based classifiers.

With technology becoming ubiquitous, having programming skills are highly sought after. In a University or MOOC setting, 'Introduction to Programming' courses typically have a large class size, and with a limited number of Teaching Assistants, providing individual help becomes a difficult task. The work in this paper focuses on attempting to assist in helping students learn Java programming with a data-driven tutorial question answering system.

This work attempts to build the tutorial question-answering system as both a retrieval-based question answering system (Ji et al., 2014) via the

Proceedings of the Thirteenth Workshop on Innovative Use of NLP for Building Educational Applications, pages 273–283
New Orleans, Louisiana, June 5, 2018. ©2018 Association for Computational Linguistics

Dual Encoder architecture (Medsker and Jain, 2001; Bromley et al., 1994) and as a generative question answering system (Ritter et al., 2011) via the Sequence-to-Sequence architecture (Sutsveker et al., 2014; Cho et al., 2014). The retrieval-based model answers the user's question by predicting the most relevant answer from a set of predefined answers. In contrast to the retrieval-based model, the generative model answers the user's question by generating new answers based on the data on which the model was trained. Both of these approaches rely on building good semantic representations of the input in the vector space using word embeddings (Mikolov et al., 2013; Mikolov et al., 2013).

This work also explores the usefulness of a hybrid approach involving the combination of the retrieval-based and generative models. This paper thus represents the first work to explore deep learning techniques for data-driven tutorial dialogue for Java programming.

2 Related Work

Recently, there has been work using natural language processing and machine learning techniques within tools for programming support and computer science education. Zhang et al. (2016) explored using Deep Belief Networks to grade short-answer texts and showed that this approach outperformed conventional machine learning models. They also explored using student modeling and clustering based on engineered features to predict the grades with reasonable success. Wang et al. (2017) used a recurrent neural network to attempt to represent a student's knowledge states for programming exercises and found that the model was able to successfully identify students with knowledge gaps and provide indications that assistance may be necessary.

Work is also being done to build models from data that can generate their own answers to questions. Bengio et al. (2003) and Mikolov (2012) (Mikolov et al., 2010) were able to successfully construct a neural language model using recurrent neural networks, further reinforcing the prevailing conclusion that recurrent neural networks are the architecture of choice for this task. Sordoni et al. (2015) and Shang et al. (2015) were also able to model short conversations using a recurrent neural network.

A critical turning point for generative models was when Sutskever et al. (2014) & Cho et al.

(2014) introduced the sequence-to-sequence framework in the domain of machine translation. The authors proposed an architecture to convert one sequence to another sequence using recurrent neural networks as encoders and decoders. Inspired by the previous success of recurrent neural networks and the sequence-to-sequence framework, Vinyals and Le (2015) proposed applying this framework to conversational modeling, framing question answering as a machine translation problem. While Vinyals and Le (2015) showed that the model was able to give short, coherent answers for queries in a variety of settings, they also mentioned limitations of the system: it is restricted to short answers and lacks a personality.

In addition to generative systems, retrieval-based systems have also shown success in the recent past. Kannan et al. (2016) used semi-supervised learning with an LSTM RNN along with semantic intent clustering to generate high-quality responses for the Google Smart Reply system. Lu et al. (2017) explored how to generate responses from a large answer space by using a dual encoder LSTM network and employing clustering to generate templates from their large answer set, reducing the answer set space for a customer support question answering system. Jeon et al. (2005) investigated how to find question similarity using word translation probabilities. Lowe et al. (2015) constructed a corpus of one million multi-turn dialogues from the Ask Ubuntu forum, then performed experiments with retrieval-based models that demonstrated that a useful question answering system could be built using a dataset sampled from a community-based question answering forum. These techniques helped us gain insight on how to identify the most appropriate responses from a knowledge base.

The work in this paper attempts to employ deep learning techniques to support computer science education by developing a programming support tool for Java Programming that provides automated tutorial question answering. The work builds upon recent work in retrieval-based and generative models to construct answers that combine the English language with the Java programming language.

3 Dataset

Stack Exchange is a set of community-based question answering websites, with each website covering a specific topic. Stack Overflow deals

Figure 1: Sample Stack Overflow question[1]

with programming questions and relies on self-moderation through peer upvoting mechanisms. The user who posts the question can select the answer that they deem most appropriate. In some cases, the original poster does not select an answer, and in these cases the highest upvoted answer could be considered the best answer.

A typical Stack Overflow question can be seen in Figure 1. We see a title for the question at the top "Java String Declaration", followed by a description, "What is the difference between ... performance variation." An important piece of information is the meta tags seen underneath the description. We see the meta tags of "java" and "string", which describe on a high level to what the post is related. We see an upvote count to the left of the answer, a measure of how many other users agree with this answer. For the question in Figure 1, we see that there is an answer that has received the user's accepted answer status as well as 29 upvotes by the community.

Stack Exchange provides an anonymized data dump of all the user-contributed content, with the most recent version published on Dec 1, 2017. The data dump is in the format of a SQL database consisting of various components of the website represented in the form of SQL tables such as the Posts table, Users table, and Comments table. For the purposes of this work we consider only the Stack Overflow data and the Posts table.

---

[1] https://stackoverflow.com/questions/3652369/

3.1 Working with the Stack Exchange Database

The Posts table contained about 38 million posts, i.e. all the post data on Stack Overflow as of the data dump publication date. Every question and answer posted on the website is part of the Posts table, with different identifiers to signify the type of Post and relationships between the Posts. The question-answer relationship was defined as follows: the original question had a post ID, and answers corresponding to this question had the same post ID in their parentID column.

3.2 Filtering Posts

This work focuses on Java programming questions, which required us to narrow our search to Java-related questions from the Posts table. We first filtered to ignore questions containing the '<code>' tag in the 'Body' column, as our present goal is to answer general questions within a future tutorial system.

In order to obtain posts related to Java, we used the Post table's 'Tags' column, which contained meta tags related to the post, as seen in Figure 1. In order to ignore technology-specific questions such as a question about 'Spring' or 'Hibernate', we created a list of tags to ignore based on frequency counts and prefixes (such as 'google-api-xx' or 'facebook-api-xx'). Once these filters were in place, we filtered to ignore all unanswered questions based on the 'AnswerCount' column in the Posts table. Another filtering step was to take all the answers that contained code snippets defined by the <code> token and replace the tokens with 'CODE_START' and 'CODE_END' as labels to mark the beginning and end of the code snippet.

3.3 Dataset Statistics

We collected all corresponding answers from our set of filtered questions to create an initial corpus. This corpus contained 107,961 question-description-answer triplets, of which 47,220 questions did not have a 'user accepted best answer'. A statistical analysis based on a naive word split showed that there were outliers in the corpus, with very large maximum lengths of up to 10,000 words in an answer. We identified and removed the outliers in the corpus by removing the current largest sample and monitoring the average length of the corpus. We continued to remove the largest sample till we obtained a rela-

Average Question Length	8.68013
Average Description Length	71.45428
Average Answer Length	87.54342
Vocabulary Size	284,827

Table 1: Final Dataset Statistics

tively stable average value. This outlier determination was performed for each sample type of question, description and answer separately. Ultimately, we removed questions longer than 19 words, or whose descriptions were longer than 125 words, or with answers longer than 175 words.

The questions, descriptions and answers in the dataset were then converted into a sequence of numbers using word indexing techniques, in order to be usable by a machine learning model. The word indexing techniques involved first tokenizing the sentences into word tokens by using an open-source tokenizer (Python NLTK).[2] Each word was labelled with a unique index and stored as a key-value pair in a data structure. Secondly, the words in each sentence were replaced by the corresponding indexes using the data structure created above to obtain a sequence of numbers which corresponded to the original sentence. A total of 284, 827 words were obtained through tokenization and subsequently indexed in the data structure.

To maintain the uniformity of sentence length, we 'pre-pad' the sequence with 0 before the original sequence. Adding zeros at the start of the original sequence (if required) allows the network to accept a fixed sequence length and the nature of the number zero also allows us to denote that the element in the sequence is an empty space. We 'pre-pad' and thus structure the sequence with actual content towards the end of the sequence because a time-based neural network is more likely to 'remember' time steps towards the end of the sequence, as those would be stored in the more recent memory which is captured by the network.

The filtering of the sentences with length thresholds is important, as it is difficult to capture semantic representations for lengthy text using word embeddings. Setting these thresholds resulted in a reduced dataset of 106,386 questions. The

statistics for the final dataset are shown in Table 1. We also make this dataset available for public use as a contribution of this paper.[3]

4 Methods and Techniques

With the future objective of building a data-driven tutorial question-answering system, we first explore three overarching approaches of retrieval-based models, generative models, and hybrid models for Java programming-based tutorial question answering.

The challenges associated with this dataset are that unlike traditional question answering datasets, this dataset has three streams of inputs. Each stream has its own unique descriptors such as vocabulary and length. The answers in the dataset contain interspersed English and Java, which could make building meaningful word vector representations difficult. Long sentences are typically more difficult to represent in a vector space and this dataset contains longer typical sentences for the description and answer than those seen in previous work of Lowe et al. (2015) and Lu et al. (2017). As a part of this work, we investigate which combinations of inputs from the dataset yield the most optimal results.

4.1 Dual Encoder LSTM (Siamese network)

The Siamese Network or Dual Encoder architecture (Medsker and Jain, 2001; Bromley et al., 1994) has shown success in the recent past to build a retrieval-based question answering system (Lowe et al., 2015; Lu et al., 2017).

To use the dataset with the Dual Encoder architecture, we needed to perform some additional pre-processing. We first built a dataset containing the question along with its description and the corresponding correct answer, and we assigned a label of 1 to these samples. We then created a sample containing the incorrect answer for a given question and description pair. This was done by randomly choosing another answer from the rest of the answer set and assigning a label of 0 to these samples.

Description & Answer Dual Encoder (DADE): This architecture consisted of a Dual Encoder Bidirectional LSTM network, where the first encoder encoded the description of the question and the second encoder encoded the answer

---

[2] NLTK implementation: https://www.nltk.org/

[3] https://cise.ufl.edu/research/learndialogue/data/java-stackoverflow-QA-dec2017.zip

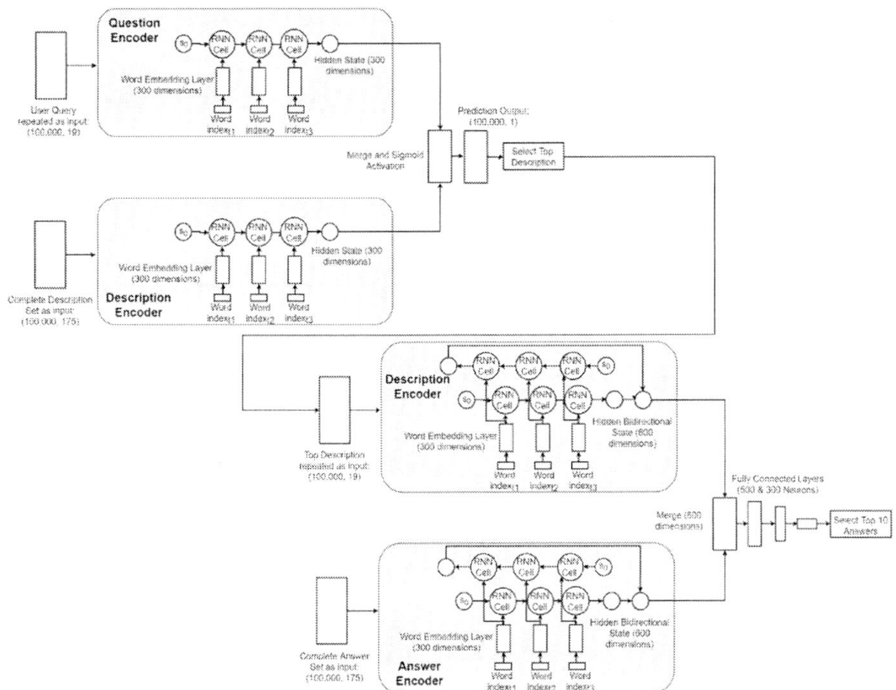

Figure 2. Question Description Matching followed by Description Answer Matching

statement. The large maximum sequence lengths influenced us to choose to use a Bidirectional LSTM (Schuster and Paliwal, 1997) as it allows the network to understand the context of a word with respect to both previous and next words and thus build better vector representations of the words. Each bidirectional encoder's output was merged together to obtain a single 600-dimensional output, and then this output was fed to a fully connected network of two layers, with the first layer containing 500 neurons and the second layer containing 300 neurons. This was then run through a sigmoid activation function in order to obtain the result.

This architecture used pre-trained GloVe word embeddings which were updated during the training phase. The LSTM cells contained 300 hidden units and 2 layers and optimized the binary cross-entropy loss function.

Question & Description Dual Encoder (QDDE): This architecture was similar to the Description and Answer Dual Encoder in that it consisted of a Dual Encoder LSTM network, where the first encoder encoded the question statement and the second encoder encoded the description statement. Each encoder's outputs were merged together to obtain a single 300-dimensional output and then this output was run through a sigmoid activation function in order to obtain the result.

Again, this architecture also used pre-trained GloVe word embeddings which were updated during the training phase. The LSTM cells contained 300 hidden units and a single layer and optimized the binary cross-entropy loss function.

The rationale for this architecture was to build a dual encoder that would be able to predict a description given a question. We wanted to investigate whether the dual encoder could learn relationships between smaller questions and longer descriptions. If we could successfully predict the description for a given question, it would allow us to leverage the similar lengths of the description and answer to obtain better results.

4.2 Techniques to answer queries

The aforementioned architectures were able to determine answers for the given training, validation and testing sets, where the correct answers are predetermined. To extend our model's use to the real world, we needed to define a different set of strategies to answer questions for which we do not know the predetermined answer. We explore our proposed strategies in the following section.

Question Description Matching followed by Description Answer Matching: This approach attempted to find a similarity measure between a given user question and a description of the given

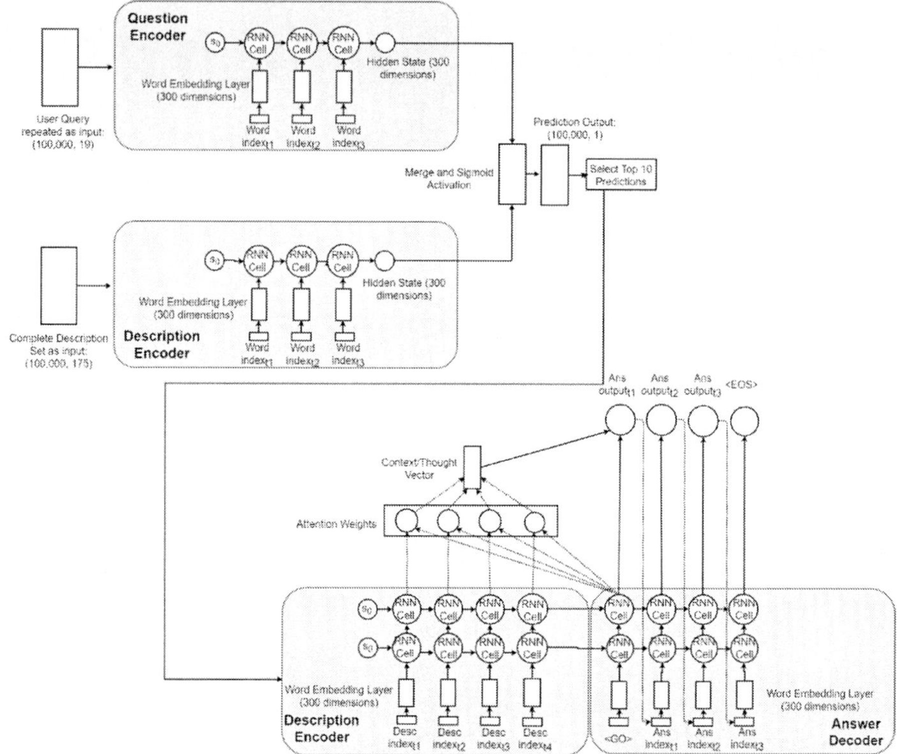

Figure 3. Hybrid Architecture Combining Dual Encoder with Sequence-to-Sequence Model

question via QDDE. The best matching description was then run against all the answers to determine the top 10 best possible answers, as seen in Figure 2. The intuition behind using this approach was that the description-answer dual encoder should provide better results as it used a bidirectional LSTM network and both sequence lengths were approximately the same.

4.3 Sequence-to-Sequence Models

Sequence-to-Sequence models are generative models that, unlike their retrieval-based counterparts, do not rely on choosing from an existing set of answers but rather generate answers on their own.

The preprocessing steps for the sequence-to-sequence model were identical to the preprocessing steps specified for the dual encoder model.

Description to Answer Encoder - Decoder: This architecture used the description of a question as the input to the encoder and attempted to match the actual answer to the question using the decoder. The intuition behind matching a description to the answer was that as the sequences are of almost equal length, this could then be framed as a machine translation problem, which has seen significant success with the sequence-to-sequence model (Sutskever et al., 2014; Cho et al., 2014; Vinyals and Le, 2015).

The encoder was a bidirectional recurrent neural network using LSTM cells. We chose bidirectionality for better sentence vector representation, and LSTM cells for their ability to capture long-term dependencies. The decoder is a standard recurrent neural network with LSTM cells.

The LSTM cells contained 512 hidden units and 2 layers. We used a dropout (Srivastava et al, 2014) probability of 0.2 and gradient normalization (Pascanu et al., 2013) of 3.6. We used 15 buckets, as the length of 175 (maximum answer length) would then be equally split into smaller chunks of size 12 increments. The Luong attention mechanism (Luong et al., 2015) was implemented in order to boost accuracy, as was beam search (Wiseman and Rush, 2016) of beam width 10 in order to obtain a better output for a given input. The vocabulary had to be reduced to 60,000 due to memory constraints.

All the hyperparameters stated for the networks discussed above were determined by performing a

Model Name		recall@1	recall@2	recall@5
DA	TF-IDF	0.7837	0.8437	0.9137
	DADE	0.7052	**0.8672**	**0.9798**
QA	TF-IDF	0.9483	0.9685	0.9785
	QDDE	0.8542	0.951	**0.9928**

Table 2. Testing recall@k for group size 10

grid search and cross-validating with the validation dataset.

4.4 Hybrid architecture (Dual Encoder + Sequence-to-Sequence)

In this work, we built a hybrid structure that combined both the retrieval-based model of the dual encoder with the generative model of the sequence-to-sequence model. The intuition behind building this model was that a user typically asks questions with a length of fewer than 20 words and may not necessarily have enough of a description to fit the 125-word limit sufficiently. The proposed architecture combats this issue by obtaining the user question and trying to find the most appropriate description from a set of prefixed descriptions, this is done by the question and description dual encoder mentioned earlier. The entire workflow can be seen in Figure 3.

We take the top 10 predicted descriptions and feed these descriptions as input to the description to answer sequence-to-sequence model.

The Description to Answer model would result in 10 different generated answers and the answers were ranked based on the input descriptions ranking. This architecture also lets us leverage the nature of the dataset, in that it contains a question, a description and an answer as opposed to a traditional question-answer pair dataset.

5 Experiments

All the experiments performed as a part of this work were done on a desktop with the following specification i7 8-core CPU, 32GB RAM, and NVIDIA GTX 1070 8GB VRAM.

The dataset of 106,386 was split into separate training, testing and validation sets. Given the large network sizes used in the experiments, there were a correspondingly large number of parameters to be trained for each network, which in turn

required a sufficiently large dataset to train on. Taking this into consideration we chose to not follow the traditional 80-20 train-test split but rather maintain a large enough training set and use the rest of the data for testing and validation. The training set thus contained 100,000 questions and corresponding description and answers triplets, the test dataset contained 5,000 triplets and the validation set contained 1,386 triplets.

For the dual encoder experiments, the training set size was 200,000 as we had to use both positive and negative samples while training. Whereas for the sequence-to-sequence model training we used only 100,000 description and answer pairs.

5.1 Quantitative Analysis

Dual Encoder: The recall@k metric works in conjunction with the group size. Given that we have a group size of 5, recall@1 tells us that if we had the option to choose 1 out of the 5 options, what is the probability that it would be correct. We take a look at Table 2, where the group size is 10 and we compare another popular retrieval-based method, TF-IDF (Ramos, 2003), to our obtained results. TF-IDF has been outperformed by dual encoders for conversational models in the past (Lowe et al., 2015), but we see some interesting results for our dataset.

We see that for DADE, TF-IDF is able to slightly outperform the dual encoder at the recall@1 scores, but the dual encoder outperforms TF-IDF for recall@2 and recall@5. We further see that QDDE is outperformed by TF-IDF in both recall@1 and recall@2, only for QDDE to do better in recall@5.

We believe that we see this behavior because TF-IDF works based on word similarity and rates rare words between two documents as highly related (Ramos, 2003). Questions and descriptions containing common phrases are better perceived by TF-IDF than by the dual encoders. In addition, previous results like Lowe et al. (2015), worked on a corpus with an average word count of 10 words where they showed that the dual encoder architecture significantly outperformed TF-IDF, whereas our work deals with much longer utterances. In spite of long utterances, we see that the dual encoders do a comparable or better job than TF-IDF.

Sequence-to-Sequence: We followed Google's Neural Machine Translation tutorial (Luong et al., 2017) to build our sequence-to-sequence models.

Model:	Best Output:
QDDE + DADE	you can use an arraylist or a list of integers instead so that you can add items to the list as and when required also the list would then have only as many elements as the number of inputs syntax CODE_START List<Integer> = new ArrayList<Integer>() CODE_END to add elements to the list use CODE_START elements.add(new Item()) CODE_END to access members of the list use CODE_START elements.get(index) CODE_END

Hybrid Model (Response #1)	```
	CODE_START
	public static void main (string args)
	list<integer> list = new arraylist<integer>
	for (int i = 0; i < list.size(); i++){
	        system.out.println(list.get(i));
	}
	CODE_END[4]
	``
	Actual output: code start list lt integer gt list new arraylist lt integer gt for int i 0 i lt list size i system out println list get i code end

Hybrid Model (Response #2)	```
	CODE_START
	public static void main(string args) {
	list<integer> list = new arraylist<integer>
	for (int i = 0; i < 10; i++){
	        list.add(i);
	        system.out.println(list.get(i));
	}
	CODE_END[3]
	``
	Actual output: code start public static void main string args list lt integer gt list new arraylist lt integer gt for int i 0 i lt 10 i list add i system out println list get i code end

Table 3. Top Responses for "how can we create an integer array in java"

An important point to note is that while traditional machine translations are judged based on BLEU score (Papineni et al., 2002) and perplexity, a conversational model cannot be judged on BLEU and hence we used perplexity as the primary measure of judgment (Shao et al., 2017).

Description to Answer Sequence-to-Sequence Model: The perplexity for the dev set continued to decrease, thus we could assume no overfitting had occurred over the epochs of training this network. The dev and test perplexity scores were better than the previous model, with scores of 68.91 and 70.15 respectively, and this is also reflected in the coherent responses made by the model.

5.2   Qualitative Analysis

We chose a question which was neither part of the training, development nor test corpus to analyze the qualitative results. The reason these results are presented as qualitative is that since its part of neither of the corpus we do not have the actual expected response. The question that we chose is a fairly simple and straightforward question:

"How can we create an integer array in java"

We take a look at the responses given by the models in Table 3. As the models provide multiple answers, we have handpicked the answer that we thought was most relevant from the top 10. We have also cleaned the answer by referring the original post on Stack Overflow for readability.

The QDDE+DADE model produces a response that suggests using Java collections to achieve the same purpose of the array. The drawback here is that it diverges from the actual answer but is still relevant nonetheless. Another one of the top ten answers suggested looking at some of the Java documentation related to arrays.

We now take a look at the responses generated by sequence-to-sequence models and the hybrid model. While the hybrid model suggests using an 'ArrayList' instead of an array, it was able to form different codes for the condition of the 'for' loop in both the answers, suggesting that it may understand a relationship between functions such as 'get' and 'add' and the 'for' loop condition.

It is also interesting to see the response generated by the Description to Answer sequence-to-sequence model. We can analyze some of the aforementioned testing responses generated via the Description to Answer Sequence-to-Sequence model as can be seen in Table 4.

By analyzing the generated responses for the samples above, we can see that the model has learned how to create new objects and has also learned what kind of commands are related to a given object, such as the date in Java needs simpledateformat class or that the file could need a file path. Perhaps the most notable was the crea-

---

[4] The sequence-to-sequence model does not include non-word tokens such as '=' or '{'. These have been added for readability.

	Question:	how to format a date in java
1	Description:	how can change this date format 2011 09 07...[5]
	Generated Response:	CODE_START simpledateformat sdf new simpledateformat yyyy mm dd hh mm ss ......
	Question:	java does not recognize a file when it begins with file
2	Description:	java says a file does not exist when it is a valid file path ...[6]
	Generated Response:	CODE_START file file new file path to file CODE_END
	Question:	how to track of other application's memory and cpu usage by java coding
3	Description:	i want to show cpu and memory utilization of any application...[7]
	Generated Response:	you can take a look at the CODE_START java util concurrent CODE_END package http docs oracle com javase tutorial essential environment sysprop html

Table 4: Sample Sequence-to-Sequence Generated Responses from Test Set

tion of a coherent 'for' loop using the previously created object and referencing the appropriate method.

We also see that the models are able to successfully combine the English language along with java code, starting answers with phrases such as "you can use...", "i dont think there is a way...", "i am not sure but try…" and so on. The models are also able to draw a clear line between code snippets and English language and code start labels are mostly correctly completed with code end la-

bels. There have also been instances where English phrases such "you can also try" are used between two code snippets.

While these examples have been sampled from a much larger set in which not all the responses are as appropriate, this still shows promise in using this architecture to build models that can appropriately respond to a query by generating their own response.

6 Conclusion

This work has examined how we can leverage community-based question answering forums as a source of data to build a dataset specific to general Java-based programming questions. We have seen that retrieval-based models obtain high recall rates on the testing set but are restricted only to the answer set available. On the other hand, generative models are able to successfully combine the English language along with Java code to make coherent responses at times, but the responses are small and do not completely answer the question. We found reasonable success with the hybrid model by combining the retrieval-based approach with the generative approach. The proposed approaches show promise in building a useful tutorial system based on the sampled dataset. These are the first steps made in that direction.

This work could be furthered by investigating jointly training the hybrid model to improve description selection and answer generation. One could also frame this task as a machine comprehension task, where the entire answer set could be used as the context. Doing so would allow us to leverage the memory network architecture, which performs better at tasks involving storing long-term memory. Finally, we could explore using adversarial training, as it has seen success on conversational models in the recent past (Li et al., 2017).

7 Acknowledgments

The authors wish to thank the members of the LearnDialogue group at the University of Florida for their helpful input. This work is supported in part by the National Science Foundation through grant CNS-1622438. Any opinions, findings, conclusions, or recommendations expressed in this report are those of the authors, and do not necessarily represent the official views, opinions, or policy of the National Science Foundation.

---

[5] https://stackoverflow.com/questions/7631470

[6] https://stackoverflow.com/questions/40983790

[7] https://stackoverflow.com/questions/6390581

References

Yoshua Bengio, Réjean Ducharme, Pascal Vincent and Christian Jauvin. 2003. A neural probabilistic language model. *Journal of Machine Learning Research, 3(Feb), pp. 1137-1155.*

Jane Bromley, Isabelle Guyon, Yann LeCun, Eduard Säckinger and Roopak Shah. 1994. Signature verification using a "siamese" time delay neural network. *In Advances in Neural Information Processing Systems, pp. 737-744.*

Brock Angus Campbell and Christoph Treude. 2017. NLP2Code: Code snippet content assist via natural language tasks. *In Software Maintenance and Evolution (ICSME), 2017 IEEE International Conference on, pp. 628-632. IEEE.*

Eduardo C. Campos, Lucas BL Souza and Marcelo de A. Maia. 2016. Searching crowd knowledge to recommend solutions for API usage tasks. *Journal of Software: Evolution and Process 28, no. 10: 863-892*

Kyunghyun Cho, Bart Van Merriënboer, Caglar Gulcehre, Dzmitry Bahdanau, Fethi Bougares, Holger Schwenk and Yoshua Bengio. 2014. Learning phrase representations using RNN encoder-decoder for statistical machine translation. *In Proceedings of the 2014 Conference on Empirical Methods in Natural Language Processing (EMNLP), pp. 1724–1734.*

Jiwoon Jeon, W. Bruce Croft and Joon Ho Lee. 2005. Finding similar questions in large question and answer archives. *In Proceedings of the 14th ACM International Conference on Information and Knowledge Management, pp. 84-90. ACM.*

Zongcheng Ji, Zhengdong Lu and Hang Li. 2014. An information retrieval approach to short text conversation. *arXiv preprint arXiv:1408.6988.*

Anjuli Kannan, Karol Kurach, Sujith Ravi, Tobias Kaufmann, Andrew Tomkins, Balint Miklos, Greg Corrado et al. 2016. Smart reply: Automated response suggestion for email. *In Proceedings of the 22nd ACM SIGKDD International Conference on Knowledge Discovery and Data Mining, pp. 955-964. ACM.*

Jiwei Li, Michel Galley, Chris Brockett, Georgios P. Spithourakis, Jianfeng Gao and Bill Dolan. 2016. A persona-based neural conversation model. *In Proceedings of 54th Annual Meeting of Association for Computational Linguistics, pp. 994–1003.*

Jiwei Li, Will Monroe, Tianlin Shi, Alan Ritter and Dan Jurafsky. 2017. Adversarial learning for neural dialogue generation. *arXiv preprint arXiv:1701.06547.*

Ryan Lowe, Nissan Pow, Iulian Serban and Joelle Pineau. 2015. The ubuntu dialogue corpus: A large dataset for research in unstructured multi-turn dialogue systems. *In Proceedings of the SIGDIAL 2015 Conference, pp. 285–294.*

Yichao Lu, Phillip Keung, Shaonan Zhang, Jason Sun and Vikas Bhardwaj. 2017. A practical approach to dialogue response generation in closed domains. *arXiv preprint arXiv:1703.09439.*

Minh-Thang Luong and Eugene Brevdo and Rui Zhao. 2017. Neural Machine Translation (seq2seq) Tutorial, *https://github.com/tensorflow/nmt.*

Minh-Thang Luong, Hieu Pham and Christopher D. Manning. 2015. Effective approaches to attention-based neural machine translation. *In Proceedings of the 2015 Conference on Empirical Methods in Natural Language Processing, pp. 1412–1421.*

L. R. Medsker and L. C. Jain. 2001. Recurrent neural networks. *Design and Applications 5.*

Tomáš Mikolov. 2012. Statistical language models based on neural networks. *PhD thesis, PhD Thesis, Brno University of Technology, 2012.*

Tomáš Mikolov, Ilya Sutskever, Kai Chen, Greg S. Corrado, and Jeff Dean. 2013. Distributed representations of words and phrases and their compositionality. *In Advances in Neural Information Processing Systems (pp. 3111-3119).*

Tomáš Mikolov, Kai Chen, Greg Corrado, and Jeffrey Dean. 2013. Efficient estimation of word representations in vector space. *arXiv preprint arXiv:1301.3781.*

Tomáš Mikolov, Martin Karafiát, Lukáš Burget, Jan Černocký and Sanjeev Khudanpur. 2010. Recurrent neural network based language model. *In Eleventh Annual Conference of the International Speech Communication Association, pp. 1045-1048.*

Lili Mou, Zhao Meng, Rui Yan, Ge Li, Yan Xu, Lu Zhang and Zhi Jin. 2016. How Transferable are Neural Networks in NLP Applications?. *In Proceedings of the 2016 Conference on Empirical Methods in Natural Language Processing, pp. 479–489.*

Kishore Papineni, Salim Roukos, Todd Ward and Wei-Jing Zhu. 2002. Bleu: a method for automatic evaluation of machine translation. *In Proceedings of the 40th Annual Meeting on Association for Computational Linguistics, pp. 311–318.*

Razvan Pascanu, Tomas Mikolov, and Yoshua Bengio. 2013. On the difficulty of training recurrent neural networks. *In International Conference on Machine Learning (pp. 1310-1318)*

Juan Ramos. 2003. Using tf-idf to determine word relevance in document queries. *In Proceedings of the First Instructional Conference on Machine Learning, vol. 242, pp. 133-142.*

Alan Ritter, Colin Cherry and William B. Dolan. 2011. Data-driven response generation in social media. *In Proceedings of the Conference on Empirical Methods in Natural Language Processing, pp. 583-593.*

Mike Schuster and Kuldip K. Paliwal. 1997. Bidirectional recurrent neural networks. *IEEE Transactions on Signal Processing 45, no. 11: 2673-2681.*

Lifeng Shang, Zhengdong Lu and Hang Li. 2015. Neural responding machine for short-text conversation. *In Proceedings of the 53rd Annual Meeting of the Association for Computational Linguistics and the 7th International Joint Conference on Natural Language Processing, pp. 1577–1586.*

Yuanlong Shao, Stephan Gouws, Denny Britz, Anna Goldie, Brian Strope and Ray Kurzweil. 2017. Generating high-quality and informative conversation responses with sequence-to-sequence models. *In Proceedings of the 2017 Conference on Empirical Methods in Natural Language Processing, pp. 2210-2219.*

Alessandro Sordoni, Michel Galley, Michael Auli, Chris Brockett, Yangfeng Ji, Margaret Mitchell, Jian-Yun Nie, Jianfeng Gao and Bill Dolan. 2015. A neural network approach to context-sensitive generation of conversational responses. *In Proceedings of Human Language Technologies: The 2015 Annual Conference of the North American Chapter of the ACL, pp. 196–205.*

Nitish Srivastava, Geoffrey Hinton, Alex Krizhevsky, Ilya Sutskever, and Ruslan Salakhutdinov. 2014. Dropout: A simple way to prevent neural networks from overfitting. *The Journal of Machine Learning Research, 15(1), 1929-1958.*

Ilya Sutskever, Oriol Vinyals and Quoc V. Le. 2014. Sequence to sequence learning with neural networks. *In Advances in Neural Information Processing Systems, pp. 3104-3112.*

Oriol Vinyals and Quoc Le. 2015. A neural conversational model. *Proceedings of the 31st International Conference on Machine Learning, JMLR: W&CP volume 37.*

Lisa Wang, Angela Sy, Larry Liu, Chris Piech. 2017. Learning to represent student knowledge on programming exercises using deep learning. *In Proceedings of the 10th International Conference on Educational Data Mining; Wuhan, China (pp. 324-329).*

Jason D. Williams, Kavosh Asadi and Geoffrey Zweig. 2017. Hybrid code networks: practical and efficient end-to-end dialog control with supervised and reinforcement learning. *In Proceedings of 55th*

Annual Meeting of Association for Computational Linguistics, pp. 665-677.

Sam Wiseman and Alexander M. Rush. 2016. Sequence-to-sequence learning as beam-search optimization. *In Proceedings of the 2016 Conference on Empirical Methods in Natural Language Processing, pp. 1296–1306.*

Yuan Zhang, Rajat Shah and Min Chi. 2016. Deep Learning+ Student Modeling+ Clustering: a Recipe for Effective Automatic Short Answer Grading. *In Proceedings of the 9th International Conference on Educational Data Mining (pp. 562-567).*

Distractor Generation for Multiple Choice Questions Using Learning to Rank

Chen Liang[1], Xiao Yang[2], Neisarg Dave[1], Drew Wham[3], Bart Pursel[3], C. Lee Giles[1]
[1]Information Sciences and Technology
[2]Computer Science and Engineering
[3]Teaching and Learning with Technology
Pennsylvania State University
{cul226,xuy111,nud83,fcw5014,bkp10}@psu.edu, giles@ist.psu.edu

Abstract

We investigate how machine learning models, specifically ranking models, can be used to select useful distractors for multiple choice questions. Our proposed models can learn to select distractors that resemble those in actual exam questions, which is different from most existing unsupervised ontology-based and similarity-based methods. We empirically study feature-based and neural net (NN) based ranking models with experiments on the recently released SciQ dataset and our MCQL dataset. Experimental results show that feature-based ensemble learning methods (random forest and LambdaMART) outperform both the NN-based method and unsupervised baselines. These two datasets can also be used as benchmarks for distractor generation.

1 Introduction

Multiple choice questions (MCQs) are widely used as an assessment of students' knowledge and skills. A MCQ consists of three elements: (i) *stem*, the question sentence; (ii) *key*, the correct answer; (iii) *distractors*, alternative answers used to distract students from the correct answer. Among all methods for creating good MCQs, finding reasonable distractors is crucial and usually the most time-consuming. We here investigate automatic *distractor generation* (DG), i.e., generating distractors given the stem and the key to the question. We focus on the case where distractors are not limited to single words and can be phrases and sentences.

Rather than generate trivial wrong answers, the goal of DG is to generate plausible false answers - good distractors. Specifically, a "good" distractor should be at least semantically related to the key (Goodrich, 1977), grammatically correct given the stem, and consistent with the semantic context of the stem. Taking these cri-

terion into consideration, most existing methods for DG are based on various similarity measures. These include WordNet-based metrics (Mitkov and Ha, 2003), embedding-based similarities (Guo et al., 2016; Kumar et al., 2015; Jiang and Lee, 2017), n-gram co-occurrence likelihood (Hill and Simha, 2016), phonetic and morphological similarities (Pino and Eskenazi, 2009), structural similarities in an ontology (Stasaski and Hearst, 2017), a thesaurus (Sumita et al., 2005), context similarity (Pino et al., 2008), context-sensitive inference (Zesch and Melamud, 2014), and syntactic similarity (Chen et al., 2006). Then distractors are selected from a candidate distractor set based on a weighted combination of similarities, where the weights are determined by heuristics.

In contrast to the above-mentioned similarity-based methods, we apply learning-based ranking models to select distractors that resemble those in actual exam MCQs. Specifically, we propose two types of models for DG: feature-based and NN-based models. Our models are able to take existing heuristics as features and learn from these questions a function beyond a simple linear combination. Learning to generate distractors has been previously explored in a few studies. Given a blanked question, Sakaguchi et al. (2013) use a discriminative model to predict distractors and Liang et al. (2017) apply generative adversarial nets. They view DG as a multi-class classification problem and use answers as output labels while we use them as input. Other related work (Welbl et al., 2017) uses a random forest. However, with the reported binary classification metrics, the quality of the top generated distractors is not quantitatively evaluated. Here we conduct a more comprehensive study on various learning models and devise ranking evaluation metrics for DG.

Machine learning of a robust model usually requires large-scale training data. However, to

Proceedings of the Thirteenth Workshop on Innovative Use of NLP for Building Educational Applications, pages 284–290
New Orleans, Louisiana, June 5, 2018. ©2018 Association for Computational Linguistics

the best of our knowledge, there is no benchmark dataset for DG, which makes it difficult to directly compare methods. Prior methods were evaluated on different question sets collected from textbooks (Agarwal and Mannem, 2011), Wikipedia (Liang et al., 2017), ESL corpuses (Sakaguchi et al., 2013), etc. We propose to evaluate DG methods with two datasets: the recently released SciQ dataset (Welbl et al., 2017) (13.7K MCQs) and the MCQL dataset (7.1K MCQs) that we made. These two datasets can be used as benchmarks for training and testing DG models. Our experimental results show that feature-based ensemble learning methods (random forest and LambdaMART) outperform both the NN-based method and unsupervised baselines for DG.

2 Learning to Rank for Distractor Generation

We solve DG as the following ranking problem:
Problem. Given a candidate distractor set $\mathcal{D}$ and a MCQ dataset $\mathcal{M} = \{(q_i, a_i, \{d_{i1}, ..., d_{ik}\})\}_{i=1}^{N}$, where q_i is the question stem, a_i is the key, $D_i = \{d_{i1}...d_{ik}\} \subseteq \mathcal{D}$ are the distractors associated with q_i and a_i, find a point-wise ranking function r: $(q_i, a_i, d) \rightarrow [0, 1]$ for $d \in \mathcal{D}$, such that distractors in D_i are ranked higher than those in $\mathcal{D} - D_i$.

This problem formulation is similar to "learning to rank" (Liu et al., 2009) in information retrieval. To learn the ranking function, we investigate two types of models: feature-based models and NN-based models.

2.1 Feature-based Models

2.1.1 Feature Description

Given a tuple (q, a, d), a feature-based model first transforms it to a feature vector $\phi(q, a, d) \in \mathbb{R}^d$ with the function ϕ. We design the following features for DG, resulting in a 26-dimension feature vector:

- *Emb Sim.* Embedding similarity between q and d and the similarity between a and d. We use the average GloVe embedding (Pennington et al., 2014) as the sentence embedding. Embeddings have been shown to be effective for finding semantically similar distractors (Kumar et al., 2015; Guo et al., 2016).

- *POS Sim.* Jaccard similarity between a and d's POS tags. The intuition is that ditractors

might also be noun phrases if the key is a noun phrase.

- *ED*. Edit distance between a and d. This measures the spelling similarity and is useful for cases such as selecting "RNA" as a distractor for "DNA".

- *Token Sim.* Jaccard similarities between q and d's tokens, a and d's tokens, and q and a's tokens. This feature is motivated by the observation that distractors might share tokens with the key.

- *Length.* a and d's character and token lengths and the difference of lengths. This feature is designed to explore whether distractors and the key are similar in terms of lengths.

- *Suffix.* The absolute and relative length of a and d's longest common suffix. The key and distractors often have common suffixes. For example, "maltose", "lactose", and "suctose" could be good distractors for "fructose".

- *Freq.* Average word frequency in a and d. Word frequency has been used as a proxy for words' difficulty levels (Coniam, 1997). This feature is designed to select distractors with a similar difficulty level as the key.

- *Single.* Singular/plural consistency of a and d. This checks the consistency of singular vs. plural usage, which will select grammatically correct distractors given the stem.

- *Num.* Whether numbers appear in a and d. This feature will cover cases where distractors and keys contain numbers, such as "90 degree", "one year", "2018", etc.

- *Wiki Sim.* If a and d are Wikipedia entities, we calculate their Wiki embedding similarity. The embedding is trained using word2vec (Mikolov et al., 2013) on Wikipedia data with each Wiki entity treated as an individual token. This feature is a complement to Emb Sim where sentence embedding is a simple average of word embeddings.

2.1.2 Classifiers

We study the following three feature-based classifiers: (i) Logistic Regression: an efficient generalized linear classification model; (ii) Random Forest (Breiman, 2001): an effective ensemble classification model; (iii) LambdaMART (Burges, 2010): a gradient boosted tree based learning-to-rank model. To train these models, following previous notations, we use D_i as positive examples and sample from $\mathcal{D} - D_i$ to get negative examples.

2.2 NN-based Models

Based on the recently proposed method IR-GAN (Wang et al., 2017), we propose an adversarial training framework for DG. Our framework consists of two components: a generator G and a discriminator D. G is a generative model that aims to capture the conditional probability of generating distractors given stems and answers $P(d|q, a)$. D is a discriminative model that estimates the probability that a distractor sample comes from the real training data rather than G.

Assume that the discriminator is based on an arbitrary scoring function $f_\phi(d, q, a) \in \mathbb{R}$ parameterized by ϕ, then the objective for D is to maximize the following log-likelihood:

$$\max_\phi \; \mathbb{E}_{d \sim P_{\text{true}}(d|q,a)}[\log(\sigma(f_\phi(d, q, a)))]$$
$$+ \; \mathbb{E}_{d \sim P_\theta(d|q,a)}[\log(1 - \sigma(f_\phi(d, q, a)))] \quad (1)$$

where σ is the sigmoid function. For the generator G, we choose another scoring function $f_\theta(d, q, a) \in \mathbb{R}$ parameterized by θ, evaluate it on every possible distractor d_i given a (q, a) pair, and sample generated distractors based on the discrete probability after applying softmax:

$$p_\theta(d_i|q, a) = \frac{\exp(\tau \cdot f_\theta(d_i, q, a))}{\sum_j \exp(\tau \cdot f_\theta(d_j, q, a))} \quad (2)$$

where τ is a temperature hyper-parameter.

In practice, since the total size of distractors is large, it is very time-consuming to evaluate on every possible d_i. Following the common practice as in (Wang et al., 2017; Cai and Wang, 2018), we uniformly sample K candidate distractors for each (q, a) pair and evaluate f_θ on each $d_i, \forall i \in [1, K]$. The objective for G is to "fool" D so that D misclassifies distractors generated by G as positive:

$$\min_\theta \; \mathbb{E}_{d \sim P_\theta(d|q,a)}[\log(1 - \sigma(f_\phi(d, q, a)))] \quad (3)$$

The training procedure follows a two-player minimax game, where D and G are alternatively optimized towards their own objective.

The scoring function f_ϕ and f_θ can take arbitrary forms. IRGAN utilizes a convolutional neu-

Dataset	$|\mathcal{D}|$	# MCQs	# Train	# Valid	# Test	Avg. # Dis
SciQ	22379	13679	11679	1000	1000	3
MCQL	16446	7116	5999	554	563	2.91

Table 1: Dataset Statistics.

ral network based model to obtain sentence embeddings and then calculates the cosine similarities. However, such a method ignores the word-level interactions, which is important for the DG task. For example, if the stem asks "which physical unit", good distractors should be units. Therefore, we adopt the Decomposable Attention model (DecompAtt) (Parikh et al., 2016) proposed for Natural Language Inference to measure the similarities between q and d. We also consider the similarities between a and d. Since they are usually short sequences, we simply use the cosine similarity between summed word embeddings. As such, the scoring function is defined as a linear combination of DecompAtt(d, q) and Cosine(d, a).

2.3 Cascaded Learning Framework

To make the ranking process more efficient and effective, we propose a cascaded learning framework, a multistage ensemble learning framework that has been widely used for computer vision (Viola and Jones, 2001). We experiment with 2-stage cascading, where the first stage ranker is a simple model trained with part of the features in Sec. 2.1.1 and the second stage ranker can be any aforementioned ranking model. Such cascading has two advantages: (i) The candidate size is significantly reduced by the first stage ranker, which allows the use of more expensive features and complex models in the second stage; (ii) The second stage ranker can learn from more challenging negative examples since they are top predictions from previous stage, which can make the learning more effective.

3 Experiments

3.1 Datasets

We evaluate the proposed DG models on the following two datasets: (i) **SciQ** (Welbl et al., 2017): crowdsourced 13.7K science MCQs covering biology, chemistry, earth science, and physics. The questions span elementary level to college introductory level in the US. (ii) **MCQL**: 7.1K MCQs crawled from the Web. Questions are about biology, physics, and chemistry and at the Cambridge

O level and college level.

For SciQ, we follow the original train/valid/test splits. For MCQL, we randomly divide the dataset into train/valid/test with an approximate ratio of 10:1:1. We convert the dataset to lowercase, filter out the distractors such as "all of them", "none of them", "both A and B", and keep questions with at least one distractor. We use all the keys and distractors in the dataset as candidate distractor set $\mathcal{D}$. Table 1 summarizes the statistics of the two datasets after preprocessing. $|\mathcal{D}|$ is the number of candidate distractors. # MCQs is the total number of MCQs. # Train/Valid/Test is the number of questions in each split of the dataset. Avg. # Dis is the average number of distractors per question.

3.2 Experiment Settings

We use Logistic Regression (**LR**) as the first stage ranker. As for the second stage, we compare LR, Random Forest (**RF**), LambdaMART (**LM**), and the proposed NN-based model (**NN**). Specifically, we set C to 1 for LR, use 500 trees for RF, and 500 rounds of boosting for LM. For first stage training, the number of negative samples is set to be equal to the number of distractors, which is 3 for most questions. And we sample 100 negative samples for second stage training. More details can be found in the supplementary material. In addition, we also study the following unsupervised baselines that measure similarities between the key and distractors: (i) pointwise mutual information (**PMI**) based on co-occurrences; (ii) edit distance (**ED**), which measures the spelling similarity; and (iii) GloVe embedding similarity (**Emb Sim**). For evaluation, we report top recall (R@10), precision (P@1, P@3), mean average precision (MAP@10), normalized discounted cumulative gain (NDCG@10), and mean reciprocal rank (MRR).

3.3 Experimental Results

First Stage Ranker The main goal of the first stage ranker is to reduce the candidate size for the later stage while achieving a relatively high recall. Figure 1 shows the Recall@K for the first stage ranker on the two datasets. Validation set is used for choosing top K predictions for later stage training. We empirically set K to 2000 for SciQ and 2500 for MCQL to get a recall of about 90%.

Distractor Ranking Results Table 2 lists the ranking results for DG. From the table we observe

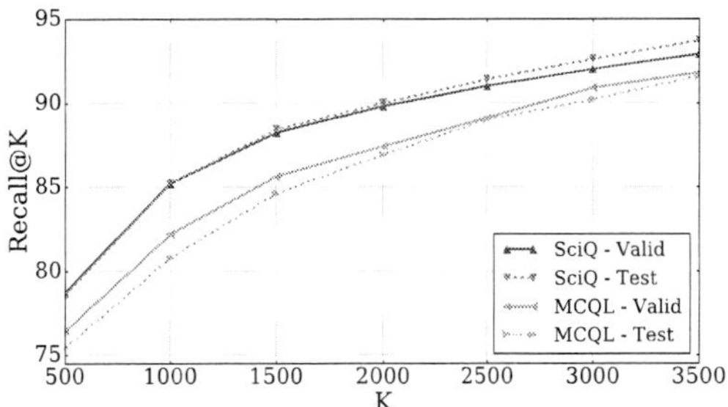

Figure 1: Recall@K for the first stage ranker.

1st Stage Ranker	2nd Stage Ranker	R@10	P@1	P@3	MAP @10	NDCG @10	MRR
LR	PMI	11.0	2.1	3.1	3.6	6.8	8.8
	ED	14.3	12.6	9.2	8.7	12.5	18.9
	Emb Sim	19.3	9.3	9.0	9.6	14.2	17.5
	LR	29.7	14.8	14.1	14.7	22.1	27.6
	RF	44.1	36.8	27.0	28.4	38.0	49.2
	LM	43.3	37.2	26.4	28.0	37.5	49.3
	NN	24.6	11.7	11.7	11.6	23.1	25.7
RF	—	41.4	31.2	23.7	25.0	34.4	44.0
LM	—	39.1	26.5	22.6	22.9	31.8	40.4

(a) SciQ

1st Stage Ranker	2nd Stage Ranker	R@10	P@1	P@3	MAP @10	NDCG @10	MRR
LR	PMI	20.7	5.9	6.8	7.8	13.5	16.2
	ED	32.1	34.6	23.6	23.7	30.5	42.8
	Emb Sim	32.1	25.6	18.4	20.4	26.9	33.9
	LR	42.9	29.3	24.5	26.6	35.1	42.2
	RF	48.4	45.5	32.7	35.4	43.8	54.8
	LM	49.4	42.8	31.5	34.5	43.4	53.6
	NN	36.5	22.9	22.5	22.7	34.6	36.7
RF	—	48.0	40.9	30.4	33.6	42.0	51.1
LM	—	46.7	42.5	30.6	33.0	41.6	52.7

(b) MCQL

Table 2: Ranking results (%) for DG.

the following: (i) The proposed ranking models perform better than unsupervised similarity-based methods (PMI, ED, and Emb Sim) most of the time, which is expected since similarity-based heuristics are used as features. (ii) Ensemble models - RF and LM - have comparable performance and are significantly better than other methods. These ensemble methods are more suitable for capturing the nonlinear relation between the proposed feature set and distractors. (iii) NN performs worse than feature-based models. The main reason is that NN is solely based on word embeddings. Although embedding similarity is the most important feature, information provided by other top features such as ED, Suffix, Freq is missing in NN. Given the limited training examples (11.6K for SciQ and 6K for MCQL), it is difficult to learn a robust end-to-end NN-based model.

#	SciQ	MCQL
1	Emb Sim (a, d)	Emb Sim (a, d)
2	Freq d	Token Sim (a, d)
3	Freq a	ED
4	Wiki Sim	Suffix
5	Emb Sim (q, d)	Suffix / len(d)
6	Suffix	Freq a
7	Suffix / len(d)	Wiki Sim
8	Suffix / len(a)	Freq d
9	Token Sim (a, d)	Emb Sim (q, d)
10	ED	Suffix / len(a)

Table 3: Top 10 important features.

Feature Analysis We conduct a feature analysis to have more insights on the proposed feature set. Feature importance is calculated by "mean decrease impurity" using RF. It is defined as the total decrease in node impurity, weighted by the probability of reaching that node, averaged over all trees of the ensemble. Table 3 lists the top 10 important features for SciQ and MCQL datasets. We find that: (i) the embedding similarity between a and d is the most important feature, which shows embeddings are effective at capturing semantic relations between a and d. (ii) String similarities such as Token Sim, ED, and Suffix are more important in MCQL than those in SciQ. This is consistent with the observation that ED has relatively good performance as seen in Table 2b. (iii) The set of top 10 features is the same for SciQ and MCQL, regardless of order.

Effects of Cascaded Learning Since we choose the top 2000 for SciQ and 2500 for MCQL from first stage, the ranking candidate size is reduced by 91% for SciQ and 85% for MCQL, which makes the second stage learning more efficient. To study whether cascaded learning is effective, we experiment with RF and LM without 2-stage learning, as shown as the bottom two rows in Table 2. Here we sample 100 negative samples for training models in order to make a fair comparison with other methods using 2-stage learning. We can see that the performance is better when cascaded learning is applied.

4 Conclusion

We investigated DG as a ranking problem and applied feature-based and NN-based supervised ranking models to the task. Experiments with the SciQ and the MCQL datasets empirically show that ensemble learning models (random forest and LambdaMART) outperform both the NN-based

method and unsupervised baselines. The MCQL data is publicly available upon request. The two datasets can be used as benchmarks for further DG research. Future work will be to design a user interface to implement the proposed models to help teachers with DG and collect more user data for model training.

Acknowledgments

We gratefully acknowledge partial support from the Pennsylvania State University Center for Online Innovation in Learning and helpful comments from the reviewers.

A   Training and Implementation Details

Feature-based Models. We use the implementations of scikit-learn (Pedregosa et al., 2011) for logistic regression and random forest experiments. For LambdaMART experiments, we use the XGBoost library (Chen and Guestrin, 2016). For both SCIQ and MCQL datasets we train with 500 rounds of boosting, step size shrinkage of 0.1, maximum depth of 30, minimum child weight of 0.1 and minimum loss reduction of 1.0 for partition. For calculating Wiki Sim features, we use a Wikipedia dump of Oct. 2016. Part of speech tags are calculated with NLTK (Bird and Loper, 2004).

The logistic regression used for the first stage ranker is based on features including: Emb Sim, POS Sim, ED, Token Sim, Length, Suffix, and Freq. Models for the second stage ranker is based on all features described in Sec. 2.1.1.

NN-based Models. Our NN-based models are implemented with TensorFlow (Abadi et al., 2016). When training the generator, we first uniformly select $K = 512$ candidates and then sample 16 distractors according to Equation 2. The temperature τ is set to 5. Our scoring functions are based on Decomposable Attention Model (Parikh et al., 2016). The word embeddings are initialized using the pre-trained GloVe (Pennington et al., 2014) (840B tokens), and the embedding size is 300. Our model is optimized using Adam algorithm (Kingma and Ba, 2015) with a learning rate of 1e-4 and a weight decay of 1e-6.

Since the sampling process in G is not differentiable, the gradient-decent-based optimization in the original GAN paper (Goodfellow et al., 2014) is not directly applicable. To tackle this problem, we use policy gradient based reinforcement learning as in IRGAN.

References

Martín Abadi, Paul Barham, Jianmin Chen, Zhifeng Chen, Andy Davis, Jeffrey Dean, Matthieu Devin, Sanjay Ghemawat, Geoffrey Irving, Michael Isard, et al. 2016. Tensorflow: A system for large-scale machine learning. In *OSDI*, volume 16, pages 265–283.

Manish Agarwal and Prashanth Mannem. 2011. Automatic gap-fill question generation from text books. In *BEA*, pages 56–64. ACL.

Steven Bird and Edward Loper. 2004. Nltk: the natural language toolkit. In *Proceedings of the ACL 2004 on Interactive poster and demonstration sessions*, page 31. ACL.

Leo Breiman. 2001. Random forests. *Machine learning*, 45(1):5–32.

Chris J.C. Burges. 2010. From ranknet to lambdarank to lambdamart: An overview. Technical report.

Liwei Cai and William Yang Wang. 2018. Kbgan: Adversarial learning for knowledge graph embeddings. In *NAACL*. ACL.

Chia-Yin Chen, Hsien-Chin Liou, and Jason S Chang. 2006. Fast: an automatic generation system for grammar tests. In *Proceedings of the COLING/ACL on Interactive presentation sessions*, pages 1–4. ACL.

Tianqi Chen and Carlos Guestrin. 2016. Xgboost: A scalable tree boosting system. In *KDD*, pages 785–794. ACM.

David Coniam. 1997. A preliminary inquiry into using corpus word frequency data in the automatic generation of english language cloze tests. *Calico Journal*, 14(2-4):15–33.

Ian Goodfellow, Jean Pouget-Abadie, Mehdi Mirza, Bing Xu, David Warde-Farley, Sherjil Ozair, Aaron Courville, and Yoshua Bengio. 2014. Generative adversarial nets. In *NIPS*, pages 2672–2680.

Hubbard C Goodrich. 1977. Distractor efficiency in foreign language testing. *TESOL Quarterly*, pages 69–78.

Qi Guo, Chinmay Kulkarni, Aniket Kittur, Jeffrey P. Bigham, and Emma Brunskill. 2016. Questimator: Generating knowledge assessments for arbitrary topics. In *IJCAI*, pages 3726–3732.

Jennifer Hill and Rahul Simha. 2016. Automatic generation of context-based fill-in-the-blank exercises using co-occurrence likelihoods and google n-grams. In *BEA@NAACL*, pages 23–30. ACL.

Shu Jiang and John Lee. 2017. Distractor generation for chinese fill-in-the-blank items. In *BEA@EMNLP*, pages 143–148. ACL.

Diederik P Kingma and Jimmy Ba. 2015. Adam: A method for stochastic optimization. In *ICLR*.

Girish Kumar, Rafael E Banchs, and Luis Fernando D'Haro Enriquez. 2015. Revup: Automatic gap-fill question generation from educational texts. In *BEA*. ACL.

Chen Liang, Xiao Yang, Drew Wham, Bart Pursel, Rebecca Passonneau, and C. Lee Giles. 2017. Distractor generation with generative adversarial nets for automatically creating fill-in-the-blank questions. In *Proceedings of the Knowledge Capture Conference*, page 33. ACM.

Tie-Yan Liu et al. 2009. Learning to rank for information retrieval. *Foundations and Trends® in Information Retrieval*, 3(3):225–331.

Tomas Mikolov, Ilya Sutskever, Kai Chen, Greg S Corrado, and Jeff Dean. 2013. Distributed representations of words and phrases and their compositionality. In *NIPS*, pages 3111–3119.

Ruslan Mitkov and Le An Ha. 2003. Computer-aided generation of multiple-choice tests. In *BEA@NAACL*, pages 17–22. ACL.

Ankur Parikh, Oscar Täckström, Dipanjan Das, and Jakob Uszkoreit. 2016. A decomposable attention model for natural language inference. In *EMNLP*, pages 2249–2255. ACL.

Fabian Pedregosa, Gaël Varoquaux, Alexandre Gramfort, Vincent Michel, Bertrand Thirion, Olivier Grisel, Mathieu Blondel, Peter Prettenhofer, Ron Weiss, Vincent Dubourg, et al. 2011. Scikit-learn: Machine learning in python. *Journal of machine learning research*, 12(Oct):2825–2830.

Jeffrey Pennington, Richard Socher, and Christopher Manning. 2014. Glove: Global vectors for word representation. In *EMNLP*, pages 1532–1543. ACL.

Juan Pino and Maxine Eskenazi. 2009. Semi-automatic generation of cloze question distractors effect of students' l1. In *SLaTE*, pages 65–68.

Juan Pino, Michael Heilman, and Maxine Eskenazi. 2008. A selection strategy to improve cloze question quality. In *Proceedings of the Workshop on Intelligent Tutoring Systems for Ill-Defined Domains. 9th International Conference on Intelligent Tutoring Systems.*, pages 30–42.

Keisuke Sakaguchi, Yuki Arase, and Mamoru Komachi. 2013. Discriminative approach to fill-in-the-blank quiz generation for language learners. In *ACL*, volume 2, pages 238–242. ACL.

Katherine Stasaski and Marti A Hearst. 2017. Multiple choice question generation utilizing an ontology. In *BEA@EMNLP*, pages 303–312. ACL.

Eiichiro Sumita, Fumiaki Sugaya, and Seiichi Yamamoto. 2005. Measuring non-native speakers' proficiency of english by using a test with automatically-generated fill-in-the-blank questions. In *BEA*, pages 61–68. ACL.

Paul Viola and Michael Jones. 2001. Rapid object detection using a boosted cascade of simple features. In *CVPR*, volume 1, pages 511–518. IEEE.

Jun Wang, Lantao Yu, Weinan Zhang, Yu Gong, Yinghui Xu, Benyou Wang, Peng Zhang, and Dell Zhang. 2017. Irgan: A minimax game for unifying generative and discriminative information retrieval models. In *SIGIR*, pages 515–524. ACM.

Johannes Welbl, Nelson F. Liu, and Matt Gardner. 2017. Crowdsourcing multiple choice science questions. In *Proceedings of the 3rd Workshop on Noisy User-generated Text, NUT@EMNLP*, pages 94–106. ACL.

Torsten Zesch and Oren Melamud. 2014. Automatic generation of challenging distractors using context-sensitive inference rules. In *BEA*, pages 143–148. ACL.

A Portuguese Native Language Identification Dataset

Iria del Río[1], Marcos Zampieri[2], Shervin Malmasi[3,4]
[1]University of Lisbon, Center of Linguistics-CLUL, Portugal
[2]University of Wolverhampton, United Kingdom
[3]Harvard Medical School, United States
[4]Macquarie University, Australia
`igayo@letras.ulisboa.pt`

Abstract

In this paper we present NLI-PT, the first Portuguese dataset compiled for Native Language Identification (NLI), the task of identifying an author's first language based on their second language writing. The dataset includes 1,868 student essays written by learners of European Portuguese, native speakers of the following L1s: Chinese, English, Spanish, German, Russian, French, Japanese, Italian, Dutch, Tetum, Arabic, Polish, Korean, Romanian, and Swedish. NLI-PT includes the original student text and four different types of annotation: POS, fine-grained POS, constituency parses, and dependency parses. NLI-PT can be used not only in NLI but also in research on several topics in the field of Second Language Acquisition and educational NLP. We discuss possible applications of this dataset and present the results obtained for the first lexical baseline system for Portuguese NLI.

1 Introduction

Several learner corpora have been compiled for English, such as the International Corpus of Learner English (Granger, 2003). The importance of such resources has been increasingly recognized across a variety of research areas, from Second Language Acquisition to Natural Language Processing. Recently, we have seen substantial growth in this area and new corpora for languages other than English have appeared. For Romance languages, there are a several corpora and resources for French[1], Spanish (Lozano, 2010), and Italian (Boyd et al., 2014).

Portuguese has also received attention in the compilation of learner corpora. There are two corpora compiled at the School of Arts and Humanities of the University of Lisbon: the cor-

pus *Recolha de dados de Aprendizagem do Português Língua Estrangeira*[2] (hereafter, Leiria corpus), with 470 texts and 70,500 tokens, and the Learner Corpus of Portuguese as Second/Foreign Language, COPLE2[3] (del Río et al., 2016), with 1,058 texts and 201,921 tokens. The *Corpus de Produções Escritas de Aprendentes de PL2*, PEAPL2[4] compiled at the University of Coimbra, contains 516 texts and 119,381 tokens. Finally, the *Corpus de Aquisição de L2*, CAL2[5], compiled at the New University of Lisbon, contains 1,380 texts and 281,301 words, and it includes texts produced by adults and children, as well as a spoken subset.

The aforementioned Portuguese learner corpora contain very useful data for research, particularly for Native Language Identification (NLI), a task that has received much attention in recent years. NLI is the task of determining the native language (L1) of an author based on their second language (L2) linguistic productions (Malmasi and Dras, 2017). NLI works by identifying language use patterns that are common to groups of speakers of the same native language. This process is underpinned by the presupposition that an author's L1 disposes them towards certain language production patterns in their L2, as influenced by their mother tongue. A major motivation for NLI is studying second language acquisition. NLI models can enable analysis of inter-L1 linguistic differences, allowing us to study the language learning process and develop L1-specific pedagogical methods and materials.

However, there are limitations to using existing Portuguese data for NLI. An important issue is that the different corpora each contain data col-

---

[1]https://uclouvain.be/en/research-institutes/ilc/cecl/frida.html

[2]http://www.clul.ulisboa.pt/pt/24-recursos/350-recolha-de-dados-de-ple

[3]http://alfclul.clul.ul.pt/teitok/learnercorpus

[4]http://teitok.iltec.pt/peapl2/

[5]http://cal2.clunl.edu.pt/

Proceedings of the Thirteenth Workshop on Innovative Use of NLP for Building Educational Applications, pages 291–296
New Orleans, Louisiana, June 5, 2018. ©2018 Association for Computational Linguistics

lected from different L1 backgrounds in varying amounts; they would need to be combined to have sufficient data for an NLI study. Another challenge concerns the annotations as only two of the corpora (PEAPL2 and COPLE2) are linguistically annotated, and this is limited to POS tags. The different data formats used by each corpus presents yet another challenge to their usage.

In this paper we present NLI-PT, a dataset collected for Portuguese NLI. The dataset is made freely available for research purposes.[6] With the goal of unifying learner data collected from various sources, listed in Section 3.1, we applied a methodology which has been previously used for the compilation of language variety corpora (Tan et al., 2014). The data was converted to a unified data format and uniformly annotated at different linguistic levels as described in Section 3.2. To the best of our knowledge, NLI-PT is the only Portuguese dataset developed specifically for NLI, this will open avenues for research in this area.

2 Related Work

NLI has attracted a lot of attention in recent years. Due to the availability of suitable data, as discussed earlier, this attention has been particularly focused on English. The most notable examples are the two editions of the NLI shared task organized in 2013 (Tetreault et al., 2013) and 2017 (Malmasi et al., 2017).

Even though most NLI research has been carried out on English data, an important research trend in recent years has been the application of NLI methods to other languages, as discussed in Malmasi and Dras (2015). Recent NLI studies on languages other than English include Arabic (Malmasi and Dras, 2014a) and Chinese (Malmasi and Dras, 2014b; Wang et al., 2015). To the best of our knowledge, no study has been published on Portuguese and the NLI-PT dataset opens new possibilities of research for Portuguese. In Section 4.1 we present the first simple baseline results for this task.

Finally, as NLI-PT can be used in other applications besides NLI, it is important to point out that a number of studies have been published on educational NLP applications for Portuguese and on the

compilation of learner language resources for Portuguese. Examples of such studies include grammatical error correction (Martins et al., 1998), automated essay scoring (Elliot, 2003), academic word lists (Baptista et al., 2010), and the learner corpora presented in the previous section.

3 Corpus Description

3.1 Collection methodology

The data was collected from three different learner corpora of Portuguese: (i) COPLE2; (ii) Leiria corpus, and (iii) PEAPL2[7] as presented in Table 3.

	COPLE2	LEIRIA	PEAPL2	TOTAL
Texts	1,058	330	480	1,868
Tokens	201,921	57,358	121,138	380,417
Types	9,373	4,504	6,808	20,685
TTR	0.05	0.08	0.06	0.05

Table 1: Distribution of the dataset: Number of texts, tokens, types, and type/token ratio (TTER) per source corpus.

The three corpora contain written productions from learners of Portuguese with different proficiency levels and native languages (L1s). In the dataset we included all the data in COPLE2 and sections of PEAPL2 and Leiria corpus.

The main variable we used for text selection was the presence of specific L1s. Since the three corpora consider different L1s, we decided to use the L1s present in the largest corpus, COPLE2, as the reference. Therefore, we included in the dataset texts corresponding to the following 15 L1s: Chinese, English, Spanish, German, Russian, French, Japanese, Italian, Dutch, Tetum, Arabic, Polish, Korean, Romanian, and Swedish. It was the case that some of the L1s present in COPLE2 were not documented in the other corpora. The number of texts from each L1 is presented in Table 2.

Concerning the corpus design, there is some variability among the sources we used. Leiria corpus and PEAPL2 followed a similar approach for data collection and show a close design. They consider a close list of topics, called "stimulus", which belong to three general areas: (i) the individual; (ii) the society; (iii) the environment.

[6]NLI-PT is available at: http://www.clul.ulisboa.pt/en/resources-en/11-resources/894-nli-pt-a-portuguese-native-language-identification-dataset

[7]In the near future we want to incorporate also data from the CAL2 corpus.

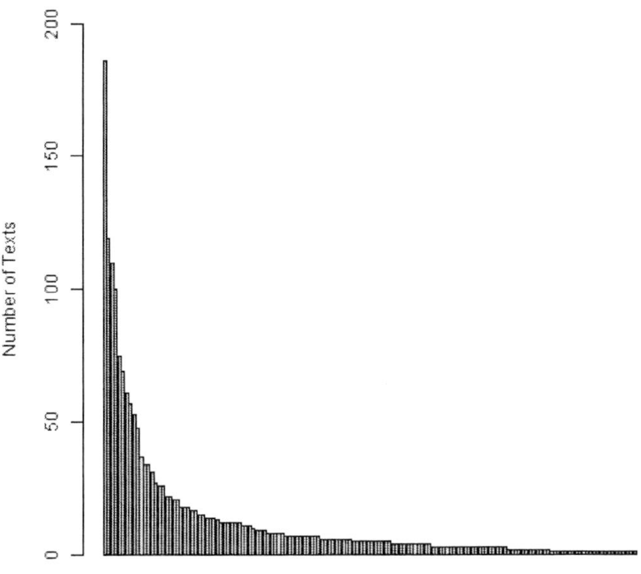

Figure 1: Topic distribution by number of texts. Each bar represents one of the 148 topics.

	COPLE2	PEAPL2	LEIRIA	TOTAL
Arabic	13	1	0	14
Chinese	323	32	0	355
Dutch	17	26	0	43
English	142	62	31	235
French	59	38	7	104
German	86	88	40	214
Italian	49	83	83	215
Japanese	52	15	0	67
Korean	9	9	48	66
Polish	31	28	12	71
Romanian	12	16	51	79
Russian	80	11	1	92
Spanish	147	68	56	271
Swedish	16	2	1	19
Tetum	22	1	0	23
Total	1,058	480	330	1,868

Table 2: Distribution by L1s and source corpora.

Those topics are presented to the students in order to produce a written text. As a whole, texts from PEAPL2 and Leiria represent 36 different stimuli or topics in the dataset. In COPLE2 corpus the written texts correspond to written exercises done during Portuguese lessons, or to official Portuguese proficiency tests. For this reason, the topics considered in COPLE2 corpus are different from the topics in Leiria and PEAPL2. The number of topics is also larger in COPLE2 corpus: 149 different topics. There is some overlap between the different topics considered in COPLE2, that is, some topics deal with the same subject. This overlap allowed us to reorganize COPLE2 topics in our dataset, reducing them to 112.

	Number of topics
COPLE2	112
PEAPL2+Leiria	36
Total	148

Table 3: Number of different topics by source.

Due to the different distribution of topics in the source corpora, the 148 topics in the dataset are not represented uniformly. Three topics account for a 48.7% of the total texts and, on the other hand, a 72% of the topics are represented by 1-10 texts (Figure 1). This variability affects also text length. The longest text has 787 tokens and

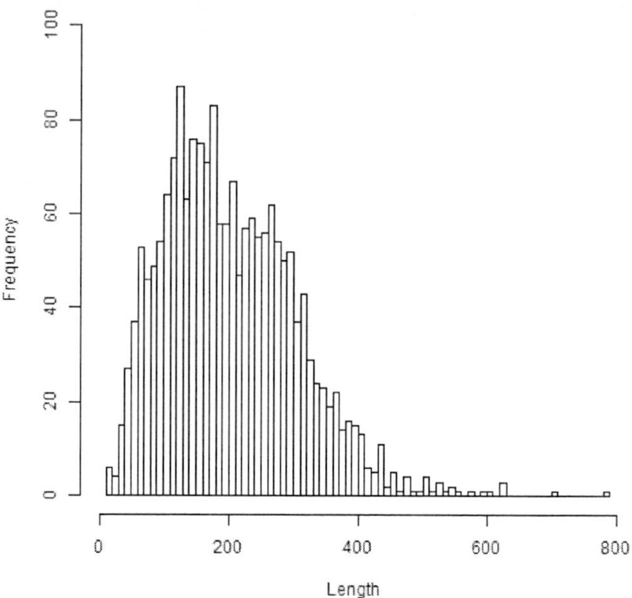

Figure 2: Histogram of document lengths, as measured by the number of tokens. The mean value is 204 with standard deviation of 103.

the shortest has only 16 tokens. Most texts, however, range roughly from 150 to 250 tokens. To better understand the distribution of texts in terms of word length we plot a histogram of all texts with their word length in bins of 10 (1-10 tokens, 11-20 tokens, 21-30 tokens and so on) (Figure 2).

The three corpora use the proficiency levels defined in the Common European Framework of Reference for Languages (CEFR), but they show differences in the number of levels they consider. There are five proficiency levels in COPLE2 and PEAPL2: A1, A2, B1, B2, and C1. But there are 3 levels in Leiria corpus: A, B, and C. The number of texts included from each proficiency level is presented in Table 4.

3.2 Preprocessing and annotation of texts

As demonstrated earlier, these learner corpora use different formats. COPLE2 is mainly codified in XML, although it gives the possibility of getting the student version of the essay in TXT format. PEAPL2 and Leiria corpus are compiled in TXT format.[8] In both corpora, the TXT files contain the student version with special annotations from the

	COPLE2	LEIRIA	PEAPL2	TOTAL
A1	91	n/a	78	169
A2	414	n/a	89	503
A	505	203	167	875
B1	312	n/a	203	515
B2	202	n/a	70	272
B	514	89	273	876
C1	39	n/a	40	79
C	39	38	40	117

Table 4: Distribution by proficiency levels and by source corpus.

transcription. For the NLI experiments we were interested in a clean txt version of the students' text, together with versions annotated at different linguistics levels. Therefore, as a first step, we removed all the annotations corresponding to the transcription process in PEAPL2 and Leiria files. As a second step, we proceeded to the linguistic annotation of the texts using different NLP tools.

We annotated the dataset at two levels: Part of Speech (POS) and syntax. We performed the annotation with freely available tools for the Portuguese language. For POS we added a simple POS, that is, only type of word, and a fine-

---

[8]Currently there is a XML version of PEAPL2, but this version was not available when we compiled the dataset.

grained POS, which is the type of word plus its morphological features. We used the LX Parser (Silva et al., 2010), for the simple POS and the Portuguese morphological module of Freeling (Padró and Stanilovsky, 2012), for detailed POS. Concerning syntactic annotations, we included constituency and dependency annotations. For constituency parsing, we used the LX Parser, and for dependency, the DepPattern toolkit (Otero and González, 2012).

4 Applications

NLI-PT was developed primarily for NLI, but it can be used for other research purposes ranging from second language acquisition to educational NLP applications. Here are a few examples of applications in which the dataset can be used:

- Computer-aided Language Learning (CALL): CALL software has been developed for Portuguese (Marujo et al., 2009). Further improvements in these tools can take advantage of the training material available in NLI-PT for a number of purposes such as L1-tailored exercise design.

- Grammatical error detection and correction: as discussed in Zampieri and Tan (2014), a known challenge in this task is acquiring suitable training data to account for the variation of errors present in non-native texts. One of the strategies developed to cope with this problem is to generate artificial training data (Felice and Yuan, 2014). Augmenting training data using a suitable annotated dataset such as NLI-PT can improve the quality of existing grammatical error correction systems for Portuguese.

- Spellchecking: Studies have shown that general-purpose spell checkers target performance errors but fail to address many competence errors committed by language learners (Rimrott and Heift, 2005). To address this shortcoming a number of spell checking tools have been developed for language learners (Ndiaye and Faltin, 2003). Suitable training data is required o develop these tools. NLI-PT is a suitable resource to train learner spell checkers for Portuguese.

- L1 interference: one of the aspects of non-native language production that can be stud-

ied using data-driven methods is the influence of L1 in non-native speakers production. Its annotation and the number of second languages included in the dataset make NLI-PT a perfect fit for such studies.

4.1 A Baseline for Portuguese NLI

To demonstrate the usefulness of the dataset we present the first lexical baseline for Portuguese NLI using a sub-set of NLI-PT. To the best of our knowledge, no study has been published on Portuguese NLI and our work fills this gap.

In this experiment we included the five L1s in NLI-PT which contain the largest number of texts in this sub-set and run a simple linear SVM (Fan et al., 2008) classifier using a bag of words model to identify the L1 of each text. The languages included in this experiment were Chinese (355 texts), English (236 texts), German (214 texts), Italian (216 texts), and Spanish (271 texts).

We evaluated the model using stratified 10-fold cross-validation, achieving 70% accuracy. An important limitation of this experiment is that it does not account for topic bias, an important issue in NLI (Malmasi, 2016). This is due to the fact that NLI-PT is not balanced by topic and the model could be learning topic associations instead.[9] In future work we would like to carry out using syntactic features such as function words, syntactic relations and POS annotation.

5 Conclusion and Future Work

This paper presented NLI-PT, the first Portuguese dataset compiled for NLI. NLI-PT contains 1,868 texts written by speakers of 15 L1s amounting to over 380,000 tokens.

As discussed in Section 4, NLI-PT opens several avenues for future research. It can be used for different research purposes beyond NLI such as grammatical error correction and CALL. An experiment with the texts written by the speakers of five L1s: Chinese, English, German, Italian, and Spanish using a bag of words model achieved 70% accuracy. We are currently experimenting with different features taking advantage of the annotation available in NLI-PT thus reducing topic bias in classification.

In future work we would like to include more texts in the dataset following the same methodology and annotation.

---

[9]See Malmasi (2016, p. 23) for a detailed discussion.

Acknowledgement

We want to thank the research teams that have made available the data we used in this work: Centro de Estudos de Linguística Geral e Aplicada at Universidade de Coimbra (specially Cristina Martins) and Centro de Linguística da Universidade de Lisboa (particularly Amália Mendes).

This work was partially supported by Fundação para a Ciência e a Tecnologia (postdoctoral research grant SFRH/BPD/109914/2015).

References

Jorge Baptista, Neuza Costa, Joaquim Guerra, Marcos Zampieri, Maria Cabral, and Nuno Mamede. 2010. P-AWL: academic word list for Portuguese. In *Proceedings of PROPOR*.

Adriane Boyd, Jirka Hana, Lionel Nicolas, Detmar Meurers, Katrin Wisniewski, andrea Abel, Karin Schöne, Barbora Štindlová, and Chiara Vettori. 2014. The MERLIN corpus: Learner Language and the CEFR. In *Proceedings of LREC*.

Scott Elliot. 2003. IntelliMetric: From here to validity. *Automated essay scoring: A cross-disciplinary perspective*, pages 71–86.

Rong-En Fan, Kai-Wei Chang, Cho-Jui Hsieh, Xiang-Rui Wang, and Chih-Jen Lin. 2008. LIBLINEAR: A Library for Large Linear Classification. *Journal of Machine Learning Research*, 9(Aug):1871–1874.

Mariano Felice and Zheng Yuan. 2014. Generating Artificial Errors for Grammatical Error Correction. In *Proceedings of the EACL Student Research Workshop*.

Sylviane Granger. 2003. The international corpus of learner english: A new resource for foreign language learning and teaching and second language acquisition research. *TESOL Quarterly*, 37(3):538–546.

Cristóbal Lozano. 2010. *CEDEL2, Corpus Escrito del Español L2*. Department of English, Universidad Autónoma de Madrid, Madrid.

Shervin Malmasi. 2016. *Native Language Identification: Explorations and Applications*. Ph.D. thesis.

Shervin Malmasi and Mark Dras. 2014a. Arabic Native Language Identification. In *Proceedings of the Arabic Natural Language Processing Workshop*.

Shervin Malmasi and Mark Dras. 2014b. Chinese Native Language Identification. In *Proceedings of EACL*.

Shervin Malmasi and Mark Dras. 2015. Multilingual Native Language Identification. In *Natural Language Engineering*.

Shervin Malmasi and Mark Dras. 2017. Native Language Identification using Stacked Generalization. *arXiv preprint arXiv:1703.06541*.

Shervin Malmasi, Keelan Evanini, Aoife Cahill, Joel Tetreault, Robert Pugh, Christopher Hamill, Diane Napolitano, and Yao Qian. 2017. A Report on the 2017 Native Language Identification Shared Task. In *Proceedings of BEA*.

Ronaldo Teixeira Martins, Ricardo Hasegawa, Maria das Graças Volpe Nunes, Gisele Montilha, and Osvaldo Novais De Oliveira. 1998. Linguistic issues in the development of ReGra: A grammar checker for Brazilian Portuguese. *Natural Language Engineering*, 4(4):287–307.

Luís Marujo, José Lopes, Nuno Mamede, Isabel Trancoso, Juan Pino, Maxine Eskenazi, Jorge Baptista, and Céu Viana. 2009. Porting REAP to European Portuguese. In *Proceedings of the International Workshop on Speech and Language Technology in Education*.

Mar Ndiaye and Anne Vandeventer Faltin. 2003. A Spell Checker Tailored to Language Learners. *Computer Assisted Language Learning*, 16(2-3):213–232.

Pablo Gamallo Otero and Isaac González. 2012. DepPattern: a Multilingual Dependency Parser. In *Proceedings of PROPOR*.

Lluís Padró and Evgeny Stanilovsky. 2012. Freeling 3.0: Towards wider multilinguality. In *Proceedings LREC*.

Anne Rimrott and Trude Heift. 2005. Language Learners and Generic Spell Checkers in CALL. *CALICO journal*, pages 17–48.

Iria del Río, Sandra Antunes, Amália Mendes, and Maarten Janssen. 2016. Towards error annotation in a learner corpus of portuguese. In *Proceedings of the NLP4CALL workshop at SLTC*, pages 8–17.

João Ricardo Silva, António Branco, Sérgio Castro, and Ruben Reis. 2010. Out-of-the-Box Robust Parsing of Portuguese. In *Proceedings of PROPOR*, pages 75–85.

Liling Tan, Marcos Zampieri, Nikola Ljubešic, and Jörg Tiedemann. 2014. Merging Comparable Data Sources for the Discrimination of Similar Languages: The DSL Corpus Collection. In *Proceedings of the BUCC Workshop*.

Joel Tetreault, Daniel Blanchard, and Aoife Cahill. 2013. A report on the first native language identification shared task. In *Proceedings of BEA*.

Maolin Wang, Shervin Malmasi, and Mingxuan Huang. 2015. The Jinan Chinese Learner Corpus. In *Proceedings of BEA*.

Marcos Zampieri and Liling Tan. 2014. Grammatical Error Detection with Limited Training Data: The Case of Chinese. In *Proceedings of ICCE*.

OneStopEnglish corpus: A new corpus for automatic readability assessment and text simplification

Sowmya Vajjala
Iowa State University, USA
sowmya@iastate.edu

Ivana Lučić
Iowa State University, USA
ilucic@iastate.edu

Abstract

This paper describes the collection and compilation of the OneStopEnglish corpus of texts written at three reading levels, and demonstrates its usefulness for through two applications - automatic readability assessment and automatic text simplification. The corpus consists of 189 texts, each in three versions (567 in total). The corpus is now freely available under a CC by-SA 4.0 license[1] and we hope that it would foster further research on the topics of readability assessment and text simplification.

1 Introduction

Automatic Readability Assessment (ARA), the task of assessing the reading difficulty of a text, is a well-studied problem in computational linguistics (cf. Collins-Thompson, 2014). A related problem is Automatic Text Simplification (cf. Siddharthan, 2014) which aims to generate simplified texts from complex versions. While most of the research on these problems focused on feature engineering and modeling, there is very little reported work about the creation of open access corpora that supports this research.

Corpora used in ARA were primarily derived from textbooks or news articles written for different target audiences. In most of the cases, the texts at different levels in these corpora are not comparable versions of each other, which would not help us develop fine-grained readability models which can identify what parts of texts are difficult compared to others, instead of having a single score for the whole text. Corpora of parallel texts simplified for different target reading levels can solve this problem, and support better ARA models. On the other hand, ATS systems by default need parallel corpora, and primarily relied on parallel sentence pairs from Wikipedia-Simple Wikipedia for

training and evaluating the simplification models. While the availability and suitability of this corpus is definitely a positive aspect, the lack of additional corpora makes an evaluation of the generalizability of simplification approaches difficult.

In this background, we created a corpus aligned at text and sentence level, across three reading levels (beginner, intermediate, advanced), targeting English as Second Language (ESL) learners. To our knowledge, this is the first such free corpus in any language for readability assessment research. While a sentence aligned corpus from the same source was discussed in previous research, the current corpus is larger, and cleaner. In addition to describing the corpus, we demonstrate the usefulness of this corpus for automatic readability classification and text simplification. The corpus is freely available[2]. Its creation and relevance are described in the sections that follow: Section 2 describes other relevant corpus creation projects. Section 3 describes our corpus creation. Section 4 describes some preliminary experiments with readability assessment and text simplification using this corpus. Section 5 concludes the paper with pointers to future work.

2 Related Work

Washburne and Vogel (1926) and Vogel and Washburne (1928) can be considered one of the early works on corpora creation for readability research, where they collected a corpus of 700 books annotated by children in terms of reading difficulty. While there are other such efforts in the past century, corpora from those early projects are not available for current use. Contemporary approaches to readability assessment typically rely on compiling large corpora from the Web. The WeeklyReader magazine was used as a source

---

[1] https://creativecommons.org/licenses/by-sa/4.0/

[2] https://zenodo.org/record/1219041

297

Proceedings of the Thirteenth Workshop on Innovative Use of NLP for Building Educational Applications, pages 297–304
New Orleans, Louisiana, June 5, 2018. ©2018 Association for Computational Linguistics

for graded news texts in past ARA research (Petersen, 2007; Feng, 2010). Petersen and Ostendorf (2009) described a corpus of articles from Encyclopedia Britannica, where each article had a comparable "Elementary Version", which, however, is not freely available as far as we know. Vajjala and Meurers (2012) compiled WeeBit corpus, combining WeeklyReader with BBC Bite-Size, and this corpus was used in several ARA approaches in the past few years. (Vajjala and Meurers, 2013) described a large corpus of age specific TV program transcripts from BBC, and (Napoles and Dredze, 2010) used a corpus of Wikipedia-Simple Wikipedia articles. (Hancke et al., 2012; Dell'Orletta et al., 2011; Gonzalez-Dios et al., 2014), describe such web-based corpus compilation efforts for German, Italian and Basque respectively.

Textbooks from school curricula were also used as training corpora for readability assessment models in the past (e.g., Heilman et al. (2008) for English, Berendes et al. (2017) for German, (Islam et al., 2012) for Bangla). In all these cases, the grade level of the text was decided based on the target reader group (according to the website/textbook) which was decided by either publishers or authors. Another way of creating such corpora is through human annotations. DeLite corpus Vor der Brück et al. (2008) for German legal texts, and van Oosten and Hoste (2011); Clercq et al. (2014) for Dutch texts describe crowd annotated resources whereas the common core standards corpus described in Nelson et al. (2012) is annotated by experts according to the common core guidelines on text complexity. Corpora created with such human annotations are expensive to obtain and hence, are generally smaller in size. Therefore, such corpora may not be sufficient to build new models, although they can serve as good evaluation datasets.

Primary concern with all these corpora is that the articles in different reading levels are not comparable versions of each other (except Encyclopedia Britannica). The only other publicly and/or freely accessible readability corpus that potentially has parallel and comparable texts in multiple reading levels is the NewsEla[3] corpus which is a corpus of manually simplified news texts. While the corpus is available for research under some license restrictions, it also addresses a different tar-

get audience, young L1 English learners. In this background, we release an openly accessible corpus of texts with text and sentence level mapping across three reading levels, targeting L2 learners of English.

In terms of sentence aligned corpora for text simplification, different versions of aligned Wiki-Simple Wikipedia sentences have been used in NLP research (Zhu et al., 2010; Coster and Kauchak, 2011; Hwang et al., 2015). Different supervised and unsupervised approaches were proposed to construct such corpora (Bott and Saggion, 2011; Klerke and Søgaard, 2012; Klaper et al., 2013; Brunato et al., 2016). Our corpus adds a new resource for the English text simplification task.

3   Corpus

Our corpus was compiled from onestopenglish.com over the period 2013–2016. onestopenglish.com is an English language learning resources website run by MacMillan Education, with over 700,000 users across 100 countries. One of the features of the website is a weekly news lessons section, which contains articles sourced from The Guardian newspaper, and rewritten by teachers to suit three levels of adult ESL learners (elementary, intermediate, and advanced). That is, content from the same original article is rewritten in three versions, to suit three reading levels. The advanced version is close to the original article, although not with exact same content. Texts from this source were previously used for training sentence level readability models (Vajjala and Meurers, 2016; Ambati et al., 2016; Howcroft and Demberg, 2017), for performing corpus analysis about the characteristics of simplified text (Allen, 2009), and in user studies about the relationship between text complexity and reading comprehension (Crossley et al., 2014; Vajjala et al., 2016), although the corpus was not publicly available in the past.

Original articles from the website consisted of pdf files containing the article text, some pre/post test questions, and other additional material. So, the first step in the corpus creation process involved removing the irrelevant content. We first explored off-the-shelf pdf to text converters, and while they worked, they did not always result in a clean text, sometimes missing entire pages of content. While this may not be a significant issue for

---

Reading Level	Example
Advanced (Adv)	*Amsterdam still looks liberal to tourists, who were recently assured by the Labour Mayor that the city's marijuana-selling coffee shops would stay open despite a new national law tackling drug tourism. But the Dutch capital may lose its reputation for tolerance over plans to dispatch nuisance neighbours to scum villages made from shipping containers.*
Intermediate (Int)	*To tourists, Amsterdam still seems very liberal. Recently the city's Mayor assured them that the city's marijuana-selling coffee shops would stay open despite a new national law to prevent drug tourism. But the Dutch capitals plans to send nuisance neighbours to scum villages made from shipping containers may damage its reputation for tolerance.*
Elementary (Ele)	*To tourists, Amsterdam still seems very liberal. Recently the city's Mayor told them that the coffee shops that sell marijuana would stay open, although there is a new national law to stop drug tourism. But the Dutch capital has a plan to send antisocial neighbours to scum villages made from shipping containers, and so maybe now people wont think it is a liberal city any more.*

Table 1: Example sentences for three reading levels

doing text level classification, it becomes important when we try to align sentences or use this corpus for any qualitatiokave analyses. Hence, one of the authors manually went through all the files, comparing with the pdf version, to ensure there are no missing pages/content, resulting in a clean corpus[4]. An example of the degree of simplification performed is shown in Table 1.

Table 2 contains some descriptive statistics about the final corpus. As expected, advanced texts are much longer than elementary texts. However, the standard deviation for each level is also high, indicating that text length may not be the deciding factor in terms of reading level.

Reading level	Avg. Num. Words	Std. Dev
Elementary	533.17	103.79
Intermediate	676.59	117.15
Advanced	820.49	162.52

Table 2: Descriptive Statistics about the corpus

We performed some preliminary corpus analysis of the three reading levels in terms of some common features used in readability literature. Table 3 shows the summary of these results, using traditionally used features such as Flesch-Kincaid Grade Level (FKGL) (Kincaid et al., 1975) and

Type-token ratio (TTR), and occurrences of different phrases, as given by Stanford Parser (Chen and Manning, 2014). In general, all feature values decrease from ADV to ELE, which is expected, if we assume all these features to be indicative of reading level of text.

Feature	ADV	INT	ELE
FKGL	9.5	8.2	6.4
TTR	0.56	0.432	0.42
avg num. NP	6.08	5.52	4.92
avg num. VP	4.49	4.03	3.49
avg num. PP	2.72	2.30	1.82

Table 3: Some of the features across reading levels

Sentence Alignment: A sentence aligned version was created using cosine similarity, taking one pair of reading levels at a time and performing a one-to-all comparison of sentences in both texts. We chose a similarity range of [0.7-0.95] for pairing sentences, after experimenting with several thresholds. The reason for choosing 0.95 instead of 1 is that there were some sentences with only a change of punctuation, which we did not want in our sentence aligned data. The final sentence aligned corpus had 1674 pairs for ELE-INT, 2166 pairs for ELE-ADV and 3154 pairs for INT-ADV. On an average, INT-ADV sentence pairs had a higher degree of similarity (0.9) than ELE-ADV (0.77) or ELE-INT (0.85).

---

[4]We acquired permission both from Onestopenglish.com and The Guardian to release this plain-text version of the corpus.

4   Experiments

We demonstrate the usefulness of this corpus for two applications: readability assessment and text simplification.

4.1   Readability Assessment

We modeled this as a classification problem using both generic text classification features such as word ngrams as well as features typically used in readability classification research[5]. Generic text classification features include:

1. Word n-grams: Uni, Bi, Trigram features

2. POS n-grams: Bi and Trigrams of POS tags from Stanford tagger (Toutanova et al., 2003)

3. Character n-grams: 2–5 character n-grams, considering word boundaries

4. Syntactic production rules: phrase structure production rules from Stanford parser (Klein and Manning, 2003)

5. Dependency relations: Dependency relation triplets of the form (relation, head, word) from Stanford dependency parser (Chen and Manning, 2014)

All n-gram features and grammar rules/relations that occurred at least 5 times in the entire corpus were retained for the final feature set. All these features were extracted using LightSide text mining workbench (Mayfield and Rosé, 2013). Table 4 shows the classification results with these features, using Sequential Minimal Optimization (SMO) classifier with linear kernel (with a random baseline of 33% as all classes are represented equally in the data).

Features	Accuracy
Word n-grams	61.38%
POS n-grams	67.37%
Char n-grams	**77.25%**
Syntactic Production Rules	54.67%
Dependency Relations	27.16%

Table 4: Text Classification Results with generic features

Character ngrams seem to be the best performing group of generic features, achieving 77% accuracy. Data-driven features that rely on deeper

linguistic representations seem to perform poorly compared to these simple features. Particularly, dependency relations perform worse than the random baseline. Since we are working with parallel texts, there will be a lot of word level overlap across reading levels, and hence, it is not entirely surprising to see word n-grams not doing well. However, despite this, character n-grams seems to do well. We speculate they capture sub-word simplified text information such as usage of certain suffixes or prefixes, which has to be further explored in future.

In addition to the generic features, we also trained classifiers with features that are typically used in ARA research. These are:

1. Traditional features and formulae, that have been used in all the ARA models in the past

2. lexical variation, type token ratio, and POS tag ratio based features

3. Features based on psycholinguistic databases

4. Features based on constituent parse trees

5. Discourse features include:

   - overlap measures among sentences in a document as used in Coh-Metrix (Graesser et al., 2014)
   - usage of different kinds of connectives obtained from the discourse connectives tagger (Pitler and Nenkova, 2009)
   - coreference chains in the text from Stanford CoreNLP

Table 5 summarizes the results from these experiments[6].

Feature Group	Num. Feats.	Accuracy
Traditional	10	58.5%
Word	10	67.19&
Psycholinguistic	11	52.02%
LexVar, POS	29	72.48%
Syntactic Features	28	73.89%
Discourse Features	67	63.66%
Total	**155**	**78.13%**

Table 5: Text Classification Results with specific linguistic complexity features

---

[5]full feature file is provided in the supplementary material.

[6]Code for feature extraction is available at: https://bitbucket.org/nishkalavallabhi/complexity-features

Highest classification accuracy is achieved when all the features are put together, as shown in Table 5. However, this only results in a less than 1% improvement over character n-grams. Character n-grams as features for readability assessment were not explored in the past, and these results would lead us to explore that in future. In terms of comparison with existing work on ARA, highest accuracies reported are close to 90% on WeeBit dataset (Vajjala and Meurers, 2012). However, considering that we are comparing texts on the same topic, differing primarily in terms of style rather than content, this is perhaps a difficult dataset to model, compared to other existing readability datasets.

Since we now have a corpus with parallel versions of sentences and paragraphs at different reading levels, one idea to explore further is to model readability assessment as a sentence and paragraph level pair-wise ranking problem, and then use those "local" readability assessments to infer "global" text level readability (e.g., Chapter 5.5, Vajjala (2015)). Previous research also (Ma et al., 2012) showed that pair-wise ranking resulted in better readability models than classification. A combination of both these approaches would be an interesting dimension to explore in future.

4.2 Text Simplification

Automatic Text Simplification (ATS) has been commonly modeled as a Phrase Based Machine Translation (PBMT) problem in the literature. To demonstrate the usefulness of this corpus for ATS experiments, we used the *adv-ele* sentence aligned version of the OSE corpus and treated it as a phrase based machine translation problem. We split the dataset with 2166 sentence pairs into - 1000 sentence pairs for training, 500 for development, and the remaining 666 pairs for testing. We did not explore a neural model, due to the size of the dataset considered. We used Moses (Hoang et al., 2007) to train the model, and evaluated the model performance on test data in terms of various evaluation metrics used in MT research, comparing machine generated and human translations.

This model resulted in a BLEU (Papineni et al., 2001) score of 54.45 and METEOR (Denkowski and Lavie, 2014) score of 46. While the scores are not interpretable by themselves, general guidelines by Lavie (2011) suggest that BLEU and METEOR scores above 50 indicate understandable translations. Comparing with existing results on ATS, Zhang and Lapata (2017) trained a neural network based MT model with 300K sentence pairs as training data, and reported a much higher BLEU score of 88.85. The results on current dataset (with 1000 sentence training data and PBMT) cannot be compared with this result though, especially considering the size of the dataset. However, previous research showed that a high BLEU score with one corpus did not generalize when the test set came from another source (Chapter 6 in Vajjala, 2015). While our dataset may not be sufficient to build robust text simplification models, it can be used to test the generalizability of such state of the art text simplification approaches, or to be combined with a larger dataset while training a simplification model.

5 Conclusion

In this paper, we described the creation of a new corpus for readability assessment and text simplification research, and demonstrated its usefulness for readability assessment and text simplification research. The corpus is released with this paper, and we hope it will foster further research into readability assessment and text simplification systems aimed at ESL learners.

Beyond researchers interested in computational modeling, this corpus is also useful for other groups such as: a) researchers interested in conducting user studies about the relationship between text simplification and reader comprehension, or between expert annotated readability labels and target reader comprehension of texts (e.g., Vajjala et al. (2016)) and b) researchers interested in doing corpus studies with simplified and unsimplified texts, which can give insights into creating both manual and automatically simplified texts (e.g., (Allen, 2009)).

Acknowledgements:

We thank the onestopenglish.com team, and The Guardian, for allowing us to release the corpus for research use, and the anonymous reviewers for their useful comments. We also thank Detmar Meurers, University of Tübingen, for supporting the corpus creation in early stages.

References

David Allen. 2009. A study of the role of relative clauses in the simplification of news texts for learners of English. *System*, 37(4):58–599.

Bharat Ram Ambati, Siva Reddy, and Mark Steedman. 2016. Assessing relative sentence complexity using an incremental ccg parser. In *Proceedings of the 2016 Conference of the North American Chapter of the Association for Computational Linguistics: Human Language Technologies*, pages 1051–1057, San Diego, California. Association for Computational Linguistics.

Karin Berendes, Sowmya Vajjala, Detmar Meurers, Doreen Bryant, Wolfgang Wagner, Maria Chinkina, and Ulrich Trautwein. 2017. Reading demands in secondary school: Does the linguistic complexity of textbooks increase with grade level and the academic orientation of the school track? *Journal of Educational Psychology*.

S Bott and H Saggion. 2011. An unsupervised alignment algorithm for text simplification corpus construction. In *ACL Workshop on Monolingual Text-to-Text Generation*.

Tim Vor der Brück, Hermann Helbig, and Johannes Leveling. 2008. The readability checker delite. Technical Report Technical Report 345-5/2008, Fakultät für Mathematik und Informatik, FernUniversität in Hagen.

Dominique Brunato, Andrea Cimino, Felice Dell'Orletta, and Giulia Venturi. 2016. Paccss-it: A parallel corpus of complex-simple sentences for automatic text simplification. In *Proceedings of the 2016 Conference on Empirical Methods in Natural Language Processing*, pages 351–361.

Danqi Chen and Christopher Manning. 2014. A fast and accurate dependency parser using neural networks. In *Proceedings of the 2014 Conference on Empirical Methods in Natural Language Processing (EMNLP)*, pages 740–750, Doha, Qatar. Association for Computational Linguistics.

Orphée De Clercq, Véronique Hoste, Bart Desmet, Philip Van Oosten, Martine De Cock, and Lieve Macken. 2014. Using the crowd for readability prediction. *Natural Language Engineering*, -:1–33.

Kevyn Collins-Thompson. 2014. Computational assessment of text readability: A survey of past, present, and future research. *International Journal of Applied Linguistics*, 165(2):97–135.

William Coster and David Kauchak. 2011. Simple English wikipedia: A new text simplification task. In *Proceedings of the 49th Annual Meeting of the Association for Computational Linguistics: Human Language Technologies*, pages 665–669, Portland, Oregon, USA. Association for Computational Linguistics.

Scott A. Crossley, Hae Sung Yang, and Danielle S. McNamara. 2014. What's so simple about simplified texts? a computational and psycholinguistic investigation of text comprehension and text processing. *Reading in a Foreign Language*, 26(1):92–113.

Felice Dell'Orletta, Simonetta Montemagni, and Giulia Venturi. 2011. Read-it: Assessing readability of Italian texts with a view to text simplification. In *Proceedings of the 2nd Workshop on Speech and Language Processing for Assistive Technologies*, pages 73–83.

Michael Denkowski and Alon Lavie. 2014. Meteor universal: Language specific translation evaluation for any target language. In *Proceedings of the ninth workshop on statistical machine translation*, pages 376–380.

Lijun Feng. 2010. *Automatic Readability Assessment*. Ph.D. thesis, City University of New York (CUNY).

Itziar Gonzalez-Dios, María Jesús Aranzabe, Arantza Díaz de Ilarraza, and Haritz Salaberri. 2014. Simple or complex? assessing the readability of basque texts. In *Proceedings of COLING 2014, the 25th International Conference on Computational Linguistics: Technical Papers*, pages 334–344, Dublin, Ireland. Dublin City University and Association for Computational Linguistics.

Arthur C. Graesser, Danielle S. McNamara, Zhiqang Cai, Mark Conley, Haiying Li, and James Pennebaker. 2014. Coh-metrix measures text characteristics at multiple levels of language and discourse. *The Elementary School Journal*, 115(2):pp. 210–229.

Julia Hancke, Detmar Meurers, and Sowmya Vajjala. 2012. Readability classification for German using lexical, syntactic, and morphological features. In *Proceedings of the 24th International Conference on Computational Linguistics (COLING)*, pages 1063–1080, Mumbai, India.

Michael Heilman, Kevyn Collins-Thompson, and Maxine Eskenazi. 2008. An analysis of statistical models and features for reading difficulty prediction. In *Proceedings of the 3rd Workshop on Innovative Use of NLP for Building Educational Applications at ACL-08*, Columbus, Ohio.

Hieu Hoang, Alexandra Birch, Chris Callison-burch, Richard Zens, Rwth Aachen, Alexandra Constantin, Marcello Federico, Nicola Bertoldi, Chris Dyer, Brooke Cowan, Wade Shen, Christine Moran, and Ondřej Bojar. 2007. Moses: Open source toolkit for statistical machine translation. In *Proceedings of the 45nd Annual Meeting of the Association for Computational Linguistics (ACL '07)*.

David M Howcroft and Vera Demberg. 2017. Psycholinguistic models of sentence processing improve sentence readability ranking. In *Proceedings of the 15th Conference of the European Chapter of the Association for Computational Linguistics: Volume 1, Long Papers*, volume 1, pages 958–968.

William Hwang, Hannaneh Hajishirzi, Mari Ostendorf, and Wei Wu. 2015. Aligning sentences from standard wikipedia to simple wikipedia. In *Human Language Technologies: The 2015 Annual Conference of the North American Chapter of the ACL*, pages 211–217.

Zahurul Islam, Alexander Mehler, and Rashedur Rahman. 2012. Text readability classification of textbooks of a low-resource language. In *26th Pacific Asia Conference on Language,Information and Computation pages*.

J. P. Kincaid, R. P. Jr. Fishburne, R. L. Rogers, and B. S Chissom. 1975. Derivation of new readability formulas (Automated Readability Index, Fog Count and Flesch Reading Ease formula) for Navy enlisted personnel. Research Branch Report 8-75, Naval Technical Training Command, Millington, TN.

David Klaper, Sarah Ebling, and Martin Volk. 2013. Building a german/simple German parallel corpus for automatic text simplification. In *Proceedings of the Second Workshop on Predicting and Improving Text Readability for Target Reader Populations (PITR)*.

Dan Klein and Christopher D. Manning. 2003. Accurate unlexicalized parsing. In *Proceedings of the 41st Meeting of the Association for Computational Linguistics (ACL 2003)*, pages 423–430, Sapporo, Japan.

Sigrid Klerke and Anders Søgaard. 2012. Danish parallel corpus for text simplification. In *In Proceedings of Language Resources and Evaluation Conference (LREC), 2012*.

Alon Lavie. 2011. Evaluating the output of machine translation systems. *MT Summit Tutorial*, page 86.

Yi Ma, Eric Fosler-Lussier, and Robert Lofthus. 2012. Ranking-based readability assessment for early primary children's literature. In *Proceedings of the 2012 Conference of the North American Chapter of the Association for Computational Linguistics: Human Language Technologies*, NAACL HLT '12, pages 548–552, Stroudsburg, PA, USA. Association for Computational Linguistics.

Elijah Mayfield and Carolyn Penstein Rosé. 2013. Open source machine learning for text. *Handbook of automated essay evaluation: Current applications and new directions*.

Courtney Napoles and Mark Dredze. 2010. Learning simple wikipedia: a cogitation in ascertaining abecedarian language. In *Proceedings of the NAACL HLT 2010 Workshop on Computational Linguistics and Writing: Writing Processes and Authoring Aids*, CL&W '10, pages 42–50, Stroudsburg, PA, USA. Association for Computational Linguistics.

J. Nelson, C. Perfetti, D. Liben, and M. Liben. 2012. Measures of text difficulty: Testing their predictive value for grade levels and student performance. Technical report, The Council of Chief State School Officers.

Philip van Oosten and Véronique Hoste. 2011. Readability annotation: replacing the expert by the crowd. In *Proceedings of the 6th Workshop on Innovative Use of NLP for Building Educational Applications*, IUNLPBEA '11, pages 120–129, Stroudsburg, PA, USA. Association for Computational Linguistics.

Kishore Papineni, Salim Roukos, Todd Ward, and Wei-Jing Zhu. 2001. Bleu: A method for automatic evaluation of machine translation. Technical report, IBM Research Division, Thomas J. Watson Research Center.

Sarah E. Petersen. 2007. *Natural Language Processing Tools for Reading Level Assessment and Text Simplification for Bilingual Education*. Ph.D. thesis, University of Washington.

Sarah E. Petersen and Mari Ostendorf. 2009. A machine learning approach to reading level assessment. *Computer Speech and Language*, 23:86–106.

Emily Pitler and Ani Nenkova. 2009. Using syntax to disambiguate explicit discourse connectives in text. In *Proceedings of the ACL-IJCNLP 2009 Conference Short Papers*, pages 13–16. Association for Computational Linguistics.

Advaith Siddharthan. 2014. A survey of research on text simplification. *International Journal of Applied Linguistics: Special issue on Recent Advances in Automatic Readability Assessment and Text Simplification*, 165:2:259–298.

K. Toutanova, D. Klein, C. Manning, and Y. Singer. 2003. Feature-rich part-of-speech tagging with a cyclic dependency network. In *HLT-NAACL*, pages 252–259, Edmonton, Canada.

Sowmya Vajjala. 2015. *Analyzing Text Complexity and Text Simplification: Connecting Linguistics, Processing and Educational Applications*. Ph.D. thesis, University of Tübingen.

Sowmya Vajjala and Detmar Meurers. 2012. On improving the accuracy of readability classification using insights from second language acquisition. In *In Proceedings of the 7th Workshop on Innovative Use of NLP for Building Educational Applications*, pages 163–173, Montréal, Canada. Association for Computational Linguistics.

Sowmya Vajjala and Detmar Meurers. 2013. On the applicability of readability models to web texts. In *Proceedings of the Second Workshop on Predicting and Improving Text Readability for Target Reader Populations*, pages 59–68.

Sowmya Vajjala and Detmar Meurers. 2014. Readability assessment for text simplification: From analyzing documents to identifying sentential simplifications. *International Journal of Applied Linguistics, Special Issue on Current Research in Readability and Text Simplification*, 165(2):142–222.

Sowmya Vajjala and Detmar Meurers. 2016. Readability-based sentence ranking for evaluating text simplification. *arXiv preprint arXiv:1603.06009*.

Sowmya Vajjala, Detmar Meurers, Alexander Eitel, and Katharina Scheiter. 2016. Towards grounding computational linguistic approaches to readability: Modeling reader-text interaction for easy and difficult texts. In *Proceedings of the Workshop on Computational Linguistics for Linguistic Complexity (CL4LC)*, pages 38–48, Osaka, Japan. The COLING 2016 Organizing Committee.

Mabel Vogel and Carleton Washburne. 1928. An objective method of determining grade placement of children's reading material. *Elementary School Journal*, 38:58–66.

Carleton Washburne and Mabel Vogel. 1926. *Winnetka graded book list*, volume 1. American Library Association.

Xingxing Zhang and Mirella Lapata. 2017. Sentence simplification with deep reinforcement learning. In *Proceedings of the 2017 Conference on Empirical Methods in Natural Language Processing*, pages 584–594.

Zhemin Zhu, Delphine Bernhard, and Iryna Gurevych. 2010. A monolingual tree-based translation model for sentence simplification. In *Proceedings of The 23rd International Conference on Computational Linguistics (COLING), August 2010. Beijing, China*, pages 1353–1361.

A   Supplemental Material

The corpus, and some processed output files are available at: `https://github.com/nishkalavallabhi/OneStopEnglishCorpus`. An example is shown below:

The Effect of Adding Authorship Knowledge in Automated Text Scoring

Meng Zhang[1], Xie Chen[2], Ronan Cummins[3], Øistein Andersen[1], and Ted Briscoe[1]

[1,3]ALTA Institute, Department of Computer Science and Technology, University of Cambridge, UK
[1]{*mz342, oa223, ejb1*}*@cam.ac.uk*
[3]*Ron.Cummins@gmail.com*
[2]Department of Engineering, University of Cambridge, UK
[2]*xc257@cam.ac.uk*

Abstract

Some language exams have multiple writing tasks. When a learner writes multiple texts in a language exam, it is not surprising that the quality of these texts tends to be similar, and the existing automated text scoring (ATS) systems do not explicitly model this similarity. In this paper, we suggest that it could be useful to include the other texts written by this learner in the same exam as extra references in an ATS system. We propose various approaches of fusing information from multiple tasks and pass this authorship knowledge into our ATS model on six different datasets. We show that this can positively affect the model performance in most cases.

1 Introduction

The existence of various English exam products provides a useful and fair way for language learners to measure their English skills accurately. It also offers a well-accepted standard to help schools and companies to quantitatively judge whether their non-native English applicants meet the compulsory language requirements they set up. Many learners have taken different English exams to get the qualifications required by different organisations. For example, more than two million International English Language Testing System (IELTS) exam sessions have been taken in 2012-2013[1], and more than 30 million people have taken the Test of English as a Foreign Language (TOEFL) exam[2].

English exams like IELTS and TOEFL have free-text writing tasks to evaluate a learner's writing ability. For a writing task, each learner needs to write a text to answer the prompt in the task. Appropriately assessing the quality of free-text

writings requires highly proficient human examiners, and the lack of professional and qualified examiners makes it hard for learners to get accurate feedback on the quality of their writings in a timely fashion. Consequently, it is hoped that an ATS system can possibly act as a kind of examiner to mitigate this problem, which offers an assistance to both learners and educators. The goal of ATS is to improve consistency and reduce human resource overheads. ATS usually utilises machine learning techniques to build a model to learn the underlying relationship between texts and scores. ATS is often used as the second marker in high-stakes exams, the only marker in practice and tutoring software products.

1.1 Multiple Writing Tasks

To evaluate a learner's writing skill more thoroughly, many English exams like IELTS and TOEFL ask them to answer multiple writing tasks. These tasks are drawn from different topics and genres, and each learner is required to write a text for each task. In practice, human judges score each text with an **individual score**, and these scores are aggregated to obtain an **overall score**, which reflects their writing skills. We also define the ATS model predicting the individual score of a text and the overall score of all the texts as the **individual-level** and **overall-level** models, respectively.

When an individual-level ATS model scores texts, previous work has made an implicit assumption that all responses to all tasks are composed independently. This is not true for exams requiring responses to multiple tasks. The writing skill exemplified by a learner during the same exam session will not normally vary greatly, so the texts written by one learner may share some commonalities, such as preferential word usages and common mistakes, and should also approximately

---

[1]https://www.britishcouncil.org/organisation/press/record-two-million-ielts-tests

[2]https://www.ets.org/toefl/ibt/about

305

Proceedings of the Thirteenth Workshop on Innovative Use of NLP for Building Educational Applications, pages 305–314
New Orleans, Louisiana, June 5, 2018. ©2018 Association for Computational Linguistics

equally reflect their writing skills. We suggest that when an individual-level model predicts the score of a text written by a learner, it is helpful to use their other texts as a reference and pass it as an extra piece of information to the model. We refer to this information as **authorship knowledge**.

We suggest that the potential benefit of passing this authorship knowledge to an ATS model might come from a reduction of data sparsity and improvement in the robustness and reliability of feature extraction. Normally the text length for each task is limited, and so there may be insufficient features exemplified in a single response to differentiate language proficiency levels. It can be challenging for an ATS model to learn the mapping between texts and scores accurately, and adding authorship knowledge might provide additional salient features to learn the mapping.

In this paper, we test the hypothesis that authorship knowledge can improve individual-level model performance. We pass this authorship knowledge to an individual-level model in two independent ways: feature fusion and score fusion. When the model predicts text scores, both methods pass all the texts written by the same learner to the model as an extra reference. It is shown that adding this knowledge is helpful in an individual-level ATS model in most cases. To the best of our knowledge, this is the first study that studies how authorship knowledge affects ATS system performance.

2   Related Work

In most previous work, text features are defined manually and automatically extracted from each text. A machine learning model is then applied to learn the mapping from features to scores. Many different machine learning models have been used, including regression (Page, 2003; Attali and Burstein, 2006; Phandi et al., 2015), classification (Larkey, 1998; Rudner and Liang, 2002) and ranking (Chen and He, 2013; Cummins et al., 2016b). The features used in previous work range from shallow textual features to discourse structure and semantic coherence (Higgins et al., 2004; Yannakoudakis and Briscoe, 2012; Somasundaran et al., 2014), and from prompt independent to dependent features (Cummins et al., 2016a). Some recent models have dispensed with feature engineering and utilised word embeddings and neural networks (Alikaniotis et al., 2016; Dong and

Zhang, 2016; Taghipour and Ng, 2016).

However, no previous work has investigated the utility of authorship knowledge in ATS. One possible reason is that most datasets only have one text written by each learner. The First Certificate in English (FCE) dataset released by Yannakoudakis et al. (2011), on the other hand, contains two texts per learner. We primarily focus on the FCE dataset in this paper, but also utilise other datasets to corroborate our results. Yannakoudakis et al. defined all the texts written by a learner as a **script**. They extracted features from each text and then combined the features of the two texts within the same script together. A support vector machine (SVM) ranking model was trained to learn the relationship between features and overall scores.

3   Datasets

In this paper, we require a dataset that includes more than one text written by each learner, where each text is scored with an individual-level score. We finally get six datasets in total for our experiments. Each dataset is a set of texts collected from a real exam, and each exam is targeted at one or more Common European Framework of Reference for Languages (CEFR) [3] levels in English. There are six CEFR levels in total: A1, A2, B1, B2, C1 and C2 arranged from lowest to highest.

In each dataset, each script consists of the answers to two tasks. The answers to both tasks were scored on the same grading scale. Each script was written on the same day so we can safely assume no dramatic variation in the writing skill for each learner. The FCE dataset discussed in Section 2 was collected from the FCE exam. The other five datasets were provided by Cambridge Assessment collected from different years.

We need to choose the score for each text for an ATS model to learn. As the original score for each text in the FCE is not reported on a numerical scale, Cambridge Assessment helped us convert the grades to integers between 0 and 20. This mapping is available in Table 2. All the texts from the B2-U, B2-S, C1-U and C1-S datasets are evaluated in terms of four aspects: content, communicative achievement, language quality and organisation. Each aspect is scored as an integer in the range 0-5. We add the scores of these four aspects of a text together to obtain a total score in the range 0-20, and we use this total score as the score for

---

[3]http://www.coe.int/t/dg4/linguistic/Cadre1_en.asp

Exam	CEFR	Score Range	MEAN	STD	# prompts	# scripts	# train	# dev	# test
FCE	B2	0-20	13.92	2.92	31	1212	822	293	97
B2-U	B2	0-20	14.51	2.18	37	2047	1447	300	300
C1-U	C1	0-20	13.20	2.69	50	2088	1488	300	300
AL-U	A1-C2	0-9	5.78	0.96	58	1604	1004	300	300
B2-S	B2	0-20	13.72	2.41	67	6584	5984	300	300
C1-S	C1	0-20	12.77	2.73	35	1910	1310	300	300

Table 1: The details of the six datasets. FCE is the dataset released by Yannakoudakis et al.. For the other five datasets, the name of each dataset encodes its target CEFR level learners with whether it is **unshuffled** or **shuffled**. B2-U means that it aims at **B2** level learners and is **unshuffled**. MEAN and STD describe the mean and standard deviation of the scores. All the datasets have two writing tasks, and for each writing task, each learner is required to write an answer to one prompt. # prompts describes how many prompts exist in each dataset.

this text for our study. In contrast, AL-U is marked on a scale of 0-9 at 0.5 mark intervals, where each text also receives a score for each of four aspects including task achievement, coherence, word usage and grammar. The total score is aggregated from the scores on all four aspects by Cambridge Assessment, and it is still normalised to 0-9 at 0.5 mark intervals. In this case, we directly use the existing total score as the individual score for a text in AL-U for our study.

Original $\to$ New	Original $\to$ New
0,0 $\to$ 0	3,2 $\to$ 13
1,1 $\to$ 1	3,3 $\to$ 14
1,2 $\to$ 4	4,1 $\to$ 15
1,3 $\to$ 7	4,2 $\to$ 16
2,1 $\to$ 9	4,3 $\to$ 17
2,2 $\to$ 10	5,1 $\to$ 18
2,3 $\to$ 11	5,2 $\to$ 19
3,1 $\to$ 12	5,3 $\to$ 20

Table 2: The score mapping in the FCE dataset

We summarise the six datasets in Table 1. The difference between the shuffled and unshuffled datasets in Table 1 is how texts are presented to human judges to score. For the four unshuffled datasets, each human judge marks the first and second text written by a learner in sequence, so the score of the second text might be affected by the first marked text. In comparison, the texts in B2-S and C1-S are shuffled and randomly displayed to human judges. Hence, this removes any grading bias due to knowing the authorship.

Due to transcription errors, we only kept scripts which do not contain any invalid individual score.

After we cleaned the text scores, each dataset was then split into training, development and test sets. The total number of scripts in each dataset, and the number of scripts in the training, development and test sets are summarised in Table 1. The test set for FCE is the same in Yannakoudakis et al. (2011).

4   Notations

Let us introduce some notations to facilitate our discussion. Each dataset consists of M tasks for each learner to answer, and there are J learners in one dataset. We assume that each learner only takes any exam once. All the datasets we described in Section 3 require learners to write two texts. Hence, $M = 2$ in each dataset. $t_{m,j}$ denotes the mth text written by learner l_j, which answers the mth task $task_m$ in a dataset. text $t_{m,j}$ can be represented as a sequence of words written by learner l_j. The individual score for text $t_{m,j}$ marked by a human examiner is $s_{m,j}$.

$TL_j = \{t_{m,j} | m = 1, ..., M\}$ denotes the set of all the texts written by l_j in a dataset. In other words, TL_j is equivalent to the script answered by learner l_j.

$TN_{m,j} = TL_j \setminus t_{m,j}$ denotes the neighbouring text set of $t_{m,j}$, which is all the texts written by learner l_j except for $t_{m,j}$. In this section, since each dataset only contains 2 texts per learner, the number of texts in $TN_{m,j}$ is always 1, and the only text in this set is $t_{(M+1-m),j}$, which denotes the neighbouring text of $t_{m,j}$.

$TT_m = \{t_{m,j} | j = 1, ..., J\}$ denotes the sequence of all the texts to the mth task $task_m$ answered by all learners in the same exam.

5 Assumptions

There are two assumptions behind authorship knowledge and ATS we want to validate.

The first assumption is that there is a variable $skill_j$ which can describe the writing skill of each learner l_j, and $skill_j$ is approximately constant during an exam. If we believe the skill of a learner could be measured by the English exam they take, $s_{m,j}$ for any m will be a sample from a distribution constrained by $skill_j$ during the exam. We also assume that no learner will behave totally differently on the two tasks during the same exam. In this case, these individual text scores should be close and correlate well with their skill $skill_j$, and this correlation might be helpful in training an individual-level model.

However, the first assumption is not always correct. In some circumstances, learners will perform really well on some tasks, but fail to finish other tasks to the same quality, and they can get low scores on these tasks. An obvious reason for this is that some learners may have managed their time badly and failed to finish the second task; some may also be better prepared for the topic and genre elicited by one of the prompts.

To verify and measure this assumption, we calculate root-mean-squared error (RMSE), quadratic weighted kappa (κ), Pearson (ρ_{prs}) and Spearman correlation (ρ_{spr}) between all the responses to the first task TT_1, and the second task TT_2 answered by all learners. The results are given in Table 3.

Dataset	RMSE	κ	ρ_{prs}	ρ_{spr}
unshuffled datasets				
FCE	2.264	0.700	0.706	0.704
B2-U	1.902	0.620	0.630	0.607
C1-U	2.148	0.680	0.684	0.670
AL-U	0.716	0.726	0.746	0.735
shuffled datasets				
B2-S	2.566	0.434	0.440	0.416
C1-S	2.984	0.408	0.419	0.394

Table 3: The relation between TT_1 and TT_2 to check how the scores of the first and second text written by each learner are correlated

As we can see, κ, ρ_{prs} and ρ_{spr} are above 0.6 in the four unshuffled datasets, and about 0.4 in the two shuffled datasets. It is suggested by Landis and Koch (1977) that there is a substantial agreement between two sequences if Cohen's Kappa is above 0.6 and a moderate agreement when Cohen's Kappa is between 0.4 to 0.6 [4]. We use their interpretation to describe our results, and there is at least a moderate correlation and agreement between the scores of TT_1 and TT_2. This verifies our first assumption to some degree. Whether this amount of agreement can affect the performance of an ATS model is further investigated in the following sections.

The second assumption concerns whether passing authorship knowledge to an ATS model truly improves the model performance by bringing more reliable features and better understanding about each learner's writing skill. An alternative explanation for the possible improvement, if it exists, is brought by the bias during the marking procedure. When comparing RMSE for the unshuffled and shuffled datasets as shown in Table 3, we can see that RMSE is higher for BS-2 than for B2-U, and higher for C2-S than for C2-U. This suggests that human judges might be biased when marking the second text after the first. Hence, we aim to determine whether authorship knowledge truly improves ATS performance by looking at the shuffled dataset, since any improvement on the unshuffled dataset might be the result of grading bias.

6 Methods

To study how authorship knowledge affects ATS, we first need a baseline model.

6.1 Baseline

In the baseline model, a feature vector $f_{m,j}$, extracted from text $t_{m,j}$ written by learner l_j, is used to train an individual-level model to learn the relationship between feature vector space F and text score space S. The model finally predicts the score of text $t_{m,j}$ as $\hat{s}_{m,j}$. The predicted score $\hat{s}_{m,j}$ might be invalid on the given grading scale. For example, an ATS model might predict a score of 4.3, but the grading scale requires an integer. Hence, we round $\hat{s}_{m,j}$ to the nearest valid score on the given grading scale as $\hat{rs}_{m,j}$, which is 4 in this case.

6.1.1 Features

The features for the baseline model we use are similar to those of Yannakoudakis et al. mentioned in Section 2. More specifically, we use features including word and POS n-grams, script

---

[4]Although Landis and Koch claimed that this interpretation is clearly arbitrary.

length, the n-gram missing rate estimated on a background corpus, phrase structure rules, and grammatical dependency distances between any two words within the same sentence, though we only use the top parse result for grammatical relation distance measures. The n-gram missing rate is estimated on UKWaC (Ferraresi et al., 2008). Besides that, we also include the number of words misspelt, the count of grammatical relation types, and the minimum, maximum and average sentence and word lengths. The POS tags, grammatical relations and phrase structure rules are derived from the RASP (robust accurate statistical parsing) toolkit (Briscoe et al., 2006). We remove any feature whose frequency in the training set is below 4, and keep the top 25,000 features that have the highest absolute Pearson correlation with text scores. Each feature vector is normalised to $||f_{m,j}|| = 1$.

6.2 Benchmark

Yannakoudakis et al. (2011) only built an overall-level model and evaluated it in terms of ρ_{prs} and ρ_{spr}. As we use more features and also a global feature selection step, we should ensure that our model is relatively optimal and thus a challenging baseline.

We firstly concatenate all the texts in script TL_j together as **concatenated text** ct_j so that

$$ct_j := t_{1,j} \oplus t_{2,j} \oplus ... \oplus t_{M,j}$$

We extract the script feature vector cf_j from the concatenated text ct_j based on the features defined in Section 6.1.1. We define the combined script score cs_j as the sum of the individual text scores to represent the overall score of each script: $cs_j := \sum_{m=1}^{M} s_{m,j}$

The FCE dataset has another overall script score ss_j for script TL_j used by Yannakoudakis et al. (2011). In order to benchmark with Yannakoudakis et al.'s work, we train an overall-level model by means of support vector regression (SVR) and SVM ranking between cf_j and its script score ss_j rather than cs_j together with a linear kernel. In order to get the valid predicted score on given the grading scale for SVM ranking, we train another linear regression model on the training set between the ranking scores and the actual text scores. For both SVR and SVM ranking, we then round the scores predicted from their corresponding regressors to the nearest valid integers on the given grading scale.

We tune the regularization hyper-parameter on the development set and report the results achieving the lowest RMSE on the development set. The results are included in Table 4. The upper part of the table shows previous results. UKWaC and CLC are the results reported in Yannakoudakis et al. (2011) on SVM ranking models which use the UKWaC and the Cambridge Learner Corpus (CLC) (Nicholls, 2003) as the background corpus for n-gram missing rate estimation respectively. DISCOURSE is the CLC version with extra discourse features. In the DISCOURSE version, Yannakoudakis and Briscoe (2012) investigated different features to measure the coherence of a text and how these features affect the overall score of the texts in the FCE dataset. They showed that the coherence feature based on incremental semantic analysis (Baroni et al., 2007) measuring average adjacent sentence similarity can help their ATS system improve in terms of the Pearson and Spearman correlations.

Table 4 does not include any recent neural model on the FCE dataset, because the neural model developed by Farag et al. (2017) shows that there is still a performance gap between the neural model and the models built on hand-crafted features.

Our models achieve relatively good performance, and we also found that by selecting appropriate features and hyper-parameters, the difference between using ranking and regression to train an ATS model is relatively small. This contrasts with Yannakoudakis et al. (2011)'s finding that ranking is much better than regression on this task. Therefore, we use SVR (BASE) in the following experiments.

Model	RMSE	κ	ρ_{prs}	ρ_{spr}
UKWaC	X	X	0.735	0.758
CLC	X	X	0.741	0.773
DISCOURSE	X	X	0.749	**0.790**
SVR (BASE)	**3.988**	**0.657**	**0.761**	0.787
SVM RANKING	4.123	0.646	0.735	0.766

Table 4: The comparison of the previous work and our baseline models on the FCE test set.

6.3 Model Fusion

There are two ways in which we can pass authorship knowledge in our ATS model. We refer to them as **score fusion** and **feature fusion**.

For **score fusion**, we concatenate all the texts within the same script together as ct_j written by learner l_j. We extract the script feature vector cf_j from ct_j. An overall-level model is trained on cf_j and its combined script score cs_j, which is the sum of all the individual scores of one script. This overall-level model predicts the combined script score of ct_j as $\hat{cs}_j$, and the predicted normalised combined score $\frac{\hat{cs}_j}{M}$ is fused with the predicted individual score $\hat{s}_{m,j}$ by linear interpolation to get the predicted fused score $\hat{fs}_{m,j}$:

$$\hat{fs}_{m,j} := (1 - \alpha)\hat{s}_{m,j} + \alpha\frac{\hat{cs}_j}{M}$$

The interpolation hyper-parameter α is tuned on the development set, and $\hat{fs}_{m,j}$ is then rounded to the nearest valid score on the given grading scale as the final predicted individual-level score for $t_{m,j}$.

For **feature fusion**, we still extract the script feature vector cf_j from ct_j. Then, we define the fused feature vector $ff_{m,j}$ of $t_{m,j}$ as the vector concatenated by $f_{m,j}$ and cf_j together as follows:

$$ff_{m,j} := (1 - \beta)f_{m,j} \oplus \beta cf_j$$

where β is the concatenation weighting hyper-parameter to be tuned on the development set. We train an individual-level model on the fused feature vector $ff_{m,j}$ and text score $s_{m,j}$, and the predicted score $\hat{s}_{m,j}$ is rounded to the nearest valid score $\hat{rs}_{m,j}$ on the given grading scale.

Another question raised by the discussion here is what to fuse. For text $t_{m,j}$ in score fusion, instead of fusing the individual score $\hat{s}_{m,j}$ with the combined script score $\hat{cs}_j$, we can also fuse $\hat{s}_{m,j}$ with the individual predicted score $\hat{s}_{(M-m+1),j}$ from the other text within the same script, which is the neighbouring text $t_{(M-m+1),j}$.

For feature fusion, when we are augmenting text feature vector $f_{m,j}$ to $ff_{m,j}$, we can concatenate it with the feature vector $f_{(M-m+1),j}$ from the neighbouring text $t_{(M-m+1),j}$ instead of the script feature vector cf_j derived from the concatenated text ct_j. Therefore, we have two different fusion approaches, and each approach also has two different sources to fuse.

It should be noticed that the two questions for each dataset are designed on a similar difficulty level. The fusion approach can easily be made to work even if these questions are not on the same difficulty level. If the difficulty difference between the targeted question and the neighbouring question is too large, we can penalise the neighbouring question so that the ATS model mainly look at the targeted question. This is straightforward to do in our method by adjusting the weight of the neighbouring question. We will investigate questions from different difficulty levels in future work once we have a suitable dataset.

7 Results and Discussion

In this section, we evaluate the baseline model and the fusion approaches to study the influence of authorship knowledge. For each setup, we train an individual-level model for each dataset. The model for each setup is optimised on each development set in terms of RMSE. We tune the SVR regularisation and interpolation hyper-parameters on each development set. We report RMSE, κ, ρ_{prs} and ρ_{spr} in Table 6 for each test set. The optimal interpolation hyper-parameters for each fusion approach are reported as α/β in Table 6.

Some readers might notice that there is a numerical difference between Table 4 and Table 6 for the same baseline model evaluated on the FCE test set. The reason for the difference here is that these two tables correspond to two different tasks. The task in Table 4 is predicting the overall-level score, and Table 6 is the individual-level score of a text. It seems that predicting the individual-level scores is a harder task as there is less text to assess (Section 1.1).

For feature fusion, feature fusion with neighbouring text (FF-NT) and concatenated text (FF-CT) is consistently better than the baseline (BASE) on all the datasets except for the B2-U on κ, ρ_{prs} and ρ_{spr}. For score fusion, score fusion with concatenated text (SF-CT) is better than BASE on all the six datasets except for κ in AL-U. In contrast, score fusion with neighbouring text (SF-NT) is better than BASE on all the datasets regarding RMSE except for FCE, but κ is only better than BASE on C1-S. Both SF-CT and SF-NT are better than BASE in terms of ρ_{prs} and ρ_{spr}. The improvement is also visible on the two shuffled datasets, and we suggest that adding authorship knowledge is not merely the result of modelling grading bias, which answers the second assumption in Section 5.

To give a better global understanding of how each approach performs, we conduct the Wilcoxon signed-rank test (Wilcoxon, 1945; Demšar, 2006) across the six datasets to see whether any setup is significantly better or worse than BASE at a global level. We use the SciPy implementation to run the test[5], and the p-values of all the metrics across all the six datasets are listed in Table 5. Based on the result in Table 5, there is a significant difference between all the fusion approaches ($p < 0.05$) and BASE on all the metrics except for SF-NT on κ across multiple datasets.

Setup	RMSE	κ	ρ_{prs}	ρ_{spr}
SF-NT	0.046	**0.058**	0.028	0.028
SF-CT	0.028	0.046	0.028	0.028
FF-NT	0.028	0.046	0.046	0.046
FF-CT	0.028	0.046	0.046	0.046

Table 5: p-value for each approach estimated by the Wilcoxon signed-rank test across all the six datasets. The value bigger than 0.05 is in **bold**

7.1 Hyper-parameters

$\alpha, \beta > 0.5$ in each fusion approach tells the ATS model that it should favour the information from the other source over the current individual text $t_{m,j}$ being marked, and vice versa. We also visualise the relation between β and RMSE for the feature fusion approaches in Figure 1 and 2.

For the fusion with concatenated text ct_j, $\alpha > 0.5$ on FCE and C1-S in SF-CT. $\beta > 0.5$ for all the datasets except for B2-U in FF-CT. Furthermore, if we tune β on the test sets, we can find the optimal β for all the six datasets are bigger than 0.5. On the one hand, we are a little bit surprised that the fusion approaches with concatenated text favour ct_j, and it might mean that ct_j is more salient compared to the original text $t_{m,j}$ in ATS. On the other hand, it is still to be expected to observe these results, because ct_j also contains $t_{m,j}$, and the information from $t_{m,j}$ is still dominant in the model even if $\alpha, \beta > 0.5$.

In contrast, we expect that the model fused with neighbouring text achieves the best performance on each dataset when α or β is smaller than 0.5, as the model should focus on the text $t_{m,j}$ being marked. For SF-NT in Table 6, the optimal α is always smaller than 0.5. However, for FF-NT, the optimal $\beta = 0.5$ for AL-U and C1-U in Table 6. Furthermore, if we choose the test sets to tune β instead of the development sets, we can see that

[5]https://www.scipy.org

$\beta > 0.5$ on the FCE, C1-U and AL-U dataset in Figure 2. Based on these results, we suggest that in some cases, the features from two tasks written by the same learner could be highly similar and shared to some extent in an ATS model.

7.2 Score Difference

Although positive effects are observed in most cases, no method is significantly better than BASE on every dataset and metric we used. One reason might be that it is not ideal to aggregate the two texts written by the same learner together if the performance difference between these texts is big. For example, some learners might perform well on the first task, but fail to complete the second task. This is what we have discussed in the first assumption in Section 5, and this assumption might be invalid in some cases. So, we conduct another study to see how the score difference between the two texts in each script affects the model performance.

We define the script score difference sd_j as the score difference between two texts $t_{1,j}$ and $t_{2,j}$ within the same script TL_j: $sd_j := |s_{1,j} - s_{2,j}|$.

The text score difference of text $t_{m,j}$ is defined as the score difference of the script to which it belongs: $sd_{m,j} := sd_j$.

The text score error $error_{m,j}$ denotes the difference between the predicted score and the gold score of $t_{m,j}$: $error_{m,j} := |\hat{rs}_{m,j} - s_{m,j}|$.

The text score errors $error_{m,j}$ produced by BASE and any fusion approach on text $t_{m,j}$ denote $error_{m,j}^{\text{BASE}}$ and $error_{m,j}^{\text{FUSION}}$, respectively.

The performance difference $PD_{m,j}$ between BASE and any fusion approach for text $t_{m,j}$ denotes the difference between the errors made by the two setups:

$$PD_{m,j} := error_{m,j}^{\text{BASE}} - error_{m,j}^{\text{FUSION}} \quad (1)$$

$PD_{m,j} > 0$ means that the fusion approach is better than BASE at predicting the score of $t_{m,j}$, and vice versa.

We calculate the Pearson correlation ρ_{prs} between $PD_{m,j}$ and $sd_{m,j}$ for each test set in Table 7. Although we do not find any interesting relation between the correlation here and the performance variation in Table 6, Table 7 does reveal some patterns. On the one hand, most values are negative, and the five positive values in bold tend to be close to 0, and p is always bigger than 0.05 for all the positive values. We suggest that there is a negative correlation between performance dif-

Setup	RMSE	κ	ρ_{prs}	ρ_{spr}	α/β	RMSE	κ	ρ_{prs}	ρ_{spr}	α/β
	FCE					AL-U				
BASE	2.569	0.511	0.662	0.652	X	0.693	0.620	0.684	0.659	X
SF-NT	2.572	0.490	0.693	0.696+	0.35	0.686	0.603	0.704	0.687+	0.34
SF-CT	2.495	0.533	**0.696**	**0.702+**	0.70	0.691	0.610	0.689	0.667	0.33
FF-NT	2.529	**0.554+**	0.688	0.688+	0.30	0.683	0.634	0.698	0.680	0.50
FF-CT	**2.460+**	**0.554+**	0.694	0.695	0.67	**0.664+**	**0.649+**	**0.720+**	**0.710+**	0.70
	B2-U					B2-S				
BASE	1.991	0.246	0.359	0.339	X	2.085	0.386	0.476	0.442	X
SF-NT	1.979	0.241	0.371	0.347	0.18	2.050+	0.384	0.501+	0.463	0.23
SF-CT	**1.954+**	**0.271+**	**0.398+**	**0.377+**	0.32	2.029+	0.400	0.510+	0.476+	0.33
FF-NT	1.982	0.242	0.348	0.324	0.20	**1.983+**	**0.430+**	**0.541+**	**0.511+**	0.33
FF-CT	1.974	0.241	0.354	0.333	0.25	2.017+	0.415	0.506	0.481	0.80
	C1-U					C1-S				
BASE	2.405	0.269	0.411	0.410	X	2.421	0.341	0.504	0.471	X
SF-NT	2.387	0.260	0.438	0.433	0.37	2.413	0.343	0.511	0.480	0.02
SF-CT	2.366+	0.288	0.453+	0.451+	0.37	**2.346+**	0.378+	**0.567+**	**0.523+**	0.78
FF-NT	**2.350+**	**0.304+**	**0.462+**	**0.455+**	0.50	2.370+	**0.389+**	0.529	0.498	0.40
FF-CT	2.378	0.296+	0.428	0.420	0.60	2.361+	0.381+	0.548+	0.513+	0.67

Table 6: The results of different setups on the test sets. The best setup per dataset is in **bold**. GREEN means improvement and RED means degradation over BASE. The optimal interpolation hyper-parameters for each fusion approach are reported as α/β. + means significantly better ($p < 0.05$) than BASE using the permutation randomisation test (Yeh, 2000) with 2,000 samples. No metric is found significantly worse than BASE.

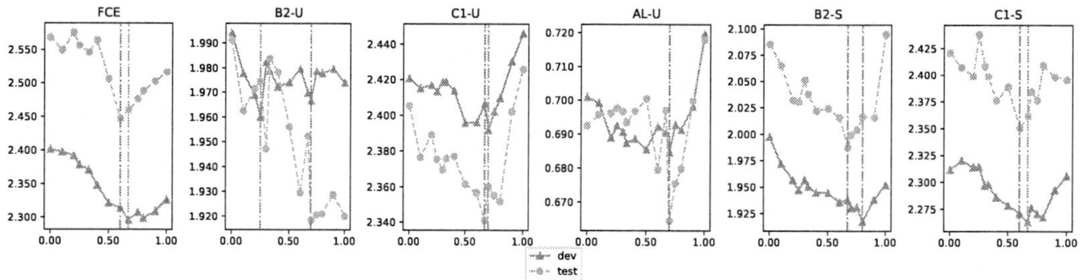

Figure 1: How RMSE (y-axis) changes with β (x-axis) in FF-CT. The vertical RED and GREEN dashed-dot lines in each graph represent that the model achieves the lowest RMSE on the development and test sets at the corresponding β.

ference $PD_{m,j}$ and text score difference $sd_{m,j}$ on some datasets.

On the other hand, only the p-values for six negative values in Table 7 are smaller than 0.05. We think the negative influence brought by the score difference is not huge, because the scores of the two texts written by the same learners are at least moderately correlated in Table 3. This correlation might reduce the negative influence of score difference here.

In some operational settings, it might be consid-ered unfair to use other responses to score a new response, and grading guidelines usually require texts to be marked independently. Nevertheless, we found a clear improvement when making use of such information, and no approach is significantly worse than BASE on any metric or dataset. In other words, the positive influence brought by our fusion approaches is stronger than any possible negative effects.

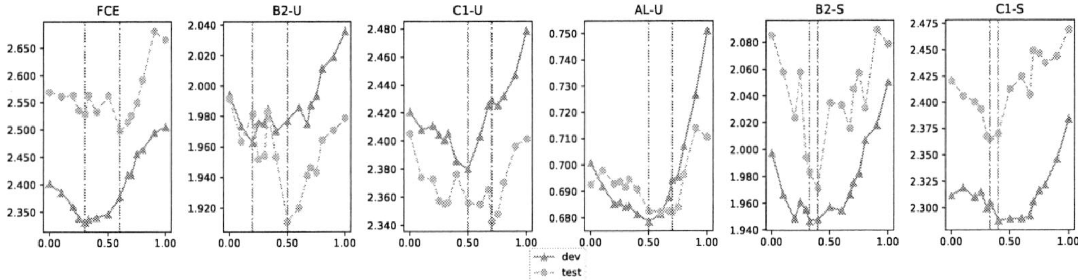

Figure 2: How RMSE (y-axis) changes with β (x-axis) in FF-NT. The vertical RED and GREEN dashed-dot lines in each graph represent that the model achieves the lowest RMSE on the development and test sets at the corresponding β.

Setup	SF-NT	SF-CT	FF-NT	FF-CT
FCE	-0.102	-0.156*	**0.002**	-0.162*
B2-U	-0.034	-0.009	**0.036**	**0.012**
C1-U	-0.060	-0.018	**0.034**	-0.005
AL-U	-0.188*	-0.107*	-0.021	-0.108*
B2-S	-0.039	-0.039	**0.014**	-0.074
C1-S	-0.074	-0.102*	-0.032	-0.048

Table 7: The Pearson correlation between performance difference $PD_{m,j}$ and script score difference $sd_{m,j}$ on the test sets. * denotes p-value < 0.05, and **bold** denotes a positive correlation.

8 Conclusion

In this paper, we studied how authorship knowledge, by means of score fusion and feature fusion, is a useful feature in ATS. We showed that including such information improves model performance at in most datasets, and that improvement is not only from modelling grading bias. One possible topic for future work is to study whether the target CEFR level of each dataset affects the influence of adding authorship knowledge.

9 Acknowledgement

This work is funded by the Institute for Automated Language Teaching and Assessment (ALTA). Special thanks to Christopher Bryant, Yimai Fang, Helen Yannakoudakis, Nanyang Ye and Ann Copestake, as well as the anonymous reviewers for their valuable suggestions at various stages.

References

Dimitrios Alikaniotis, Helen Yannakoudakis, and Marek Rei. 2016. Automatic text scoring using neural networks. In *Proceedings of the 54th Annual Meeting of the Association for Computational Linguistics (Volume 1: Long Papers)*. Association for Computational Linguistics, Berlin, Germany, pages 715–725. http://www.aclweb.org/anthology/P16-1068.

Yigal Attali and Jill Burstein. 2006. Automated essay scoring with e-rater® v. 2. *The Journal of Technology, Learning and Assessment* 4(3).

Marco Baroni, Alessandro Lenci, and Luca Onnis. 2007. Isa meets lara: An incremental word space model for cognitively plausible simulations of semantic learning. In *Proceedings of the Workshop on Cognitive Aspects of Computational Language Acquisition*. Association for Computational Linguistics, pages 49–56.

Ted Briscoe, John Carroll, and Rebecca Watson. 2006. The second release of the RASP system. In *Proceedings of the COLING/ACL 2006 Interactive Presentation Sessions*. Association for Computational Linguistics, Sydney, Australia, pages 77–80. https://doi.org/10.3115/1225403.1225423.

Hongbo Chen and Ben He. 2013. Automated essay scoring by maximizing human-machine agreement. In *Proceedings of the 2013 Conference on Empirical Methods in Natural Language Processing*. Association for Computational Linguistics, Seattle, Washington, USA, pages 1741–1752. http://www.aclweb.org/anthology/D13-1180.

Ronan Cummins, Helen Yannakoudakis, and Ted Briscoe. 2016a. Unsupervised modeling of topical relevance in l2 learner text. In *Proceedings of the 11th Workshop on Innovative Use of NLP for Building Educational Applications*. pages 95–104.

Ronan Cummins, Meng Zhang, and Ted Briscoe. 2016b. Constrained multi-task learning for automated essay scoring. In *Proceedings of the 54th Annual Meeting of the Association for Computational Linguistics (Volume 1: Long Papers)*. Association for Computational Linguistics, Berlin, Germany, pages 789–799. http://www.aclweb.org/anthology/P16-1075.

Janez Demšar. 2006. Statistical comparisons of classifiers over multiple data sets. *Journal of Machine learning research* 7(Jan):1–30.

Fei Dong and Yue Zhang. 2016. Automatic features for essay scoring – an empirical study. In *Proceedings of the 2016 Conference on Empirical Methods in Natural Language Processing*. Association for Computational Linguistics, Austin, Texas, pages 1072–1077. https://aclweb.org/anthology/D16-1115.

Youmna Farag, Marek Rei, and Ted Briscoe. 2017. An error-oriented approach to word embedding pre-training. In *Proceedings of the 12th Workshop on Innovative Use of NLP for Building Educational Applications*. Association for Computational Linguistics, Copenhagen, Denmark, pages 149–158. http://www.aclweb.org/anthology/W17-5016.

Adriano Ferraresi, Eros Zanchetta, Marco Baroni, and Silvia Bernardini. 2008. Introducing and evaluating ukwac, a very large web-derived corpus of english. In *Proceedings of the 4th Web as Corpus Workshop (WAC-4) Can we beat Google*. pages 47–54.

Derrick Higgins, Jill Burstein, Daniel Marcu, and Claudia Gentile. 2004. Evaluating multiple aspects of coherence in student essays. In *HLT-NAACL*. pages 185–192.

J Richard Landis and Gary G Koch. 1977. The measurement of observer agreement for categorical data. *biometrics* pages 159–174.

Leah S Larkey. 1998. Automatic essay grading using text categorization techniques. In *Proceedings of the 21st annual international ACM SIGIR conference on Research and development in information retrieval*. ACM, pages 90–95.

Diane Nicholls. 2003. The cambridge learner corpus: Error coding and analysis for lexicography and elt. In *Proceedings of the Corpus Linguistics 2003 conference*. volume 16, pages 572–581.

Ellis Batten Page. 2003. Project essay grade: Peg. *Automated essay scoring: A cross-disciplinary perspective* pages 43–54.

Peter Phandi, Kian Ming A. Chai, and Hwee Tou Ng. 2015. Flexible domain adaptation for automated essay scoring using correlated linear regression. In *Proceedings of the 2015 Conference on Empirical Methods in Natural Language Processing*. Association for Computational Linguistics, Lisbon, Portugal, pages 431–439. http://aclweb.org/anthology/D15-1049.

Lawrence M Rudner and Tahung Liang. 2002. Automated essay scoring using bayes' theorem. *The Journal of Technology, Learning and Assessment* 1(2).

Swapna Somasundaran, Jill Burstein, and Martin Chodorow. 2014. Lexical chaining for measuring discourse coherence quality in test-taker essays. In *Proceedings of COLING 2014, the 25th International Conference on Computational Linguistics: Technical Papers*. Dublin City University and Association for Computational Linguistics, Dublin, Ireland, pages 950–961. http://www.aclweb.org/anthology/C14-1090.

Kaveh Taghipour and Hwee Tou Ng. 2016. A neural approach to automated essay scoring. In *Proceedings of the 2016 Conference on Empirical Methods in Natural Language Processing*. Association for Computational Linguistics, Austin, Texas, pages 1882–1891. https://aclweb.org/anthology/D16-1193.

Frank Wilcoxon. 1945. Individual comparisons by ranking methods. *Biometrics bulletin* 1(6):80–83.

Helen Yannakoudakis and Ted Briscoe. 2012. Modeling coherence in esol learner texts. In *Proceedings of the Seventh Workshop on Building Educational Applications Using NLP*. Association for Computational Linguistics, Montréal, Canada, pages 33–43. http://www.aclweb.org/anthology/W12-2004.

Helen Yannakoudakis, Ted Briscoe, and Ben Medlock. 2011. A new dataset and method for automatically grading esol texts. In *Proceedings of the 49th Annual Meeting of the Association for Computational Linguistics: Human Language Technologies*. Association for Computational Linguistics, Portland, Oregon, USA, pages 180–189. http://www.aclweb.org/anthology/P11-1019.

Alexander Yeh. 2000. More accurate tests for the statistical significance of result differences. In *Proceedings of the 18th conference on Computational linguistics-Volume 2*. Association for Computational Linguistics, pages 947–953.

SB@GU at the Complex Word Identification 2018 Shared Task

David Alfter
Språkbanken
University of Gothenburg
Sweden
david.alfter@gu.se

Ildikó Pilán
Språkbanken
University of Gothenburg
Sweden
ildiko.pilan@gu.se

Abstract

In this paper, we describe our experiments for the Shared Task on Complex Word Identification (CWI) 2018 (Yimam et al., 2018), hosted by the 13th Workshop on Innovative Use of NLP for Building Educational Applications (BEA) at NAACL 2018. Our system for English builds on previous work for Swedish concerning the classification of words into proficiency levels. We investigate different features for English and compare their usefulness using feature selection methods. For the German, Spanish and French data we use simple systems based on character n-gram models and show that sometimes simple models achieve comparable results to fully feature-engineered systems.

1 Introduction

The task of identifying complex words consists of automatically detecting lexical items that might be hard to understand for a certain audience. Once identified, text simplification systems can substitute these complex words by simpler equivalents to increase the comprehensibility (*readability*) of a text. Readable texts can facilitate information processing for language learners and people with reading difficulties (Vajjala and Meurers, 2014; Heimann Mühlenbock, 2013; Yaneva et al., 2016).

Building on previous work for classifying Swedish words into different language proficiency levels (Alfter and Volodina, 2018), we extend our pipeline with English resources. We explore a large number of features for English based on, among others, length information, parts of speech, word embeddings and language model probabilities. In contrast to this feature-engineered approach, we use a word-length and n-gram probability based approach for the German, Spanish and French data.

Our interest for participation in this shared task is connected to the ongoing development of a complexity prediction system for Swedish (Alfter and Volodina, 2018). In contrast to this shared task, we perform a five-way classification corresponding to the first five levels of the CEFR scale of language proficiency (Council of Europe, 2001). We adapted the pipeline to English, and included some freely available English resources to see how well these would perform on the CWI 2018 task and to gain insights into how we could improve our own system.

2 Data

There were four different tracks at the shared task. Table 1 shows the number of annotated instances per language. For the French sub-task, no training data was provided. Each instance in the English dataset was annotated by 10 native speakers and 10 non-native speakers. For the other languages, 10 annotators (native and non-native speakers) annotated the data. An item is considered complex if at least one annotator annotates the item as complex.

Language	Training	Development
English	27299	3328
Spanish	13750	1622
German	6151	795
French	/	/

Table 1: Number of instances per language

In the dataset, information about the total number of native and non-native annotators and how many of each category considered a word complex is also available.

A surprising aspect of the 2018 dataset was the presence of multi-word expressions (MWE), which were not part of the 2016 shared task. For

Proceedings of the Thirteenth Workshop on Innovative Use of NLP for Building Educational Applications, pages 315–321
New Orleans, Louisiana, June 5, 2018. ©2018 Association for Computational Linguistics

the 2018 task, the training data contains 14% of
MWEs while the development data contains 13%.

3   Features

We extract a number of features from each target
item, either a single word or a multi-word expression. The features can be grouped into: (i) count
and word form based features, (ii) morphological
features, (iii) semantic features and (iv) context
features. In addition, we use psycholinguistic features extracted by N-Watch (Davis, 2005). In Table 2, we list the complete set of features used for
English.

Count features

Length (number of characters)
Syllable count (S1)
Contains non-alphanumeric character
Is number
Is MWE
Character bigrams (B1)
N-gram probabilities (Wikipedia)
In Ogden list
AWL distribution
CEFRLex distribution

Morphological features

Part-of-speech
Suffix length

Semantic features

Number of synsets
Number of hypernyms
Number of hyponyms
Sense id

Context features

Topic distributions
Word embeddings

N-Watch features

British National Corpus frequency (BNC)
CELEX frequency (total, written, spoken)
In Kučera Francis (KF) list
Sydney Morning Herald frequency (SMH)
Reaction time
Bigram frequency (B2)
Trigram frequency (T2)
Syllable count (S2)

Table 2: Overview of features

Word length in terms of number of characters
has been shown to correlate well with complexity
in a number of studies (Smith, 1961; Björnsson,
1968; O'Regan and Jacobs, 1992).

Besides the number of characters, we also consider the number of syllables (S1 and S2). As the
calculation of syllables in English is not straightforward, we use a lookup-based method for S1. In
case the word is not present in the lookup list, we
apply a heuristic approach as a fall-back. A high
number of multi-syllabic words has been shown to
increase the overall complexity of a text (Flesch,
1948; Kincaid et al., 1975), so we assume it could
also be helpful in predicting the complexity of
smaller units.

The feature related to bigrams (B1) indicates
which character bigrams occur in the target item.
We calculate all character-level bigrams in the
training data and only retain the 36 most predictive bigrams using Correlation-based Feature Subset Selection (Hall, 1999).

N-gram probabilities are based on language
models trained on the English Wikipedia dumps
from June and July 2015[1]. We calculate character-
level unigram, bigram and trigram probabilities.

The Ogden list contains 850 words from Basic
English (Ogden, 1944) and this feature indicates
whether a word is part of this list.

AWL distribution considers the ten Academic
Word List (AWL) sublists (Coxhead, 1998) and indicates in which lists the word occurs. The AWL
list contains word families which appear often in
academic texts but excludes general English vocabulary, making it specific to the academic context. The ten sub-lists are ordered according to frequency, so that words from the first sub-list are
more frequent than words from the second sub-
list, and so forth.

CEFRLex distribution indicates the pres-
ence/absence in the 5th, 10th and 20th percentile
English CEFRLex lists[2]. These lists are obtained
by aligning and sorting four different vocabulary
lists for English (EFLLex) (Dürlich and François,
2018), French (FLELex) (François et al., 2014),
Swedish (SVALex) (François et al., 2016) and
Dutch (NT2Lex) (François and Fairon, 2017) by
frequency and only taking words which occur in

---

[1] We already had these pre-calculated language models
from previous experiments. For simplicity and time reasons, we chose not to retrain them on more recent Wikipedia
dumps.

[2] http://cental.uclouvain.be/cefrlex/

the 5th, 10th and 20th percentile across all languages.

Morphological features include information about parts of speech and suffix length. Suffix length is calculated by stemming the word using the NLTK stemmer (Bird et al., 2009) and substracting the length of the identified stem from the length of the original word.

Semantic features are: number of synsets, number of hyponyms, number of hypernyms and sense id. These features are calculated from WordNet (Miller and Fellbaum, 1998). The first three are obtained by calculating how many items WordNet returns for the word in terms of synsets, hyponyms and hypernyms. Sense id is obtained by using the Lesk algorithm (Lesk, 1986) on the sentence the target item occurs in.

Context features consist of topic distribution and word embeddings. For word embeddings, we use the pre-trained Google News dataset embeddings. We calculate the word context of a word w_i in a sentence $S \in w_1...w_n$ as the sum of word vectors from w_{i-5} to w_{i+5}, excluding the vector for w_i. In case there is not enough context, the available context is used instead. Topic distributions are calculated by first collecting Wikipedia texts about 26 different topics such as animals, arts, education or politics. These texts are tokenized and lemmatized. We then exclude words which occur across all topic lists. Topic distribution indicates in which of these topic lists the target item occurs.

Features from N-Watch include frequency information from the British National Corpus (BNC), the English part of CELEX, the Kučera and Francis list (KF), the Sydney Morning Herald (SMH); reaction times and bi- and trigram character frequencies (B2 and T2). While these features are redundant in some case, such as number of syllables (S1 and S2), their values can differ due to being calculated differently.

Since our pipeline was not designed to handle multi-word expressions, we address this by a two-pass approach. First, we extract all features for single words and store the resulting vector representations. Then, for each multi-word expression, if we have feature vectors for all constituents making up the MWE, we sum the vectors for count-based features such as length and number of syllables and average the vectors for frequency counts. We have experimented with adding all vectors and averaging all vectors, but found that summing some features and averaging other features not only yields higher scores but also is linguistically more plausible. Context vectors for MWEs are not added but calculated separately as described above with the difference that for a multi-word expression MWE $\in w_i, ..., w_{i+k}$ occurring in a sentence $S \in w_1, ..., w_n$ as the sum of vectors from w_{i-5} to w_{i-1} and w_{i+k+1} to w_{i+k+5}. In case not all constituents of a multi-word expression have corresponding vectors from phase 1, we set all feature values to zero and only use the context.

4 Experiments on the English data

We tried three different configurations for the English data set, namely context-free, context-only and context-sensitive. For context-free, we use the features described above, excluding word embedding context. For context-only, we only use the word embedding context vectors.For context-sensitive, we concatenate the context-free and context-only features.

4.1 Classification

We tried different classifiers, among others Random Forest (Breiman, 2001), Extra Trees (Geurts et al., 2006), convolutional neural networks and recurrent convolutional neural networks implemented in Keras (Chollet et al., 2015) and PyTorch (Paszke et al., 2017). For Random Forest and Extra Trees, we tried different numbers of estimators in the interval $[10, 2000]$ and found that generally either 500 or 1000 estimators reached the best results on the development set. For neural networks, we tried different combinations of hyperparameters such as the type of layers, number of convolution filters, adding LSTM layers, varying the number of neurons in each layer. We tried two different architectures, one taking as input the features extracted as described below and convolving over these features, the other taking both the features and word embeddings as separate inputs and merging the separate layers before the final layer.

5 Experiments on other languages

5.1 Predicting the German and the Spanish test set

During testing, we noticed that using the character-level n-gram model trained on the English Wikipedia and using only unigram, bigram and trigram probabilities and word length as features yielded scores in the vicinity of our best-performing feature-engineered models at that time (0.81 F1 vs 0.82 F1).

Following this finding, we used character-level n-gram models trained on Wikipedia dumps[3] for Spanish, German and French and calculated unigram, bigram and trigram probabilities for these languages. In addition, we used target item length in characters as additional feature.

5.2 Predicting the French test set

As there was no training or development data for the French test set, we used the n-gram language model to convert each French entry into n-gram probabilities. We then used the n-gram classifiers for English, German and Spanish to predict labels for each word. We tested two configurations:

1. Predict with English, German and Spanish classifier and use majority vote to get the final label

2. Predict with Spanish classifier and use label as final label

The rationale behind the second configuration is that French and Spanish are both Romance languages. The single Spanish classifier might thus model French data better than incorporating also the English and the German classifiers, as German and English are both Germanic languages.

6 Results

Table 3 shows the results of the best classifiers on both the development data and the test data. For the English News and WikiNews, the best classifier is an Extra Trees classifier with 1000 estimators with the reduced feature set (see subsection 6.1) and trained on each genre separately, as opposed to the general English classifier trained on all three genres. For all other tasks, the best classifier is an Extra Trees classifier with 500 estimators with the reduced feature set.

6.1 Feature selection for English

Out of the set of features proposed for a certain task, usually some features are more useful than others. Eliminating redundant features can result not only in simpler models, but it can also improve performance (Witten et al., 2011, 308). We

---

[3]See footnote 1

	F1 (dev)	F1 (test)
EN News	0.8623	0.8325
EN WikiNews	0.8199	0.8031
EN Wikipedia	0.7666	0.7812
German	0.7668	0.7427
Spanish	0.7261	0.7281
French	/	0.6266

Table 3: Results of best classifiers

therefore run feature selection experiments in order to identify the best performing subset of features. We use the SelectFromModel[4] feature selection method as implemented in scikit-learn (Pedregosa et al., 2011). This method selects features based on their importance weights learned by a certain estimator. We base our selection on the development data and the Extra Trees learning algorithm, since it performed best with the full set of features. We use the median of importances as threshold for retaining features. For the other parameters, the default values were maintained for the selection.

The feature selection method identified a subset of 64 informative features. We list these features in Table 4, indicating in parenthesis the amount of features per feature type where it is relevant.

Selected features	
Length	Sense id
Is adjective	# Syllable count S2
Is noun	BNC freq.
Is verb	CELEX freq. (3)
Syllable count S1	KF list
Suffix length	Reaction time
# synsets	SMH
# hypernyms	Bigram B2 freq (4)
# hyponyms	Trigram T2 freq (4)
Topic distr. (22)	Is MWE
Char. bigram B1 (8)	Unigram prob
In Ogden list	Bigram prob
CEFRLex distr. (3)	Trigram prob

Table 4: Selected subset of features

The best performing features included, among others, features based on word frequency, infor-

---

[4]We also tested other feature selection methods, namely an ANOVA-based univariate feature selection and recursive feature elimination, but we omit the results of these since they were inferior.

mation based on words senses and topics as well as language model probabilities.

As only lexical classes were annotated for complexity, it is not surprising to see that, even though our pipeline considers all part-of-speech classes, the feature selection picked adjectives, nouns and verbs.

7 Additional experiments on English

7.1 Native vs non-native

Since we had information about how many native speakers and non-native speakers rated target items as complex, we experimented with training classifiers separately for these two categories of raters. We applied the native-only classifier on the native judgments of the development set, as well as on the non-native judgments, and similarly the non-native classifier on native judgments and non-native judgments. In all four configurations, we found accuracy to be the same, at about 75%.

7.2 2016 vs 2018

Before this shared task, we experimented with the 2016 CWI shared task data and trained classifiers on it. We tried applying the best-performing classifier trained on the 2016 data on the 2018 development data, but results were inferior to training on the 2018 training data and predicting 2018 development data. The same is true in the other direction; applying the best-performing 2018 classifier on the 2016 data yields inferior results. Table 5 shows the result of these experiments. This raises the question of how generalizable these complex word identification systems are and how dependent they are on the data, the annotation and the task at hand.

Configuration	Accuracy	Recall	F1
2016 on 2018	0.6499	0.7463	0.6948
2018 on 2018	0.7992	0.7269	0.7613
2018 on 2016	0.6610	0.6335	0.6470
2016 on 2016	0.8062	0.6511	0.7204

Table 5: Results of 2016/2018 comparison

7.3 Genre dependency

During the training phase, we concatenated the English training files for News, WikiNews and Wikipedia into one single training file. We did the same with the development data. We trained

a single, genre-agnostic English classifier on this data. During the submission phase, we used the single classifier but also split the data into the three sub-genres News, WikiNews and Wikipedia again and retrained our systems, which improved performance. This hints at the genre-dependency of the concept of *complex* words.

7.4 Context

As the notion of complexity may be context-dependent, i.e. a word might be perceived as more complex in a certain context, we used word embedding context vectors as features. However, our feature selection methods show that these context vectors do not contribute much to the overall classification results. Indeed, of the 300-dimensional word embedding vectors representing word context, not a single dimension was selected by our feature selection.

However, if we only look at features which can be derived from isolated words, we also have a problem of contradictory annotations. This means that representing isolated words as vectors can lead to the same vector representation of different instances of a word with different target labels. We calculated the number of contradictions and found that representing each word as a vector leads to 5% of contradictory data points.

8 Discussion

One interesting aspect of the data is the separation of annotators into native and non-native speakers. However, while it can be interesting to try and train separate classifiers for modeling native and non-native perceptions of complexity, and this information can be exploited at training time, using features that rely on the number of native and non-native annotators could not be used on the test data, as the only information given at test time is the total number of native and non-native annotators, and these numbers do not vary for the English data.

Our best classifiers are all Extra Trees. All other classifiers that we tested, especially convolutional neural networks and recurrent convolutional neural networks, reached lower accuracies. This might be due to insufficient data to train neural networks, a suboptimal choice of hyperparameters or the type of features used.

While our systems did not reach high ranks on the English datasets (ranks 13, 13 and 6 on

News, WikiNews and Wikipedia respectively), we reached place 2 on the German data set and place 3 on the French data set. Given the simplicity of the chosen approach, this is slightly surprising. However, we surmise that n-gram probabilities implicitly encode frequency among other things, and frequency-based approaches generally perform well.

Further, we found that using only the Spanish classifier on the French data lead to better scores than using all three classifiers and majority vote. This speaks in favor of the hypothesis that closely related languages model each other better. This can be interesting for low-resource languages if there is a related language with more resources.

9 Conclusion

We presented our systems and results of the 2018 shared task on complex word identification. We found that simple n-gram language models perform similarly well to fully-feature engineered systems for English. Our submission for the non-English tracks were based on this observation, circumventing the need for more language-specific feature engineering.

10 Acknowledgements

We would like to thank our anonymous reviewer for their helpful comments and the organizers of the shared task for the opportunity to work on this problem.

References

David Alfter and Elena Volodina. 2018. Towards Single Word Lexical Complexity Prediction. In *Proceedings of the 13th Workshop on Innovative Use of NLP for Building Educational Applications*.

Steven Bird, Ewan Klein, and Edward Loper. 2009. *Natural language processing with Python: analyzing text with the natural language toolkit*. O'Reilly Media, Inc.

Carl Hugo Björnsson. 1968. *Läsbarhet*. Liber.

Leo Breiman. 2001. Random forests. *Machine Learning*, 45(1):5–32.

François Chollet et al. 2015. Keras. https://keras.io.

Council of Europe. 2001. *Common European Framework of Reference for Languages: Learning, Teaching, Assessment*. Press Syndicate of the University of Cambridge.

Averil Coxhead. 1998. *An academic word list*, volume 18. School of Linguistics and Applied Language Studies.

Colin J Davis. 2005. N-Watch: A program for deriving neighborhood size and other psycholinguistic statistics. *Behavior research methods*, 37(1):65–70.

Luise Dürlich and Thomas François. 2018. EFLLex: A Graded Lexical Resource for Learners of English as a Foreign Language. In *11th International Conference on Language Resources and Evaluation (LREC 2018)*.

Rudolph Flesch. 1948. A new readability yardstick. *Journal of applied psychology*, 32(3):221.

Thomas François and Cédrick Fairon. 2017. Introducing NT2Lex: A Machine-readable CEFR-graded Lexical Resource for Dutch as a Foreign Language. In *Computational Linguistics in the Netherlands 27 (CLIN27)*.

Thomas François, Nuria Gala, Patrick Watrin, and Cédrick Fairon. 2014. FLELex: a graded lexical resource for French foreign learners. In *LREC*, pages 3766–3773. Citeseer.

Thomas François, Elena Volodina, Ildikó Pilán, and Anaïs Tack. 2016. SVALex: a CEFR-graded Lexical Resource for Swedish Foreign and Second Language Learners. In *LREC*.

Pierre Geurts, Damien Ernst, and Louis Wehenkel. 2006. Extremely randomized trees. *Machine Learning*, 63(1):3–42.

Mark Andrew Hall. 1999. Correlation-based feature selection for machine learning.

Katarina Heimann Mühlenbock. 2013. I see what you meanAssessing readability for specific target groups. *Data linguistica*, (24).

J Peter Kincaid, Robert P Fishburne Jr, Richard L Rogers, and Brad S Chissom. 1975. Derivation of new readability formulas (automated readability index, fog count and flesch reading ease formula) for navy enlisted personnel. Technical report, Naval Technical Training Command Millington TN Research Branch.

Michael Lesk. 1986. Automatic sense disambiguation using machine readable dictionaries: how to tell a pine cone from an ice cream cone. In *Proceedings of the 5th annual international conference on Systems documentation*, pages 24–26. ACM.

George Miller and Christiane Fellbaum. 1998. Wordnet: An electronic lexical database.

Charles Kay Ogden. 1944. *Basic English: A general introduction with rules and grammar*, volume 29. K. Paul, Trench, Trubner.

J Kevin O'Regan and Arthur M Jacobs. 1992. Optimal viewing position effect in word recognition: A challenge to current theory. *Journal of Experimental Psychology: Human Perception and Performance*, 18(1):185.

Adam Paszke, Sam Gross, Soumith Chintala, Gregory Chanan, Edward Yang, Zachary DeVito, Zeming Lin, Alban Desmaison, Luca Antiga, and Adam Lerer. 2017. Automatic differentiation in PyTorch. In *NIPS-W*.

Fabian Pedregosa, Gaël Varoquaux, Alexandre Gramfort, Vincent Michel, Bertrand Thirion, Olivier Grisel, Mathieu Blondel, Peter Prettenhofer, Ron Weiss, Vincent Dubourg, et al. 2011. Scikit-learn: Machine learning in Python. *Journal of Machine Learning Research*, 12(Oct):2825–2830.

Edgar A Smith. 1961. Devereux Readability Index. *The Journal of Educational Research*, 54(8):298–303.

Sowmya Vajjala and Detmar Meurers. 2014. Assessing the relative reading level of sentence pairs for text simplification. In *Proceedings of the 14th Conference of the European Chapter of the Association for Computational Linguistics*.

Ian H Witten, Eibe Frank, Mark A Hall, and Christopher J Pal. 2011. *Data Mining: Practical machine learning tools and techniques*. Morgan Kaufmann.

Victoria Yaneva, Irina P Temnikova, and Ruslan Mitkov. 2016. Evaluating the Readability of Text Simplification Output for Readers with Cognitive Disabilities. In *LREC*.

Seid Muhie Yimam, Chris Biemann, Shervin Malmasi, Gustavo Paetzold, Lucia Specia, Sanja Štajner, Anaïs Tack, and Marcos Zampieri. 2018. A Report on the Complex Word Identification Shared Task 2018. In *Proceedings of the 13th Workshop on Innovative Use of NLP for Building Educational Applications*, New Orleans, United States. Association for Computational Linguistics.

Complex Word Identification:
Convolutional Neural Network vs. Feature Engineering

Segun Taofeek Aroyehun
CIC, Instituto Politécnico Nacional
Mexico City, Mexico
aroyehun.segun@gmail.com

Jason Angel
CIC, Instituto Politécnico Nacional
Mexico City, Mexico
ajason08@gmail.com

Daniel Alejandro Pérez Alvarez
CIC, Instituto Politécnico Nacional
Mexico City, Mexico
daperezalvarez@gmail.com

Alexander Gelbukh
CIC, Instituto Politécnico Nacional
Mexico City, Mexico
www.gelbukh.com

Abstract

We describe the systems of NLP-CIC team that participated in the Complex Word Identification (CWI) 2018 shared task. The shared task aimed to benchmark approaches for identifying complex words in English and other languages from the perspective of non-native speakers. Our goal is to compare two approaches: feature engineering and a deep neural network. Both approaches achieved comparable performance on the English test set. We demonstrated the flexibility of the deep-learning approach by using the same deep neural network setup in the Spanish track. Our systems achieved competitive results: all our systems were within 0.01 of the system with the best macro-F1 score on the test sets except on Wikipedia test set, on which our best system is 0.04 below the best macro-F1 score.

1 Introduction

Complex Word Identification (CWI) is an important step in text simplification. The ability to accurately identify word(s) as complex or not in a given context for a given target population significantly impacts subsequent processing steps such as lexical substitution in the simplification pipeline.

The organizers of the 2018 CWI shared task (Yimam et al., 2018) provided participants with multilingual human-annotated datasets (Yimam et al., 2017a,b) for the identification of complex words. Training and development data were provided for three languages: English, Spanish, and German. In the case of English, three genres were covered: news, Wikinews, and Wikipedia.

Some of the participants of the previous CWI shared task used neural network-based approaches. For instance, Bingel et al. (2016) used

a simple feed-forward neural network, while Nat (2016) used an ensemble of recurrent neural networks (RNN). The performance of the neural network approaches was not impressive. The RNN achieved the best result among all the submissions that used neural networks (Paetzold and Specia, 2016b).

In this paper, we report further experiments with the efficacy of deep neural networks for CWI, using another deep neural network architecture— Convolutional Neural Network (CNN). Namely, we compare two approaches for the task of CWI: one based on an extensive feature engineering and the tree ensembles classifier, and another one based on deep neural network using the word embedding representation. The latter approach is, to the best of our knowledge, the first attempt to apply CNNs to the task of CWI. Apart from comparing the performance of the two approaches on the classification subtask of CWI on English, we demonstrate the flexibility of the CNN-based approach by applying it to another language— Spanish in our case.

The remainder of the paper is organized as follows. Section 2 outlines relevant work. Sections 3 and 4 present our two approaches. Section 5 gives some details on the datasets used. Results of our experiments are in Section 6. Section 7 presents error analysis. Finally, Section 8 concludes the paper and outlines future work directions.

2 Related Work

The majority of works on CWI are related to feature engineering at various linguistic levels. Section 2.1 below discusses existing approaches to feature engineering for machine-learning models used for CWI. On the other hand, Section 2.2 men-

Proceedings of the Thirteenth Workshop on Innovative Use of NLP for Building Educational Applications, pages 322–327
New Orleans, Louisiana, June 5, 2018. ©2018 Association for Computational Linguistics

tions some relevant applications of CNNs to natural language processing (NLP).

2.1 Feature Engineering for he CWI Task

Participants of the first edition of CWI shared task have experimented with various linguistic features. These linguistic features span various linguistic levels: morphological, syntactic, semantic, and psycholinguistic. Paetzold and Specia (2016c) used morphological, lexical, and semantic features to train frequency-based, lexicon-based, and machine-learning models for CWI. Konkol (2016) used only frequency of occurrence of a word in Wikipedia as the only feature to train a Max entropy classifier. Davoodi and Kosseim (2016) experimented with the degree of abstractness of a word as a psycholinguistic feature for CWI.

In this work, we used some of these features and experimented with some new features, such as contextual and entity information and additional psycholinguistic scores.

2.2 CNNs in NLP

Convolutional neural networks have shown notable results in the fields of computer vision, speech recognition and recently in NLP.

CNN models achieve state-of-the-art results in NLP tasks such as clause coherence (Yin and Schütze, 2015b), paraphrase identification (Yin and Schütze, 2015b,a) and Twitter sentiment analysis (Severyn and Moschitti, 2015).

Kim (2014) presents a CNN fed with word2vec word embedding vectors (Mikolov et al., 2013) used for detection of positive and negative reviews, as well as sentence classification. Their results suggest that pre-trained vectors encode generic semantic features, which can benefit various NLP classification tasks. In our work, we used a similar model with slight additions to the architecture of the network and a different preprocessing step.

3 Feature-Engineering Approach

In this section, we present the set of features used to build one of our CWI systems.

Morphological Features Most of the morphological features we used consist of frequency count of target text on large corpora such as Wikipedia and Simple Wikipedia. We computed term frequency, inverse term frequency, document frequency and term document entropy. Also, the

tf-idf values were calculated. In addition, we used characteristics of each target text such as number of characters, vowels, and syllables.

Syntactic and Lexical Features We used OpenNLP[1] part-of-speech (POS) tagger to determine the target word's POS in the context. We used the POS as a parameter to filter the possible meanings of the target word. With this, we obtained the number of senses, lemmas, hyponyms, and hypernyms given by WordNet.[2]

Psycholinguistic and Entity Features We included some psycholinguistic scores provided by the improved MRC psycholinguistics database (Paetzold and Specia, 2016a) as features. The database provides familiarity, age of acquisition, concreteness, and imagery scores for each word. We hypothesized that these scores would be useful to identify complex word. Unfortunately, many target words were absent in this database. We used OpenNLP and Stanford CoreNLP[3] to tag target words as organization, person, location, date, and time. The resulting tag was used as an *entity* feature.

Word Embedding Distances as Features Beyond these classic linguistic features, we used word embeddings. Namely, we downloaded the pre-trained Word2vec (Mikolov et al., 2013) vectors of 300 dimensions to measure the distance between the sentence and the target word. The distance was computed using cosine similarity and Euclidean similarity over the average of the vector representation of the words in the sentence and the target text.

Classical Machine Learning Models We noticed that for this task (with our features), the tree learner offered better performance than other models. Thus, we tried several settings for the tree learner model provided by KNIME (Berthold et al., 2009), as well as more complex variations such as random forest, gradient boosted, and tree ensembles. The best obtained result was given by the tree ensembles with 600 models.

4 Deep-Learning Approach

In this section, we present our deep-learning approach. It is based on 2D convolution and word-

---

[1] http://opennlp.apache.org/
[2] https://wordnet.princeton.edu/
[3] https://stanfordnlp.github.io/CoreNLP

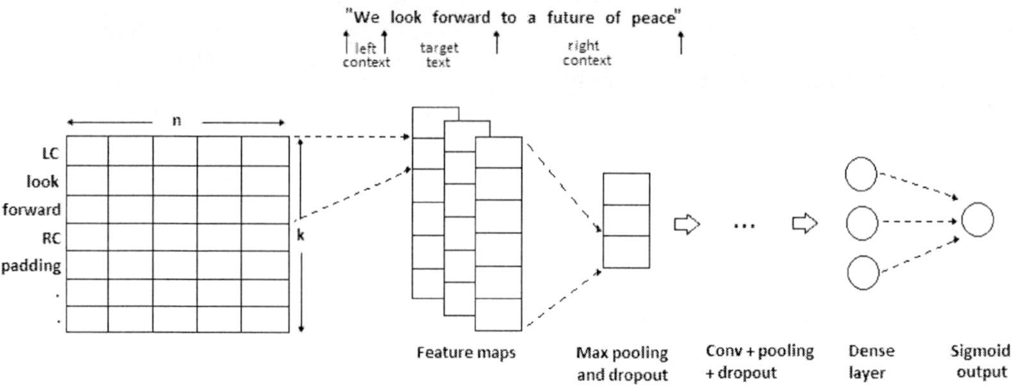

Figure 1: The architecture of our network

embedding representation of the target text fragment and its context.

Since text is one-dimensional, we applied a preprocessing step described in Section 4.1 prior to the application of convolution layer. Section 4.2 describes our network architecture, and Section 4.3 presents the training procedure.

4.1 Preprocessing

As a first step, we removed punctuation marks, digits, and special characters. Each word was then replaced by its vector representation using the pre-trained word vectors from the Word2vec model (Mikolov et al., 2013) for English and fastText model (Grave et al., 2018) for Spanish. A min-max normalization was applied to every vector to convert the values from the range $[-1, 1]$ to $[0, 1]$. We assigned a zero vector to the words missing in the pre-trained embeddings.

We defined the left context (LC) and the right context (RC) as those words that appear to the left and the right of the target text, respectively. As a compact representation of the left or right context, we used one 300-dimensional vector calculated as the average of the vectors of all the words in the LC and RC, respectively (if the target text was located at the beginning or the end of the sentence, we used a zero vector as the respective context representation). Next, we generated a matrix where the first row corresponds to the LC vector, the next k rows are given by the embedding vectors of the words contained in the target text, where k is the number of words in the target text, and the last row corresponds to the RC vector. In order to have a regular representation, we padded the matrix with

$p = m - k$ zero vectors, where m is the maximum value of k in the training set.

Figure 1 illustrates the preprocessing step on the sentence of an example in the English training set. The output of the preprocessing step is the input of the network.

We believe that the averaging operation on the words in the contexts allowed differentiating between cases where the same sentence has distinct target texts. Those words included or excluded in the context will slightly modify the representation of the context, which will help the model to learn some relationships between the target text and the rest of the sentence. We could have compressed the representation matrix by combining the vector representation of the words in the target text instead of stacking them. However, this could dramatically reduce the valuable information pertaining to the target text.

4.2 Architecture of our Network

In our architecture, we used an input, convolution, pooling, and fully-connected layers; see Figure 1. Below we describe each of these layers except the input layer, which was described in Section 4.1.

Convolution The number of filters in this layer varied from 16 to 256 with a convolution stride of 1 and kernel size in the range of 2 to 4. We applied the rectified linear unit activation function to the output of this layer in order to introduce non-linearity. This layer is central to the idea of CNN, which enables the network to identify the most important features in the input. The output of this layer is often referred to as feature maps. Our net-

Source	Training Set				Test Set		
	Avg. Length Target Text	Avg. Sentence Length	Examples	Positive	Avg. Length Target Text	Avg. Sentence Length	Examples
Wikinews	8	168	7746	42%	8	166	1287
News	8	174	14002	40%	8	153	2095
Wikipedia	8	175	5551	45%	9	194	870
Spanish	9	193	13750	40%	9	190	2233

Table 1: English and Spanish datasets

work included four convolutional layers.

Pooling Max pooling was applied to the output of the convolution layer to downsample the feature maps. The feature maps of the last pooling layer were flattened.

Fully-Connected Layer We used three fully-connected layers (FC). The first FC took as input the flattened output of the last pooling layer. The first two FCs used a linear activation function and the third applied the sigmoid activation function. The last FC gave a number in the range $[0, 1]$, which was the final output of the network. By a threshold (we found 0.5 to be optimal), we determined whether the output on a given example implied a label of 0 (simple) or 1 (complex).

4.3 Training

We used the binary cross-entropy as our objective function for training the network. We experimented with various types of optimizers. We chose optimizers with static learning rate and those with adaptive learning rate schedules. Based on the performance of the model on the validation set, we found RMSprop to be the best on updating the network parameters and minimizing the loss function while using 100 epochs.

The dataset is imbalanced: it contains unequal proportion of examples by class labels, roughly 60% negative examples and 40% positive examples. So, we introduced class weights in our training procedure, which resulted in performance improvement. We computed class weights using scikit-learn (Pedregosa et al., 2011).

To mitigate overfitting, we tried several regularization alternatives (Goodfellow et al., 2016) including kernel and weight regularization, batch normalization, dropout, and early stopping. We found dropout and early stopping useful. Our final model included dropout (Srivastava et al., 2014) after every layer with dropout probability of 0.25.

5 Datasets

Table 1 shows some statistics on the corpora we used: the average length of the target text and sentences and the number of examples in the training and test sets, with the percentage of positive examples (target texts labeled as complex) in the training set. The table shows that the datasets are skewed towards negative examples: the percentage of positive examples on the datasets did not exceed 45%. The Wikipedia dataset has the smallest number of training examples, 5551. The average length of target text in the training examples and test examples are comparable. One can see some variations in the average length of sentences in the training and test sets. These variations are remarkable for the Wikipedia and News datasets.

6 Results

This section presents the performance of both models on the English test set and that of the CNN model on the Spanish test set.

Table 2 shows the macro-F1 and accuracy scores as well as the respective ranks of both CNN and TreeE models on the English test set. The performance measures are given per genre in the English test set. Out of 11 teams, our best model places fifth on News; second on Wikinews, and seventh on Wikipedia. All our systems were within 0.01 of the system with the best macro-F1 score on the test sets except on Wikipedia test set. On the Wikipedia test set, our best system was 0.04 below the best macro-F1 score.

On the Spanish test set, we submitted only the CNN-based system. Table 3 shows its macro-precision, macro-recall, macro-F1, and accuracy scores. Our best submission ranks third among seven teams that participated in the Spanish track.

The main advantage of the CNN model is that it can be applied to any language for which an embedding can be easily created given the availability of sufficient electronic textual resources.

Models	News			Wikinews			Wikipedia		
	Macro-F1	Accuracy	Rank	Macro-F1	Accuracy	Rank	Macro-F1	Accuracy	Rank
NLP-CIC-TreeE	0.851	0.859	9	**0.831**	**0.837**	3	0.772	**0.774**	11
NLP-CIC-CNN	**0.855**	**0.863**	8	0.824	0.828	7	0.772	0.772	12

Table 2: Accuracy and macro-F1 scores by genres on the English test set

Model	Macro-Recall	Macro-Precision	Macro-F1	Accuracy	Rank
NLP-CIC-CNN	0.765	0.772	0.767	0.772	3

Table 3: CNN performance scores on the Spanish test set

Source	NLP-CIC-TreeE Model		NLP-CIC-CNN Model	
	Correct	Wrong	Correct	Wrong
Wikinews	0.94 ± 0.53	1.10 ± 0.65	0.94 ± 0.51	1.12 ± 0.72
News	0.97 ± 0.55	1.21 ± 0.75	0.97 ± 0.55	1.17 ± 0.75
Wikipedia	1.05 ± 0.65	1.04 ± 0.68	1.04 ± 0.66	1.08 ± 0.65

Table 4: Target text Normalized character count BY model performance on English test set

7 Discussion

We observed a relationship between the length of the target text—character count—and the performance of our models.

On the News genre dataset of the English test set, our CNN model tends to show better performance on target texts with fewer words compared to Tree Ensembles. When the target text contains more than three words, Tree ensembles perform better than CNN. Similarly, both models tend to make mistakes when the average character count in the target text is higher. Table 4 shows the normalized mean character count of the target text in the English test set when each of our models made correct and wrong predictions.

We believe that this behavior is a reflection of the training examples: there are fewer examples with longer target texts.

8 Conclusion and Future Work

We have described two approaches for the classification subtask of the CWI 2018 shared task: one using feature engineering with Tree Ensembles and one using CNN. We compared them on the test set provided for the CWI 2018 shared task. On the English test set, the two approaches showed comparable performance: the difference between the performance scores was within 0.01. On the English test set, our best model placed fifth on News, second on Wikinews, and seventh on Wikipedia. On the Spanish test set, the CNN model ranked third. This result demonstrates the flexibility of applying CNN to CWI on any language for which pre-trained embeddings are available.

Our models behaved differently depending on the length of the target text: they tend to make mistakes on longer target texts. We attribute this behavior to the skewness of the training set.

In the future, it would be interesting to evaluate the impact of domain-specific features, as well as of different vector operations used to generate context vectors, on the performance of our models.

Acknowledgements

Thanks to the CWI 2018 task organizers. We appreciate the anonymous reviewers for their useful comments on this paper. The last author acknowledges the support of the Mexican government via CONACYT (SNI) and the Instituto Politécnico Nacional grant SIP-20181792.

References

Michael R Berthold, Nicolas Cebron, Fabian Dill, Thomas R Gabriel, Tobias Kötter, Thorsten Meinl, Peter Ohl, Kilian Thiel, and Bernd Wiswedel. 2009. KNIME-the Konstanz information miner: version 2.0 and beyond. *ACM SIGKDD explorations Newsletter*, 11(1):26–31.

Joachim Bingel, Natalie Schluter, and Héctor Martínez Alonso. 2016. CoastalCPH at SemEval-2016 Task 11: The importance of designing your Neural Networks right. In *Proceedings of the 10th International Workshop on Semantic Evaluation (SemEval-2016)*, pages 1028–1033, San Diego, California. Association for Computational Linguistics.

Elnaz Davoodi and Leila Kosseim. 2016. CLaC at SemEval-2016 Task 11: Exploring linguistic and psycho-linguistic Features for Complex Word Identification. In *Proceedings of the 10th International Workshop on Semantic Evaluation (SemEval-2016)*, pages 982–985, San Diego, California. Association for Computational Linguistics.

Ian Goodfellow, Yoshua Bengio, and Aaron Courville. 2016. *Deep Learning*. MIT Press, Cambridge, Massachusetts. `http://www.deeplearningbook.org`.

Edouard Grave, Piotr Bojanowski, Prakhar Gupta, Armand Joulin, and Tomas Mikolov. 2018. Learning word vectors for 157 languages. In *Proceedings of the International Conference on Language Resources and Evaluation (LREC 2018)*, Miyazaki, Japan.

Yoon Kim. 2014. Convolutional neural networks for sentence classification. In *Proceedings of the 2014 Conference on Empirical Methods in Natural Language Processing (EMNLP)*, pages 1746–1751, Doha, Qatar.

Michal Konkol. 2016. UWB at SemEval-2016 Task 11: Exploring Features for Complex Word Identification. In *Proceedings of the 10th International Workshop on Semantic Evaluation (SemEval-2016)*, pages 1038–1041, San Diego, California. Association for Computational Linguistics.

Tomas Mikolov, Kai Chen, Greg Corrado, and Jeffrey Dean. 2013. Efficient estimation of word representations in vector space. *arXiv preprint arXiv:1301.3781*.

Gillin Nat. 2016. Sensible at SemEval-2016 Task 11: Neural Nonsense Mangled in Ensemble Mess. In *Proceedings of the 10th International Workshop on Semantic Evaluation (SemEval-2016)*, pages 963–968, San Diego, California. Association for Computational Linguistics.

Gustavo Paetzold and Lucia Specia. 2016a. Inferring psycholinguistic properties of words. In *Proceedings of the 2016 Conference of the North American Chapter of the Association for Computational Linguistics: Human Language Technologies*, pages 435–440, San Diego, California. Association for Computational Linguistics.

Gustavo Paetzold and Lucia Specia. 2016b. SemEval 2016 Task 11: Complex Word Identification. In *Proceedings of the 10th International Workshop on Semantic Evaluation (SemEval-2016)*, pages 560–569, San Diego, California. Association for Computational Linguistics.

Gustavo Paetzold and Lucia Specia. 2016c. SV000gg at SemEval-2016 Task 11: Heavy Gauge Complex Word Identification with System Voting. In *Proceedings of the 10th International Workshop on Semantic Evaluation (SemEval-2016)*, pages 969–974, San Diego, California. Association for Computational Linguistics.

Fabian Pedregosa, Gaël Varoquaux, Alexandre Gramfort, Vincent Michel, Bertrand Thirion, Olivier Grisel, Mathieu Blondel, Peter Prettenhofer, Ron Weiss, Vincent Dubourg, et al. 2011. Scikit-learn: Machine learning in python. *Journal of machine learning research*, 12(Oct):2825–2830.

Aliaksei Severyn and Alessandro Moschitti. 2015. Twitter sentiment analysis with deep convolutional neural networks. In *Proceedings of the 38th International ACM SIGIR Conference on Research and Development in Information Retrieval*, pages 959–962, Santiago, Chile. ACM.

Nitish Srivastava, Geoffrey Hinton, Alex Krizhevsky, Ilya Sutskever, and Ruslan Salakhutdinov. 2014. Dropout: A simple way to prevent neural networks from overfitting. *The Journal of Machine Learning Research*, 15(1):1929–1958.

Seid Muhie Yimam, Chris Biemann, Shervin Malmasi, Gustavo Paetzold, Lucia Specia, Sanja Štajner, Anaïs Tack, and Marcos Zampieri. 2018. A Report on the Complex Word Identification Shared Task 2018. In *Proceedings of the 13th Workshop on Innovative Use of NLP for Building Educational Applications*, New Orleans, United States. Association for Computational Linguistics.

Seid Muhie Yimam, Sanja Štajner, Martin Riedl, and Chris Biemann. 2017a. CWIG3G2-Complex Word Identification Task across Three Text Genres and Two User Groups. In *Proceedings of the Eighth International Joint Conference on Natural Language Processing (Volume 2: Short Papers)*, volume 2, pages 401–407, Taipei, Taiwan. Asian Federation of Natural Language Processing.

Seid Muhie Yimam, Sanja Štajner, Martin Riedl, and Chris Biemann. 2017b. Multilingual and cross-lingual complex word identification. In *Proceedings of RANLP*, pages 813–822, Varna, Bulgaria. INCOMA Ltd.

Wenpeng Yin and Hinrich Schütze. 2015a. Convolutional neural network for paraphrase identification. In *Proceedings of the 2015 Conference of the North American Chapter of the Association for Computational Linguistics: Human Language Technologies*, pages 901–911, Denver, Colorado. Association for Computational Linguistics.

Wenpeng Yin and Hinrich Schütze. 2015b. Multigrancnn: An architecture for general matching of text chunks on multiple levels of granularity. In *Proceedings of the 53rd Annual Meeting of the Association for Computational Linguistics and the 7th International Joint Conference on Natural Language Processing (Volume 1: Long Papers)*, pages 63–73, Beijing, China. Association for Computational Linguistics.

Deep Learning Architecture for Complex Word Identification

Dirk De Hertog
ITEC, imec, KU Leuven
`dirk.dehertog@kuleuven.be`

Anaïs Tack
CENTAL, Univ. catholique de Louvain
ITEC, imec, KU Leuven
F.R.S.-FNRS Research Fellow
`anais.tack@uclouvain.be`

Abstract

We describe a system for the CWI-task that includes information on 5 aspects of the (complex) lexical item, namely distributional information of the item itself, morphological structure, psychological measures, corpus-counts and topical information. We constructed a deep learning architecture that combines those features and apply it to the probabilistic and binary classification task for all English sets and Spanish. We achieved reasonable performance on all sets with best performances seen on the probabilistic task, particularly on the English news set (MAE 0.054 and F1-score of 0.872). An analysis of the results shows that reasonable performance can be achieved with a single architecture without any domain-specific tweaking of the parameter settings and that distributional features capture almost all of the information also found in hand-crafted features.

1 Introduction

In general, complex word identification (CWI) aims to identify words that are perceived as difficult for a given target audience. As such, children (De Belder and Moens, 2010), foreign language learners (Paetzold and Specia, 2016c) and readers suffering from aphasia (Devlin and Tait, 1998), dyslexia (Rello et al., 2013) or autism spectrum disorder (Štajner et al., 2017) will struggle with different words.

The goal of the current CWI shared task (Yimam et al., 2018) is to predict which words can be difficult for a non-native speaker, based on annotations collected from a mixture of native and non-native speakers. The instructions for the English dataset are formulated so that the annotator marks the words he thinks are problematic for children, non-native speakers, or people with language disabilities.

Having such a diverse target audience requires a system that includes a variety of information at different levels of linguistic description. We include information that covers 5 aspects of the lexical item at hand, namely distributional information of the item itself, morphological structure, psychological measures, corpus-counts and topical information. With the exception of the psychological measures, all can be readily trained by an appropriate neural network architecture and/or acquired from large-scale corpora.

We train a neural network to integrate said sources of information and apply it to the probabilistic and the binary complexity assessment for the three English datasets and the Spanish one.

2 Related Work

2.1 Complex Word Identification

The task of complex word identification has often been regarded as a critical first step for automatic lexical simplification (Shardlow, 2014). Indeed, erroneously identifying or failing to identify words as complex is likely to trigger important errors in the simplification pipeline. As a result, a growing number of studies have been dedicated specifically to complex word identification and have focused on developing accurate statistical learning methods and on collecting appropriate gold standards (Paetzold and Specia, 2016a; Yimam et al., 2017a,b; Štajner et al., 2017)

Complex word identification has only relatively recently been framed as a machine learning (ML) problem (Zeng et al., 2005; Shardlow, 2013). Indeed, before any gold-standard datasets were made available, the early approaches to the identification of complex words in a text included, on the one hand, readability measures determining complex words based on word familiarity (Dale and Chall, 1948) or on syllable count (Gunning, 1952; Mc Laughlin, 1969) and, on the other hand, simplification methods which plainly considered all words as complex and simplified every-

Proceedings of the Thirteenth Workshop on Innovative Use of NLP for Building Educational Applications, pages 328–334
New Orleans, Louisiana, June 5, 2018. ©2018 Association for Computational Linguistics

thing (Devlin and Tait, 1998) or simplified words based on a threshold on word familiarity (Elhadad, 2006).

The SemEval-2016 shared task on complex word identification (described in detail in Paetzold and Specia, 2016a) was the first evaluation campaign which provided a gold-standard dataset as well as an extensive comparison of different machine learning approaches for the task at hand. The submitted systems included different types of classifiers such as SVMs, random forests, maximum entropy systems, ... which combined different types of features, ranging from linguistic information (on a lexical, morphological, semantic and syntactic level), over psycholinguistic measures to corpus-based information such as frequencies. The results on the shared task showed how ensemble methods (Paetzold and Specia, 2016b) outperformed any other ML technique and neural approaches in particular (Bingel et al., 2016). The task also showed however how a lack of annotation standards made it difficult for any ML-approach to model the rather inconsistent human assessment (Zampieri et al., 2017).

2.2 Deep Learning Architectures

The system we describe likewise inscribes itself in the ML-approach to CWI and draws inspiration from neural network literature in NLP. We adapt the architectures' initial purposes and apply it to the task at hand. Collobert et al. (2011) show how distributional information from words, called word embeddings, can be used in combination with a neural network architecture to largely replace hand-crafted features for learning NLP-related tasks such as POS-tagging and NER. The embeddings capture fine-grained information covering its linguistic behavior and the neural network model successfully teases out the relevant properties from that representation for the given task. Character embeddings (Zhang et al., 2015; Zhang and LeCun, 2015) take it one step further and also make it possible to encode and capture subword information in the modeling process.

3 Methods, Data, etc.

3.1 Data sources

The English datasets cover 3 informationally dense target domains for which to assess lexical complexity, namely news, Wikipedia and Wikipedia news. The Spanish dataset contains data taken from Spanish Wikipedia pages. Table 1 summarizes the number of training, development and test items for each dataset we used in the experiment. We combined training and development sets and used it as a single training set.

As a general domain corpus we use the COW-corpora (Schäfer, 2015; Schäfer and Bildhauer, 2012). The corpora are gathered online and cover a wide scope of topics. The English corpus contains well over 13 billion tokens, the Spanish one over 4 billion tokens.

We have at our disposal psychological measures for English from the MRC Psycholinguistic Database (Wilson, 1988). Measures include age of acquistion, imageability, concreteness, familiarity and meaningfulness and covers 150837 words. The overlap between the training dataset is however limited to approximately 1500 words.

Dataset	Train	Dev	Test
English News	14002	1764	2095
English Wikipedia	5551	694	870
English Wikinews	7746	870	1287
Spanish	13750	1622	2233

Table 1: CWI training, development and test sets

3.2 Feature operationalization

Psychological measures Psychological measures are used for the words found in the available dataset. Missing values were extrapolated based on findings that psychological measures correlate (inversely) to frequency. As such, less frequent words tend for instance to have a higher age of acquisition, and a lower imageability and concreteness rating. We therefore chose to respectively use third and first quartile values. In order to accommodate the neural network architecture all values have been normalized by dividing by the maximum value.

Frequency counts Frequency counts are calculated from the general corpus for all experiments. To avoid skewness we perform a rank transformation, with equal ranks being given the first encountered rank, and normalize again by dividing by the highest rank.

Word length Word length is also determined.

Word embeddings Word embeddings are pretrained using the COW-corpora and are used to initialize several of our input layers in the neural network. We use the gensim implementation of word2vec to construct a 300 dimensional embedding space, based on a window-size of 5 including words that reach a minimum frequency threshold of 20.

Character embeddings Character embeddings are trained on the train and development set of all target words. Each character is replaced by a 16-dimensional encoding which has been randomly initialized. Each word consists of a concatenation of its character representations.

3.3 Architecture

Figure 1 shows the general architecture for the CWI-task. The model has been constructed with the Keras deep learning library (Chollet et al., 2015) with tensorflow-gpu as a backend. It includes the 5 sources of information we discussed in the previous section/ which are used as features to represent information at the word and the sentence level. At the word level, we include engineered features (psychological measures, corpus-counts and word length) and distributional information (word and character embeddings). At the sentence level we concatenate embeddings to capture topical information.

3.3.1 Input Layers

We include **engineered features** for the English dataset following the idea that they correlate with cognitive complexity. The features include psychological information, corpus-counts and word length. Corpus-counts measure familiarity and infrequent words are attributed a higher degree of complexity. Word length then has been shown to be related to processing difficulties and is relevant for instance to determine which words pose problems for persons with dyslexia.

Each target word is encoded by its **word embedding**, or in the case of word groups by their concatenated embeddings. The idea is that words with similar distributional patterns might have a comparable complexity. An LSTM layer with a dimensionality of 64 compacts the dimensionality of the representation.

Each target is also encoded as a sequence of its **character embeddings**. This input encoding is meant to capture morphological information as well as cues from letter sequences which might be perceived as difficult. The character embeddings

are trained through 2 convolutional layers (4 filters, kernel size of 4, stride of 1) followed by max pooling (with a size of 2). An LSTM of size 64 is the final layer that directly encodes the character information.

The entire **sentence** is encoded as a concatenation of word embeddings and serves as a sort of topical approximation using contextual cues. An LSTM of 128 finalizes the information captured in this layer.

3.3.2 Dense Layers

All inputs are then concatenated and run through a shallow 3 layered fully connected network (each consisting of 32 nodes) with a moderate dropout rate of 0.3. A final dense layer predicts the output. 2 auxiliary loss functions are provided to ensure smooth training of the character and the topic model. We use binary cross-entropy as the loss function for the binary outcome task and mean squared error rate for the probabilistic one. We applied the architecture to the English datasets and, with the exception of the psychological measures, also to the Spanish one.

4 Results

Dataset	Result	Rank	Maximum-score
English News (Acc)	0.872	2	0.879
English Wikipedia (Acc)	0.782	5	0.812
English Wikinews (Acc)	0.815	6	0.843
Spanish (Acc)	0.777	2	0.784
English News (MAE)	0.054	2	0.051
English Wikipedia (MAE)	0.081	2	0.074
English Wikinews (MAE)	0.071	3	0.067
Spanish (MAE)	0.073	2	0.072

Table 2: Results, Rank and Maximum scores for the CWI identification task

The results in Table 2 show reasonably good performance for all tasks. Our architecture seems to work especially well for the regression task, but shows its aptitude for the classification task as well. The size of the training data seems to play a direct role in the system's ability for accurate predictions. This is in line with other deep learning literature. This does not hold for the Spanish set however, which might be due to a slight difference in apprehension during the data collection phase. The inclusion of corpus-counts and pre-trained embeddings from a general corpus, rather than a wikipedia corpus shows directly

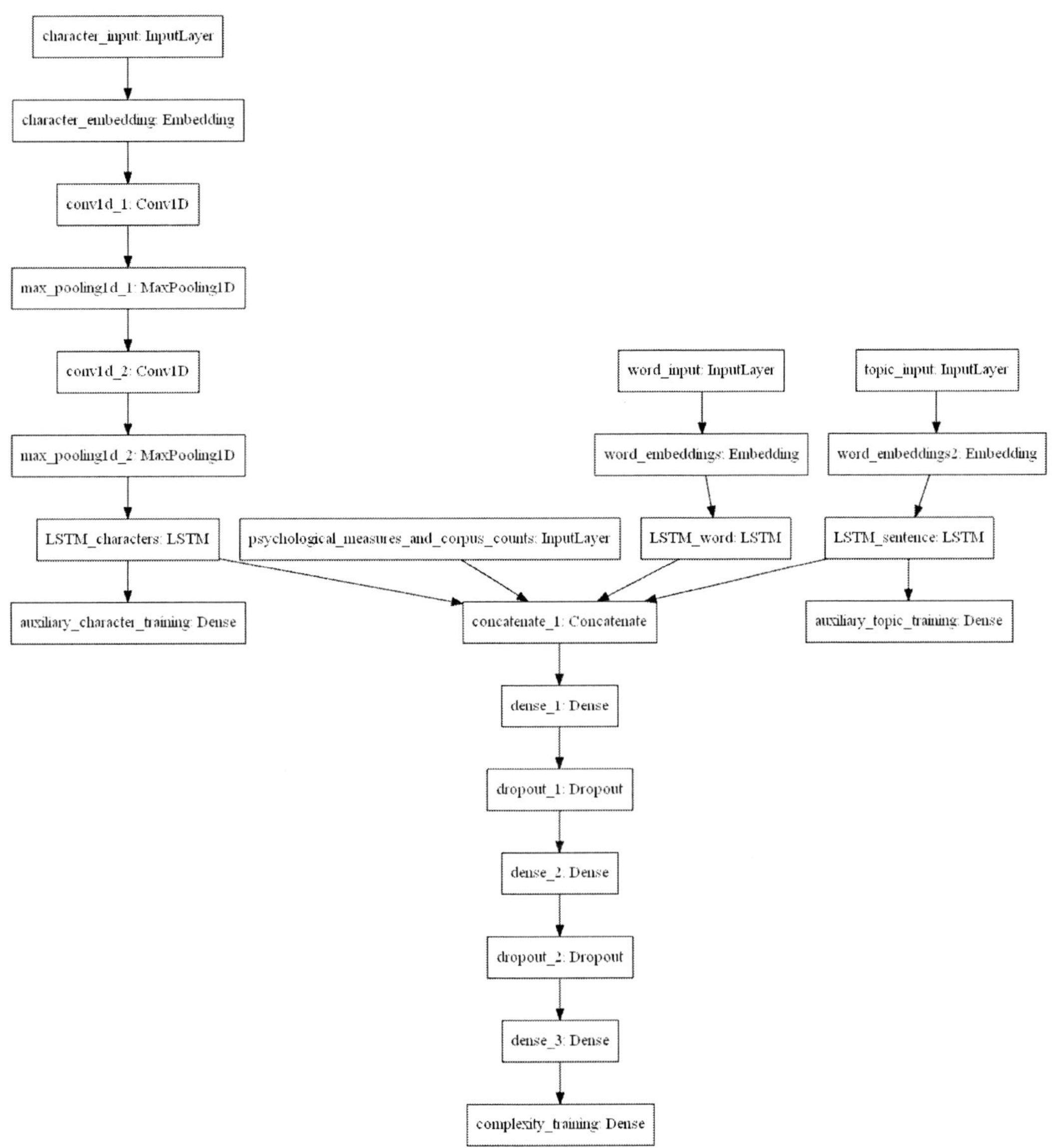

Figure 1: Neural Network Architecture

Input	Precision Non-complex	Precision Complex	Recall Non-complex	Recall Complex
Character encoding (C)	0.876	0.757	0.839	0.809
Engineered features (E)	0.853	0.755	0.846	0.764
Word embeddings (W)	0.892	0.813	0.882	0.829
Sentences (S)	0.617	0	1	0
W + C	0.897	0.829	0.893	0.835
W + C + E	0.902	0.825	0.888	0.845

Table 3: Precision and Recall for different input layers

in the performance of the respective tasks. Using a wikipedia corpus will probably positively influence the results for those particular sets. Yet, the inclusion of general corpus-information proves to be a valid alternative in lack of specialized corpora. The inclusion of the engineered features does not seem to affect the obtained scores much.

Table 3 provides an overview of the relative contribution of each input layer to the final result for the English news dataset. The models were trained for 50 epochs. Considering each input layer separately, the word embeddings are the best estimator for the complexity task, followed closely by the character embeddings. Engineered features capture some information on the word's complexity, yet not as much as the embedding layers. Interestingly, sentence information does not outperform the baseline.

The combination of input layers shows the relative improvement that can be achieved by adding more information to the best performing input layer. The results indicate that combining information only marginally improves performance. They also confirm that the engineered features in combination with the embeddings do not contribute much to the final score.

This leads to the following conclusions for the current dataset. First, complexity is best determined by including focused information of the target word itself. The inclusion of contextual, topical information does not show any noticeable advantage. Looking at the combination of input layers, we can derive that the engineered features only add marginally different information from other input sources. This could be due to the limited number of words that are actually covered by the psychological dataset, but it also implies that the information from the corpus-counts is indirectly captured by the embeddings and from the word length by the character encodings. It is a case in point for replacing manual feature engineering by word and character embeddings. Based on these results we cannot conclude whether the word embeddings' better performance over the character embeddings is due to pre-training.

5 Conclusion

Reasonable performance can be achieved with a single architecture including information from different levels of linguistic description. Information derived from large scale corpora makes it possible to include them as a starting point on which to build a general architecture that learns the appropriate weights for the specific problem, in our case, the CWI-task. Embeddings at the word and the character level seem to contain sufficient information to model the problem well.

Future work will include an exploration to find optimal hyperparameter settings to optimize the identification task. We will likewise explore whether pre-training the character embeddings on a larger corpus will put its performance on par with the pre-trained word embeddings. The latter would pave the way for a model with less training parameters and would significantly reduce complexity.

References

Joachim Bingel, Natalie Schluter, and Héctor Martínez Alonso. 2016. CoastalCPH at SemEval-2016 Task 11: The importance of designing your Neural Networks right. In *Proceedings of the 10th International Workshop on Semantic Evaluation (SemEval-2016)*, pages 1028–1033, San Diego, California. Association for Computational Linguistics.

François Chollet et al. 2015. Keras. `https://keras.io`.

Ronan Collobert, Jason Weston, Léon Bottou, Michael Karlen, Koray Kavukcuoglu, and Pavel Kuksa. 2011. Natural Language Processing (Almost) from Scratch. *Journal of Machine Learning Research*, 12:2493–2537.

Edgar Dale and Jeanne S. Chall. 1948. A Formula for Predicting Readability. *Educational Research Bulletin*, 27(1):11–28.

Jan De Belder and Marie-Francine Moens. 2010. Text Simplification for Children. In *Proceedings of the SIGIR workshop on accessible search systems*, pages 19–26. ACM.

Siobhan Devlin and John Tait. 1998. The Use of a Psycholinguistic Database in the Simplification of Text for Aphasic Readers. In John Nerbonne, editor, *Linguistic Databases*, number 77 in CSLI Lecture Notes, pages 161–173.

N. Elhadad. 2006. Comprehending technical texts: predicting and defining unfamiliar terms., Comprehending Technical Texts: Predicting and Defining Unfamiliar Terms. *AMIA Annual Symposium Proceedings, AMIA Annual Symposium Proceedings*, 2006:239, 239–243.

Robert Gunning. 1952. *The Technique of Clear Writing*. McGraw-Hill, New York.

G. Harry Mc Laughlin. 1969. SMOG Grading—a New Readability Formula. *Journal of Reading*, 12(8):639–646.

Gustavo Paetzold and Lucia Specia. 2016a. SemEval 2016 Task 11: Complex Word Identification. In *Proceedings of the 10th International Workshop on Semantic Evaluation (SemEval-2016)*, pages 560–569, San Diego, California. Association for Computational Linguistics.

Gustavo Paetzold and Lucia Specia. 2016b. SV000gg at SemEval-2016 Task 11: Heavy Gauge Complex Word Identification with System Voting. In *Proceedings of the 10th International Workshop on Semantic Evaluation (SemEval-2016)*, pages 969–974, San Diego, California. Association for Computational Linguistics.

Gustavo Henrique Paetzold and Lucia Specia. 2016c. Understanding the Lexical Simplification Needs of Non-Native Speakers of English. In *Proceedings of COLING 2016, the 26th International Conference on Computational Linguistics: Technical Papers*, pages 717–727, Osaka, Japan.

Luz Rello, Ricardo Baeza-Yates, Stefan Bott, and Horacio Saggion. 2013. Simplify or Help?: Text Simplification Strategies for People with Dyslexia. In *Proceedings of the 10th International Cross-Disciplinary Conference on Web Accessibility*, W4A '13, pages 15:1–15:10, New York, NY, USA. ACM.

Roland Schäfer. 2015. Processing and querying large web corpora with the COW14 architecture. In *Proceedings of Challenges in the Management of Large Corpora 3 (CMLC-3)*, Lancaster. UCREL, IDS.

Roland Schäfer and Felix Bildhauer. 2012. Building Large Corpora from the Web Using a New Efficient Tool ChainNo Title. In *Proceedings of the Eight International Conference on Language Resources and Evaluation (LREC'12)*, pages 486–493.

Matthew Shardlow. 2013. A Comparison of Techniques to Automatically Identify Complex Words. In *51st Annual Meeting of the Association for Computational Linguistics Proceedings of the Student Research Workshop*, pages 103–109, Sofia, Bulgaria. Association for Computational Linguistics.

Matthew Shardlow. 2014. Out in the Open: Finding and Categorising Errors in the Lexical Simplification Pipeline. In *LREC 2014*, pages 1583–1580. European Language Resources Association (ELRA).

Sanja Štajner, Victoria Yaneva, Ruslan Mitkov, and Simone Paolo Ponzetto. 2017. Effects of Lexical Properties on Viewing Time per Word in Autistic and Neurotypical Readers. In *Proceedings of the 12th Workshop on Innovative Use of NLP for Building Educational Applications*, pages 271–281, Copenhagen, Denmark. Association for Computational Linguistics.

Michael Wilson. 1988. MRC Psycholinguistic Database: Machine Usable Dictionary, version 2.00. *Behavior Research Methods, Instruments, & Computers*, 20(1):6–10.

Seid Muhie Yimam, Chris Biemann, Shervin Malmasi, Gustavo Paetzold, Lucia Specia, Sanja Štajner, Anaïs Tack, and Marcos Zampieri. 2018. A Report on the Complex Word Identification Shared Task 2018. In *Proceedings of the 13th Workshop on Innovative Use of NLP for Building Educational Applications*, New Orleans, United States. Association for Computational Linguistics.

Seid Muhie Yimam, Sanja Štajner, Martin Riedl, and Chris Biemann. 2017a. CWIG3g2 - Complex Word Identification Task across Three Text Genres and Two User Groups. In *Proceedings of the Eighth International Joint Conference on Natural Language Processing (Volume 2: Short Papers)*, pages 401–407, Taipei, Taiwan. Asian Federation of Natural Language Processing.

Seid Muhie Yimam, Sanja Štajner, Martin Riedl, and Chris Biemann. 2017b. Multilingual and Cross-Lingual Complex Word Identification. In *Proceedings of Recent Advances in Natural Language Processing*, pages 813–822, Varna, Bulgaria. Incoma Ltd. Shoumen, Bulgaria.

Marcos Zampieri, Shervin Malmasi, Gustavo Paetzold, and Lucia Specia. 2017. Complex Word Identification: Challenges in Data Annotation and System Performance. In *Proceedings of the 4th Workshop on Natural Language Processing Techniques for Educational Applications (NLPTEA 2017)*, pages 59–63, Taipei, Taiwan. Asian Federation of Natural Language Processing.

Qing Zeng, Eunjung Kim, Jon Crowell, and Tony Tse.
2005. A Text Corpora-Based Estimation of the Familiarity of Health Terminology. In *Biological and Medical Data Analysis*, Lecture Notes in Computer Science, pages 184–192. Springer, Berlin, Heidelberg.

Xiang Zhang and Yann LeCun. 2015. Text Understanding from Scratch. *arXiv:1502.01710 [cs].* ArXiv: 1502.01710.

Xiang Zhang, Junbo Zhao, and Yann LeCun. 2015. Character-level Convolutional Networks for Text Classification. pages 1–9.

NILC at CWI 2018: Exploring Feature Engineering and Feature Learning

Nathan Siegle Hartmann[1,2] and Leandro Borges dos Santos[1,2]
[1]Data Science Team, Itaú-Unibanco, São Paulo, Brazil[*]
[2]Institute of Mathematics and Computer Science, University of São Paulo, São Carlos, Brazil
`nathansh@icmc.usp.com.br, leandrobs@usp.br`

Abstract

This paper describes the results of NILC team at CWI 2018. We developed solutions following three approaches: (i) a feature engineering method using lexical, n-gram and psycholinguistic features, (ii) a shallow neural network method using only word embeddings, and (iii) a Long Short-Term Memory (LSTM) language model, which is pre-trained on a large text corpus to produce a contextualized word vector. The feature engineering method obtained our best results for the classification task and the LSTM model achieved the best results for the probabilistic classification task. Our results show that deep neural networks are able to perform as well as traditional machine learning methods using manually engineered features for the task of complex word identification in English.

1 Introduction

Research efforts on text simplification have mostly focused on either lexical (Devlin and Tait, 1998; Biran et al., 2011; Glavaš and Štajner, 2015; Paetzold and Specia, 2016b) or syntactic simplification (Siddharthan, 2006; Kauchak, 2013). Lexical simplification involves replacing specific words in order to reduce lexical complexity. Lexical simplification is an open problem, as identifying and simplifying complex words in a given context is not straightforward. Although very intuitive, this is a challenging task since the substitutions must preserve both the original meaning and the grammaticality of the sentence being simplified. Complex word identification is part of the usual lexical simplification pipeline (Paetzold and Specia, 2015), which is illustrated in Figure 1.

For the challenge, we focused on the English monolingual CWI track. We implemented three

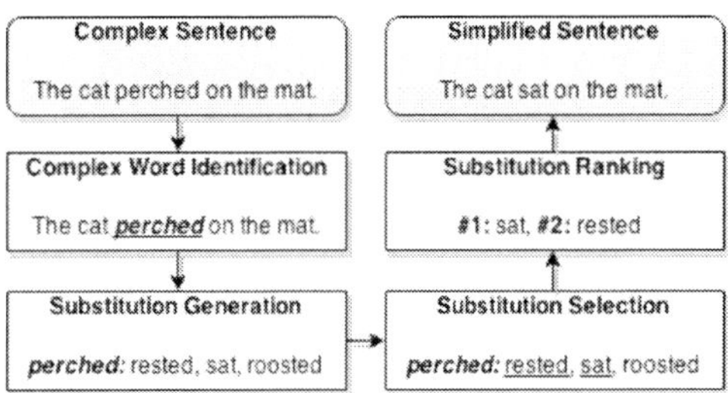

Figure 1: Lexical Simplification pipeline.

approaches using machine learning: the first one uses feature engineering; the second one takes the average embedding of target words as input to a neural network; and the third approach models the context of the target words using an LSTM (Gers et al., 1999). Our code is publicly available at github[1].

2 Task Description

The setup of the CWI Shared Task 2018 is as follows: given a target word (or a chunk of words) in a sentence, predict whether or not a non-native English speaker would be able to understand it. These predictions are based on annotations collected from a mixture of 10 native and 10 non-native speakers. The labels in the binary classification task were assigned "1" if at least one of the 20 annotators did not understand it (complex), and "0" otherwise (simple). The labels in the probabilistic classification task were assigned as the number of annotators who marked the word as difficult divided by the total number of annotators.

In this edition a multilingual dataset was available and participants could choose to participate in one or more of the following tracks: English monolingual CWI, German monolingual

---

[1]`https://github.com/nathanshartmann/NILC-at-CWI-2018`

Proceedings of the Thirteenth Workshop on Innovative Use of NLP for Building Educational Applications, pages 335–340
New Orleans, Louisiana, June 5, 2018. ©2018 Association for Computational Linguistics

CWI, Spanish monolingual CWI, Multilingual CWI shared task with French test set. Also, the participants could choose between binary classification or probabilistic classification task. We chose to participate in the English monolingual track and in both classification tasks (see in Table 1 the dataset distribution for the track).

Dataset	Train	Dev	Test
News	14,002	1,764	2,095
WikiNews	7,746	870	1,287
Wikipedia	5,551	694	870
Total	27,299	3,328	4,252

Table 1: CWI 2018 english dataset distribution.

More relevant task description, data and results are available in Yimam et al. (2018).

3 Datasets

In this work, we used two extra corpora to train language models, one of these to train a neural language model:

- BookCorpus dataset: which has 11,038 free books written by yet unpublished authors (Zhu et al., 2015);

- One Billion Word dataset: which is the largest public benchmark for language modeling (Chelba et al., 2013).

4 Proposed Methods

In this section we show our developed methods, following three approaches: feature engineering, feature learning and ensembles.

4.1 Methods based on Feature Engineering

We used linguistic, psycholinguistic and language model features to train several classification and probabilistic classification methods. Our feature set consists of three groups of features:

- LEX: includes word length, number of syllables, number of senses, hypernyms and hyponyms in WordNet (Fellbaum, 1998);

- N-gram: includes log probabilities of an n-gram containing target words in two language models trained on BookCorpus and One Billion Word datasets using SRILM (Stolcke, 2002);

- PSY: contains word-level psycholinguistic features such as familiarity, age of acquisition, concreteness and imagery values for every target word (Paetzold and Specia, 2016a).

Because an instance can contain more than a target word, mean, standard deviation, min and max values were calculated for each feature. A total of 38 features are extracted for each instance. We also normalized features using Z-score.

We trained Linear Regression, Logistic Regression, Decision Trees, Gradient Boosting, Extra Trees, AdaBoost and XGBoost methods for both classification and probabilistic classification tasks.

4.2 Methods based on Feature Learning and Transfer Learning

An alternative approach to feature engineering is to make the machine learning model itself create a data representation. This is the principle of feature learning. In this scenario, all elements of the vector contain an independent value, which has some meaning for the model (LeCun et al., 2015).

Most importantly, we can reuse this representation in another tasks, which is called transfer learning or domain adaptation. This strategy is already used with success in Computer Vision, where deep neural networks are pre-trained in large supervised training sets like ImageNet (Girshick et al., 2014; Esteva et al., 2017).

It is common in Natural Language Processing (NLP) tasks to use pre-trained word embeddings with models like Word2Vec (Mikolov et al., 2013) or GloVe (Pennington et al., 2014). However, more recently some studies have used distributed sentences to produce contextualized embeddings, from a language model, machine translation model, or auto-encoder (Dai and Le, 2015; Kiros et al., 2015; Yuan et al., 2016; Le et al., 2017; Peters et al., 2017, 2018; McCann et al., 2017; Howard and Ruder, 2018).

In the next section we will explain how we used both strategies.

4.2.1 Average Embedding Method

Word embedding is a technique to represent words into dense real vectors, that helps NLP tasks and improves neural networks models (Collobert et al., 2011; Kim, 2014; Bowman et al., 2015), because this dense representation captures semantic and morphological information of the words. In this work, we obtained word vector representations for complex words. When a complex word was a chunk of words, we took the average of their vectors. We used word vectors from GloVe (6B tokens (Pennington et al., 2014)).

The resulting vector was passed on to a neural network with two ReLU layers (Nair and Hinton, 2010) followed by a Sigmoid layer, which predicted the probability of whether or not the word was complex (Figure 2).

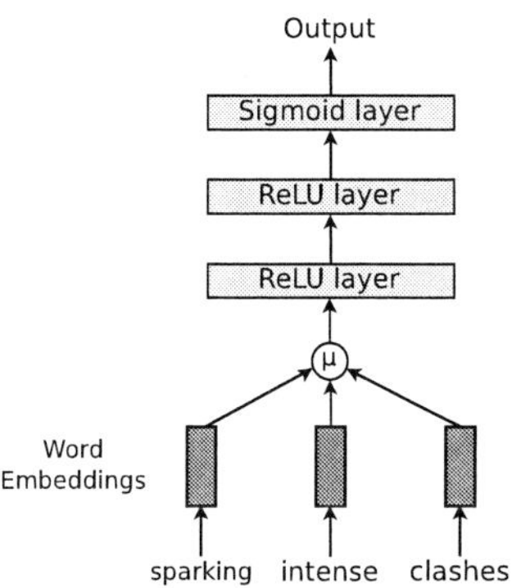

Figure 2: Example of average embedding method processing target words.

4.2.2 LSTM Method

LSTM is a powerful tool for modeling sequential data. This type of neural network architecture can learn to map an input sentence of variable length into a fixed-dimensional vector representation. For this reason, a lot of state-of-the-art systems in several NLP tasks incorporate an LSTM, for example, language modeling (Jozefowicz et al., 2016; Melis et al., 2017), machine translation (Di Gangi et al., 2017), textual inference (Tay et al., 2017), and others.

Some studies used a pre-trained LSTM language model (Dai and Le, 2015; Yuan et al., 2016; Le et al., 2017; Peters et al., 2017, 2018) to represent a sentence/document and used this representation to improve their results.

Therefore, we trained a language model in the One Billion Word dataset using similar parameters from Le et al. (2017): one-layer LSTM with 512 units, 128 embedding size, and sampled softmax loss (Jean et al., 2015). However, we used weight tying, which means the weights between the embedding and softmax layer are shared, consequently reducing the total parameters of the model (Melis et al., 2017). For the CWI task, the LSTM read five words before the complex word, then the complex word itself (or the chunk

of words). We took the last hidden vector from the LSTM and passed it through a Sigmoid layer.

In Figure 3 we show the pipeline where the blue boxes represent the context words and red boxes represents the complex word, which is a chunk in this example.

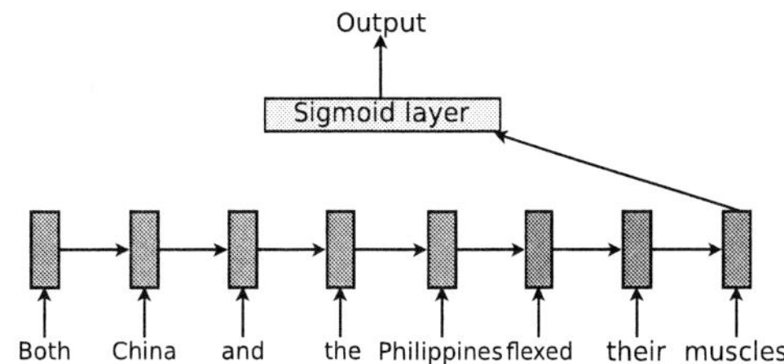

Figure 3: Example of a LSTM processing target words.

4.2.3 Sent2Vec

We also used sentence embeddings generated by Skip-thought (Kiros et al., 2015). This model produces a sentence representation of 2,400 dimensions. We trained two models using sentence embedding. In the first, we passed the embedding through a sigmoid layer and in the second, we used two layers with ReLUs of 1,200 and 600 dimensions respectively, followed by a Sigmoid layer. In the last model we employed a dropout layer (0.7) between all of the layers. Both models obtained good results in the training set, however, the models had poor results in the development set.

4.3 Ensembles

We combined our three best systems: Feature Engineering, MLP Average Embedding and LSTM Transfer Learning. For the binary classification task, we combined the system by majority voting rule. For the probabilistic classification task we used stacking with Linear Regression as a base learner, which took the probabilities from our three best system as features.

5 Results

For the binary classification task, we first evaluated the ROC-AUC in the development set for all methods. For the Feature Engineering method, we decided to use an XGBoost classifier which achieved the best AUC in development set (0.91). Although we selected the threshold which maximizes the F1 in the training set for each Feature Engineering, Shallow and Deep Neural network method, it is important to mention that these

	News			WikiNews			Wikipedia		
	F1	#Subm.	#Author	F1	#Subm.	#Author	F1	#Subm.	#Author
XGBoost Linguistics	0.8606	9th		**0.8277**	7th	3rd	0.7918	4th	
MLP Avg. Embeddings	0.8467	15th		0.7977	16th		0.7360	26th	
LSTM Transfer Learning	0.8173	27th		0.7961	17th		0.7528	20th	
Voting	**0.8636**	5th	4th	0.8270	8th		**0.7965**	2nd	2nd
Best competition results	0.8736			0.8400			0.8115		

Table 2: F1 (macro) for English monolingual classification task.

	News			WikiNews			Wikipedia		
	MAE	#Subm.	#Author	MAE	#Subm.	#Author	MAE	#Subm.	#Author
XGBoost Linguistics	0.2978	14th		0.3203	15th		0.3819	7th	
MLP Avg. Embeddings	0.2958	13th		0.3240	16th		0.3578	7th	
LSTM Transfer Learning	**0.0588**	7th	4th	0.0742	7th		0.0822	7th	
Stacking	0.0590	8th		**0.0733**	6th	4th	**0.0819**	6th	3rd
Best competition results	0.0510			0.0674			0.0739		

Table 3: MAE for English monolingual probabilistic classification task.

thresholds were found for the whole training set and not for each subset. This guarantees that we are not overfitting our method to test data or to a specific dataset. Our results for the English monolingual classification task are described in Table 2. The Feature Engineering method itself achieved by far our best results for the three test sets. In order to achieve better results, we submitted a fourth system which calculated the majority voting of our three methods. This voting system surpassed our individual methods in two test sets, but was inferior compared to the Feature Engineering method by less than 1^{-3} F1 in the WikiNews dataset. Majority voting was our best method for the classification task.

For the probabilistic classification task, our Feature Engineering method used also an XGBoost classifier which achieved the best MAE in development set (0.28). Our results for English monolingual probabilistic classification task are described in Table 3. While both Feature Engineering and Average Embedding did not perform well, our best individual system by a large margin was the LSTM method. In order to achieve better results, we used stacking of our three models. The stacking performed better than individual methods in two datasets, but was not better than LSTM for the News test set (2^{-4} gap).

6 Conclusion

For the binary classification task, majority voting achieved our best results, although only slightly better than the standalone Feature Engineering model.

For the probabilistic classification task, LSTM had better results in one data set, but the stacking method performed slightly better in the other data sets. The deep learning method showed its potential when contrasted with the feature engineering method.

In the future, we intend to explore more powerful neural language models, such as encoding characters embeddings (Jozefowicz et al., 2016), bidirectional language model (Peters et al., 2017, 2018), and other transfer learning methods (Howard and Ruder, 2018).

Acknowledgments

This work was supported by CAPES, CNPq and Google Research Awards in Latin America. We would like to thank NVIDIA for their donation of Titan X. Research carried out using the computational resources of the Center for Mathematical Sciences Applied to Industry (CeMEAI) funded by FAPESP (grant 2013/07375-0).

References

Or Biran, Samuel Brody, and Noémie Elhadad. 2011. Putting it simply: a context-aware approach to lexical simplification. In Proceedings of the 49th Annual Meeting of the Association for Computational Linguistics: Human Language Technologies: short papers-Volume 2, pages 496–501. Association for Computational Linguistics.

Samuel R Bowman, Gabor Angeli, Christopher Potts, and Christopher D Manning. 2015. A large annotated corpus for learning natural language inference. arXiv preprint arXiv:1508.05326.

Ciprian Chelba, Tomas Mikolov, Mike Schuster, Qi Ge, Thorsten Brants, Phillipp Koehn, and Tony Robinson. 2013. One billion word benchmark for measuring progress in statistical language modeling. Technical report, Google.

Ronan Collobert, Jason Weston, Léon Bottou, Michael Karlen, Koray Kavukcuoglu, and Pavel Kuksa. 2011. Natural language processing (almost) from scratch. Journal of Machine Learning Research, 12(Aug):2493–2537.

Andrew M Dai and Quoc V Le. 2015. Semi-supervised sequence learning. In Advances in Neural Information Processing Systems, pages 3079–3087.

Siobhan Devlin and John Tait. 1998. The use of a psycholinguistic database in the simplification of text for aphasic readers. Linguistic databases, pages 161–173.

Mattia Antonino Di Gangi, Nicola Bertoldi, and Marcello Federico. 2017. Fbk's participation to the english-to-german news translation task of wmt 2017. In Proceedings of the Second Conference on Machine Translation, pages 271–275.

Andre Esteva, Brett Kuprel, Roberto A Novoa, Justin Ko, Susan M Swetter, Helen M Blau, and Sebastian Thrun. 2017. Dermatologist-level classification of skin cancer with deep neural networks. Nature, 542(7639):115.

Christiane Fellbaum. 1998. WordNet. Wiley Online Library.

Felix A Gers, Jürgen Schmidhuber, and Fred Cummins. 1999. Learning to forget: Continual prediction with lstm.

Ross Girshick, Jeff Donahue, Trevor Darrell, and Jitendra Malik. 2014. Rich feature hierarchies for accurate object detection and semantic segmentation. In Proceedings of the 2014 IEEE Conference on Computer Vision and Pattern Recognition, pages 580–587. IEEE Computer Society.

Goran Glavaš and Sanja Štajner. 2015. Simplifying Lexical Simplification: Do We Need Simplified Corpora? In Proceedings of the 53rd Annual Meeting of the Association for Computational Linguistics and the 7th International Joint Conference on Natural Language Processing (ACL-IJCNLP-2015), volume 2, pages 63–68.

Jeremy Howard and Sebastian Ruder. 2018. Fine-tuned language models for text classification. arXiv preprint arXiv:1801.06146.

Sébastien Jean, Kyunghyun Cho, Roland Memisevic, and Yoshua Bengio. 2015. On using very large target vocabulary for neural machine translation. In Proceedings of the 53rd Annual Meeting of the Association for Computational Linguistics and the 7th International Joint Conference on Natural Language Processing (Volume 1: Long Papers), volume 1, pages 1–10.

Rafal Jozefowicz, Oriol Vinyals, Mike Schuster, Noam Shazeer, and Yonghui Wu. 2016. Exploring the limits of language modeling. arXiv preprint arXiv:1602.02410.

David Kauchak. 2013. Improving Text Simplification Language Modeling Using Unsimplified Text Data. In Proceedings of the 51st Annual Meeting of the Association for Computational Linguistics (ACL-2013), pages 1537–1546.

Yoon Kim. 2014. Convolutional neural networks for sentence classification. In Proceedings of the 2014 Conference on Empirical Methods in Natural Language Processing (EMNLP), pages 1746–1751.

Ryan Kiros, Yukun Zhu, Ruslan R Salakhutdinov, Richard Zemel, Raquel Urtasun, Antonio Torralba, and Sanja Fidler. 2015. Skip-thought vectors. In Advances in neural information processing systems, pages 3294–3302.

Minh Le, Marten Postma, and Jacopo Urbani. 2017. Word sense disambiguation with lstm: Do we really need 100 billion words? arXiv preprint arXiv:1712.03376.

Yann LeCun, Yoshua Bengio, and Geoffrey Hinton. 2015. Deep learning. nature, 521(7553):436.

Bryan McCann, James Bradbury, Caiming Xiong, and Richard Socher. 2017. Learned in translation: Contextualized word vectors. In Advances in Neural Information Processing Systems, pages 6297–6308.

Gábor Melis, Chris Dyer, and Phil Blunsom. 2017. On the state of the art of evaluation in neural language models. arXiv preprint arXiv:1707.05589.

Tomas Mikolov, Kai Chen, Greg Corrado, and Jeffrey Dean. 2013. Efficient estimation of word representations in vector space. arXiv preprint arXiv:1301.3781.

Vinod Nair and Geoffrey E Hinton. 2010. Rectified linear units improve restricted boltzmann machines. In Proceedings of the 27th International Conference on International Conference on Machine Learning, pages 807–814. Omnipress.

Gustavo Paetzold and Lucia Specia. 2015. Lexenstein: A framework for lexical simplification. Proceedings of ACL-IJCNLP 2015 System Demonstrations, pages 85–90.

Gustavo Paetzold and Lucia Specia. 2016a. Inferring psycholinguistic properties of words. In Proceedings of the 2016 Conference of the North American Chapter of the Association for Computational Linguistics: Human Language Technologies, pages 435–440.

Gustavo Henrique Paetzold and Lucia Specia. 2016b. Benchmarking lexical simplification systems. Proceedings of the 10th International Conference on Language Resources and Evaluation (LREC-2016), pages 3074–3080.

Jeffrey Pennington, Richard Socher, and Christopher Manning. 2014. Glove: Global vectors for word representation. In Proceedings of the 2014 conference on empirical methods in natural language processing (EMNLP), pages 1532–1543.

Matthew Peters, Waleed Ammar, Chandra Bhagavatula, and Russell Power. 2017. Semi-supervised sequence tagging with bidirectional language models. In Proceedings of the 55th Annual Meeting of the Association for Computational Linguistics (Volume 1: Long Papers), volume 1, pages 1756–1765.

Matthew E Peters, Mark Neumann, Mohit Iyyer, Matt Gardner, Christopher Clark, Kenton Lee, and Luke Zettlemoyer. 2018. Deep contextualized word representations. arXiv preprint arXiv:1802.05365.

Advaith Siddharthan. 2006. Syntactic simplification and text cohesion. Ph.D. thesis, University of Cambridge, Inglaterra.

Andreas Stolcke. 2002. Srilm-an extensible language modeling toolkit. In Seventh international conference on spoken language processing.

Yi Tay, Luu Anh Tuan, and Siu Cheung Hui. 2017. A compare-propagate architecture with alignment factorization for natural language inference. arXiv preprint arXiv:1801.00102.

Seid Muhie Yimam, Chris Biemann, Shervin Malmasi, Gustavo Paetzold, Lucia Specia, Sanja Štajner, Anaïs Tack, and Marcos Zampieri. 2018. A Report on the Complex Word Identification Shared Task 2018. In Proceedings of the 13th Workshop on Innovative Use of NLP for Building Educational Applications, New Orleans, United States. Association for Computational Linguistics.

Dayu Yuan, Julian Richardson, Ryan Doherty, Colin Evans, and Eric Altendorf. 2016. Semi-supervised word sense disambiguation with neural models. In Proceedings of COLING 2016, the 26th International Conference on Computational Linguistics: Technical Papers, pages 1374–1385.

Yukun Zhu, Ryan Kiros, Richard Zemel, Ruslan Salakhutdinov, Raquel Urtasun, Antonio Torralba, and Sanja Fidler. 2015. Aligning books and movies: Towards story-like visual explanations by watching movies and reading books. arXiv preprint arXiv:1506.06724.

Complex Word Identification Using Character n-grams

Maja Popović
Humboldt University of Berlin
Berlin, Germany
`maja.popovic@hu-berlin.de`

Abstract

This paper investigates the use of character n-gram frequencies for identifying complex words in English, German and Spanish texts. The approach is based on the assumption that complex words are likely to contain different character sequences than simple words. The multinomial Naive Bayes classifier was used with n-grams of different lengths as features, and the best results were obtained for the combination of 2-grams and 4-grams. This variant was submitted to the Complex Word Identification Shared Task 2018 for all texts and achieved F-scores between 70% and 83%. The system was ranked in the middle range for all English tracks, as third of fourteen submissions for German, and as tenth of seventeen submissions for Spanish. The method is not very convenient for the cross-language task, achieving only 59% on the French text.

1 Introduction

Complex Word Identification (CWI) refers to identification of words which are considered by readers from a specific target audience to be complex. The CWI task is the first step towards the lexical simplification task which aims at improving the readability of texts: a lexical simplification system should replace the identified complex words with their simpler synonyms. Some of these systems have a CWI module at the beginning of their pipeline, e.g. (Paetzold and Specia, 2015) whereas some perform the CWI task implicitly, such as (Glavaš and Štajner, 2015).

The first shared task on CWI was organized at the SemEval 2016 (Paetzold and Specia, 2016) where 21 teams submitted 42 systems trained to predict whether words in a given context were complex for a non-native English speaker. Following the success of the first CWI shared task and additional findings reported in (Zampieri et al.,

2017), the second shared task has been organised at the BEA workshop 2018 (Yimam et al., 2018) featuring a multilingual dataset. The dataset consists of training and testing sets for three languages: English, German and Spanish, as well as French test set for cross-lingual CWI. The goal was to predict which words could be difficult for a non-native speaker, based on annotations collected from a mixture of native and non-native speakers. The predictions could be submitted in the form of class labels (complex or simple) and/or in the form of complexity probabilities.

This work proposes the use of character n-grams for complex word identification. The main assumption is that complex words contain different character sequences than simple words, i.e. that the combination of particular characters is related to the complexity of a word. Additional motivation is the successful use of character n-grams for machine translation evaluation metrics in recent years (Stanojević and Sima'an, 2014; Popović, 2015; Wang et al., 2016). The results of Machine Translation Metrics Shared Tasks[1] (Bojar et al., 2017) have shown that these metrics correlate very well with human judgments for all analysed target languages, which indicates that character sequences carry some important information.

We used the multinomial Naive Bayes classifier, although the assumption about independence between different n-grams was certainly not valid. The motivation to conduct our first experiments with character n-grams using this classifier was its often use as a baseline for text classification (McCallum and Nigam, 1998; Kibriya et al., 2004; Lohar et al., 2017). Since Naive Bayes probabilities are generally not reliable, we participated only in the binary classification task.

---

[1]http://www.statmt.org/wmt17/metrics-task.html

341

Proceedings of the Thirteenth Workshop on Innovative Use of NLP for Building Educational Applications, pages 341–348
New Orleans, Louisiana, June 5, 2018. ©2018 Association for Computational Linguistics

Although the relation between character n-grams and word complexity intuitively depends on the language, we still decided to investigate cross-lingual CWI and to participate in this track.

1.1 Related work

Several different techniques for identifying complex words were investigated by (Shardlow, 2013) which include word frequency, word length and syllable counts among others, but no character sequences.

The first CWI shared task (Paetzold and Specia, 2016) featured 42 systems based on different techniques and using different features such as semantic, morphological, lexical, as well as word frequencies which are reported to be a very important factor for CWI.

One of the submitted systems (Mukherjee et al., 2016) used Naive Bayes classifier with morphological, semantic and lexical features, however no character n-grams were investigated.

Another system (Zampieri et al., 2016) used probabilities of word character trigrams and sentence character trigrams together with word length and sentence length to measure orthographic difficulty. These features together with the word frequency features are used for three classifiers: Random Forest, Nearest neighbour and SVM. Nevertheless, no results regarding the contribution of character trigram features were reported.

Number of vowels, number of syllables and number of characters (word length) together with word frequencies in corpora were investigated in (Yimam et al., 2017b), but no experiments with character n-grams were conducted.

2 Character n-grams and multinomial Naive Bayes classifier

For each labelled word, all character n-grams of given length(s) and their frequencies were extracted and the word was represented as a "bag of n-grams". Decision on which n-gram length(s) to concentrate is far from trivial since, to our best knowledge, no similar experiments have been conducted before. Therefore, we started with individual n-gram lengths from 2 to 6, following the findings from machine translation metric task where lenghts above 6 did not bring any improvements. Our preliminary experiments showed that introducing six-grams degraded the performance so we kept the lengths up to 5. As for mixed lengths, the

best preliminary results were obtained for 2-gram, 3-gram and 4-gram combinations, so we concentrated on these variants.

Table 1 presents two complex and three simple English words with their 2-grams, 3-grams and 4-grams and corresponding frequencies. Under the (very) naive assumption of conditional independence between individual n-grams, these frequencies are then used for estimating the class-contidition probabilities of the Naive Bayes multinomial model:

$$\hat{c} = \arg\max_c P(c) \prod_{i=1}^{N_{ngr}} P(ngr_i \mid c) \qquad (1)$$

where $P(ngr_i|c)$ is the conditional probability that the n-gram ngr_i occurs in a word with the class value c, and N_{ngr} is the total number of distinct n-grams, i.e. the dimension of the feature vector. $P(c)$ is the prior probability that a word has class label c.

For the multinomial model, these two probabilities can be estimated as relative frequencies in the following way:

$$\hat{P}(ngr_i \mid c) = \frac{count(ngr_i, c)}{\sum_{i=1}^{Ngr} count(ngr_i, c)} \qquad (2)$$

where the numerator represents the number of occurences of the n-gram ngr_i in a word with class label c, and the denominator represents the number of occurences of all n-grams in this class. The smoothing probability for unseen n-grams was set to 0.001.

The prior class probability can be estimated as:

$$\hat{P}(c) = \frac{count(c)}{count(words)} \qquad (3)$$

where $count(c)$ represents the number of words with class label c and $count(words)$ represents the total number of labelled words.

If the words in Table 1 and their 4-grams were used for training, the prior class probabilities for simple ("S") and complex ("C") words would be $P(S) = 3/5 = 0.60$ and $P(C) = 2/5 = 0.4$. Class condition probabilities for the 4-gram "frug" would be $P(frug|S) = 0$ and $P(frug|C) = 1/5 = 0.2$, and for the 4-gram "real" $P(real|S) = 0.25$, $P(real|C) = 0$. The 4-ram "lity" would have similar probabilities for the complex and for

word	"bag of n-grams": 2-grams, 3-grams, 4-grams and their frequencies	class
frugality	fr:1 ru:1 ug:1 ga:1 al:1 li:1 it:1 ty:1 fru:1 rug:1 uga:1 ali:1 lit:1 ity:1 frug:1 ruga:1 ugal:1 gali:1 lity:1	C
reefs	re:1 ee:1 ef:1 fs:1 ree:1 eef:1 efs:1 reef:1 eefs:1	C
banana	ba:1 an:2 na:2 ban:1 ana:2 nan:1 bana:1 anan:1 nana:1	S
coral	co:1 or:1 ra:1 al:1 cor:1 ora:1 ral:1 cora:1 oral:1	S
reality	re:1 ea:1 al:1 li:1 it:1 ty:1 rea:1 eal:1 ali:1 lit:1 ity:1 real:1 eali:1 alit:1 lity:1	S

Table 1: Examples of two complex and three simple words with their 2-grams, 3-grams and 4-grams and corresponding frequencies.

the simple class since it appears both in "frugality" and in "reality": $P(lity|S) = 1/4 = 0.25$, $P(lity|C) = 1/5 = 0.20$.

3 Data

The organisers of the shared CWI task provided all participants with training and test data sets for English, German and Spanish. For French, only test data set was provided since it was intended for the cross-lingual CWI task. The English data set consists of mixture of professionally written news (News), non-professionally written news (WikiNews), and Wikipedia articles (Wiki). German, Spanish and French data sets contain data taken from German, Spanish and French Wikipedia pages. Data statistics is presented in Table 2.

Each sentence in the English data set was annotated by 20 people, 10 native and 10 non-native speakers. Each sentence in the German, Spanish and French data sets was annotated by 10 people, a mixture of native and non-native speakers. Annotators were provided with the surrounding context of each sentence, i.e. a paragraph, then asked to mark words they think would be difficult to understand for children, non-native speakers, and people with language disabilities. Annotators were enabled not only to annotate individual words, but also several consecutive words as complex. The details about the data sets can be found in (Yimam et al., 2017b) and (Yimam et al., 2017a).

4 Results

As mentioned in Section 2, the main part of our experiments was to determine which n-gram lenghts to include in the classifier. Preliminary experiments showed that the individual lengths of 2,3,4 and 5 should be further investigated, as well as combinations of 2- and 4-grams, 3- and 4-grams, as well as 2-, 3- and 4-grams.

All these variants were investigated for three scenarios: (i) standard classification, where each training set corresponds to the development set, (ii) classification with the extended English training corpus, where all English training corpora were concatenated and used for classifying each of the development sets, and (iii) cross-lingual classification, where training sets of other two languages were used for each language.

The comparison of the methods was carried out on the development sets in terms of complex word F-score and overall accuracy.

4.1 Standard set-up

In the standard set-up, each development set was classified using its corresponding training set, both in terms of domain and of language. Table 3 represents the obtained resuls, with best F-scores / accuracies in bold.

It can be noted that the combination of 2-grams and 4-grams is the best option for allmost all texts. It is second ranked (and very close to the best one) only for the accuracy of English news. As for the individual n-grams, the best performance is obtained by 4-grams. The scores are improving when increasing n-gram length up to 4, and then drop for 5-grams (except for the accuracy of English News and German Wikipedia). It can also be seen that in general, combining different n-gram lenghts works better than using the individual ones.

4.2 Concatenated English training corpus

Since the English data set contained three domains: Wikipedia, News and WikiNews, the question about effects of enlarging the training set arised: will the use of a larger training corpus from

#words	English			German	Spanish	French
domain	Wiki	News	WN	Wiki	Wiki	Wiki
Train	5551	14002	7746	6151	13750	0
Dev	694	1764	870	795	1622	0
Test	870	2095	1287	959	2233	2251

Table 2: Data statistics: the number of instances for each training, development and test set used in the CWI 2018 shared task.

n-gram length(s)	English			German	Spanish
	Wiki	News	WikiNews	Wiki	Wiki
2	64.7 / 64.8	63.2 / 70.5	61.8 / 67.6	60.7 / 69.6	55.9 / 68.2
3	67.5 / 68.7	72.6 / 77.8	64.8 / 71.5	62.5 / 68.6	62.0 / 70.3
4	67.5 / 69.3	75.9 / 81.2	68.9 / 75.4	60.9 / 69.9	63.4 / 73.1
5	61.1 / 67.3	75.0 / **81.7**	64.5 / 74.6	57.3 / 70.2	58.2 / 72.6
24	**69.9 / 70.9**	**76.7** / 81.3	**69.9 / 75.7**	**65.3 / 72.6**	**64.7 / 73.6**
34	68.3 / 69.2	75.9 / 80.4	68.5 / 74.0	62.2 / 69.2	**64.7** / 72.4
234	68.4 / 69.4	75.4 / 79.6	**69.9** / 75.0	62.9 / 69.4	64.4 / 72.1

Table 3: F-score for complex word class / accuracy for English, German and Spanish development sets.

different domains lead to better results or not? In order to answer this question, each of the three English development sets was also classified using the concatenated English training corpus containing all three domains and the results are presented in Table 4. These results show that enlarging the training corpus generally helps.

The smallest improvements can be observed for the News text, probably because the News training corpus is the largest one, as can be noted in Table 2. Another finding is that for the larger training set, individual 3-grams, 4-grams and 5-grams can outperform the n-gram combinations. A possible explanation is that the reliability of longer character sequences is increased when a larger training corpus with more instances is used. When the three n-gram length combinations are compared on the larger training set, "24" still outperforms the other two except for the Wikipedia set.

4.3 Cross-lingual classification

In order to explore cross-language classification, each of the Wikipedia development sets was classified using the training corpora of another two languages. English News and WikiNews development sets were not used in order to avoid possible effects of domain mixing. The results in Table 5 show that the method is, as mentioned in Section 1, indeed not very appropriate for cross-lingual classification since the character combina-

tions are generally language dependent – the drop in F-score and accuracy is large, in the range of 10 to 15 absolute points.

As for the n-gram lengths, combination "24" is useful, although mostly for English. For German and Spanish, 3-grams and 5-grams outperformed the n-gram combinations. As for the usage of different languages, no advantage of one "foreign" language over another was observed – the best results are rather similar for both "external" languages. For example, the F-score for English is slightly better when the German training set is used, and accuracy is slightly better when the system was trained on the Spanish text. The fact that none of the language pairs is closely related might have an important influence on these results.

4.4 Confusion analysis

The results described in previous sections have shown the following:

- combination of 2-grams and 4-grams is the best option for the standard setting, and performs decently also for enlarged English training corpus as well as for cross-lingual classification;

- individual 3-grams, 4-grams and 5-grams outperform the combinations when a larger English corpus is used.

n-gram	Wiki dev		News dev		WikiNews dev	
length(s)	Wiki train	all train	News train	all train	WN train	all train
2	64.7 / 64.8	61.2 / 63.6	63.2 / 70.5	61.9 / 69.8	61.8 / 67.6	63.0 / 68.8
3	67.5 / 68.7	68.6 / 69.7	72.6 / 77.8	71.5 / 77.5	64.8 / 71.5	**73.4** / 74.0
4	67.5 / 69.3	**73.5 / 74.6**	75.9 / 81.2	76.0 / 81.3	68.9 / 75.4	**73.4** / 78.4
5	61.1 / 67.3	66.8 / 71.8	75.0 / **81.7**	75.9 / **82.4**	64.5 / 75.6	71.2 / **79.0**
24	**69.9 / 70.9**	70.9 / 72.0	**76.7** / 81.3	**76.4** / 81.3	**69.9 / 75.7**	73.3 / 77.9
34	68.3 / 69.2	73.3 / 74.1	75.9 / 80.4	76.2 / 81.0	68.5 / 74.0	72.8 / 77.2
234	68.4 / 69.4	71.4 / 72.2	75.4 / 79.6	75.4 / 80.2	**69.9** / 75.0	72.5 / 77.0

Table 4: F-score for English complex word class / accurracy for domain-specific and concatenated training set.

n-gram	English development		German development		Spanish development	
length(s)	es-train	de-train	en-train	es-train	en-train	de-train
2	50.7 / 59.4	60.1 / 59.5	48.9 / 54.3	49.9 / 62.6	55.4 / 55.7	53.9 / 57.4
3	58.0 / 60.5	60.4 / 58.6	**55.6** / 55.0	49.6 / 56.5	**55.8** / 54.2	55.0 / 58.6
4	57.3 / 62.5	51.7 / 57.2	53.8 / 61.2	55.6 / **64.0**	51.8 / 58.4	45.8 / 59.7
5	41.7 / 59.6	38.2 / 57.5	34.9 / **62.5**	33.3 / 63.1	38.2 / **61.0**	24.4 / **61.8**
24	58.9 / **63.0**	**61.4 / 61.4**	53.3 / 56.7	**57.0** / 63.9	53.4 / 54.4	52.5 / 57.2
34	**59.7** / 61.7	59.6 / 57.1	53.7 / 53.0	53.9 / 58.0	54.6 / 53.1	54.7 / 57.1
234	59.3 / 61.4	61.1 / 58.2	51.6 / 51.6	56.0 / 60.9	54.8 / 53.4	**55.4** / 56.7

Table 5: Cross-language classification: F-score for complex word class / accurracy for cross-language classification.

In order to better understand the above findings, confusion analysis was carried out for all n-gram lengths and for all Wikipedia development sets in all three set-ups.

Table 6 shows the percentages of (non-)confusions: C-C and S-S represent correctly classified instances, C-S stands for complex words classified as simple, and S-C for simple words classified as complex. The results show the following:

- 5-grams are very good in identifying simple words: less than 10% of them are classified as complex. Nevertheless, they are absolutely the worse in labelling complex words: for German and Spanish texts, they even label more complex instances incorrectly than correctly (red numbers).

- the combination "24" is very good in labelling complex words, although often outperformed by one of the other two combinations; the percentages in the majority of those cases are very close, though.

- the same combination, "24", is the best of all three combinations for labelling simple words, although clearly outperformed by 5-grams and 4-grams.

The described findings indicate that the combination "24", despite not always yielding the best scores, is the most balanced and the most stable one over all set-ups. Therefore, this variant was submitted for all shared task tracks.

It should be noted that the confusions were also analysed for the cross-lingual classification showing the very same behaviour for 5-grams and for the "24" variant. As for other n-gram lenghts, a number of different large confusion percentages was observed, indicating once again that the method is not convenient for cross-lingual CWI.

5   Official shared task results

Following all the findings described in previous sections, we decided to submit the "24" variant, i.e. the combination of 2-grams and 4-grams, to all shared task tracks. For each of the three English test sets, we sent two submissions: one classified using the corresponding in-domain training corpus, and one classified using the concatenated training corpus. For the French test set, we sent four submissions: one classified using English

(a) English – in-domain training corpora

n-gram	Wiki				News				WikiNews			
order(s)	C-C	C-S	S-C	S-S	C-C	C-S	S-C	S-S	C-C	C-S	S-C	S-S
2	32.3	16.6	18.6	32.6	25.3	14.1	15.4	45.2	26.2	14.4	18.0	41.4
3	32.4	16.4	14.8	36.3	29.5	10.0	12.2	48.3	26.2	14.4	14.1	45.3
4	31.8	17.0	13.7	37.5	29.6	9.8	9.0	51.5	27.2	13.3	11.3	48.2
5	25.6	23.2	**9.5**	**41.7**	27.4	12.0	**6.2**	**54.3**	23.1	17.4	**7.9**	**51.5**
24	**33.9**	**15.0**	14.1	37.0	30.7	8.8	9.9	50.7	28.2	12.4	11.8	47.6
34	33.3	15.6	15.3	35.9	30.8	8.6	11.0	49.6	28.3	12.3	12.7	45.7
234	33.1	15.7	14.8	36.3	**31.3**	**8.2**	12.2	48.3	**29.0**	**11.6**	13.3	46.1

(b) English – concatenated training corpus

n-gram	Wiki				News				WikiNews			
order(s)	C-C	C-S	S-C	S-S	C-C	C-S	S-C	S-S	C-C	C-S	S-C	S-S
2	28.7	20.2	16.1	35.0	24.5	14.9	15.3	45.2	26.6	14.0	17.1	42.3
3	33.1	15.7	14.6	36.6	28.7	10.8	12.1	48.5	28.0	12.5	13.4	46.0
4	35.2	13.7	11.7	39.5	29.5	10.0	8.7	51.9	29.9	10.7	10.9	48.5
5	28.4	20.5	**7.8**	**43.4**	28.2	11.2	**6.6**	**53.9**	26.0	14.6	**6.4**	**53.0**
24	34.0	14.8	13.1	38.0	30.3	9.1	9.6	51.0	30.2	10.3	11.7	47.7
34	**36.0**	**13.2**	12.7	38.5	**30.4**	**9.0**	10.0	50.6	**30.4**	**10.1**	12.6	46.8
234	34.7	14.1	13.7	37.5	30.3	9.1	10.7	49.9	30.3	10.2	12.8	46.7

(c) German

n-gram order(s)	C-C	C-S	S-C	S-S
2	23.5	18.5	11.9	46.1
3	26.2	15.8	15.6	42.4
4	23.4	18.6	11.4	46.5
5	20.0	22.0	**8.8**	**50.2**
24	25.8	16.2	11.2	46.8
34	25.4	16.6	14.2	43.8
234	**25.9**	**16.1**	14.5	43.5

(d) Spanish

n-gram order(s)	C-C	C-S	S-C	S-S
2	20.2	20.1	11.6	48.1
3	24.2	16.1	13.6	46.2
4	23.3	17.0	10.0	49.7
5	19.0	21.2	**6.2**	**53.6**
24	24.2	16.0	10.4	49.4
34	**25.3**	**14.9**	12.7	47.0
234	25.2	15.0	12.9	46.9

Table 6: Confusion analysis for the English, German and Spanish development sets: C-C and S-S are correctly classified complex and simple words, C-S stands for complex words classified as simple, and S-C for simple words classified as complex.

Wikipedia training corpus, one classified using the concatenated English training corpus, one classified using the Spanish training corpus, and one using the German training corpus. For the German and Spanish test sets, one submission was sent for each.

The official accurracies for the best system, for all our submissions and for the worst system are shown in Table 7 together with the ranks (in parenthesis).

All our monolingual submissions were ranked in the middle, some better than others. The best rank is achieved for German (3 of 14) and the worst for Spanish (10 from 17). The obtained accurracies are all above 70%, the German being the lowest one and the English News the highest one. For the cross-lingual task, our submissions were ranked very low, with one of the submissions being the worst one. However, it should be noted that the use of the Spanish training set yielded the best result: this indicates that the method could potentially be used for closely related languages, however this should be further examined in future work.

All the results indicate that there is a potential for using character n-grams for complex word identification, however more experiments should be carried out and several refinements should be applied.

6   Summary and outlook

In this paper, we have proposed the use of character n-grams for complex word idenfitication starting from the assumption that character sequences in complex words are often different than those in simple words. We carried out extensive experiments with multinomial Naive Bayes classifier with n-grams of different lengths as features, and found out that using 2-grams and 4-grams is the most stable option in this configuration. Our system was ranked in a middle-range position for all tracks except for the cross-lingual track where it was ranked very low – this was not surprising since frequencies of character sequences in words are intuitively rather language-dependent. Our official accuracy scores range from 70% to 83% for English, German and Spanish texts and from 50% to 59% for French cross-lingually classified text.

Our experiments described in this work together with the official shared task results indicate that the use of character n-grams for complex word

identification has a potential, but the methods should be further investigated and improved. First of all, other classifiers without independency assumption should be investigated. In addition, using context (surrounding words and their n-grams) should be investigated as well.

References

Ondřej Bojar, Yvette Graham, and Amir Kamran. 2017. Results of the WMT17 Metrics Shared Task. In *Proceedings of the Second Conference on Machine Translation (WMT 17)*, pages 489–513, Copenhagen, Denmark.

Goran Glavaš and Sanja Štajner. 2015. Simplifying lexical simplification: do we need simplified corpora? In *Proceedings of 53rd annual meeting of the Association for Computational Linguistics and 7th International Joint Conference on Natural Language Processing of the Asian Federation of Natural Language Processing*, pages 63–68, Beijing, China.

Ashraf M. Kibriya, Eibe Frank, Bernhard Pfahringer, and Geoffrey Holmes. 2004. Multinomial Naive Bayes for Text Categorization Revisited. In *Proceedings of the 17th Australian Joint Conference on Advances in Artificial Intelligence*, pages 488–499.

Pintu Lohar, Koel Dutta Chowdhury, Haithem Afli, Mohammed Hasanuzzaman, and Andy Way. 2017. ADAPT at IJCNLP-2017 Task 4: A Multinomial Naive Bayes Classification Approach for Customer Feedback Analysis task. In *Proceedings of the IJCNLP 2017, Shared Tasks*, pages 161–169.

Andrew D McCallum and Kamal Nigam. 1998. A Comparison of Event Models for Naive Bayes Text Classification. In *Proceedings of ICML/AAAI 98 Workshop on Learning of Text Categorisation*, pages 41–48, Madison, Wisconsin.

Niloy Mukherjee, Braja Gopal Patra, Dipankar Das, and Sivaji Bandyopadhyay. 2016. JU-NLP at Semeval-2016 task 11: Identifying complex words in a sentence. In *Proceedings of the 10th International Workshop on Semantic Evaluation (SemEval-2016)*, pages 986–990, San Diego, California.

Gustavo Paetzold and Lucia Specia. 2015. Lexenstein: A framework for lexical simplification. In *Proceedings of the System Demonstrations at the 53rd Annual Meeting of the Association for Computational Linguistics and the 7th International Joint Conference on Natural Language Processing of the Asian Federation of Natural Language Processing*, pages 85–90, Beijing, China.

Gustavo Paetzold and Lucia Specia. 2016. SemEval 2016 Task 11: Complex Word Identification. In *Proceedings of the 10th International Workshop on Semantic Evaluation (SemEval-2016)*, pages 560–569, San Diego, California.

| | English | | | German | Spanish | French |
system	Wiki	News	WikiNews	Wiki	Wiki	Wiki
best	81.2	87.9	84.3	76.2	78.4	80.2
nb24	**74.6 (16)**	82.8 (21)	75.4 (24)	70.9 (3)	72.6 (10)	/
nb24-allen	73.0 (20)	**83.5 (17)**	**77.2 (20)**	/	/	53.0 (8)
nb24-en	/	/	/	/	/	51.8 (9)
nb24-de	/	/	/	/	/	55.1 (7)
nb24-es	/	/	/	/	/	**59.8 (5)**
worst	34.1 (28)	17.6 (34)	56.8 (31)	58.1 (14)	701 (17)	51.8 (9)

Table 7: Official accurracies and ranks (in parenthesis) for English, German, Spanish and French test sets used in the CWI shared task 2018: the best system, all our submissions, and the worst system.

Maja Popović. 2015. chrF: character n-gram F-score for automatic MT evaluation. In *Proceedings of the 10th Workshop on Statistical Machine Translation (WMT 15)*, pages 392–395, Lisbon, Portugal.

Matthew Shardlow. 2013. A comparison of techniques to automatically identify complex words. In *Proceedings of the Student Research Workshop at the 51st Annual Meeting of the Association for Computational Linguistics (ACL 2013*, Sofia, Bulgaria.

Miloš Stanojević and Khalil Sima'an. 2014. BEER: BEtter Evaluation as Ranking. In *Proceedings of the Ninth Workshop on Statistical Machine Translation (WMT 14)*, pages 414–419, Baltimore, Maryland, USA.

Weiyue Wang, Jan-Thorsten Peter, Hendrik Rosendahl, and Hermann Ney. 2016. CharacTer: Translation Edit Rate on Character Level. In *Proceedings of the First Conference on Machine Translation (WMT 16)*, pages 505–510, Berlin, Germany.

Seid Muhie Yimam, Chris Biemann, Shervin Malmasi, Gustavo Paetzold, Lucia Specia, Sanja Štajner, Anaïs Tack, and Marcos Zampieri. 2018. A Report on the Complex Word Identification Shared Task 2018. In *Proceedings of the 13th Workshop on Innovative Use of NLP for Building Educational Applications*, New Orleans, United States.

Seid Muhie Yimam, Sanja Štajner, Martin Riedl, and Chris Biemann. 2017a. CWIG3G2 - Complex Word Identification Task across Three Text Genres and Two User Groups. In *Proceedings of the Eighth International Joint Conference on Natural Language Processing (Volume 2: Short Papers)*, pages 401–407, Taipei, Taiwan.

Seid Muhie Yimam, Sanja Štajner, Martin Riedl, and Chris Biemann. 2017b. Multilingual and Cross-Lingual Complex Word Identification. In *Proceedings of the International Conference Recent Advances in Natural Language Processing, RANLP 2017*, pages 813–822, Varna, Bulgaria.

Marcos Zampieri, Shervin Malmasi, Gustavo Paetzold, and Lucia Specia. 2017. Complex Word Identification: Challenges in Data Annotation and System Performance. In *Proceedings of the 4th Workshop on Natural Language Processing Techniques for Educational Applications (NLPTEA 2017)*, pages 59–63, Taipei, Taiwan.

Marcos Zampieri, Liling Tan, and Josef van Genabith. 2016. MacSaar at SemEval-2016 Task 11: Zipfian and Character Features for Complex Word Identification. In *Proceedings of the 10th International Workshop on Semantic Evaluation (SemEval-2016)*, pages 1001–1005, San Diego, California.

Predicting Second Language Learner Successes and Mistakes by Means of Conjunctive Features

Yves Bestgen

Centre for English Corpus Linguistics
Université catholique de Louvain
Place Cardinal Mercier, 10 1348 Louvain-la-Neuve
`yves.bestgen@uclouvain.be`

Abstract

This paper describes the system developed by the Centre for English Corpus Linguistics for the 2018 Duolingo SLAM challenge. It aimed at predicting the successes and mistakes of second language learners on each of the words that compose the exercises they answered. Its main characteristic is to include conjunctive features, built by combining word ngrams with metadata about the user and the exercise. It achieved a relatively good performance, ranking fifth out of 15 systems. Complementary analyses carried out to gauge the contribution of the different sets of features to the performance confirmed the usefulness of the conjunctive features for the SLAM task.

1 Introduction

This paper presents the participation of the Centre for English Corpus Linguistics (CECL) in the 2018 Duolingo shared task on Second Language Acquisition Modeling (SLAM) which was held in conjunction with the 13th Workshop on Innovative Use of NLP for Building Educational Applications. The objective of the task is to build a model to predict whether second language learners will make a mistake on each of the words (tokens) that compose the exercises they answered. There were three tracks: English speakers learning Spanish (es_en), Spanish speakers learning English (es_en) and English speakers learning French (en_en).

To develop the model, the organizers of the challenge made available a very large number of exercises carried out by a large number of learners of Duolingo, a free online language-learning platform, which attracted more than 200 million learners since its launching in 2012 (see Settles et al. (2018) for details). In this training set, the tokens on which each learner made a mistake were marked, but the error itself was not provided. This

task is thus very different from the one at the root of many applications of natural language processing in the field of education that aim to automatically evaluate texts produced by second language learners (Weigle, 2013). The traditional approach for the latter, which relies on linguistic indices more or less strongly correlated with text quality such as lexical richness, syntactic complexity and especially the presence of errors of different types (e.g., Burstein et al., 2004; Futagi et al., 2008; Yannakoudakis et al., 2011; Santos et al., 2012; Ramineni and Williamson, 2013; Somasundaran et al., 2015; Bestgen, 2016, 2017), is obviously not applicable to the SLAM challenge.

Compared to the automatic evaluation of learner texts, the SLAM task has several advantages (+), but also several disadvantages (-):

+ Each learner produced a relatively large number of responses allowing to estimate his or her level of competence;

+ The learners' responses are spaced out in time making possible to try to model the evolution of their competence throughout their learning;

+ The same exercises were presented to a large number of different learners making it possible to get a relatively good estimate of the difficulty of each of them;

− The exercises are very short, as 99% of the utterances consist of no more than six tokens, which strongly limits the linguistic context available for any NLP procedure;

− And above all, as indicated above, the prompt to be processed by the learner is provided, but not the actual answer.

As previous research of the CECL in this field deals with the question of automatic evaluation

Proceedings of the Thirteenth Workshop on Innovative Use of NLP for Building Educational Applications, pages 349–355
New Orleans, Louisiana, June 5, 2018. ©2018 Association for Computational Linguistics

and only partially took into account the temporal dimension of learning (Bestgen and Granger, 2014), I chose to break down the problem in two steps:

- Try to get the best prediction without using the sequential information available in the dataset.

- Add the sequential information and see whether it can improve the prediction.

Having not been successful in the second step, I focused this report on the first. It is therefore not really an attempt to model second language acquisition, but to predict the successes and mistakes of second language learners. The proposed system can be seen as a baseline system since it does not take into account the richest information made available.

The developed system achieved a relatively good performance since it ranks fifth out of 15 systems, but nevertheless at a respectable distance from the best systems. Its main characteristic is to include conjunctive features, built by combining several primitive features. In machine learning, these conjunctive features are classically obtained by means of a polynomial kernel, but this has the effect of greatly lengthening the time needed to learn the model (Fan et al., 2008; Yoshinaga and Kitsuregawa, 2012). It was more efficient to obtain them manually and to use a (much faster) linear approach to learn the model.

The remainder of this report describes the datasets made available for this challenge, the system developed and the results obtained as well as the analyzes performed to get a better idea of the usefulness of the various components of the system.

2   Data

As explained in Settles et al. (2018), each instance to be categorized corresponded to a token of an exercise that has been presented to a user in one of three possible types of exercise, in one of three possible types of session and at a given time of his or her participation in the learning activities of the Duolingo platform. Several other metadata were provided for each exercise such as the country from which a user had done it. For each token, a series of morpho-syntactic features were also provided. The datasets were very large.

The fr_en dataset, which was by far the smallest, contained more than 410 000 exercises and almost 1 200 000 tokens. The other data sets were approximately 2.12 times (es_en) and 2.83 times (en_es) larger.

These datasets were divided by the organizers into three sets, the TRAIN set with 80% of the data, the DEV set with 10% and the TEST set with remaining 10%. The final results of the challenge were determined by the organizers on the TEST set. In this report, all the developments that led to the predictive models were only done on the fr_en dataset because its smaller size allowed the fastest processing. They were based on the TRAIN set to build the models and on the DEV set for evaluation.

3   System

3.1   Main Features Used

As a quick glance at the exercises, undertaken by students during their first 30 days of learning with the Duolingo platform (Settles et al., 2018), suggested that they were relatively simple from a lexical and syntactical point of view, I chose to base the features on the tokens and to disregard morpho-syntactic information.

Each instance (i.e., a token in an exercise) was encoded as a vector of 47 binary features, consisting of the following three feature sets:

- The main part (5 features) was composed of the target token and the tokens (T) that surround it in the exercise. For a token such as "pas" (not) in the exercise "Ce n' est pas un sandwich" (This is not a sandwich), the following five features were encoded: the trigram including the two tokens that precede it (n'_est_pas), the bigram including the token that precedes it (est_pas), the token itself (pas), the bigram including the next token (pas_un) and the trigram including the two following tokens (pas_un_sandwich)[1]. When a ngram is incomplete because a token is too close to the beginning or to end of the exercise, the missing element is replaced by the pseudo-token "<s>".

---

[1]The trigram composed of the preceding token, the target token and the following token (est_pas_un) was not encoded. This was an oversight, fortunately without consequences since the analyzes carried out after the end of the challenge showed that taking into account this trigram and the conjunctive features derived from it (8 features, see below) did not improve the performances.

- The second set of features (7 features) was based on three metadata: the unique identifier for each student (U), the exercise format (F: three different values), and the session type (S: three different values). These features were encoded alone and in conjunction, producing the following features: U, F, S, UF, US, FS and UFS.

- Finally, the conjunction of each token feature[2] with each of the metadata feature, such as n'_est_pas_UFS, was encoded (35 features).

Each different type of feature was prefixed with a unique character sequence to avoid any collision between features of different types. Of the 47 features used to encode each instance, some were very common in the dataset, such as the format, the session and their conjunctions, others were moderately frequent such as a user id or a token, but the majority was much rarer such as the conjunction of a user, a format, a session and a trigram.

3.2 Sequential Information Use

All the features, which included a target token and had been previously seen by a user, were duplicated with a new value that reflected the number of times it had been seen, the proportion of mistakes this user made on it, and the time that had elapsed since he or she had seen it for the last time. These values were transformed by means of an exponential[3] function. More details are not given on these features because they were very inefficient as shown in the analyzes reported below.

3.3 Procedure to Build the Models

The feature extraction was performed by means of a series of custom SAS programs running in SAS University (freely available for research at http://www.sas.com/en_us/software/university-edition.html). The predictive models used during the development phase were built on the fr_en dataset by means of the L1-regularized logistic regression (L1-LR) available in the LIBLINEAR package (-s 6, Fan et al., 2008). The only meta-parameter that can be optimized was the regular-

ization parameter C. A series of tests carried out on the TRAIN and DEV fr_en sets led to setting it to 0.75. It was also the L1-LR with this same C parameter that was used in all the analyzes reported here, except for the models used for the final submission that were build by means of the L2-regularized logistic regression (-s 7, L2-LR) because it appeared while preparing the submission that it produced slightly higher performances.

4   Analyses and Results

All the performances are summarized in terms of the area under the receiver operating characteristic curve (AUROC), the challenge main evaluation metric. The F1 score was also proposed as a secondary metric by the challenge organizers, but it is not reported here because no attempt was made to optimize it[4].

In the tables presented below, T stands for the Token ngrams, M for the Metadata, with U for User, F for Format and S for Session, Mc for the conjunctive features derived from the metadata and TM for the conjunctive features derived from the token ngrams and the metadata.

4.1   Performance on the Test Set

The performance and ranking of the base model and of the model that takes into account the sequential information is given in Table 1 along with the performances of the systems ranked first, those of the two closest teams in the ranking and those of the baseline provided by the organizers. As a reminder, the proposed models were developed for the fr_en dataset and simply applied to the two other tracks. For the three tracks, the regularization parameter C for the L2-LR was set on the basis of the TRAIN and DEV sets at the following values: 0.10 for fr_en and es_en and 0.05 for en_es. The final models were learned on the concatenated TRAIN and DEV sets.

The performances of the proposed models were significantly better than the baseline, but not as good as the best system. They were lower than those of the team ranked fourth in two tracks, but higher in the fr_en track on the basis of which they

---

[2]Technically, bigrams and trigrams can also be seen as conjunctive features.

[3]Following a reviewer's suggestion, a logarithm transformation was also tried, but it did not improve the performance on the TRAIN and DEV fr_en datasets.

[4]Furthermore, simple tricks allow, at least in the present case, to strongly improve it without harming the AUROC. For example, the base model described in this paper gets an AUROC of 0.8367 and an F1 of 0.4796 when C is set at 0.75 (on fr_en TRAIN and DEV sets, see Table 2). If C is set at 0.30 for the correct instances and at 0.84 for the mistakes (using LIBLINEAR -wi parameter), the model keeps exactly the same AUROC, but the F1 is now 0.5409.

System	en_es	es_en	fr_en
First	0.861	0.838	0.857
Fourth	0.848	0.824	0.839
Sequential	0.846	0.818	0.843
Base	0.845	0.817	0.842
Sixth	0.841	0.807	0.835
Baseline	0.774	0.746	0.771

Table 1: Final performances (AUROC) for several systems.

T	M	Mc	TM	AUROC
x	x	x	x	0.8367
x	x	x		0.8167
x	x			0.8078
x				0.7488

Table 2: AUROC for several sets of features in the base model.

were developed. The benefits brought by using the sequential information were very small, probably because the procedure employed did not introduce new features, but duplicated a number of them with different values.

4.2 In-depth Analysis of the Feature Sets

The remainder of this report analyzes in detail the contribution of the different sets of features to the performance of the base model. All these analyses were conducted on the TRAIN and DEV fr_en dataset as explained above.

First, the ablation approach was used to assess the independent contribution of each set of features to the overall performance of the system. It consists in removing some sets of features of the model and re-evaluating it.

As Table 2 shows, the conjunctive features, including those built from the metadata alone, made a significant contribution to performance. The model that only includes the token ngrams clearly underperformed. The metadata are thus necessary to achieve an acceptable performance.

A second analysis was conducted to evaluate the impact of the three lengths of ngrams in the base model (Table 3). The results indicated that the trigrams were not very useful contrarily to the bigrams.

To get a better idea of the usefulness of the conjunctive features, Table 4 presents the number of features of each type to which the L1-LR assigned a non-zero weight (Andrew and Gao, 2007). It also indicates how many of these features were

Unigram	Bigram	Trigram	AUROC
x	x	x	0.8367
x	x		0.8340
x			0.8130

Table 3: AUROC for the three ngram lengths (base model).

Type	#	# in Dev	% in Dev
TU	14 996	4 975	33.2
TUS	10 651	2 396	22.5
TUF	9 507	2 643	27.8
TUFS	6 597	1 382	20.9
TF	6 436	5 993	93.1
TFS	5 854	5 072	86.6
T	4 938	4 717	95.5
TS	4 830	4 343	89.9
UFS	2 181	1 772	81.2
UF	1 948	1 877	96.4
US	1 151	990	86.0
U	854	849	99.4
FS	9	9	100.0
F	3	3	100.0
S	3	3	100.0
Total	70 624	37 668	53.3

Table 4: Number of features of each type selected by the L1-LR. Note: The conjunctive features are represented by the concatenation of the corresponding symbols.

present in the DEV set.

This table shows that the conjunctive features, including the more complex ones, were frequently selected by the L1-LR and that a non-negligible proportion of them were present in the DEV set. These are of course the types that encompassed the largest number of different features.

However, an ablation approach on these feature subtypes suggests that many conjunctive features are not truly essential as shown in Table 5. The first row of the table reports the performance of the base model. The second section shows that the conjunctions of four and three types of features are not necessary for achieving this performance. The third section indicates that it is the conjunctive features including the tokens and the exercise format on the other hand that make the most important contribution (see below for instances). With regard to the conjunctive features based on the metadata only, UF (alone or with Session in UFS) is the most useful. The last line of the table corresponds to the model without conjunctive features (except the token ngrams). Overall, it appears that the Ses-

T	M	UF	US	FS	UFS	TU	TF	TS	TUF	TUS	TFS	TUFS	AUROC
X	X	X	X	X	X	X	X	X	X	X	X	X	0.8367
X	X	X	X	X	X	X	X	X	X	X	X		0.8371
X	X	X	X	X	X	X	X	X		X	X		0.8367
X	X	X	X	X	X	X	X	X	X		X		0.8372
X	X	X	X	X	X	X	X	X	X	X			0.8368
X	X	X	X	X	X	X	X	X					0.8368
X	X	X	X	X	X		X	X					0.8334
X	X	X	X	X	X	X		X					0.8214
X	X	X	X	X	X	X	X						0.8357
X	X	X	X	X	X	X							0.8203
X	X	X	X	X	X		X						0.8324
X	X	X	X	X	X			X					0.8178
X	X	X	X	X	X								0.8167
X	X		X	X	X								0.8161
X	X	X		X	X								0.8170
X	X	X	X		X								0.8169
X	X	X	X	X									0.8175
X	X	X											0.8187
X	X		X										0.8075
X	X			X									0.8079
X	X				X								0.8165
X	X												0.8078

Table 5: AUROC for several subsets of features in the base model.

sion metadata are not very useful.

All these observations confirm the interest of some of the conjunctive features for the SLAM task, the token ngrams being a specific type of conjunctive features whose usefulness is well established in NLP. Their interest can be illustrated concretely by the two following examples. In the fr_en TRAIN set, users made 78% of errors on the token "-" when it is preceded by the token "après" (after), forming the bigram "après_-" (N = 198) found in "après-midi" (afternoon). This overall percentage hides a large difference between the reverse-tap exercises (N = 91) on which 100% of errors were made and the reverse-translate exercises (N = 51) in which 49% of errors were made. The opposite profile is observed for the bigram "Vous_connaissez" (You_know), whose target token is "connaissez", for which there were in general 66% of errors (N = 73). When presented in the reverse-translate format, there were 94% of errors (N = 48) while there were only 9% of errors in the reverse-tap format (N = 22).

4.3 Conclusion

The base model presented in this paper does not take into account the longitudinal nature of the data made available by the organizers. Despite this, it achieved relatively high performances, ranking fifth out of 15 teams with an average of 0.016 AUROC point less than the best team, but it also outperformed nine team by more than 0.016 AUROC point. It must however be recognized that the inclusion of longitudinal information in this approach was inefficient. A psycholinguistically motivated approach would have probably produced better results (Settles and Meeder, 2016). The papers of the best teams participating in this challenge should allow to determine whether they have used non-sequential features that are identical or similar to those used here. If it is not the case, it might be interesting to determine whether the conjunctive features used here would allow to further improve their system performances.

It would also be interesting to look at other metadata provided by the organizers. In particular, the country from which a user has done the exercises could perhaps allow to take into account the

L1 transfer, which is known to affect the type of errors produced by learners of a foreign language (Wong and Dras, 2009; Jarvis et al., 2013).

In a future edition of the challenge, it might be interesting to include in the test set a larger proportion of tokens that do not appear (or very rarely) in the training set and to carry out part of the evaluation separately on those tokens. In the current datasets, only 116 of the 1 920 different tokens present in the fr_en TEST set were absent from the TRAIN and DEV sets. Even more, these 116 different tokens represented only 0.12% of the instances to categorize (168 out of 135 525). It should be noted that the datasets included a sizable proportion of rarely seen tokens (i.e. 27% of the different tokens in fr_en TRAIN and DEV sets were present at most 3 times), but they represented only a very small fraction of the TEST set (less than 0.5%). Increasing the proportion of new or infrequently seen tokens in the test materials could favor the use of features that can be generalized to unseen tokens. If this path is followed, it could be interesting to provide, in the training datasets, the exercises and the mistakes actually produced to further the development of predictive models that try to figure out the relation between a token and the mistake (while providing only the exercises for the test material to avoid the use of simple error detection systems).

Acknowledgments

The author wishes to thank the organizers of the 2018 SLAM challenge for putting together this valuable event and the reviewers for their very constructive comments. This work was supported by the Fonds de la Recherche Scientifique - FNRS (grant number J.0025.16). The author is a Research Associate of this institution.

References

Galen Andrew and Jianfeng Gao. 2007. Scalable training of L1-regularized log-linear models. In *Proceedings of the 24th International Conference on Machine Learning*, ICML '07, pages 33–40, New York, NY, USA. ACM.

Yves Bestgen. 2016. Using collocational features to improve automated scoring of EFL texts. In *Proceedings of the 12th Workshop on Multiword Expressions*, pages 84–90.

Yves Bestgen. 2018. Beyond single-word measures: L2 writing assessment, lexical richness and formulaic competence. *System*, 69:65–78.

Yves Bestgen and Sylviane Granger. 2014. Quantifying the development of phraseological competence in L2 English writing: An automated approach. *Journal of Second Language Writing*, 26:28–41.

Jill Burstein, Martin Chodorow, and Claudia Leacock. 2004. Automated essay evaluation: The criterion online writing service. *AI Magazine*, 25:27–36.

Martin Chodorow and Claudia Leacock. 2000. An unsupervised method for detecting grammatical errors. In *Proceedings of the Conference of the North American Chapter of the Association of Computational Linguistics (NAACL)*, pages 140–147.

Yoko Futagi, Paul Deane, Martin Chodorow, and Joel Tetreault. 2008. A computational approach to detecting collocation errors in the writing of non-native speakers of English. *Computer Assisted Language Learning*, 21:353–367.

Scott Jarvis, Yves Bestgen, and Steve Pepper. 2013. Maximizing classification accuracy in native language identification. In *Proceedings of The 8th Workshop on Innovative Use of NLP for Building Educational Applications (NAACL-HLT)*, pages 111–118.

Chaitanya Ramineni and David M. Williamson. 2013. Automated essay scoring: Psychometric guidelines and practices. *Assessing Writing*, 18(1):25–39.

Victor Santos, Marjolijn Verspoo, and John Nerbonne. 2012. Identifying important factors in essay grading using machine learning. In Dina Sagari, Salomi Papadima-Sophocleous, and Sophie Ioannou-Georgiou, editors, *International Experiences in Language Testing and Assessment—Selected Papers in Memory of Pavlos Pavlou*, pages 295–309. Peter Lang, Frankfurt au Main, Germany.

Burr Settles, Chris Brust, Erin Gustafson, Masato Hagiwara, and Nitin Madnani. 2018. Second language acquisition modeling. In *Proceedings of the NAACL-HLT Workshop on Innovative Use of NLP for Building Educational Applications (BEA)*. ACL.

Burr Settles and Brendan Meeder. 2016. A trainable spaced repetition model for language learning. In *Proceedings of the 54th Annual Meeting of the Association for Computational Linguistics (Volume 1: Long Papers)*, pages 1848–1858. Association for Computational Linguistics.

Swapna Somasundaran, Chong M. Lee, Martin Chodorow, and Xinhao Wang. 2015. Automated scoring of picture-based story narration. In *Proceedings of the Tenth Workshop on Innovative Use of NLP for Building Educational Applications*, pages 42–48.

Sara Cushing Weigle. 2013. English language learners and automated scoring of essays: Critical considerations. *Assessing Writing*, 18(1):85–99.

Sze-Meng Jojo Wong and Mark Dras. 2009. Contrastive analysis and native language identification. In *Proceedings of the Australasian Language Technology Association Workshop*, pages 53–61.

Helen Yannakoudakis, Ted Briscoe, and Ben Medlock. 2011. A new dataset and method for automatically grading ESOL texts. In *The 49th Annual Meeting of the Association for Computational Linguistics: Human Language Technologies*, pages 180–189.

Naoki Yoshinaga and Masaru Kitsuregawa. 2012. Efficient classification with conjunctive features. *Journal of Information Processing*, 20(1):228–237.

Feature Engineering for Second Language Acquisition Modeling

Guanliang Chen, Claudia Hauff, Geert-Jan Houben
Delft University of Technology
Delft, The Netherlands
{guanliang.chen, c.hauff, g.j.p.m.houben}@tudelft.nl

Abstract

Knowledge tracing serves as a keystone in delivering personalized education. However, few works attempted to model students' knowledge state in the setting of Second Language Acquisition. The Duolingo Shared Task on Second Language Acquisition Modeling (Settles et al., 2018) provides students' trace data that we extensively analyze and engineer features from for the task of predicting whether a student will correctly solve a vocabulary exercise. Our analyses of students' learning traces reveal that factors like exercise format and engagement impact their exercise performance to a large extent. Overall, we extracted 23 different features as input to a Gradient Tree Boosting framework, which resulted in an AUC score of between 0.80 and 0.82 on the official test set.

1 Introduction

Knowledge Tracing plays a crucial role in providing adaptive learning to students (Pelánek, 2017): by estimating a student's current knowledge state and predicting her performance in future interactions, students can receive personalized learning materials (e.g. on the topics the student is estimated to know the least about).

Over the years, various knowledge tracing techniques have been proposed and studied, including Bayesian Knowledge Tracing (Corbett and Anderson, 1994), Performance Factor Analysis (Pavlik Jr et al., 2009), Learning Factors Analysis (Cen et al., 2006) and Deep Knowledge Tracing (Piech et al., 2015). Notable is that most of the existing works focus on learning performance within mathematics in elementary school and high school due to the availability of sufficiently large datasets in this domain, e.g. ASSISTment and OLI (Piech et al., 2015; Xiong et al., 2016; Zhang et al., 2017; Khajah et al., 2016). The generalization

to other learning scenarios and domains remains under-explored.

Particularly, there are few studies attempted to explore knowledge tracing in the setting of Second Language Acquisition (SLA) (Bialystok, 1978). Recent studies showed that SLA is becoming increasingly important in people's daily lives and should gain more research attention to facilitate their learning process (Larsen-Freeman and Long, 2014). It remains an open question whether the existing knowledge tracing techniques can be directly applied to SLA modeling—the release of the Duolingo challenge datasets now enables us to investigate this very question.

Thus, our work is guided by the following research question: **What *factors* impact students' language learning performance?**

To answer the question, we first formulate six research hypotheses which are built on previous studies in SLA. We perform extensive analyses on the three SLA Duolingo datasets (Settles et al., 2018) to determine to what extent they hold. Subsequently, we engineer a set of 23 features informed by the analyses and use them as input for a state-of-the-art machine learning model, *Gradient Tree Boosting* (Ye et al., 2009; Chen and Guestrin, 2016), to estimate the likelihood of whether a student will correctly solve an exercise.

We contribute the following major findings: (i) students who are heavily engaged with the learning platform are more likely to solve words correctly; (ii) contextual factors like the device being used and learning format impact students' performance considerably; (iii) repetitive practice is a necessary step for students towards mastery; (iv) Gradient Tree Boosting are demonstrated to be an effective method for predicting students' future performance in SLA.

Proceedings of the Thirteenth Workshop on Innovative Use of NLP for Building Educational Applications, pages 356–364
New Orleans, Louisiana, June 5, 2018. ©2018 Association for Computational Linguistics

2 Data Analysis

Before describing the six hypotheses we ground our work in as well as their empirical validation, we first introduce the Duolingo datasets.

2.1 Data Description

To advance knowledge modeling in SLA, Duolingo released three datasets[1], collected from students of English who already speak Spanish (EN-ES), students of Spanish who already speak English (ES-EN), and students of French who already speak English (FR-EN), respectively, over their first 30 days of language learning on the Duolingo platform (Settles et al., 2018). The task is to predict what mistakes a student will make in the future. Table 1 shows basic statistics about each dataset. Interesting are in particular the last two rows of the table which indicate the unbalanced nature of the data: across all languages correctly solving an exercise is far more likely than incorrectly solving it. Note that the datasets contain rich information not only on students, words and exercises[2] but also on students' learning process, e.g., the amount of time a student required to solve an exercise, the device being used to access the learning platform and the countries from which a student accessed the Duolingo platform.

Table 1: Statistics of the datasets.

	FR-EN	ES-EN	EN-ES
#Unique students	1,213	2,643	2,593
#Unique words	2,178	2,915	2,226
#Exercises	326,792	731,896	824,012
#Words in all exercises	926,657	1,973,558	2,622,958
#Avg. words / exercise	2.84	2.7	3.18
%Correctly solved words	84%	86%	87%
%Incorrectly solved words	16%	14%	13%

In our work, we use *learning session* to denote the period from a student's login to the platform until the time she leaves the platform. We use *learning type* to refer to the "session" information in the original released datasets, whose value can be *lesson*, *practice* or *test*.

2.2 Research Hypotheses

Grounded in prior works we explore the following hypotheses:

H1 A student's *living community* affects her language acquisition performance.
Previous works, e.g., (Dixon et al., 2012) demonstrated that the surrounding living community is a non-negligible factor in SLA. For instance, a student learning English whilst living in an English-speaking country is more likely to practice more often and thus more likely to achieve a higher learning gain than a student not living in one.

H2 The more *engaged* a student is, the more words she can master.
Educational studies, e.g., (Carini et al., 2006), have shown that a student's engagement can be regarded as a useful indicator to predict her learning gain, which is the number of mastered words in our case.

H3 The *more time* a student spends on *solving an exercise*, the more likely she will get it wrong.

H4 *Contextual factors* such as the device being used (e.g. iOS or Android), learning type (lesson, practice or test) and exercise format (such as transcribing an utterance from scratch or formulating an answer by selecting from a set of candidate words) will impact a student's mastery of a word.
We hypothesize that, under specific contexts, a student can achieve a higher learning gain due to the different difficulty level of exercises. For instance, compared to transcribing an utterance from scratch, a student is likely to solve more exercises correctly when being provided with a small set of candidate words.

H5 *Repetition* is useful and necessary for a student to master a word (Young-Davy, 2014; Gu and Johnson, 1996; Lawson and Hogben, 1996).

H6 Students with a high-spacing learning routine are more likely to learn more words than those with a low-spacing learning routine.
Here, high-spacing refers to a larger number of discrete learning sessions. Correspondingly, low-spacing refers to relatively few learning sessions, which usually last a relatively long time. In other words, students with a low-spacing routine tend to acquire words in a "cramming" manner (Miyamoto et al., 2015; Donovan and Radosevich, 1999; Bjork, 1994).

---

[1] http://sharedtask.duolingo.com/#task-definition-data

[2] An exercise usually contains multiple words.

2.3 Performance Metrics

We now define four metrics we use to measure a student's exercise performance.

Student-level Accuracy (Stud-Acc) measures the overall accuracy of a student across all completed exercises. It is calculated as the ratio between the number of words correctly solved by a student and the total number of words she attempted.

Exercise-level Accuracy (Exer-Acc) measures to what extent a student answers a particular exercise correctly. It is computed as the number of correctly solved words divided by the total number of words in the exercise.

Word-level Accuracy (Word-Acc) measures the percentage of times of a word being answered correctly by students. For a word, it is calculated as the number of times students provided correct answers divided by the total number of attempts.

Mastered Words (Mast-Word) measures how many words have been mastered by a student. As suggested in (Young-Davy, 2014), it takes about 17 exposures for a student to learn a new word. Thus, we define a word being mastered by a student only if (i) it has been exposed to the student at least 17 times and (ii) the student answered the word accurately in the remaining exposures.

2.4 From Hypotheses To Validation

To verify **H1**, we use the location (country) from where a student accessed the Duolingo platform as an indicator of the student' living community. We first bin students into groups according to their locations. Next, we calculate the average student-level accuracy and the number of mastered words of students in each group. We report the results in Table 2. Here we only consider locations with more than 50 students. If a student accessed the platform from more than one location, the student would be assigned to all of the identified location groups. In contrast to our hypothesis, we do not observe the anticipated relationship between living community and language learning (e.g. Spanish-speaking English-students living in the US do not perform better than other students).

For **H2** (student engagement), we consider three ways to measure engagement with the platform: (i) number of attempted exercises, (ii) number of attempted words and (iii) amount of time spent learning. To quantify the relationship between students' engagement and their learning gain, we report the Pearson correlation coefficient between

Table 2: Avg. student-level accuracy (%) and the number of mastered words of students living in different locations (approximated by the countries from which students have finished the exercises). Significant differences (compared to *Avg.*, according to Mann-Whitney) are marked with $*$ ($p < 0.001$).

Datasets	Locations	Stud-Acc	Mast-Word
	Avg.	83.57	3.37
	CA	84.12	3.13
FR-EN	US	83.01	3.40
	GB	83.66	3.46
	AU	85.69	3.70
	Avg.	85.91	2.74
	CA	84.89	3.26
ES-EN	US	86.22	2.58
	AU	85.82	3.50
	GB	83.94 $*$	3.30
	NL	87.15	2.86
	Avg.	87.62	4.39
	CO	87.49	4.14
	US	87.98	5.02
	ES	87.85	5.66 $*$
	MX	86.92 $*$	3.71 $*$
EN-ES	CL	88.95	4.42
	DO	87.26	4.40
	AR	89.58	4.75
	VE	89.47 $*$	4.99
	PE	88.83	4.37

the three engagement metrics and Stud-Acc as well as Mast-Word (Table 3). We note a consistent negative correlation between accuracy and our engagement metrics. This is not surprising, as more engagement also means more exposure to novel vocabulary items. When examining the number of mastered words, we can conclude that—as stated in **H2**—higher engagement does indeed lead to a higher learning gain. This motivates us to design engagement related features for knowledge tracing models.

To determine the validity of **H3**, in Table 4 we report the Pearson correlation coefficient between the amount of time spent in solving each exercise and the corresponding exercise-level accuracy. The moderate negative correlation values indicate that the hypothesis holds to some extent.

For **H4**, we investigate three types of contextual factors: (i) device used (i.e., Web, iOS, Android); (ii) learning type (i.e., Lesson, Practice, Test) and (iii) exercise format (i.e., Reverse Translate, Listen, Reverse Tap). To verify whether these contextual factors impact students' exercise performance, we partition exercises into different groups

Table 3: Pearson Correlation between student engagement (measured by # attempted exercises/words and the amount of time spent in learning) and student-level accuracy as well as # mastered words. Significant differences are marked with $*$ ($p < 0.001$).

	Stud-Acc			Mast-Word		
	FR-EN	ES-EN	EN-ES	FR-EN	ES-EN	EN-ES
# Exercises Attempted	-0.05 *	-0.09 *	-0.08 *	0.85 *	0.87 *	0.79 *
# Words Attempted	-0.06 *	-0.08 *	-0.08 *	0.85 *	0.86 *	0.80 *
Time Spent	-0.13 *	-0.14 *	-0.22 *	0.73 *	0.79 *	0.61 *

Table 4: Pearson Correlation between the amount of time spent in solving each exercise and exercise-level accuracy. Significant differences are marked with $*$ ($p < 0.001$).

	FR-EN	ES-EN	EN-ES
Correlation	-0.16 *	-0.18 *	-0.18 *

Table 5: Average exercise-level accuracy (%) in different contextual conditions. Significant differences (compared to *Avg.*, according to Mann-Whitney) are marked with $*$($p < 0.001$).

	FR-EN	ES-EN	EN-ES
Avg.	84.29	86.31	87.96
Client			
Web	80.64 *	85.44 *	85.68 *
iOS	86.45 *	87.90 *	88.10 *
Android	83.92 *	84.88 *	88.92 *
Session			
Lesson	85.43 *	87.23 *	88.76 *
Practice	80.94 *	83.92 *	84.19 *
Test	82.19 *	84.34 *	84.66 *
Format			
Reverse Translate	77.92 *	85.88 *	85.42 *
Listen	78.30 *	77.01	82.78 *
Reverse Tap	92.51 *	94.84 *	95.48 *

according to the contextual condition in which they were completed and calculate the average of their exercise-level accuracy within each group. Table 5 shows the results. Interestingly, students with *iOS* devices perform better than those using *Web* or *Android*. Students' learning accuracy is highest in the *Lesson* type. Learning formats also have an impact: *Reverse Tap* achieves the highest accuracy followed by *Reverse Translate* and then *Listen*. This result is not surprising as active recall of words is more difficult than recognition. Finally, we note for English students who speak Spanish (EN-ES) and Spanish students who speak English (ES-EN), the accuracy of *Reverse Trans-*

late is considerably higher than *Listen*, which is not the case in FR-EN (where both are comparable). These results suggest that contextual factors should be taken into account in SLA modeling.

Table 6: Avg. word-level accuracy (%) of words with different number of exposures.

	# Words	Word-Acc	Correlation
FR-EN			
≥ 1	2,178	72.30	-0.08 *
≥ 10	1,007	75.01	0.13 *
≥ 20	756	75.78	0.15 *
≥ 50	756	76.41	0.19 *
≥ 100	580	77.47	0.25 *
ES-EN			
≥ 1	2,915	75.33	-0.10 *
≥ 10	1,798	77.10	0.12 *
≥ 20	1,511	77.29	0.19 *
≥ 50	1,163	77.92	0.25 *
≥ 100	900	78.67	0.31 *
EN-ES			
≥ 1	2,226	75.58	0.00
≥ 10	1,587	77.12	0.25 *
≥ 20	1,401	77.88	0.28 *
≥ 50	1,171	78.90	0.28 *
≥ 100	963	79.57	0.34 *

Table 7: Pearson Correlation between student performance and the number of previous attempts and the amount of time elapsed since the last attempt for a word.

	FR-EN	ES-EN	EN-ES
# Previous attempts	-0.05 *	-0.04 *	-0.07 *
Time elapsed	0.05 *	0.06 *	0.07 *

We investigate **H5** from two angles. Firstly, we investigate whether words with very different exposure amounts will differ from each other in terms of word-level accuracy as they are practiced by students to different degrees. For this purpose, we only retain words with more than n exposures (with n being ≥ 1, ≥ 10, ≥ 20, ≥ 50, ≥ 100)

and calculate Pearson correlation coefficient between the word-level accuracy and their number of exposures (Table 6). As expected, the more low-exposure words we filter out, the higher the average word-level accuracy and the stronger the correlation scores (albeit at best these are moderate correlations).

Secondly, we believe that whether a student will solve a word correctly (0 mean solving correctly and 1 incorrectly) is affected by two factors related to word repetition. One factor is the number of previous attempts that a student has for a word, and the other is the amount of time elapsed since her last attempt at the word. Therefore, we compute Pearson correlation coefficient between students' performance on exercises and the two repetition related factors (Table 7). The resulting correlations are even weaker than in our preceding analysis, though they do point towards a (very) weak relationship: if a student gets more exposed to a word or practices the word more frequently, she is more likely to get it correct. Clearly, the results indicate that other factors at play here too.

Lastly, to study **H6**, we partition all students into low-spacing and high-spacing groups according to (Miyamoto et al., 2015). Initially, all students are sorted in ascending order according to their total time spent in learning words. Subsequently, these students are binned into ten equally-sized groups labeled from 0 (spending the least amount of time) to 9 (spending the most amount of time). Therefore, we can regard students from the same group as learning roughly the same amount of time. Next, within each group, the students are sorted based on their number of distinct learning sessions[3], and we further divide them into two equally-sized subgroups: students with few sessions (low-spacing) and students with many sessions (high-spacing). In this way, students spending similar total amounts of time can be compared with each other. We plot the average student-level accuracy as well as the number of mastered words within each low-spacing and high-spacing subgroup in Figure 1. We do not observe consistent differences between low-spacing and high-spacing groups. Therefore, we conclude **H6** to not hold.

---

[3]Here we consider all learning activities occurring within 60 minutes as belonging to the same learning session.

3 Knowledge Tracing Model

We now describe the machine learning model we adopt for knowledge tracing and then introduce our features.

3.1 Gradient Tree Boosting

Various approaches have been proposed for modeling student learning. Two representatives are Bayesian Knowledge Tracing (Corbett and Anderson, 1994) and Performance Factor Analysis (Pavlik Jr et al., 2009), both of which have been studied for years. Inspired by the recent wave of deep learning research in different domains, deep neural nets were also recently applied to track the knowledge state of students (Piech et al., 2015; Xiong et al., 2016; Zhang et al., 2017). In principal, all of these methods can be adapted to predict students' performance in SLA. As our major goal is to investigate the usefulness of the designed features, we selected a robust model that is able to take various types of features as input and works well with skewed data. Gradient Tree Boosting (GTB) is a machine learning technique which can be used for both regression and classification problems (Ye et al., 2009). It is currently one of the most robust machine learning approaches that is employed for a wide range of problems (Chen and Guestrin, 2016). It can deal with various types of feature data and has reliable predictive power when dealing with unbalanced data (as in our case). We selected it over a deep learning approach as we aim to built an interpretable model.

3.2 Feature Engineering

Based on the results in §2.4, we designed 23 features. The features are categorized into two groups: features directly available in the datasets (7 *given features*) and features derived from the datasets (16 *derived features*). Note that the features differ in their granularity—they are computed per student, or per word, per exercise or a combination of them, as summarized in Table 8.

Given features:

- *Student ID*: the 8-digit, anonymized, unique string for each student;

- *Word*: the word to be learnt by a student;

- *Countries*: a vector of dimension N (N denotes the total number of countries) with

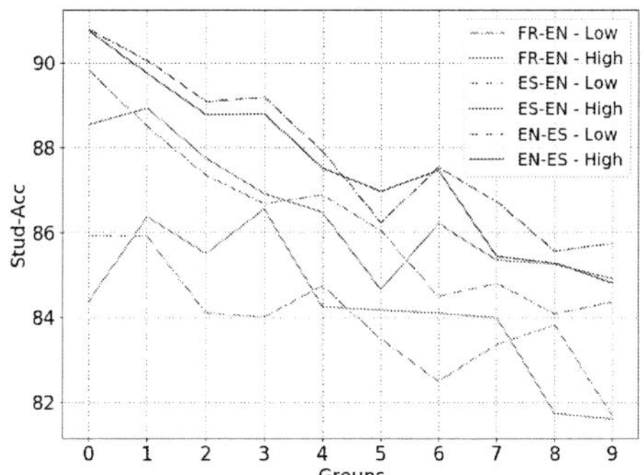 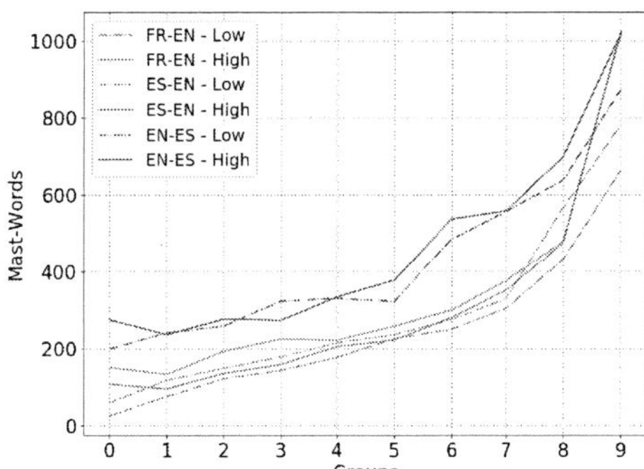

Figure 1: The average student-level accuracy, i.e., Stud-Acc (Left), and the average number of mastered words, i.e., Mast-Word (Right), of students in high-spacing and low-spacing groups.

Table 8: Granularity levels on which each feature is retrieved or computed. Features marked with b are used as input in the baseline provided by the benchmark organizers.

Features	Granularity Level		
	User	Word	Exercise
Student ID[b]	✓		
Word[b]		✓	
Countries	✓		
Format[b]			✓
Type			✓
Device			✓
Time spent (exercise)			✓
# Exercises attempted	✓		
# Words attempted	✓		
# Unique words attempted	✓		
# sessions	✓		
Time spent (learning)	✓		
# Previous attempts	✓	✓	
# Correct times	✓	✓	
# Incorrect times	✓	✓	
Time elapsed	✓	✓	
Word-Acc	✓	✓	
Std. timestamps (exercise)	✓		✓
Std. timestamps (word)	✓	✓	
Std. timestamps (session)	✓		
Std. timestamps (word-session)	✓	✓	
Std. timestamps (word-correct)	✓	✓	
Std. timestamps (word-incorrect)	✓	✓	

binary values indicating whether a student complete an exercise in one or multiple countries;

- *Format*: the exercise format in which a student completed an exercise, i.e., Reverse Translate, Reverse Tap and Listen;

- *Type*: the learning type in which a student completed an exercise, i.e., Lesson, Practice and Test;

- *Device*: the device platform which is used by a student to complete an exercise, i.e., iOS, Web and Android;

- *Time spent (exercise)*: the amount of time a student spent in solving an exercise, measured in seconds;

Derived features:

- *# Exercises attempted*: the number of exercises that a student has attempted in the past;

- *# Words attempted*: the number of words that a student has attempted in the past;

- *# Unique Words attempted*: the number of unique words a student has attempted in the past;

- *# Sessions*: the number of learning sessions a student completed;

- *Time spent (learning)*: the total amount of time a student spent learning, measured in minutes;

- *# Previous attempts*: a student's number of previous attempts at a specific word;

- *# Correct times*: the number of times that a student correctly solved a word;

- *# Incorrect times*: the number of times that a student incorrectly solved a word;

- *Time elapsed*: the amount of time that elapsed since the last exposure of a word to a student;

- *Word-Acc*: the word-level accuracy that a student gained for a word in the training dataset;

- *Std. timestamps (exercise)*: the standard deviation of the timestamps that a student solved exercises;

- *Std. timestamps (word)*: the standard deviation of the timestamps that a student solved a word;

- *Std. timestamps (session)*: the standard deviation of timestamps that a student logged in to start a learning session;

- *Std. timestamps (word-session)*: the standard deviation of session starting timestamps that a student solved a word;

- *Std. timestamps (word-correct)*: the standard deviation of timestamps that a student answered a word correctly;

- *Std. timestamps (word-incorrect)*: the standard deviation of timestamps that a student answered a word incorrectly.

Finally, we note that none of the features in our feature set make use of external data sources. We leave the inclusion of additional data sources to future work.

4 Experiments

In this section, we first describe our experimental setup and then present the results.

4.1 Experimental Setup

Each of the three Duolingo datasets consists of three parts: TRAIN and DEV sets for offline experimentations and one TEST set for the final evaluation. We use the TRAIN and DEV sets to explore features that are useful in predicting a student's exercise performance and then combine TRAIN and DEV sets to train the GTB model; we report the model's performance on the TEST set.

We trained the GTB model using XGBoost, a scalable machine learning system for tree boosting (Chen and Guestrin, 2016). All model parameters[4] were optimized through grid search and are reported in Table 9.

---

[4]For a detailed explanation of the parameters, please refer to `https://github.com/dmlc/xgboost/blob/v0.71/doc/parameter.md`.

We also report the official baseline provided by the benchmark organizers as comparison. The baseline is a logistic regression model which takes six features as input, which include student ID, word, format and three morpho-syntactic features of the word (e.g., Part of Speech). As suggested by the benchmark organizers, we use the AUC and F1 scores as our evaluation metrics.

Table 9: Model parameters of the GTB model; determined by using grid search per dataset.

	FR-EN	ES-EN	EN-ES
learning_rate	0.4	0.5	0.6
n_estimatorss	800	1100	1550
max_depth	6	6	5
min_child_weight	7	8	13
gamma	0.0	0.0	0.1
subsample	1.0	1.0	1.0
colsample_bytree	0.7	0.7	0.85
reg_alpha	4	6	5

4.2 Results

In order to evaluate the impact of the features described in §3.2, we report in Table 10 different versions of GTB training, starting with three features (Student ID, Word, Format) and adding additional features one at a time. We incrementally added features according to the order presented in Section 3.2 and only kept features that boost the prediction performance (i.e. the AUC score improves on the DEV set). Among all 23 evaluated features, seven are thus useful for SLA modeling. Here, we only report the results in the ES-EN dataset; we make similar observations in the other two datasets. In contrast to our expectations, a large number of the designed features did not boost the prediction accuracy. This implies that further analyses of the data and further feature engineering efforts are necessary. The extraction of features from external data sources (which may provide insights in the difficulty of words, the relationship between language families and so on) is also left for future work.

In our final prediction for the TEST set, we combine the TRAIN and DEV data to train the GTB model with the nine features listed in Table 10 and student ID as well as the word as input. The results are shown in Table 11. Compared to the logistic regression baseline, GTB is more effective with a 6% improvement in AUC and 83% improvement in F1 on average.

Table 10: Experimental results reported in AUC on ES-EN. Each row indicates a feature added to the GBT feature space; the model of row 1 has three features.

	TRAIN	DEV
Student ID & Word & Format	0.8095	0.7758
Mode	0.8111	0.7780
Client	0.8137	0.7790
Time spent (exercise)	0.8270	0.7828
# Previous attempts	0.8323	0.7835
# Wrong times	0.8348	0.7871
Std. time (word-session)	0.8348	0.7871

Table 11: Final prediction results on the TEST data. Significant differences (compared to Baseline, according to paired t-test) are marked with $*$ ($p < 0.001$).

	Methods	AUC	F1
FR-EN	Baseline	0.7707	0.2814
	GTB	0.8153 *	0.4145 *
ES-EN	Baseline	0.7456	0.1753
	GTB	0.8013 *	0.3436 *
EN-ES	Baseline	0.7737	0.1899
	GTB	0.8210 *	0.3889 *

5   Conclusion

Knowledge tracing is a vital element in personalized and adaptive educational systems. In order to investigate the peculiarities of SLA and explore the applicability of existing knowledge tracing techniques for SLA modeling, we conducted extensive data analyses on three newly released Duolingo datasets. We identified a number of factors affecting students' learning performance in SLA. We extracted a set of 23 features from student trace data and used them as input for the GTB model to predict students' knowledge state. Our experimental results showed that (i) a student's engagement plays an important role in achieving good exercise performance; (ii) contextual factors like the device being used and learning format should be taken into account for SLA modeling; (iii) repetitive practice of words and exercises affect students performance considerably; (iv) GTB can effectively use some of the designed features for SLA modeling and there is a need for further investigation on feature engineering. Apart from the future work already outlined in previous sections, we also plan to investigate deep knowledge tracing approaches and the inclusion of some of our rich features into deep models, inspired by (Zhang et al., 2017). Also, instead of developing a one-size-fits-all prediction model, it will be interesting to explore subsets of students that behave similarly and develop customized models for different student groups.

References

Ellen Bialystok. 1978. A theoretical model of second language learning. *Language learning*, 28(1):69–83.

Robert A. Bjork. 1994. Memory and metamemory considerations in the training of human beings. *Metacognition: Knowing about knowing*, pages 185–205.

Robert M. Carini, George D. Kuh, and Stephen P. Klein. 2006. Student engagement and student learning: Testing the linkages*. *Research in Higher Education*, 47(1):1–32.

Hao Cen, Kenneth Koedinger, and Brian Junker. 2006. Learning factors analysis–a general method for cognitive model evaluation and improvement. In *International Conference on Intelligent Tutoring Systems*, pages 164–175. Springer.

Tianqi Chen and Carlos Guestrin. 2016. Xgboost: A scalable tree boosting system. In *Proceedings of the 22nd acm sigkdd international conference on knowledge discovery and data mining*, pages 785–794. ACM.

Albert T Corbett and John R Anderson. 1994. Knowledge tracing: Modeling the acquisition of procedural knowledge. *User modeling and user-adapted interaction*, 4(4):253–278.

L Quentin Dixon, Jing Zhao, Blanca G Quiroz, and Jee-Young Shin. 2012. Home and community factors influencing bilingual childrens ethnic language vocabulary development. *International Journal of Bilingualism*, 16(4):541–565.

John J. Donovan and David J. Radosevich. 1999. A meta-analytic review of the distribution of practice effect: Now you see it, now you don't. *Journal of Applied Psychology*, 84(5):795–805.

Yongqi Gu and Robert Keith Johnson. 1996. Vocabulary learning strategies and language learning outcomes. *Language learning*, 46(4):643–679.

Mohammad Khajah, Robert V. Lindsey, and Michael C. Mozer. 2016. How deep is knowledge tracing? *CoRR*, abs/1604.02416.

Diane Larsen-Freeman and Michael H Long. 2014. *An introduction to second language acquisition research*. Routledge.

Michael J Lawson and Donald Hogben. 1996. The vocabulary-learning strategies of foreign-language students. *Language learning*, 46(1):101–135.

Yohsuke R. Miyamoto, Cody A. Coleman, Joseph J. Williams, Jacob Whitehill, Sergiy O. Nesterko, and Justin Reich. 2015. Beyond time-on-task: The relationship between spaced study and certification in moocs. *SSRN 2547799*.

Philip I Pavlik Jr, Hao Cen, and Kenneth R Koedinger. 2009. Performance factors analysis–a new alternative to knowledge tracing. *Online Submission*.

Radek Pelánek. 2017. Bayesian knowledge tracing, logistic models, and beyond: an overview of learner modeling techniques. *User Modeling and User-Adapted Interaction*, 27(3):313–350.

Chris Piech, Jonathan Bassen, Jonathan Huang, Surya Ganguli, Mehran Sahami, Leonidas J Guibas, and Jascha Sohl-Dickstein. 2015. Deep knowledge tracing. In *Advances in Neural Information Processing Systems*, pages 505–513.

B. Settles, C. Brust, E. Gustafson, M. Hagiwara, and N. Madnani. 2018. Second language acquisition modeling. In *Proceedings of the NAACL-HLT Workshop on Innovative Use of NLP for Building Educational Applications (BEA)*. ACL.

Xiaolu Xiong, Siyuan Zhao, Eric Van Inwegen, and Joseph Beck. 2016. Going deeper with deep knowledge tracing. In *EDM*, pages 545–550.

Jerry Ye, Jyh-Herng Chow, Jiang Chen, and Zhaohui Zheng. 2009. Stochastic gradient boosted distributed decision trees. In *Proceedings of the 18th ACM Conference on Information and Knowledge Management*, CIKM '09, pages 2061–2064, New York, NY, USA. ACM.

Belinda Young-Davy. 2014. Explicit vocabulary instruction. *ORTESOL Journal*, 31:26.

Liang Zhang, Xiaolu Xiong, Siyuan Zhao, Anthony Botelho, and Neil T. Heffernan. 2017. Incorporating rich features into deep knowledge tracing. In *Proceedings of the Fourth (2017) ACM Conference on Learning @ Scale*, L@S '17, pages 169–172, New York, NY, USA. ACM.

TMU System for SLAM-2018

Masahiro Kaneko[†]   **Tomoyuki Kajiwara**[††]   **Mamoru Komachi**[†]

[†]Graduate School of Systems Design, Tokyo Metropolitan University, Tokyo, Japan
[‡]Institute for Datability Science, Osaka University, Osaka, Japan
`kaneko-masahiro@ed.tmu.ac.jp`
`kajiwara@ids.osaka-u.ac.jp`
`komachi@tmu.ac.jp`

Abstract

We introduce the TMU systems for the second language acquisition modeling shared task 2018 (Settles et al., 2018). To model learner error patterns, it is necessary to maintain a considerable amount of information regarding the type of exercises learners have been learning in the past and the manner in which they answered them. Tracking an enormous learner's learning history and their correct and mistaken answers is essential to predict the learner's future mistakes. Therefore, we propose a model which tracks the learner's learning history efficiently. Our systems ranked fourth in the English and Spanish subtasks, and fifth in the French subtask.

1   Introduction

The second language acquisition modeling (SLAM) is an interesting research topic in the fields of psychology, linguistics, and pedagogy as well as engineering. Popular language learning applications such as Duolingo accumulate learning data of language learners on a large-scale; thus, there has been an increasing interest for SLAM using machine learning using such data. In this study on SLAM, we aim to clarify both: (1) the inherent nature of second language learning, and (2) effective machine learning/natural language processing (ML/NLP) engineering strategies to build personalized adaptive learning systems.

In order to predict the learner's future mistakes, it is important to track a huge history of what and how exercises were solved by that learner and be able to model it. Therefore, we propose a model that can efficiently track a learner's learning history. (Piech et al., 2015; Khajah et al., 2014, 2016)

correct: She is my mother and he is my father
learner: she is   mother and he is   fhader
label: 0 0 1   0   0 0 0 1   1

Figure 1: An exercise example. Given exercise is a "correct" input. Outputs are "1" each time a learner makes a mistake

2   2018 Duolingo Shared Task on SLAM

We used data from Duolingo in this shared task. Duolingo is the most popular language-learning online application. Learners solve the exercises and this shared task use only 3 type of exercises. Exercise (a) is a *reverse_translate* item, where learners translate written prompt from the language they know into the language they are learning. Exercise (b) is a *reverse_tap* item, where learners construct an answer given a set of words and distractors in the second language. Exercise (c) is a *listen* item, where learners listen and transcribe an utterance in the second language. In this shared task, There are 3 exercise data of the following groups of second language learners:

- English learners (who already speak Spanish)

- Spanish learners (who already speak English)

- French learners (who already speak English)

The Duolingo data set, which contains more than 2 million annotated words, is created from the answers submitted by more than 6,000 learners during their first 30 days. In the related exercises, learners answer questions related to the second language they are learning; thus, they inevitably make various mistakes during the course. In this task, we predict mistakes on word level given an exercise. Figure 1 is an exercise example. Given a "correct" exercise as input a system has to predict labels as output.

Proceedings of the Thirteenth Workshop on Innovative Use of NLP for Building Educational Applications, pages 365–369
New Orleans, Louisiana, June 5, 2018. ©2018 Association for Computational Linguistics

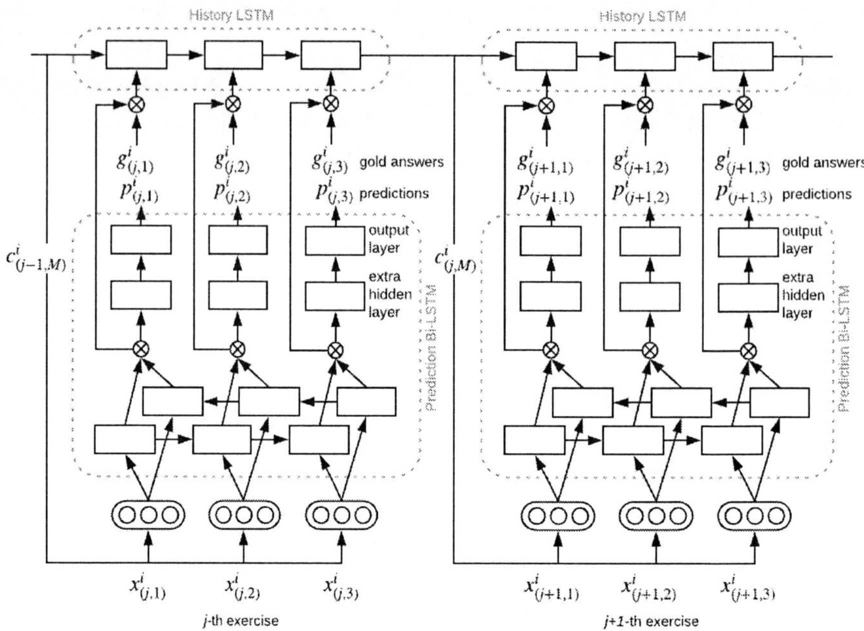

Figure 2: Architecture of the proposed TMU system.

In general, most tokens are perfect matches; however, the remainder of the tokens are either missing or spelled incorrectly (ignoring capitalization, punctuation, and accents). The former is assigned the label "0" (OK), while the latter is assigned the label "1" (Mistake).

3 TMU System

To track a lot of learner's histories, our proposed TMU system has two components: (1) a base component that predicts whether a learner has made a mistake for the given word in an exercise (Fig. 2, Prediction Bi-LSTM) and (2) a component that tracks a specific learner's information regarding the learned exercises and the words that he or she might have mistaken (Fig. 2, History LSTM). It is expected to track huge history of the learned exercise by inputting the hidden state of the Prediction model to the History LSTM.

In prediction, we receive exercise as input and make predictions on word-level. Using Bi-LSTM for sequence labeling on exercise level, e.g., information as POS tags or dependency edge labels, allows us to share information within each exercise for better prediction. We perform training by feeding input exercises arranged in a chronologi-

cal order for each learner.

3.1 Features

Table 1 lists all the features used by our system. We use features (1-7) included in the dataset distributed by the task organizers as well as the tracking history (8) (Section 3.3) and labels for language identification (9). We trained a single model with three languages, including English, Spanish, and French; in addition, we used the language identification feature to distinguish them.

There are three types of inputs for the Bi-LSTM. The first input includes word-level features that indicate information changing for each word in an exercise. In particular, word surface and POS are used as word-level features. The second input consists of exercise-level features. In particular, days, session, format, time, and history are used as exercise-level features. The third input includes learner-level features. For this, learner and language features are extracted for each learner.

3.2 Prediction Bidirectional LSTM

We used bidirectional LSTM (Bi-LSTM) to predict whether a learner has mistaken each word in an exercise. The k-th word and POS of the j-th exercise of the i-th learner are converted into $e^i_{(j,k)}$

	Feature	Embeddings	Description
1	Word	$e^i_{(j,k)} \in \mathbb{R}^{d_e \times 1}$	Word Surface
2	POS	$p^i_{(j,k)} \in \mathbb{R}^{d_p \times 1}$	Part of Speech
3	Session	$s^i_j \in \mathbb{R}^{d_s \times 1}$	Lesson, Practice or Test
4	Format	$f^i_j \in \mathbb{R}^{d_f \times 1}$	Reverse_translate, Reverse_tap, or Listen
5	Days	$b^i_j \in \mathbb{R}^{1 \times 1}$	Number of Days Since the Start for Each Learner
6	Time	$t^i_j \in \mathbb{R}^{1 \times 1}$	Amount of Time to Construct and Submit Answers for Each Learner
7	User	$u^i \in \mathbb{R}^{d_u \times 1}$	Unique Identifier for Each Learner
8	History	$c^i_{(j-1,M)} \in \mathbb{R}^{d_c \times 1}$	Last Hidden Layer of History LSTM
9	Language	$l^i \in \mathbb{R}^{d_l \times 1}$	English, Spanish, French

Table 1: Features used in our system. i: Learner's ID; j: Exercise Number of the i-th Learner; k: Word's and POS's index of the j-th Exercise. d_e: Word Embedding Size; d_p: POS Embedding Size; d_s: Session Embedding Size; d_f: Format Embedding Size; d_u: User Embedding Size; d_c: History Embedding Size; M: Total Sentence Length of All Previous Exercises; d_l: Language Embedding Size.

and $p^i_{(j,k)}$ distributed representations, respectively. Further, the session and format of the j-th exercise of the i-th learner are converted into s^i_j and f^i_j distributed representations, respectively. Days and time are represented as b^i_j and t^i_j, respectively. User and language are converted into u^i and l^i distributed representations, respectively. History is the last hidden state $c^i_{(j-1,M)}$ of the History LSTM, which will be described later (Section 3.3).

The inputs of the Bi-LSTM are given as $x^i_{(j,1)}, x^i_{(j,2)}, \cdots, x^i_{(j,N)}$. where, $x^i_{(j,k)} = [e^i_{(j,k)}; p^i_{(j,k)}; s^i_j; f^i_j; b^i_j; t^i_j; c^i_{(j-1,M)}; u^i; l^i]$ is the concatenation of all features and N is the length of the j-th exercise. $x^i_{(j,k)}$ is converted into the forward hidden state $\overrightarrow{h^i_{(j,k)}} \in \mathbb{R}^{d_h \times 1}$ and backward hidden state $\overleftarrow{h^i_{(j,k)}} \in \mathbb{R}^{d_h \times 1}$ using LSTM, where d_h is the hidden size. The final hidden state $h^i_{(j,k)} \in \mathbb{R}^{2d_h \times 1}$ is acquired by concatenating $\overrightarrow{h^i_{(j,k)}}$ and $\overleftarrow{h^i_{(j,k)}}$. Further, $h^i_{(j,k)}$ is fed into the extra hidden layer:

$$\hat{h}^i_{(j,k)} = \mathrm{ReLU}(W_h h^i_{(j,k)} + b_h) \qquad (1)$$

where $\hat{h}^i_{(j,k)} \in \mathbb{R}^{d_{\hat{h}} \times 1}$ is an extra hidden layer output, $W_h \in \mathbb{R}^{d_{\hat{h}} \times d_h}$ is a weighting matrix, and $b_h \in \mathbb{R}^{d_{\hat{h}} \times 1}$ is a bias. The extra hidden layer output $\hat{h}^i_{(j,k)}$ is linearly transformed using the output layer as follows and the probability distribution $p^i_{(j,k)} \in \mathbb{R}^{t \times 1}$ of the true/false tag is acquired using the softmax function, where t is the size of the tag, which is set to 2 in our study.

$$p^i_{(j,k)} = \mathrm{softmax}(W_{\hat{h}} \hat{h}^i_{(j,k)} + b_{\hat{h}}) \qquad (2)$$

where $W_{\hat{h}} \in \mathbb{R}^{t \times d_{\hat{h}}}$ is a weighting matrix and $b_{\hat{h}} \in \mathbb{R}^{t \times 1}$ is a bias.

3.3 History LSTM

As previously mentioned, to correctly predict each learner's mistakes, it is important to consider not only the history of learned exercises, but also the learner's answers to exercises. Thus, the History LSTM tracks all previous information regarding the learned exercises and how they were answered by each learner.

For each j-th exercise, $o^i_{(j,1)}, o^i_{(j,2)}, \cdots, o^i_{(j,N)}$ is given as an input to the j-th History LSTM, where $o^i_{(j,k)} = [h^i_{(j,k)}; g^i_{(j,k)}]$. $h^i_{(j,k)}$ (Section 3.2) is considered as information about the j-th exercise of the i-th learner and $g^i_{(j,k)} \in \mathbb{R}^{1 \times 1}$ is the gold answer of the i-th learner to the j-th exercise. In addition, the first hidden state and cell memory of the j-th History LSTM is initialized with the last hidden state and cell memory of the previous j-1-th History LSTM. The hidden state $c^i_{(j,1)}$ is created from $o^i_{(j,1)}$ using the LSTM for the next step of the Prediction Bi-LSTM.

3.4 Training

The objective function is defined as follows:

$$L_\theta = \frac{1}{|D|} \sum_{(x,y) \in D} \log p(y|x; \theta) \qquad (3)$$

where D is the training data and θ represents model parameters. We use Backpropagation Through Time (BPTT) for training.

In general, low-frequency words are replaced by *unk* word to learn *unk* vector. However, in our study, unknown words appear not because they

Language	Train	Dev	Test
English	936,782	3,000	114,586
Spanish	824,899	3,000	93,145
French	367,402	3,000	41,753

Table 2: Number of exercises for each language.

have low-frequency, but because they have not been learned yet. Hence, we use words that appear for the first time in an exercise to be replaced by *unk* word to learn *unk* vector. In addition, we use words without *unk* replacement to track the history for the History LSTM.

The final loss is calculated as follows:

$$\overline{L_\theta} = \alpha L_\theta^{unk} + (1 - \alpha)L_\theta^{orig} \qquad (4)$$

where αL_θ^{unk} is calculated by replacing the word appearing for the first time with *unk*, while $(1 - \alpha)L_\theta^{orig}$ is calculated using this word itself. In particular, α expresses the degree of emphasis placed on *unk* and a learned word. For example, when a word "Japanese" appears for the first time, then:

Original exercise: *I am Japanese*
Replaced by *unk*: *I am <unk>*

If the *unk* does not exist in any exercise, $\overline{L_\theta}$ has the same value as L_θ^{orig}.

3.5 Testing

During our test, predictions were made on exercises of the test data arranged in chronological order for each learner. We update History LSTM using output and hidden state of Prediction Bi-LSTM. Test data does not have gold answers unlike training data. Hence, each system used its own converted probability outputs of the Prediction Bi-LSTM component with arg max as gold answers.

In addition, we performed ensemble predictions. The parameters of ensemble models are initialized with different values. As the final prediction result, we used the average of the probability outputs of each Prediction Bi-LSTM. Each system used its own converted probability outputs of the Prediction Bi-LSTM component as gold answers.

4 Experiments

4.1 Experiment settings

Table 2 shows the number of exercises for train, dev and test data for each language. The hyper parameters of our model are listed in Table 3. All

Parameter	Value
d_e: Word Embedding Size	100
d_p: POS Embedding Size	20
d_s: Session Embedding Size	20
d_f: Format Embedding Size	20
d_u: User Embedding Size	50
d_l: Language Embedding Size	20
d_c: Hidden Size (History)	200
d_h: Hidden Size (Prediction)	100
$d_{\hat{h}}$: Extra Hidden Size	50
Minibatch size	32
BPTT	18
Optimizer	Adadelta
Learning rate	0.1
Initialization parameters	[-0.1, +0.1]
α, Eq. (4)	0.01
Dev, (Section 3.5)	3,000
Ensemble, (Section 3.5)	10

Table 3: Hyper parameter values.

words that appeared in the training data were included in the vocabulary. Preliminary experiments showed that the AUROC of the one model trained on data of three languages was higher than those models trained for each language. Therefore, we trained a single model with three language tracks, including English, Spanish and French. Especially, AUROC increased for low-resource French language.

Each model of the ensemble uses different dev and training sets randomly sampled from the data. In particular, since we needed to evaluate the learning results of Future Days of each learner, we combined the provided official training and dev sets and arranged exercises in chronological order of Days for each learner. Next, we randomly sampled exercises from final learning exercises of learners to create a dev set and the remaining data were used as training data.

4.2 Results

Table 4 lists the results of SLAM for English learners, Spanish learners, and French learners. The systems are ranked by their AUROC. The TMU system ranked fourth in English and Spanish subtasks, while it ranked fifth in the French subtask.

4.3 Analysis of Tracking History

In order to confirm the importance of history tracking, we compared the model that considers history (W/ History Model) with the model that

English	Spanish	French
0.861 SanaLabs	0.838 SanaLabs	0.857 SanaLabs
0.860 singsound-xushuyao	0.835 alexrich	0.854 singsound-xushuyao
0.858 alexrich	0.834 singsound-xushuyao	0.858 alexrich
0.848 TMU	**0.823 TMU**	0.843 zz
0.846 zz	0.818 zz	**0.839 TMU**
0.841 Cam	0.807 Cam	0.834 Cam
0.828 btomosch	0.802 btomosch	0.822 btomosch
0.821 nihalnayak	0.801 LambdaLearning	0.815 LambdaLearning
0.821 LambdaLearning	0.790 Grotoco	0.813 Grotoco
0.816 Grotoco	0.790 nihalnayak	0.811 nihalnayak
0.815 jilljenn	0.788 ymatusevich	0.808 jilljenn
0.813 ymatusevich	0.787 jilljenn	0.808 ymatusevich
0.796 renhk	0.773 renhk	0.806 caseykennington
0.787 zlb241	0.745 SLAM_baseline	0.795 renhk
0.773 SLAM_baseline	0.681 zlb241	0.770 SLAM_baseline

Table 4: SLAM official evaluation results. Systems are ranked by AUROC.

Model	AUROC
W/ History Model	0.834
W/O History Model	0.648

Table 5: The history model has an effect to improve AUROC on English subtask.

does not consider history (W/O History Model) on the dev set for English. The W/O History Model used only the Prediction Bi-LSTM component which does not use the history feature. For experiments using this model, we used a single model trained only on the English corpus. The default split of training set and dev set was 824,012 exercises and 115,770 exercises, respectively. Both aforementioned models used the same parameters as listed in Table 3.

Table 5 lists our evaluation results[1]. It can be observed that the AUROC of prediction of the W/ History Model case is considerably higher than that of the W/O History Model. As we expected, it is important to consider what learner have learned in the past and how they responded to it in order to improve future predictions.

5 Conclusion

In this study, we described the TMU system for the 2018 SLAM Shared Task. Our system is based on RNN; It has two components: (1) Bi-LSTM for predicting learners' error and (2) LSTM for tracking learners' learning history.

In this work, we have not used any language-specific information. As future work, we plan to exploit additional data for each language, such as pre-trained word representations, n-grams, and character-based features. Additionally, we hope to incorporate word difficulty features (Kajiwara and Komachi, 2018). In particular, the more complex a word is, the more difficult it likely is to be learned.

References

T. Kajiwara and M. Komachi. 2018. Complex Word Identification Based on Frequency in a Learner Corpus. In *Proceedings of The 13th Workshop on Innovative Use of NLP for Building Educational Applications (BEA)*.

M. Khajah, R. V. Lindsey, and M. C. Mozer. 2016. How Deep Is Knowledge Tracing? *CoRR*.

M. Khajah, R. Wing, R. V. Lindsey, and M. C. Mozer. 2014. Integrating Latent-Factor and Knowledge-Tracing Models to Predict Individual Differences in Learning. In *Educational Data Mining 2014*. Citeseer.

C. Piech, J. Bassen, J. Huang, S. Ganguli, M. Sahami, L. Guibas, and J. Sohl-Dickstein. 2015. Deep Knowledge Tracing. In *Advances in Neural Information Processing Systems 28*, pages 505–513.

B. Settles, C. Brust, E. Gustafson, M. Hagiwara, and N. Madnani. 2018. Second Language Acquisition Modeling. In *Proceedings of the NAACL-HLT Workshop on Innovative Use of NLP for Building Educational Applications (BEA)*.

---

[1]The performance is slightly different from the one reported in Table 3 because of the difference in models and ensembling.

Deep Factorization Machines for Knowledge Tracing

Jill-Jênn Vie
RIKEN Center for Advanced Intelligence Project
Nihonbashi 1-4-1, Mitsui Building 15F
Chuo-ku, 103-0027 Tokyo, Japan
`vie@jill-jenn.net`

Abstract

This paper introduces our solution to the 2018 Duolingo Shared Task on Second Language Acquisition Modeling (SLAM). We used deep factorization machines, a wide and deep learning model of pairwise relationships between users, items, skills, and other entities considered. Our solution (AUC 0.815) hopefully managed to beat the logistic regression baseline (AUC 0.774) but not the top performing model (AUC 0.861) and reveals interesting strategies to build upon item response theory models.

1 Introduction

Given the massive amount of data collected by online platforms, it is natural to wonder how to use it to personalize learning. Students should receive, based on their estimated knowledge, tailored exercises and lessons, so they can be guided through databases of potentially millions of exercises.

With this objective in mind, numerous models have been designed for student modeling (Desmarais and Baker, 2012). Based on the outcomes of students, one can infer the parameters of these so-called student models, measure knowledge, and tailor instruction accordingly.

In the 2018 Duolingo Shared Task on Second Language Acquisition Modeling (Settles et al., 2018), we had access to attempts of thousands of students over sentences (composed of thousands of possible words, each of these being labeled as correct or incorrect), and we had to predict whether a student would write correctly or not the words of a new sentence. Sentences were annotated with precious side information such as lexical, morphological, or syntactic features. This problem is coined as knowledge tracing (Corbett and Anderson, 1994) or predicting student performance (Minaei-Bidgoli et al., 2003) in the litera-

ture. In this particular challenge, it is done at the word level.

In this paper, we explain the motivations that led us to our solution, and show how our models handle typical models in educational data mining as special cases. In Section 2, we show related work. In Section 3, we present the existing model of DeepFM and clarify how it can be applied for knowledge tracing, notably the SLAM task. In Section 4, we detail the data preparation, in order to apply DeepFM. Finally, we expose our results in Section 5 and further work in Section 6.

2 Related Work

Item Response Theory (IRT) models (Hambleton et al., 1991) have been extensively studied and deployed in many real-world applications such as standardized tests (GMAT). They model the ability (level information) of students, and diverse parameters of items (such as difficulty), and involve many criteria for the selection of items to measure the ability of examinees.

Related work in knowledge tracing consists in predicting the sequence of outcomes for a given learner. Historically, Bayesian Knowledge Tracing (BKT) modeled the learner as a Hidden Markov model (Corbett and Anderson, 1994), but with the advent of deep learning, a Deep Knowledge Tracing (DKT) model has been proposed (Piech et al., 2015), relying on long short-term memory (Hochreiter and Schmidhuber, 1997). However, Wilson et al. (2016) have shown that a simple variant of IRT could outperform DKT models.

All of these IRT, BKT or DKT models do not consider side information, such as knowledge components, which is why new models naturally rose. Vie and Kashima (2018) have used Bayesian factorization machines for knowledge tracing, and

Proceedings of the Thirteenth Workshop on Innovative Use of NLP for Building Educational Applications, pages 370–373
New Orleans, Louisiana, June 5, 2018. ©2018 Association for Computational Linguistics

recovered most student models as special cases.

Wide and deep learning models have been proposed by Google (Cheng et al., 2016) to learn lower-order and higher-order features. Guo et al. (2017) have proposed a variant where they replace the wide linear model by a factorization machine, and this is the best model we got for the Shared Task challenge.

3 DeepFM for knowledge tracing

We now introduce some vocabulary. We assume that our observed instances can be described by C *categories* of discrete or continuous features (such as `user_id`, `item_id` or `country`, but also `time`). *Entities* denote couples of categories and discrete values (such as `user=2`, `country=FR` or again `time` if the category is continuous). We denote by N the number of possible entities, number them from 1 to N. The DeepFM model we are describing will learn an embedding for each of those entities[1].

Each instance can be encoded as a sparse vector x of size N: each component will be set at a certain value (for example, 1 if the category of the corresponding entity is discrete, the value itself if it is continuous, and 0 if the entity is not present in the observation). For each instance, our model will output a probability $p(x) = \psi(y_{FM} + y_{DNN})$, where ψ is a link function such as the sigmoid σ or the cumulative distribution function (CDF) Φ of the standard normal distribution.

The DeepFM model is made of two components, the FM component and the Deep component.

3.1 FM component

Given an embedding size $d \in \mathbf{N}$, the output of a factorization machine is the following:

$$y_{FM} = \sum_{k=1}^{N} w_k x_k + \sum_{1 \le k < l \le N} x_k x_l \langle v_k, v_l \rangle$$

The first term shows that a bias $w_k \in \mathbf{R}$ is learned for each entity k. The second term models the pairwise interactions between entities by learning a vector $v_k \in \mathbf{R}^d$ for each entity k.

3.1.1 Relation to existing student models

If $d = 0$ and ψ is the sigmoid function σ, $p(x) = \sigma(\langle w, x \rangle)$ and the FM component behaves like logistic regression.

In particular, if there are two fields users (of n possible values) and items, then each instance encoding x_{ij} of user i and item j is a concatenation of two one-hot vectors, and $p(x_{ij}) = \sigma(w_i + w_{n+j}) = \sigma(\theta_i - d_j)$ for appropriate values of w, which means the Rasch model is recovered.

As pointed out by Settles et al. (2018), their baseline model is a logistic regression with side information, which makes it similar to an additive factor model. To see more connections between our FM component and existing educational data mining models, see Vie and Kashima (2018).

3.2 Deep component

The deep component is a L-layer feedforward neural network that outputs:

$$y_{DNN} = \text{ReLU}(W^{(L)} a^{(L)} + b^{(L)})$$

where each layer $0 \le \ell < L$ verifies:

$$a^{(\ell+1)} = \text{ReLU}(W^{(\ell)} a^{(\ell)} + b^{(\ell)})$$

for learned parameters W, a, b for each layer, and the first layer is given by the corresponding v_{i_c} embeddings of the activated entities (the ones for each category $c = 1, \ldots, C$, which correspond to the nonzero entries of x):

$$a^0 = (v_{i_1}, \ldots, v_{i_C}).$$

In order to select the hyperparameters, we followed the instructions of (Guo et al., 2017) and the default values of the available implementation on GitHub[2].

3.3 Training

Training is performed by minimizing the log loss of the output probabilities compared to the true outcomes of the students over the tokens. For all models trained, the optimizer was Adam (Kingma and Ba, 2014), with learning rate $\gamma = 10^{-3}$ and minibatches of size 1024.

4 Encoding the Duolingo Dataset

4.1 Fundamental, discrete categories

Fundamental categories (`<fundamental>`) refer to the features that have discrete values, such as

---

[1] The original DeepFM paper (Guo et al., 2017) chooses *fields* and *features* in lieu of *categories* or *entities*, but we prefer to use our own formulation (Vie and Kashima, 2018) because we usually agree with ourselves.

[2] https://github.com/ChenglongChen/tensorflow-DeepFM

user (which refer to the user ID) or countries (which can be in a many-to-many relationship).

- user
- token
- part_of_speech
- dependency_label
- exercise_index
- countries
- client
- session
- format

4.2 Noisy discrete categories

Duolingo was providing the SyntaxNet features (morphosyntactic rules) such as:

- Definite
- Gender
- Number
- fPOS
- Person
- PronType
- Mood
- Tense
- VerbForm

We call them noisy (<noisy> below), because they are the output of another algorithm. Also, not all of them were specified, there were some missing entries.

4.3 Continuous categories

- time for answering the question
- days since when the user subscribed the Duolingo platform.

4.4 Encoding

In the baseline model provided by Duolingo, all fundamental features were encoded as a concatenation of n-hot encoders[3]. Then they used logistic regression and achieved AUC 0.772.

Here are the models we considered.

- IRT: user + token, $d = 0$
- Logistic regression baseline: <fundamental>
- Vanilla FM: <fundamental>
- DeepFM: <fundamental>
- DeepFM*: <fundamental> + <noisy> + <continuous>

The implementation of Deep Factorization Machines we used needed a concatenation of one-hot encoders. So we picked the first country among the list of countries for each instance. Also, it could not handle missing entries, so for the noisy partial categories, we used a None entity.

---

[3] For this reason, the continuous features could not be used for the baseline.

	ACC	AUC	NLL	F1
IRT + attempts	0.833	0.739	0.411	
Basic IRT	0.838	0.752	0.399	
LR baseline	0.838	0.772	0.391	0.284
Vanilla FM	0.824	0.773	0.414	
DeepFM*		0.811		**0.382**
DeepFM		**0.815**		0.329

Table 1: Performance of all tested algorithms on the en_es dataset.

5 Results

We first tried different models on a validation set. All models were trained using 500 epochs for the vanilla FM, or 100 epochs for DeepFM with early stopping, and refit on the validation set.

5.1 On validation set

A vanilla FM was used considering $\psi = \Phi$ the CDF of the standard normal distribution as link function, like in the implementation of[4] (Rendle, 2012). Then, for our experiments, we used the TensorFlow implementation of DeepFM provided by Alibaba on GitHub[5]. Our encoding is available on GitHub[6].

Vanilla FM had comparable performance of the LR baseline. It agrees with the findings of Vie and Kashima (2018) that a bigger dimension may not necessarily help.

5.2 On test set

The DeepFM model managed to improve the baseline by 3 points AUC. We got AUC 0.815, while the top performing solution had AUC 0.861.

Our best performing model was DeepFM: using only the discrete features, train a model of latent embedding size 10 during a fixed number of epochs (50). DeepFM* using all features was slightly worse.

6 Further Work

We could embed the dependency graph provided by Duolingo in the encoding of the vanilla FM.

Ensemble methods such as xgboost (Chen and Guestrin, 2016) could be considered, as typically encountered in challenges.

---

[4] http://www.libfm.org
[5] https://github.com/ChenglongChen/tensorflow-DeepFM
[6] https://github.com/jilljenn/ktm

Here we want to combine information of the student which is quite poor (almost only their outcomes), compared to the knowledge of tokens (syntactic trees, or word2vec, etc.). This is why we could use extra embeddings, such as a LSTM encoding of the sentence as feature for the token.

The performance of DeepFM* that was using all features was slightly worse than DeepFM that was limited to the fundamental features. We might mitigate this problem by using a field-aware factorization machine (Juan et al., 2016) that learns a parameter per category of feature in order to draw more importance on some category (such as `user`) than others (such as `date`).

7 Conclusion

In this paper, we showed how to use deep factorization machines for knowledge tracing. Our findings show interesting combinations of features, together with embeddings provided by deep neural networks. In some way, it shows how to learn dense embeddings from the sparse features typically encountered in learning platforms.

References

Tianqi Chen and Carlos Guestrin. 2016. Xgboost: A scalable tree boosting system. In *Proceedings of the 22nd acm sigkdd international conference on knowledge discovery and data mining*, pages 785–794. ACM.

Heng-Tze Cheng, Levent Koc, Jeremiah Harmsen, Tal Shaked, Tushar Chandra, Hrishi Aradhye, Glen Anderson, Greg Corrado, Wei Chai, Mustafa Ispir, et al. 2016. Wide & deep learning for recommender systems. In *Proceedings of the 1st Workshop on Deep Learning for Recommender Systems*, pages 7–10. ACM.

Albert T Corbett and John R Anderson. 1994. Knowledge tracing: Modeling the acquisition of procedural knowledge. *User modeling and user-adapted interaction*, 4(4):253–278.

Michel C. Desmarais and Ryan S. J. D. Baker. 2012. A review of recent advances in learner and skill modeling in intelligent learning environments. *User Modeling and User-Adapted Interaction*, 22(1-2):9–38.

Huifeng Guo, Ruiming Tang, Yunming Ye, Zhenguo Li, and Xiuqiang He. 2017. Deepfm: a factorization-machine based neural network for ctr prediction. In *Proceedings of the 26th International Joint Conference on Artificial Intelligence*, pages 1725–1731. AAAI Press.

Ronald K. Hambleton, Hariharan Swaminathan, and H. Jane Rogers. 1991. *Fundamentals of item response theory*. Sage.

Sepp Hochreiter and Jürgen Schmidhuber. 1997. Long short-term memory. *Neural computation*, 9(8):1735–1780.

Yuchin Juan, Yong Zhuang, Wei-Sheng Chin, and Chih-Jen Lin. 2016. Field-aware factorization machines for ctr prediction. In *Proceedings of the 10th ACM Conference on Recommender Systems*, pages 43–50. ACM.

Diederik P Kingma and Jimmy Ba. 2014. Adam: A method for stochastic optimization. *arXiv preprint arXiv:1412.6980*.

Behrouz Minaei-Bidgoli, Deborah A Kashy, Gerd Kortemeyer, and William F Punch. 2003. Predicting student performance: an application of data mining methods with an educational web-based system. In *Frontiers in education, 2003. FIE 2003 33rd annual*, volume 1, pages T2A–13. IEEE.

Chris Piech, Jonathan Bassen, Jonathan Huang, Surya Ganguli, Mehran Sahami, Leonidas J Guibas, and Jascha Sohl-Dickstein. 2015. Deep knowledge tracing. In *Advances in Neural Information Processing Systems (NIPS)*, pages 505–513.

Steffen Rendle. 2012. Factorization machines with libfm. *ACM Transactions on Intelligent Systems and Technology (TIST)*, 3(3):57:1–57:22.

B. Settles, C. Brust, E. Gustafson, M. Hagiwara, and N. Madnani. 2018. Second language acquisition modeling. In *Proceedings of the NAACL-HLT Workshop on Innovative Use of NLP for Building Educational Applications (BEA)*. ACL.

Jill-Jênn Vie and Hisashi Kashima. 2018. Knowledge tracing machines.

Kevin H. Wilson, Yan Karklin, Bojian Han, and Chaitanya Ekanadham. 2016. Back to the basics: Bayesian extensions of IRT outperform neural networks for proficiency estimation. In *Proceedings of the 9th International Conference on Educational Data Mining (EDM)*, pages 539–544.

CLUF: a Neural Model for Second Language Acquisition Modeling

Shuyao Xu
Singsound Inc.
Beijing, China
xushuy@singsound.com

Jin Chen
Singsound Inc.
Beijing, China
chenjin@singsound.com

Long Qin
Singsound Inc.
Beijing, China
qinlong@singsound.com

Abstract

Second Language Acquisition Modeling is the task to predict whether a second language learner would respond correctly in future exercises based on their learning history. In this paper, we propose a neural network based system to utilize rich contextual, linguistic and user information. Our neural model consists of a Context encoder, a Linguistic feature encoder, a User information encoder and a Format information encoder (CLUF). Furthermore, a decoder is introduced to combine such encoded features and make final predictions. Our system ranked in first place in the English track and second place in the Spanish and French track with an AUROC score of 0.861, 0.835 and 0.854 respectively.

1 Introduction

Education systems that can adapt to the presenting of educational materials according to students' personal learning needs have great potential. Specifically, in the area of second language learning, we try to predict whether the learning materials are too easy or too hard for language learners. Therefore, we study the Second Language Acquisition Modeling (SLAM) task to build a model of the language learning process.

Bayesian Knowledge Tracing (BKT) (Corbett and Anderson, 1994; Pardos and Heffernan, 2010; Pelánek, 2017) that models students' knowledge over time is a well-established problem. It takes a Hidden Markov Model (HMM) with binary hidden states to represent knowledge acquisition for each concept separately. BKT had been successfully applied to subjects like mathematics and programming, where a limited number of concepts can be predefined. However, in language learning, it's difficult to define a small number of concepts, especially when the vocabulary size increases over time. Deep Knowledge Tracing (DKT) (Piech

et al., 2015; Wilson et al., 2016) is a recent implementation of knowledge tracing which uses Recurrent Neural Networks (RNNs) to model student's learning trace. Although RNNs and its commonly used variants, such as Gated Recurrent Units (Cho et al., 2014) and Long Short-Term Memory (LSTM) (Hochreiter and Schmidhuber, 1997), are capable of exploring dynamic temporal behavior for a time sequence, it's hard to model extremely long learning history that can range over months even years. Half-life Regression (Settles and Meeder, 2016) is a novel approach for the SLAM task, which combines a psycholinguistic model of human memory with modern machine learning techniques. It had demonstrated state-of-art performance for predicting student recall rates.

Mapping symbols, such as characters or words, into a continuous space is a popular method in natural language processing (Hinton, 1986; Mikolov et al., 2013; Pennington et al., 2014; Mikolov et al., 2017). It achieved remarkable success in many tasks, for example, neural language modeling (Bengio et al., 2003; Collobert and Weston, 2008; Mikolov et al., 2010), machine translation (Sutskever et al., 2014; Bahdanau et al., 2015), text classification (Lai et al., 2015; Zhang et al., 2015; Conneau et al., 2017), sentiment analysis (dos Santos and Gatti, 2014; Poria et al., 2015) and machine reading comprehension (Xiong et al., 2017; Hu et al., 2017). In this work, we introduce a similar neural approach for the SLAM task, where we use neural encoders to extract features from each exercise as well as metadata about student and session. To be specific, we build a Context encoder, a Linguistic feature encoder, a User information encoder and a Format information encoder (CLUF) to calculate high-level representations from characters, words, part-of-speech (POS) labels, syntactic dependency labels, user id and country, exercise type, client, etc.

374

Proceedings of the Thirteenth Workshop on Innovative Use of NLP for Building Educational Applications, pages 374–380
New Orleans, Louisiana, June 5, 2018. ©2018 Association for Computational Linguistics

Track	Set	Users	Exercises	Unique Tokens	Positive Ratio (%)	OOV Ratio (%)
en_es	Train	2593	824012	1967	12.6	-
	Dev	2592	115770	1839	14.3	3.4
	Test	2593	114586	1879	-	4.5
es_en	Train	2643	731896	2525	14.1	-
	Dev	2640	96003	2353	15.7	7.6
	Test	2641	93145	2459	-	10.0
fr_en	Train	1213	326792	1941	16.2	-
	Dev	1206	43610	1671	17.6	7.1
	Test	1206	41753	1707	-	5.9

Table 1: The SLAM dataset statistics

2 Dataset

The Duolingo SLAM dataset (Settles et al., 2018) is organized into three language tracks:

- en_es: English learners (who already speak Spanish)

- es_en: Spanish learners (who already speak English)

- fr_en: French learners (who already speak English)

According to Table 1, most tokens (more than 80%) are perfect matches and are given the label 0 for "OK". Tokens that are missing or spelled incorrectly (ignoring capitalization, punctuation, and accents) are given the label 1 denoting a mistake. Across the three language tracks, en_es has the lowest positive ratio, while es_en has the highest out-of-vocabulary (OOV) ratio.

Table 2 shows the features provided with the SLAM dataset. In our system, we used all features except the morphology features and syntactic dependency edges, as we did not get any improvement during experiments. Perhaps it is because that the neural networks already encoded similar information from characters, words and their syntactic dependency labels.

3 Method

We used in total four encoders to model the students' learning behavior. Inputs to these encoders are embeddings learned from one-hot representations of raw features. The context encoder consists of a character level LSTM encoder and a word level LSTM encoder. The linguistic feature encoder is also a LSTM model, where POS and syn-

Category	Features
Context	word surface form
Linguistic	part of speech
	morphology features
	syntactic dependency edges
	syntactic dependency labels
User	user id
	countries
	days in course
Format	client
	session type
	exercise format
	response time

Table 2: Features provided with the SLAM task

tactic dependency embedding are concatenated together and then fed into a multilayer LSTM unit. At last, user encoder and format encoder are both fully-connected neural networks. The user encoder takes account of user id, users' nationality and other user related information, while the format encoder encodes exercise format, session type, client type and time used for the exercise. The decoder combines the outputs of these encoders and then makes predictions through a sigmoid unit.

3.1 Context Encoder

The context encoder operates at both the word level and the character level. The word level encoding is capable of capturing better semantics and longer dependency than the character level encoding. But learning new words is a key part in language learning. By modeling the character sequence, we may be able to learn certain word

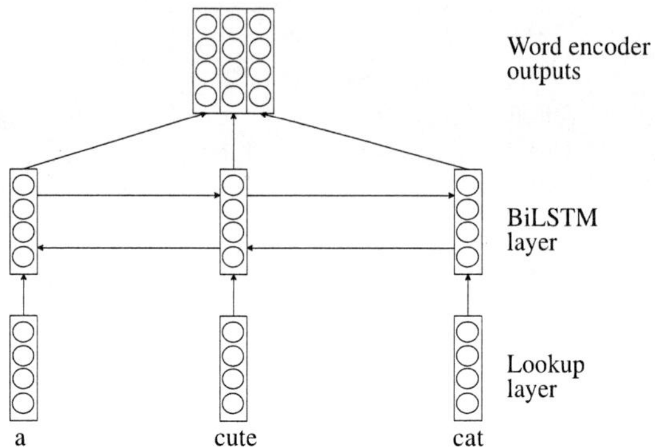

Figure 1: The Word Level Context Encoder

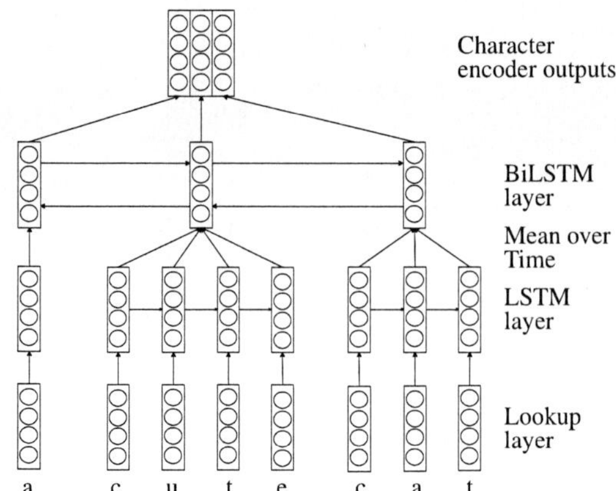

Figure 2: The Character Level Context Encoder

formation rules, therefore partially avoid the OOV problem.

The word level context encoder is a Bidirectional LSTM model. Given a sequence of words represented as one-hot vectors $(w_1, w_2, ..., w_N)$, we can get the word embedding of w_t as

$$x_t = E_w \cdot w_t,$$

where E_w is the word embedding matrix, which is learned during training.

Given the input vector x_t, the forward, backward, and combined activations of the j-th hidden layer are computed as

$$f_t^j = LSTM(f_{t-1}^j, \ f_t^{j-1})$$
$$b_t^j = LSTM(b_{t+1}^j, \ b_t^{j-1})$$
$$g_t = [f_t^{K_0}, \ b_t^{K_0}],$$

where K_0 is the number of layers of the network, $j = 1, 2, ..., K_0$.

The character level context encoder is a hierarchical LSTM model. Given a sequence of one-hot representations of characters in word w_t, $(c_1, c_2, ..., c_M)$, we can get the embedding of c_i as

$$h_i^0 = E_c \cdot c_i,$$

where E_c is the character embedding matrix, which is learned during training.

The outputs of the lookup layer are then fed into a multilayer LSTM unit

$$h_i^j = LSTM(h_{i-1}^j, \ h_i^{j-1})$$
$$H_{w_t} = (h_1^{K_1}, \ h_2^{K_1}, \ ..., \ h_M^{K_1}),$$

where K_1 is the number of layers of the LSTM, $j = 1, 2, ..., K_1$.

The mean-over-time (MoT) layer takes H_{w_t} as inputs

$$h_{w_t} = \frac{1}{M} \sum_{i=1}^{M} h_i^{K_1},$$

Then the outputs of the MoT layer $(h_{w_1}, h_{w_2}, ..., h_{w_N})$ are inputs to a Bidirectional LSTM model,

$$\hat{f}_t^j = LSTM(\hat{f}_{t-1}^j, \ \hat{f}_t^{j-1})$$
$$\hat{b}_t^j = LSTM(\hat{b}_{t+1}^j, \ \hat{b}_t^{j-1})$$
$$\hat{g}_t = [\hat{f}_t^{K_2}, \ \hat{b}_t^{K_2}],$$

where K_2 is the number of layers of the BiLSTM, $j = 1, 2, ..., K_2$.

The final outputs of the context encoder are computed as:

$$O = (o_1, \ o_2, \ ..., \ o_N),$$

where $o_t = g_t + \hat{g}_t$.

3.2 Linguistic Feature Encoder

The linguistic feature encoder is also a LSTM model. Similar to the context encoder, we trained embedding representations of the POS labels and the syntactic dependency labels. The POS embeddings and syntactic dependency embeddings are concatenated together and then fed into a LSTM unit,

$$l_t^0 = [pos_t, \ dep_t]$$
$$l_t^j = LSTM(l_{t-1}^j, \ l_t^{j-1})$$
$$L = (l_1^{K_3}, \ l_2^{K_3}, \ ..., \ l_N^{K_3}),$$

where pos_t is the POS embedding of word w_t and dep_t is the syntactic dependency label embedding of word w_t. j is the layer index, and we have K_3 layers in this LSTM unit.

3.3 User Encoder

The user encoder is a one-layer fully-connected feedforward network. The encoder takes user metadata as inputs

$$\mu^0 = [u, \ s, \ days]$$
$$\mu^1 = tanh(W_\mu \cdot \mu^0 + b_\mu),$$

where u is the embedding of the user id, s is the embedding of the user's nationality and $days$ is the time since the student started learning this language. W_μ, b_μ are trained network parameters. We used the tanh activation function for the user encoder.

3.4 Format Encoder

Similar to the user encoder, the format encoder is also a one-layer fully-connected feedforward network. The inputs are format, session, client, and the response time,

$$f^0 = [format, \ session, \ client, \ time]$$
$$f^1 = tanh(W_f \cdot f^0 + b_f),$$

where W_f, b_f are trainable parameters.

3.5 Decoder

The decoder takes the outputs (O, L, μ^1, f^1) of the context encoder, linguistic encoder, user encoder and format encoder as inputs. The prediction for word w_t in the given sequence $(w_1, \ w_2, \ ..., \ w_N)$ is computed as

$$\nu = \sigma(W_\nu \cdot [\mu^1, \ f^1] + b_\nu)$$
$$\gamma_t = \sigma(W_\gamma \cdot [l_t^{K_3}, \ o_t] + b_\gamma)$$
$$p_t = \sigma(W_p \cdot (\nu \odot \gamma_t) + b_p),$$

where W_ν, b_ν, W_γ, b_γ, W_p, and b_p are trainable parameters. For decoding, we used the sigmoid activation function σ.

3.6 Training

The model is trained to minimize the following loss function

$$Loss = -\frac{1}{N} \sum_{t=1}^{N} (\alpha y_t \cdot log(p_t) +$$
$$(1 - \alpha)(1 - y_t) \cdot log(1 - p_t)),$$

Team	AUROC	F1
SanaLabs	0.861	0.561
our model	0.861	0.559
alexrich	0.859	0.468
Masahiro	0.848	0.476
zz	0.846	0.414
Cam	0.841	0.479
btomosch	0.829	0.424
LambdaLearning	0.821	0.389
nihalnayak	0.821	0.376
...	...	...
baseline	0.774	0.190

Table 3: Results of the en_es track.

Team	AUROC	F1
SanaLabs	0.838	0.530
our model	0.835	0.524
alexrich	0.835	0.420
Masahiro	0.824	0.439
zz	0.818	0.390
Cam	0.807	0.435
btomosch	0.803	0.375
LambdaLearning	0.801	0.344
Grotoco	0.791	0.452
...	...	...
baseline	0.746	0.175

Table 4: Results of the es_en track.

where α is the hyper parameter to balance the negative and positive samples and y_t is the label of the time step t. In our experiment, we set α to 0.7.

4 Experiments and Results

4.1 Experiments

We considered the words that appear less than five times in the training data as unknown token. For students with more than one nationality, only the first one was used.

The embedding size was set to 100, and the Dropout (Srivastava et al., 2014) regularization was applied, where the dropout rate was set to 0.5. We used the Adam optimization algorithm (Kingma and Ba, 2014) with a learning rate of 0.001. The word level context encoder was a two-layer Bidirectional LSTM. The character level context encoder had one LSTM layer for encoding each word and three Bidirectional LSTM layers above the MoT layer. Furthermore, the linguistic

Team	AUROC	F1
SanaLabs	0.857	0.573
our model	0.854	0.569
alexrich	0.854	0.493
zz	0.843	0.487
Masahiro	0.839	0.502
Cam	0.835	0.508
btomosch	0.823	0.442
LambdaLearning	0.815	0.415
Grotoco	0.813	0.502
...	...	...
baseline	0.771	0.281

Table 5: Results of the fr_en track.

Term	en_es	es_en	fr_en
Relative impr (%)	11.24	11.93	9.72

Table 6: The relative improvement over the baseline

encoder was a two-layer LSTM. Both of the user encoder and format encoder were one-layer fully-connected feedforward networks.

4.2 Results

The evaluation metrics for the SLAM task were the Area Under the Receiver Operation Characteristic (AUROC) curve and the F1 score.

As provided in Table 3, Table 4 and Table 5, our model achieved the AUROC score of 0.861, 0.835, and 0.854 and the F1 score of 0.559, 0.524 and 0.569 for the en_es, es_en, and fr_en track, respectively. We ranked in first place in the en_es track and second place in the es_en and fr_en track.

Table 6 shows that CLUF gained significant improvements on all tracks compared to the baseline model. The improvement on the en_es and es_en track were close, while the improvement on the fr_en track was a bit lower. We think this is because the fr_en (327k exercises) track has much less training data than the en_es (824k exercises) and es_en (732k exercises) track.

4.3 Discussion

Our intuition behind CLUF is to factorize raw features into four independent parts: 1) word surface form models the word formation rules; 2) the linguistic encoder is to provide linguistic and syntactic dependency information; 3) the user part explores students' second language acquisition skills

Model	AUROC	F1
CLUF	0.846	0.554
LUF	0.775	0.446
CUF	0.843	0.552
CLF	0.813	0.501
CLU	0.779	0.467

Table 7: Encoder analysis. LUF has no context encoder; CUF has no linguistic encoder; CLF has no user encoder; CLU is the model without format encoder.

over time; 4) the format encoder measures the difficulty level of different exercises on various clients.

Table 7 shows the performance of our CLUF model when excluding one of the context, linguistic, user and format encoder. We can see that the performance drops substantially if we don't use the contextual or format features. On the other hand, excluding the linguistic features does not affect the performance much. At last, we can achieve fairly good performance even if we don't use any user information.

5 Conclusion

We presented a neural network based model, CLUF, for the SLAM task. We encoded the contextual, linguistic, user and format features separately. Our system achieved one of the best results in this task. Moreover, our CLUF model was language invariant, as it performed approximately equally well across three language tracks. We further explored how effective each encoder was. We found that the context encoder was the most effective one, while the linguistic encoder was the least effective one.

Acknowledgments

We thank Duolingo and Educational Testing Service for organizing this novel and interesting task and releasing the SLAM dataset.

References

Dzmitry Bahdanau, Kyunghyun Cho, and Yoshua Bengio. 2015. Neural machine translation by jointly learning to align and translate. *international conference on learning representations.*

Yoshua Bengio, Réjean Ducharme, Pascal Vincent, and Christian Jauvin. 2003. A neural probabilistic language model. *Journal of machine learning research*, 3(Feb):1137–1155.

Kyunghyun Cho, Bart Van Merriënboer, Dzmitry Bahdanau, and Yoshua Bengio. 2014. On the properties of neural machine translation: Encoder-decoder approaches. *arXiv preprint arXiv:1409.1259*.

Ronan Collobert and Jason Weston. 2008. A unified architecture for natural language processing: Deep neural networks with multitask learning. In *Proceedings of the 25th international conference on Machine learning*, pages 160–167. ACM.

Alexis Conneau, Holger Schwenk, Loïc Barrault, and Yann Lecun. 2017. Very deep convolutional networks for text classification. In *Proceedings of the 15th Conference of the European Chapter of the Association for Computational Linguistics: Volume 1, Long Papers*, volume 1, pages 1107–1116.

Albert T Corbett and John R Anderson. 1994. Knowledge tracing: Modeling the acquisition of procedural knowledge. *User modeling and user-adapted interaction*, 4(4):253–278.

Geoffrey E Hinton. 1986. Learning distributed representations of concepts. In *Proceedings of the eighth annual conference of the cognitive science society*, volume 1, page 12. Amherst, MA.

Sepp Hochreiter and Jürgen Schmidhuber. 1997. Long short-term memory. *Neural computation*, 9(8):1735–1780.

Minghao Hu, Yuxing Peng, and Xipeng Qiu. 2017. Reinforced mnemonic reader for machine comprehension. *CoRR, abs/1705.02798*.

Diederik P Kingma and Jimmy Ba. 2014. Adam: A method for stochastic optimization. *arXiv preprint arXiv:1412.6980*.

Siwei Lai, Liheng Xu, Kang Liu, and Jun Zhao. 2015. Recurrent convolutional neural networks for text classification. In *AAAI*, volume 333, pages 2267–2273.

Tomas Mikolov, Edouard Grave, Piotr Bojanowski, Christian Puhrsch, and Armand Joulin. 2017. Advances in pre-training distributed word representations. *arXiv preprint arXiv:1712.09405*.

Tomáš Mikolov, Martin Karafiát, Lukáš Burget, Jan Černockỳ, and Sanjeev Khudanpur. 2010. Recurrent neural network based language model. In *Eleventh Annual Conference of the International Speech Communication Association*.

Tomas Mikolov, Ilya Sutskever, Kai Chen, Greg S Corrado, and Jeff Dean. 2013. Distributed representations of words and phrases and their compositionality. In C. J. C. Burges, L. Bottou, M. Welling, Z. Ghahramani, and K. Q. Weinberger, editors, *Advances in Neural Information Processing Systems 26*, pages 3111–3119. Curran Associates, Inc.

Zachary A Pardos and Neil T Heffernan. 2010. Modeling individualization in a bayesian networks implementation of knowledge tracing. In *International Conference on User Modeling, Adaptation, and Personalization*, pages 255–266. Springer.

Radek Pelánek. 2017. Bayesian knowledge tracing, logistic models, and beyond: an overview of learner modeling techniques. *User Modeling and User-Adapted Interaction*, 27(3-5):313–350.

Jeffrey Pennington, Richard Socher, and Christopher Manning. 2014. Glove: Global vectors for word representation. In *Proceedings of the 2014 conference on empirical methods in natural language processing (EMNLP)*, pages 1532–1543.

Chris Piech, Jonathan Bassen, Jonathan Huang, Surya Ganguli, Mehran Sahami, Leonidas J Guibas, and Jascha Sohl-Dickstein. 2015. Deep knowledge tracing. In C. Cortes, N. D. Lawrence, D. D. Lee, M. Sugiyama, and R. Garnett, editors, *Advances in Neural Information Processing Systems 28*, pages 505–513. Curran Associates, Inc.

Soujanya Poria, Erik Cambria, and Alexander Gelbukh. 2015. Deep convolutional neural network textual features and multiple kernel learning for utterance-level multimodal sentiment analysis. In *Proceedings of the 2015 conference on empirical methods in natural language processing*, pages 2539–2544.

Cicero dos Santos and Maira Gatti. 2014. Deep convolutional neural networks for sentiment analysis of short texts. In *Proceedings of COLING 2014, the 25th International Conference on Computational Linguistics: Technical Papers*, pages 69–78.

B. Settles, C. Brust, E. Gustafson, M. Hagiwara, and N. Madnani. 2018. Second language acquisition modeling. In *Proceedings of the NAACL-HLT Workshop on Innovative Use of NLP for Building Educational Applications (BEA)*. ACL.

Burr Settles and Brendan Meeder. 2016. A trainable spaced repetition model for language learning. In *Proceedings of the 54th Annual Meeting of the Association for Computational Linguistics (Volume 1: Long Papers)*, volume 1, pages 1848–1858.

Nitish Srivastava, Geoffrey Hinton, Alex Krizhevsky, Ilya Sutskever, and Ruslan Salakhutdinov. 2014. Dropout: A simple way to prevent neural networks from overfitting. *The Journal of Machine Learning Research*, 15(1):1929–1958.

Ilya Sutskever, Oriol Vinyals, and Quoc V Le. 2014. Sequence to sequence learning with neural networks. In Z. Ghahramani, M. Welling, C. Cortes, N. D. Lawrence, and K. Q. Weinberger, editors, *Advances in Neural Information Processing Systems 27*, pages 3104–3112. Curran Associates, Inc.

Kevin H Wilson, Xiaolu Xiong, Mohammad Khajah, Robert V Lindsey, Siyuan Zhao, Yan Karklin, Eric G Van Inwegen, Bojian Han, Chaitanya Ekanadham, Joseph E Beck, et al. 2016. Estimating student proficiency: Deep learning is not the panacea. In *In Neural Information Processing Systems, Workshop on Machine Learning for Education*.

Caiming Xiong, Victor Zhong, and Richard Socher. 2017. Dynamic coattention networks for question answering. *international conference on learning representations*.

Xiang Zhang, Junbo Zhao, and Yann LeCun. 2015. Character-level convolutional networks for text classification. In *Advances in neural information processing systems*, pages 649–657.

Neural sequence modelling for learner error prediction

Zheng Yuan

The ALTA Institute

Department of Computer Science and Technology

University of Cambridge

zheng.yuan@cl.cam.ac.uk

Abstract

This paper describes our use of two recurrent neural network sequence models: sequence labelling and sequence-to-sequence models, for the prediction of future learner errors in our submission to the 2018 Duolingo Shared Task on Second Language Acquisition Modeling (SLAM). We show that these two models capture complementary information as combining them improves performance. Furthermore, the same network architecture and group of features can be used directly to build competitive prediction models in all three language tracks, demonstrating that our approach generalises well across languages.

1 Introduction

Most recent work on second language acquisition (SLA) has focused on intermediate-to-advanced learners in assessment settings driven by a series of shared tasks (Dale and Kilgarriff, 2011; Dale et al., 2012; Ng et al., 2013, 2014; Lee et al., 2015, 2016; Daudaravicius et al., 2016). The 2018 Duolingo Shared Task on Second Language Acquisition Modeling (SLAM) (Settles et al., 2018) targets early stage learners and aims to provide personalised learning instructions. Participating teams are provided with transcripts from exercises submitted by learners over their first 30 days of learning on Duolingo,[1] which are annotated for token (word) level errors. The task is to predict what errors each learner will make in the future based on their learning history. There are three language tracks in this shared task:

- *en_es*: native Spanish speakers learning English;

- *es_en*: native English speakers learning Spanish;

- *fr_en*: native English speakers learning French.

Teams can either focus on a particular language track, or explore generalised models and features across all three languages.

Inspired by the success of neural sequence models in grammatical error detection and correction (Yuan and Briscoe, 2016; Rei and Yannakoudakis, 2016; Yannakoudakis et al., 2017; Schmaltz et al., 2017), we propose two recurrent neural network sequence models for this problem: sequence labelling and sequence-to-sequence modelling. We demonstrate the utility of these two models for the future learner error prediction task. We also provide evidence of performance gains by using an ensemble of these two models, suggesting that they are complementary to each other.

For model development, we focus on the English track only and language-specific features are introduced and studied. When it comes to official evaluation, two new prediction systems, one for the *es_en* track and another for the *fr_en* track, are built using the same network architecture and the same (hyper-)parameter setting, without tuning for new datasets or languages. Competitive results on all three language tracks show that our approach generalises well and might be used as a generic solution across different languages.

The remainder of this paper is organised as follows: Section 2 describes our approach and two neural sequence models in detail, Section 3 discusses the feature types that we exploit in our models, Section 4 reports our experiments and results on the development set for the *en_es* track, Section 5 presents our official results on the test sets for all three language tracks. Finally, Section 6 provides conclusions and ideas for future work.

---

[1] https://www.duolingo.com

381

Proceedings of the Thirteenth Workshop on Innovative Use of NLP for Building Educational Applications, pages 381–388
New Orleans, Louisiana, June 5, 2018. ©2018 Association for Computational Linguistics

2 Approach

We introduce two models for the task of future learner error prediction: a sequence labelling model and a sequence-to-sequence model. The following sections describe these two models.

2.1 Neural sequence labelling

We treat error prediction as a sequence labelling problem. Similar to Yannakoudakis et al. (2017), we construct a bidirectional recurrent neural network for detecting future learner errors. Unlike their system, error-free and correct sequences are fed into our model, and the goal is to predict where a learner is likely to make token-level errors based on their learning history. The model receives a sequence of tokens $\mathbf{x} = (x_1, x_2, ..., x_T)$ as input, and assigns a label y to each input token x. A bidirectional long short-term memory (LSTM) (Hochreiter and Schmidhuber, 1997) is used to learn context-specific representations:

$$\overrightarrow{h_t} = \text{LSTM}(x_t, \overrightarrow{h_{t-1}}) \qquad (1)$$

$$\overleftarrow{h_t} = \text{LSTM}(x_t, \overleftarrow{h_{t+1}}) \qquad (2)$$

$$h_t = [\overrightarrow{h_t}; \overleftarrow{h_t}] \qquad (3)$$

where $\overrightarrow{h_t}$ is the hidden state of the forward-moving LSTM at time t, that reads the input sequence from the first token to the last; $\overleftarrow{h_t}$ is the hidden state of the backward-moving LSTM at time t, which reads the input sequence in reverse order; and h_t is the concatenation of both hidden states, that captures both historical and future sequential information.

A softmax output layer predicts the label distribution for each input token, given the whole input sequence $\mathbf{x}$:

$$p(y_t|\mathbf{x}) = \text{softmax}(W_o h_t) \qquad (4)$$

where W_o is an output weight matrix.

We optimise the model by minimising categorical cross-entropy between the predicted label distributions and the gold labels:

$$E = -\sum_{t=1}^{T} \log p(y_t|\mathbf{x}) \qquad (5)$$

2.2 Sequence-to-sequence modelling

We utilise a sequence-to-sequence model with a soft attention mechanism similar to that of Yuan and Briscoe (2016), which contains a bidirectional LSTM encoder and an attention-based LSTM decoder. An encoder first reads and encodes an input sequence $\mathbf{x} = (x_1, x_2, ..., x_T)$ into hidden state representations $\mathbf{h} = (h_1, h_2, ..., h_T)$, which is the same as the one used in our sequence labelling model (see Section 2.1, Equation 3). A decoder then generates an output sequence $\mathbf{y} = (y_1, y_2, ..., y_T)^2$ by predicting the next token y_t based on the input sequence $\mathbf{x}$ and all the previously generated tokens $\{y_1, y_2, ..., y_{t-1}\}$:

$$p(y_t|\{y_1, ..., y_{t-1}\}, \mathbf{x}) = \text{softmax}(W_o s_t) \qquad (6)$$

where W_o is a decoder output weight matrix, and s_t is the hidden state of the LSTM decoder at decoding time t:

$$s_t = \text{LSTM}(s_{t-1}, y_{t-1}, c_t) \qquad (7)$$

where c_t is the input sequence representation for predicting the output token y_t, and is calculated using a soft attention mechanism:

$$c_t = \sum_{j=1}^{T} (\alpha_{tj} h_j) \qquad (8)$$

The weight α_{tj} is computed with a softmax function:

$$\alpha_{tj} = \frac{\exp(e_{tj})}{\sum_{k=1}^{T} \exp(e_{tk})} \qquad (9)$$

A feedforward neural network is used to represent the energy function:

$$e_{tj} = \tanh(W_\alpha s_{t-1} + U_\alpha h_j) \qquad (10)$$

where W_α and U_α are attention weight matrices.

3 Feature space

Besides original word tokens, new features (in the form of discrete labels) are introduced, which provide additional exercise and learner information. These features are described briefly below.

---

[2] For the error prediction task, the number of tokens generated in the output sequence $\mathbf{y}$ must equal the number of tokens in the input sequence $\mathbf{x}$.

3.1 Exercise-level feature set

user: a unique identifier for each learner;

format: the exercise format (*reverse_translate*, *reverse_tap*, or *listen*);[3]

session: the exercise session type (*lesson*, *practice*, or *test*);[4]

client: the learner's device platform (*android*, *ios*, or *web*);

country: the country from which the learner has done the exercise.

3.2 Token-level feature set

part of speech (POS): the POS tag of the word;

dependency edge label (DEP): the grammatical relation (GR) between the word and its head.

3.3 Language-specific feature set

CEFR word level: The Common European Framework of Reference (CEFR) (Council of Europe, 2011) describes what language learners can do at different stages of their learning and defines language proficiency in six levels: A1, A2, B1, B2, C1 and C2, with A1 being the lowest and C2 the highest. These six CEFR levels can be grouped into three broad levels: basic (A1 and A2), independent (B1 and B2) and proficient (C1 and C2).

The CEFR levels for all the English words appeared in the dataset are extracted from the English Vocabulary Profile (EVP),[5] which is based on the 50-million word Cambridge Learner Corpus (CLC) and the 1.2-billion word Cambridge English Corpus (CEC). The EVP is a free online vocabulary resource that contains information about which words and phrases are known and used by learners at each CEFR level (Capel, 2012).

Even though we only focus on English words here, it is worth noting that the CEFR levels were designed in a way that can be applied to all languages. Therefore, if resources for other languages similar to the EVP became available, we can then make use of this feature for other languages.

CLC error rate: We collect error rate information from the CLC, which is a large annotated corpus of learner English developed by Cambridge University Press and Cambridge English Language Assessment since 1993 (Nicholls, 2003). It comprises examination scripts written by learners of English who took Cambridge English examinations around the world with over 80 L1s and representing all six CEFR levels.

Two criteria are applied to create two sub corpora:

- CLC(KET): contains examination scripts for A2 Key, formerly known as Cambridge English: Key (KET)[6]; and A2 Key for Schools, formerly known as Cambridge English: Key for Schools (KETfS)[7].

  KET is the lowest level General English examination in the Cambridge English range, which targets at A2 level. KETfS is at the same level as KET, but its examination content is targeted at the interests and experiences of schoolchildren.

- CLC(ES): contains examination scripts written by native speakers of Spanish, which account for around 24.6% of the non-native speakers represented in the CLC.

For every word w, an error rate $E(w)$ is defined as:

$$E(w) = \frac{\text{count}(s \neq w, t = w)}{\text{count}(t = w)} \quad (11)$$

where $\text{count}(t = w)$ is the number of times the word w is seen in the target side (*i.e.* corrected version) of the corpus, and $\text{count}(s \neq w, t = w)$ is the number of times any word except w in the source side (*i.e.* original version) has been corrected to the word w in the target side.

We compute $E(w)$ from the CLC, CLC(KET) and CLC(ES); and then create two new features **CLC-KET** and **CLC-ES**:

---

[3] *reverse_translate*: learners are asked to read a sentence written in their L1, and then translate it into L2; *reverse_tap*: an easier version of *reverse_translate*, where learners are given a bank of words and distractors; *listen*: learners are asked to listen to an utterance in L2, and then transcribe it.

[4] The *lesson* sessions (about 77% of all the data) introduce new words; the *practice* sessions (22%) contain only previously-seen words; and the *test* sessions (1%) are quizzes that allow learners to "skip" a particular skill unit of the curriculum.

[5] http://www.englishprofile.org/wordlists

[6] http://www.cambridgeenglish.org/exams-and-tests/key

[7] http://www.cambridgeenglish.org/exams-and-tests/key-for-schools

$$
\text{CLC-KET} = \begin{cases} 1 & \text{if } \frac{E_{\text{CLC(KET)}}}{E_{\text{CLC}}} > 1 \\ 0 & \text{otherwise} \end{cases} \quad (12)
$$

$$
\text{CLC-ES} = \begin{cases} 1 & \text{if } \frac{E_{\text{CLC(ES)}}}{E_{\text{CLC}}} > 1 \\ 0 & \text{otherwise} \end{cases} \quad (13)
$$

All the exercise-level and token-level features are directly extracted from the metadata and pre-processed data provided by the shared task organisers. The language-specific features are only generated for the English data to be used in the *en_es* track.

4 Experiments and results

4.1 Dataset and evaluation

The shared task dataset comprises answers submitted by more than 6,000 Duolingo users over the course of their first 30 days. Token-level binary labels are provided:

Correct reference :	*She*	*is*	*my*	*mother*
Learner answer:	*She*	*is*		*mader*
Label:	0	0	1	1

Matched tokens are given the label '0'; and missing or misspelt tokens (ignoring capitalisation, punctuation and accents) are given the label '1' to indicate an error. Only correct references and label sequences are provided, not original learners' responses. Therefore, in our experiments, we map **correct** reference to its **label** sequence.

The dataset is partitioned sequentially into training, development and test sets, which all contain the same group of learners. The training set contains the first 80% of the sessions for each learner, followed by the next 10% for development and the final 10% for testing. Each learner's test items are subsequent to their development items, which in turn are all subsequent to their training items.

During development, we focus on learners of English. The training set provided for the *en_es* track contains approximately 2,622,958 tokens (however, only 13% are labelled with '1') in about 824,012 sentences. The development set includes additional 387,374 tokens in 115,770 sentences. All the data has been pre-processed using the Google SyntaxNet dependency parser[8] by the shared task organisers.

System performance is evaluated in terms of area under the ROC curve (AUROC) and F1 (with a threshold of 0.5).

4.2 Training

All our models are built using OpenNMT (Klein et al., 2017). For the sequence labelling model, our training procedure is similar to Yannakoudakis et al. (2017)); while for the sequence-to-sequence model, we follow Yuan and Briscoe (2016). Additionally, we set the source and target word embedding sizes to 750, as well as the LSTM hidden layer size. We no longer limit the vocabulary size or the maximum sentence length as both of them are small enough to train effectively. New features defined in Section 3 are added to the models incrementally and results are presented in the next section.

4.3 Results

Evaluation results on the development set for the *en_es* track are reported. We also include a baseline model provided by the shared task organisers for comparison purposes. The baseline model uses L2-regularised logistic regression, trained with stochastic gradient descent (SGD) weighted by frequency (Settles et al., 2018).

Sequence labelling model Results for the sequence labelling models are presented in Table 1, and all our models outperform the baseline (Table 1 #0). We start by adding exercise-level features incrementally (Table 1 #1-5). Introducing new exercise-level features yields consistent improvements in overall performance. The one trained on all our exercise-level features gives the best AUROC and F1 scores (Table 1 #5).

Token-level features (Table 1 #6-7) and language-specific features (Table 1 #8-10) are then added to the current best model. However, none of them yields further gains. A closer inspection of the training data reveals a number of cases where **POS** and **DEP** tags provided by the shared task organises are not reliable, as in the following examples (incorrect tags are marked in red):

384

#	Feature	AUROC	F1
0	baseline	0.776	0.173
1	token + user	0.784	0.421
2	token + user + format	0.809	0.453
3	token + user + format + session	0.825	0.470
4	token + user + format + session + client	0.834	0.476
5	token + user + format + session + client + country	**0.837**	**0.480**
6	token + user + format + session + client + country + POS	0.807	0.447
7	token + user + format + session + client + country + DEP	0.830	0.474
8	token + user + format + session + client + country + CEFR	0.823	0.469
9	token + user + format + session + client + country + CLC-KET	0.825	0.471
10	token + user + format + session + client + country + CLC-ES	0.825	0.470

Table 1: Results of our sequence labelling models on the *en_es* development set. The results of our best model are marked in **bold**.

Token	POS	DEP	Label
A	DET	det	0
man	NOUN	ROOT	0
a	PUNCT	punct	0
woman	DET	det	0

Token	POS	DEP	Label
The	DET	det	1
judge	ADJ	amod	1
returns	NOUN	ROOT	1

Since we use the tags in the dataset directly, without cleaning any noisy data or pre-processing the data again, it is not surprising that adding these features yields worse performance.

In terms of the language-specific features, we also notice that the **CEFR word level** feature is not very informative as not all the words in the dataset are also in the EVP; and for words that are, most of them turn out to be at either A1 or A2 level.

Sequence-to-sequence model We follow the same training procedure to build sequence-to-sequence models - see Table 2. Similar results are observed: all our models perform better than the baseline (Table 2 #0); exercise-level features contribute to the overall performance improvements (Table 2 #1-5); and token-level and language-specific features seem to be detrimental and bring performance down (Table 2 #6-10). The best sequence-to-sequence model uses all the exercise-level features, achieving an AUROC score of 0.837 and an F1 score of 0.464 - see Table 2 #5.

Combining two sequence models Our best sequence labelling model (seqlabel) and our best sequence-to-sequence model (seq2seq) achieve the same AUROC score of 0.837; while seqlabel yields a better F1 score of 0.480, compared to an F1 score of 0.464 for seq2seq.

We further combine these two best models using linear interpolation:

$$P_{combined} = (1 - \lambda)P_{seqlabel} + \lambda P_{seq2seq} \quad (14)$$

where $P_{seqlabel}$ represents the score from the sequence labelling model, $P_{seq2seq}$ represents the score from the sequence-to-sequence model, and λ is a parameter that controls the impact the sequence-to-sequence model has on the final score. After tuning λ on the development set, we set it to 0.5.

Results of our best individual models and the final combined model are reported in Table 3. We can see that the combined model yields the overall best results, which suggests that our two individual neural sequence models capture complementary information even though they are both trained on the same group of features.

5 Official evaluation results

Our submissions to the shared task are the results of our best systems. As each participating team is allowed to submit up to 10 runs, we first run our best sequence labelling, sequence-to-sequence and combined systems from the previous section on the *en_es* test set.

After determining that our language-specific features are not helpful, we train new models for

#	Feature	AUROC	F1
0	baseline	0.776	0.173
1	token + user	0.787	0.353
2	token + user + format	0.800	0.431
3	token + user + format + session	0.811	0.441
4	token + user + format + session + client	0.825	0.448
5	token + user + format + session + client + country	**0.837**	**0.464**
6	token + user + format + session + client + country + POS	0.829	0.460
7	token + user + format + session + client + country + DEP	0.823	0.448
8	token + user + format + session + client + country + CEFR	0.805	0.433
9	token + user + format + session + client + country + CLC-KET	0.804	0.433
10	token + user + format + session + client + country + CLC-ES	0.805	0.433

Table 2: Results of our sequence-to-sequence models on the *en_es* development set. The results of our best model are marked in **bold**.

Model	AUROC	F1
seqlabel	0.837	0.480
seq2seq	0.837	0.464
combined	**0.843**	**0.481**

Table 3: Results of our best models on the *en_es* development set. The best results are marked in **bold**.

the *es_en* and *fr_en* tracks using the same network architecture and the same group of features as for *en_es*. No tuning of (hyper-)parameters is performed for new datasets or languages.

The official results of our submissions for all three language tracks are reported in Table 4. Results on the *en_es* test set are similar to those on the *en_es* development set (see Table 3) - no significant drop is observed. The `combined` model produces the best overall performance, and the `seqlabel` model outperforms the `seq2seq` model. In the *fr_en* track, the `combined` model again yields the highest AUROC and F1 scores, followed by the `seq2seq` model and the `seqlabel` model. Our *es_en* `seq2seq` model had not finished training by the shared task submission deadline, therefore, we only submit the *es_en* `seqlabel` model. Based on the results for the other two language tracks, we expect our *es_en* results might be further improved by combining a `seqlabel` model and a `seq2seq` model.

6   Conclusions and future work

In this paper, we have described the use of recurrent neural sequence labelling and sequence-to-sequence models for future learner error predic-tion. We have provided evidence of further performance gains by combining them together, showing that these two types of sequence models are complementary. We have also explored different types of features, which capture exercise-level, token-level and language-specific information. Furthermore, we have demonstrated that the same network architecture and group of features can be applied directly to build competitive prediction systems across all three languages, without the need for language-specific parameter tuning.

Results of our best systems on the official test sets yield: AUROC=0.841 (ranked sixth out of the fifteen participating teams) and F1=0.479 (ranked third) for the *en_es* track; AUROC=0.835 (ranked sixth) and F1=0.508 (ranked third) for *fr_en*; and AUROC=0.807 (ranked sixth) and F1=0.435 (ranked fifth) for *es_en*.

Plans for future work include combining the training and development sets to train new models, using better quality token-level features, and exploring other exercise-level features like the amount of **time** it took for the learner to construct and submit their answer and the number of **days** since the learner started using Duolingo. We would also like to test our approach as well as our language-specific features on a broader scale (*i.e.* using corpora which cover language learners at different levels, ideally ranging from basic to proficient).

Acknowledgments

We would like to thank Ted Briscoe and Meng Zhang for their valuable comments and suggestions. We are also grateful to Christopher Bryant

	en_es		fr_en		es_en	
Model	**AUROC**	**F1**	**AUROC**	**F1**	**AUROC**	**F1**
seqlabel	0.836	0.467	0.825	0.498	0.807	0.435
seq2seq	0.830	0.465	0.830	0.500	-	-
combined	0.841	0.479	0.835	0.508	-	-
baseline	0.774	0.190	0.771	0.281	0.746	0.175
top-performing	0.861	0.561	0.857	0.573	0.838	0.530

Table 4: Official results of our submitted systems on the test sets for all three tracks: `seqlabel` is our best sequence labelling model, `seq2seq` is our best sequence-to-sequence model, and `combined` is the combination of these two models. For comparison, we also include the `baseline` results provided by the shared task organisers and the results from the `top-performing` systems.

and Ahmed Zaidi for providing us with the CLC and EVP resources. Our gratitude goes also to the shared task organisers for coordinating the task. We acknowledge NVIDIA for an Academic Hardware Grant.

References

Annette Capel. 2012. Completing the English Vocabulary Profile: C1 and C2 vocabulary. *English Profile Journal*, 3(e1).

Council of Europe. 2011. *Common European Framework of Reference for Languages: Learning, Teaching, Assessment*. Cambridge University Press.

Robert Dale, Ilya Anisimoff, and George Narroway. 2012. HOO 2012: A Report on the Preposition and Determiner Error Correction Shared Task. In *Proceedings of the 7th Workshop on Innovative Use of NLP for Building Educational Applications*, pages 54–62, Montréal, Canada. Association for Computational Linguistics.

Robert Dale and Adam Kilgarriff. 2011. Helping Our Own: The HOO 2011 Pilot Shared Task. In *Proceedings of the 13th European Workshop on Natural Language Generation*, pages 242–249, Nancy, France. Association for Computational Linguistics.

Vidas Daudaravicius, Rafael E. Banchs, Elena Volodina, and Courtney Napoles. 2016. A Report on the Automatic Evaluation of Scientific Writing Shared Task. In *Proceedings of the 11th Workshop on Innovative Use of NLP for Building Educational Applications*, pages 53–62, San Diego, CA. Association for Computational Linguistics.

Sepp Hochreiter and Jürgen Schmidhuber. 1997. Long Short-Term Memory. *Neural Computation*, 9(8):1735–1780.

Guillaume Klein, Yoon Kim, Yuntian Deng, Jean Senellart, and Alexander Rush. 2017. OpenNMT: Open-Source Toolkit for Neural Machine Translation. In *Proceedings of ACL 2017, System Demonstrations*, pages 67–72, Vancouver, Canada. Association for Computational Linguistics.

Lung-Hao Lee, Gaoqi RAO, Liang-Chih Yu, Endong XUN, Baolin Zhang, and Li-Ping Chang. 2016. Overview of NLP-TEA 2016 Shared Task for Chinese Grammatical Error Diagnosis. In *Proceedings of the 3rd Workshop on Natural Language Processing Techniques for Educational Applications*, pages 40–48, Osaka, Japan. The COLING 2016 Organizing Committee.

Lung-Hao Lee, Liang-Chih Yu, and Li-Ping Chang. 2015. Overview of the NLP-TEA 2015 Shared Task for Chinese Grammatical Error Diagnosis. In *Proceedings of the 2nd Workshop on Natural Language Processing Techniques for Educational Applications*, pages 1–6, Beijing, China. Association for Computational Linguistics.

Hwee Tou Ng, Siew Mei Wu, Ted Briscoe, Christian Hadiwinoto, Raymond Hendy Susanto, and Christopher Bryant. 2014. The CoNLL-2014 Shared Task on Grammatical Error Correction. In *Proceedings of the Eighteenth Conference on Computational Natural Language Learning: Shared Task*, pages 1–14, Baltimore, Maryland. Association for Computational Linguistics.

Hwee Tou Ng, Siew Mei Wu, Yuanbin Wu, Christian Hadiwinoto, and Joel Tetreault. 2013. The CoNLL-2013 Shared Task on Grammatical Error Correction. In *Proceedings of the Seventeenth Conference on Computational Natural Language Learning: Shared Task*, pages 1–12, Sofia, Bulgaria. Association for Computational Linguistics.

Diane Nicholls. 2003. The Cambridge Learner Corpus - error coding and analysis for lexicography and ELT. In *Proceedings of the Corpus Linguistics 2003 Conference*, pages 572–581.

Marek Rei and Helen Yannakoudakis. 2016. Compositional Sequence Labeling Models for Error Detection in Learner Writing. In *Proceedings of the 54th Annual Meeting of the Association for Computational Linguistics (Volume 1: Long Papers)*, pages 1181–1191, Berlin, Germany. Association for Computational Linguistics.

Allen Schmaltz, Yoon Kim, Alexander Rush, and Stuart Shieber. 2017. Adapting Sequence Models for Sentence Correction. In *Proceedings of the 2017 Conference on Empirical Methods in Natural Language Processing*, pages 2807–2813, Copenhagen, Denmark. Association for Computational Linguistics.

Burr Settles, Chris Brust, Erin Gustafson, Masato Hagiwara, and Nitin Madnani. 2018. Second Language Acquisition Modeling. In *Proceedings of the 13th Workshop on Innovative Use of NLP for Building Educational Applications*. Association for Computational Linguistics.

Helen Yannakoudakis, Marek Rei, Øistein E. Andersen, and Zheng Yuan. 2017. Neural Sequence-Labelling Models for Grammatical Error Correction. In *Proceedings of the 2017 Conference on Empirical Methods in Natural Language Processing*, pages 2795–2806, Copenhagen, Denmark. Association for Computational Linguistics.

Zheng Yuan and Ted Briscoe. 2016. Grammatical error correction using neural machine translation. In *Proceedings of the 2016 Conference of the North American Chapter of the Association for Computational Linguistics: Human Language Technologies*, pages 380–386, San Diego, California. Association for Computational Linguistics.

Automatic Distractor Suggestion for Multiple-Choice Tests Using Concept Embeddings and Information Retrieval

Le An Ha and Victoria Yaneva
Research Institute in Information and Language Processing,
University of Wolverhampton, UK
`ha.l.a@wlv.ac.uk, v.yaneva@wlv.ac.uk`

Abstract

Developing plausible distractors (wrong answer options) when writing multiple-choice questions has been described as one of the most challenging and time-consuming parts of the item-writing process. In this paper we propose a fully automatic method for generating distractor suggestions for multiple-choice questions used in high-stakes medical exams. The system uses a question stem and the correct answer as an input and produces a list of suggested distractors ranked based on their similarity to the stem and the correct answer. To do this we use a novel approach of combining concept embeddings with information retrieval methods. We frame the evaluation as a prediction task where we aim to "predict" the human-produced distractors used in large sets of medical questions, i.e. if a distractor generated by our system is good enough it is likely to feature among the list of distractors produced by the human item-writers. The results reveal that combining concept embeddings with information retrieval approaches significantly improves the generation of plausible distractors and enables us to match around 1 in 5 of the human-produced distractors. The approach proposed in this paper is generalisable to all scenarios where the distractors refer to concepts.

1 Introduction

Multiple-choice tests are one of the most widely used forms of both formative and summative assessment and are a probably the most prominent feature of high-stakes standardized exams (Gierl et al., 2017). Administering such exams requires the development of a large number of good-quality multiple-choice questions (MCQs). To illustrate the need to have a large number of questions, Breithaupt et al. (2009) report that a 40-item computer adaptive test for high-stakes examination administered twice a year would require a bank with 2,000

items and Gierl et al. (2017) estimate that the cost of developing an item bank of this size would be between 3,000,000 and 5,000,000 USD. Naturally, this creates the incentive to automate the test production as much as possible and has resulted in a large number of papers on the topic of automatic MCQ generation.

An important aspect of MCQ development is the generation of plausible distractors (wrong answer options), as they can help control for the difficulty of the item, reduce random guessing and discriminate properly between different levels of student ability (Alsubait et al., 2013). This task poses a challenge to both humans and machines and is especially demanding in the field of medical exams. For example, an analysis of 514 human-produced items including 2056 options (1542 distractors and 514 correct responses), administered to undergraduate nursing students, indicated that "Only 52.2% (n = 805) of all distractors were functioning effectively and 10.2% (n = 158) had a choice frequency of 0." (Tarrant et al., 2009). Items with more functioning distractors were found to be more difficult and more discriminating.

A particular challenge for the automatic development of MCQ distractors for the medical domain is the coverage of the ontologies, which could be too narrow in some cases, and too broad in others, and the need to rank the candidates in order to select the best ones. At the same time, this domain is of particular need of automated assistance, as the requirement for a very specialized knowledge makes the recruitment of item-writers and the test development procedure even more costly.

To address this issue we propose a method to fully automatically suggest distractors for MCQs given a stem[1] and a correct answer. The data used

---

[1] In this study we refer to the following components of an MCQ. The *stem* denotes the part that identifies the question or problem; *answer options* refer to all possible answers that an

Proceedings of the Thirteenth Workshop on Innovative Use of NLP for Building Educational Applications, pages 389–398
New Orleans, Louisiana, June 5, 2018. ©2018 Association for Computational Linguistics

in this study features two sets of 1,441 MCQs and 369 MCQs from the United States Medical Licensing Examination (USMLE) for which we have the stem, all answer options and information on which the correct answer is. We compare two approaches to suggesting distractors based on: i) concept embeddings only and ii) concept embeddings reranked using information retrieval techniques. The evaluation of these approaches is formulated as a prediction task, where each system uses the stem and the correct answer as an input and tries to predict the existing distractor options for each item as an output. The contributions of this study are as follows:

- We propose a novel method for distractor generation and selection based on concept embeddings reranked using information retrieval, which can successfully suggest relevant distractors given an item stem and the correct answer option.

- We show that the ranking based on information-retrieval methods improves the distractor prediction significantly.

- The approach used in this study is generalisable to all scenarios where the answer options refer to concepts. Furthermore, it can generate distractors for any item given that the correct answer features as an entry in the ontology, as opposed to only items generated by a specific method.

The rest of this paper is organised as follows. The next section presents related work on automatic item generation with special emphasis on distractor generation and evaluation. Section 3 describes the data sets used in this study and Section 4 describes our method. The results are reported in Section 6, discussed in Section 6 and summarised in Section 7.

2   Related Work

The automatic generation of multiple-choice questions (MCQs) has received a lot of attention in the past two decades, offering a range of approaches such as template-based item generation (Gierl et al., 2015, 2016; Lai et al., 2016), ontology-based item generation (Holohan et al., 2006; Papasalouros et al., 2008; Alsubait et al., 2014),

examinee can choose from; *distractors* are the wrong answer options, and the *correct answer* is the correct answer option. Please refer to Table 1 for an example of a MCQ item.

and generation of items from unstructured text (Mitkov and Ha, 2003; Brown et al., 2005; Heilman, 2011; Hoshino and Nakagawa, 2005; Majumder and Saha, 2015).

The work most relevant to the field of MCQ generation for the medical education domain relies on a semi-automatic approach for template-based language generation, where variations of items are produced based on an item template (Gierl et al., 2016; Lai et al., 2016). An item template is a model that highlights the features which can be manipulated in order to generate a variation of the MCQ (e.g. strings and numerals) and thus increase the item bank for an exam. The method is semi-automatic in that it requires content developers to specify the initial item template and the information which could potentially be varied. For numeric options, the distractors are generated based on a pre-defined formula for each distractor candidate. For key feature options, the distractors may be from the same category as the correct answer, such as the same concept, topic, or idea at varying hyponymic or hypernymic levels. Evaluation of 13 MCQs generated in this way by 455 Canadian and international medical graduates revealed that the generated items were consistently discriminative in measuring the different levels of abilities of the students (Lai et al., 2016).

In terms of automatic distractor generation, systems which generate MCQs based on unstructured text have a limited ability to infer implicit relations within the text and generate plausible distractors (Alsubait et al., 2013). However, Mitkov and Ha (2003) select distractors by using WordNet to compute concepts semantically close to the correct answer by retrieving hypernyms, hyponyms, and coordinates of the term. In the event of WordNet returning too many concepts, preference is given to those appearing in the corpus and in the event that no concepts are returned the corpus is searched for noun phrases with the same head which are then used as distractors. Evaluation of 24 MCQs with test-takers revealed that the distractors were able to discriminate between high and low-ability students, where only 3 distractors were selected by no student and 6 were classed as *poor*, for misleading high-ability students.

Finally, most ontology-based MCQ generation systems output distractors based on hierarchical parent and sibling relations between the correct answer and the candidates (Papasalouros et al.,

An example of an item from the public data set
A 55-year-old woman with small cell carcinoma of the lung is admitted to the hospital to undergo chemotherapy. Six days after treatment is started, she develops a temperature of 38C (100.4F). Physical examination shows no other abnormalities. Laboratory studies show a leukocyte count of 100/mm3 (5% segmented neutrophils and 95% lymphocytes). Which of the following is the most appropriate pharmacotherapy to increase this patient's leukocyte count? (A) Darbepoetin (B) Dexamethasone (C) Filgrastim (D) Interferon alfa (E) Interleukin-2 (IL-2) (F) Leucovorin

Table 1: An example of an item from the USMLE exam

2008). Different strategies are then employed to select the most plausible distractors and the generated MCQs are most commonly evaluated by experts, and in more rare cases given to students or crowd workers. For example, Papasalouros et al. (2008) present a rule-based approach for selecting the distractors, mostly limiting them to siblings of the correct answer. In another study Žitko et al. (2009) use ontologies to generate the question stems and then propose a random list of alternative answers. More recent approaches make use of the semantics of the domain represented as mapped axioms (Vinu and Kumar, 2015b). Another approach called pattern-based MCQ generation utilizes different combinations of predicates associated with the instances of an ontology to generate the stems (Vinu and Kumar, 2015a). The distractors are selected from the list of instances in the ontology within the intersection classes of the domain or range of the predicates in the stem and are presented in a random order. In a follow-up study, Vinu et al. (2016) manipulate the difficulty of the stem and choice set based on similarity measure called *Instance Similarity Ratio* which takes into consideration the similarity between instances with regards to the conditions in the stem. The system then varies the question difficulty based on the similarity between the distractors, the correct answer and the stem (higher similarity indicates a more difficult question). Evaluation with test-takers revealed a correlation of .79 between the predicted and the actual difficulty levels.

The studies mentioned so far describe automatic and semi-automatic approaches for distractor generation in scenarios where the system generates the entire MCQ (i.e. it controls the stem). In the experiments presented in this paper we introduce a fully automatic approach to distractor generation and selection based on embedding vectors and information retrieval techniques, which can be used for any given stem and correct answer pair. The next section presents the data used in our study.

3 Data

In this study we use multiple-choice questions administered by the United States Medical Licensing Examination (USMLE). The USMLE exam is a high-stakes examination for medical licensure in the United States, the outcome of which is recognised by all medical boards in the USA. The goal of the licensure and certification examination is to ensure that medical professionals have met the required standards and are qualified to engage in practice. The data has been provided by the National Board of Medical Examiners (NBME) who develop and manage the USMLE.

We use two separate data sets of questions where each test item is a single-best-answer multiple-choice question consisting of a stem followed by four or more response options. An example of such item is provided in Table 1.

Our main data set consists of 1,441 multiple choice test items that have been administered or pretested during the 2008 administration of the USMLE. These questions are not available to the public due to test security reasons and are henceforth referred to as the private data set. An additional 369 items which are publicly available[2] have also been used in this study and are referred to as the public data set. The public data set contains 132 questions from the USMLE Step 1 2015 sample booklet, 117 questions from the USMLE Step 1 2016 sample booklet, and 120 questions

---

[2]The items can be accessed at the USMLE web site, for example: `http://www.usmle.org/pdfs/step-1/2017samples_step1.pdf`

from the USMLE Step 2 2017 sample booklet. The main characteristics of the test items and their options within both sets are presented in Table 3.

Dataset	Public	Private
Total number of items	369	1441
Total number of options	1728	7664
Total number of distractors	1359	6223
Options per item	4.68	5.32

Table 2: Item characteristics for the two data sets

4 Method

Content specialists are instructed to create distractors that are similar in content and structure relative to the correct options (Ascalon et al., 2007; Gierl et al., 2017; Case and Swanson, 2001). The similarity can be quantified using either ontologies or computational models such as distributional similarity ones. For example, according to embedding vectors which represent the state-of-the-art in distributional similarity, distractors found in actual items are more similar to the correct answers than random concepts; they are also more similar to their stem than a random concept as well (this is also empirically tested further in the paper, see tables 3 and 4). As a result, we extend the instruction that distractors should be similar to the correct answers to computer models used to suggest distractors: distractor candidates are those that are similar to the correct answers and stems, measured using various models of similarity, and specifically, embedding vectors and information retrieval based similarity (Sections 4.1 and 4.3).

We first describe the lexicons, the embedding vectors derived from them (Section 4.1) and how they are used to calculate the similarity between different item parts (e.g. stem, correct answer, answer options, etc.) (Section 4.2). We then describe the methodology for ranking the suggested distractors using information retrieval techniques in Section 4.3.

4.1 The concept embeddings

We use embedding vectors to quantify the similarity between correct answers, distractors, and stems. Precomputed embedding vectors are available for various lexical databases such as Freebase and UMLS. We use the embedding vectors based on data from two lexical-semantic databases:

- Unified Medical Language System (UMLS) [3] 2012. We use the concept embedding vectors provided by Yu et al. (2017). These vectors are built using Pubmed citations published before 2016, bag-of-words model, and 200 dimensions.

- Freebase entities[4]. Freebase is a large collaborative knowledge base containing more than 39 million topics and more than 1.9 billion "facts". We use pretrained vectors for 1.4M entities, trained using 100B words from various news articles[5]. Each vector has 1000 dimensions.

Table 5 shows the number of USMLE item options that are also entries in the two lexical-semantic databases: UMLS and Freebase entities. As can be seen from the table, the UMLS database is a promising source for option candidates, as more than half of the options from both data sets can also be found in this database. On the other hand, Freebase vectors have been derived from much more data compared to UMLS vectors (approximately 100 billion of tokens). Nevertheless, even though Freebase has more concepts than UMLS (the Freebase vectors represent 1.4M entities, whereas UMLS vectors represent 300K concepts), its coverage is poorer in the medicine domain, and only 32% of distractors can be found in the Freebase, versus 56% coverage of UMLS (see Table 5). Based on this comparison, we focus on experimenting with the UMLS vectors and all results reported in the remainder of this paper were obtained using UMLS vectors.

4.2 Similarity calculation

We then calculate the similarity between:

1. The options themselves

2. Distractors and correct answers

3. Stems and options

4. Stems and correct answers

The similarities are calculated using embedding vectors as follows. The embedding vectors map an entity to a vector of n dimensions. In the case of the Freebases entities, n = 1000, and in the case of the UMLS concepts, n = 200. These vectors

---

[3] https://www.nlm.nih.gov/research/umls/
[4] https://developers.google.com/freebase/
[5] https://code.google.com/archive/p/word2vec/

	Mean	STD	Min	Max	N
Distractor-CorrectAnswer	0.34	0.15	-0.10	0.82	1341
Option-Option (Dist-CorrAns + DistDist)	0.33	0.15	-0.10	0.82	3674
Random pair of entities	0.09	0.13	-0.09	0.92	10000
Stem-Option	0.17	0.08	-0.02	0.53	1860
Stem-CorrectAnswer	0.18	0.08	-0.01	0.53	519
Stem-Random entity	0.05	0.06	-0.13	0.34	1860

Table 3: Cosine similarity between different item-part configurations calculated using Freebase vectors, using the private dataset.

	Mean	STD	Min	Max	N
Distractor-CorrectAnswer	0.41	0.17	-0.12	0.98	2849
Option-Option (Dist-CorrAns + DistDist)	0.39	0.19	-0.21	0.98	7981
Random pair of entities	0.03	0.17	-0.40	0.99	10000
Stem-Option	0.30	0.15	-0.24	0.71	4408
Stem-CorrectAnswer	0.34	0.14	-0.08	0.69	806
Stem-Random entity	0.02	0.17	-0.42	0.64	4408

Table 4: Cosine similarity between different item-part configurations calculated using UMLS vectors, using the private dataset.

	Total hits (%)	
Lexicon	Public	Private
UMLS concepts	964 (56%)	4408 (57%)
Freebase entities	562 (32%)	2734 (36%)
In either	980 (57%)	4448 (58%)

Table 5: Number of USMLE item options that are also entries in the two lexical-semantic databases

represent the distributional information of the entities with regard to some training objective and the cosine distance between two vectors is a good estimation of the similarity between the two entities. Here, "similarity" is defined as the similarity of information the two entities contain that is useful for the objective of the models used to acquire these vectors. The training objectives of the two sets of embedding vectors are to predict the context in which an entity would appear.

The representative embedding of a stem is computed by first translating the stem into a list of Concept Unique Identifiers (CUIs) using Metamap[6]. In cases where numerals were present in the stem (e.g. 100/mm3, 95%), these were excluded. We then sum the CUIs in the stem in the following way[7]:

$$S = L^2 - norm\left(\sum_{CUI in S} V_{CUI}\right)$$

We only choose options that appear in the respective databases. Table 3 shows the cosine similarities calculated using Freebase entities' embedding vectors, whereas Table 4 shows the calculations using UMLS concepts' vectors. We also perform calculations using random entities as a baseline. N represents the number of pairs.

As shown in Table 3, options that are found within the Freebase database are more similar to each other and to the stems, compared to random entities. This suggests that Freebase vectors can be used to suggest option candidates by suggesting entities which are similar to the correct answer. As can be seen from Table 4, options that are found within the UMLS database are also more similar to each other and to the stems than random entities are. The above observations confirm the premise that measurable similarity between distractors and the correct answers as well as the stems can be used as a criterion to suggest distractor candidates. They serve as a basis for our proposed method of predicting which distractor candidates would actually be used, as detailed below.

4.3 Predicting distractors using embedding vector similarity and information retrieval

In order to predict which distractor candidates would actually be used in an item, we first get the list of candidates, and then rank these candidates according to their similarity to the options and stems. The list of candidates could be entire UMLS, or only those that share the same semantic

---

⁶https://metamap.nlm.nih.gov/
[6]https://metamap.nlm.nih.gov/

[7]OOV rate: About 8% of the CIUs returned by Metamap do not feature in UMLS embedding

type[8] with the correct answers (STY), are marked as sibling of the correct answer (SIB), or are built using a graph walking method starting from the correct answers, then walk up to their broader concepts and then walk down to the narrower concepts of these broader concepts (RB_RN). For each of these choices there is a trade-off between coverage and precision. Using sibling relation only will produce the least number of candidates, at the expense of having the least coverage (only around 20% of potential matches). On the other hand, using the entire UMLS as candidates would ensure maximum coverage, at the expense of having to consider hundreds of thousands of candidates for each correct answer.

We then sort the candidates according to their similarity to the correct answers combined with the stem. This similarity is measured as the cosine similarity between the embedding vectors of the candidates, and those that represent the sums of the embedding vectors of the correct answer and those of the stem.

Top 10, 20, and 100 are called "predictions", and the number of correct "predictions" (i.e. the number of candidates that actually features as real distractors) is recorded as hits.

We also incorporate information retrieval. We first get the top n suggestions (in our experiment, we use $n = 500$), as previously described, we then rerank the candidates according to the rank of the first document in which they appear, when we use the stems as the query as we search our text collection, in our case, 2013 MEDLINE citations[9]. We use Lucene[10] for indexing and retrieving documents. The premise for this reranking is similar to that of Mitkov and Ha (2003): distractor candidates that appear in the same document that contains fragments of the stem would be prioritised over other candidates. Documents that contain fragments of the stem are retrieved by querying the text collection with the stem as the query.

To the best of our knowledge, a similar set up for the generation and evaluation of distractors has not been proposed before, which is why we are not able to compare our results to baselines from previous studies. We do, however, compare the performance of our system to a baseline of random hit prediction. Furthermore, the concept-embedding

approach can be viewed as a baseline compared to the approach using concept embeddings combined with IR techniques.

5 Evaluation

In order to evaluate our approach and the usefulness of the suggestions in the generated list, we describe an evaluation procedure where our system takes existing items together with all their options and tries to "predict" one or more of the existing distractors. In other words, if the system comes up with one or more of the same distractors as the ones produced by the human item-writers, then the approach could be considered useful for the generation of suitable distractor suggestions for new items. To do this, for each item, we get the first n concepts that are most similar to the combination of stem and the correct answer, and see how many of these concepts actually feature as distractors in that item (hits). The number of hits provides an estimation of the usefulness of the suggested list.

The results are presented in Table 6. Within that table, *Applicable items* are the ones whose correct answers could produce distractor candidates using the specific ontology relation. *Number of all candidates* reflects the number of candidates suggested by the specific ontology relation. *Maximum number of hits* refers to the number of hits if all the suggested candidates are considered, *Random N hits* is the number of hits if random N candidates are picked for each item. *Recall at N* signifies the total number of hits if the top N candidates are considered, divided by the total number of distractors that also feature in UMLS. In terms of ontology relations, SIB includes only candidates that are considered to be the siblings of the correct answer (according to UMLS). RN_RB means that only candidates that share a broader or narrower concept with the correct answer are considered, and STY means that all candidates that share the same semantic type with the correct answer are considered. The precision and recall relation is presented in Figure 1, while Figures 2 and 3 present the recall for the private and public data sets respectively.

As can be seen from Table 6, the suggested list outperformed the baseline of random hits in all three types of relations (SIB, RB_RN and STY), where best result (in terms of trade off between precision and recall) is achieved for the top 20 hits. Using the broadest ontology relation, namely

---

By approach (the relation used is STY)

		Public	Private
	Embedding only	73	319
Top 10	IR reranking	76	325
	Improvement	4%	2%
	Embedding only	99	492
Top 20	IR reranking	142	572
	Improvement	43%	16%
	Embedding only	190	811
Top 100	IR reranking	275	1242
	Improvement	45%	53%

By Ontology relation (IR reranking is used)

	Public			Private		
Ontology relations	SIB	RB_RN	STY	SIB	RB_RN	STY
Applicable items	143	165	181	640	756	806
Number of all candidates	3657	63998	10804667	18660	327623	48539316
Maximum number of hits	85	208	473	424	942	2360
Top 10 hits baseline	75	70	76	333	290	325
Random 10 hits	57	11	1	275	64	2
Recall at 10 (over all possible UMLS distractors, see last row)	0.13	0.12	0.13	0.12	0.10	0.11
Top 20	82	120	142	382	450	572
Recall at 20	0.14	0.20	0.24	0.13	0.16	0.20
Top 50	85	165	233	410	750	968
Recall at 50	0.14	0.28	0.39	0.14	0.26	0.34
Top 100	85	191	275	415	844	1242
Recall at 100	0.14	0.32	0.46	0.15	0.30	0.44
Distractors that belong to items whose correct answers feature in UMLS, and themselves also feature in UMLS	592			2831		

Table 6: Evaluation results: distractor hits.

same semantic type (STY), performs as well as the *sibling* (SIB) relation for the top 10 hits (i.e. 76 vs. 75, respectively, for the public data set and 325 vs. 333 for the private one). From the top 20 hits onwards, the STY relation outperforms SIB (i.e. for 20 hits we have STY hits= 142 and SIB = 82 for the public data set and STY = 572 and SIB = 382 for the private data set).

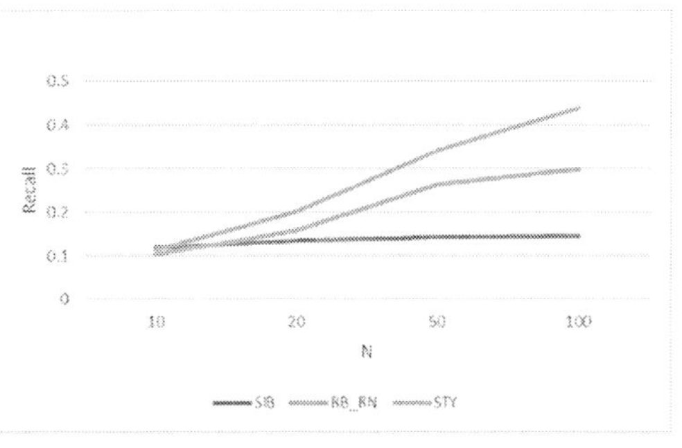

Figure 2: Recall at N, Private Data Set

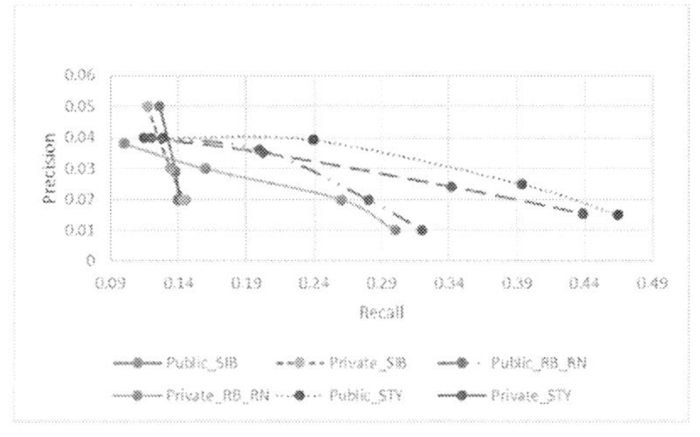

Figure 1: Precision - Recall Relation Graph

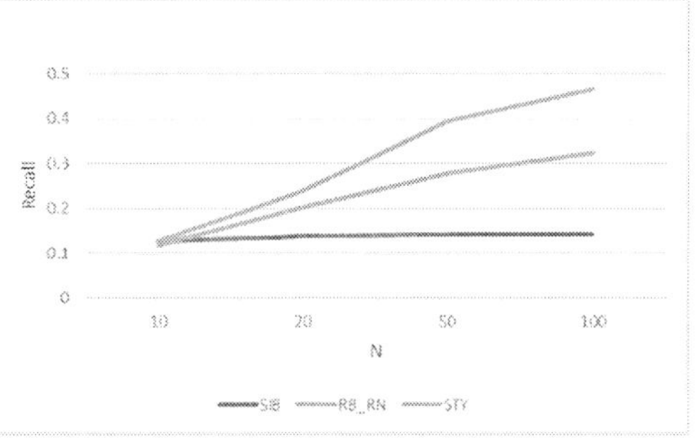

Figure 3: Recall at N, Public Data Set

An example of a question and the list of generated distractors and their ranking is presented in Table 7. As can be seen from the table, the

Example Question 85, 2015 Booklet

A 30-year-old man with peptic ulcer disease suddenly develops pain, redness, and swelling of his right first metatarsophalangeal joint. There is no history of injury. Serum uric acid concentration is 8 mg/dL. Examination of joint aspirate shows birefringent crystals.
Which of the following drugs is most appropriate to treat the acute symptoms in this patient?
(A) Allopurinol;
(B) Colchicine (correct answer)
(C) Morphine;
(D) Probenecid;
(E) Sulfinpyrazone

SIB Top 10	SIB Top 10 IR	RB_RN top 10	RB_RN top 10 IR	STY top 10	STY top 10 IR
Vinca alkaloid	Allopurinol*	Desacetylcolch.	Allopurinol*	Colchicoside	Probenecid*
Castanospermine	Probenecid*	Colchamine	Morphine*	Cornigerine	Indomethacin
Emetine	Opioid	Vinca alkaloid	Probenecid*	Vinblastine sulf.	Benemid
Probenecid*	Quinine	Thiocolchicoside	Indomethacin	Desacetylcolch.	Sulfinpyrazone*
Cyproheptadine	Dl-hyoscyam.	Desmethylphall.	Naproxen	Oncodazole	Gabexate Mesylate
Strychnine	Amitriptyline	O-methylandroc.	Sulfinpyrazone*	Lumicolchicine	Deltahydrocort.
Swainsonine	Cocaine	Isocolchicine	Uricosuric agent	VLB	Cholestyramine res.
Staurosporine	Emetine	Chelidonine	Methyl morphine	Oryzalin	Methotrexate
Paclitaxel	Hyoscine	Tropone	Opioid	Demecolcine	6-alpha-Methylp.
Aconitine	Nicotine	Paclitaxel	Quinine	Colchicine analog	Ursodeoxycholic Ac.

Table 7: Example of the Top 10 candidates suggested by various ontological relations and rankings for Question 85 from the 2015 booklet. Suggestions that also feature in the item are marked with *.

information-retrieval ranking improves the number of hits in all types of relations (SIB, RB_RN, and STY). It should be noted that the improvement we notice in this example is not as significant in other examples but the general trend is the same. The average improvement across of all items can be seen in Table 6.

6   Discussion

The results presented above indicate that best performance is achieved when combining the two approaches, namely generating distractors using concept embedding similarity to provide the initial list, and then using a re-ranking approach from information retrieval in order to improve the prediction. Using this combined approach, our system can hit around 1 in 5 distractors produced by the human-item writers when producing 20 candidates for each item. It should be noted that a random pick in the case of "predicting" distractors has a very low chance of being correct. For example, using the STY relation, a random 10 chosen distractor candidates for each item will probably produce *one* hit for the whole public dataset, and *two* hits for the whole private dataset. It is also worth noting that the proposed method does not rely on training data.

It was shown that the *STY* relation outperformed the *SIB* relation in the samples of top 20, top 50,

top 100 hits. The reason for this result is the ability of the *STY* relation to consider more candidates. Based on these results, we recommend the use of a broader ontology relation. Further to this, the results presented in Table 6 indicate that the longer the list of suggested ditractors, the smaller the return. As can be seen, the return diminishes when having a list of more than 20 suggested distractors.

One limitation of the current evaluation is the fact that it assumes that the distractors developed by the human item-writers are the best ones. As shown in the introduction section, this may not necessarily be the case since item-writers also find the selection of plausible distractors a challenging task. It is also quite possible that some of the automatically generated distractors are suitable enough even though they were not included as an item option and in this sense it is possible that our evaluation has been too conservative and that more distractor candidates are in fact feasible options. To address this we plan a future evaluation where human item-writers will be presented with a list of automatically generated distractors that they can choose from. An even longer term evaluation would be to assess the quality of the distractors by collecting data from examinees and using the item response theory (Embretson and Reise, 2013). Another limitation is that since we do not have control over the stem, we do not control for cases where a plausible distractor candidate may in fact be an alternative correct answer. To a certain extent this is mitigated by the condition that no synonyms of the correct answer can feature as distractors and that, ultimately, there would be a human item-writer who selects the most suitable distractors proposed by the system.

To the best of our knowledge, the experiments presented in this paper are the first fully automatic approach for distractor generation which relies on the combination between concept embeddings and IR. The benefit of this approach is not only its performance but that it can also be generalized to other domains where the distractors are concepts.

Directions for improvement include experimenting with different embedding vectors or ontological relations (such as RO (other relation) in UMLS). In addition, instead of using the whole stem as the query to search the text collection, one could break the stem into smaller components, and search using these components[11] Last but not least, the number of prediction hits could be enhanced through other machine learning models.

7   Conclusion

We presented an experiment for the automatic suggestions of distractors for multiple-choice questions given a question stem and the correct answer option. Our method was based on concept embeddings and re-ranking of the distractors candidates using an information retrieval approach. To evaluate the output, we compare the existing human-generated distractors and the automatic suggestions in two sets of items. The results indicate that the concept embeddings can correctly predict one in five possible distractors, which otherwise has a very low chance of being predicted randomly. Re-ranking of the candidates boosts the performance significantly, which shows that approaches from IR can contribute to the task of automatic distractor generation.

References

Tahani Alsubait, Bijan Parsia, and Uli Sattler. 2014. Generating multiple choice questions from ontologies: Lessons learnt. In *OWLED*, pages 73–84. Citeseer.

Tahani Alsubait, Bijan Parsia, and Ulrike Sattler. 2013. A similarity-based theory of controlling mcq difficulty. In *e-Learning and e-Technologies in Education (ICEEE), 2013 Second International Conference on*, pages 283–288. IEEE.

M Evelina Ascalon, Lawrence S Meyers, Bruce W Davis, and Niels Smits. 2007. Distractor similarity and item-stem structure: Effects on item difficulty. *Applied Measurement in Education*, 20(2):153–170.

Krista Breithaupt, Adelaide A Ariel, and Donovan R Hare. 2009. Assembling an inventory of multistage adaptive testing systems. In *Elements of adaptive testing*, pages 247–266. Springer.

Jonathan C Brown, Gwen A Frishkoff, and Maxine Eskenazi. 2005. Automatic question generation for vocabulary assessment. In *Proceedings of the conference on Human Language Technology and Empirical Methods in Natural Language Processing*, pages 819–826. Association for Computational Linguistics.

Susan M Case and David B Swanson. 2001. *Constructing written test questions for the basic and clinical sciences*. 3rd edition. National Board of Medical Examiners Philadelphia.

Susan E Embretson and Steven P Reise. 2013. *Item response theory*. Psychology Press.

Mark J Gierl, Okan Bulut, Qi Guo, and Xinxin Zhang. 2017. Developing, analyzing, and using distractors for multiple-choice tests in education: a comprehensive review. *Review of Educational Research*, 87(6):1082–1116.

Mark J Gierl, Hollis Lai, James B Hogan, and Donna Matovinovic. 2015. A method for generating educational test items that are aligned to the common core state standards. *Journal of Applied Testing Technology*, 16(1):1–18.

Mark J Gierl, Hollis Lai, Debra Pugh, Claire Touchie, André-Philippe Boulais, and André De Champlain. 2016. Evaluating the psychometric characteristics of generated multiple-choice test items. *Applied Measurement in Education*, 29(3):196–210.

Michael Heilman. 2011. *Automatic factual question generation from text*. Ph.D. thesis, Carnegie Mellon University.

Edmond Holohan, Mark Melia, Declan McMullen, and Claus Pahl. 2006. The generation of e-learning exercise problems from subject ontologies. In *Advanced Learning Technologies, 2006. Sixth International Conference on*, pages 967–969. IEEE.

Ayako Hoshino and Hiroshi Nakagawa. 2005. A real-time multiple-choice question generation for language testing: a preliminary study. In *Proceedings of the second workshop on Building Educational Applications Using NLP*, pages 17–20. Association for Computational Linguistics.

---

[11]In the case of our sets of items, the components could be "chief complaint, further history, significant positives, significant negatives, medical history, medications, physical examination, lab values".

Hollis Lai, Mark J Gierl, Claire Touchie, Debra Pugh, André-Philippe Boulais, and André De Champlain. 2016. Using automatic item generation to improve the quality of mcq distractors. *Teaching and learning in medicine*, 28(2):166–173.

Mukta Majumder and Sujan Kumar Saha. 2015. A system for generating multiple choice questions: With a novel approach for sentence selection. In *Proceedings of the 2nd Workshop on Natural Language Processing Techniques for Educational Applications*, pages 64–72.

Ruslan Mitkov and Le An Ha. 2003. Computer-aided generation of multiple-choice tests. In *Proceedings of the HLT-NAACL 03 workshop on Building educational applications using natural language processing-Volume 2*, pages 17–22. Association for Computational Linguistics.

Andreas Papasalouros, Konstantinos Kanaris, and Konstantinos Kotis. 2008. Automatic generation of multiple choice questions from domain ontologies. In *e-Learning*, pages 427–434. Citeseer.

Marie Tarrant, James Ware, and Ahmed M Mohammed. 2009. An assessment of functioning and non-functioning distractors in multiple-choice questions: a descriptive analysis. *BMC medical education*, 9(1):40.

Ellampallil Venugopal Vinu, Tahani Alsubait, and P Sreenivasa Kumar. 2016. Modeling of item-difficulty for ontology-based mcqs. *arXiv preprint arXiv:1607.00869*.

Ellampallil Venugopal Vinu and P Sreenivasa Kumar. 2015a. Improving large-scale assessment tests by ontology based approach. In *FLAIRS Conference*, page 457.

EV Vinu and Sreenivasa Kumar. 2015b. A novel approach to generate mcqs from domain ontology: Considering dl semantics and open-world assumption. *Web Semantics: Science, Services and Agents on the World Wide Web*, 34:40–54.

Zhiguo Yu, Byron Wallace, Todd Johnson, and Trevor Cohen. 2017. Retrofitting concept vector representations of medical concepts to improve estimates of semantic similarity and relatedness. In *Proceedings of MedInfo - World Congress on Medical and Health Informatics*, pages 657–661. International Medical Informatics Association.

Branko Žitko, Slavomir Stankov, Marko Rosić, and Ani Grubišić. 2009. Dynamic test generation over ontology-based knowledge representation in authoring shell. *Expert Systems with Applications*, 36(4):8185–8196.

Co-Attention Based Neural Network for Source-Dependent Essay Scoring

Haoran Zhang
Department of Computer Science
University of Pittsburgh
Pittsburgh, PA 15260
`colinzhang@cs.pitt.edu`

Diane Litman
Department of Computer Science & LRDC
University of Pittsburgh
Pittsburgh, PA 15260
`litman@cs.pitt.edu`

Abstract

This paper presents an investigation of using a co-attention based neural network for source-dependent essay scoring. We use a co-attention mechanism to help the model learn the importance of each part of the essay more accurately. Also, this paper shows that the co-attention based neural network model provides reliable score prediction of source-dependent responses. We evaluate our model on two source-dependent response corpora. Results show that our model outperforms the baseline on both corpora. We also show that the attention of the model is similar to the expert opinions with examples.

1 Introduction

Manually grading students' essays is labor intensive. Therefore, many automated essay scoring (AES) methods have been developed to support grading essays at scale. However, in different grading tasks, the information required by an AES system is different. For example, if a system needs to assign a holistic score to the essay, the system needs to take all information into account. In contrast, if a system needs to assign a score for one specific aspect of the essay (e.g. use of evidence), the system needs to ignore some information. Also, if an essay is a source-dependent essay, the system needs to exploit knowledge of the source article.

This paper focuses on source-dependent essay assessment. In this task, students read a source article before writing the essay, and assessment involves recognizing and analyzing references to the article in the essay. We propose a new type of co-attention based neural network model tailored to source-dependent grading, then use two source-dependent essay corpora to evaluate our model. Our first corpus contains the four source-dependent essay sets in the Automated Student Assessment Prize (ASAP) corpus[1]. The ASAP grading task is to assign a holistic score to each essay. The second corpus uses the Response to Text Assessment (RTA) (Correnti et al., 2013) to assess students' analytic writing skills. Instead of evaluating holistic writing skills, the RTA was designed to evaluate students' writing skills along five dimensions: Analysis, Evidence, Organization, Style, and MUGS (Mechanics, Usage, Grammar, and Spelling). Our grading task for this corpus is to assign an Evidence score to each essay, by evaluating students' ability to find and use evidence from a source article to support their claims.

The main contributions of this paper are as follows. First, we introduce a co-attention based neural network model that is fully automated and does not need any expert effort to encode knowledge of a source article. Second, our co-attention based neural network model extends prior work by designing the model to take a source article into account during grading. Third, we apply our model to the subset of source-dependent responses tasks in the ASAP corpus and show that the model outperforms a previous neural network model developed for the full corpus. Fourth, we show that our model also performs well on the RTA task and again significantly outperforms our baseline neural net model. Last, we use examples to show that our model can assign reasonable attention scores to different sentences in the essay.

In the following sections, we first present related research. Then we describe our tasks by introducing the ASAP corpus and the RTA corpus. Next, we explain the structure of our co-attention based neural network model. Finally, we discuss the results of our experiments and future plans.

---

[1] https://www.kaggle.com/c/asap-aes

Proceedings of the Thirteenth Workshop on Innovative Use of NLP for Building Educational Applications, pages 399–409
New Orleans, Louisiana, June 5, 2018. ©2018 Association for Computational Linguistics

2   Related Work

Previous research in AES needed feature engineering. In very early work, Page (1968) developed an AES tool named Project Essay Grade (PEG) by only using linguistic surface features. A more recent well-known AES system is E-Rater (Burstein et al., 1998), which employs many more natural language processing (NLP) technologies. Later, Attali and Burstein (2004) released E-Rater V2, where they created a new set of features to represent linguistic characteristic related to organization and development, lexical complexity, prompt-specific vocabulary usage, etc. Similarly to Page (1968), this system used regression equations for assessment of student essays. One limitation of all of the above models is that all need handcrafted features for training the model. In contrast, our model uses a neural network for the AES task and thus does not require feature engineering.

Recently, neural network models have been introduced into AES, making the development of handcrafted features unnecessary or at least optional. Alikaniotis et al. (2016) and Taghipour and Ng (2016) presented AES models that used Long Short Term Memory (LSTM) networks. Differently, Dong and Zhang (2016) used a Convolutional Neural Network (CNN) model for essay scoring by applying two CNN layers on both the word level and then sentence level. Later, Dong et al. (2017) presented another work that uses attention pooling to replace the mean over time pooling after the convolutional layer in both word level and sentence levels. However, none of these neural network grading models consider the source article if it exists. In this paper, we introduce a neural network model that takes the source article into account by using a co-attention mechanism instead of the self-attention mechanism of prior work.

Our work not only focuses on essay assessment using a holistic score, but also evaluates a particular dimension of argument-oriented writing skills, namely use of Evidence. Louis and Higgins (2010) analyze only the content of essays by detecting off-topic essays. Ong et al. (2014) used argumentation mining techniques to evaluate if students use enough evidence to support their positions. However, these two prior studies are not suitable for our task because they did not measure the use of content or evidence from a source article. With respect to source-based dimensional

essay analysis, Rahimi et al. (2014, 2017) developed a set of rubric-based features that compared a student's essay and a source article in terms of number of related words or paraphrases. Zhang and Litman (2017) improved their model by introducing word embedding into the feature extraction process to extract relationships previously missed due to lexical errors or use of different vocabulary. However, in both of these studies, human effort was still necessary for pre-processing the source article, for example, by having experts manually create a list of important words and phrases in the article which the system would compare with features extracted from the student's essay. In contrast, our work does not need any human effort to analyze the source article before essay grading. Although Rahimi and Litman (2016) investigated extracting example lists by using LDA (Blei et al., 2003) model, the data-driven model missed an example when there was no essay mentioning the example. Klebanov et al. (2014) predicted which parts of the source material were important and that students needed to use in their essays. The essay score is required to obtain the content importance for their work, but our work does not need to know the essay score while identifying the content importance.

3   Data

We use two different essay corpora in our experiments: source-based essays from the ASAP corpus, and source-based RTA essays. While the full ASAP corpus contains essays in response to 8 different prompts, we use only essays in response to the 4 source-dependent prompts. The gold standard ASAP assessment is a holistic score. In contrast, the gold standard assessment in the RTA corpus is an Evidence score. In particular, the assessment only considers how students use evidence from a source article to support their claims; the assessement thus ignores the lexical and syntactic mistakes made by students and the organization of the essay when assessing the evidence dimension.

3.1   ASAP

The Automated Student Assessment Prize (ASAP) corpus consists of written responses to 8 prompts. Among them, prompts 3, 4, 5, and 6 are source-dependent which means students read an article before writing their essays. Since the scores assigned to essays are holistic, assessment considers

Source Excerpt: My mother and father had come to this country with such courage, without any knowledge of the language or the culture. They came selflessly, as many immigrants do, to give their children a better life, even though it meant leaving behind their families, friends, and careers in the country they loved.

Essay Prompt: Describe the mood created by the author in the memoir. Support your answer with relevant and specific information from the memoir.

Figure 1: A source excerpt for ASAP Prompt 5.

the overall quality of the essay, not just a specific dimension. Figure 1 contains an excerpt from an ASAP source article and the associated Prompt 5.

Prompt	3	4	5	6
Score 0	39	311	24	44
	(2%)	(18%)	(1%)	(3%)
Score 1	607	636	302	167
	(35%)	(36%)	(17%)	(9%)
Score 2	657	570	649	405
	(38%)	(32%)	(36%)	(23%)
Score 3	423	253	572	817
	(25%)	(14%)	(32%)	(45%)
Score 4	NA	NA	258	367
			(14%)	(20%)
Total	1726	1770	1805	1800

Table 1: The holistic score distribution of ASAP.

In this paper, we only focus on prompts 3, 4, 5, and 6 (denoted by $ASAP_3$, $ASAP_4$, $ASAP_5$, and $ASAP_6$ respectively), because they are source-dependent responses. In ASAP, different prompts have different score ranges. The score range of $ASAP_3$ and $ASAP_4$ is 0 to 3, while the range of $ASAP_5$ and $ASAP_6$ is 0 to 4. Figure 2 shows an excerpt of an essay with score of 4 for $ASAP_5$. The score distribution is shown in Table 1.

3.2 RTA

The RTA corpora were collected from upper elementary level students, as described by Correnti et al. (2013). There are two forms of RTA based on different articles that students read before writing essays. The first article is from *Time for Kids*

Essay Excerpt: The author of the memoir, Narciso Rodriguez creates a caring, happy, and thoughtful mood. By mentioning the Cuban traditions shared in the neighborhood between close friends, and cooking in the kitchen to share a great meal with one another the mood is happy. When Narciso talks about the great friends he made from different heritages and knowing the entire community like family the mood is thoughtful and caring because it shows that the people really appreciated each other's company...

Figure 2: Excerpt of an essay with score of 4 for ASAP Prompt 5.

about the Millennium Villages Project, an effort by the United Nations to end poverty in a rural village in Sauri, Kenya; we refer to it as RTA_{MVP}. The other article talks about the importance of space exploration; we refer to refer it as RTA_{Space}. Figure 3 shows an excerpt from the RTA_{MVP} article and the associated essay writing prompt. Bolded text spans in the article excerpt are pieces of evidence that our experts (School of Education RTA team members) manually labeled as being important for students to include in their essays.

Source Excerpt: Today, Yala Sub-District **Hospital has medicine, free of charge, for all of the most common diseases. Water is connected to the hospital**, which also has a **generator for electricity. Bed nets are used** in every sleeping site in Sauri...

Essay Prompt: The author provided one specific example of how the quality of life can be improved by the Millennium Villages Project in Sauri, Kenya. Based on the article, did the author provide a convincing argument that winning the fight against poverty is achievable in our lifetime? Explain why or why not with 3-4 examples from the text to support your answer.

Figure 3: A source excerpt for the RTA_{MVP} prompt.

Evidence usage in each RTA essay was scored

on a scale of 1 to 4 (low to high). The distribution of Evidence scores is shown in Table 2. Figure 4 shows a student essay with a score of 3. Our experts manually bolded all pieces of evidence found in this essay.

> **Essay:** In my opinion I think that they will **achieve it in lifetime**. During the years threw **2004 and 2008 they made progress**. People didnt have the money to buy the stuff in 2004. **The hospital was packed with patients** and they didnt have alot of treatment in 2004. In 2008 it changed the **hospital had medicine, free of charge**, and **for all the common dieases**. **Water was connected to the hospital** and has a **generator for electricity**. **Everybody has net** in their site. **The hunger crisis has been addressed** with **fertilizer and seeds**, as well as the **tools needed to maintain the food**. **The school has no fees** and **they serve lunch**. To me thats sounds like it is going achieve it in the lifetime.

Figure 4: A RTA_{MVP} essay with score of 3.

Prompt	RTA_{MVP}	RTA_{Space}
Score 1	852	538
	(29%)	(26%)
Score 2	1197	789
	(40%)	(38%)
Score 3	616	512
	(21%)	(25%)
Score 4	305	237
	(10%)	(11%)
Total	2970	2076

Table 2: The Evidence score distribution of RTA.

4 Model

Our network is inspired by the hierarchical neural network model presented by Dong et al. (2017). In their model, they considered each essay as a sequence of sentences rather than a sequence of words. Their model has three parts. First, they used a convolutional layer and attention pooling layer to get sentence representation. Second, they used an LSTM layer and another attention pooling layer for document representation. Finally, they used a sigmoid layer for score prediction.

Differently from their model, our model replaces the attention pooling layer for document representation with a bi-directional attention flow layer and an additional modeling layer (Seo et al., 2017). By doing so, our model considers students' essays associated with a source article and this attention mechanism captures the relationship between the essay and the source article. In particular, a higher attention score will be assigned to sentences that are mentioned in the article but less mentioned in other essays. Our model is a hierarchical neural network and consists of seven layers. Figure 5 shows the structure of our network. The layers in the dashed box were presented by Dong et al. (2017). The sentence level co-attention layer was presented by Seo et al. (2017).

4.1 Word Embedding Layer

This layer maps each word in sentences to a high dimension vector. We use the GloVe pre-trained word embeddings (Pennington et al., 2014) to obtain the word embedding vector for each word. It was trained on 6 billion words from Wikipedia 2014 and Gigaword 5. It has 400,000 uncased vocabulary items. The dimensionality of GloVe in our model is 50 dimensions. The outputs of this layer are two matrices, $L_E \in \mathbb{R}^{S_e \times W_e \times d_L}$ for the essay and $L_A \in \mathbb{R}^{S_a \times W_a \times d_L}$ for the article, where S_e, S_a, W_e, W_a, and d_L are number of sentences of the essay and the article, length of sentences of the essay and the article, and the embedding size, respectively. Same to Dong et al. (2017), a dropout is applied after the word embedding layer.

4.2 Word Level Convolutional Layer

In this layer, we perform 1D convolution over the word representations of both L_E and L_A, so that we can get local representation of each sentence. For each word w_i in each sentence, we perform 1D convolution:

$$p_i = g([w_i : w_{i+k-1}] \cdot U_p + b_p) \tag{1}$$

where g is a nonlinear activation, k is the kernel size, U_p is the filter weight matrix, and b_p is the bias vector. The outputs of this layer are $C_e \in \mathbb{R}^{S_e \times P_e \times d_C}$ for the essay and $C_a \in \mathbb{R}^{S_a \times P_a \times d_C}$ for the article, where P_e and P_a are filtered lengths of sentences of the essay and the article, respectively. d_C is the number of filters of the 1D convolution layer.

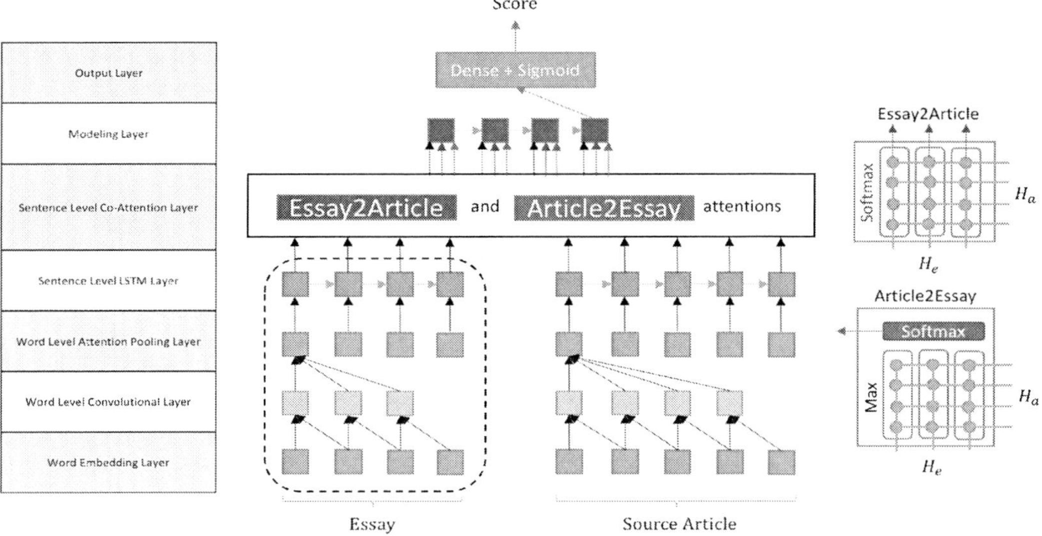

Figure 5: The Co-Attention Based Neural Network Structure.

4.3 Word Level Attention Pooling Layer

After the convolutional layer, a pooling layer is demanded to obtain the sentence representations. In this layer, we follow the same design presented by Dong et al. (2017). The attention pooling is defined as equations below:

$$m_i = tanh(U_m \cdot p_i + b_m) \quad (2)$$

$$v_i = \frac{e^{u_v \cdot m_i}}{\sum e^{u_v \cdot m_j}} \quad (3)$$

$$s = \sum v_i p_i \quad (4)$$

where U_m, u_v and b_m are weight matrix, vector, and bias vector, respectively. m_i and v_i are attention vector and attention weight for p_i. The outputs of this layer are $A_e \in \mathbb{R}^{S_e \times d_C}$ for the essay and $A_a \in \mathbb{R}^{S_a \times d_C}$ for the article.

4.4 Sentence Level LSTM Layer

In this layer, we use a Long Short-Term Memory Network (LSTM) (Hochreiter and Schmidhuber, 1997) over the sentence representations of the essay and the article to capture contextual evidence from previous sentences to refine the sentence representation.

The LSTM unit is a special kind of RNN unit which has long-term dependency learning ability. LSTMs use three gates to control information flow to avoid the long-term dependency problem by forgetting or remembering information in each LSTM unit. They are an input gate, a forget gate, and an output gate. The following equations define the LSTM unit:

$$f_t = \sigma(W_f \cdot [h_{t-1}, s_t] + b_f) \quad (5)$$

$$i_t = \sigma(W_i \cdot [h_{t-1}, s_t] + b_i) \quad (6)$$

$$\tilde{c}_t = tanh(W_c \cdot [h_{t-1}, s_t] + b_c) \quad (7)$$

$$c_t = f_t * c_{t-1} + i_t * \tilde{c}_t \quad (8)$$

$$o_t = \sigma(W_o \cdot [h_{t-1}, s_t] + b_o) \quad (9)$$

$$h_t = o_t * tanh(c_t) \quad (10)$$

where s_t and h_t are the input sentence and the output state of time t, respectively. W_f, W_i, W_c, and W_o are weight matrices. b_f, b_i, b_c, and b_o are bias vectors. σ is the sigmoid function, and $*$ is element-wise multiplication. The output of this layer are $H_e \in \mathbb{R}^{S_e \times d_H}$ for the essay and $H_a \in \mathbb{R}^{S_a \times d_H}$ for the article, where d_H is the dimensionality of the output.

4.5 Sentence Level Co-Attention Layer

The concept of this layer is presented by Seo et al. (2017) in the part of attention flow layer. This layer links information from H_e and H_a, and generates a collection of article aware features vector of essay sentences. The attention is computed in two directions, from essay to article, and vice versa. Both attention scores are figured from a similarity matrix by the following equation:

$$Sim = W_{sim}^T \cdot [he_t; ha_j; ha_t * ha_j^T] + b_{sim} \quad (11)$$

where W_{sim} is weight matrix, he_t and ha_j are t_{th} row vector of H_e and j_{th} row vector of H_a, b_{sim} is bias vector. $*$ is element-wise multiplication. $[;]$ is vector concatenation. After obtaining the similarity matrix $Sim \in \mathbb{R}^{S_e \times S_a}$, we compute the attention in two directions.

Essay to Article Attention measures which sentences in the article are similar to each sentence in students' essays. The following equations define the essay to article attention:

$$a_{ea} = softmax(Sim) \tag{12}$$

$$\tilde{H}_a = a_{ea}H_a \tag{13}$$

where $a_{ea} \in \mathbb{R}^{S_e \times S_a}$ represents the attention score of each sentence in the article associate with each sentence in the essay, $softmax$ is performed across each row. The output of this $\tilde{H}_a \in \mathbb{R}^{S_e \times d_H}$.

Article to Essay Attention measures which sentences in the essay have the closest meaning to one of the sentences in the article. The following equations define the article to essay attention:

$$a_{ae} = softmax(max_{col}(Sim)) \tag{14}$$

$$\tilde{h}_e = a_{ae}^T H_e \tag{15}$$

where $a_{ae} \in \mathbb{R}^{S_e}$, max_{col} is a maximum function performed across the column, and $\tilde{h}_e \in \mathbb{R}^{d_H}$. Because max_{col} will find out which sentence in the article has the closest meaning to each sentence in the essay, so $\tilde{h}_e$ represents the attention score of the most important sentence in the essay associated with the article. After tiling S_e times, the final output of this layer is $\tilde{H}_e \in \mathbb{R}^{S_e \times d_H}$.

The final output G is a concatenated matrix of H_e, $\tilde{H}_e$, and $\tilde{H}_a$ defined by:

$$G = [H_e; \tilde{H}_a; H_e * \tilde{H}_a; H_e * \tilde{H}_e] \tag{16}$$

where $*$ is element-wise multiplication, and $[;]$ is concatenation, H_e is the original representation of essay, $\tilde{H}_a$ is the essay to article attention, $H_e * \tilde{H}_a$ is the self-aware representation, and $H_e * \tilde{H}_e$ is article-aware representation. Therefore, the output of this layer is $G \in \mathbb{R}^{S_e \times 4d_H}$, the article-aware representation of each sentence in the essay.

4.6 Modeling Layer

G is the representation of each sentence, and we need the representation of the essay. Therefore, we introduce another LSTM layer for modeling the essay and only use the output of the final LSTM unit as the output of this layer $M \in \mathbb{R}^{d_M}$, where d_M is the dimensionality of the output of LSTM units.

4.7 Output Layer

After obtaining the essay representation M, a linear layer with sigmoid activation will predict the final output. The following equation defines the output layer:

$$y = sigmoid(W_o M + b_o) \tag{17}$$

where W_o is weight vector, and b_o is bias vector. y is the final predicted score of the essay.

5 Training

Loss. Dong et al. (2017) used mean squared error (MSE) loss, thus we use the same loss function. MSE evaluates the average of squared error between the predicted score and the gold standard. Thus it is widely used in regression tasks. The following equation defines MSE:

$$mse(y, y') = \frac{1}{N} \sum_{i=1}^{N} (y_i - y_i')^2 \tag{18}$$

where y_i is the predicted score, y_i' is the gold standard, N it the total number of samples.

Optimization. The optimizer we use is RMSprop (Dauphin et al., 2015). The initial learning rate is 0.001, momentum is 0.9, and Dropout rate is 0.5 for preventing overfitting. These setting are the same as used by Dong et al. (2017).

6 Experimental Setup

We configure experiments to test three hypotheses:

H1: the model we proposed (denoted by CO-ATTN) will outperform or at least perform equally well as the baseline (denoted by SELF-ATTN) presented by Dong et al. (2017) on four ASAP essay corpora in the holistic score prediction task.

H2: the model we proposed will outperform or at least perform equally well as the baseline on two RTA corpora in the Evidence score prediction task.

H3: the model we proposed will outperform or at least perform equally well as the non-neural network baselines on both corpora.

We use NLTK (Bird et al., 2009) for text preprocessing. The vocabulary size of the data is limited to 4000, and all scores are scaled to the range [0, 1], following Taghipour and Ng (2016) and Dong et al. (2017). In particular, the 4000 most frequent words are preserved, with all other words treated as unknowns. The assessment scores will be converted back to their original range during evaluation. We use Quadratic Weighted Kappa (QWK) to evaluate our model. QWK is not only the official criteria of ASAP corpus, but also adopted as evaluation metric in Rahimi et al. (2014); Taghipour and Ng (2016); Dong et al. (2017); Rahimi et al. (2017); Zhang and Litman (2017) for both ASAP and RTA corpora.

We use 5-fold cross-validation because both RTA and ASAP corpora have no released labeled test data. We split all corpora into 5 folds. For the ASAP corpus, the partition is the same as the setting presented by Taghipour and Ng (2016). For the RTA corpus, since there is no prior work to split the corpus, we separate it into 5 folds randomly. In each fold, 60% of the data are used for training, 20% of the data are the development set, and 20% of the data are used for testing.

To select the best model, we trained each model on 100 epochs and evaluated on the development set after each epoch. The best model is the model with the best QWK on the development set. This is done five times, once for each partition in the cross-validation. Then the average QWK score from these five evaluations on the test set is reported. Paired t-tests are used for significance tests with $p < 0.05$. Table 3 shows all hyper-parameters for training.

The code of SELF-ATTN are provided by Dong et al. (2017), they used Keras (Chollet et al., 2015) 1.1.1 and Theano (Theano Development Team, 2016) 0.8.2 as the backend. Because we are using Keras 2.1.3 and TensorFlow (Abadi et al., 2015) 1.4.0 as the backend, we ran all experiments with our frameworks. Therefore, the numbers of SELF-ATTN have small differences to the numbers reported by the baseline model.

For non-neural network baselines, we introduce the SVR and BLRR baselines presented by Phandi et al. (2015) for the ASAP corpus, and SG baseline presented by Zhang and Litman (2017) for the RTA corpus.

SVR and BLRR models use Enhanced AI Scoring Engine (EASE)[2] to extract four types of features, such as length, part of speech, prompt, and the bag of words. Then they use SVR and BLRR as the classifiers, respectively. We do not perform

any significance test on both SVR and BLRR because we do not have detailed experiment data. Therefore, we only report the result presented in Phandi et al. (2015).

SG model extracts evidence features based on hand-crafted topic and example lists, and uses random forest tree as the classifier. We follow the same data partition. However, we only use the training set for training and the testing set for testing while ignoring the development set so that we can perform the same paired t-tests in the experiments.

Layer	Parameter Name	Value
Embedding	Embedding dimension	50
Word-CNN	Kernel size	5
	Number of filters	100
Sent-LSTM	Hidden units	100
Modeling	Hidden units	100
Dropout	Dropout rate	0.5
Others	Epochs	100
	Batch size	100
	Initial learning rate	0.001
	Momentum	0.9

Table 3: Hyper-parameters of training.

7 Results

We first examine H1. The results shown in Table 4 support this hypothesis. The CO-ATTN model yields higher performance than the SELF-ATTN model on all ASAP prompts. However, the CO-ATTN model only significantly outperforms the SELF-ATTN model on Prompt 3.

Second, we examine H2. Again, the results shown in Table 4 support this hypothesis. The CO-ATTN model yields higher performance than the SELF-ATTN model, significantly on both of the RTA corpora.

Last, we examine H3. The results shown in Table 4 still support this hypothesis. The CO-ATTN model yields higher performance than all non-neural network baselines.

The results show that in our tasks, the neural network approaches are better than non-neural network baselines. One possible reason is the final representation of the essay from neural network contains more information. However, some of the information might be ignored by hand-crafted features. For example, the importance of different evidence in RTA task is not considered in the SG

Prompts	SVR	BLRR	SG	SELF-ATTN	CO-ATTN
RTA_{MVP}	NA	NA	0.653	0.701†	**0.718∗†**
RTA_{Space}	NA	NA	0.632	0.690†	**0.702∗†**
$ASAP_3$	0.630	0.621	NA	0.677	**0.697∗**
$ASAP_4$	0.749	0.784	NA	0.807	**0.809**
$ASAP_5$	0.782	0.784	NA	0.806	**0.815**
$ASAP_6$	0.771	0.775	NA	0.809	**0.812**

Table 4: The performance (QWK) of the baselines and our model. ∗ indicates that the model QWK is significantly better than the SELF-ATTN ($p < 0.05$). † indicates that the model QWK is significantly better than the SG ($p < 0.05$). The best results in each row are in bold.

model. It treats all evidence equally. However, the neural network models capture this information automatically.

Apparently, the CO-ATTN model performs better in the RTA tasks, because it always significantly outperforms the SELF-ATTN model. One possible reason is that the RTA task only considers the Evidence score. The CO-ATTN model is more suitable for the Evidence score prediction task because it can find pieces of evidence that appear in both students' essays and the source article better. In contrast, the SELF-ATTN model only considers students' essays associated with the scores. In this case, if a piece of evidence is not mentioned by students, this data-driven model cannot distinguish it. Consequently, some important pieces of evidence will be assigned to a lower weight. However, the CO-ATTN model considers not only the students' essays but also the source article. In other words, if an important piece of evidence is not mentioned by too many students, but it is in the source article, the CO-ATTN model will assign this sentence higher attention.

In the ASAP holistic score prediction task, although we still see a benefit in using the CO-ATTN model, it is reduced. In this case, the benefit we saw in the Evidence dimension from the CO-ATTN model becomes less significant because the model also needs to consider more aspects of the essay, such as organization, grammar mistakes, and so on. Our results suggest that the co-attention mechanism of the CO-ATTN model cannot capture these aspects significantly better than the SELF-ATTN model. Therefore, the CO-ATTN model only significantly outperforms the SELF-ATTN model on Prompt 3.

8 Discussion

In Table 5, we list 10 sentences from student RTA_{MVP} essays and their associated attention scores. Because we have a list of examples manually extracted by our experts as important evidence from the RTA_{MVP} source article, examining RTA data helps us understand the attention score assigned by our model. Bolded are examples extracted by the expert from the source article that the student includes in the essay. A lower attention score means this sentence is less important. Otherwise, the score is high. As we can see, sentences 1, 2, 3, and 4 are low attention sentences, sentences 5, 6, and 7 are mid attention sentences, and sentences 8, 9, and 10 are high attention sentences. The attention scores reflect the importance of these sentences accurately.

Sentence 1 is a short and general sentence related to the source article, but it has no specific evidence from it. Sentence 2 even has no content related to the source article. Sentence 3 has many details related to the source article. However, it still has no evidence directly from the source article. Sentence 4 mentions *"The author did convince me that winning the fight against poverty is achievable in our lifetime"* which comes from both the prompt and the source article, but this statement is so general that almost every student mentions this statement in the essay which makes this statement not distinguishable. For these reasons, these four sentences receive low attention scores.

Although sentence 5 is short, it mentions one piece of evidence. Sentence 6 talks about farming which is a topic from the source article. In the article, the things listed in this sentence are things the farmer needs to worry about. However, this sentence indicates *"the farmer don't have to worry"* because of the MVP project. Sentence 7 also mentions conditions of hospitals nowadays.

However, it mentions not only water but also electricity which is more than Sentence 5. For these reasons, these three sentences receive mid attention scores from low to high.

The last three sentences receive high attention scores because they all use more pieces of evidence directly from the source article. Sentence 8 talks about the school, and Sentence 9 talks about the hospital. Sentence 10 talks about farming. However, sentence 10 receives the highest attention score, because it mentions evidence from both before and after the MVP project.

No.	Sentences	Attention
1	Life in Kenya is hard.	0.00173
2	In this essay I will give my top 3 reasons why.	0.00174
3	Because like I said, we have more advanced & better & more qualified materials than them, and these days kids & adults are spoiled, we have phones stores, houses & even shoes and clothes.	0.00243
4	The author did **convince me that winning the fight against poverty is achievable in our lifetime** because she showed me how many people in Sauri, Kenya need our help against poverty.	0.00229
5	**Water is connected to the hospitals.**	0.02936
6	So the farmer don't have to worry all the time that him or his **family won't have enough food** to eat and the farmer have to worry that their kids will get hungry and then sick.	0.05580
7	**The hospital aslo has water and electricity.**	0.07746
8	Also, there were **no school fees**, and **the school now serves lunch** for the students because they **didn't have any midday meals** to provide them with **energy they need** to help them with the rest of their days.	0.19483
9	In 2008 though, when they **checked for progress, the hospital had medicine, free of charge**, with **running water and electricty**.	0.20177
10	Also **farmers could not afford fertilizer and irrigation** but now **they placed irrigation** and have them **fertilizer for the crops**.	0.25855

Table 5: Example attention scores of essay sentences.

From these sentences, we can also see that the attention score depends on neither the length of the sentence nor only the specificity of the sentence. It instead depends on how many important pieces of evidence there are in the sentence. For example, Sentence 3 is long and talks about some details of our modern life. Although it also talks about quality materials or better housing and clothing compared to people living in Kenya, it receives a low attention score because there is no specific evidence directly from the source article. In contrast, Sentence 9 is shorter than Sentence 3. However, it receives a higher attention score because it mentions many pieces of evidence from the source article.

Overall, the CO-ATTN model seems to capture the importance of sentences by assigning reasonable attention scores based on the relevance of the sentence to the source article.

9 Conclusion and Future Work

In this paper, we presented a co-attention based neural network model that outperforms a state of the art attention based neural network model for essay scoring, not only for RTA Evidence assessment but also for holistic assessment of ASAP source-dependent responses. Advantages of our model are that it does not need any expert preprocessing of the source article; the input of this model is only the raw student essay and its source article. Moreover, our model somewhat captures the importance of different pieces of evidence, although it is not specifically designed for this purpose. However, quantitative experiments that can answer whether the attention scores are correlated to the importance of different pieces of evidence need to be done. Also, this leads to an interesting future investigation, development of a neural network approach that both has an acceptable score prediction, and can simultaneously generate evidence lists from the source article. Another interesting future investigation could be examining the ability of this model to generalize to a new prompt.

Acknowledgments

We would like to show our appreciation to Tazin Afrin and Luca Lugini for their comments on an earlier version of the paper. We are also immensely grateful to every member of the RTA group for sharing their pearls of wisdom with us.

The research reported here was supported, in whole or in part, by the Institute of Education Sciences, U.S. Department of Education, through Grant R305A160245 to the University of Pittsburgh. The opinions expressed are those of the authors and do not represent the views of the Institute or the U.S. Department of Education.

References

Martín Abadi, Ashish Agarwal, Paul Barham, Eugene Brevdo, Zhifeng Chen, Craig Citro, Greg S. Corrado, Andy Davis, Jeffrey Dean, Matthieu Devin, Sanjay Ghemawat, Ian Goodfellow, Andrew Harp, Geoffrey Irving, Michael Isard, Yangqing Jia, Rafal Jozefowicz, Lukasz Kaiser, Manjunath Kudlur, Josh Levenberg, Dandelion Mané, Rajat Monga, Sherry Moore, Derek Murray, Chris Olah, Mike Schuster, Jonathon Shlens, Benoit Steiner, Ilya Sutskever, Kunal Talwar, Paul Tucker, Vincent Vanhoucke, Vijay Vasudevan, Fernanda Viégas, Oriol Vinyals, Pete Warden, Martin Wattenberg, Martin Wicke, Yuan Yu, and Xiaoqiang Zheng. 2015. TensorFlow: Large-scale machine learning on heterogeneous systems. Software available from tensorflow.org.

Dimitrios Alikaniotis, Helen Yannakoudakis, and Marek Rei. 2016. Automatic text scoring using neural networks. In *Proceedings of the 54th Annual Meeting of the Association for Computational Linguistics (Volume 1: Long Papers)*, volume 1, pages 715–725.

Yigal Attali and Jill Burstein. 2004. Automated essay scoring with e-rater® v. 2.0. *ETS Research Report Series*, 2004(2).

Steven Bird, Ewan Klein, and Edward Loper. 2009. *Natural language processing with Python: analyzing text with the natural language toolkit.* ” O’Reilly Media, Inc.”.

David M Blei, Andrew Y Ng, and Michael I Jordan. 2003. Latent dirichlet allocation. *Journal of machine Learning research*, 3(Jan):993–1022.

Jill Burstein, Karen Kukich, Susanne Wolff, Chi Lu, Martin Chodorow, Lisa Braden-Harder, and Mary Dee Harris. 1998. Automated scoring using a hybrid feature identification technique. In *Proceedings of the 17th international conference on Computational linguistics-Volume 1*, pages 206–210. Association for Computational Linguistics.

François Chollet et al. 2015. Keras. https://keras.io.

Richard Correnti, Lindsay Clare Matsumura, Laura Hamilton, and Elaine Wang. 2013. Assessing students’ skills at writing analytically in response to texts. *The Elementary School Journal*, 114(2):142–177.

Yann Dauphin, Harm de Vries, and Yoshua Bengio. 2015. Equilibrated adaptive learning rates for non-convex optimization. In *Advances in neural information processing systems*, pages 1504–1512.

Fei Dong and Yue Zhang. 2016. Automatic features for essay scoring–an empirical study. In *Proceedings of the 2016 Conference on Empirical Methods in Natural Language Processing*, pages 1072–1077.

Fei Dong, Yue Zhang, and Jie Yang. 2017. Attention-based recurrent convolutional neural network for automatic essay scoring. In *Proceedings of the 21st Conference on Computational Natural Language Learning (CoNLL 2017)*, pages 153–162.

Sepp Hochreiter and Jürgen Schmidhuber. 1997. Long short-term memory. *Neural computation*, 9(8):1735–1780.

Beata Beigman Klebanov, Nitin Madnani, Jill Burstein, and Swapna Somasundaran. 2014. Content importance models for scoring writing from sources. In *Proceedings of the 52nd Annual Meeting of the Association for Computational Linguistics (Volume 2: Short Papers)*, volume 2, pages 247–252.

Annie Louis and Derrick Higgins. 2010. Off-topic essay detection using short prompt texts. In *Proceedings of the NAACL HLT 2010 Fifth Workshop on Innovative Use of NLP for Building Educational Applications*, pages 92–95. Association for Computational Linguistics.

Nathan Ong, Diane Litman, and Alexandra Brusilovsky. 2014. Ontology-based argument mining and automatic essay scoring. In *Proceedings of the First Workshop on Argumentation Mining*, pages 24–28.

Ellis B Page. 1968. The use of the computer in analyzing student essays. *International review of education*, 14(2):210–225.

Jeffrey Pennington, Richard Socher, and Christopher D. Manning. 2014. Glove: Global vectors for word representation. In *Empirical Methods in Natural Language Processing (EMNLP)*, pages 1532–1543.

Peter Phandi, Kian Ming A Chai, and Hwee Tou Ng. 2015. Flexible domain adaptation for automated essay scoring using correlated linear regression. In *Proceedings of the 2015 Conference on Empirical Methods in Natural Language Processing*, pages 431–439.

Zahra Rahimi and Diane Litman. 2016. Automatically extracting topical components for a response-to-text writing assessment. In *Proceedings of the 11th Workshop on Innovative Use of NLP for Building Educational Applications*, pages 277–282.

Zahra Rahimi, Diane Litman, Richard Correnti, Elaine Wang, and Lindsay Clare Matsumura. 2017. Assessing students use of evidence and organization in response-to-text writing: Using natural language processing for rubric-based automated scoring. *International Journal of Artificial Intelligence in Education*, pages 1–35.

Zahra Rahimi, Diane J Litman, Richard Correnti, Lindsay Clare Matsumura, Elaine Wang, and Zahid Kisa. 2014. Automatic scoring of an analytical response-to-text assessment. In *International Conference on Intelligent Tutoring Systems*, pages 601–610. Springer.

Minjoon Seo, Aniruddha Kembhavi, Ali Farhadi, and
Hannaneh Hajishirzi. 2017. Bidirectional attention
flow for machine comprehension. In *Proceedings of
the International Conference on Learning Representations (ICLR)*.

Kaveh Taghipour and Hwee Tou Ng. 2016. A neural
approach to automated essay scoring. In *Proceedings of the 2016 Conference on Empirical Methods
in Natural Language Processing*, pages 1882–1891.

Theano Development Team. 2016. Theano: A Python
framework for fast computation of mathematical expressions. *arXiv e-prints*, abs/1605.02688.

Haoran Zhang and Diane Litman. 2017. Word embedding for response-to-text assessment of evidence. In
*Proceedings of ACL 2017, Student Research Work-
shop*, pages 75–81.

Cross-Lingual Content Scoring

Andrea Horbach, Sebastian Stennmanns, Torsten Zesch
Language Technology Lab, Department of Computer Science and Applied Cognitive Science,
University of Duisburg-Essen, Germany
{andrea.horbach|torsten.zesch}@uni-due.de
sebastian.stennmanns@stud.uni-due.de

Abstract

We investigate the feasibility of cross-lingual content scoring, a scenario where training and test data in an automatic scoring task are from two different languages. Cross-lingual scoring can contribute to educational equality by allowing answers in multiple languages. Training a model in one language and applying it to another language might also help to overcome data sparsity issues by re-using trained models from other languages. As there is no suitable dataset available for this new task, we create a comparable bi-lingual corpus by extending the English ASAP dataset with German answers. Our experiments with cross-lingual scoring based on machine-translating either training or test data show a considerable drop in scoring quality.

1 Introduction

Automatically scoring the content of student answers is a well-established research field (see, e.g., Sukkarieh and Blackmore (2009); Ziai et al. (2012); Higgins et al. (2014)). However, content scoring is usually restricted to training a model on labeled answers in one language and then applying it to unseen student answers in the same language. In this paper, we examine how well the scoring models transfer when being applied cross-lingually, i.e., whether data in one language can be used for training a model to score data in another language.

The motivation for our study is two-fold: First, cross-lingual scoring can contribute to **educational equality**. In a realistic educational setting, scores assigned to an answer given in the language of instruction can discriminate against non-native students who might conceptually understand the topic in question, but are unable to express their understanding in that language. One solution to this problem could be that students are allowed

to answer a question in a language they are proficient in. As only the content matters, the form, including the language, is unimportant. Such a setting would of course require that a teacher scoring an item is also proficient in the language used by the student, which would still restrict the available language options for the student. In such a scenario, automatic scoring of answers in different languages can help to treat students equally.

Second, cross-lingual scoring can help to **overcome data sparsity**. Existing short-answer datasets have mainly been collected in English. If a researcher or practitioner wants to work on a different language, little annotated data is available. Cross-lingual approaches can help in such a scenario to re-use trained models from different languages or to combine data from several languages to train a new model.

In our study, we investigate whether cross-lingual scoring is possible using state-of-the-art machine translation techniques. We translate either training or test data from one language to another, such that both training and test data are available in the same language. We then build prompt-specific models for each prompt and compare the performance to a monolingual approach. Figure 1 illustrates the different approaches.

It is likely that machine translation will negatively impact scoring quality due to translation errors. Additionally, student answers often contain language errors that might further decrease translation quality. However, translation might also have a positive effect on automatic scoring in case of typos being corrected during translation (e.g. *seperate* correctly translated as *getrennt*).

Datasets in more than one language might also differ depending on different teaching or learning traditions in the environments where they are collected, so that a new dataset collection has to be carefully planned to control such influence factors.

Proceedings of the Thirteenth Workshop on Innovative Use of NLP for Building Educational Applications, pages 410–419
New Orleans, Louisiana, June 5, 2018. ©2018 Association for Computational Linguistics

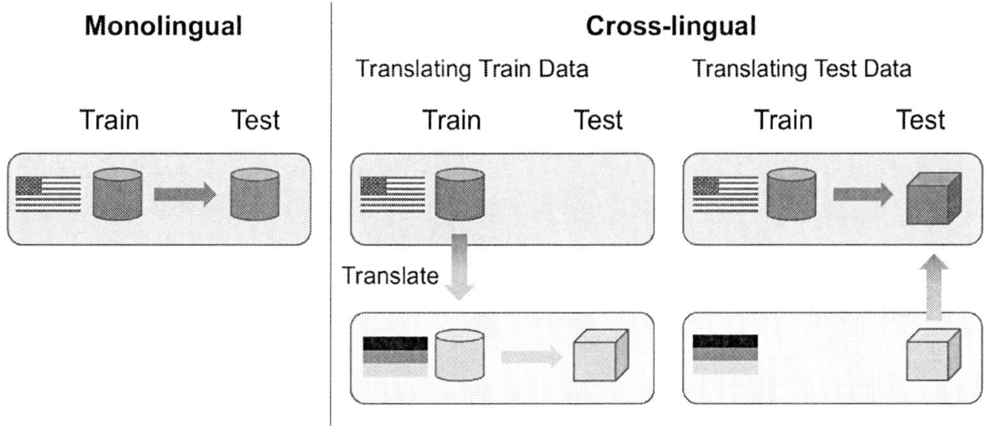

Figure 1: Monolingual vs. cross-lingual scoring

To the best of our knowledge, we are the first to investigate the feasibility of cross-lingual scoring. As our approach relies heavily on the availability of machine-translation methods, we also assess whether state-of-the-art machine translation methods perform well enough to be used in automatic scoring. To evaluate cross-lingual scoring in a realistic scenario, we collect and release a new dataset ASAP-DE that consists of three prompts from the ASAP corpus for which we collect answers in German.[1] In our experiments, we find that cross-lingual scoring using machine-translation is feasible, but –unsurprisingly– at the cost of a decrease in performance. Preliminary analyses showed that his performance drop varies across prompts and is only in part due to artifacts of machine translation, but it rather results from differences between the two datasets involved.

2 Pilot Study

Machine translation nowadays has good quality in general, but we need to assess its performance with respect to the language used in content scoring datasets. In contrast to standard newspaper data, answers in such datasets have been written by non-professional writers, so they may contain typos and ungrammaticalities. These datasets can thus be harder to translate than newspaper text.

To examine the impact of these issues, we conduct monolingual scoring experiments with the English ASAP dataset. We translate both the training and the test section of the ASAP data into a dif-

ferent language and build and train a model in that language. For the moment, we do not change the score an answer receives after translation because we assume that translating an answer preserves its meaning. We will revisit this issue later.

We automatically translate the English ASAP dataset using two different translation frameworks: Google Translate API[2] and DeepL[3]. As target languages, we use German as a closely related language and Russian as a more distantly related language. Table 2 shows the results of a state-of-the-art scoring system applied in this setting measured as quadratically weighted kappa.. We can see that there is a performance drop when translating to a different language, but that the change is within a reasonable margin, such that we can assume that machine translation is good enough for our purposes. We select Google Translate for all further experiments in this paper, as it produces on average better results than DeepL.

Influence of Spelling Errors Translating misspelled words is especially challenging, and we expect two different types of influence on the results. There could be a normalizing effect when wrong forms are translated into correct ones, or a noise-introducing effect when a wrong form from one language leaks into the other. We observe both effects in the data. First, some errors are corrected by the translation, mainly for very common misspellings, which a machine translation system might have encountered during training, such as

---

Domain	Prompt ID	EN	DE^T Google	DE^T DeepL	RU^T Google
Science	1	.72	.69	.64	.66
	2	.68	.64	.52	.57
	10	.65	.66	.67	.64
Biology	5	.75	.70	.70	.71
	6	.80	.75	.73	.79
ELA	3	.59	.60	.54	.59
	4	.66	.67	.54	.60
	7	.62	.50	.50	.55
	8	.51	.53	.50	.53
	9	.75	.75	.70	.71

Table 1: Monolingual scoring

Domain	Prompt ID	EN	DE^T Google	DE^T DeepL	RU^T Google
Science	1	.69	.69	.63	.65
	2	.69	.64	.52	.57
	10	.66	.64	.68	.64
Biology	5	.75	.71	.69	.70
	6	.81	.76	.74	.79
ELA	3	.59	.58	.53	.58
	4	.66	.67	.54	.60
	7	.62	.47	.50	.54
	8	.51	.53	.47	.54
	9	.75	.76	.69	.71

Table 2: Monolingual scoring

seperate instead of *separate*, which are both correctly translated to the German *getrennt*. Second, the less frequent misspellings are often preserved, although nouns are capitalized and inflected in German. An example would be the phrase *the temperature of vineger* which is translated to *die Temperatur des Vinegers* using the correct German inflected form, but not translating the word to the correct German *Essig*. Another is the misspelled word *diffrence* which is translated to the similarly misspelled form *Diffrenz* (instead of *Differenz*), i.e., the affix *-ence* is correctly translated while keeping the misspelled stem of the word.

Influence of Translation on Human Scores So far, we have simply assumed that the machine translation process is good enough that it does not affect the score assigned to an answer. We examine whether this assumption is valid by re-scoring a small sample of 50 answers each from ASAP prompts 1, 2 and 10, which have been machine translated to German. The annotator also scored the original English data (with some delay time in between to avoid memory effects) so that we can compare scores in different languages assigned by

the same annotator. We found the annotation to be consistent between different language versions. (Quadratically weighted kappa (Cohen, 1968) of between .75 and .94 for the agreement of the same annotator between the original version and the one translated using google translate. Inter-annotator agreement on this sample between the original annotation and our annotator is between .66 and .84.) If machine translation introduced a lot of noise, one would expect scores to differ more between the two versions. One would especially assume that translated answers might make less sense, and would therefore receive lower scores, but we do not see such a phenomenon in the data.

3 Collecting a Cross-lingual Dataset

For our cross-lingual experiments, we need a dataset that contains answers to the same prompt in at least two different languages. As no such dataset is publicly available so far, we decided to create and release a new dataset.

3.1 Selecting a Source Dataset

We decided to extend an existing monolingual dataset instead of collecting a new dataset from scratch, as it provides the advantage that larger amounts of data are already available in one language. The majority of datasets is available in English, so this is a realistic option for the source language. We use German as the target language due to familiarity with the language, as we need to be able to manually score the new dataset. Also, the expected translation quality between English and German is rather high providing a good test case for the feasibility of the approach in general.

There is a set of publicly available English datasets that we could base our experiments on: The ASAP-2 short answer scoring dataset [4], the Powergrading dataset by (Basu et al., 2013), the computer science dataset by (Mohler and Mihalcea, 2009), and the SemEval2013 dataset (Dzikovska et al., 2013). When deciding for a dataset, we took the following criteria into account: First, all necessary **prompt material has to be completely available**, including reading texts or connected images. This requirement rules out the SemEval2013 data, where the prompt contains pictures and graphs (such as a drawing of a electrical circuit) that are necessary to answer the questions but that are not included in the dataset.

---

[4] https://www.kaggle.com/c/asap-sas

Second, the prompts should be **language and culture-independent** so that speakers of a different language or from a different culture have similar chances to answer the questions correctly. This requirement rules out the Powergrading data, as this dataset contains solely questions from US immigration tests like, *If both the President and the Vice President can no longer serve, who becomes President?* German participants are rather unlikely to correctly answer those questions.

Third, the prompts should be **curriculum-independent**, i.e., they should not be based on a specific university course, as we expect answers in those settings to be heavily influenced by what exactly was taught in the corresponding course. Thus, we excluded the computer science dataset, which was targeted at students from a specific computer science class. (In addition, the number of only 30 answers per prompt is relatively small.)

Last, in order to be able to score the newly collected data, **scoring guidelines** for the original dataset have to be **available** and we must be able to apply them with a reasonable inter-annotator-agreement.

Re-scoring Study The ASAP dataset is the only dataset fulfilling the first two requirements and seems relatively curriculum-independent as well. We tested in an annotation study, whether we are able to apply the available annotation guidelines. We selected one prompt for each of the three domains covered by the dataset (science, biology, English Language Arts (ELA)). Two German native speakers with a good command in English annotated a subset of 50 answers for each prompt. For the science prompt, the pairwise inter-annotator agreement between our two annotators and the original English annotators, measured by quadratically weighted kappa, was between .70 and .79 for the science prompt, between .60 and .78 for biology, and between .26 and .63 for ELA. IAA between the two German annotators lies in similar regions. The agreement between the two original annotations was .95 for science, .98 for biology and .77 for ELA. Based on these numbers, we deemed ELA prompts unsuitable for re-collection.

3.2 Dataset Collection & Annotation

As described above, we find the science and biology prompts from ASAP to be suitable for the re-collection process. An exploratory data collec-

	ASAP	ASAP-De
Language	English	German
#Prompts	10	3
#Answers / prompt	>2000	300
Domains	Science ELA Biology	Science

Table 3: Dataset statistics

tion for the three science and two biology prompts revealed that the knowledge tested in the biology prompts was more course-specific than we thought and most participants were unable to answer these questions. Therefore, we restricted ourselves to the three science prompts, which we translated into German. We collect answers from the crowd-sourcing platform CrowdFlower,[5] as well as by directly asking colleagues and students, with the majority of answer (>90%) originating from Crowd-Flower. We excluded answers in any language different from German and obvious non-answers, such as copying the prompt.[6] Overall, we collect a total of 301 answers per prompt. Table 3 compares the resulting German dataset with the original English one.

All answers have been annotated by two German annotators (one being one of the authors of this paper). We found an inter-annotator agreement per prompt between .58 and .84 quadratically weighted kappa. Figure 2 shows some exemplary answers from Prompt 1 both for the original English and the newly collected German dataset.

3.3 Dataset Analysis

We provide a corpus analysis to get further insights into the differences between the two language versions of the dataset.

Label distribution A first indicator as to whether the two language versions are comparable is the label distribution as shown in Table 3. We see that the distribution in the German dataset is skewed towards lower scores, which could be an artifact of our assessment situation. While we tried to avoid questions answerable only by a certain group of learners, it might still be that the original English test taker population was either better prepared or more motivated to answer the ques-

---

[5] https://www.crowdflower.com

[6] We needed to do so because of a relatively high number of such non-answers. However, we kept other non-answers such as *"Ich weiß es nicht"* (*I don't know.*)

ENGLISH	GERMAN
QUESTION: After reading the groups procedure, describe what additional information you would need in order to replicate the experiment. Make sure to include at least three pieces of information.	**QUESTION:** Nachdem Sie die Prozedur der Gruppe gelesen haben, beschreiben Sie, welche zusätzlichen Informationen nötig sind, um das Experiment zu wiederholen. Geben Sie mindestens drei benötigte Informationen an.
LEARNER ANSWERS:	**LEARNER ANSWERS:**

ENGLISH

LEARNER ANSWERS:

- **3 points:** Some additional information you will need are the material. You also need to know the size of the contaneir to measure how the acid rain effected it. You need to know how much vineager is used for each sample. Another thing that would help is to know how big the sample stones are by measureing the best possible way.

- **1 point:** After reading the expireiment, I realized that the additional information you need to replicate the expireiment is one, the amant of vinegar you poured in each container, two, label the containers before you start yar expirement and three, write a conclusion to make sure yar results are accurate.

- **0 points:** The student should list what rock is better and what rock is the worse in the procedure.

GERMAN

LEARNER ANSWERS:

- **3 points:** Es fehlt der Säuregehalt des Essigs. Die Menge Essig die verwendet wurde. Und welche Holzart da Holzsorten unterschiedliche Säureresistenz aufweist.

- **2 points:** Wie viel Essig wurde verwendet? Aus welchem Material waren die Behälter? Wurden die Behälter verschlossen?

- **0 points:** Wir müssen wissen, wie viel Wasser wir sammeln müssen, um die Probe zu machen

Figure 2: Exemplary answers for prompt 1 from the English and the German datasets.

Language	Prompt		
	1	2	10
EN			
DE			

Figure 3: Label distribution for each prompt in the German and English version of the data.

tions correctly than the crowd-workers providing the German answers.

Average Length   Figure 4 shows that answers in the English dataset are considerably longer than in the German one. This difference can be due to two parameters. One is the learner population from which the data is collected, the other is idiosyncrasies of the language itself. To differentiate between the influence of these two effects as far as possible, we also run our comparisons on versions of each dataset that have been automatically translated into the other language (EN^T and DE^T). Thus, comparing the English dataset to DE^T should only display effects of having different datasets, not different languages, while comparing the English dataset to EN^T should show differences between languages but is the same data.

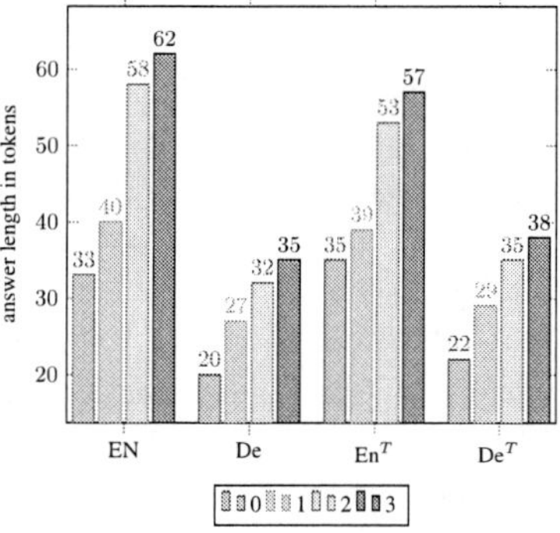

Figure 4: Answer length in tokens averaged over all answers with a certain score.

Figure 4 shows that the difference in length observed between English and German is not an effect of the different languages, but of the different datasets. Additionally, we observe in both datasets that answers with a higher score tend to be longer than incorrect answers.

Linguistic diversity   Next, we look at the linguistic diversity in both datasets. We compute the type-token-ratio (TTR) for each dataset, by randomly sampling chunks of 100 tokens and averaging over the individual values to avoid effect of different corpus sizes, shown in Figure 5. The two main findings from this analysis are: First,

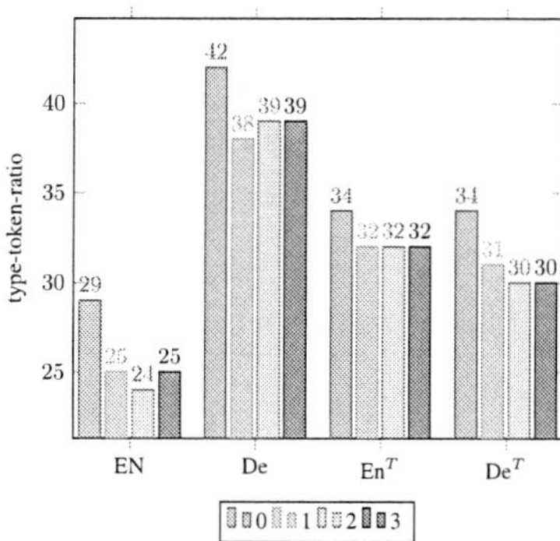

Figure 5: Type-token-ratio for the four datasets computed for all labels with a particular score.

	Prompt		
Compared datasets	**1**	**2**	**10**
EN (train) / EN (test)	.68	.68	.62
EN (train) / DE^T	.45	.49	.45
EN^T (train) / DE	.43	.48	.43

Table 4: Lexical overlap measured on the type level for the top 1000 unigrams for each prompt.

TTR is slightly higher for low scoring answers. This fits the observation that there are often more ways to get an answer wrong than ways to formulate the correct answer. (Note that annotators ignore spelling errors when scoring an answer, and we found that low-scoring answers do not contain more errors than high-scoring answers.) Second, TTR is higher for the original German than for the original English dataset. This is in part due to the language difference. German has a much richer morphology than English, and translating data from German to English reduces TTR while translating from English to German increases it.

Some part of the difference, however, cannot be explained by the different languages and must come from the learner population, which is more homogeneous in the English version (high-school students) as compared to the German version (crowd-workers).

Vocabulary overlap Here, we compute the overlap between the vocabulary used in the English data and the vocabulary of the German dataset. Table 4 shows the comparison measuring the overlap of types on the unigram level. As a baseline, we compute the overlap between training and test data from the English dataset. Next we compare the English training data with the German dataset by either translating the English or the German data to the respective other language. We find a much lower lexical overlap across all prompts.

We therefore expect a decrease in performance when using n-grams as features in a cross-lingual setup compared to the monolingual case.

Summary Overall we observe differences between the datasets in terms of answer length, label distribution, linguistic diversity and used vocabulary. They can only be partially explained by the language difference and seem to be mostly due to differences between the datasets themselves or rather between the learner populations that produced theses answers. In the next section, we examine the effect these differences have on automatic scoring.

4 Cross-lingual Scoring Experiments

After finding in the previous monolingual pilot study that machine translation quality is good enough for our purposes, we now present in this section our cross-lingual experiments. We assume that training data in one language is used to score test data in another language by means of translating either the test or the training data.

4.1 Experimental setup

For our scoring experiments, we use a standard supervised machine learning setup with Weka's SVM classifier in standard configuration as classification backbone, implemented using free-text scoring toolkit ESCRITO (Zesch and Horbach, 2018). We use token uni-, bi- and trigrams as well as character bi- to five-grams as features and evaluate our results using accuracy and quadratically weighted Kappa (Cohen, 1968).

The English ASAP dataset comes with an established split into train and test data, which we reuse. The German dataset is very small in direct comparison, so that we cannot use a fixed split into training and test data. Therefore, we use 10-fold cross-validation for the German dataset.

Experimental conditions We conduct experiments falling into four groups:

(1) for the **baseline** experiments, we train and test models on monolingual datasets and use either the English or German dataset exclusively. These two datasets have very different sizes. For the original English data, we have over 2000 answers per prompt. For the re-collected German set, we

only have 300 answers per prompt, 270 of which are used for training in our cross-validation setup. This difference in size might also reflect in different performances. To eliminate such effects, we conduct experiments on the English training data in a variant that uses only 270 training items, sampled from the training data section. For comparison, we also conduct the baseline experiment on the full English train data (EN_{all}). To avoid sampling artifacts, we repeat the experiment 100 times with different splits and report the average of all runs.

(2) In the **monolingual** condition, we translate both the training and the test data, similar to our experiments in the pilot study, but using data sampling that makes sure that training data sizes are comparable. Differences to the baseline are thus only due to the machine translation process.

(3) In the **translate train** experiments, we combine the original English test data with the German training data automatically translated to English, as well as original German test data with the English training data translated to German.

(4) In the **translate test** condition, we use test data translated into the other language with the original test data from that language. In these last two conditions, differences to the baseline result either from machine translation or from differences inherent to the datasets.

			QWK			
	Train	**Test**	**1**	**2**	**10**	**∅**
baselines	EN_{all}	EN	.72	.68	.65	.68
	EN	EN	.64	.56	.64	.61
	DE	DE	.78	.61	.63	.67
translate both	EN^T	EN^T	.63	.49	.64	.58
	DE^T	DE^T	.84	.62	.54	.66
translate train	EN^T	DE	.49	.08	.46	.34
	DE^T	EN	.41	.39	.39	.40
translate test	EN	DE^T	.35	.08	.43	.29
	DE	EN^T	.26	.35	.33	.31

Table 5: Content scoring performance measured in quadratically weighted kappa for different cross-lingual setups.

4.2 Results

Table 5 shows our results measured in quadratically weighted kappa. When looking at the baselines first, we see that automatic scoring in this monolingual case works comparably well for En-

		QWK			
Train	**Test**	**1**	**2**	**10**	**∅**
EN	EN	.64	.56	.64	.61
EN	EN^{2T}	.50	.40	.55	.48
EN^{2T}	EN	.64	.52	.62	.60

Table 6: Double translation in monolingual setting

glish and German. This shows that our manual scoring of the German data set is reliable enough to learn a competitive model. In the second monolingual case, when we translate both training and test data, we only observe moderate losses or for some prompts even small improvements compared to the original language version.

When turning towards the cross-lingual results, where we either only translate train or test data, the picture looks quite different: in all four conditions, scoring performance is considerably lower compared to the monolingual settings. The loss is especially pronounced for prompt 2. This difference between prompts cannot be explained by our corpus analysis in Section 3, especially the vocabulary overlap between English and German datasets, which were in the same range for all three prompts (and even slightly higher for prompt 2 than for the other two prompts).

Differences between Prompts To investigate the apparent differences in similarity between training and test data for the individual prompts further, we analyze the data using language models. We build a trigram language model per prompt for the English data using the SRILM toolkit (Stolcke, 2002) and measure the perplexity of translated German answers under that language model. We find the perplexity of answers to prompt 2 to be higher than answers to prompt 1 and 10, indicating that German answers to prompt 2 fit the model of the English answer worse than the other prompts. Considering that using n-grams as classification features as well as for language models are quite related tasks, these results are not surprising but do not provide a full explanation to our observations. Further investigations into the differences between prompts are definitely necessary

4.3 Follow-up Experiment: The Influence of Machine Translation

As discussed in the introduction, the difference between the baseline and cross-lingual scoring performance can originate from two sources: different learner populations and effects of machine translation. In order to assess the individual contributions of these two factors, we propose a variant of our experiment that operates on only one dataset but still uses machine translation on either the test **or** the training data, so that the delta in performance is due to translation and not to different learner populations. We achieve this by *double-translating* the training or test data of the English ASAP dataset, i.e., we have the data automatically translated from English to German and then back to English (marked as EN^{2T}). Table 6 shows the performance in comparison to the monolingual baseline experiments where we see that double-translating the test data decreases performance considerably while –surprisingly– double-translating the training data leaves performance unaffected.

A naive approach to factor out artifacts from translationese, while keeping effects stemming from the differences between the datasets, would be to use translated datasets in the cross-lingual case both for training and testing, i.e., we double-translate one dataset and translate the other one only once. In this setup, shown in Table 7, performance benefits only slightly, if at all, from double-translation (with the exception of double translated train data in prompt 1).

Consider the following example of an answer from the original English dataset:

(A) Plastic type B was the superior in both trial 1 and trial 2. (B) Record the weight that was put on to show how much effected each plastic. Also conducting more trials (. . .)

After translating the answer automatically to German and back to English it looks like this:

Type B plastic was the supervisor in both Trial 1 and Trial 2. (B) Write down the weight that was put on to show how much each one has made plastic. Also do more experiments (. . .)

Apart from obvious translation errors (*superior–supervisor*), we see a simplifying effect of translation: *record–write down*, *effect–make*, and *conduct–do*. Such simplifications might on the one hand normalize over different paraphrases of the same content, but could on the other hand also remove meaningful differences between correct and incorrect answers.

	Train	Test	QWK			
			1	2	10	$\varnothing$
translate train	EN^T	DE	.49	.08	.46	.34
	EN^T	DE^{2T}	.49	.07	.46	.34
	DE^T	EN	.41	.39	.39	.40
	DE^T	EN^{2T}	.43	.36	.44	.41
translate test	EN	DE^T	.35	.08	.43	.29
	EN^{2T}	DE^T	.55	.03	.46	.35
	DE	EN^T	.26	.35	.33	.31
	DE^{2T}	EN^T	.41	.38	.32	.37

Table 7: Double translation in cross-lingual setting

5   Related Work

To the best of our knowledge, there are no previous approaches to cross-lingual scoring in the educational domain. However, cross-lingual NLP approaches have been successfully used for a variety of tasks, including information retrieval (Oard and Diekema, 1998), sentiment analysis (Mihalcea et al., 2007) and textual similarity (Mohammad et al., 2007; Potthast et al., 2008). While in some of these approaches, dictionaries are used as the bridge the gap between languages to translate search queries (e.g. by Ballesteros and Croft (1996) for cross-lingual information retrieval) or translate features in a learned model ((Shi et al., 2010)), many approaches rely on having similar training data in both languages, often by means of parallel or comparable corpora (Gliozzo and Strapparava, 2006). If such corpora are not available, as is the case for our scenario, leveraging machine translation to create training data for handling a new language or to transfer test data into a language for which training data exists has been explored for example by Fortuna and Shawe-Taylor, while other approaches use cross-lingual word embeddings (Klementiev et al., 2012).

6   Conclusion

In this paper we showed the general feasibility of cross-lingual short-answer scoring. We also identified a number of challenges: One is that artifacts from machine translation seem to produce a language that is substantially different from genuine text, and that this translationese poses a problem, as highlighted by our experiments with double-translated items. Second, the two datasets bear differences that go beyond differences in language. In a real-life application scenario, this problem might be less severe, e.g. in a class where everyone received the same instructions and just answers an exam in different languages, where answers can be expected to be more consistent than the two versions of the ASAP corpus in our experiments.

For future work, we want to explore more sophisticated approaches going beyond our straightforward procedure of automatically translating test or training data, such as translation of word features or using cross-lingual embeddings in a neural network approach as well as extending our experiments to a broader variety of data.

Acknowledgments

This work has been funded by the German Federal Ministry of Education and Research under grant no. FKZ 01PL16075.

References

Lisa Ballesteros and Bruce Croft. 1996. Dictionary methods for cross-lingual information retrieval. In *International Conference on Database and Expert Systems Applications*. Springer, pages 791–801.

Sumit Basu, Chuck Jacobs, and Lucy Vanderwende. 2013. Powergrading: a Clustering Approach to Amplify Human Effort for Short Answer Grading. *Transactions of the Association for Computational Linguistics (TACL)* 1:391–402.

Jacob Cohen. 1968. Weighted kappa: Nominal scale agreement provision for scaled disagreement or partial credit. *Psychological bulletin* 70(4):213.

Myroslava O. Dzikovska, Rodney Nielsen, Chris Brew, Claudia Leacock, Danilo Giampiccolo, Luisa Bentivogli, Peter Clark, Ido Dagan, and Hoa Trang Dang. 2013. SemEval-2013 Task 7: The Joint Student Response Analysis and 8th Recognizing Textual Entailment Challenge. **SEM 2013: The First Joint Conference on Lexical and Computational Semantics* .

Blaz Fortuna and John Shawe-Taylor. ????? The use of machine translation tools for cross-lingual text mining. In *Proceedings of the Workshop on Learning with Multiple Views*.

Alfio Gliozzo and Carlo Strapparava. 2006. Exploiting comparable corpora and bilingual dictionaries for cross-language text categorization. In *Proceedings of the 21st International Conference on Computational Linguistics and the 44th annual meeting of the Association for Computational Linguistics*. Association for Computational Linguistics, pages 553–560.

Derrick Higgins, Chris Brew, Michael Heilman, Ramon Ziai, Lei Chen, Aoife Cahill, Michael Flor, Nitin Madnani, Joel Tetreault, Daniel Blanchard,

et al. 2014. Is getting the right answer just about choosing the right words? the role of syntactically-informed features in short answer scoring. *arXiv preprint arXiv:1403.0801* .

Alexandre Klementiev, Ivan Titov, and Binod Bhattarai. 2012. Inducing crosslingual distributed representations of words. *Proceedings of COLING 2012* pages 1459–1474.

Rada Mihalcea, Carmen Banea, and Janyce Wiebe. 2007. Learning multilingual subjective language via cross-lingual projections. In *Proceedings of the 45th annual meeting of the association of computational linguistics*. pages 976–983.

Saif Mohammad, Iryna Gurevych, Graeme Hirst, and Torsten Zesch. 2007. Cross-lingual distributional profiles of concepts for measuring semantic distance. In *Proceedings of the 2007 Joint Conference on Empirical Methods in Natural Language Processing and Computational Natural Language Learning (EMNLP-CoNLL)*.

Michael Mohler and Rada Mihalcea. 2009. Text-to-text semantic similarity for automatic short answer grading. In *Proceedings of the 12th Conference of the European Chapter of the Association for Computational Linguistics*. Association for Computational Linguistics, Stroudsburg, PA, USA, EACL '09, pages 567–575. http://dl.acm.org/citation.cfm?id=1609067.1609130.

Douglas W Oard and Anne R Diekema. 1998. Cross-language information retrieval. *Annual Review of Information Science and Technology (ARIST)* 33:223–56.

Martin Potthast, Benno Stein, and Maik Anderka. 2008. A wikipedia-based multilingual retrieval model. In *European conference on information retrieval*. Springer, pages 522–530.

Lei Shi, Rada Mihalcea, and Mingjun Tian. 2010. Cross language text classification by model translation and semi-supervised learning. In *Proceedings of the 2010 Conference on Empirical Methods in Natural Language Processing*. Association for Computational Linguistics, pages 1057–1067.

Andreas Stolcke. 2002. Srilm – an extensible language modeling toolkit. In *In proceedings of the 7th International Conference on Spoken Language Processing (ICSLP 2002*. pages 901–904.

Jana Zuheir Sukkarieh and John Blackmore. 2009. C-rater: Automatic content scoring for short constructed responses. In *FLAIRS Conference*. pages 290–295.

Torsten Zesch and Andrea Horbach. 2018. ESCRITO An NLP-Enhanced Educational Scoring Toolkit. In *Proceedings of the Eleventh International Conference on Language Resources and Evaluation (LREC 2018)*.

Ramon Ziai, Niels Ott, and Detmar Meurers. 2012. Short answer assessment: Establishing links between research strands. In *Proceedings of the Seventh Workshop on Building Educational Applications Using NLP*. Association for Computational Linguistics, pages 190–200.

Author Index